# Russian Politics and Society

Having been fully revised and updated to reflect the considerable changes in Russia over the last decade, the fourth edition of this classic text builds on the strengths of the previous editions to provide a comprehensive and sophisticated analysis on Russian politics and society.

In this edition, Richard Sakwa seeks to evaluate the evidence in a balanced and informed way, denying simplistic assumptions about the inevitable failure of the democratic experiment in Russia while avoiding facile generalisations on the inevitable triumph of global integration and democratisation. New to this edition:

- Extended coverage of electoral laws, party development and regional politics
- New chapter on the 'phoney democracy' period, 1991–3
- Historical evaluation of Yeltsin's leadership
- Full coverage of Putin's presidency
- Discussion of the development of civil society and the problems of democratic consolidation
- Latest developments in the Chechnya conflict
- More on foreign policy issues such as Russia's relationship with NATO and the EU after enlargement, Russia's relations with other post-Soviet states and the problem of competing 'near abroads' for Russia and the West
- The re-introduction of the Russian constitution as an appendix
- An updated select bibliography
- More focus on the challenges facing Russia in the twenty-first century

Written in an accessible and lively style, this book is packed with detailed information on the central debates and issues in Russia's difficult transformation. This makes it the best available textbook on the subject and essential reading for all those concerned with the fate of Russia, and with the future of international society.

**Richard Sakwa** is Professor of Russian and European Politics at the University of Kent.

# Russian Politics and Society

## Fourth edition

**Richard Sakwa**

Routledge
Taylor & Francis Group

LONDON AND NEW YORK

First published 1993
Second edition, 1996
Third edition, 2002
Fourth edition, 2008
by Routledge
2 Park Square, Milton Park, Abingdon, Oxon, OX14 4RN

Simultaneously published in the USA and Canada
by Routledge
270 Madison Ave, New York NY 10016

Routledge is an imprint of the Taylor & Francis Group, *an informa business*

Transferred to Digital Printing 2009

Typeset in Times New Roman by Keyword Group Ltd.

*British Library Cataloguing in Publication Data*
A catalogue record for this book is available from the British Library

*Library of Congress Cataloging in Publication Data*
Sakwa, Richard.
Russian politics and society/Richard Sakwa.–4th ed.
p. cm.
Includes bibliographical references and index.
1. Russia (Federation)–Politics and government–1991– 2. Post-communism–
Russia (Federation). 3. Former Soviet republics–Politics and government.
4. Post-communism–Former Soviet republics. I. Title.
JN6695.S28 2008
320.947–dc22   2007032799


ISBN 10: 0-415-41527-6 (hbk)
ISBN 10: 0-415-41528-4 (pbk)
ISBN 10: 0-203-93125-4 (ebk)


ISBN 13: 978-0-415-41527-9 (hbk)
ISBN 13: 978-0-415-41528-6 (pbk)
ISBN 13: 978-0-203-93125-7 (ebk)

# Contents

# Figures

# Tables

# Preface to the fourth edition

Nearly two decades have passed since the fall of the Soviet communist system in 1991. Russia remains balanced between consolidating the democratic aspirations that accompanied the fall of the old regime and reproducing in new forms the authoritarianism that was overthrown at that time. There are undoubtedly major achievements recorded in these years. The basic framework of a democratic law-governed state has been established, enshrined in the constitution adopted in December 1993. Some of the fundamental institutions of such a state have also been established, notably a differentiated legal system, authoritative executive institutions, a functioning legislature and a viable representative system, together with a market-oriented economy. Relations with the former members of the Soviet Union have been strained, but no Yugoslav-style inter-state wars involving Russia have broken out, while Russia's relations with the rest of the world are now probably more stable than at any time in the past, although characterised by persistent tensions. There are, however, many aspects of Russia's post-communist evolution that give concern. Although the framework and institutions of a democratic society have been established, political practices of leaders at all levels often undermine the spirit of democracy. This is most in evidence during elections, where the weakness of an independent media and civil society allows executive authorities considerable leeway. Above all, the wars in Chechnya (1994–6, 1999–2003) entailed untold suffering and abuse of human rights.

This book will try to provide a balanced and informative analysis of post-communist Russian institutional, political and social development. The structure of this version substantially follows that of the third edition, published in 2002, although there have been some changes. Chapter 1 now contains a revised summary of Soviet politics, providing some historical context as background to contemporary developments. Detailed analysis of the events leading up to the violent confrontation of October 1993, and details of the evolution of the current constitution, can be found in a new Chapter 3, which brings together discussion of the 'phoney democracy' period between 1991 and 1993. The chapters in Part II have been reordered, while the material in Part VI has been much condensed. The focus of this book is less on the presidency of Boris Yeltsin (1991–9) and more focused on that of Vladimir Putin (2000–8). A further major change is the addition of the Russian constitution as an appendix, which was removed from the third edition to save space, a move that was much criticised. Overall, the material has been updated to reflect events up to the end of Vladimir Putin's two-term presidency. Plenty of echoes of the earlier versions remain, but this edition focuses on the challenges facing Russia in the twenty-first century.

The restructuring and updating have been the relatively easy part. Far harder has been the attempt to make sense of it all. Already in the preface to the second edition in 1996

I noted that the glad days of the early post-communist years (reflected to a degree in the tone of the first edition of 1993) had given way to foreboding about the erosion of Russia's tenuous democratic gains. I argued in 1996 that between the people and the state a 'regime system' based on Yeltsin personally had emerged that undermined the consolidation of the constitutional state and the autonomy of social institutions in one direction, and stunted the growth of an active civil society, accountability and representative system on the other. In 1996 only the outlines of a type of oligarchical capitalism that funded the regime and blurred the distinction between particularistic economic and general state interests were visible. The heyday of oligarchical capitalism and regime elitism lasted a bare two years, between Yeltsin's re-election for a second term in 1996 and the financial crash of August 1998. The appointment of Yevgeny Primakov as prime minister in September 1998, and even more the emergence of Putin as Yeltsin's successor in 1999, signalled the reassertion of a 'statist' line that sought to regain a relative autonomy for the state, freed from the deathly embrace from the oligarchs and Yeltsin's personalised 'courtly' style of regime rule. The reassertion of the state in the early 2000s, however, threatened further to undermine the free development of autonomous political institutions in society. Putin's advocacy of a liberal economic model appeared balanced by a rather more traditional monocentric model of politics and a distinctively Russian type of neo-patrimonialism in the economy. State capture by big business gave way to elements of business capture by the state. At the same time, a more assertive foreign policy provoked confrontational echoes of the Cold War era.

This is the stage in which we now find ourselves. The question 'is Russia a democracy?' resounds ever more insistently as press freedom appears under attack, political pluralism is restricted and elections are hedged in by growing restrictions. The anarchic pluralism of the Yeltsin years has given way to a more stable but exclusive state-centred system. This book promises no simple answer to questions about the nature of Russian democracy or the meaning of contemporary political developments, but it does argue that the potential for democratic political evolution remains strong. The story of post-communist Russian political reconstitution is far from over, and although Russia may well revert to some kind of authoritarianism, more likely will be renewed democratic advance, occasioned by leadership change and elite renewal. This book provides the historical and institutional framework to help understand the dynamics of development, some of the economic and social context, and presents the key debates and issues within which the reader can make up his or her mind on the way that Russia has developed. If the book allows the reader to take a balanced and informed view of contemporary Russian politics, then it will have succeeded in its purpose.

Canterbury
November 2007

# Acknowledgements

The debts incurred in preparing a work of this size are too numerous to list. In addition to thanking all those who helped in the preparation of the first three editions of this book, I would like in particular to mention Mikhail Afanas'ev, Vladimir Amelin, Edwin Bacon, Yitzhak Brudny, Philip Boobbyer, Archie Brown, Paul Chaisty, Tim Colton, Artour Demtchouk, Alexander Doroshchenko, Peter Duncan, Gilles Favarel-Garrigue, Vladimir Gel'man, Philip Hanson, Yuri Igritskii, Mikhail Il'in, David Johnson, Svyatoslav Kaspe, Vladimir Kolosov, Anatoly Kulik, Bobo Lo, Luke March, Alexander Markarov, Sergei Markov, Andrei Medushevskii, Lena Meleshkina, Andrei Melville, Valentin Mikhailov, Alexei Mukhin, Georges Nivat, James Nixey, Oksana Oracheva, Vladimir Pastukhov, Nicolai Petro, Nikolai Petrov, Yurii Pivovarov, Sergei Prozorov, Thomas Remington, Neil Robinson, Cameron Ross, Viktor Rudenko, Peter Rutland, Andrei Ryabov, Helena Rytovuori-Apunen, Thomas Saalfeld, Jutta Scherrer, Elena Shestopal, Elizabeth Teague, Vera Tolz-Zilitinkevich, Joan Barth Urban, David White, Stephen White and Andrei Zagorskii. Collaboration with the Institute of Law and Public Policy in Moscow, under the directorship of Olga Sidorovich, has been particularly fruitful, and I thank all there who have helped in the development of this work. The workshops of the Eurasian Political Studies Network, directed by Vitaly Merkushev and generously supported by the HESP programme of the Open Society Institute, Budapest, have provided a stimulating forum for discussion and learning with young scholars from post-Soviet Eurasia and Western Europe. The faults, of course, remain my own. Craig Fowlie and Natalja Mortensen at Routledge, like their predecessors who have tussled with the gigantism inherent in Russian studies, once again displayed great patience and understanding as I tried to cut a crystal goblet out of jelly. The technical support of Ulrike Swientek at Routledge is greatly appreciated. I am most grateful for the secretarial and other assistance of Gemma Chapman, Nicola Cooper, Ann Hadaway and Suzanne Robinson, together with the constant support of Jean Hudson, in the Department of Politics and International Relations at the University of Kent. It is my pleasure to acknowledge the support of INTAS grant No. 04-79-7284, 'Eurasian Political Studies Network: developing comparative studies of regime transformations in multicultural societies and the state and nation building process in the post-soviet region' in the preparation of this edition.

# Note on style, spelling and transliteration

Words like Party are capitalised to indicate that the proper noun referred to is a concrete entity that existed or exists in the Soviet Union or Russia. The word 'democrat' is usually used without inverted commas, although the attempt by a particular group to appropriate the term for themselves is clearly problematical; similarly, for stylistic reasons, the use of 'self-styled democrat' or 'so-called democrat' is kept to a minimum.

The spelling of geographical areas tries to follow the changes since the late 1980s, but in most cases has resisted the conversion back to Sovietised forms. Moldavia has thus become Moldova, and its capital Kishinev has become Chisinau, and there they stay despite the reversion to the earlier usage in the Russian media. The same goes for Belorussia's conversion to Belarus; Kirghizia's to Kyrgyzstan; Tataria's to Tatarstan; and Alma Ata's change to Almaty. However, where there is a standard American/British rendition of a name, this is the one used here. For example, Kiev rather than the Ukrainised Kyiv, and Lvov rather than Lviv.

The transliteration system is the standard British one (a modified version of the Library of Congress system), used in most cases except when convention has decreed otherwise. The 'iu' letter becomes 'yu', 'ia' becomes 'ya', and at the beginning of names 'e' become 'ye' (Yevgeny rather than Evgeny). Thus, El'tsin becomes Yeltsin, Ekaterinburg is Yekaterinburg, and Riiazan is Ryazan. For the sake of reader-friendliness the 'ii' at the end of words is usually rendered as 'y' – Yevgeny rather than Yevgenii, Yuri rather than Yury and Valeri rather than Valery. The diacritical (representing the soft sign) in the text is also omitted from the end of frequently used words like *oblast'* (region) and Belarus', and from the end of place names and proper nouns, thus Lebed rather than the more strictly accurate Lebed' and Rossel rather than Rossel', although when the soft sign is in the middle of a name (e.g. Luk'yanov, Zor'kin) it is retained. When transliterated from the Russian, footnotes will tend to follow the more accurate form, and thus there may be a variance between the spelling of a word in the text and in the references.

# Glossary of acronyms, acrostics and terms

| | |
|---|---|
| ABM | Anti-Ballistic Missile treaty (1972) |
| *Afghantsy* | Those who fought in the Afghan war, 1979–89 |
| APEC | Asia-Pacific Economic Cooperation forum |
| *Apparatchik* | Worker in the Communist Party's Central Committee apparatus |
| ASEAN | Association of South-East Asian Nations |
| ASSR | Autonomous Soviet Socialist Republic |
| CC | Central Committee |
| CEC | Central Electoral Commission |
| Cheka | *Chrezvychainaya Komissiya*, Extraordinary Commission, Soviet security organ 1918–22, although the name lived on to describe the various Soviet security agencies |
| CMEA | Council for Mutual Economic Assistance, Comecon |
| CEE | Central and Eastern Europe |
| CFE | Conventional Forces in Europe treaty (1990) |
| CFSP | Common Foreign and Security Policy |
| *Chinovnik* | (Tsarist) civil servant |
| CIS | Commonwealth of Independent States |
| CFDP | Council for Foreign and Defence Policy (in Russian: SVOP) |
| CPD | Congress of People's Deputies |
| CPRF | Communist Party of the Russian Federation |
| CPSU | Communist Party of the Soviet Union |
| CSCE | Conference on Security and Cooperation in Europe, established in Helsinki in 1975 (see also OSCE) |
| *Dedovshchina* | Bullying, hazing |
| EAPC | Euro-Atlantic Partnership Council |
| EBRD | European Bank for Reconstruction and Development |
| ECHR | European Convention on Human Rights and Fundamental Freedoms |
| ECtHR | European Court of Human Rights |
| ECJ | European Court of Justice |
| ESDI | European Security and Defence Identity |
| EU | European Union |
| FC | Federation Council |
| FD | Federal district |
| FDI | Foreign Direct Investment |

| | |
|---|---|
| FIS | Foreign Intelligence Service (see SVR) |
| FSB | *Federal'naya sluzhba bezopasnosti*, Federal Security Service |
| FSK | *Federal'naya sluzhba kontrrazvedki*, Federal Counter-Intelligence Service |
| FEC | Fuel and Energy Complex (in Russian: TEK) |
| GDP | Gross Domestic Product |
| GKChP | *Gosudarstvennyi komitet cherezvychainoi polozhenie*, established during the attempted coup of August 1991 (see also SCSE below) |
| GKU | Main Monitoring Department (of the Presidential Administration) |
| *Glasnost* | Openness |
| GNP | Gross National Product |
| *Grazhdanin* | Citizen |
| GRP | Gross Regional Product |
| *Guberniya* | Province, unit of Tsarist administration |
| GU(U)AM | Georgia, Ukraine, (Uzbekistan), Azerbaijan and Moldova grouping |
| IFIs | International Financial Institutions |
| IMF | International Monetary Fund |
| INF | Intermediate Nuclear Forces Treaty (1987) |
| *Ispolkom* | *Ispolnitel'nyi komitet*, Executive committee (of the soviets) |
| JR | *Spravedlivaya Rossiya*, political party Just Russia |
| KGB | *Komitet gosudarstvennogo bezopasnosti*, Committee of State Security |
| *Kolkhoz* | Collective farm |
| Komsomol | *Kommunisticheskii soyuz molodezhi*, Young Communist League |
| *Korenizatsiya* | Indigenisation, nativisation |
| *Krai* | Territory, province |
| LDPR | Liberal Democratic Party of Russia |
| MD | Military District |
| MFA | Ministry of Foreign Affairs (see also MID) |
| MID | *Ministerstvo inostrannykh del*, Ministry of Foreign Affairs |
| MVD | *Ministerstvo vnutrennykh del*, Ministry of Internal Affairs |
| NACC | North Atlantic Cooperation Council |
| NATO | North Atlantic Treaty Organisation |
| *Neformaly* | Informals |
| NMD | National Missile Defence |
| *Nomenklatura* | The Communist system of political appointments, came to designate the class of office-holders |
| NPT | Non-proliferation Treaty (1968) |
| *Obkom* | *Oblastnoi komitet*, *oblast* committee (of the CPSU) |
| *Oblast* | Region |
| OECD | Organisation for Economic Cooperation and Development |
| *Okrug* | District |
| OMON | Special-purpose riot police |
| OSCE | Organisation for Security and Cooperation in Europe (the name for the CSCE from December 1994) |
| OVR | Fatherland–All Russia electoral bloc |
| PCA | Partnership and Cooperation Agreement |

| | |
|---|---|
| *Perestroika* | Restructuring |
| PfP | Partnership for Peace |
| PL | Party list electoral system |
| *Postanovlenie* | Directive |
| *Raion* | District, borough |
| *Rasporyazhenie* | Executive order |
| RF | Russian Federation |
| *Rossiyanin* | Russian (in the civic sense, although now used more broadly) |
| RSFSR | Russian Soviet Federated Socialist Republic |
| *Russkii* | Russian (in the ethnic sense) |
| SALT | Strategic Arms Limitation (Talks) Treaty |
| SCO | Shanghai Cooperation Organisation |
| SCSE | State Committee of the State of Emergency (see also GKChP) |
| SMD | Single-member districts in elections |
| *Sootechestvenniki* | Compatriots |
| SPS | *Soyuz pravykh sil*, Union of Right Forces political party |
| SSR | Soviet Socialist Republic |
| START | Strategic Arms Reduction (Talks) Treaty |
| SVR | *Sluzhba vneshnoi razvedky*, Foreign Intelligence Service |
| TLE | Treaty Limited Equipment |
| UES | United Energy Systems, the electricity monopoly |
| *Ukaz* | Decree |
| UN | United Nations |
| UNDP | United Nations Development Programme |
| USSR | Union of Soviet Socialist Republics |
| Vesenkha | Supreme Council of the Economy |
| VTsIOM | All-Russian Centre for the Study of Public Opinion |
| VV | Interior Troops |
| WEU | Western European Union |
| WGF | Western Group of Forces |
| WTO | Warsaw Treaty Organisation, Warsaw Pact |
| WTO | World Trade Organisation |
| Zastoi | Stagnation |
| *Zemlya* (pl. *zemli*) | Territory, comparable to the German *Länder* |
| Zemstvo | Unit of Tsarist local administration |

# Part I

# The fall of communism and the rebirth of Russia

In this part we will examine two associated but nevertheless distinct processes. The first is the *dissolution* of the system of Soviet communism. We will provide a brief overview of the trajectory of Soviet politics, noting both its achievements and identifying some of its main failings, before examining the rise of Russia and its role in the breakdown of Soviet communism. In the second chapter the emphasis shifts from issues of political organisation to the shape of the state itself. The focus will be on the *disintegration* of the Union of Soviet Socialist Republics (USSR), a process entwined with the dissolution of the communist order but analytically distinct. The USSR was established in December 1922 as a union of allegedly sovereign republics to give political form to the diversity of the new republic's peoples and nations, and this was then given juridical form in the adoption of the Soviet Union's first constitution in January 1924. The system worked as long as there was a force standing outside the ethno-federal framework; and this force was the All-Union Communist Party (Bolsheviks) (VKP(b)), renamed the Communist Party of the Soviet Union (CPSU) at the Nineteenth Party Congress in 1952. With the launching of *perestroika* (restructuring) by the new General Secretary of the CPSU, Mikhail Gorbachev, in 1985, the Party gradually lost its integrative capacity as its own internal coherence dissolved, precipitating by late 1991 the disintegration of the state that it had overseen. The dynamics of the relationship between dissolution and disintegration and the reconstitution of Russia is our central concern in this part. Between the disintegration of the USSR in December 1991 and the adoption of a new constitution in December 1993, Russia entered a period of crisis when democratic institutions and practices failed to take root.

# 1 Soviet communism and its dissolution

> But what I believe to be certain is this: if you were to give all these grand, contemporary teachers full scope to destroy the old society and build it anew, the result would be such obscurity, such chaos, something so crude, blind, and inhuman that the whole structure would collapse to the sound of humanity's curses before it could ever be completed.
>
> (Fyodor Dostoyevsky)[1]

Soviet communism was one of the most ambitious attempts at social engineering known to history. Coming to power in October 1917, the Bolshevik party under the leadership of Vladimir Il'ich Lenin sought to change every aspect of Russian politics and society. Armed with the ideology of Marxism, they launched the great communist experiment to build a society on fundamentally different principles from those that humanity had hitherto experienced. The ideology proclaimed the abolition of the private ownership of the means of production, the rejection of Russia's imperial legacy by granting autonomy to many of the peoples making up the nation, the repudiation of the whole tradition of Western state and law, the introduction of the unmediated power of the working masses, and the spread of the revolution to all corners of the earth. In practice, of course, these ideals were tempered by the harsh realities of trying to build socialism in a relatively backward and isolated society. Communism in Russia was a social experiment in the most profound sense, in that untested principles of social organisation were applied by one group over the rest of the community.[2] For seventy-four years the Soviet Union sought to create an alternative social order, in effect an alternative modernity, to that predominant in the West. In the event, what was established was a *mismodernised* society, creating institutions that were modern in form but repudiating modernity's spirit, above all political liberty, economic entrepreneurialism and free thought. The Soviet system endured far longer than most of its early critics thought possible, but ultimately in 1991 came crashing down. The legacy of the failed experiment lives on in Russia today. Although the old system collapsed, great wedges of the old institutional and informal structures survived intact into the post-communist era. The relatively soft transition into the post-communist era meant that the successor regime did not enjoy a *tabula rasa* on which to build a new system. What emerged out of the fall of communism is a unique and fascinating hybrid. The bulk of this book is devoted to analysing the nature of this hybrid new political order, but this chapter will focus on the nature and fall of the communist system itself.

## The Soviet system

We will provide here no more than a brief outline of the main phases of Soviet power. The periodisation is used only to highlight key developments. The last Tsar, Nicholas II, was overthrown by what was in effect a palace coup in February 1917. The Provisional Government, led in its final period by Alexander Kerensky, replaced imperial rule, but itself lasted a mere eight months. This period is known in Marxist terminology as 'bourgeois democratic', but as even Lenin acknowledged, it made Russia the freest country in the world. At Lenin's insistence the Bolsheviks seized power on 25 October 1917 (7 November in the new-style calendar), and thus put an end to Russia's first democratic 'transition'. The October revolution was effectively six revolutions rolled into one.

1   The mass social revolution, in which peasants sought land, soldiers (peasants in another guise) struggled for peace, and workers for greater recognition in the labour process.
2   The democratic revolution, expressing aspirations for the development of political accountability and popular representation, although not necessarily in classic liberal democratic forms.
3   The radical counter-elite revolution, in which the alienated Russian intelligentsia repudiated the absolutist claims of divine rule by the monarchy and fought to apply what they considered to be more enlightened forms of government. The Bolsheviks from this perspective were only the most ruthless and effective part of this counter-elite, challenging the bases of the old order in the name of the radical emancipation of the people in the name of a new set of social ideals. This radical emancipatory agenda stemmed from the Enlightenment as reworked with a social agenda by Karl Marx.
4   The national revolution, which confirmed the independence of Poland and Finland, saw the rapid fragmentation of the Russian empire. However, the Provisional Government's failure to respond to the national aspirations of Ukraine, the South Caucasian and the Central Asian republics was one of the reasons for its downfall.
5   The revolution of internationalism. The Russian revolution reflected a trend of thought, exemplified by Marx, which suggested that the old-style nation-state was redundant and as capitalism became a global system, so social orders would gradually lose their national characteristics. From this perspective the revolution could just as easily have taken place in Berlin or Paris; it just happened to start in what Lenin called 'the weakest link in the imperialist chain', in St Petersburg and Moscow, but would according to him inevitably spread.
6   The revolution within the revolution, as the most extreme wing of the Bolsheviks usurped the agenda of the moderate socialists, mobilised workers and revolutionary idealists (such as the anarchists) to establish their own political dictatorship.

The inter-relationship and tension between these six levels of revolution are what make the Russian revolution so perennially fascinating, but these contradictions, as we shall explore below, were ultimately never resolved. The Bolshevik seizure of power was followed by seven recognisable phases before the final period of reform and collapse from 1985.

### Consolidation and compromise, October 1917–June 1918

The weeks following the revolution were followed by decrees granting the peasants land and declaring Russia's withdrawal from the First World War. This was accompanied by an assault on big business ('the Red Guard attack on capital'), as well as against the free press. The secret police, the Cheka, was established in December 1917, the forerunner of many Soviet repressive agencies. In the Treaty of Brest-Litovsk of March 1918 the Germans imposed crushing terms on Russia as Lenin gave up territory to buy time. This was a period in which various oppositional groupings *within* the revolution, like the coalitionists (in favour of broadening the government to include all parties represented in the soviets (councils)) and the Left Communists (who urged Lenin to wage a revolutionary war against Germany in the name of the internationalist principles of October) were defeated. It was also the period when movements *against* the revolution began to mobilise, precipitating the Civil War. Between March and June 1918 Lenin sought to find a compromise with big business through his programme of 'state capitalism', an attempt that revealed his ruthless pragmatism (as the peace of Brest-Litovsk had done earlier) as the emancipatory goals of the mass revolution came into contradiction with the developmental goals of the regime. The independent workers' movement was ruthlessly crushed by Bolshevik power. Lenin's model of socialism appeared to be that of the German war economy without capitalists, a type of state capitalism where the state fulfilled the role of capitalists.

### Civil War and War Communism, June 1918–March 1921

The attempts at compromise (and there remain questions over the degree of Lenin's commitment to broadening the base of the new regime) came to an end when the incipient Civil War broadened into full-scale armed confrontation. The system known as War Communism developed, partially in response to the exigencies of fighting the war and the concomitant need to centralise authority and resources, but also reflecting aspects of Bolshevik utopianism such as the attempt to abolish private property over the means of production in its entirety. Nationalisation of enterprises was accompanied by the establishment of a Supreme Council of the Economy (Vesenkha) that tried, in Lenin's words, to hold the entire economic life of the country in its fist. To feed the cities and the Red Army (established on 23 February 1918) a harsh system of grain expropriation operated against the peasantry. The new political system also became increasingly centralised, provoking the emergence of the Democratic Centralist opposition that demanded the introduction of the separation of powers within the regime itself, with greater autonomy for local soviets and lower-level party committees. This was a period characterised by an unstable mix of ideological extremism and pragmatism, reflected in 1920, for example, by the attempt to abolish money, which had become largely worthless anyway. With the Civil War effectively over by mid-1920, the momentum of Bolshevik ideological extremism continued for another few months, showing itself, for example, in the war against Poland in 1920 that sought to spread the revolution at the point of the Red Army's bayonets. The intensification of grain requisitioning, the militarisation of labour (a policy advocated by the commissar of war, Leon Trotsky), and the closure of urban markets provoked peasant uprisings (notably in Tambov region) and, most significantly, demands by workers at the Kronstadt naval base in the Gulf of Finland in March 1921 for 'soviets without Bolsheviks'.

### The New Economic Policy (NEP), March 1921–9

In response to the threat to the regime, Lenin at the Tenth Party Congress in March 1921 convinced his party to reverse its policies and make concessions to the peasantry. Compulsory grain deliveries were now replaced by a tax in kind, allowing peasants to sell grain surpluses in a restored market. A limited degree of producer autonomy was introduced as part of the New Economic Policy. To secure the regime's flanks in this 'retreat', however, Lenin imposed draconian discipline within the party through a 'ban on factions', adopted at the same congress. Although the Workers' Opposition since 1920 had been complaining about the curbs on free speech within the Party and had tried to broaden the base of the regime by restoring elements of the mass revolution by granting broad economic rights to the trade unions, they were now not only defeated but the very idea of opposition and legal debate within the Party was proscribed. The distinction between opposition *to* the revolution, by various forces outside the regime, and opposition *within* the system by those seeking to explore alternative policy options, was extinguished, and the door opened to Stalin's monocratic rule.

The establishment of the USSR in December 1922 reflected a peculiar type of ethno-federalism, where the 'union republics' of Ukraine, Belorussia (as it was known before changing its name to Belarus in 1991), the Russian Soviet Federated Soviet Republic (RSFSR) and the Transcaucasian Federation came together to form a new state whose legacy of dual federalism (with representation based on both territorial and ethno-federal principles) lives on to this day. By the time the USSR disintegrated in 1991 the number of union republics had risen to 15 (Figure 1.1). Lenin himself died in January 1924, and in the jockeying for power that followed Stalin proved the most adept at exploiting the political closure of the regime bequeathed by Lenin to secure his power against Trotsky, Nikolai Bukharin and other Bolshevik leaders. At first Stalin supported Bukharin's moderate policies within the framework of NEP, but by the late 1920s, despite the evident success of NEP in restoring industry and prosperity to the countryside, sought ways to go beyond its limitations. The regime was effectively hostage to the peasants' willingness to sell grain on the market. At the same time, already in 1924 Stalin had announced the idea of 'socialism in one country', effectively renouncing Lenin's internationalism and establishing the priority of Soviet state interests above those of the international revolution. Stalin insisted that Russia could not only *begin* the transition to socialism, but could go on to *complete* its construction by its own efforts. To do this required resources from the countryside to pay for the investment required.

### Revolution from above and Stalin's rule, 1929–53

Stalin's 'third revolution' (following those of 1905 and 1917) was directed initially against the peasantry, forcing them into collective farms (*kolkhozy*), making it easier to extract grain from them in order to fund industrialisation. The five-year plans for crash industrialisation were launched within the framework of the state planning agency, Gosplan. The principles of command and administer were now universalised to every

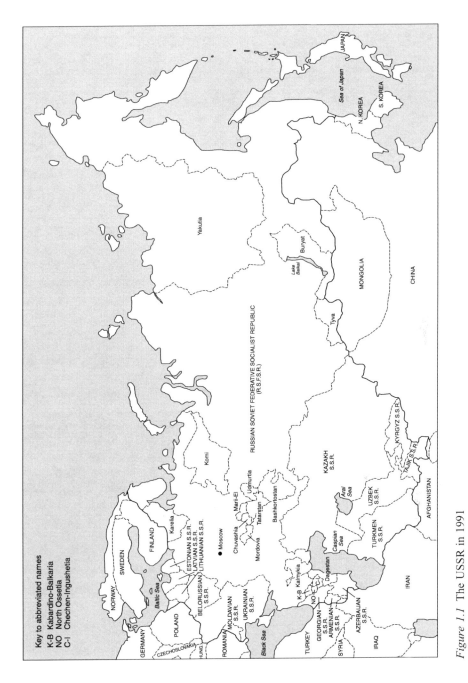

*Figure 1.1* The USSR in 1991

aspect of economic and social life, including the arts and personal life. The power of the secret police climaxed in the purges and great terror of 1937–8. Nevertheless, the rudiments of a modern industrial economy were built, although at great cost. The distortions of the Stalinist command economy, the destruction of the most active people in the countryside, the neglect of the service sector, the reduction of money to an internal accounting unit, and the relative isolation of the Soviet economy from world development, all left the post-communist Russian economy with severe structural problems. It was this economy, nevertheless, that provided the sinews of war to defeat the Nazi German invasion of 22 June 1941, and the USSR emerged victorious in May 1945 as part of the winning alliance with the Western powers. This alliance soon crumbled into the Cold War as it became clear that Soviet power had come to stay in the Eastern European countries liberated from fascism by the Red Army, but now to be subordinated to the great Soviet communist experiment.

### Khrushchev and attempts at reform, 1953–64

Stalin's death on 5 March 1953 left his successors with several major dilemmas. The country had been governed by the personalised rule of a morbidly suspicious dictator for several decades, and the institutions of governance, including the CPSU, had been reduced to little more than shells. In the economy, Stalinist command methods were clearly stifling innovation and preventing the system from moving beyond the primary phase of industrialisation to become more complex, intensive and technologically sophisticated. At the same time, millions remained incarcerated in the *gulag*, the term used by Alexander Solzhenitsyn to describe the great archipelago of labour camps that stretched across the country. In his 'Secret Speech' of 25 February 1956 at the Twentieth Party Congress Nikita Khrushchev began to lift the lid on some of Stalin's crimes, including the deportation of whole peoples in 1944 (the Chechens, the Ingush, the Balkars and others). Destalinisation recognised the need for change, but it was also an attempt to limit the change to a condemnation of the man, Joseph Vissarionovich Stalin, and not of the system that had allowed such a man to terrorise his own population for so long. In the event Khrushchev's reforms, conducted under the slogan of returning to the alleged original purity of the revolution under Lenin, were deeply ambiguous and flawed, if for no other reason than (as we have seen) the October revolution consisted of at least six levels that were in tension with each other. There was no original grail to which Stalin's successors could return, as Gorbachev was to discover later. Khrushchev's erratic style of rule, moreover, had so thoroughly alarmed the defenders of the elite revolution that in October 1964 they ousted him.

### Brezhnev and stagnation, 1964–82

Although in retrospect we view the long rule of Leonid Il'ich Brezhnev as General Secretary of the CPSU as a period of retrenchment and conservative reaction, some of the key features of the Khrushchev era were maintained, such as more attention to the needs of agriculture and the attempt to shift from producer to consumer goods. Nevertheless, most of the institutional innovations of the Khrushchev era, like the creation of some one hundred regional economic councils (*sovnarkhozy*) in an attempt to improve economic coordination, and initiatives to stimulate popular participation, were reversed: the Stalinist centralised ministries were restored and the stifling rule of local Party committees, where jobs were effectively for life, was restored. The 'stability of cadres' policy fostered complacency and corruption. Extensive patronage networks ultimately even came to challenge the prerogatives of the party in making personal appointments (the *nomenklatura* system). The Brezhnev years can be seen as the Soviet system at its most 'normal', with no system-threatening external or internal threats. The challenge represented by the 'Prague Spring' of 1968 to democratise Soviet-style communism by introducing 'socialism with a human face', where the party's legitimacy to rule was to be achieved through effective policies and not to be derived in perpetuity from the very act of seizing power, was crushed by the Soviet-led Warsaw Pact invasion of 20–1 August 1968. The crushing of reform communism in Czechoslovakia was followed by a period of 'normalisation', and the stifling of sources of innovation and dynamism was carried over into Soviet domestic policy. Soviet renewal and 'dissent' was persecuted with single-minded ruthlessness by Yuri Andropov, at the head of the Committee for State Security (KGB) from 1967. Soviet-style communism was condemned now to an extended period of entropy, with no self-sustaining mechanism of growth or regeneration allowed to revitalise the system. A type of neo-Stalinism was restored, without mass terror but where the suffocating rule of the petty bureaucracy inhibited initiative and imbued the whole era with an aura of stagnation (*zastoi*).

### The interregnum, 1982–5

Brezhnev's death in November 1982 provided his successor, Andropov, with the opportunity to experiment with ways of regenerating the system. His approach was that of 'authoritarian modernisation' employing the heavy-handed tactics of the secret policeman to defeat corruption and to kick-start the engine of economic growth. Fate, however, intervened to cut Andropov's innovations short, and his death in February 1983 allowed Konstantin Chernenko, one of the worst, oldest and most complacent of Brezhnev's accolytes, a brief period to restore the glories of the stagnation era before his own death in March 1985 inaugurated an exhilarating period of change.

### Perestroika

Gorbachev came to power committed to revitalising the Soviet Union. Within months he launched the programme that he called *perestroika* (restructuring), which in the space of six years moved from attempts to rationalise the system to a phase of liberalisation, and then on to a democratisation phase that began to transform the society and polity but that culminated in a final stage of disintegration. Once changes began they could not be constrained by regime-led reform, and by 1991 pressure for a radical change of system became overwhelming. The attempt in August 1991 by a group to hold back the tide of change precipitated the result that they had sought to avert: the dissolution of the communist system of government and, by the end of the year, the disintegration of the USSR.

*Perestroika* was the last great attempt at communist reform. Even before coming to power Gorbachev realised that the system was suffering from major problems, with declining economic growth, stultifying secrecy in scientific and political life, and with politics dominated by a corrupt elite. Visiting Canada in May 1983 Gorbachev shared his concerns with the Soviet ambassador there, Alexander Yakovlev, who would later become one of the architects of *perestroika*. Yakovlev reports that they spent hours discussing the disasters awaiting the Soviet Union if nothing was done: 'The most important common understanding ... was the idea that we could not live this way anymore.'[3] By starting a 'revolution within the revolution' Gorbachev hoped to save the essentials of the system, above all the leading role of the party and the planned economy. Greater responsiveness would be achieved by the use of *glasnost* (openness) and elements of competition through democratisation and limited marketisation.

Gorbachev believed that the old system remained viable; that it was a powerful motor that required only some fine tuning. *Perestroika*, he insisted, has 'been prompted by an awareness that the potential of socialism has been underutilized'.[4] The remoralising strain in *perestroika* was crucial. Gorbachev noted that the decision to launch *perestroika* was prompted in part by 'our troubled conscience'.[5] Despite the revolutionary language, his was essentially a reformist programme, to save the system rather than to transform it. In the event, his tragic fate was to act as the destroyer rather than the builder; the more that he tinkered with the system, the deeper the crisis. His policies became increasingly radical, in part to stay ahead of his opponents. His reform communism only exacerbated the problems of what was already a system in crisis, and worsened the legacy facing the post-communist governments. It fell to his successors in Russia and the other republics to rebuild economies and to nourish the fragile shoots of democracy that *perestroika* had encouraged. We shall examine below the three main phases of the old regime in its death agonies.

### *Rationalisation, 1985–6*

In this phase some of the themes of Andropov's authoritarian reform programme were revived. Andropov's management of the KGB informed him about the real state of affairs in the country, and in the fifteen months of his leadership he launched a campaign against corruption and attempted to tighten up on labour and social discipline. To Andropov's programme Gorbachev added the notion of *uskorenie* (acceleration), seeking to rejuvenate the economy by the vigorous application of old remedies. The government led by Nikolai Ryzhkov devoted yet more resources to investment and reinvestment (the improvement of old plant and facilities), imports were cut back and once again the needs of the long-suffering Soviet consumer were neglected. During this period grand and ultimately meaningless programmes were announced, such as the promise that by the year 2000 every Soviet citizen would have an apartment of their own. The programme of acceleration sought both to reform the economy and increase output at the same time, contradictory demands that failed to achieve either.[6] The misconceived anti-alcohol campaign launched at this time, inspired by the 'conservative reformer' Yegor Ligachev, led to the increased production of bootleg liquor (*samogon*) and devastating losses to the budget revenues of central and regional authorities.

Rationalisation, according to László Póti, entails 'a series of superficial, partial and non-conceptual measures that, however, indicate a certain degree of unintentional discontent with the system'.[7] The period of rationalisation entailed recognition of the problem accompanied by the belief that the solution lay within the framework of the existing system. Gorbachev, however, soon came to understand that more radical measures were required.

### Reform, January 1987–March 1990

The second phase of *perestroika* can be divided into two sub-periods: a discussion phase from January 1987 to the Nineteenth Party Conference (28 June–1 July 1988) marked by debates over *demokratizatsiya* (democratisation) and the revelations of *glasnost*, a period which proved to be the high point of *perestroika*; and an implementation phase from summer 1988 to March 1990, which proved far more difficult than the reform communists anticipated. This reform phase corresponds to the stage of liberalisation discussed in the literature on transitions.[8]

In the discussion period increasingly bold strategies for the political regeneration of the political system were debated in an attempt to tap the alleged hidden potential of the Soviet model of development. The January 1987 plenum of the Central Committee (CC) of the CPSU marked a watershed in the move away from authoritarian towards democratic reform. The plenum called for the extension of competitive elections in the workplace, the soviets and in the Party itself. In June 1987 a further plenum of the CC adopted a plan for the economic transformation of the country that focused on greater autonomy for enterprises and increased rights for workers to elect their own managers. Rather than strengthening the system, however, the revelations made possible by *glasnost* about the crimes of past and the inadequacies of the present only undermined the legitimacy of the regime as a whole.

The Nineteenth Party Conference in June–July 1988 marked the transition to the implementation of programmes of reform. Attempts were made to formulate a grand strategy of political reform to modernise the entire system within the framework of one-party democracy and one-Party parliamentarianism. Gorbachev's strategy was based on the CPSU retaining a predominant role;[9] but the Party was now to guide rather than to lead. The overall principle aim was to create a 'socialist legal state', with the separation of powers and a revived legislature. In December 1988 the USSR Supreme Soviet created a three-chamber Congress of People's Deputies (CPD), two chambers of which (the Soviet of the Union and the Soviet of Nationalities) were to be chosen in multi-candidate elections, while the third (what can be called the Soviet of Representatives) was to be made up of delegates from social organisations, including 100 guaranteed seats for the Communist Party. The full Congress was to meet twice a year while current parliamentary business was to be conducted by a smaller Supreme Soviet drawn from the CPD. This strange parliamentary model, devised by Gorbachev's old friend from his Moscow University days Anatoly Luk'yanov, represented a return to the dual system of a large and rather irrelevant Congress and smaller Central Executive Committee (VtsIK) that operated in the early Soviet years before abolished by Stalin in 1936.

The semi-free elections of March 1989 for the new assembly saw the defeat of many communist officials and the return of around 400 democrats out of a total of 2,250 CPD deputies (see Table 1.1). At the first convocation of the CPD in May 1989 Gorbachev was elected chairman of its new 542-member Supreme Soviet, a post he had achieved without facing the electorate at any stage. Power began to shift from the Party to the protofipresidency, but the lack of electoral legitimacy would ultimately cripple Gorbachev's ambitions. The Congress was the scene of vigorous debates, televised live

*Table 1.1* Election to the USSR Congress of People's Deputies, 26 March 1989

---

*Background*

- There were 2,250 seats, but only 1,500 were contested, the rest (750) were reserved for social organisations.
- The CPSU was allocated 100 seats, and the CPSU Central Committee drew up a list of exactly 100 (including Gorbachev).
- 85% of the candidates were communists, whereas in the previous election for the old Supreme Soviet they had comprised only 71.4%. Thus 'democratisation' at this time had the paradoxical result of increasing the proportion of communists.

*Electoral system*

- Candidates had to obtain an absolute majority of the votes cast. If none achieved the threshold of 50%, a run-off election was held between the two candidates with the most votes. The second vote usually took place a fortnight after the first ballot.

*Result*

- CPSU 1,931, non-CPSU 319.

*Organisation*

- In June 1989 the Congress elected a permanent Supreme Soviet of 542 members.
- The CPSU gained 475 seats, non-CPSU 67.
- The Supreme Soviet was divided into two equal chambers with 271 seats apiece, the Council of the Union and the Council of the Nationalities.

---

to an enthralled nation, and appeared to mark the onset of effective parliamentary politics. The CPD and its Supreme Soviet passed a significant body of reformist legislation, with new laws on freedom of conscience and religious belief, and freedom of the press. The first steps were taken towards creating a law-governed state (*Rechtsstaat*), if not a democracy, something that distinguished *perestroika* from the rest of Soviet history. The structure of the new parliament, however, was deeply flawed – perhaps intentionally so. The Congress was unwieldy and, lacking the necessary committee structure, could not focus on key issues or set a coherent legislative agenda, while the Supreme Soviet became a permanent forum for wide-ranging debates but failed to establish the necessary routines for effective legislative activity (adoption *and* implementation) or oversight over the executive.

The attempt to reconcile representative democracy with a leading role for the CPSU only rendered government incoherent. One-Party democracy was a contradiction in terms, and the attempt to achieve the 'socialist pluralism of opinions' was challenged by the growth of genuine political pluralism in society. The very existence of the Soviet state in its old borders was challenged by the Baltic republics and others. Already in the final speech to the First Soviet Congress, Andrei Sakharov (an outstanding nuclear physicist who had worked to develop the Soviet atom bomb, but who had then become increasingly critical of the lack of political freedom in the system and consequently spent several years in internal exile in Gorky, now Nizhny Novgorod), outlined a 'Decree on Power' that called for the repeal of the Party's constitutionally guaranteed right to a leading role, enshrined in Article 6 of the 1977 Soviet constitution (see p. 54), and sought to invert the relationship between the centre and the localities to guarantee that the laws of the former could only be implemented in the latter with their explicit authorisation.[10] The Decree on Power represented a revolutionary programme for the liquidation of the power of the *apparatchiki* (full-time Communist Party officials), insisting that:

> Any anti-legal interference by political parties, party-political organs and other social organisations in the work of state power and administration, the economic and socio-cultural activity of state enterprises, institutions and organisations must cease immediately and absolutely decisively.[11]

The Decree sought to separate the Communist Party from state management, and in particular tried to end the practice whereby local Party leaders were simultaneously chairmen of local soviets. Although challenged in the courts by Gorbachev, several local soviet chairmen resigned their Party posts.[12] In the great majority of cases, however, local soviet leaders right up to the coup of August 1991 were members of the local Party committee, and in numerous cases local Party leader as well.

The period was marked by accumulating failures, above all in the economic sphere. Reform plan followed reform plan, but none were consistently implemented. The country became increasingly ungovernable as Ryzhkov's relatively conservative government was unable to implement its own version of reform, in part because of Gorbachev's lack of support, while more radical alternatives were equally unacceptable. The emergence of an active workers' movement in the form of miners' strikes from June 1989 marked the point at which Gorbachev's strategy of reform from above was transformed into a revolution from below.

The reforms of this period can be defined as 'the substantial extension of the rationalisation measures in depth and rate with increased awareness of the tensions of the system, but still within that framework'.[13] Gorbachev's attempt to implement reforms within the framework of the one-party system proved unfeasible; the strategy of reform communism known as *perestroika* was not implemented because it sought to achieve contradictory goals. The period was characterised by a mass of contradictions, and it soon became obvious that one-party parliamentarianism was self-defeating. A 'socialist' legal state appeared to be an obstacle to the development of a genuine legal state in which the rights of citizens could be defended by law and in which powers were separated and defined. The reform consensus that existed in 1985 was undermined; by implementing self-defeating reforms, Gorbachev undermined the very concept of reform itself.

### Transformation, March 1990–August 1991

The third phase was characterised by the dissolution of Gorbachev's definition of *perestroika* as a party-led programme of reform and culminated in the coup of August 1991. From mid-1989 miners' strikes had demonstrated that new independent forces were entering the stage of Soviet politics. The 'vodka' riots of the New Year of 1990 were followed by a wave of demonstrations and the dismissal of unpopular regional Party leaders in Volgograd, Murmansk, Sverdlovsk, Tyumen and elsewhere under the pressure of mass protest. The politics of resentment against elite privileges was as strong as the hunger for democratic ideals.[14] This wave of protest culminated in a demonstration of perhaps half a million people in Moscow on 4 February 1990 calling for multi-party democracy.

The revolutions in Eastern Europe in the last months of 1989, following the inauguration of the first post-war non-communist government in Poland led by Tadeusz Mazowiecki in August 1989, swept away the communist regimes in East Germany, Czechoslovakia, Bulgaria and Romania. Afraid that this might happen to them too, the Central Committee plenum of 5–7 February 1990 agreed to modify Article 6 to remove the constitutional monopoly of the CPSU on political power. This was confirmed by the third (emergency) meeting of the CPD on 14 March, which the next day strengthened Gorbachev's presidential powers. Thus the era of one-Party rule, that had in effect lasted since October 1917, came to an end: free elections were introduced, the half-truths of *glasnost* gave way to genuine freedom of speech, and Party *perestroika* gave way to presidential *perestroika*. The transformation of the political system at last allowed liberalisation to give way to genuine democratisation.

This phase of *perestroika* could not be anything but a transitional period. It was characterised by intensified conflicts over economic policy, national issues and political strategies. Gorbachev had been able to consolidate his power faster than any previous Soviet leader, yet he still faced formidable opposition. Above all, the very forces he hoped to use to implement his reforms, the Party and the ministerial bureaucracy, resisted his policies, while he himself gave conflicting signals of what precisely these policies should be. In the early years of *perestroika* Gorbachev had been able to mobilise a reform coalition of groups (including the military and the KGB) who, if not welcoming change, realised that some reform of the economy and the political system was essential if the Soviet Union was to meet the challenge of technological and social modernisation and to maintain its status in the international system. However, by 1990 it was clear that the reform coalition was disintegrating and Gorbachev's own brand of communist reformism was losing support. Political life was becoming increasingly polarised, and Gorbachev's centrism was eroded from both sides.

A group of diehard reactionaries emerged, warning that Gorbachev's policies would lead to the betrayal of socialism and the destruction of the country. Already the letter in March 1988 by a Leningrad chemistry teacher, Nina Andreeva, had expressed the anger of the old generation. It urged a 'balanced' assessment of Stalinism and condemned the classless 'humanism' espoused by *perestroika*.[15] Conservatives like Ligachev were willing to accept some change, but were adamantly opposed to transforming the fundamentals of the Soviet system. The growing democratic movement also now diverged from *perestroika*'s centrist reformism and was united on the need to transform the old structures of Soviet power and to introduce the basic features of a modern democratic system. Looming over all of these, however, was the growing unrest in the republics. The three Baltic republics (Estonia, Latvia and Lithuania) had never reconciled themselves to their incorporation into the Soviet Union in 1940 as part of the deal between Stalin and Hitler in August 1939 (the Nazi-Soviet Pact, and its various secret protocols), and now frustration with *perestroika* encouraged them to think of secession. Moldova had also been a victim of the Nazi-Soviet pact, while the Caucasian republics of Armenia and Georgia still hankered after the independence that they had lost as a result of Soviet invasions in 1921 (see Chapter 2).

The democratic and national currents critical of Gorbachev's policies in 1988 found an individual around which opposition could focus. Already at the Twenty-seventh Party Congress in February–March 1986 Boris Yeltsin, at the time Party leader in Sverdlovsk *oblast* (region) and soon to be transferred to head the Moscow Party Organisation, had been the first top Party leader openly to condemn the privileges of the Party elite, and his stress on social justice earned him the soubriquet of a populist. Yeltsin's attack on the leading conservative, Ligachev, at the CC plenum on 21 October 1987 signalled the end of the monolithic rule of the CPSU and resulted in his dismissal as head of the Party in Moscow. His open confrontation with Ligachev, broadcast to millions on television, at the Nineteenth Party Conference on 1 July 1988 revealed the deep splits in the Party.[16] In the elections of March 1989 a tired and angry people gave him overwhelming (89 per cent of the vote) support in Moscow. In the Congress he was one of the leaders of the 400-strong Interregional Deputy's Group advocating the radicalisation of the reforms.

*Perestroika*-style institutions were duplicated in each of the USSR's 15 republics. The elections to the Russian CPD of 4 March 1990 were relatively more democratic (although by no means free) than the Soviet elections of 1989, with nomination through social organisations dropped and district registration meetings, used by officials in the 1989 Soviet elections to screen out undesirable candidates, abolished (see Chapter 5). Democratic groups achieved significant victories, assisted by the Democratic Russia electoral bloc established in January 1990 with branches in all major Russian towns. Some 20 per cent of the seats in the Russian Congress were won by democrats,[17] taking 63 out of 65 seats assigned to Moscow in the Russian parliament, and 25 out of 34 in Leningrad.[18] The economist Gavriil Popov came to head the Moscow Soviet, in Leningrad the law professor Anatoly Sobchak came to power, and in Sverdlovsk (Yeltsin's home town), the democrats took control. There was a marked regional dynamic to the elections, with half of the establishment candidates North of Moscow's latitude suffering defeat, whereas South of that line hardly any. The pattern of the 1990s whereby voters above the 55th parallel tended to vote for reformists while those in the South for conservatives was already established.

As long as the struggle was between a decaying old regime and a rising new order, the democrats could muster a majority against the communist old guard. Even before August 1991 the second and third echelons of the ruling elite began to throw in their lot with the rising alternative as the rule of the *nomenklatura* (the class of people appointed by or deriving their status from the Communist Party), ebbed away: 'workers and intelligentsia, collective farmers and military officers, militiamen and former dissidents, Party secretaries in enterprises and non-party informals', were all moving over to the other side of the barricades against the higher officials of state and Party who, because of the distorted electoral process of 1990, were elected in almost equal numbers to the Congress.[19] The 'new class' of which Milovan Djilas had spoken was finally coming into its own;[20] born under Stalin, freed from the terror under Khrushchev, given job security under Brezhnev, harangued by Gorbachev in the cause of a restructured humane socialism, this class now cast aside the final shreds of communist ideology and claimed the role of the universal (middle) class of modernity.

## The emergence of Russia

Russian predominance in the USSR did not necessarily mean that the Soviet state governed in the interests of Russia – a point made with great force by 'dissidents' like Solzhenitsyn and then taken up by the democratic insurgency in the late 1980s with Yeltsin at their head.[21] In institutional terms the RSFSR had been dissolved into the amorphous USSR. The other fourteen republics had been endowed with the attributes of statehood in the form of republican governments, parliaments and Communist Party organisations, and had developed distinct national identities even within the centralised framework. Russia, however, lacked its own Academy of Sciences, its KGB, its Ministry of Internal Affairs (MVD), its trade union or Komsomol organisations, its own national television and radio stations or even its own national capital. Its Council of Ministers was firmly subordinated to the Soviet government and lacked many of the ministries and departments present in other republics.

Above all, until 1990 the RSFSR had no Party organisation of its own, even though it made up 58 per cent (10.6 million) of the CPSU's membership of nineteen million members. A separate Russian Party organisation had been abolished with the adoption of the Union Treaty in December 1922 setting up the USSR, when Lenin had argued that the threat of 'great Russian chauvinism' would thus be diminished. The problem of the political representation of Russians themselves was ignored until Khrushchev in 1956 established a Russian Bureau, but this also was abolished in 1966. Russian communists lacked direct representation and were managed by All-Union Party bodies,[22] reinforcing the view in other republics that 'Soviet' meant 'Russian' while adding to the sense of grievance felt in Russia itself. As Ruslan Khasbulatov, the speaker of the Russian parliament in 1991–3, notes: 'The lack of rights and the grievous condition of Russia itself was a result of the deliberate policy of the central administration, which "dissolved" the republic in All-Union Party, economic and administrative structures.'[23] The history and traditions of Russia and its peoples were distorted and specifically Russian interests overlain by those of the Soviet system.

Already towards the end of *perestroika*, in response to stirrings of national consciousness, attempts were made to give shape to the aspirations for Russian statehood. On 27 July 1989 Russia's last communist prime minister, Alexander Vlasov, informed the Russian Supreme Soviet of plans to give greater economic autonomy to Russia, reminding deputies that Russia accounted for 60 per cent of Soviet GNP yet less than half of the wealth produced by Russia was left in the republic, whereas other union republics retained virtually all the national income they produced. He informed deputies of plans to increase Russia's sovereignty by the creation of new institutions that existed at the All-Union level but not yet at the republican level. These included a separate Russian Academy of Sciences, various social institutions, ministries, as well as a new television channel to cater to Russian needs.[24] The Leningrad Party organisation on 26 August called for the creation of a separate Russian Party organisation, but warned against any attempts to convert the CPSU into a confederation of republican parties.[25] In response to these demands in December 1989 a 'Russian Bureau' of the CPSU was once again created, headed by Gorbachev himself. This half-measure satisfied few since the structural asymmetries between Russia and the other republics remained. It was this that provided the impetus for the establishment of Russian sovereignty.

At the first meeting of the Soviet Congress in May 1989 the idea that Russia itself could leave the Union was first mooted. In an impassioned speech the writer Valentin Rasputin spoke of environmental and moral issues and warned of the growing anti-Russian sentiments in some of the other republics:

> Russophobia is spreading in the Baltic and Georgia, and it has penetrated other republics as well ... Anti-Soviet slogans are combined with anti-Russian ones, and

emissaries from Lithuania and Estonia travel about with such slogans, seeking to create a united front.

In such circumstances, he warned the non-Russian republics:

> Perhaps it is Russia which should leave the Union, since you hold her responsible for all your misfortunes ... Without fear of being called nationalists, we [Russians] could then pronounce the word *Russian* and speak openly about our national self-awareness; we could end the mass corruption of the soul of our youth, and we could finally create our own Academy of Sciences.[26]

Such sentiments inspired deputies at the first convocation of the Russian Congress on 29 May 1990 to elect Yeltsin, after three ballots and by a margin of only four votes, chairman of the Russian parliament.[27] Gorbachev had bitterly opposed such an outcome, not trusting Yeltsin's political judgment and fearing that he would use Russian aspirations to further his own ambitions. His concern was justified, and henceforth the search for union-wide solutions to the country's problems would give way to each republic trying to find its own way. It was clear that Gorbachev's attempts to revive the Soviet system through reform communism had failed; the union republics of the USSR began to take responsibility for their own affairs. The blockage on democratic breakthrough at the all-union centre encouraged the insurgency against the communist regime to take on national forms.

The most important manifestation of this was the adoption by the Russian legislature on 12 June 1990, by an overwhelming majority, of the Declaration of State Sovereignty of the RSFSR, whose principles were to lie at the basis of post-communist government in Russia. The Declaration stated that Russia was 'a sovereign state, created by historically united nations'; that 'RSFSR sovereignty is the unique and necessary condition for the existence of Russian statehood'; that 'the RSFSR retains for itself the right of free departure from the USSR'; and stressed the priority of the Russian constitution and laws over Soviet legislation.[28] The proclamation of state sovereignty, in Zverev's words, was 'psychologically rooted in the Russian people's unwillingness to carry the burden of empire'.[29] To paraphrase Stalin, Russia's insurgency was national in form but democratic in content. Gorbachev took a very different view, arguing later that 'Yeltsin's irresponsible actions' triggered the ensuing avalanche of sovereignty declarations – known as the 'parade of sovereignties' and the accompanying 'war of the laws' – that precipitated the disintegration of the Soviet Union.[30]

Gorbachev and others insist that the Declaration laid the foundations for the disintegration of the USSR. This interpretation is categorically rejected by Khasbulatov (at the time Yeltsin's deputy chairman of the Russian Supreme Soviet), who insisted 'The Declaration [did] not, in essence, deal with sovereignty at all, but only with decentralisation of the excessively centralised Union state.' He noted how much remained under Soviet control: 'the combined armed forces, common rail network, airlines, defence' and much more, 'practically all the basic functions which make a state a state'.[31] This may well be true, but the Declaration acted as a spur to the other union republics (as well as to the autonomous republics within Russia) to adopt their own sovereignty declarations. By the autumn of 1990 the 'war of the laws' between the union authorities and components of the USSR was in full spate, ultimately destroying the state. The assertion that in his struggle with Gorbachev Yeltsin destroyed the Soviet Union exaggerates the role of personalities in the titanic shift of geopolitical relations in Eurasia.

The centre of political life gradually shifted to Russia and the other republics as politics became 'renationalised'. The creation in June 1990 of the hardline Communist Party of the RSFSR (CP RSFSR), headed by Ivan Polozkov, finally gave separate representation for CPSU members in Russia; but it was also an attempt by the conservatives to build a separate power base to thwart Gorbachev's more radical reforms. In the event, they achieved little except to encourage Yeltsin and the Russian parliament to redouble their efforts to strengthen the Russian state as an instrument in the struggle against the Soviet Party regime. In 1990 Russia also gained its own Academy of Sciences, trade union and Komsomol organisations, and in May 1991 a Russian republic KGB was established. The struggle against the communist monopoly increasingly focused on 'democracy in one republic' rather than on Gorbachev's apparently futile attempts to democratise the union and its institutions. The Declaration of State Sovereignty of 12 June 1990, as noted, marked the turning point in relations between the republics and the union as Russian statehood was formally reborn and Russian laws were to take precedence over union legislation.

The Decree on Power that followed achieved what the democrats had earlier hoped that the Soviet Congress would do, namely assume the full powers of the state. The decree stipulated the separation of the Communist Party from the government in Russia and outlawed the 'party-political system of leadership' in the state, in enterprises, the KGB and the army. A resolution adopted at the same time forbade leading state officials to hold other posts, including those in political or social organisations.[32] On 24 October 1990 the Russian parliament adopted a law stipulating that RSFSR legislation would take priority over USSR laws, and that all Soviet laws had to be ratified by Russia's Supreme Soviet.[33] Russia became a state-in-waiting, and thus rather than a democratic movement taking the lead against the dissolving communist system, this role was taken by a nascent state. State institutions rather than social organisations took the lead in the revolution against the old order in Russia. This was to have momentous consequences for the later development of democracy in Russia.

Other republics followed Russia's lead, and on 16 July Ukraine adopted an extremely radical declaration of sovereignty, passed unanimously by its parliament, calling for respect for human rights, multi-party democracy, and a separate national army. The precise meaning and juridical status of these declarations remained unclear, but they demonstrated that Gorbachev's attempts to negotiate a new 'Union Treaty' for the USSR would have to take into account the aspirations of the republics for autonomy. Declarations of sovereignty were not restricted to union republics but began to be adopted by autonomous republics and even by regions and boroughs in Moscow and other cities. The 'war of the laws' revealed just how far the old system had decayed. As the Soviet administrative system came apart at the seams, both the republics and the centre claimed priority for their laws, leading in most cases to the implementation of neither.

The nascent Russian state became the main opposition to the decaying Soviet regime, and as Khasbulatov noted, 'we find ourselves in an unprecedented situation in world history: a legitimate government in opposition'.[34] Gorbachev had planned a gradual liberalisation of the regime, yet his hesitancy in relinquishing the concept of Party rule, and indeed his failure to split the CPSU at the Twenty-eighth Party Congress in July 1990 and place an avowedly Social Democratic party at the head of the democratic transformation of the USSR, meant that as power leaked away from the old 'administrative-command' system (as the Soviet order was dubbed by democrats at this time) it was absorbed by the republics. As in 1917, the many layers of the revolution interacted in unpredictable ways. There was an upsurge of civic activity as a plethora of social organisations, known as *neformaly* (informals), were established. The rebirth of civil society was accompanied by the growth of pathological aspects of 'uncivil society', including virulently nation-alist and racist movements. At the same time, the remnants of official structures used the new freedom to engage in the spontaneous privatisation of state property. Solnick likens the 'breakdown of hierarchy' at this time to a 'bank run' as Party officials began to prepare their 'golden parachutes' by 'stealing the state'.[35] In most republics, moreover, old communist elites managed to convert themselves into nationalists and continued to rule as national leaders.

## Popular insurgency and regime decay

Despite a host of difficulties, such as complex registration laws and harassment, numer-ous parties were established in this period of insurgency. Gorbachev's 'socialist pluralism of opinions' was now superseded by structured political conflict and the veritable rebirth of politics.[36] The problem soon became one not of the lack of alternatives but the sheer abundance of new parties that failed to coalesce into a coherent force that could challenge the CPSU or provide the basis for viable government.[37] The decline of the Interre-gional Group of Deputies prefigured the decline of the USSR CPD itself. The democratic deputies, led by Yeltsin and Sakharov, were greatly outnumbered by the rest of the 2,250 deputies, whom the radical democrat Yuri Afanas'ev dubbed the 'aggressively obedient majority'.[38] The group was weakened by splits over national issues, with the Baltic del-egation barely participating at all; and over tactics – the degree to which reform should remain within the one-Party system. By late 1990 they had lost direction and coherence, especially with the death of Sakharov in December 1989.

Gorbachev's inability to convert the CPSU into a genuine instrument of reform was one of the main reasons for the failure of *perestroika*.[39] Although the party had given up its monopoly of power in March 1990, this did not indicate a sudden conversion to democracy. As late as March 1991 the CPSU was still giving orders to government ministries, a year after having given up its constitutional 'leading role'. The old regime at this time tried to co-opt the resurgent Russian nationalism for its own purposes, but succeeded only in stimulating reactionary Russian nationalism and awakening the aspira-tions to statehood of some of the minorities within Russia. The CPSU sponsored various 'front' organisations, like the United Front of Workers (OFT), which tried to appeal to the loyalist instincts of blue-collar workers, and sought to influence the new parties established after March 1990. The USSR had moved from one-Party rule to a limbo of non-party governance as the CPSU refused to move out of the way to allow new forces to take over. The Communist Party still claimed to be the only force that could fill the political vacuum, although it was now as fragmented as the rest of society.

One of the cardinal principles that had kept the Party together was democratic centralism, an institutional theory that suggested participation of lower bodies in the deci-sions of higher ones but which in practice imposed a rigid hierarchical subordination.[40] Lenin's 1921 'ban on factions', as we have seen, prohibited horizontal contacts between Party cells. Gorbachev now weakened this element of democratic centralism, allowing an upsurge in factional activity. A Democratic Platform emerged calling for the radical democratisation of the CPSU, while the Marxist Platform demanded a return to a purer form of Marxian socialism.[41] The Party also began to split into its constituent national parts. In December 1989 the Lithuanian Communist Party under Algirdas Brazauskas broke away from the national CPSU in the belief that only by allying with domestic nationalists could it hope to retain a voice in Lithuanian politics. At the Twenty-eighth Party Congress in July 1990 Gorbachev had to fight hard to have his draft democratic programme of the Party adopted, with the CP RSFSR distinguishing itself by its dogged conservatism. The Party seemed constitutionally unable to reform itself, and thus far from being in the vanguard of reform it lagged behind and indeed obstructed change.

The Central Committee of the CPSU, although much changed at the Congress, remained solidly conservative. At the same Congress the Politburo, a body that had in effect been the supreme government of the country, was radically transformed. Membership shifted from professional-territorial to largely territorial representation, comprised now of the heads of the republican and some regional Party organisations, and certain key officials. At a stroke the Politburo was reduced in power, and the Party was crippled as a functioning political machine. As the linchpin of the Soviet political system, the CPSU had always been more than a political party. It was the Party's full-time apparatus, staffed by half a million *apparatchiki*, that was the effective core both of the Party and the state, while a million more were on the Party's teaching staff in the dense network of Party schools and departments of 'social science' in colleges. The ability of the rest of the membership to influence policy was severely limited by democratic centralism. During *perestroika* Gorbachev tried to broaden the influence of the rank-and-file by democratising the Party through the use of elections, and at the same time sought to weaken the grip of the Party bureaucracy by strengthening state bodies and the legislature.[42]

The CPSU's popularity fell sharply from its peak at the height of *perestroika*, and by May 1990 only 18.8 per cent of the electorate would have voted for it if there had been elections.[43] The Party began for the first time to suffer a financial crisis.[44] Party members themselves were disillusioned, and only 27 per cent stated that if given a choice they would join a second time.[45] Party membership peaked in October 1988 when it stood at 18.9 million members and 416,000 candidates, a total of 19.3 million.[46] In 1989 for the first time since the purges membership actually fell;[47] in the last quarter of 1989 alone 279,000 communists failed to renew their membership, and another 670,000 failed to do so by 1 April 1990.[48] Communists in Armenia and Azerbaijan left *en masse*, and few in the rest of the country felt moved to join what was increasingly perceived as a discredited organisation. Mass defections saw membership fall to some 15 million by August 1991.

By the time of the August 1991 coup the CPSU had lost its ideological and organisational integrity and had failed in its attempts to convert itself from a state structure to a campaigning political organisation, that is, to become once again a normal political party.[49] The CPSU was marginalised, its membership was falling, it was splitting into various factions, and communist dominance was challenged by numerous informal groups and movements, accompanied by the emergence of genuine pluralism in intellectual and political life. The Communist Party was by definition an expansive and monopolistic body that had left civil society, the proper sphere for political parties, after October 1917 and had occupied the state; it was now faced with the prospect of being ousted from its strongholds in the factories, the army and the KGB to become a normal parliamentary party subject to the vagaries of electoral politics. Gorbachev on this crucial issue could not follow his usual centrist position, because the centre had disappeared and he had to come off the fence: either Party rule or genuine multi-party politics. His failure to choose in time only protracted the crisis, preventing either side from taking the initiative and weakening his own position.

Gorbachev's economic policy was marked by similar equivocations. By 1990 he had broadly decided in favour of establishing a market economy, but like most of the population he was unwilling to face the hardships – or the political price – that would inevitably accompany the transition. Gorbachev's failure in September 1990 to support the plan proposed by the team led by Stanislav Shatalin, Grigory Yavlinsky (a young economist who served as deputy chair of the RSFSR Council of Ministers from July to November 1990) and Yegor Gaidar, envisaging a rapid transition to the market in '500 days', was in retrospect probably the moment when the USSR passed the point of no return and could no longer be held together. The plan called for an end to price controls, fiscal and monetary discipline to contain inflation, and rapid privatisation. It envisaged the conversion of the USSR into an economic union with only loose political ties between the constituent republics. Under pressure from conservatives, the plan was rejected by Gorbachev in favour of a much-diluted programme proposed by a different team. Yeltsin had supported the Shatalin plan, and its failure led him to launch Russia's own economic reforms in November 1990. It appeared that no single economic programme could work for all of the USSR; but if every republic had to devise its own reform plan, then what was the point of Gorbachev's 'renewed union'?

Communist hardliners now launched the so-called 'winter offensive' of 1990–1. Isolated from the radical democrats and fearing the hardline reactionaries, Gorbachev became hostage to the conservatives. This was reflected in personnel policy. The liberal Vadim Bakatin was replaced as minister of the interior (MVD) by the pugnacious Boris Pugo, and on 27 December 1990 Gorbachev forced parliament to accept Gennady Yanaev as his vice-president. Even the usually compliant Soviet legislature, now chaired by Luk'yanov, baulked at ratifying the appointment of an official who epitomised the stagnation of the Soviet bureaucratic system. On 20 December 1990 Eduard Shevardnadze, who had been foreign minister since July 1985, resigned, warning darkly of the threat of a coup.

The conservative offensive was not limited to displacing liberal officials in Moscow but attempted to crush the nationalists in the republics. The low point of this period came with the storming of the Lithuanian TV building on 13 January 1991, in which 15 people were killed. Gorbachev's role in these events is still not clear, publicly defending the ministers responsible for the bloodshed but denying any responsibility. He might well have gone along with what turned out to be a dress rehearsal for the events of August, and then at the last minute repudiated the attempt by the conservatives to seize power in Lithuania. In economic policy this period was if anything more catastrophic than what had come before. In December 1990 Ryzhkov was replaced as prime minister by Valentin Pavlov, a man who had earlier been minister of finance and had almost single-handedly destroyed the rouble by printing money as fast as the budget deficit grew. He now set about destroying the whole economy by his refusal to countenance a rapid advance to the market and by his poorly planned currency reform and price rises.

At the time of the crisis of January 1991 Yeltsin had not hesitated to rush to the Baltic countries to declare his support for their independence. While often seen as no more than a ploy in his struggle with Gorbachev, Yeltsin's action nevertheless represented a remarkable repudiation of Moscow's traditional empire-building role and created the conditions for the relatively peaceful dissolution of what now came to be known as the Soviet 'empire'. Gorbachev's attempt to relegitimise the authority of the Soviet Union in the following months by renegotiating the federation was always a fragile affair, having been delayed too long while he had been distracted by the excitement of foreign affairs and the struggle with his Party opponents. The referendum on 17 March 1991 on a renewed union gave a notably ambiguous response (see Table 1.2). While 71.3 per cent of the RSFSR's 79.4 million turnout (75.1 per cent of the total electorate) voted 'yes' to a renewed federation, almost exactly the same number (69.6 per cent) voted in favour of a second question added to the ballot in Russia, the creation of a Russian presidency, which implicitly challenged the postulates of the first.

The counter-attack of the conservatives was halted by a renewed wave of labour unrest. On 1 March 1991 a national strike of miners began with economic and political demands, including calls for the resignation of Gorbachev and Pavlov, and the dissolution

---

*Table 1.2* Referendum on 'renewed union' and a presidency in Russia, 17 March 1991

*The question*

- Voters were asked: 'Do you consider necessary the preservation of the Union of Soviet Socialist Republics as a renewed federation of equal sovereign republics, in which the rights and freedom of the individual of any nationality will be fully guaranteed?'.

*Participation*

- Six republics boycotted the referendum: Armenia, Georgia, Moldova, and the three Baltic republics of Estonia, Latvia, Lithuania.
- This signified the *de facto* division of the USSR into at least two parts.

*Turnout and results (USSR)*

- In the USSR 147 million voted, 75.4% of the electorate.
- Of those who voted, 112 million supported the idea of a 'renewed union'.
- Thus 76.2% of turnout supported the union.

*Turnout and results (Russia)*

- In Russia out of a total registered electorate of 105.6 million, 79.7 million took part, 75.4%.
- Of those who voted, 56,860,783 voted 'yes' and 21,030,753 voted 'no'.
- Thus 71.3% supported the union and 26.4% did not.
- 2.3% of ballots were spoiled.

*On whether to establish a presidency in Russia*

- A supplementary question was added in Russia: 'Do you consider necessary the introduction of the post of president of the RSFSR, elected by universal suffrage?'
- 69.85 % of the ballot voted for Russia to have a president.
- Of those who took part, 28% voted against a presidency for Russia and for a renewed union.
- 23.4% voted for a Russian president but against the union.
- 45.6% voted for a president and for the union.
- 2.1% of votes were spoiled.

---

*Sources*: *Izvestiya*, 26 March 1991, p. 2; *Pravda*, 27 March 1991; M. Gorbachev, *Soyuz mozhno bylo sokhranit'* (Moscow, 'Aprel'-85', 1995), pp. 148–9.

of the USSR Supreme Soviet. Many mines continued to strike until early May 1991, and they were joined by workers in other industries in Belarus in April. All of this warned Gorbachev that alliance with the conservatives eroded his position. At the opening on 28 March of the Third Russian (Emergency) Congress of People's Deputies, called by the conservatives in an attempt to oust Yeltsin, Gorbachev ordered 50,000 MVD troops into Moscow to prevent a demonstration in support of Yeltsin, yet perhaps a quarter of a million people defied his ban. Gorbachev at this point turned once again to the reformists, and in the 'nine-plus-one' agreement of 23 April at his dacha at Novo-Ogarevo conceded greater power to the leaders of the nine republics involved and an accelerated transition to the market economy. Yeltsin went on to pacify the miners, and announced that the mines were to be transferred to Russia. The new Union Treaty between the republics of what had been the Soviet Union would be built from the bottom up, founded on the sovereignty of the republics and relegating Gorbachev and the central government to a secondary role. The treaty was formalised on 23 July 1991 and was to have been signed by the republics on 20 August.

At the same time Yeltsin was strengthening his position. On 12 June 1991 Russia for the first time in its history chose its leader in a popular vote (see Table 1.3), with Alexander Rutskoi (the leader of the Communists for Democracy faction that had emerged at the Third CPD) selected as his vice-president. On the same day Popov was elected mayor of Moscow with 65 per cent of the vote; in Leningrad Sobchak was elected mayor with 69 per cent (soon recruiting Vladimir Putin as his adviser and later deputy), and at the same time 54 per cent voted to rename the city St Petersburg. At his inauguration on 10 July 1991 Yeltsin proclaimed his readiness to embark on a far-reaching democratic transformation and the fundamental renewal of the Russian Federation (RF). He supported the plan for a restructured union and promised cooperation with the other republics, but at the same time he stressed the sovereignty of the RSFSR

*Table 1.3* First Russian presidential election, 12 June 1991

*Turnout and participation*

- The total number of registered electors was 106,484,518 and turnout was 74.7%.
- With the exception of Tatarstan, where a boycott of the elections was organised resulting in a 40% turnout, participation ranged from 65% in Moscow and St Petersburg to 85% in Kursk and Belgorod *oblasts*.
- Yeltsin won over 50% of the vote in the first round so no second round was required.

*Result*

| Candidate | Votes cast | % |
| --- | --- | --- |
| 1. Yeltsin, Boris | 45,552,041 | 57.30 |
| 2. Ryzhkov, Nikolai | 14,395,335 | 16.85 |
| 3. Zhirinovsky, Vladimir | 6,211,007 | 7.81 |
| 4. Tuleev, Aman | 5,417,464 | 6.81 |
| 5. Makashov, Al'bert | 2,969,511 | 3.74 |
| 6. Bakatin, Vadim | 2,719,757 | 3.42 |
| Invalid votes | 3,242,167 | 4.10 |
| *Total votes cast* | 79,507,282 | 100.00 |

*Sources*: 'Soobshchenie tsentral'noi izbiratel'noi komissii po vyboram Prezidenta RSFSR', *Izvestiya*, 20 June 1991; *Pravda*, 20 June 1991.

and its role in the world, not simply as part of the USSR but as a sovereign state in its own right. He painted a vision of a rejuvenated Russia 'rising from her knees' and drawing on its cultural and spiritual heritage and its great past, re-entering the world community freed of imperialist ambitions and embracing the principles of freedom, property, the rule of law and openness to the world.[50] Yeltsin appealed to Russian patriotism against the communist regime, but at the same time offered a new synthesis of national self-affirmation and democratic aspirations.

# 2 The disintegration of the USSR

Nothing destroyeth authority so much as the unequal and untimely interchange of power pressed too far, and relaxed too much.

(Francis Bacon)[1]

At the beginning of the 1990s Henry Kissinger observed that 'The borders between the "centre" and the republics do not necessarily coincide with the borders between totalitarianism and democracy.'[2] This view was certainly at the core of Gorbachev's attempts to save the union. Yeltsin, meanwhile, continued the assault on the CPSU, and its demise in August 1991 left the USSR vulnerable to the increasingly sovereign republics. On 20 July 1991 Yeltsin issued a decree banning party structures in government offices and enterprises, and he also proposed legislation that would ban the Party from the armed forces.[3] The legal basis for the decree was dubious, since the USSR law on public associations stated that only the courts could outlaw a party (presumably including its branches). 'Departification' meant that communist officials would have to choose between their party and jobs. The depoliticisation decree came into effect on 4 August, and the CPSU was still considering its response when the coup intervened. Even Gorbachev appeared to lose patience with the dogged unreformability of the Party, vividly in evidence at the last plenum of the CPSU's Central Committee on 25–6 July, and announced that an emergency Party congress would be held in December 1991 to adopt a radical new programme that would return the Party to its social democratic roots. The draft of the new Party programme had been published on 23 July (the same day as the publication of the draft federal treaty), not in *Pravda* as would be expected but in the liberal *Nezavisimaya gazeta*.[4] The draft was a thoroughly revisionist document, repudiating basic elements of communist theory and practice, including the notion of a vanguard role for the party and stressed the universal nature of individual freedom. Gorbachev at last appeared to accept the necessity of splitting the Party and placing himself at the head of the radical reforming faction. In the event, conservatives sought to halt the dissolution of communist power by forceful means, but succeeded only in precipitating the disintegration of the country that they tried to save.

## The August coup

Conservatives realised that the Union Treaty, due to be signed on 20 August, would make the old structures of power redundant. In July twelve leading politicians, writers and generals signed a 'Word to the People', written among others by Gennady Zyuganov who would go on to lead the revived Communist Party of the Russian Federation (CPRF), that served as the manifesto of the coup. In emotional language the address warned of the

> enormous, unprecedented misfortune that has befallen us ... Why is it that sly and pompous rulers, intelligent and clever apostates and greedy and rich moneygrubbers, mocking us, scoffing at our beliefs and taking advantage of our naïveté, have seized power and are pilfering our wealth, taking homes, factories and land away from the people, carving the country up into separate parts ... excommunicating us from the past and debarring us from the future ... our differences are nothing in the face of the general calamity and distress, in the face of the general love for the homeland, which we see as a single, indivisible entity that has united fraternal peoples in a mighty state, without which we would have no existence.[5]

The address urged the creation of a nationwide movement of resistance to enemies like 'thoughtless and inept parliamentarians' but was vague on what form this should take.

The attempted coup of August 1991 sought to resolve by forceful means the crisis of power and end the struggle of conflicting ideologies. The leading conspirators were Pavlov (prime minister), Vladimir Kryuchkov (head of the KGB), Dmitry Yazov (minister of defence), and Yanaev (vice-president). On Saturday 17 August they met and discussed the implications of the new Union Treaty. They were joined by Luk'yanov, who realised that the devolution of power to the republics would in effect mean the end of the old centralised structures, including probably the national parliament and with it his own job. On learning that Gorbachev was unaware of their plans, he refused formally to join them but agreed to write against the treaty and at the same time assisted the putschists by delaying the convocation of the Soviet parliament for a week.[6]

On Sunday 18 August the plotters sent a delegation to Gorbachev in his holiday home in Foros in the Crimea. The group included Valeri Boldin, on Gorbachev's personal staff since 1981 and accepted almost as one of the family, Oleg Shenin, a member of the CC Secretariat, Oleg Baklanov, first vice-chairman of the Defence Council, and General Valentin Varennikov, commander-in-chief of ground forces. They sought a presidential decree establishing a state of emergency or agreement to hand over power to the vice-president. Gorbachev condemned their actions and refused to have anything to do with the plot, warning that 'You and the people who sent you are irresponsible. You will destroy yourselves, but that's your business and to hell with you. But you will also destroy the country and everything we have already done.'[7] Gorbachev's communications with the outside world were cut off, but there remains a suggestion that Gorbachev might have done more to try to prevent the coup; indeed, Amy Knight asserts that 'Gorbachev's claims that he was an innocent victim of the coup ha[ve] lost all credibility.'[8] Others argue that in the circumstances he could have done little more.[9]

On Monday 19 August the country woke up to endlessly repeated announcements by the mass media about the imposition of a state of emergency. A declaration by the State Committee for the State of Emergency (SCSE; GKChP in Russian) was read out, signed by the original four plotters now joined by another four: Pugo, the hardline minister of the interior; Baklanov; Alexander Tizyakov, president of the Association of State Enterprises; and Vasily Starodubtsev, chair of the government-sponsored Peasant's Union. Yanaev announced that Gorbachev was ill and unable to fulfil his duties, and thus he was taking over in the interim. Troops entered Moscow, and for three days the Russian White House, the seat of parliament and the presidency, was defended by citizens. The plotters had stumbled into launching the coup with very little real preparation, and they had sent the troops into Moscow with no detailed instructions about what they were supposed to do once they got there. As Yazov admitted during later interrogations, 'We had no real plan.'[10] The coup had been organised with the same level of incompetence as the country had been run for the last few years. The Russian leadership acted far more resolutely. On 19 August Yeltsin, Khasbulatov and Ivan Silaev (the Russian prime minister) drafted an 'Appeal to the Citizens of Russia', condemning the coup in no uncertain terms as 'a right-wing, reactionary, unconstitutional coup' and branding the SCSE an illegal body.[11]

Within three days it was all over, defeated by the opposition of the Russian leadership, the heroism of the people who took to the streets unarmed against tanks, the resistance in the army, the media and the factories, and by the lack of resolution of the plotters themselves. For the first time since Stalin a major initiative had been launched by-passing the Communist leadership, and thus the coup revealed the degree to which the Party had been marginalised. At the same time, neither the Politburo nor the Central Committee and its Secretariat defended their own General Secretary imprisoned in the Crimea. However paradoxical it might appear, this was in a sense a 'constitutional coup'. The plotters tried to present their actions as being in conformity with the constitution and thus sought to draw legitimacy from their formal legality. The 'manifesto' of the putschists played down the ideological appeal to communist values. Instead, they sought to ground their venture on Soviet nationalism, the attempt to maintain the Soviet Union as a centralised state, and hoped to gain popular support by playing on populist emotions, above all by denouncing the unpopular cooperatives and other new forms of business activity, which the address quoted above had termed 'bloodsuckers'. The plotters were not reactionaries, realising that the clock could not be turned back to before 1985. They were willing to accept some of Gorbachev's reforms but insisted that the time had come to stop the retreat. They represented a return to Andropov's authoritarian reform and a rejection of Gorbachev's democratising reforms. The attempted coup was therefore a conservative one, trying to preserve the USSR and its political system but ready to accept some necessary changes. The plotters sought to find a path midway between the out-and-out reactionaries, who would not have objected to Stalin's return, and the reform communists of Gorbachev's ilk who were allegedly betraying the achievements of Soviet socialism.

They hoped that Luk'yanov's delay in convening the USSR Supreme Soviet would allow the country to settle down and accept the coup as a *fait accompli*. There was only one problem for the plotters, and that was that Gorbachev refused to step down, even temporarily. In any event, Yeltsin and his colleagues in the Russian government insisted that the coup subverted the constitution, and on that basis launched a counter-coup that not only defeated the putschists but also destroyed the whole system of Soviet power. On 22 August anti-communist demonstrations took place around the country, and the headquarters of the CPSU in Old Square in Moscow was in danger of being stormed. The statue of Felix Dzerzhinsky, the founder of the Cheka, in front of the KGB's headquarters in the Lubyanka was removed with the assistance of the Moscow city authorities. The demonstrations on that day looked as if they might turn into a popular revolution against Party officials and institutions. In Moldova and the Baltic republics statues of Lenin were dismantled, and one after another the republics announced their independence.

Yeltsin transformed the coup into a revolution. At a session of the Russian parliament the next day the CPSU was suspended in Russia by a stroke of Yeltsin's pen. The CC and Moscow City Communist Party offices in Old Square were sealed to stop documents being destroyed, and Yeltsin ordered a number of communist newspapers to stop publication, including *Pravda* and *Sovetskaya Rossiya*. The retreat of the Party turned into a rout. On 24 August Gorbachev resigned as General Secretary of the CPSU and called for the dissolution of the Central Committee. On 29 August the USSR Supreme Soviet suspended the CPSU, and on 6 November 1991 Yeltsin banned the Party in Russia.[12] Party organisations were forbidden in military units and state institutions, and the property and bank accounts of the CPSU were placed under the control of the Russian authorities. Details emerged of a Party-funded shadow economy, a secret financial empire organised by a Business Directorate in the Central Committee to maintain its financial position when the Party lost political power.[13] Amid revelations of the abuse of state and Party funds, on 26 August N. Kruchina, a key worker in the CC's International Department which had been illicitly funding foreign communist parties, committed suicide, as did some other Party administrators involved in this activity. The Party's links with other communist parties and its subversive activities became known.[14] Some of the old guard in state posts also committed suicide, notably Marshal S. F. Akhromeev on 24 August, in despair at seeing the destruction of his life's work in building the USSR.[15]

The attempt by conservatives to halt the tide of disintegration by staging a coup only accelerated the demise of the old system and the state. While the nature of the August coup remains controversial, its effect is clear; the collapse of the once all-powerful Communist Party and the disintegration of the Soviet Union itself. The coup was the final act of 'one of the cruellest regimes in human history'.[16] The Soviet system had destroyed the old Russian middle class and the cultural intelligentsia; it had destroyed the self-sufficient peasantry and Russia's agriculture; the system had squandered the vast natural resources of the country and the wealth accumulated from the past; and in its final act the cannibalistic regime devoured itself.

## The disintegration of the USSR

The defeat of the coup reinvigorated democratic aspirations and instilled a new pride in Russian statehood, symbolised by the ubiquitous presence of the pre-revolutionary Russian tricolour (white, blue and red), which became the symbol of Russian democracy and was later adopted as the official Russian flag. At the funeral of the three young men who had died in the defence of the White House Yeltsin stressed that 'this conspiracy, this coup, was directed above all at Russia, the federation, the parliament, the president. But the whole of Russia stood up in its defence.'[17] The coup was followed by what can be considered the fourth and final phase of *perestroika*: disintegration.

The coup justified a series of formally anti-constitutional measures adopted by the Russian and other republican governments. All the major institutions of the Soviet state were discredited, with the partial exception of the military. The system was no longer in crisis but in a condition of catastrophic breakdown; few of its institutions were capable of reform or regeneration and after the coup were destroyed in their entirety. There was an immediate sense of popular relief that at last some of the problems facing the country could be resolved. A poll conducted by the All-Union (Russian) Centre for the Study of Public Opinion (VTsIOM) on 7 September 1991 found that 46 per cent of Muscovites were more optimistic than in early August, 32 per cent were as before, and only 15 per cent less optimistic.[18] However, for the new system to be considered secure it had to base itself not only on the negative legitimacy of having withstood the coup, but also on a positive programme. With the destruction of the common enemy, the communist regime, the democratic and national coalition in Russia disintegrated. How was the country to be governed, and indeed, what country, Russia or the Soviet Union?

On his return from the Crimea early on 22 August Gorbachev remarked that he felt as if he was returning to 'a different country',[19] although he reaffirmed his commitment to reform communism. Political life had indeed changed radically, and the next few months revealed that Gorbachev increasingly failed to adapt to the new circumstances, and became increasingly marginalised. The centre had in effect destroyed itself, and the coup transformed the declarations of sovereignty of the republics into declarations of independence. Lithuania had declared its independence on 11 March 1990 and Georgia on 9 April 1991, and even as the coup progressed other republics joined them: Estonia on 20 August; Latvia on the 21st; Ukraine on the 24th; Belarus on the 25th; Moldova on the 27th; Azerbaijan on the 30th; Kyrgyzstan and Uzbekistan on the 31st; Tajikistan on 9 September; Armenia on 23 September and Turkmenistan on 27 October. This formally left only Russia and Kazakhstan in the Soviet Union. Kazakhstan favoured a union because of its own delicate ethnic balance, split almost equally between Russians and Kazakhs, and because of its high degree of economic integration with the rest of the country.

Following the suspension of the CPSU its property was sequestered, and the democratic forces indulged in a rather undignified scramble for the pickings. The magnificent headquarters of the Central Committee on Old Square was taken over by the Russian government, and sessions of the Russian Council of Ministers would henceforth be held in the former offices of the Politburo. Up and down the country former Party headquarters were taken over by local administrations and organisations, and the Party's offices in factories and offices were turned over to new purposes. Very soon the ubiquitous presence of the Communist Party, once feared but more recently reviled, was but a fading memory.

The next casualty after the CPSU was the semi-democratic USSR Congress of People's Deputies, inaugurated in a fanfare of enthusiasm less than two years earlier. Rather than dismantling the apparatus of communist power, the Congress had provided a patina of democratic legitimacy for that authority.[20] An Emergency Congress from 2–5 September put an end to itself and thus also to one of the major elements of *perestroika*-style politics. Its last act was a Declaration of Human Rights and Freedoms, which committed the country to international standards of legal, citizenship, property, and social rights, including the right to work, and religious freedom and the right to use one's own language.[21] In the context, however, it was meaningless since there were no institutions that could guarantee these rights; and how could the rights of citizenship be defended in a country that increasingly existed only in name? Hopes for a democratic USSR were disappointed, and in the opinion of the self-styled democrats were probably unrealisable since empires and democracy are by definition incompatible. But the question that was to haunt post-communist state-building immediately arose: what if the

USSR was not an empire in anything like the traditional colonial sense but the core of a multinational community that could have survived as a democratic, confederal state? The latter was Gorbachev's view, that of a broad nationalist-leftist bloc, and increasingly of many ordinary citizens.

The bankruptcy of existing union institutions had been vividly exposed by the coup. The logic of the struggle against the communist 'centre' had undermined all attempts to create alternative *national democratic* institutions and had focused attention instead on establishing the *state* organisations of individual republics. In these circumstances only a strong centre could have managed the transition from Soviet unitarism to a genuine confederation, but in this matter (as in so many others), Gorbachev had equivocated for too long and lost the opportunity that might have existed in 1988–9. The absence of a clear demarcation between union and Russian institutions now gave rise to a dangerous vacuum of authority. Russia in effect suffered from a form of dual power, with two presidents and two parliaments, which gave rise to a type of 'dual powerlessness' and a paralysis of government.[22] This hesitancy was illustrated by Yeltsin's own behaviour. Instead of taking advantage of the enormous boost to his own popularity given by victory over the coup by launching decisive measures (including possibly pre-term elections to Russia's parliament and regional soviets), to consolidate the democratic revolution, he went on vacation to Sochi to ponder the future and thus missed the opportunity. Khasbulatov notes that 'The extraordinary passivity of the state during this period [from August to late October] remains a mystery to me.'[23]

It is precisely Yeltsin's failure to dissolve the Russian parliament, ironically, for which he is most condemned. In his second volume of memoirs, however, Yeltsin questions whether elections at that time would really have brought forward 'good' deputies, and notes that his resistance to the sort of acts suggested by the democrats, like the abolition of the state security system and vigorous 'decommunisation' measures, was based on the fear of provoking popular violence against the old regime, an approach that might have 'turned August into another October 1917', with all of the attendant violence and bloodshed.[24] The spectre of October and the fear of popular mobilisation inhibited the deepening of the democratic revolution. Yeltsin was making a powerful normative point, that the exit from communism should entail not just a change of system but also a new style of politics. However, by compromising with so much of the old order, the enthusiasm of August to build a new system was dissipated. Rather than representing a radical break with the past, 1991 has now come to symbolise little more than a change of regime. Politics focused on intra-elite intrigues and institutional wrangling, soon provoking, not surprisingly, popular disillusionment.

The Russian authorities now stumbled into a war of manoeuvre with Gorbachev and what remained of the USSR. Russia took over the powers of the union, slice by slice, in a new form of 'salami tactics'. Four main provisional structures operated to fill the vacuum resulting from the collapse of the old regime:

1   The Congress was replaced by a new USSR Supreme Soviet made up of representatives from the republics. If nothing else, the new parliament was intended to act as a counterweight to the Russian parliament.[25] The modified Supreme Soviet had the right to call a full Congress but never did so. Several republics failed to send delegates to the new USSR legislature, and few regretted its abolition in December 1991.

2   The most important body was the 12-member State Council made up of the leaders of eleven republics (the three Baltic republics and Georgia did not participate) with Gorbachev in the chair as president of what remained of the USSR. Gorbachev's acceptance of the new system ranks amongst his highest achievements, but his position would have been stronger if he had accepted more emphatically the confederalisation of the union before the coup rather than after. During the coup all the structures on which he had relied betrayed him (the CPSU, the army, the KGB and the MVD), but even earlier Gorbachev's instincts led him to try to find a new power base, the collective authority of the presidents of the republics in the Novo-Ogarevo process that had given rise to the Union Treaty, and this was now formalised by the creation of the State Council. Leaders of the democratic opposition had long called for a 'round table' conference of the Eastern Europe sort, but the coup made it clear that the only round table that would have any meaning in the USSR would be one involving not political movements but the leaders of the republics (yet again revealing the displacement of post-authoritarian energies from the democratic to the statist). The State Council took the key strategic decisions in the interim, recognising the independence of the three Baltic republics, but delayed the recognition of the independence of Armenia, Georgia and Moldova or that of Ukraine.

3   The third transitional body was the State Council's Inter-Republican Economic Committee, headed from 16 September by the former prime minister of Russia, Ivan Silaev. The committee acted as the government of the USSR to provide central direction in the transition to the market. Silaev's appointment reflected tensions within Yeltsin's camp, especially since he was, together with the reform economist Yavlinsky, convinced of the need to maintain a single economic space in the old union. To this end an economic accord between ten of the former Soviet republics (excluding the three newly independent Baltic states, and Armenia and Georgia) was signed in the Kazakhstani capital, Almaty (formerly Alma Ata) in October 1991.

4   The USSR presidency itself was the fourth transitional structure. Gorbachev in the immediate post-coup period looked out of touch with current realities, reiterating his commitment to the renewal of the Communist Party and to notions of a renewed socialism. He had expected to carry on as before, but he was soon disabused of this illusion. He was harried and bullied by Yeltsin in the Russian parliament on 23 August, and popular opinion held him responsible for the coup because of his appointment of conservatives and his equivocation over economic reform. Gorbachev's mastery of compromise now worked to his advantage as he tried to achieve some sort of centrist democratic consensus in the post-communist era, as reflected in his appointments to the new Political Consultative Council under the presidency. Moreover, it now seemed to be in the interests of the non-Russian republics to keep an independent centre alive, if only to act as a counter-weight to Russia's growing power.

By the end of 1991 it was clear that the old centre could play only a very limited role in post-communist politics. Gorbachev's authority was increasingly over-shadowed by the Russian government and by Yeltsin personally. The republics were unwilling to delegate functions to the centre now that they themselves could decide the terms and intensity of the relationship with each other and the federal state. In the early post-coup days the republics reached agreements on cooperation in economic, scientific, ecological and human rights matters and, above all, the principles of collective security and defence. But these commitments, like the economic accords, remained vague and gave way to republican politics. The creeping Russification of all-union institutions, evident even before the coup, now accelerated as Russian normative acts increasingly replaced union laws. Already in April 1991 the coal industry had been transferred to the control of the Russian government in exchange for ending the miners' strikes, and now the process of Russia 'gathering in' economic responsibilities gathered pace. The federal budget was largely funded by transfers from the Russian treasury, and when in late October the Russian Congress decided to stop financing most union bodies (with the exception of the foreign, defence, railways and atomic industries ministries), the union effectively came to an end. In mid-November Yeltsin took over Soviet oil exports and the gold and diamond industries, most of which are on Russian territory. The transitional institutions had little authority to take, let alone implement, decisions. The union presidency headed by Gorbachev and the old institutions continued as if by sufferance from Yeltsin, and enjoyed only as much authority as he was willing to grant. To the alarm of the other republics, Russia began to take on the mantle of the old union centre.

Since Russia had led the democratic struggle against the coup and against the communist regime as a whole, it came as a surprise to find that the hostility of the other republics was now directed against itself. Instead of reaping gratitude for defeating the communist regime, Russia found itself isolated. What Russia had started was now completed by Ukraine in its refusal to be associated with the recreation of a new union or any other centre in Moscow. As the Ukrainian leader, Leonid Kravchuk, put it on 8 November:

> We will oppose any attempt to create central government bodies. We will not ratify a treaty if central government bodies of any kind whatsoever are hidden behind it. Indeed no Center of any kind should exist other than coordinating bodies that would be established by the states participating in the treaty process.[26]

Russia's failure quickly enough to realise the depth of the distrust that existed towards any strong power in Moscow, be it in a Soviet authoritarian guise or a Russian democratic one, led to several ill-considered acts. Yeltsin's press secretary, Pavel Voshchanov, for example announced on 28 August that the borders of republics that declared their independence would be questioned. Russia, moreover, was in the process of swallowing up the Soviet state apparatus, raising fears that it sought to absorb territory as well. This only seemed to confirm the suspicions of the republics that Russia was the new imperial hegemon replacing the Soviet one, and put paid to Russia's hopes of establishing a genuine confederation to replace the USSR. Moreover, the republican leaderships that had wavered during the coup sought to protect themselves from Moscow's retribution by wrapping themselves in anti-Russian and nationalist flags, a ploy that was remarkably successful in allowing renamed neo-communist regimes to remain in power in many republics.

The West favoured the continuation of the USSR in order to maintain a single economic and political space and to minimise the dangers of conflicts and the proliferation of nuclear weapons. Gorbachev's domestic position, however, became increasingly untenable and ultimately he failed to find a role either for himself or for the union bureaucracy. He tried to reconstitute the centre by offering the leaders of the republics seats on the State Council, but the leaders themselves were under pressure in their own republics. The increasingly bankrupt union bureaucracy remained in business by printing money, stoking inflation and making a dire economic situation even worse, prompting the republics (above all Russia, see Chapter 12) to pursue their own economic reform plans. Silaev was given the impossible task of initiating reform from within the existing structures in a way that would suit both the republics and the centre.

These contradictions came to a head over attempts to negotiate a new Union Treaty of 12 sovereign states in a reconstituted entity that would be the subject of international law. Gorbachev insisted on the continuation of what he called 'the Novo-Ogarevo process', the search for a new Union of Sovereign States (USS), and on 14 November 1991 this resulted in the fifth draft of the Union Treaty which conceded yet more powers to the union republics while retaining some central institutions such as a directly elected president and a bicameral legislature.[27] Support for confederation came from the president of Kazakhstan, Nursultan Nazarbaev, and Yeltsin, who considered the maintenance of some sort of union in Russia's interests. Only the Central Asian states, Belarus and Russia were willing to attend the initialling ceremony to be held on 25 November. The problem was noted by Yeltsin at this meeting: 'Signing the treaty without Ukraine is useless. There would be no Union. Let's wait for Ukraine.'[28] The other republics, above all Ukraine, in the event refused to have anything to do with a renewed centre and the ceremony never took place. Hopes for a new Union Treaty foundered on the rocks of Ukrainian aspirations, and ultimately the whole union, already weakened by Baltic independence, was broken by the attempt to keep Ukraine part of it. While Gorbachev, and indeed Yeltsin, insisted that a union without Ukraine was meaningless, Ukraine nevertheless abstained from all active participation in negotiations until the presidential elections and referendum of 1 December 1991. Policy within Ukraine was led by its western regions, above all Lvov, taken from Poland in 1945. According to Szporluk, it was at that time that ethnicity took precedence over modernisation in Soviet development: 'The seeds of the Soviet Union's decline were thus planted at the moment of the Soviet Union's greatest triumph – 1945.'[29] As Napoleon put it, 'All empires die of indigestion.' Already by late 1991 there were plans to issue a separate Ukrainian currency. The overwhelming vote on 1 December 1991 to confirm the provisional declaration of independence of 24 August, and the election of Kravchuk as president, demonstrated that the initiative had irrevocably passed to the republics.

If Ukraine and other republics refused to have anything to do with a new Union Treaty, then what was Russia to do? If Ukraine became independent and began to issue its own currency, there was a danger that Russia would be flooded by the surplus roubles of 52 million Ukrainians. In the event, Yeltsin adopted the strategy long advocated by his close adviser, Gennady Burbulis, namely the development of specifically Russian, as opposed to Soviet, policies.[30] A number of consequences followed from this, including the appointment of a new radical government headed by Yeltsin personally in early November 1991, with Gaidar placed in charge of economic reform; he later became acting prime minister. Another was the pronunciation of the death sentence on the Soviet Union. All this was tantamount to a Russian declaration of independence.

On 7–8 December 1991 the leaders of the three Slavic republics (Russia, Ukraine and Belarus) met to discuss the future of the union in a hunting lodge in the Belovezh Pushcha nature reserve in Western Belarus. Since the three countries were the original signatories of the Union Treaty of December 1922, they claimed the right to dissolve what they had once formed; although according to the Soviet constitution the only way that a republic could secede was by referendum.[31] The Belovezh Accords declared that 'The USSR as a subject of international law and as a geopolitical entity has ceased to exist' and announced the formation of a Commonwealth of Independent States (CIS).[32] The Accords were ratified by the Russian Supreme Soviet on 12 December. While coming as a shock to the rest of the world, the Ukrainians had long been considering the option: their ideas for a confederation had been dismissed by Gorbachev, and they plainly considered that attempts now to renegotiate the Union Treaty were futile.[33] No records of the meeting survive, but two factors clearly precipitated the decision: the need to accommodate Ukraine's drive for independence; and the perception of Russia's 'government of reforms' that the only way forwards was on their own. For Yeltsin, moreover, the act of dissolution had two advantages: it put a summary end to the Gorbachev era; and he apparently believed that the CIS would become a new union with a new president, himself.[34]

The signatories reaffirmed their commitment to 'the goals and principles of the UN Charter, of the Helsinki Final Act and of other CSCE [Conference on Security and Cooperation in Europe] documents' (Preamble). Despite the commitment to 'universally recognised norms concerning human rights', no method of implementing these goals was indicated. Article 3 expressed the commitment to the 'preservation and progress of the ethnic, cultural, linguistic and religious identity of national minorities', but stopped short of recognising their right to political self-determination. The agreement attempted to maintain the territorial *status quo*, and Article 5 forcefully committed the member states to 'recognise and respect the territorial integrity of each other and the inviolability of the existing borders within the Commonwealth', although there was to be free movement of people and information within the Commonwealth. Above all, Article 6 committed the member states to 'maintain a common military-strategic space under joint command, including unified control over nuclear weapons.'[35]

The Central Asian leaders, and in particular Nazarbaev, were angered by the creation of an exclusively Slavic union. They met on 12 December in Ashgabat, the capital of Turkmenistan, and resolved to join the new body. On 21 December all 11 republics that would make up the new enlarged Commonwealth met in Almaty. The eight that had not met in Belarus (Armenia, Azerbaijan, Kazakhstan, Kyrgyzstan, Moldova, Tajikistan, Turkmenistan and Uzbekistan; but not Georgia) signed a Protocol making them equal High Contracting Parties with the original signatories. The Protocol committed them to the Belovezh Accords and rendered them founder members of the Commonwealth. On that day Nazarbaev announced that the USSR was no more, although formally it ended on 31 December 1991. The presidents signed six documents addressing some of the key problems facing the post-USSR world. They committed themselves to a single economic space, unified control of nuclear arms and strategic forces, and pledged that the international treaties of the USSR would be upheld and that the existing borders would be respected. The documents, however, were declarations of intent rather than binding treaties. Above all, the Almaty Accords declared that the new Commonwealth 'is neither a state nor a supra-state entity'.[36] It lacked serious central coordinating institutions and in effect abolished 'the centre' altogether, facilitating the ratification of the accords by the respective republican parliaments. It appeared that the CIS was to be a transitional phenomenon to manage the change and secure the orderly separation of military and economic structures. This at least was the view of Ukraine and some other republics, but as we shall see (Chapter 18), Russia, Kazakhstan and some others hoped for rather more.

The disappearance of the USSR meant the abolition of the post of president, and thus Gorbachev's rule was over. It would be an exaggeration to suggest that Yeltsin favoured the abolition of the USSR in order to remove his rival Gorbachev, yet the personal factor is important.[37] As time passes the depth of Gorbachev's domestic unpopularity at the time is easily forgotten. A poll in late November found that he was the seventeenth most popular politician, barely squeaking in above the populist Vladimir Zhirinovsky, and way behind the most popular figure, Yeltsin.[38] Gorbachev resigned on 25 December 1991, maintaining a statesmanlike pose and declaring his critical support for the new regime:

> There can be no justification whatsoever for my going into opposition either from a political point of view or when it comes to the interests of the country … As long as Russia follows the path of democratic change, I will not only support her I will defend her, particularly at this difficult stage.[39]

Gorbachev and Yeltsin came to an agreement whereby the former president would enjoy certain privileges as long as he kept out of active politics. He established an International Foundation for Socio-Economic and Political Studies, known as the Gorbachev Foundation, and invited many of his former colleagues to work in it, including Yakovlev and others of the *perestroika* generation. He remained a dignified elder statesman and respected international figure.

## Problems of state-building

In 1991 the communist experiment in Russia, one of the most sustained attempts in social engineering ever undertaken by humanity, came to an end. The revelations of *glasnost* encouraged the view that the whole Bolshevik period had been one gigantic 'mistake', reflected in the popular slogan of the time 'seventy years on the road to nowhere'. The Soviet Union did not just fall, it collapsed. The failure of *perestroika* turned into a catastrophic breakdown of society and economy. All the institutions that maintained Soviet statehood were shattered simultaneously: the Communist Party, the secret police, the economic apparatus and the state mechanism. All of this was in terrible fulfilment of George Kennan's prediction soon after the Second World War that 'Soviet power, like the capitalist world of its conception, bears within it the seeds of its own decay.' He warned that if 'anything were ever to disrupt the unity and the efficacy of the party as a political instrument, Soviet Russia might be changed overnight from one of the strongest to one of the weakest and most pitiable of national societies'.[40] This indeed came to pass, and the fall of the communist system in August 1991 was soon followed by the disintegration of the Soviet state.

Russia became an independent state, and the Sixth Congress in April 1992 adopted a constitutional amendment that abolished the name 'RSFSR' and introduced 'Russia' and 'Russian Federation' as names with equal legal validity. The country was faced with both a systemic and a national crisis. In systemic terms, the country's political and economic institutions had to be rebuilt, a new constitution adopted, and the basic framework of a democratic polity established. In terms of crisis, the economy was in free-fall, law and order crumbling, and society lacked unity over the nature of the new state. Basic ambiguities surround the emergence of the contemporary Russian state. We speak of an independent Russia, but at what point did it actually become independent? The other Soviet successor states in 1990–1 declared their independence, whereas Russia, while declaring its sovereignty on 12 June 1990 and effectively seceding from the USSR on 8 December 1991, was the only state simply to emerge as the residual legatee of the Soviet state following the latter's dissolution in December 1991. The reborn Russian state, moreover, had no precedents; its borders corresponded to no previous historical entity and the polity was based on entirely new principles.

The insurgency against the communist regime took the form of a struggle for the establishment of Russian statehood (*gosudarstvennost'*), and only secondarily the establishment of a democratic polity. The Russian concept of 'statehood' is alien to the Anglo-Saxon mind, suggesting both a strong state in domestic politics and a vigorous presence in foreign policy. Statehood was being returned to Russia in two senses: as a political state at last freeing itself from the suffocating tutelage of the Communist Party; and as a republic with the attributes of sovereign statehood separate from the USSR. The struggle for statehood at this time involved also a third element, the attempt to establish a democratic polity. Russia's rebirth as a political state required the development of the institutions of political sovereignty, such as an independent parliament, government and presidency, as well as the establishment of a market economy. Russia's rebirth as a democratic republic, however, was to be a complex process, involving the development of a new national identity distinct from the Tsarist or Soviet imperial past.

While 1991 represented a fundamental moment of rupture in both geopolitical and governmental terms, strong elements of continuity remained. The primordial drive for territorial consolidation was accompanied once again by attempts to strengthen the state at the centre. State-building takes four practical forms, leaving aside for the moment questions of national and cultural identity: the ability to defend the national territory; effective integration of the centre and periphery; ordered relations between the institutions of governance; and elements of reciprocity between the state and society. The Tsarist system was found wanting on all four counts, having suffered repeated defeats in the Great War; while the Soviet system was certainly able to defend itself, probably against the rest of the world combined, but it was less successful in the other three aspects. The reborn Russian state now faced these challenges, once again in the context of balancing foreign policy goals with political and economic reconstruction at home.

Russia inherited 76 per cent of the USSR's territory, 61 per cent of its GNP, and 51 per cent of its population (for map, see Figure 2.1). Over 25 million Russians, however, found themselves outside the borders of the new state, representing a large proportion of the 43 million (15 per cent of the total USSR population) who found themselves outside their titular state (see Table 2.1).

- At 148 million, Russia had the world's fifth-largest population (after China, India, the United States and Indonesia), with 128 recognised nations and ethnic groups. By 2007 Russia's population had fallen to 142 million pushing the country into seventh place.
- Russia is the world's largest country, stretching 9,000 km from east to west, and covers one-eighth of the earth's land surface (17.1 million sq km, of which 1.3 million sq km is arable).

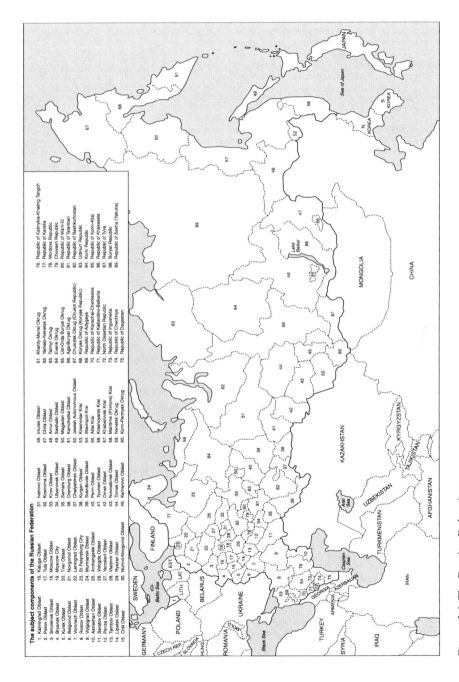

*Figure 2.1* The Russian Federation

*Table 2.1* Population of the USSR, 1989

| Republic | Population of republic | % of USSR pop. | Titular nationality | | | | | |
|---|---|---|---|---|---|---|---|---|
| | | | Living in USSR ('000) | % of USSR pop. | Living in their own titular republic | | Living outside their own titular republic | |
| | | | | | ('000) | (%) | ('000) | (%) |
| Russia | 147,386,000 | 51.4 | 145,155 | 50.6 | 119,866 | 82.6 | 25,289 | 17.4 |
| Estonia | 1,573,000 | 0.5 | 1,027 | 0.4 | 963 | 93.8 | 64 | 6.2 |
| Latvia | 2,681,000 | 0.9 | 1,459 | 0.5 | 1,388 | 95.1 | 71 | 4.9 |
| Lithuania | 3,690,000 | 1.3 | 3,067 | 1.1 | 2,924 | 95.3 | 143 | 4.7 |
| Moldova | 4,341,000 | 1.5 | 3,352 | 1.2 | 2,795 | 83.4 | 557 | 16.6 |
| Belarus | 10,200,000 | 3.6 | 10,036 | 3.5 | 7,905 | 78.8 | 2,131 | 21.2 |
| Ukraine | 51,704,000 | 18.0 | 44,186 | 15.4 | 37,417 | 82.6 | 6,767 | 15.4 |
| Armenia | 3,283,000 | 1.1 | 4,623 | 1.6 | 3,084 | 66.7 | 1,539 | 33.3 |
| Azerbaijan | 7,029,000 | 2.5 | 6,770 | 2.4 | 5,805 | 85.7 | 965 | 14.3 |
| Georgia | 5,449,000 | 1.9 | 3,981 | 1.4 | 3,787 | 95.1 | 194 | 4.9 |
| Kazakhstan | 16,538,000 | 5.8 | 8,136 | 2.8 | 6,535 | 80.3 | 1,601 | 19.7 |
| Kyrgyzstan | 4,291,000 | 1.5 | 2,529 | 0.9 | 2,230 | 88.2 | 299 | 11.8 |
| Tajikistan | 5,112,000 | 1.8 | 4,215 | 1.5 | 3,172 | 75.3 | 1,043 | 24.7 |
| Turkmenistan | 3,534,000 | 1.2 | 2,601 | 0.9 | 2,537 | 93.8 | 64 | 6.2 |
| Uzbekistan | 19,906,000 | 6.9 | 16,698 | 5.8 | 14,142 | 84.7 | 2,556 | 15.3 |
| *Total* | 286,717,000 | 100.0 | 257,965 | | 214,550 | 74.8 | 43,283 | 15.1 |

*Sources*: *SSSR v tsifrakh v 1989 godu* (Moscow, Finansy i statistika, 1990), pp. 36, 38; Alan P. Pollard (ed.), *USSR: Facts and Figures Annual*, Vol. 15 (Gulf Breeze, FL, Academic International Press, 1991), p. 504.

- Its borders stretch a total of 58,562 km, with 14,253 km bordering 16 foreign states and 44,309 km coasting 3 oceans (Atlantic, Arctic and Pacific) and 12 seas.[41]
- Russia shares borders with 16 states: 8 with former members of the Soviet Union (Estonia, Latvia, Lithuania, Belarus, Ukraine, Georgia, Azerbaijan and Kazakhstan); 2 are sea borders (Japan and USA); and the others are Norway, Finland, Poland, China, Mongolia and North Korea.
- Some 11,000 km are new boundaries, emerging as a result of the disintegration of the USSR. Lacking resources to fortify the new frontiers, which stretch 7,559 km with Kazakhstan alone and another 2,245 with Ukraine (much of it not defined, let alone demarcated), Russia at various points tried to make the outer borders of the CIS her own borders.
- The country is richly endowed with natural resources and a skilled workforce. Russia had 90 per cent of the oil, 80 per cent of the natural gas, 70 per cent of the gold production and 62 per cent of the electricity output of the former Soviet Union.
- The great majority of the research institutes and educational establishments were inherited by Russia, although the whole Soviet Union had contributed to their development.

It is this fundamental geographical and material disproportion between Russia and the other successor states that made it so difficult to establish comfortable relations between them.

Although Russia inherited the bulk of the territory and resources, the political institutions bequeathed by the old system were fragile and disordered. In his keynote speech of 28 October 1991 Yeltsin lamented the weakness of Russian statehood and stressed the need to establish the legal basis for the new Russia,[42] but the struggle to carve out a post-imperial state was to prove long and arduous. Russia had been far more subsumed into the Soviet identity than the other republics, leading them (and many outsiders) to confuse Russia with the Soviet Union. The Russian language was the official state language, and Russians predominated at all levels of government and administration: Russians traditionally were the second secretaries of the republican Party organisations and usually headed the local KGB. Native cultures had been Sovietised and the use of their languages, especially in higher educational establishments and in political life, had been stymied by the use of the imperial *lingua franca*. Russians represented Soviet power and thus Sovietisation was often perceived as synonymous with Russianisation (the cultural domination of Russia), and in places Russification (the conscious attempt to suppress other cultures in favour of Russia's) as well.

The new republic was a truncated form of the larger Russia for which the White armies had fought during the Civil War of 1918–20, and which ultimately the Bolsheviks rebuilt after their victory and which was formalised by the creation of the USSR in 1922. The rebirth of Russian statehood was accompanied by the tension between internal state-building and external withdrawal, imbuing the whole process with a sense of defeat and failure. The borders that Russia inherited in 1991 were undoubtedly arbitrary, but any attempt to recreate the 'greater Russia' that had died in 1991 would entail a level of violence comparable to that accompanying the 'greater Serbia' ambitions of the 1990s in the former Yugoslavia. Thus a smaller Russian statehood emerged in which national-patriots argued that the problems associated with building the institutions of an independent Russia internally were provoked by Russia's separation from some of its historical territories and peoples externally. It was along the line of this argument that much of post-communist Russian politics flowed.

# 3 Phoney democracy, 1991–3

Time has finally run out for communism. But its concrete edifice has not yet crumbled. May we not be crushed beneath its rubble instead of gaining liberty.

(Alexander Solzhenitsyn)[1]

In 1991 the self-declared 'democrats' came to power, but this did not necessarily entail the triumph of democracy, and it soon became clear that post-communism was a distinctive syndrome of its own and far from synonymous with democracy. The fall of the communist regime was a necessary but not a sufficient condition for the triumph of democracy. Between the collapse of the old order and the birth of the new there lay a period of disorientation and disorder, a new Time of Troubles like that in the first decade of the seventeenth century. The period between the disintegration of the USSR and the shelling of the White House, the seat of the Russian Congress of People's Deputies, was one of increasing tension as parliament and the presidency fought for supreme authority that ultimately exploded into violence in October 1993. The struggle to adopt a new constitution would take until December 1993, and included one of the most dramatic confrontations between branches of power in modern politics. The legacy of this false start in the development of Russian democracy still influences Russian political discourse.

## Phoney democracy: the road to October 1993

With the demise of Soviet power in 1991 the one-dimensional conflict between the communist 'centre' and the insurgent 'democrats' ended, revealing structural weaknesses in the organisation of legislative power and exposing a crisis in relations between executive and legislative authority. This was a period that can be described as 'phoney democracy', with the people brought on as bit players in the struggle between president and parliament. The Russian legislature elected in March 1990 was not designed to choose or control a government, let alone to act as the supreme source of sovereignty. It did not have effective means to fulfil customary parliamentary functions like approving and overseeing budgets and legislation. The absence of the separation of powers worked both to the legislature's advantage, in that it had direct control over about half of state expenditure, but also to its disadvantage, as in its weak control over the executive.[2]

### *The emergence of presidential rule*

A presidential system emerged in the last Soviet years to compensate for the decline of the CPSU and the weakness of parliament.[3] Despite the resurrection of the revolutionary slogan 'all power to the soviets', the revived legislatures failed to live up to expectations. The constitutional amendments of 1 December 1988 made the USSR Congress the highest power in the land; and following the elections of March 1989 Gorbachev was elected chair of the new body. The foundation of his rule shifted from the Party to the new parliament. On the very day that the Communist Party officially lost its monopoly on power, 14 March 1990, the powers of the Soviet presidency were strengthened. An executive presidency independent of the legislature was established, and Gorbachev was elected to this post in an uncontested ballot by the CPD on 15 March 1990. His refusal to face national elections undermined the legitimacy not only of the post but marked the point where his credibility as a democratic reformer was fatally damaged. Presidential powers were increased during the course of the year, and at the Fourth USSR CPD in December 1990 the shift to presidential power was completed by the transformation of the old Council of Ministers into a more limited 'cabinet', with the prime minister and ministers nominated by the president and accountable to him.

The powers of the prime minister remained limited and the executive powers that were more properly the prerogative of the government were devolved to the Supreme Soviet's Presidium. While the powers of the presidency were greatly increased, the powers of the Soviet legislature were not correspondingly diminished. A new type of dual power emerged that was inherently unstable but manageable as long as the chair of parliament was in safe hands. The chair of the Soviet Congress, Luk'yanov, however, betrayed Gorbachev in August 1991, and later, after much the same system was reproduced in Russia, the struggle between the presidency and parliament dominated the first phase of Russia's independent statehood. When Yeltsin became chair of the Russian Supreme Soviet in May 1990 he gained executive authority but his powers were firmly subordinated to the legislature. The strengthening of parliament, designed initially to compensate for the declining power of the CPSU, was cut short by the emergence of presidential systems rooted in the newly 'empowered' legislatures but which gradually increased their own powers at the expense of the legislatures that had given them birth.

The presidential option looked increasingly attractive to overcome the crisis of reform. At the First CPD in May-June 1990 all factions united in favour of a strong leadership, and with Yeltsin's election to chair the Supreme Soviet on 29 May a significant step was taken towards the development of the presidential system. In 1990 the Russian parliament passed some 150 acts affecting virtually every aspect of Russian life. Even so, Yeltsin insisted that the crisis of executive power remained acute.[4] Yeltsin's conservative opponents began to have second thoughts over the merits of a presidential system. They were outmanoeuvred, however, by the opportunity offered by Gorbachev's referendum of 17 March 1991 on the 'renewed Union'. As noted (see Table 1.2), a second question was added to the ballot in Russia on a directly elected president. Russians voted by the same margin for the union and a directly elected president of Russia.

At the Third (Emergency) Congress Yeltsin, in one of those reversals of fortune that mark his career, turned the tables on those who had sought to curb his powers and emerged with a mandate for a strengthened presidency. On the opening day,

28 March 1991, Gorbachev tried to enforce his ban on marches by introducing troops into Moscow, but at least half a million people took to streets in a peaceful demonstration in support of Yeltsin and Russian sovereignty. For the Congress and Yeltsin, too, the day proved decisive. The conservative 'Communists of Russia' bloc and its allies in the 'Rossiya' faction, together comprising about half the deputies, tried to block the creation of a Russian presidency. The unpopularity of the Soviet government (headed by Valentin Pavlov), and the increasingly stark conflict between allegiance to the unitary CPSU and aspirations for Russian sovereignty and statehood, led to a break in communist ranks. The Afghan war veteran and noted patriot, Alexander Rutskoi, defected and formed his own 'Communists for Democracy' faction. The balance now shifted in Yeltsin's favour, and not only were the proposed constitutional changes affecting the powers of the presidency accepted and arrangements made for elections on 12 June, but the Congress on its last day, 5 April, accepted Yeltsin's surprise demand for immediate powers to issue presidential decrees within the framework of existing legislation to accelerate economic and political reform in Russia. Soon afterwards Gorbachev signed the Novo-Ogarevo 'nine-plus-one' agreement with Russia and the other republics for a new union treaty.

The necessary constitutional amendments to create a Russian presidency were adopted by the Fourth CPD on 22 May 1991, followed by a law on the election of the president. The principle of the division of powers was ratified and executive and judicial branches of the state were to be formed. The new president, elected for no more than two consecutive five-year terms, could not be a deputy or a member of a political party. He or she would head the executive branch and would be the highest official in the land, but was obliged to report to the Congress at least once a year. The president had the right to issue binding decrees and to suspend decisions of executive bodies if they contradicted the constitution or Russian laws. Both the Supreme Soviet and the Congress, however, could revoke presidential decrees, although the actual voting procedure to do this was not specified. The Congress could impeach the president by a two-thirds vote on a report by the Constitutional Court issued at the initiative of the Congress itself, the Supreme Soviet, or one of its chambers.[5] Thus the extensive powers of an executive presidency were enshrined in law. However, unresolved issues in the relationship between president and parliament were to act as slow-acting time bombs.

After an intense two-week campaign, the first direct elections for a Russian leader were held on 12 June 1991 (see Table 1.3). Yeltsin's decisive victory, polling 57 per cent of the vote and thus winning outright in the first round,[6] endowed his presidency with a popular legitimacy that Gorbachev's had lacked and helped him withstand the August coup. Instead of the largely ceremonial presidency, as in the Czech Republic or Hungary, Russia found itself with an executive presidency on the American model. Victory gave Yeltsin freedom of manoeuvre in relations with parliament and allowed him to confront the CPSU. But, as with the Soviet parliament earlier, while the authority of the presidency had increased, the powers of parliament had not correspondingly diminished.

### The president acts

Following his inauguration on 10 July Yeltsin issued a flurry of presidential decrees, including the reappointment of Silaev as prime minister and the appointment of a number of ministers to the Russian government, the creation of a presidential administration, and a renewed onslaught against the CPSU by banning political parties from executive bodies. Yeltsin's heroic resistance to the coup seemed to justify the growth of presidential power, and the hastily reconvened Supreme Soviet in late August granted him emergency powers to deal with the situation. He was granted yet more powers by the reconvened Fifth CPD (28 October–2 November 1991), including the right to reorganise the government, but now attempts were made to define the legal relationship between the president and the Supreme Soviet. On 2 November 1991 the Congress granted Yeltsin the power for one year to appoint ministers and pass economic decrees without reference to parliament.[7] On 6 November Yeltsin assumed the post of prime minister, in addition to his other responsibilities, and placed himself at the head of a 'cabinet of reforms' (see below), with the RSFSR Council of Ministers now officially called the Russian government.

While defending strong executive authority, Yeltsin's entourage recognised the need for some separation of powers to avoid a return to a new form of despotism which would once again exclude Russia, as they put it, from 'civilised society'.[8] The idea of 'delegated legislation', in which a government is allowed to rule for a time through decrees with the force of law, is used by democratic states in times of emergency. On these occasions, however, the legislature usually establishes limits to the emergency powers, overseen by a constitutional court, and a set period that can only be renewed with the assent of parliament. In Russia no such stable system emerged; the expanding powers of the presidency were at first delegated by parliament but were thereafter converted into a self-sustaining presidential system. The appeal to the logic of the struggle against communism, already seen during the insurgency phase in the form of 'wars of the laws' and declarations of sovereignty, perpetuated the legacy of administrative arbitrariness.

When in opposition Yeltsin had assaulted the old system with a hybrid programme encompassing a populist critique of the privileges of the power elite, an appeal to social justice, economic reform, the restoration of Russian statehood, and the radicalisation of democratic change. Once in power, however, he tempered these demands; no longer the challenger but the incumbent, Yeltsin soon came to rely on the instruments of the state rather than the mass politics of the street, though on occasion he was not averse to using the crowd. Yeltsin soon freed himself from the democratic movement that had brought him to power. While this meant that he remained a free agent politically, it also suggested a failure to ensure an adequate institutional framework or political constituency to support the presidency. It also meant that the Russian presidency from the very beginning was not adequately constrained by accountability mechanisms. Yeltsin failed to consult Democratic Russia over the choice of Rutskoi as his running mate for the presidential elections, nor did he consult with them over the formation of his government. Yeltsin went on to build the presidency on the basis of his personal authority, to the detriment of institutions and mass political structures. As Gorbachev had discovered earlier, strengthened presidential power is no guarantee of legitimacy or effective government.

Even before the coup Yeltsin had prepared a series of decrees strengthening presidential power, and these were swiftly implemented in the following months. Executive authority became more independent of the legislature, though it remained constrained by law and regulated by parliament within the framework of 'delegated legislation'. Many questions remained, however, including the limits to presidential power. Would a strong executive encourage the development of democracy in society, or would it act as a sub-stitute for popular democratic organisation? Would not the 'strong hand' inevitably take on aspects of the Bolshevism which it sought to extirpate, and perpetuate rather than overcome traditions of authoritarianism and arbitrariness?

### *'Phoney democracy', August 1991–December 1993*

Schmitter has noted that 'what definitely is most peculiar about Russia's transition is the role that elections have (not) played in it'.[9] This is not quite accurate, since the elections to the Soviet Congress in March 1989, to the Russian Congress a year later, and the pres-idential elections of June 1991, were defining moments in the dissolution of the old order and the emergence of the new. Nevertheless, the absence of general elections for some two years following the coup, at a time of accelerated political development, is remark-able and this is one of the reasons why we call this period 'phoney democracy'. After August 1991 Yeltsin imposed a moratorium on elections in the regions and localities. The electoral hiatus reflected the contradictory logic of the Russian transition, above all attempts to maintain its consensual and evolutionary nature at a time of polarisation and revolution. Several by-elections to fill vacancies failed because of the inability to reach the 50 per cent threshold; voters were demobilised and disillusioned with the unseemly struggle between president and parliament.

The question remains, however, of why no elections were held after the coup in autumn 1991, when Yeltsin's popularity was at its peak and the 'democrats' could have been expected to cruise home. Fresh elections would no doubt have encouraged the devel-opment of a genuine multi-party system, legitimised the new Russian state and assisted the development of political institutions. Numerous factors inhibited this strategy. First, the Russian Supreme Soviet had played an enthusiastic part in the defeat of the coup, and it would have been a poor reward for it to be dissolved at the first opportunity. The CPD, moreover, appeared willing to go along with Yeltsin's plans, above all with his priorities for radical economic reform and a new constitution, and at its meeting from late October 1991 granted him yet more powers to impose economic reforms by decree. Second, before elections could be held it was clear that there would have had to have been a drastic reorganisation of Russian representative institutions, above all the aboli-tion of the unwieldy Congress and constitutional reform. Third, there was no guarantee that parliamentary elections would have resulted in a Congress that differed significantly from the previous one.

Fourth, and most importantly, the relegitimation of the existing representative insti-tutions would have placed the development of the presidency at risk. Russia at this time was still formally a parliamentary republic, although with an executive presidency, and Yeltsin's powers were enjoyed only in so far as they were delegated by the legislature: and what was delegated could be revoked. Finally, elections at this time would have reinforced Yeltsin's dependency on Democratic Russia and the 'democratic' movement as a whole; and as a corollary, the deepening of the democratic revolution would have entailed an assault against the *nomenklatura* class, something Yeltsin was loathe to do since he soon came to rely precisely on these managerial and administrative elites. Yeltsin tactically marginalised Democratic Russia and the democratic movement as a whole, and they exercised little influence on appointments:[10] at times of crisis, however, he was not above calling on them as his foot-soldiers in the struggle against the current enemy, as in the referendum of April 1993. The recourse to a referendum in itself suggested a failure of routine elections.

## Soviet parliamentarianism versus neo-Soviet presidentialism

The hesitant advance towards democracy of the *perestroika* years encumbered Russia with an unwieldy and largely unworkable parliamentary system. Russia was the only post-Soviet republic to retain the cumbrous two-tier legislative system for the elections of March 1990. The Russian Congress was made up of 1,068 constituencies, of which 168 (15.7 per cent) were national-territorial and 900 (84.3 per cent) territorial. The Congress was to meet twice a year to legislate on the most important constitutional and other issues. With a two-thirds majority the Congress could alter the constitution, ratify changes in the name of the republic and cities, and change the powers of the presidency.[11] The Congress selected a smaller Supreme Soviet, the body properly known as the parliament, to examine current legislation and debate policies. By September 1993 the Supreme Soviet contained 248 voting members and 138 non-voting members working in committees and commissions, and thus a total of 386 officially worked in parliament on a permanent basis, although about a quarter of Supreme Soviet deputies were inactive. All Congress deputies over a five-year period were to have the opportunity of becoming members of the Supreme Soviet, but this did not work out in practice. In the three years of the Russian parliament it was renewed only twice, at the Sixth Congress in April 1992 and again at the Seventh in December 1992.[12]

The Supreme Soviet was headed by the chair, a post that became vacant when Yeltsin was elected president in June 1991. Yeltsin's former ally Khasbulatov was the main candidate, but he encountered stiff opposition at the Fifth Congress in July 1991;[13] he was associated with the ethos of the old Party system and considered to have an abrasive personality. Having won his spurs during the coup, at the resumed Fifth Congress Khasbulatov was finally confirmed as 'speaker' (his favoured term for the post) on 28 October 1991 with 559 votes.[14] Khasbulatov's election did not put an end to Yeltsin's conflicts with the Russian parliament, and indeed intensified them as Khasbulatov, an economist by profession, sought to modify the government's economic reform programme and to defend the prerogatives of parliament – and his own.

Up to 1992 the Russian legislature was an accomplice to its own marginalisation: it voted to establish a presidential system at the Third Congress in April 1991, adopted the Law on the President at the Fourth on 24 May, and granted the presidency emergency powers to drive through reform by decree at the resumed Fifth Congress in November 1991. With the appointment in November 1991 of a non-party 'government of reforms', parliament was deprived of the right of detailed oversight over the work of the government. Although decrees and the appointment of key ministers required parliamentary approval, the legislature effectively lost control over policy and the government. Up to the Sixth Congress in April 1992 parliament largely acceded to the process of self-marginalisation. Parliament's 'marginalisation', however, was of a special type; the increased powers of the presidency were always clearly envisaged within the context of parliamentary supremacy. The Law on the President of May 1991 stipulated that 'the president does not have the right to dissolve or suspend' the Congress or Supreme Soviet; he or she was to report at least once a year to the Congress; and their decrees were not to infringe existing legislation.[15] The extraordinary powers of the president were always regarded as temporary, so that when at the height of the struggle in 1993 parliament deprived the president of these powers, they considered that they were doing no more than what they were entitled to.

The struggle between parliament and the presidency in 1992–3, however, was always about more than legal issues. Sharpening differences over economic policy and the form of the state to be consolidated in the constitution (see below) gave rise to the emergence of a 'red-brown' front (leftists and nationalists), united in their opposition to the break-up of the USSR, radical economic reforms and Yeltsin's style of leadership and the team with which he worked. They had no clear programme and instead the bloc reflected divergent interests, but a common hostility to the new order represented by the August regime was enough to unite them in opposition to Yeltsin. At the same time, although independently, Khasbulatov and his colleagues sought to reverse the marginalisation of parliament as an institution, leading to a profound political crisis at the Sixth (April 1992) and succeeding Congresses. At that Congress, for example, Khasbulatov condemned the cabinet's 'attack on democracy' and the dismissive attitude by ministers towards representative institutions.[16]

The crisis of governance derived not so much from the personal qualities of the new leaders, the social context of the new politics or even long-term factors like the weakness of liberalism in Russia. More immediate political factors allowed the emergence of a type of dual power and ultimately provoked a constitutional crisis that led to bloodshed in October 1993.[17] There remained a fundamental 'constitutional' crisis because the 1978 Russian constitution (a slightly modified version of the 1977 Soviet constitution) was heavily amended after 1990 and ended up granting both the executive and the legislative branches supreme state power.[18] Russia was *de jure* a parliamentary republic but *de facto* became a presidential republic. The balance between executive and legislative remained a matter of political struggle rather than constitutional law. The president's extraordinary powers were temporary and subject to the approval of parliament. Parliament itself enjoyed extensive powers under the existing constitution and, increasingly dominated by oppositional groups, was able to block the executive's initiatives for constitutional change and economic reform.

### Personal factors

Conflict between parliament and the presidency became endemic: personal factors played their part but structural factors were primarily responsible for the constitutional crisis that became a crisis of the state. Khasbulatov ruthlessly exploited his position as speaker to reward his supporters and make life uncomfortable for his critics. He enjoyed the power to manage the agenda, to manipulate the voting process on bills and amendments, to manage information flows; and controlled access to scarce resources and privileges such as foreign trips and offices. This did not render the Congress subservient to him, but it did mean that he exerted inordinate power to shape its actions and agendas. Already in January 1992 Khasbulatov launched the first of his many broadsides against the 'shock therapy' approach to economic reform, condemning 'anarchical, uncontrolled price rises' and insisted that 'We are fed up with experiments.' He antagonised members of parliament as much as he did the president. The main charge against him was that instead of allowing parliament to act as an impartial forum for debate, he turned it into his own power base. Deputies claimed that Khasbulatov regularly exceeded his authority, others accused him of authoritarian methods of rule, and a growing number called for his replacement.[19]

The president himself failed to build consensus in parliament, not meeting with the leaders of the democratic movement for several months after the coup, and appeared to forget their earlier efforts on his behalf. Yeltsin's own rash and often ill-considered assaults on Congress narrowed the scope for compromise. The principles of parliamentary and presidential government are both equally valid, but the tragedy for Russia was that both were being pursued with equal vigour at the same time: like two trains approaching on the same track, the collision would be disastrous for both. While Khasbulatov certainly sought to turn the Russian parliament into his personal power base, the main reason for the crisis of legislative power in Russia was structural, primarily the legacy of the anti-parliamentarian essence of Soviet power and then, during *perestroika*, the incompetent approach to institutional reform. In establishing a powerful Congress Gorbachev hoped to balance the powers of the Communist Party; but the disappearance of the latter left the field clear for the former. The structure of parliament meant that it was an anti-parliamentary parliament, unable to work like a 'normal' representative and legislative body. The constitution, although heavily amended, still gave enormous powers to parliament, but the August 1991 settlement prescribed no institutional way to fulfil this role. The biannual Congress, as the 'highest state authority' enjoyed enormous powers and when in session could alter the constitution by a simple two-thirds majority, including depriving the president of his powers, or indeed, if they dared, abolishing the presidency entirely.[20] As long as the Congress wielded the enormous power to amend the constitution at will, and as long as the floor of the Supreme Soviet could be manipulated by the Presidium (which emerged as a type of parallel government) and by the speaker, no real parliamentary politics could emerge.

The distinctive feature of the crisis was that while policy initiative lay with the presidential side, control over implementation and administration lay with parliament. This dualism was reflected in the very nature of the struggle, with parliament by necessity reduced to blocking measures: they had the power to impede presidential initiatives but lacked the power to develop policies – hence the growing irresponsibility of the Supreme Soviet's actions. The Congress and its Supreme Soviet were in the classical position of power without responsibility, but their power was essentially negative. Parliament failed to become an effective working body, with most of its legislation not direct-acting but requiring further regulations and decrees, offering enormous scope for the bureaucracy to hinder or to profit from them. The red-brown opposition, moreover, took full advantage of the moral and political collapse of the democratic challenge, intensifying the crisis of power at all levels.

## Genesis of a tragedy

The catastrophic breakdown of what some call the first Russian republic in late 1993 remains one of the great mysteries of the post-communist era. Why did a parliament that had supported the democratic cause up to 1991, and in particular the democratically elected president, Yeltsin, during the coup of August 1991, come into such violent conflict with him soon after? The answer according to an important recent study lies in the phenomenon of cycling. The institutional rules in most democratic legislatures are constructed to avoid the breakdown of majority rule; that is, a situation where fragmentation of deputy preferences establishes an idle cycle that prevents coherent majorities to coalesce and to be sustained. In Russia's under-institutionalised period of early democracy this is precisely what happened in the Supreme Soviet and the larger parent body, the Congress of People's Deputies. No adequate barriers to prevent cycling had been established. Russia's majority rule institution simply did not work in a context where parties, committees and effective rules were weak. This fluid situation allowed the parliament's speaker, Khasbulatov, to seize the initiative and impose his preferences of the parliamentary majority. Despite attempts to remove Khasbulatov by deputies, cycling did not allow them to establish a majority to vote for his removal.[21]

### Countdown to crisis

The conflict only gradually assumed the dimensions of a general crisis of power. At first Yeltsin grudgingly tolerated a degree of legislative oversight over his actions. He accepted the Supreme Soviet's repeal in November 1991 of the presidential decree imposing a state of emergency on Chechen-Ingushetia, but he over-ruled attempts by parliament to force the regional elections due on 8 December 1991. Parliament's reversal of Yeltsin's decree of 19 December 1991 merging the ministries of security and interior was allowed to stand. Parliament procrastinated over passing laws on such critical issues as privatisation, land reform and ownership, bankruptcy and the new constitution, and passed illiberal legislation on such issues as exchange controls. Deputies opposed the reformers' reliance on economic aid from the West and sought more government intervention to preserve Russian industry, and in general were wary of the 'cosmopolitan' democracy that was allegedly being introduced into Russia. Khasbulatov became increasingly critical of the president's wide powers and sought parliamentary control over the government, including the right to veto government appointments and policies.

Meetings of the Congress were times of high drama. The Sixth Congress in April 1992 failed to adopt a new constitution, placed even stricter controls over the progress of reform, and restricted the purchase and sale of land.[22] Although the Congress was able to adopt individual elements of the new constitution, no majority could be mustered to adopt the constitution as a whole, a classic example of cycling. The Russian CPD appeared to be going the same way as the old Soviet Congress, acting as a brake rather than the motor of reform. Following the Sixth Congress Yeltsin threatened to hold a nationwide referendum on the new constitution and for the early dissolution of parliament (its term was due to end in March 1995) and new elections. A referendum was allowed if one-third of Congress deputies or one million citizens asked for one. Even if Democratic Russia had collected the required signatures, the Supreme Soviet would still have had to agree to call a referendum. Thus there was stalemate and no legal way in which Yeltsin could dissolve Congress and call new elections.[23] In recognition of this Yeltsin rejoined the parliamentary process of drafting the new constitution, rather than holding a referendum and imposing his own.[24] Yeltsin, however, remained convinced that the Congress had outlived its purpose: 'In my opinion, it is an artificial, supra-parliamentary entity. Its very existence is a permanent basis for disrupting the balance between the legislative, executive and judicial branches'.[25]

Yeltsin's emergency powers had been granted for only one year and were due to expire on 1 December 1992, thus the Seventh Congress (1–14 December 1992) was if anything more tense than the Sixth. Divided into 14 fractions and with the balance of the 'marsh' (the centrist bloc comprised largely of officialdom) having tilted even further towards the conservatives,[26] the reformers faced a formidable task. On 10 December Yeltsin forced a showdown. In a short but threatening speech, he called for a referendum to decide who should have power, the president or parliament. He argued that the conservatives in the Congress had impeded the reforms, insisting that 'What they failed to achieve in August 1991, they decided to repeat now and carry out a creeping coup'.[27] On 11 December Congress passed a resolution that emasculated Yeltsin's proposed referendum, adopting a constitutional amendment which banned any plebiscite that could result in a vote of no confidence in any high state body, or which could lead to its dissolution before its term of office had expired. Under the auspices of the chairman of the Constitutional Court, Valeri Zor'kin, a deal was brokered on 12 December in the form of a nine-point agreement which stood or fell together. A referendum was to be held in April 1993 on the adoption of the new constitution, with contentious points to be placed as options, and in the meantime the existing balance between executive and legislative was to be maintained. Nominations for the post of premier were to be put to the Congress for a non-binding popularity poll, and after some complex voting Victor Chernomyrdin replaced Gaidar as prime minister.

Russia appeared to have entered a vicious circle in which it could not have elections before the adoption of a constitution, but could not adopt a constitution before elections. The weakness of party politics meant that parliament itself as an institution took on a monolithic role as an actor in politics rather than as the vessel in which politics was conducted. In other words, politics was displaced into struggle *between* institutions rather than by consensual processes *within* them. Without changes to the structure of legislative power there could be no stable political development. The unstable compromise reached at the Seventh Congress was now comprehensively repudiated. Following desultory negotiations between Yeltsin and Khasbulatov, the Eighth Congress on 10–13 March 1993 failed to sanction the referendum or to establish the framework for the adoption of a new constitution. The Congress stripped Yeltsin off many of the powers granted to him earlier to implement economic reform. He was deprived of the right to issue decrees with the same force as parliamentary laws, to appoint presidential envoys or heads of administration, or to appoint government ministers without the approval of parliament. The government was granted the right to submit legislation directly to parliament (bypassing the presidency), a privilege that the Soviet government under Pavlov had sought not long before the coup. The presidency emerged limited and damaged by this bout with Congress.

In the last months of the old parliament Khasbulatov in effect organised an insurrection against Yeltsin and sought to use the combined forces of an eclectic oppositionist front to propel himself to power. He now proposed the establishment of a parliamentary republic at the centre and the restoration of the power of the soviets in the localities. Khasbulatov declared himself in favour of the restoration of a new form of Soviet power in which local executive authorities would be subordinated to local soviets, which would in turn be subordinated to the presidium of the Supreme Soviet.[28] The president would be reduced to a figurehead, and the head of the legislature would in effect become chief executive. Khasbulatov had long advocated the municipalisation of soviets to turn them into effective bodies of local self-government,[29] but this was taking his earlier ideas much further. Khasbulatov sought to establish a type of post-communist soviet power, echoing the slogan 'soviets without communists' of the Kronstadt insurgents of March 1921. On trips to the provinces he urged local soviets to resist the executive authorities, and by April 1993 he was boasting that he had restored Soviet power in the regions, and he soon tried to restore Soviet power in the centre as well.

### The referendum of 25 April 1993

Parliament's challenge left Yeltsin facing a conundrum, and as usual in a crisis he took decisive action. In a broadcast on 20 March he announced a referendum for 25 April and the imposition of 'special rule' that would free him from legislative restraints, a declaration that was clearly unconstitutional. Despite the suggestion of a forceful res-olution to the crisis, when the decree was published on 24 March it made no mention of the dissolution of Congress or the suspension of parliament. Zor'kin's attempts to mediate this time came to nothing, having discredited himself by rushing to condemn Yeltsin's 'special rule' even before seeing the decree. The Ninth Congress, called in response to Yeltsin's démarche, nevertheless met on 26 March in an atmosphere of extreme crisis. A meeting between Yeltsin and Khasbulatov on 27 March appeared to provide a solution by stipulating early presidential and parliamentary elections in autumn 1993. However, Congress on the next day angrily rejected the deal, and turned against Khasbulatov himself, with some 300 deputies voting for his resignation, and the vote to impeach Yeltsin fell only 72 short of the required two-thirds majority. Khasbulatov's own room for manoeuvre had been drastically curtailed, and the final day of the Ninth Congress on 29 March was marked by the passage of numerous acts stripping Yeltsin off his remaining powers.

The referendum of 25 April 1993 gave people four choices: support for president Yeltsin; support for his economic policies; and whether they favoured early presidential and parliamentary elections. The Ninth CPD stipulated that the vote required 50 per cent of the registered voters (not just a simple majority of those taking part) to be binding, but following an appeal the Constitutional Court ruled that only the last two questions required the higher threshold since they involved constitutional issues. In the event both turnout (64.5 per cent) and support for Yeltsin were higher than expected (see Table 3.1). Yeltsin received a ringing personal endorsement, with some 59 per cent expressing confi-dence in him, and even his policies, despite the hardship they had caused, were supported by 53 per cent of the vote. The 49 per cent vote for pre-term presidential elections and the thumping 67 per cent (43 per cent of the electorate) for early parliamentary elections, however, were not binding since they failed to reach the required 50 per cent of registered voters.

Despite popular support for pre-term parliamentary elections, these were refused by the parliamentary leadership and the crisis deepened. While the result weakened Khasbulatov personally, the Supreme Soviet was increasingly radicalised by the conflict, and parliament as a whole over-estimated its strength, interpreting concessions as weakness. The politicisation of the struggle between parliament and presidency meant that the endemic constitutional crisis had been transformed into an overt political strug-gle for power. The extreme right, made up of nationalists and imperial restorationists, allied with the extreme left, neo-Bolshevik and Soviet rejectionists, to defeat the centre. It appeared that the parliamentary leadership was engaged in a premeditated attempt to

*Table 3.1* Referendum, 25 April 1993

*Turnout and participation*

- Out of a total of 107,310,374 eligible voters, 69,222,858 actually voted, a turnout of 64.5 per cent.
- Only Chechnya boycotted the referendum, while in Tatarstan nearly 80 per cent of the electorate ignored the vote, rendering the result there invalid.

*Result (%)*

| Yes | | No | | Spoiled ballots |
|---|---|---|---|---|
| % of vote | % of electorate | % of vote | % of electorate | |

1 Do you have confidence in the President of the Russian Federation, Boris Yeltsin?

| | | | | |
|---|---|---|---|---|
| 58.7 | 37.3 | 39.2 | 25.2 | 2.1 |

2 Do you approve of the socioeconomic policies carried out by the President of the Russian Federation and the government of the Russian Federation since 1992?

| | | | | |
|---|---|---|---|---|
| 53.0 | 34.0 | 44.6 | 28.6 | 2.4 |

3 Do you consider it necessary to hold early elections to the Presidency of the Russian Federation?

| | | | | |
|---|---|---|---|---|
| 49.5 | 31.7 | 47.1 | 30.2 | 3.4 |

4 Do you consider it necessary to hold early elections of the people's deputies of the Russian Federation?

| | | | | |
|---|---|---|---|---|
| 67.2 | 43.1 | 30.1 | 19.3 | 2.7 |

*Sources*: *Rossiiskaya gazeta*, 6 May 1993; RFE/RL, *Research Report*, Vol. 2, No. 21, 21 May 1993, p. 12.

*Note*: The Constitutional Court ruled that questions three and four involved a change in the constitution, so half the electorate would have to vote 'Yes' for them to be binding.

seize power, including the accumulation of weapons. Over the summer Khasbulatov and Rutskoi toured the provinces, hoping to garner support. On a visit to the Far East Rutskoi declared that within two months he would be president. During a visit to Orël and Bryansk he insisted that an end to the confusion had to be made during the autumn, suggesting that the Congress would call for simultaneous pre-term parliamentary and presidential elections. He announced that an alternative policy programme was being developed that would allow the rebirth of Russia from the regions up.[30] More importantly, it is clear that parliament was planning to emasculate presidential power.

Interpreting the results of the April referendum as a renewed popular mandate, Yeltsin went on the offensive and sought to break the impasse by convening a Constitutional Assembly in June 1993, a tactic (as we shall see below) that was only partially successful. The draft of a new constitution was completed in July, but its adoption was blocked by some regional leaders. Yeltsin's failure on 18 September to convert the Federation Council into a fully-fledged consultative-advisory body to replace parliament's existing Council of Nationalities triggered the final crisis.[31] On that very day Khasbulatov escalated the personal vendetta by accusing Yeltsin of being a common drunkard. Since the referendum Russian political life had descended to mutual mud-flinging amid accusations of corruption, a process encouraged by Rutskoi.[32] By a presidential decree of 1 September 1993 both Rutskoi and first deputy prime minister Vladimir Shumeiko, who had been trading insults, were suspended pending investigations into corruption.[33] The inner life of parliament itself had similarly degenerated, with a regime of fear imposed on all of Khasbulatov's opponents. The more far-seeing deputies had already resigned their mandates. Parliament appeared unable to respond to the changes taking place in Russian life.

### The new October

Finally, on 21 September 1993, Yeltsin took the dissolution option. Presidential decree No. 1400, 'On Gradual Constitutional Reform in the Russian Federation', dissolved the Supreme Soviet and the CPD, whose powers were to be transferred to a new Federal Assembly.[34] The existing Federation Council was to be vested with the functions of the upper chamber of the Assembly, while elections to the new lower chamber, the State Duma, were to take place on 12 December 1993. One of the reasons for Yeltsin's action was the failure of the Constitutional Assembly to adopt the new constitution, and it was now ordered to agree a final version with parliament's own Constitutional Commission (nominally headed by Yeltsin) by 12 December.[35]

The rejectionists greatly overplayed their hand, especially given the results of the April referendum. Khasbulatov and the deputies who supported him did not realise quite how detached they had become from popular opinion, and when they issued the call for the masses to come to defend the White House in September 1993, instead of the expected crowds a rather desultory few thousand assembled. Support for the parliamentary opposition was fragmented, and within parliament itself the picture is confused. Representatives of 13 out of the 14 factions remained in the chamber, but it is clear that the number of deputies in the White House was falling sharply, some attracted by the promise of jobs in the presidential system and by generous retirement payments. The Tenth Congress was hastily convened, but while some deputies came the Congress lacked a quorum (the required number was swiftly decreased) since, among other reasons, Yeltsin had deprived them of free travel.

In the event it was the army that saved Yeltsin's fortunes. Violent demonstrations on Sunday 3 October soon gave way to insurrection, with armed marauders from the White House seizing the Mayor's office in the old Comecon building opposite. If at that point they had turned West and marched on the Kremlin they may well have been able to seize power. Instead the insurgents turned North into the suburbs to seize the Ostankino television centre. Here they encountered stiff resistance from Interior Ministry forces defending the building, and became locked into a fire-fight lasting several hours. By the evening Yeltsin had returned to the Kremlin from his dacha, and then spent a large part of the night urging the military commanders to crush the insurgency.[36] Having learnt the pitfalls of intervening in domestic political disputes, the military leadership was wary but finally agreed to take action after Yeltsin formally signed the order. A military force was only assembled with considerable difficulty and drew on numerous units and the Alpha security force. By dawn on 4 October the White House was ringed by tanks and by the afternoon the rebel leaders headed by Rutskoi and Khasbulatov had surrendered and were incarcerated in the Lefortovo gaol. According to official statistics, 146 people died in the fighting.[37]

The results of the defeat of the Supreme Soviet were not long in coming. In the regions the traditional soviet-style legislatures were dissolved, allowing the regional executives to consolidate their powers as most created relatively subservient 'pocket' representative bodies. Putin's subsequent attempt to rein in the regional bosses was in many ways a direct legacy of the events of October 1993. In the immediate term, Yeltsin placed temporary bans on some of the more extremist parties and newspapers, but his promise to hold parliamentary elections and a referendum on the constitution on 12 December 1993 was honoured (but the presidential elections promised for six months later were forgotten).

The Russian October of 1993 can be seen, for good or ill, as completing the revolution of August 1991. The dissolution of parliament was not constitutional, but while deficient in legality it clearly commanded a high degree of popular legitimacy. There are certain similarities between Yeltsin's action and that of president Alberto Fujimori in Peru in his *autogolpe* (self-coup) of April 1992, but perhaps a better analogy is with Charles De Gaulle's démarche of 1958 leading to the end of the parliamentary Fourth Republic and the establishment of the semi-presidential Fifth Republic. Bitterly divisive though De Gaulle's action may have been, the referendum of September 1958 showed overwhelming popular support (about 80 per cent of voters) for the new presidentialist constitution. In Russia, however, the violent dénouement to the conflict irreparably damaged Yeltsin's reputation and undermined the legitimacy of the new constitutional order. Since the August 1991 coup Yeltsin had appeared as a destructive force, a *soi-disant* democrat employing Bolshevik methods to destroy Bolshevism.

## The troubled path to the constitution

In countries such as France the spirit of constitutionalism is conceptually enshrined not in any given constitution but in the constituent power (*pouvoir constituant*) of the nation. The frequency with which France has changed its constitutions reflects the belief that no given constitution can constrain the sovereign power of the French people: the French nation is considered to have existed long before any specific constitution.[38] In Russia the relationship between the constitution and the nation is far more ambiguous, reflecting the persistent syndrome of *displaced sovereignty*: instead of the basis of constitutional order being the sovereign people, it was arrogated by regimes of various types standing between the people and the state. This was evident in Russia's first experiment with constitutionalism between 1906 and the revolution, and most forcefully in the Soviet period when popular sovereignty was proclaimed but then usurped by the Communist Party in the name of the higher goal of the pursuit of socialism, and then again, in a very different way, by Yeltsin's regime that pursued the cause of 'reform' as a meta-goal over and above any institutional expression of the popular will.

### Soviet constitutionalism

Max Weber described the constitution (Basic Law) adopted for imperial Russia on 23 April 1906 as 'sham constitutionalism' (*Scheinkonstitutionalismus*), because the Tsar's power allegedly was neither reduced nor effectively constrained.[39] In fact, a constitutional monarchy was introduced abolishing 'unlimited' (*neogranichennyi*) monarchical power, although the crown retained considerable powers.[40] Sham constitutionalism took on new forms in the Soviet era, which we can call 'pseudo-constitutionalism' since the regime was quite explicit about the subordination of the constitutional state to the ideologically-driven needs of the Communist Party. The Soviet regime adopted constitutions in 1918 (for the RSFSR), 1924, 1936 and 1977, with the RSFSR adopting a slightly modified version of the latter on 12 April 1978. As the 'collective Tsar', the Party placed itself above constitutional constraints, and its Statutes were in effect more important than the constitutions themselves. As Gorbachev put it:

> Of course the totalitarian regime disguised itself with democratic decorations: a constitution, laws of various kinds, and 'representative' bodies of government. In fact all the life activity of society was dictated and guided – from beginning to end – by the party structures, by the resolutions, decisions, and orders of the top echelons of the party.[41]

The Soviet system was pseudo-constitutional because its constitutions did not do what a constitution is supposed to do, namely regulate the division of labour within the branches of the state, allocate functions between the centre and the localities, ensure systems of accountability and responsibility, and provide a normative framework for the independent operation of the legal system.

Early Soviet constitutions ignored the real balance of power in society, and in particular the leading role of the Communist Party. The 1918 constitution and its successors proclaimed 'all power to the soviets', but the actual mechanism whereby soviets were to exercise power and the role of the CPSU was left vague. Only the 1977 constitution made explicit the real dominance of the Communist Party, with Article 6 defining it as follows:

> The leading and guiding force of Soviet society and the nucleus of its political system, of all state organisations and public organisations, is the Communist Party of the Soviet Union. The CPSU exists for the people and serves the people.
>
> The Communist Party, armed with Marxism-Leninism, determines the general perspectives of the development of society and the course of the home and foreign policy of the USSR, directs the great constructive work of the Soviet people, and imparts a planned, systematic, and theoretically substantiated character to their struggle for the victory of communism.
>
> All party organisations shall function within the framework of the Constitution of the USSR.[42]

This constitution represented a significant advance towards providing a constitutional framework for Party power, and thus marked a step towards overcoming pseudo-constitutionalism. Nevertheless, the Soviet polity continued to operate according to the conventions of an 'unwritten constitution' of normative acts and administrative practices that left the formal constitution no more than declaratory window-dressing for the regime. The Soviet system had constitutions without the necessary framework of law that could achieve genuine constitutional government in which powers were defined and thus limited. The Soviet regime felt obliged to proclaim its adherence to constitutionalism in large part because the Soviet system, despite its repudiation of liberalism, felt constrained by its appeal to a democratic legitimacy.[43]

In the last years of the Soviet regime Gorbachev sought through *perestroika* to achieve the renewal of the soviet representative system, the reorganisation of the higher bodies of state power, the reform of the electoral system, and to change the judicial-legal process in its entirety. In short, Gorbachev's programme represented a profound constitutional reform but one that was to be constrained by the concept of the 'socialist legal state'.[44] This programme was given legal form in the constitutional amendments of 1 December 1988, including the creation of the partially elected USSR Congress of People's Deputies. On 9 June 1989 the CPD established a Constitutional Commission headed by Gorbachev.[45] In the event, the fall of the regime in late 1991 led to the abandonment of the Soviet constitution and the end of evolutionary reform. A precedent was set for constitutional transformation to take place in unconstitutional, indeed revolutionary, ways.

### The genesis of the Russian constitution

The task now was to write Russia's first ever democratic constitution. In the Soviet era a bureaucratic committee, with advice from experts and select groups, would propose a draft constitution, which was then publicised in a brief nationwide 'discussion' followed by a unanimous vote in the Supreme Soviet. The drafting of the new Russian constitution was to be a far more tortuous and open process, reflecting the divisions of society, and in the end taking a violent turn, as we saw above. Even in the best of times the designing of laws and institutions *ab initio* is an exhilarating but dangerous venture, likened to rebuilding a boat in the open sea.[46] Although a constitution is intended to provide a long-term framework, it is almost impossible to prevent current political concerns from intruding. Numerous choices have to be made: between a unitary or federal system; a parliamentary or a presidential republic or something in between; the balance to be drawn between limited government and effective governance; the equation to be drawn between individual and group rights, between majorities and minorities. If rights are assigned to minority groups, then is there not a danger that members will identify with that community rather than as citizens of the larger state?

The birth of the new Russian constitution was a long and painful process.[47] Four days after the revolutionary Declaration of Sovereignty of the RSFSR on 12 June 1990, the First Russian CPD on 16 June established a Constitutional Commission to prepare a document that would reflect Russia's new juridical and political status. The commission, made up of 102 MPs, was nominally chaired by Yeltsin with Khasbulatov its vice-chairman, but the main work was carried out by a smaller working group of some 15 deputies chaired by the commission's secretary, Oleg Rumyantsev. The first version, rejecting the whole notion of socialism and communism, was ready by November 1990.[48] The draft declared that 'the Russian Federation is a sovereign, democratic, social and legal state of historically united peoples' (Article 1.1) and broke decisively with Bolshevik traditions by defending the inviolable rights of the individual (Article 1.3). Russia was defined as a 'social state' guaranteeing extensive collective and welfare rights based 'on the principles of social democracy and justice' (Article 1.8). Not surprisingly, the draft was attacked as being 'anti-Soviet' and the Supreme Soviet refused to place it on the agenda for adoption by the Second CPD in December 1990.

Against the background of the 'winter offensive' by the so-called conservatives from late 1990, the Communists of Russia faction in the legislature prepared an alternative and more traditional draft constitution.[49] After much discussion the Constitutional Commission came out with a compromise in time for discussion by the Third Congress (28 March–4 April 1991); but by then the context had dramatically changed: the 17 March referendum established the post of a Russian president and the Communists of Russia split and a reformist faction (Communists for Democracy) emerged led by Rutskoi. In June 1991 the Fifth Congress (first convocation) rejected the compromise draft, insisting that it failed to formulate Russia's rights against the centre and that it was full of contradictions, and instructed the commission to prepare another version.

The August 1991 coup and the subsequent dissolution of the Soviet system added a new urgency to the constitutional question, and the commission rapidly produced a second draft,[50] which was presented by Rumyantsev to the Supreme Soviet on 10 October 1991.[51] With the fall of Soviet power ideological issues, such as individual rights, civil society and judicial reform, were no longer so contentious, but new points of disagreement had emerged. These focused above all on the separation of powers on the horizontal level (between executive and legislative power), and on the vertical level (between the central authorities and components of the federation). The territorial organisation of the state proved particularly divisive since the draft sought to move away from Bolshevik ethno-federal principles towards a classic territorial federalism (see Chapter 11). As a result, the Supreme Soviet failed to muster the required 50 per cent of deputies to place the constitution on the agenda of the reconvened Fifth Congress for approval.[52] In response, the Constitutional Commission met on 23 October and authorised Yeltsin to place a slightly revised draft before the CPD 'for discussion' (*k svedeniyu*), rather than adoption.[53] This he did on 2 November,[54] and Congress then instructed the commission to prepare yet another version in time for the Sixth Congress.

Work on the document was now torn between what appeared to be irreconcilable forces: on the one hand, most of the former autonomous republics rejected the Constitutional Commission's draft for failing to recognise their sovereign status; while, on the other, many of Russia's regions condemned it on the grounds that it gave excessive privileges to the republics. The working group sought to find a compromise, and on 2 March 1992 completed a third version which, after slight modifications, was published on 24 March.[55] This draft proposed a parliamentary republic but with broad powers for the president within the framework of parliamentary oversight and with the clear separation of powers between the executive, legislative and judiciary. As far as supporters of the legislature were concerned, 'In the absence of a civil society in our country, parliament and the Congress of People's Deputies are today virtually the only guarantors that can stop our country from plunging into a dictatorship of individuals.'[56] This was a code formulation to prevent the presidency in general, and Yeltsin in particular, from gaining strong powers. The signing of the three-tiered Federation Treaty on 31 March (Chapter 11) resolved some of the sharpest conflicts over the federation.[57]

The Supreme Soviet this time placed the constitution on the agenda, recommending that it be adopted at its first reading to avoid exhaustive debate over individual clauses. However, the Sixth CPD, while rejecting alternative drafts, merely approved the general outline (*za osnovu*) of the commission's version, calling for yet more revisions.[58] We have noted above the 'cycling' involved. Against the background of a sharp deterioration in relations between the president and parliament, including fears that Yeltsin might dissolve the legislature and put his draft to a national referendum, the Congress somewhat moderated its assault against the president's economic policies and political prerogatives, extending his right to rule by decree to the end of 1992 but forcing him to step down as prime minister. The Congress went on to make numerous amendments to the existing 'Brezhnev' constitution, including the bodily incorporation of the Federation Treaty.[59]

The constitutional process had now reached an impasse. Only the CPD had the right to amend or adopt the constitution, and Yeltsin's attempts to raise the million signatures necessary to hold a referendum did not offer a way out since adopting the constitution through a referendum was unconstitutional, and in any case required the approval of the Congress. The opposition in the Congress, on the other hand, used the right to make constitutional amendments with increasing boldness and for short-term political advantage. Of the 340 amendments made to the old constitution by early 1993, an astonishing 258 were adopted in 1992 alone.[60] The work of the commission continued, however, and a fourth version was released on 11 November 1992.[61] Work on the new constitution continued in parallel with amendments to the old, allowing, according to Rumyantsev, a gradual convergence of the two. He claimed that this permitted a 'balanced and consistent modernisation of the legal space of the Federation' rather than a constitutional revolution,[62] an assessment that was too sanguine by far.

Fearing the loss of a powerful weapon in their struggle with the president, and hesitant to commit themselves to elections, the Seventh CPD in December 1992 once again failed to adopt the prepared draft constitution. According to Rumyantsev, this was a major mistake and allowed the president to seize the initiative and encourage other drafts which, according to Rumyantsev, were inferior to the parliamentary version in that they introduced numerous 'conjunctural' elements. However long and convoluted the parliamentary version, Rumyantsev insisted, it was nevertheless permeated by a democratic spirit that was in sharp contrast to Soviet-era constitutions.[63] Agreement had been reached at the Congress on putting the basic principles of the new constitution before the people in a referendum, but Khasbulatov's call in February 1993 for pre-term presidential and parliamentary elections ruptured the fragile compromise. The president now released details of his own, much more presidential, constitutional draft on the eve of the referendum of 25 April 1993.[64] This envisaged the abolition of the old Congress and Supreme Soviet and their replacement by a bicameral legislature to be known as the Federal Assembly. The lower chamber (the State Duma) was to be elected on a proportional basis, while the upper (the Federation Council) was to be made up of the elected presidents of Russia's republics and the heads of regional administrations elsewhere. Only the president's nomination for the post of prime minister was to be ratified by parliament, while all other ministerial appointments were to be approved 'in consultation' with the chamber. The president had the power to dissolve parliament and call new elections, while only the Federation Council had the right to impeach the president. The post of vice-president was to be abolished, and it was now made more difficult to amend the constitution. These ideas lay at the basis of the constitution adopted in December 1993.

An extended process of consultation followed in which the views of members of the federation were sought.[65] The results of the April 1993 referendum were interpreted as supporting the president's accelerated programme of constitutional change; and indeed, following the referendum the struggle between the executive and the legislature now focused on the constitution.[66] By the same token, as both sides courted the regions and republics, the Russian constitutional process was ever more frequently likened to the Novo-Ogarevo process in which Gorbachev had tried to adopt a new Union Treaty, but which precipitated the union's disintegration.[67] The presidential draft was presented to the Constitutional Commission on 6 May 1993, and on the next day rejected.[68] It remained unclear how his draft, or any other, could be adopted without the support of the existing Congress and Supreme Soviet.[69]

Work had continued on the Constitutional Commission's draft, and on 7 May 1993 the Commission approved the fifth 'Khasbulatovite' parliamentary version.[70] The equality of members of the federation was stressed 'apart from those allowed by the constitution'. Republics were recognised as states, enjoying the full panoply of state powers on their territory apart from those that remained the prerogative of the Russian Federation. Other federal units were labelled simply state-territorial formations. The upper house was to be called the Federation Council, while the lower house, the State Duma, was to be elected by a simple first-past-the-post system. The president was to become merely the ceremonial head of state and not head of the executive branch.[71] The draft was to be discussed by parliamentary committees and a final version was to be published by 15 October and discussed by a special convocation of the CPD to meet on 17 November.[72]

### The Constitutional Assembly and beyond

Yeltsin could not ignore this direct challenge to his constitutional status, and on 20 May he decided to finesse the constitutional question by taking up the option long advocated by the Russian Democratic Reform Movement led by Sobchak and Popov,[73] namely the convocation of a special Constitutional Assembly to accelerate the constitutional process.[74] However, whereas Popov had insisted that the Assembly should meet for only one purpose, the adoption of a new constitution, Yeltsin's Constitutional Assembly was intended to shape a draft that could then be sent round to members of the federation for their approval. The Constitutional Assembly opened on 5 June 1993 and was composed of 762 representatives of the federation as well as from social organisations.[75] In his opening speech Yeltsin likened the period with 1917 and insisted that the new Assembly was continuing the labour of the Provisional Government in devising a democratic constitution for Russia, work brought to a violent end by the Bolshevik seizure of power and the dispersal of the Constituent Assembly in January 1918.[76] Yeltsin grounded the birth of the Russian constitutional order on the brief attempt to establish democracy in Russia in 1917, rather than the Tsarist, let alone the Soviet, experiences of 'sham' and 'pseudo' constitutionalism, and thus reinforced the link between 1917 and 1991. It symbolised the attempt to portray the Soviet period not just as an aberration but as fundamentally illegitimate; an interregnum in Russia's search for democracy. Indeed, his insistence that soviets and democracy were fundamentally incompatible was one of the factors that led to the final rift between himself and Khasbulatov.[77] Yeltsin branded the attempt by the Supreme Soviet to manage a smooth transition by maintaining continuity and observance of the existing constitution as being no more than 'a weapon in the hands of an illegitimate new ruling class, with whose assistance they try to retain their illegal power'.[78]

Despite the president's fighting talk, the work of the Constituent Assembly proceeded in a conciliatory atmosphere, and in its committees many of the ideas put forward by parliamentary representatives were adopted, giving rise to a 'mixed' form of government.[79] The Assembly came up with a new version on 12 July drawing on both the presidential draft of April 1993 and parliament's.[80] There was much on which they agreed, such as the rights and obligations of the citizen and the right to all forms of property, but they differed radically over the role of the president and parliament. The Assembly's version represented Yeltsin's last attempt to achieve some agreement with the old legislature over the constitution: the problem still remained of how to adopt it.[81] In an attempt to win over the regions a Federation Council was established at a meeting in Petrozavodsk on 13 August of the Council of the Heads of the Republics, when Yeltsin called for the creation of a type of mini-parliament to resolve the constitutional crisis. The new Council was to consist of a representative apiece from the executive and legislative powers in each region and republic, making a total of 176 from the 88 subjects of the federation willing to participate (Chechnya refused).[82] At its first meeting on 18 September, however, Yeltsin failed to get them to sign a founding document.

The Supreme Soviet was still working to its own timetable of constitutional reform, ignoring the Constitutional Assembly. This attempt to give substance to a parallel constitutional process threatened to strip the president of his powers but proved a grave miscalculation. Yeltsin struck first, and as we have seen on 21 September 1993 dissolved the legislature and suspended the constitution. His action raised grave ethical issues: to what extent are unconstitutional acts valid in the attempt to establish the rule of law? As far as he was concerned, the Soviet system could not be reformed and any attempt to smuggle back some of its principles would represent a betrayal of the democratic spirit of August 1991. With his supreme political instinct, moreover, Yeltsin was well aware that his power was at stake. In a revolutionary situation law becomes subordinate to political expediency, and by late 1993 a genuinely revolutionary danger had emerged. For the Yeltsinites, the struggle was no more than the final triumph of the 'counter-revolution' against the Bolshevik usurpation of power in October 1917; whereas for Khasbulatov and his supporters, the battle was to save something from the Soviet system and to limit the powers of the insurgent 'democratic' elite. The constitution had become a tool in the struggle for power, something that would detract from its legitimacy whichever side won. It would also diminish its efficacy, introducing an instrumental view of the constitutional process that would in the end absolve the 'reformers' of the need to subordinate themselves to the rule of law. The tradition of 'displaced sovereignty' remained strong.

# Part II

# Political institutions and processes

The dissolution of communist power was accompanied by a crisis of governance threatening chaos and social disorder. The optimal balance between stability and transformation proved elusive as the Soviet crisis of governance re-appeared in an accentuated form. The weakness of post-communist state institutions was not compensated by the growth of other mechanisms to achieve the 'reign of peace' in civil society, giving rise to an almost primeval pre-liberal struggle of all against all, as Thomas Hobbes would have put it. The distinctive feature of early post-communist Russia was the almost palpable retreat of government: the high tide of state power under the Soviet regime ebbed and society was left exposed and vulnerable to its own morbid elements; venality, criminality and corruption. Once again it appeared that decrees were issued and laws passed only to be ignored by a society apparently living according to a different set of rules. The economic collapse and the threat of social disorder accompanying the transition from communism raised fears that once again, as in 1917, the democratic experiment would be still-born.

# 4    Constitutionalism and the law

For forms of government let fools contest,
That which is best administered is best.
(Alexander Pope)[1]

The re-emergence of a separate Russia out of the Soviet shell ranks as one of the great state-building endeavours of the twentieth century. Born out of the crisis attending the collapse of the USSR, the Russian state emerged with few immediate advantages. Its system of government had to be built from scratch, its constitution had to be rewritten, its legal system needed to move away from the punitive and vindictive ethos of the Soviet period, and its officialdom had to be retrained in the ways of a modern civil service. The priority for Russia was to establish the basic framework in which politics would be conducted, to establish the 'rules of the game', but as we have seen in the previous chapter, for two years Russian political development was stymied by a period of 'phoney democracy', where the constitution became an instrument in political struggle. Now at last a constitution appropriate for a democratic republic was adopted, together with the creation of the institutional foundations for the rule of law and constitutionalism.

## The 1993 constitution

Yeltsin's decree of 21 September 1993 dissolved the Russian CPD and the Supreme Soviet and transferred their powers to a new bicameral Federal Assembly, and simultaneously suspended the operation of the old constitution. The existing Federation Council was vested with the functions of the upper chamber of the Assembly, while elections to the new lower chamber, the State Duma, were to take place on 12 December 1993. Accompanying the decree were acts establishing the electoral system.[2] The new legislature and the rules regulating its election were thus born in a process that was both unconstitutional and anti-constitutional. This irregular procedure, while breaking the impasse in the struggle between the Supreme Soviet and the presidency, undermined the development of a legal basis to Russian government. During the course of the campaign, moreover, the rules governing the election and the referendum were modified by the president, further undermining their legitimacy.[3] The duration of the new legislature, moreover, was reduced from four to two years.

### The constitutional referendum of 12 December 1993

Following the dissolution of the Supreme Soviet the Constitutional Assembly was reorganised to include a 'public chamber', and shortly afterwards a 'state chamber' (the work of both was regularised on 11 October), to complete work on the constitution. The committee drew on the Constitutional Assembly's synthesis but also borrowed directly on earlier presidential and parliamentary drafts. The draft constitution was published on 10 November and, as expected, proposed a strongly presidential system and modified some of the privileges accorded the republics and regions when they had been able to take advantage of the struggle between the president and parliament. A final section of the new version made a number of provisions for the transitional situation, stipulating that the president must serve his full term until June 1996 and thus ended speculation about pre-term presidential elections.

It was this version that was placed before the people for approval on 12 December 1993 and became Russia's first democratic constitution. By a decree of 15 October voters were asked to participate in a plebiscite on the constitution.[4] The support of the majority of the registered electorate, as stipulated by the 16 October 1990 referendum law, was no longer required for adoption but simply 50 per cent of those who voted,[5] although the minimum 50 per cent turnout was retained. The draft constitution was published on 10 November, and the question placed on the ballot paper on 12 December was a simple one: 'Do you support the adoption of the new Russian constitution?' This method of adopting the constitution is clearly open to criticism.[6] The use of the plebiscite is the favoured technique of dictators, and the judgment of a simple 'yes' or 'no' to a complex question is hardly the most democratic way of adopting such a crucial document. This was the method employed, however, by De Gaulle in 1958 to adopt the constitution establishing the Fifth Republic in France.

Official figures show that the constitution was supported by 58.43 per cent of the vote, thus exceeding the 50 per cent threshold required for adoption; while 41.6 per cent voted against (see Table 4.1).[7] The legitimacy of the constitution was weakened by the fact that only 30.7 per cent of the total electorate voted for the constitution, and in 17 republics and regions the constitution was rejected.[8] There remain doubts over the accuracy of the official turnout figures, and the way that they were achieved, especially since the evidence (the ballot papers and area tallies) were swiftly destroyed. Nevertheless, Russia at last had a constitution. The constitution came into force on 12 December 1993, although it was only officially published in the Russian media on 25 December.[9] In the Yeltsin era

*Table 4.1* Referendum on the constitution, 12 December 1993

| | |
|---|---|
| Total electorate | 106,170,835 |
| Turnout | 58,187,755 (54.8 % of registered voters) |
| Valid votes | 53,751,696 (50.6%) |
| Voting for the constitution | 32,937,630 (58.43%) |
| Voting against | 23,431,333 (41.6%) |
| Percentage of total electorate voting for the constitution | 30.7% |

*Sources*: *Rossiiskaya gazeta*, 21 December 1993, p. 1; *Byulleten' Tsentral'noi izbiratel'noi kommissii Rossiiskoi Federatsii* No. 1 (12), 1994, p. 38.

12 December was celebrated as Constitution Day, but under Putin it stopped being a national holiday.

### Basic principles of Russian constitutionalism

The Russian constitution of 1993 is liberal in its overall conception but some of the democratic procedures it proclaims are flawed (see Appendix for text). The document reflects the primacy of liberalism over democracy, a tendency typical of Yeltsin's rule. Nevertheless, the constitution upholds basic principles of democratic state-building such as the separation of powers, defining the rights and duties of various levels of government, and the independence of law. According to its critics, however, while the principle might have been upheld, the lack of balance in the separation of powers undermined the principles which it claimed to enshrine.

The new constitution is a liberal document, meeting world standards in its provisions for human and civic rights (outlined in its second chapter). It enshrines the civil rights of citizens, outlaws the incarceration of 'dissidents' and restricts the monitoring of correspondence and bugging of telephone calls. The constitution forbids censorship and guarantees freedom of the press. It allows Russians to travel abroad as a right, forbids the government from sending citizens into foreign exile or stripping Russians of their citizenship. It also promises freedom of movement within Russia, and enshrines 'the right to travel freely and choose one's place of stay and residence' (Article 27), thus making the dreaded *propiska* residence permits unconstitutional (although Moscow city continued to apply the system). It also guarantees the right to private property, and thus seals this core aspect of liberalism, including the right for citizens to buy and sell land (Articles 35, 36). Provision was made for an ombudsman for human rights, whose duties would be specified by a special 'federal constitutional law' (see below), thirteen of which are stipulated in the constitution. The constitution is direct-acting, requiring no further legal enactments for its provisions to take effect, and therefore the document remains the central reference point for legal and political processes in the country. Thus the new document sought to overcome the legacy of legal arbitrariness of the Soviet years.

The constitution explicitly repudiates the Soviet legacy, but at the same time it perpetuates its social characteristics. Russia is defined as a 'social state' (Article 7) and numerous rights and entitlements are guaranteed to its citizens, including the right to housing (Article 40). The emphasis on social as well as political rights drew on the social-democratic element in Bolshevik thinking and on the 'social liberal' tendency in pre-revolutionary Russian thought, but fundamentalist liberals insist that 'social' is no more than a tame word for 'socialist'.[10] Whatever the inspiration, the degree to which these social rights can be fulfilled is disputed since entitlements to positive rights are even more difficult to enforce in a court of law than the negative rights concerning the inviolability of the individual. The listing of entitlements is alien to the Anglo-Saxon tradition but reflects the tendency in continental social philosophy to assume that what is unregulated does not exist.

There is a more fundamental problem, however, than simply the abstract enumeration of political and social rights. Some of these rights are accompanied by qualifications that could be used to stifle political opposition. In particular, Article 29.2 forbids the incitement of social, racial, national or religious hatred and has been cited as an unwarranted limitation on political and expressional rights. More seriously, the defence of state security or the legitimate rights of others (Article 55.3) has been used for repressive purposes. Article 80 grants the president certain reserve powers as 'guarantor of the constitution', powers that could in certain circumstances be used to subvert the constitution (as has allegedly already been done in the two Chechen wars). The constitution failed to state that voting (except for the president, Article 81.1) takes place on the basis of free and *equal* representation, thus making it impossible to appeal to the constitution to prevent, for example, constituencies varying greatly in the number of electors. Moreover, the proclamation of abstract promises of social justice, such as the right to free healthcare (Article 41.1) and a 'decent environment' (Article 42) might well be seen as undermining the very basis of trust on which a constitution rests. In this category come the guarantees for trial by jury (Article 47.2), when this system came into general operation only much later, and the prohibition on 'the use of evidence obtained by violating federal law' (Article 50.2). If these are not fulfilled, then what price all the other promises?

In a sharp break with the past the constitution makes no reference to any state ideology or religion and instead guarantees freedom of conscience, religion, thought and speech (Articles 28, 29) based on political pluralism and a multi-party system. It specifically states that 'No ideology may be established as the state ideology or as a compulsory ideology' (Article 13.2). However, this does not mean that the constitution is not an ideological document: it represents a clear commitment to certain values, including the notion of a 'social' and 'secular' state based on private property, the rule of law and popular sovereignty. However, the enunciation of the rationale behind these views is no longer as explicit as in earlier drafts. The section explicitly devoted to civil society was dropped, ostensibly for the sake of brevity. What was lost, however, was a clear repudiation of Russia's statist traditions and the commitment to the development of the sphere of freedom and autonomy associated with the notion of civil society.

The political system formalised by the 1993 constitution reflected numerous conjunctural factors. A constitution, ideally, reflects a popular consensus around certain principles and values, whereas this constitution contained elements that reflected only the concerns of a particular time and the interests of a particular group. Vitaly Tret'yakov, the trenchant editor of *Nezavisimaya gazeta*, argued that 'It is a constitution for presidents in general and for president Yeltsin in particular.'[11] Rumyantsev noted that 'When the president personally formulates foreign and domestic policy, one can say that the monarchical principle outweighs the democratic principle in the constitution.'[12] Konstantin Lubenchenko went even further in claiming that the constitution not only gave an overwhelming advantage to presidential power but actually 'codifies the existence of a totalitarian state that controls all spheres of the life of society'.[13] Thus the main criticism of the 1993 constitution is its lack of balance in the separation of powers between branches of national government, above all granting the presidency excessive powers. In Russia's early post-communist years, however, the question of 'balance' was not easily resolved, since 'balance' is something derived from the alignment of social and political forces. While the constitution embodies the principles of liberalism, it is predicated on the assumption that the strong president will also be a liberal. In the event of this not being the case the authoritarian elements embedded in the constitution will come into contradiction with its liberal provisions.

Criticism of the constitution focuses on the following issues: the inadequate legal defence of the civic and human rights of individuals; the lack of balance in the relationship

between the executive and the legislative; the tension between federal and unitary principles in the relationship between the centre and localities and the large grey area of joint
jurisdiction; the large area of rules and procedures (for example, governing elections)
that are not written into the constitution but regulated by acts and decrees; excessive
social promises that are difficult to enforce; and the lack of a realistic procedure for
adopting constitutional amendments.[14] Other criticisms of the constitution include the
charge that it is too long, infringing Talleyrand's dictum that 'A constitution should be
short and unclear' (*sic*). The authors of the US constitution adhered to this principle,
but the post-war framers of the West German constitution did not. The West German
constitution (Basic Law, *Grundgesetz*) came into force on 23 May 1949 and in great
detail established the country as a federal, social, legal state based on a parliamentary
system of rule in which the president is the non-executive head of state. The constitution
sought to avoid the mistakes of the Weimar republic and enshrined the principle that
'democracy must be able to defend itself', including a ban on parties that challenge
the existing constitutional order. There was no place for referendums and other forms
of plebiscitary democracy. In terms of length the new Russian constitution veers to the
long side, but is much shorter than the unadopted Rumyantsev version.

These criticisms perhaps overstate the case. This constitution is very much a normative
document, establishing the principles on which an ethically desirable state could be established rather than suggesting that it can be achieved immediately. If we accept Bogdan
Kistiakovskii's argument that law and the state originally existed independently and that
independent courts could be introduced under conditions of absolutism, so too today
we can appreciate the new constitution in terms of asynchronicity in the introduction of
the rudiments of liberalism, democracy and, indeed, social democracy. While Western
democracies spent the better part of the twentieth century introducing a social corrective
to classical liberalism – until the rise of neo-liberalism in the 1980s – post-communist
Russia faces the problem of enormously extended social, and indeed political, demands
in conditions in which it lacks the ability to fulfil them, resulting in a gulf between
aspiration and achievement. As in pre-revolutionary Russia, however, the tendency to
subordinate law to the political struggle only creates more obstacles in the way of achieving the goal of a *pravovoe gosudarstvo* (a state ruled by law, *Rechtsstaat*), let alone a
rule of law state (see below).

### State and government

The adoption of the constitution was only the beginning of a constitutional process requiring the development of a whole system of laws and conventions. Legislative renewal
was based on a division between federal constitutional laws (those defining constitutional
principles and processes) and ordinary federal laws.[15] Federal constitutional laws are
harder to adopt or amend than routine laws, requiring a qualified majority of both houses
of parliament – a two-thirds majority in the Duma and three-quarters in the Federation
Council – and cannot be vetoed by the president, whereas ordinary laws require a simple
parliamentary majority. A vast programme of legislative activity awaited the new parliament, with the constitution itself alluding to 13 constitutional laws, 44 federal laws,
5 existing laws needing substantial changes to bring them into line with the new constitution, together with 6 acts governing the activity of the Federal Assembly itself and
4 dealing with the work of the president, a total of 72 acts that would give legislative

form to its general principles. Some of these acts were prepared by the presidential Commission for Legislative Suggestions, headed by Mikhail Mityukov, which had by 17 December 1993 drawn up a list of the required legislation.[16] The most urgent new laws were those governing states of emergency and martial law, on the prerogatives of the Constitutional and Supreme Courts, labour and tax laws, on social movements, on elections to the State Duma and on the composition of the Federation Council. Laws to be changed included those governing the status of the capital and the procuracy. To date 10 of the 13 federal constitutional laws stipulated by the constitution have been adopted.

The presidential features of the constitution attracted much criticism. Zor'kin argued that the leading role of the Communist Party had been replaced by the one-man rule of the president, while Rumyantsev argued that the constitution gave legal form to the seizure of power.[17] For Victor Ilyukhin this was a 'constitution for the fascist future', while E. Volodin saw it as inaugurating 'the banana republic of Russia'.[18] A joint declaration of party leaders insisted that the constitution 'restores the authoritarian system in the Russian Federation'.[19] The actual operation of the new system of constitutional power, however, revealed that the constitution did not establish virtually unchecked executive power, as its critics had suggested would be the case. Both Yeltsin and Putin sought to rule with the consent of the Federal Assembly; and the legislature itself for the first time in Russian history worked as a genuine parliament, adopting laws that took priority over presidential decrees. Its powers to hold the executive to account, however, are weak, and it is not clear how effective are the restraints on authoritarian rule.

For the first time in Russian history a constitution made a serious attempt to define and limit state power. The final vestiges of the communist legacy were swept away as the new document promised economic liberalism and the democratic separation of powers. Yeltsin argued that the constitution was designed to lay down a 'firm, legal order' for a democratic state, marking an end to the 'dual power' between the presidency and the legislature.[20] The constitution sought to create a 'democratic, federal, rule-of-law state with a republican form of government' (Article 1.1). The new version incorporated elements from the previous drafts, above all the section on human and civil rights, but significantly augmented presidential authority and limited the powers of parliament and the republics. The model of governance that emerges from the document is both pseudo-parliamentary and super-presidential, while the government itself has the potential to become a relatively autonomous third centre of power. (The constitution's provisions concerning the institutions of the state and federalism are discussed in the appropriate parts of this book.)

### Constitutional change

The debate over constitutional change is provoked by the perceived need to reduce the powers of the presidency. At present Russia is considered to have a 'super-presidential' system (see Chapter 5), although the degree to which there is a genuine separation of powers is sometimes under-rated. The problem is not so much that the constitution lacks a separation of powers, but that it is unbalanced – and deliberately so, given the experience of conflict in 1991–3. Among the many plans for constitutional change is the idea that the president should be selected by the Federation Council; that the prime minister should be appointed by the parliamentary majority in the Duma, which itself would enjoy enhanced powers; that the Duma should be granted the right to approve the prime minister's dismissal as well as nomination; removing the power ministries from direct subordination to the president and transferring oversight to the prime minister; and to make attendance compulsory for the prime minister and ministers when requested by the Duma (interpellation rights).

Some informal constitutional evolution has already taken place within the framework of the existing polity. During Yevgeny Primakov's premiership in 1998–9 attempts were made to hammer out cross-party agreement on constitutional reform and the redistribution of power, but no consensus was achieved. While no formal change has reduced the presidential bias of the constitution, in the late Yeltsin years there was a shift towards prime ministerial governance. Some of what becomes convention can be formalised by the adoption of federal constitutional laws by the Federal Assembly, without necessarily amending the constitution itself. According to Yegor Stroev, the second speaker of the Federation Council, 'Today, no sensible person is in any doubt that our constitution needs correction.' He noted that while in theory the president had huge powers, in practice most of these powers ended at the walls of the Kremlin. Too many decrees laws and ordinances were simply not implemented.

However, while constitutional changes may be desirable, the obstacles to their adoption are prohibitive. The constitution is much more difficult to change than Soviet-era constitutions, a feature that transforms political conflict into constitutional crises. The constitution's ninth chapter discusses amendments and revisions, in effect making it easier to abolish the constitution than to amend it. Amendments to chapters 3–8 require a two-thirds majority of the State Duma, the support of three-quarters of the members of the Federation Council, and then ratification (within a year) by the legislatures of no fewer than two-thirds of the subjects of the federation (Articles 108 and 136). Special rules apply to the 'fundamental' articles of the constitution, chapters 1 and 2, dealing with general rights, and chapter 9 itself, where change requires a three-fifths vote of both houses and a Constitutional Assembly, convened in accordance with federal constitutional law (Article 135), which has still not been adopted. In principle, it is easier to change the 'inviolable' chapters than the others, not requiring the ratification of the subjects of the federation, although it is impossible to convene a Constitutional Assembly without the appropriate law. The Constitutional Court on 28 November 1995 ruled that name changes to regions can be achieved by a simple presidential decree, while regional mergers or new regions joining Russia are entered into Article 65 of the constitution by the adoption of a federal constitutional law, without needed to be ratified by regional legislatures.[21] Overall, the difficulties attending constitutional revisions could lead to attempts to kill off the constitution as a whole and to start again.[22]

The deeper problem is that the quasi-monarchical presidential style of rule could be replaced by a form of populist and irresponsible parliamentarianism that would undermine even the existing meagre achievements in the shift towards a market economy and individual freedoms, and threaten Russia's relations with its neighbours. On many occasions the Duma passed resolutions that threatened the very basis of Yeltsin's foreign policy: for example, denouncing the dissolution of the USSR in December 1991 and claiming the return of the Crimean peninsula from Ukraine. The presence of a strong pro-presidential majority under Putin put an end to the adoption of such provocative resolutions, but the price paid was a more supine parliament. At one point even Putin considered moving towards a government of the parliamentary majority, but in the end he set his face against any constitutional change, insisting that the existing system should be allowed to bed down. He did, however, engage in considerable para-constitutional institutional development, as in the establishment of seven federal districts and a State Council in 2000 (more on this later).

## The Constitutional Court

Even the most splendid constitution on paper is valueless if there are no effective mechanisms to ensure compliance, and this was certainly the case between 1991 and 1993. In its brief existence Russia has had two sets of rules, with the first covering the phoney democracy period.

### First attempt

The Law on the Constitutional Court of 12 July 1991 established a Court of 15 independent judges, appointed for their personal qualities for a limited life term (up to the age of 65), to deal with all the main questions of constitutionality but were prohibited from examining political cases.[23] Drawing on the experience of the German Federal Constitutional Court, the Court's decisions are final and cannot be appealed. Under its chairman, Zor'kin, the Court sought to mark out the centre ground that could establish civic peace and maintain the unity of the country. The court was thus accused of placing political considerations above the defence of the laws and the constitution, although with such a malleable constitution the position of the court was unenviable. The Court asserted its authority against the executive authorities when on 14 January 1992 it overturned a presidential decree establishing a joint ministry of security and internal affairs. The court's attempt to modify the referendum held on 21 March 1992 in Tatarstan failed, although Zor'kin was vigorous in condemning the perceived threat to the unity of the country. Its ruling in November 1992 on the constitutionality of Yeltsin's ban on the Communist Party after the coup found a compromise solution that ruled that the ban on the Party apparatus had been constitutional, but not that on the rank-and-file organisations (see p. 135).

In December 1992, during Russia's first genuine *constitutional* crisis, when executive and legislative power locked in conflict, the court acted as a mediator and brokered a compromise, albeit not a durable one. The prestige of the court was undermined when in January 1993 Zor'kin changed his mind and condemned the idea of a referendum as destabilising, and confidence in his judgment was further diminished when he rushed to condemn Yeltsin's announcement on 20 March 1993 of 'special rule' before seeing the document in question.[24] An even greater challenge to the Court's authority was posed by Yeltsin's decree of 21 September 1993 suspending the constitution. The decree urged the Court not to meet until the Federal Assembly began its work, but in the event 10 out of the 14 judges condemned the presidential decree,[25] and on 17 October Yeltsin decreed the suspension of the Court. The Court had tried to assert its authority to achieve the separation of powers, but the titanic struggle between executive and legislative authority marginalised the judiciary and trampled on the rule of law in its entirety. The Constitutional Court was placed in the invidious position of defending a discredited constitution. Its procedures, moreover, encouraged acts of political adventurism. The dissolution of the old legislature and the fate of the Court appeared to illustrate the venerable Russian principle that law is subordinate to politics.[26]

### Today's system

The 1993 constitution established a new Constitutional Court of 19 judges (Article 125), with the judges appointed by the Federation Council but nominated by the president. The Law on the Constitutional Court of 21 July 1994 provided the Court with a more restricted brief than its highly politicised predecessor, depriving it of the right to initiate cases. Designed to ensure that federal laws and decrees comply with the constitution, the Court lost some of its prerogatives concerning relations between the central authorities and components of the federation. Much-needed gatekeeping mechanisms were established to make appeals to the court more difficult as part of the attempt to transform it into a more professional and less politicised body.[27] The Court now has a stable constitution to work with rather than the earlier constantly changing text.

The new law considerably reduced its scope for independent political activity. Judges are no longer allowed to accept matters for consideration on their own initiative, and the range of 'official entities' that may put matters to them has been severely restricted. Whereas earlier any deputy (and there were over a thousand of them) could send questions, now this can only be done with the approval of one-fifth of the deputies of any one chamber or by a majority vote of the Federal Assembly as a whole. In certain respects, however, its authority was increased. A ruling by the court, for example, on the constitutionality of a presidential decree, a government resolution or a parliamentary law, is final and cannot be appealed. Any legal act that is ruled as unconstitutional loses its force. The Court can deal with several cases simultaneously, usually considering similar cases together.

Some of the judges remained from the old Court, but the confirmation of the new took over a year to complete because the president's nominations were repeatedly rejected. Finally, on 7 February 1995 the Federation Council approved the nomination of the nineteenth judge and the court could commence its work.[28] Vladimir Tumanov was selected chairman of the Constitutional Court, insisting that 'in the transitional period constitutional stability is the highest value', but he feared that lack of respect for the law was the gravest challenge facing the court.[29] On 25 January 2001 the law on the Constitutional Court was amended to extend the term of its judges from 12 to 15 years and the age limit of 70 years was removed. The authority of the Constitutional Court remains high, although some of its rulings have been questioned, as over the legality of Yeltsin's war in Chechnya and Putin's abolition of gubernatorial elections. These decisions have raised doubts whether the Court is indeed Russia's last bastion against authoritarianism.[30] Yeltsin formally complied with every ruling of the Court, often instructing his representative there to withdraw proposals that were liable to be judged unconstitutional. The new chairman of the Court, Marat Baglai nevertheless in May 2001 called on the government to take additional measures to ensure that the decisions of the Court are implemented, something that was addressed in Putin's reform of the judicial system in 2001. Legislatures, which often ignore Court decisions, now have six months to respond; failure to do so after two warnings may lead to their dissolution. The new Court has focused overwhelmingly on individual rights (some three-quarters of its cases), and far less on issues dealing with the separation of powers and federalism, although under Putin the latter issue came to the fore. The Constitutional Court today, now chaired once again by Zor'kin, is the cornerstone of Russia's fragile democracy, regulating the federal, judicial and, effectively, the political system as well.[31]

## The legal system and its reform

Urban Russia since the judicial reform of 1864 had seen the development of a relatively free judiciary, Justices of the Peace (JPs) and the development of the jury system, but these achievements had been swept away by the Bolshevik revolution. The Soviet regime restored the full powers of the procuracy and emphasised the primacy of social over civil rights. Only under Gorbachev did the judiciary begin to achieve a measure of political autonomy, but this was precarious and it fell to the post-communist regime to consolidate judicial independence. Under the Soviet system each republic had its own legal code (as well as their own constitutions), but they varied little from all-union standards. The struggle for statehood from 1990 had, naturally, been accompanied by legal conflicts between republican and union legislation. During the 'war of the laws' of the late 1990s the Russian Supreme Soviet insisted that Russian laws took precedence over all-union laws.[32] Only after the August coup did Russia seriously embark upon building a new legal system. The adoption of the constitution in 1993 provides the keystone for this endeavour.

Under Putin legal reform in institutional terms accelerated, although in terms of the consolidation of the rule of law there was notable regression. Judicial reform in Putin's first years was master-minded by Dmitry Kozak, Putin's colleague from St Petersburg who had failed to become Procurator General in 2000. The laws adopted in December 2001 were designed to improve guarantees for the human and civic rights of individuals and the economic rights of citizens. The intention was to move from the Soviet-style system, weighted in favour of judges and prosecutors and based on an inquisitorial ideology, towards a more adversarial system where the rights of the defendant and the courts were more evenly balanced. The measures included greatly increased funds for the judiciary, a new Criminal Procedure Code (UPK) that would transfer power from prosecutors to judges, and attempts to boost judicial responsibility by rendering judges more accountable. In all, by 2003 eleven major laws had transformed the judicial environment, with attempts to provide adequate funds to ensure the effective implementation of the reforms.

The judicial system is divided into three main branches.

1   The courts of general jurisdiction, including military courts, are subordinated to the Supreme Court. Courts of general jurisdiction deal with cases of civil and criminal law, and include the district courts which serve local communities, regional courts, and the Supreme Court itself. Appeals against lower courts can be heard only by the immediately superior instance, unless a constitutional issue is at stake. There are 86 regional courts of general jurisdiction and 2,000 district courts, now joined by a revived system of Justices of the Peace. The latter now work throughout Russia except Chechnya. JPs deal with criminal cases involving a maximum sentence of less than three years, and with some categories of civil cases. Since the end of the 1990s a new system of administrative courts began to be introduced responsible for settling disputes over electoral law and between the federal and local authorities. The establishment of this separate system, with their own system of financing, was criticised by some civil rights activists as opening the door to kangaroo courts. The procuracy (see below) is part of this system.

   The Supreme Court is the highest body in civil, criminal and administrative law. It oversees the work of all lower courts, and its judges (of whom there are 20, assisted by 45 lay assessors) are granted personal inviolability and can only be arrested with the permission of the Constitutional Court. The Supreme Court hears appeals against judgments of lower courts, and in exceptional cases may make judgments of its own. The Court is divided into three chambers to deal with civil, criminal and military cases, respectively.

2    The *arbitrazh* courts deal with disputes between economic and other legally constituted organisations, and are in effect a system of commercial courts. The *arbitrazh* system in the Soviet era had simply arbitrated between elements of a single vast bureaucracy, and questions were raised about its suitability for market conditions. The arbitration courts now regulate disputes between legal entities as well as disputes between legal entities and the state, and like the courts of general jurisdiction, has its own system of trials, appellate courts and a supreme court, the latter known as the High Court of Arbitration.

3    The federal Constitutional Court, as well as constitutional courts in some regions and republics, constitute the third branch.

### Ministry of Justice

The judicial system is administered by the Ministry of Justice, drafting the laws and normative acts that regulate its work. The ministry is responsible for the training of judicial personnel, analysing statistics, and (under Putin) for ensuring the establishment of a 'single legal space' in Russia. The justice ministry gained extra powers as a result of the judicial reforms. In particular, one of the conditions of Russia joining the Council of Europe in February 1996 was the transfer of the penitentiary system from the procuracy to the justice ministry.

### The General Procurator's Office (GPO)

Established in 1702, the procuracy is at the heart of the Russian judicial system while at the same time it is one of its most controversial instruments. Its powers were much reduced during Alexander II's legal reforms of 1864, but they were reinstated by Lenin in 1922. The 1995 Law on the Procuracy retained this body as 'the eye of the Tsar', although proclaiming the 'supremacy of law' (*verkhovenstvo zakona*).[33] The General Procurator's Office, to give the full name, is responsible for the implementation of statutes by federal ministries, executive organs and officials, the observance of human rights by ministries and also commercial and non-commercial organisations. The Law on the Courts did not affect the GPO, which still controls itself and its hierarchy of prosecutors. The body is considered a bastion of conservatism and most plans for legal reform (as with the changes to the UPK) include attempts to erode its powers. The aim was to break its monopoly on managing a case at all stages and to restrict its supervisory functions to cases where the state's interests are involved. The GPO did not lose the power to appeal against court decisions, or to restart investigations after sentencing, but the power to issue search and arrest warrants was transferred from prosecutors to the courts. The creation of an investigation committee in the GPO, which began work on 1 September 2007, represented a major step in the reform of the system of crime investigation. The body in due course is planned to bring together all investigators from the numerous security and law enforcement agencies (the Interior Ministry, the security services and the State Narcotics Control Agency) and become an independent organisation.[34]

The Procurator General (also known as the Prosecutor General) is nominated by the president but formally his or her appointment and dismissal is the responsibility of the Federation Council. The fate of successive Procurators suggests that the independence of the judiciary remains tenuous. Valentin Stepankov resisted the dissolution of the legislature in September 1993, and was dismissed in the wake of the October events. Yeltsin bitterly opposed the Duma's 'amnesty' of 26 February 1994 for the instigators of the August 1991 coup and the October 1993 events, yet the new Procurator, Alexei Kazannik, felt it his duty to release the prisoners, but then resigned. The incident suggests scope for independence of the judiciary (and, incidentally, for parliament), but also illustrates the political pressures on the legal system. This was most apparent in Yeltsin's repeated attempts to dismiss Yuri Skuratov as Procurator General from 1998 a move that was resisted by the Federation Council until finally they agreed to Dmitry Ustinov as his replacement on 17 May 2000. Putin had hoped to appoint his ally Kozak to the post, but was forced to compromise. Ustinov's appointment in 1999 had originally been sponsored by the Yeltsinite 'family', and he had certainly not been Putin's first choice, although he agreed to the renewal of Ustinov's appointment for another five-year term in April 2005. However, Ustinov was dismissed as Procurator on 1 June 2006, and overwhelmingly approved by a surprised Federation Council on the following day. Ustinov's removal was associated with the renewed emphasis on the struggle against corruption, and was a delayed indication of Putin's consolidation of power. It also reflected faction fights in the Kremlin as the succession approached. In the event, an extraordinary swap took place – the Minister of Justice Yuri Chaika became Prosecutor General; while Ustinov took on the newly vacated post of Minister of Justice.

The procuracy remains a highly political office, even though formally the body does not have political functions. Under Chaika the prosecutor's office took the lead in a number of high-profile anti-corruption measures. Chaika insisted that his office would be more active in defending individual rights and established a department to monitor the observation of federal law to protect civil rights and liberties.[35] This applies in particular to the regions. The 1993 constitution grants considerable rights to regional leaders in judicial matters (Article 129.3). Local procurators are appointed by regional and republican authorities, facilitating corruption and undermining the independence of the judiciary. The separation of powers between the regions and the centre is flawed, and it was this that Putin sought to change.

### Civil (Criminal) Code and Criminal Procedural Code (UPK)

This is a federal law that prescribes, within the framework of the constitution, the detailed legal framework of the polity. The Duma adopted a new code, to replace the 1960 RSFSR one, on 24 May 1996 and came into force on 1 January 1997 with sections defending individual rights and freedoms and regulating economic activity.[36] The Criminal Code adds up to a vast body of normative laws regulating everything from economic activity, the behaviour of public officials to civic behaviour.

The introduction of the new UPK on 1 July 2002 represented a landmark in law reform. The new Code was a core element of the reform of the legal system and represented a major overhaul of Russia's criminal justice system, intended to defend the individual from the arbitrariness of the state. The rights of defence lawyers were increased, periods in remand were cut, and the use of jury trials was extended. Under the new law it is the courts and not the prosecutors who sanction searches, arrest and detention for longer than 48 hours, a measure that was bitterly resisted by the procuracy. Thus habeas corpus laws were reinforced, while trials *in absentia* were abolished (but restored in 2006 for suspected terrorists). The new Code grants detainees the right to a two-hour meeting with a lawyer before being questioned, and they can only be remanded for two days without an extension granted by a judge. The rules governing the use of evidence were modified to make it easier to challenge the state's evidence and that of the police. However, implementation was at best partial, notably in such high profile cases as the prosecution of Mikhail Khodorkovsky, the former head of Russia's largest oil company, Yukos. Russia's criminal justice system only fitfully protects the civil rights of the accused, the economic rights of corporate actors or the human rights of citizens.[37]

### Judges, the courts and impartiality

According to the constitution, judges of the Constitutional Court, the Supreme Court and the Supreme Arbitration Court are nominated by the president and endorsed by the Federation Council and are meant to be irremovable during their tenure of office. The constitution sought to guarantee judicial independence (Articles 10, 120 and 124) but this might appear to lack substance in the absence of life tenure for judges or of provisions for financial autonomy. When Putin came to power there was a severe lack of judges, being at least 18 per cent under strength in 2000, and they were over-burdened with cases (a five-fold increase since 1991). Under Putin the government increased the number of judges from 16,000 to about 20,000 and raised their salaries four-fold. The aim was to raise judges' 'professionalism' and 'honesty' by making them more independent of social forces, but this only increased their dependence on the central authorities. The Law on Judges regulates the activities of judges in courts of general jurisdiction and the 2,500 arbitration judges, including new procedures to bring miscreant judges to book. Large sums were also made available to train and equip court secretaries.

The court system, nevertheless, still works slowly, adding to the length of pre-trial detention. Sentences remain harsh with little concept of rehabilitation, while at the same time the number of complaints against judges witnessed a four-fold increase to 17,000 in the 1990s, above all for rude and abusive behaviour leading to the dismissal of 95 judges in 1999, 20 for falsifying records. A particular problem was the role played by the Chairs of Courts at the regional level, appointed for life and responsible for distributing cases. Although judges are appointed by the president, they can be dismissed by these Chairs. There are plans to limit their term of office to 3–5 years. A Judicial Academy is being established to remedy these problems. Thus the salaries of judges have been raised to make the job more attractive and less susceptible to bribes and their immunity to prosecution has been restricted. Although the power of judges *vis-à-vis* prosecutors increased, the establishment of a 'qualifications commission', which hires and sacks judges, increased the dependency of judges on the executive. The use of a Qualification Collegium, rather than a panel of judges, to appoint and fire judges has reduced the scope for autonomy. The executive's enhanced role in approving and reconfirming judges (after the three-year mandatory probationary period) reduced the independence of the judiciary.

The 1995 Federal Law on the Court System defended the independence of the judiciary and insisted that its rulings should conform to those legal provisions with the greatest juridical force (effectively, international law), and guaranteed judicial protection of rights and fair trial.[38] The decisions and actions (or inactions) of bodies of state power, local self-government, public associations and officials may be challenged in the courts. In practice, the lack of adequate funding of the judicial system threatened the independence of the judiciary as much as direct political interference. As for the latter, the 'telephone law' that was typical of the Soviet era, when the local party boss would inform the presiding judge of the necessary outcome in sensitive cases, has far from disappeared in post-communist Russia, and indeed some have argued that it has increased between judges and appellate judges. Regional authorities have tended to make up the shortfall in finances of the court system, provoking a dangerous dependence of the courts on local authorities. The latter, particularly in Moscow and St Petersburg, rarely lose a case. The Yukos case in 2004–5 is seen as a classic case of the continued application of 'telephone law'.

### Trial by jury, acquittals and pardons

The first ever congress of the Russian judiciary in October 1991 adopted a series of proposals for judicial reform, including the return to the jury system abolished by the Bolsheviks in October 1917.[39] A Law on Jury Trial allowed jury trials to take place in nine regions. Some leading legal experts have turned against the jury system, arguing that popular involvement in the juridical process lead to perverse outcomes.[40] The new UPK extended the system of jury trials, which had for a number of years been limited to nine regions, to the rest of the country, with Chechnya in January 2007 being the last place scheduled to introduce them (in the event postponed to 2010). In 2005, out of 1,263,000 people tried in criminal courts, 1,389 were tried by jury, usually reserved for 'especially grave' crimes such as murder in regional courts.[41] The aim was to increase the acquittal rate, which had traditionally run at a less than half of 1 per cent whereas in Western Europe it is about 15 per cent and in the United States 25 per cent. In trials conducted by a judge the acquittal rate was only 0.7 per cent, whereas in jury trials it reached 15 per cent, although a third of these were later reversed on appeal by the Supreme Court.

Some of the harshness of sentencing policy had been tempered by the Presidential Pardons Commission. Its chair, Anatoly Pristavkin, noted that in pre-1917 Russia, with roughly the same population and the same crime rate, there were only 140,000 people in prison. He hoped that reform of the judicial system would overcome the 'gulag tradition' of incarcerating everyone found guilty of a crime.[42] However, under Putin almost no pardons were granted and the Pardons Commission was disbanded. In its place a system of regional commissions was established.

### Pre-trial detention and the prison system

The civil courts are subordinate to the Ministry of Justice and have traditionally acted as branches of the state. There is now the right to appeal against arrest, but pre-trial detention centres remain over-crowded and only about a fifth of appeals lead to release. In fulfilment of commitments made on joining the Council of Europe in 1996, the prison system was transferred from the Ministry of the Interior (MVD) and placed under the jurisdiction of the Ministry of Justice, and on 15 April 2006 the Duma finally passed a law prohibiting the FSB from operating prisons, and all of its detention centres were transferred to the Ministry of Justice. There are five basic types of detention in the criminal justice system: police temporary custody centres; pre-trial detention centres, known as investigation isolation facilities (SIZOs); correctional labour colonies (ITKs); prisons for those who violate ITK rules; and educational labour colonies (VTKs) for juveniles. Some two million people are arrested each year, with some 270,000 going on to pre-trial detention in prisons (SIZOs) designed to hold 182,500, although 125,000 are released annually before going on to trial (nearly a quarter of those incarcerated).[43] The new UPK sought to reduce the number of people in pre-trial detention (about quarter of a million in 2002), who often faced years in limbo before being brought to trial. A three-year wait (and longer) is not uncommon in a system where only about 75,000 cases are heard each year and where law courts do not have to meet any deadlines. It appears that torture is widespread in these detention centres, to elicit confessions, and only after this is the suspect arrested and able to enjoy the right to legal representation. Putin's reform of the judicial system sought to reduce the time that a suspect can be kept in gaol without trial to no more than 12 months.

Lengthy gaol terms were imposed for relatively minor offences. The reforms did have an effect, and Russia's prison population began to fall. In 2001 1,084,000 people were in prison, more than the total for the whole of the USSR in the late 1980s and far higher *per capita* than all Western countries except the United States, but by 2007 the Federal Penitentiary Service announced that there were 878,000 in prison or detention facilities, about a third of whom were under 25 and about 400,000 suffering from mental illness. The prison system contained 100,000 convicted murderers. Conditions in prisons remain appalling, with infectious diseases rampant including strains of TB resistant to antibiotics affecting some 13 per cent of the prison population (over 58,000 in March 2006), while at that time there were 35,000 HIV-infected people in SIZOs and correction colonies. It appears that the incidence of torture has decreased, although 2,000 persons died in SIZOs in 2004, largely due to poor conditions and abuse by other prisoners, but abuse by officers is far from rare.

### The death penalty

Popular attitudes played their part in framing the new legal system, but law-making as such is not a democratic but an elitist pursuit; legal reform can be inhibited by venge-ful popular prejudices. This applies particularly to the question of capital punishment, with public opinion surveys showing support for the death penalty running consistently between 65–80 per cent. The number of offences liable to capital punishment had tra-ditionally been high, with some 60 capital offences in the 1960 RSFSR Criminal Code, and the USSR led the international league for the use of the death penalty. Between 1962 and 1989 21,025 people (750 a year) were executed in the USSR, though during *perestroika* the number declined to 195 in 1990.[44] Some 95 per cent of those condemned were executed for first-degree murder, but doubts were cast on the competence of the courts to categorise the offence as such, and little account was taken of the mental state of the defendants. In addition, many wrongful verdicts were passed in the absence of juries and with no courts of appeal in the USSR. A temporary moratorium was placed on the death penalty in Russia on 2 February 1991, although since then some people were executed before the moratorium became permanent in 1996 in connection with Russia's accession to the Council of Europe. Russia signed Protocol No. 6 of the ECHR on 16 April 1997, committing itself to permanently abolishing the death penalty within three years, with a moratorium to come into immediate effect. The Duma, however, refused to abolish the death penalty in 1996 and again in 1999, while the Constitutional Court on 2 February 1999 ruled that the death penalty could not be applied until every region had introduced trial by jury, due by 1 January 2007. The introduction of the jury system in Chechnya, however, has been postponed to 1 January 2010, at which point the death penalty technically becomes available once again throughout Russia. Although Putin made clear his personal opposition to the death penalty, he was not able to convince parliament to adopt the necessary law.

### Judicial independence and the rights of citizens

According to Tumanov, the first head of the new Constitutional Court, too much effort had been spent in the judicial reforms on establishing trial by jury, an aspect of criminal law covering only one per cent of the cases. The main emphasis, he argued, should have been placed on defending the rights of citizens, a much broader question. He insisted that judicial districts should not coincide with territorial areas (regions and republics), in order to preserve the independence of judicial authorities from local administrations. In pre-revolutionary Russia judicial districts encompassed several *gubernii*, and in America the 50 states are covered by only 13 federal appellate court districts. Regional bosses, however, were not in the least inclined to give up their powers.[45] The reforms of the federal system undertaken by Putin were directed precisely towards ensuring the uniformity of the exercise of law throughout the country, including plans to set up 21 federal judicial districts. Today all courts – from the top down to the regional and lower courts – are now financed solely from the federal budget, thus eliminating the courts' financial dependence on regional governments, something that obviously compromised their independence.

### International context

International law has now been adopted as domestic law (see Article 15.4 of the constitution). The international legal system is now fully part of Russian law, although there remains some discussion over what precisely is 'an international treaty of the Russian Federation' – does it mean only treaties subject to ratification, intergovernmental treaties or interdepartmental minutes and protocols (if the latter, then any ministry can make and change law). A further problem is the status of CIS agreements, particularly judgments issued by the Economic Court of the CIS. There is an emerging body of CIS law, something that is resisted by Ukraine.

Russians now have the opportunity to take their case to the European Court of Human Rights (ECtHR), and Russian cases are becoming an increasing proportion of the work facing the Court. The first six Chechen applicants against Russia won their applications to Strasbourg in February 2005, and in April 2005 Russia was condemned for failing to cooperate with the Court despite diplomatic assurances. In 2006, 10,569 of 50,500 (21 per cent) complaints were made against Russia, of which 380 were referred to the Russian government, and 151 were found to be admissible. There were 102 judgments against Russia, out of 1,498 against all Council of Europe states. Of the 90,000 cases awaiting review in 2007, a fifth concerned Russia.[46] The Russian authorities noted that this was broadly in line with Russia's population, and they stressed that Russia had been commended for fulfilling the decisions of the Court, even the most complex.[47]

### *Evaluation*

The communist system endowed Russia with an overblown administrative apparatus, which since the fall of the old system has nearly doubled in size. At the same time, officialdom is marked by what Rekosh calls 'a culture of internal political responsibility, with little or no common understanding of responsibility on the basis of professional norms, duty to the general public (taxpayers) or the rule of law'.[48] The public interest takes second place to the corporate interests of the agency itself. Financial incentives (bribes) have to be paid for the citizen to gain what is lawfully theirs. As Vladimir Pastukhov, one of Russia's leading legal experts and a practising legal consultant, notes, it is often 'necessary to pay not to obtain something contrary to the law, but in order to defend one's lawful interests. It is not the violation of the law but its fulfilment that is paid for in Russia'.[49]

Sergei Pashin, a former Moscow City judge and human rights activist (who was himself sacked as a judge), argues that the judicial reforms launched in the early 1990s have failed. He was one of the authors of the measures, and he now argues that the aims and direction of the reforms have changed. The original intention had been 'to remove the judiciary from the sphere of control of the executive, but now it has once again turned into its appendage'. Despite the introduction of jury trials and many other positive achievements, all of this remained at the formal level, while at the informal level there remain 'shadow technologies' including the falsification of court proceedings.[50] This is a judgment confirmed by the chair of the Constitutional Court, Valery Zor'kin, who has argued that the court reforms have rendered judges more corruptible and more dependent on the government.[51]

A recent study has highlighted some of the deficiencies of the Russian legal system: 'Large case backlogs, lengthy pre-trial detention, one of the highest prison populations in the world, credible reports of torture of prisoners.'[52] This is confirmed by an important report issued by the International Bar Association in June 2005. The IBA, it may be noted, is the world's largest lawyers' organisation with 16,000 members in 195 countries. The IBA report noted the attempts at judicial reform since Putin came to power, and provides a fair and objective evaluation of their achievements and failures. It does, however, single out important points that are of major concern, notably the proposals to change the method of composing the Supreme Qualification Collegium and lower level Qualification Collegia for the appointment of judges, reducing the role of judges and increasing that of politicians.[53]

## Law and constitutionalism

Ralf Dahrendorf has distinguished between constitutional and normal politics; in the former, 'the hour of the lawyers' strikes as they attempt to root modern political society in a constitutional order, whereas in the latter legislative activity concentrates on managing the established system.[54] In Russia these two types of politics were superimposed on each other, provoking the October 1993 crisis: rebuilding the boat at sea turned out indeed to be a perilous venture. Questions of 'polity', the nature of the state, and 'policy', specific problems of public policy, became entwined.[55] The new constitution had to be prepared at a time of profound political and economic changes: the work of the lawyers was overseen by politicians. Zor'kin, at the time chairman of the Court, indeed argued that the crisis of power was 'a natural result of the policy of "shock therapy"'.[56] Constitution-making became part of the political struggle, and itself became the prize in the struggle between the executive and legislative authorities.[57]

### *Concepts of law*

The late Tsarist period was marked by an important debate by legal scholars and others over the concept of *pravovoe gosudarstvo* (a 'law-based state'). The Russian notion of *pravovoe gosudarstvo* is derived from the German concept of a *Rechtsstaat* and thus differs from the Anglo-American concept of the 'rule of law'. As Donald D. Barry has noted, 'The concept of *Rechtsstaat* is based on the positivist assumption that the state itself is the highest source of law'.[58] Thus a *pravovoe gosudarstvo*, as Harold J. Berman put it, 'is rule *by* law, but not rule *of* law'; the latter is sustained by the theory of natural law suggesting that there is a law higher than statutory law governing the normative acts of society.

Many of the more notable Russian moral philosophers and legal scholars condemned the positivist tradition, so strong in Germany. Vladimir Solovyov, indeed, developed the notion of a type of social liberalism based on the idea of the 'right to a dignified existence' within the context of a society and state formally ordered by law, a view that sharply distinguished him from the revolutionary socialist challenge to Western liberalism but that brought him closer to Bismarck Germany's *Rechtstaat* liberals.[59] Strong echoes of Solovyov's thinking can be found in Russia's new constitution. At the turn of the century the name of Boris Chicherin is most strongly identified with the idea of a constitutional legal order and restraints on monarchical power, condemning the positivist tradition while calling for a type of defensive liberalism which he came to call 'liberal conservatism'. His views, also, are particularly resonant in the new constitution, as in his notion of 'liberal measures and strong government',[60] a formula adopted by Peter Stolypin when he was prime minister between 1906 and 1911, by Yeltsin's first 'government of reforms' and then by Putin. Above all, his defence of the ethical attributes of the juridical sphere encompassed by civil society and the notion of freedom that it represents went far beyond Hegel's rather grudging acceptance of this sphere of conflicting private interests and firmly rejected Marx's critique, views that in effect make Chicherin the intellectual 'godfather', albeit unacknowledged, of Russia's new constitution.

The legal revolution has a dual character. The achievement of a *Rechtsstaat* in Russia today reflects the attempt in nineteenth-century Germany to limit the arbitrariness of the absolutist *Polizeistaat* (policy state). The term *Rechtsstaat* was used to describe Germany in the second part of the nineteenth century where a legalism devoid of democratic principle (positive law) predominated. If correct bureaucratic procedures were followed, then an act was legal, and thus in these terms Hitler's regime was legal since he used the provisions of the Weimar constitution to establish his rule. The Soviet police state in its way was governed by law but public power remained arbitrary.[61] Russia now sought to combine the principles of a *Rechtsstaat* with natural law, which suggests that there is a law higher than the state to which the state itself should be subordinate. This is the heart of the concept of constitutionalism; it is more than simply rule according to a constitution – as the 'pseudo constitutionalism' of the Soviet era amply demonstrated.

The establishment of a *Rechtsstaat*, is *limiting*, but the establishment of the rule of law is *expansive*. The 'rule of law' is a concept associated with the Anglo-Saxon common law tradition, whereas Russia is part of the continental Roman law tradition: according to common law individual rights are defended by the courts; whereas in the continental tradition they are enshrined in a constitution. Thus, to the Anglo-Saxon mind the registration of political parties and religious organisations might seem superfluous, since they are protected by common law and the courts on the principle that 'everything that is not forbidden is permitted'. The continental system, however, relies on regulation to avoid conflict and to manage social affairs. The constitutional process in Russia today can therefore be seen as a dual revolution: to achieve both a *pravovoe gosudarstvo* (a state governing by law, based on the classical positivist conception of law); and to create a society governed by the rule of law to which the state itself is subordinated – in other words, genuine constitutionalism. It is this latter concept, based on the theory of natural law which has never taken root in Russia but that was acknowledged in the 1993 constitution.

For Russia the achievement of rule by law (if not yet the rule of law) would be no mean achievement. The gulf between aspiration and achievement remains large, however, but certain tangible advances have been achieved, notably the adoption of the constitution itself. The system moved beyond the nebulous concept of 'socialist legality' towards a law-based state. The concept of law of the revived Russian constitutionalism is indebted to the debates of the late Soviet period. The aim here was above all to separate the Party from the state and to remake the state as an autonomous political and ordered entity. At the same time, the overweening powers of the state were to be limited by the establishment of legal safeguards for individual rights. Associated with the second project was the discourse of civil society, a concept that figured prominently in the draft version of the CPSU's final Programme and in early drafts of the new Russian constitution. There remains, however, a tension between attempts to reconstitute and at the same time to limit the state, a contradiction that emerged with full force under Putin.

### Constitutionalism

The defeat of Khasbulatov's parliament in October 1993 put an end to a distinctive 'phoney democracy' phase, and opened the path to the establishment of a more stable political system. The adoption of a constitution is the core constitutive act of state-building and defines the ethical essence of a new state. The 1993 constitution provided Russian statehood with a coherent juridical form and stabilised the new political order. It proclaimed that 'The holder of sovereignty and the sole source of authority in the Russian Federation is its multinational people' (Article 3.1). It provides the three key elements of a modern democratic state: popular sovereignty, including extensive civil rights for citizens; the separation of powers, although the accountability of the executive to the legislature is relatively weak and the division of powers between the federal authorities and the regions remains contested; and enshrines a set of norms that provides for the choice and accountability of executive authority to citizens. Russia has finally begun to overcome the long tradition of sham and pseudo-constitutionalism to enjoy the genuine rule of law and the full exercise of constitutionalism. The Constitutional Court acts as guarantor, and its rulings have so far been authoritative if not always implemented in full.

The 1993 constitution established the foundations of the new polity, but the structure remained to be built. A constitutional system is a much broader concept than the constitution itself and reflects the ethical bases of society.[62] It is quite possible to have a constitution but no constitutional order (as under the Soviet regime); or to have a constitutional order but no constitution (as in Britain): the aim in Russia today is to combine the two. The legal functions of a constitution are only one among many, and this is particularly the case with this constitution that sought to repudiate the communist political and philosophical legacy and to establish the basis of a new constitutional order. Genuine constitutionalism entails effective mechanisms of accountability, the subordination of power to the law, and the ability of citizens to defend their rights.

Rumyantsev frequently talked about the foundations of the constitutional order in Russia, the concept of *stroi* (system) in the broadest sense,[63] and he is right to do so. As V. Leontovich argued for pre-revolutionary Russia, it was the absence of a developed civil structure, 'something that is essential for any liberal constitution', that led to the disappearance of political freedom and the destruction of the constitutional system in Russia in 1917.[64] The constitutional process in Russia reflected contradictory processes of social development; a constitution can hardly be more effective than the society which it seeks to regulate. At the same time, this constitution is an act of deliberate political intervention in the evolution of the polity. The constitution was designed not to reflect an existing social order but to mould a new one, a task very different from that confronting the Founding Fathers in Philadelphia in 1787. The instrumental and normative elements in the document, the attempt to design a new social order, raised two fundamental questions: was the constitution drafted in terms of expediency rather than right; and does the idea of order rather than freedom lie at its heart?

The adoption of the constitution represented the culmination of the democratic revolution against communism but at the same time became a casualty of this struggle. The 1993 constitution represents a conscious revolt against the alleged lack of a democratic political culture in Russia, but at the same time reflects the very cultural problematic that it sought to undermine. The constitution remains ideological (in the traditional sense) in so far as it acts as an instrument of reform in the hands of 'the Bolsheviks of the marketplace'. There remains a long way to go before Russia's political life is fully constitutionalised, with all subject equally to the rule of law. Sovereignty remains to a degree displaced, above all to executive authorities. The struggle for popular sovereignty and the full exercise of the powers of the instruments of that sovereignty (above all parliament and the courts) is at the same time a struggle for democracy, a struggle that continues to this day. As Viktor Sheinis noted, 'It is, of course, not enough to adopt a constitution in order to create a stable democratic society, but this is a necessary and, at present, urgent prerequisite'.[65] As long as the institutions of civil society and the associated 'habits of the heart', as Tocqueville put it, of a democratic and free people remain weak, the naturally predatory instincts of the state will find little resistance. Russia now has a coherent constitution, but there is still a long way to go for the achievement of genuine constitutionalism.

# 5 Crime, corruption and security

Constitutional-pluralistic systems can be corrupted by too much oligarchy or too much democracy. In the first case, they become corrupt because a minority manipulates the institutions and prevents them from reaching their highest form, which is government by the people. The second type of corruption appears, on the other hand, when oligarchy is too eroded and the different groups push their claims too far and no authority able to safeguard the general interest remains.

(Raymond Aron)[1]

A legal (positivist) state is not necessarily a democratic one, but a democratic state is by definition governed by the rule of law. The task facing the Russian legal system was nothing short of revolutionary. The old Bolshevik system of jurisprudence, and the principles on which it was based, were clearly inadequate for a democratic market-based society, and thus a new system in its entirety had to be created. Even though the constitution-adopting process was marked by crisis, the reform of the legal system was far more evolutionary and in the event judicial reform moved slowly. Freed from communism, criminality rose to the surface, while the traditional meta-corruption (of the system) took radically new forms during the grand privatisation of state assets in the 1990s. The security apparatus lost some of the prominence it had enjoyed in the communist years, but remained a significant presence. Progress towards the defence of human rights was patchy, with security agencies pursuing some high profile persecutions of civic activists.

## Crime and the mafia

The power vacuum left by the demise of the communist regime was exploited by criminal syndicates in which power, money and crime, according to Stephen Handelman, forged a 'seamless connection'. In his view, 'The Russian mafiya's [*sic*] connection with government, born of its symbiotic relationship with the former communist establishment, makes organised crime a dagger pointed at the heart of Russian democracy'.[2] The state had already been criminalised by the old elites, and now the arbitrariness of the Soviet system was converted into widespread societal lawlessnes. The criminal gangs that had emerged under Stalin, the thieves' world (*vorovskoi mir*) with a code of honour enshrined in popular song, were ideally placed to exploit the disorder associated with the turn to capitalism. As one of them told Handelman we outlasted Soviet power... The communists succeeded in grinding into powder the intelligentsia, the White Guards, the Baptists; they destroyed everything for the sake of their ideology, but they always failed to destroy us.[3]

The 'thieves in law' (*vory v zakone*, the fraternity of thieves whose strict code of criminal ethics forbade collaboration with the authorities – as opposed to the 'renegades', *suki*), were the basis for the explosion of organised crime. The authorities in many regions had effectively become mafia-like structures.[4] New and even more ruthless gangs drew freely on ex-servicemen, the KGB, the army and the militia to deal in pornography, narcotics, money laundering and protection rackets. Already in the last years of *perestroika* senior officials of the old regime, most spectacularly in the Komsomol organisation, had begun the struggle for control of Russia's financial and industrial resources, and the anarchic post-communist economy provided rich pickings for them. According to the MVD, in June 1997 there were some 9,000 organised criminal groups with some 100,000 members,[5] controlling banks, money exchanges and systematically subverting the state administration and new entrepreneurial activity. According to the Prosecutor General, Vladimir Ustinov, in early 2001 about 40,000 Russian enterprises, including a third of the country's banks, were controlled by criminal groups.[6] At least a quarter of Russia's businesspeople were linked to the criminal world.[7] Rashid Nurgaliev, the minister of the interior, provided an equally sombre evaluation in 2007, arguing that the mafia was firmly established in Moscow, St Petersburg, the South and in Siberia, posing a 'threat to the state, society and the economy'. He noted that over 3.8 million crimes had been registered in 2006, up by 8.5 per cent on 2005. Other reports suggested that a tenth of Russia's regions were in criminal hands, with up to a quarter of Russia's GDP generated by the black economy. According to Aleksei Mukhin, a specialist in the field of organised crime, Russia was home to over 10,000 criminal groups employing 300,000 people.[8]

The state weakness of the 1990s allowed a third force to emerge between debilitated governmental authority and the incipient instruments of popular representation and accountability – violent entrepreneurship. Vadim Volkov describes the development of a particular resource, organised violence, which was no longer the prerogative of the state but which had now, with the collapse of the Soviet order, dissolved back into the social body. His key point is that this was not just organised crime or even Mafia-type relations, but a substantively new type of order where the sovereign power of Hobbes's Leviathan has been rendered toothless. Instead of a Commonwealth where coercion is concentrated in a single agency, the state, a state of nature prevails. In the mid-1990s, Volkov argues, the very definition of what constituted a 'crime' was called into question, while the existence of the state as a defined entity became increasingly doubtful.[9] Volkov effectively captures the liminality of the period, when a modern state and market were only coming into being. The old Soviet state was gone, and a democratic market state was not yet born, and into this vacuum rushed the barons of the new fragmented order.

There had been a long-term rise in recorded crime since at least the mid-1970s, and this trend now accelerated. Under Gorbachev crime figures showed an alarming increase, and in the 1990s this reached awesome proportions accompanied by a sharp increase in motiveless crimes. A record 2.76 million crimes were recorded in 1992, a 27 per cent increase over the previous year, and the clear-up rate fell also,[10] and as noted above by 2005 there were 3.5 million recorded crimes.[11] The fear of crime etched itself deeply on the consciousness of the post-totalitarian society. In 1994 some 32,300 premeditated murders were recorded in Russia, double the 15,600 in 1990 and a rate considerably higher than that typical in Western Europe,[12] and in 2005 there were 31,000 homicides or attempted murders.[13] By the mid-1990s the murder rate exceeded 30 per 100,000 inhabitants, compared to 1–2 in Western Europe and 6–7 in the United States, the highest in the developed world. The Russian rate remains double that of Brazil and Mexico, and is surpassed only by South Africa and Colombia.[14] Contract killings in particular rose from 102 in 1992[15] to at least 2,500 in 1995, with some 6,500 others probably falling in this category.[16] These killings were marked by a chilling cold-bloodedness as former soldiers, accustomed to death in Russia's many 'little wars' (Afghanistan and Chechnya), profited from their 'professionalism'.

Between 1995 and 1999 there were on average 30,200 murders a year, and this if anything increased under Putin to 32,200 per annum between 2000 and 2004. Prominent victims included bankers and MPs, as well as the journalist Dmitry Kholodov, blown up by an exploding brief case in October 1994, the television star Vladislav List'ev, shot in the entrance hall to his apartment block in March 1995 and the democratic politician Galina Starovoitova, also shot in the entrance to her house in St Petersburg in October 1998. The murder of the prominent journalist Anna Politkovskaya on 7 October 2006 was particularly disturbing. The so-called mafia itself adapted to new circumstances, with criminal gangs gaining a legal foothold by registering as private detective agencies. Their international links also increased, helped by the enormous increase in the number of Russians travelling abroad. Fears of a 'tidal wave' of Russian organised crime engulfing Britain and the West, however, were exaggerated.[17]

Rising crime prompted Yeltsin in 1992 to relax the controls on the bearing of arms, thus weakening the state's monopoly on firepower that had been imposed by the Bolsheviks soon after they came to power. Citizens now had the right to bear arms to protect themselves and their property. Businesses threatened by criminal gangs were forced to pay protection money to a 'roof' (*krysha*), but this in turn stimulated the proliferation of some 8,000 private security companies employing around 1.3 million people by 1995.[18] Official anti-crime organisations lost some of their best agents as an estimated one-third of the state's policemen, security officials and professional soldiers were attracted by better wages and prestige. The work of the courts was further impeded by the threats of criminals against witnesses and their families.

The development of the market and democracy in Russia became fatefully entwined with organised crime. Criminal networks entered the banking system, were in control of many companies, and distorted the evolution of market relations by extortion and protection rackets, thus forcing costly security operations.[19] Gangs were involved not only in typically criminal behaviour but also penetrated the 'legal' open economy; indeed, in post-communist Russian conditions it was very difficult to tell where the black economy (estimated to be roughly the same size as the official economy) ended and various shades of the grey economy began. In a report delivered to the Academy of Social Sciences in July 1997, Anatoly Kulikov, then Minister for Internal Affairs and also a deputy prime minister, argued that 'Organised crime is dictating to individual Russian industries how to behave on the market and controls whole areas of the country'. According to Kulikov, 'underworld godfathers are setting up closed syndicates and have them infiltrate the state's economic institutions'.[20]

In their heyday in the 1990s a whole network emerged that impinged on all aspects of business. Volkov describes the sinuous relationship between the violent entrepreneurs and private business and the role of the police in this – which at best appears to have been marginal; at worst, they too became purveyors of violent entrepreneurship. He argues for the important analytical distinction between the world of criminals and those who protect and govern them, and it is the latter who claim a monopoly of force within their domain of operation. Volkov provides a vivid analysis of the sort of people who became racketeers, notably young men with a sporting background; indeed, some sports clubs became the organised base for this sort of activity. It appears that in the early 1980s the Communist Party was aware of the link and tried to ban the teaching of karate as a sport! Another community that had the network resources to engage in violent entrepreneurship were the veterans of the Afghanistan war.

Volkov argues that it is not adequate to consider this behaviour as 'deviant', since in a transitional society the norms and boundaries were far too fluid. For him, 'Russian criminal groups represent one of the possible institutional arrangements for the protection of property rights and form a shadow system of arbitration.'[21] However, after 1998 there has been a sustained state-building effort, notably through the establishment of an effective tax system, which has undermined the autonomy of the violence-managing agencies. The state has reasserted its prerogatives in the sphere of the management of coercion and in controlling its own agencies, a threefold process that Volkov dubs as 'neutralization', 'integration' and 'pacification'. The epoch of the violent entrepreneur is waning, and in their place the *gosudarstvenniki*, the state builders, are resurgent.

While the old regime lacked freedom, it did at least ensure a degree of security. The new freedoms after the fall of communism were accompanied by such a degree of job and physical insecurity that many yearned for the order (*poryadok*) of Soviet times. The inter-penetration of organised crime and politics led some to argue that Russia's second revolution had been 'stolen' by an unholy alliance of communists-turned-speculators and the criminal underworld. According to Handelman, whole regions and cities had fallen into the hands of criminal networks, senior officers happily traded weapons for cars, while the clandestine trade in nuclear materials threatened the rest of the world. He suggested that Russia had become a 'criminal state' run by and for criminals, while the honest lost out.[22] The Russian 'mafiya' was a distinctive product of the Soviet prison-camp system and the post-communist weakening of the state, whereas in Italy it was a well-organised product of long-term social development. The close connection between political and criminal elites originated in Soviet times but had grown in depth and scale after 1991. It would be an exaggeration, however, to argue that Russia had become a 'criminal state' since far too much remained beyond the control of criminal-political elites. It would be more accurate to say that Russia was a state marked by widespread criminality reaching into the upper echelons of central and local power; but this does not make Russia – any more than it makes Italy – a mafia state.

## Corruption, meta-corruption and anti-corruption

According to Boris Fedorov, the finance minister in the early Yeltsin years, 'Corruption has permeated our entire society... Corruption, that is a demand for remuneration, is encountered at every step.'[23] Corruption, however, is an ambiguous phenomenon.

Georgy Satarov, head of the Indem analytical agency specialising in the study of corruption, noted two meanings: it could be defined in the narrow sense as a transaction that involves a government official abusing a resource or property not in the interests of those who had placed responsibility in their hands but to the person who had bribed them (venal corruption); but it could also be defined more broadly as the degradation of power (what we call meta-corruption). He also stressed that there was a distinctively Russian phenomenon of 'corruption at the bottom', engaged in by the mass of the people to survive in a bureaucratised semi-market society, while 'corruption at the top' was the problem that usually most concerned Western writers. The two types of corruption in Russia coalesced to create a type of 'social' corruption that was prevalent in Asian societies.[24] The pollster Yuri Levada noted that in popular perceptions corruption tended to become a catch-all bogeyman to describe various social ills such as the theft of state property, tax evasion, and links between oligarchs and politicians, in addition to the more narrowly defined bribery of government officials, cronyism and nepotism. Such a conceptual lack of precision, in his view, made it more difficult to fight corruption.[25] Russia's market-oriented corruption added a new layer to a deeply embedded 'culture of favours', to use Alena Ledeneva's term, based on *blat*, the system of informal contacts and personal networks that allowed people to obtain goods and services in the Soviet system.[26] Corruption and the shadow economy fed off each other, distorting classical market relations and poisoning basic transactions in daily life.[27]

### Meta-corruption and Yeltsin's regime

Russia is moving from meta-corruption, a system which is corrupt in its very essence, to venal corruption; from a corrupt system to a system with corruption.[28] However, the inter-penetration of business and politics in the Putin years can be seen as evidence of the return of meta-corruption. The communist system was meta-corrupt in that it never subordinated itself to the rule of law (although after the initial revolutionary lawlessness it ruled by and through the law), characterised by lack of accountability and the systematic enjoyment of privileges granted its leadership by the common ownership of the means of production.[29] Corruption was one of the reasons for the fall of communism.[30] A new form of meta-corruption, however, has emerged rooted in the transition from a state-owned economy to a market-based system. The disentanglement of the political process from its deep embedment in the economy, while at the same time structuring political life as an autonomous activity governed by the impartial rule of law and accountable to the electorate, would not be achieved easily. The extrication of the Russian state from, on the one hand, deep involvement in the economy and, on the other, from its dominance by the arbitrary rule of a single Party, represents an act of political reconstitution unprecedented in its scope and complexity. What has emerged, though, is a dual system where new forms of systemic meta-corruption coexist with what we call venal corruption, the pursuit of individual gain out of the pursuit or attainment of public office. The World Bank calls the first sort 'state capture', and the second 'administrative corruption'.[31] Yeltsin's regime had the dual characteristics of both in good measure. Under Putin the meta-corrupt features have changed their form as the policy process has become less susceptible to social pressures and state capture is being reversed; but instead there are elements of 'business capture' as the state has aggressively asserted its rights over economic policy and property.[32]

No clear line can be drawn between venality and meta-corruption. The whole privatisation programme, for example, masterminded by Anatoly Chubais, was a huge exercise in transferring public goods into private assets. Privatisation favoured a small group of 'oligarchs' while reducing a large part of society to poverty. From a structural perspective privatisation was considered necessary to establish a market economy, while Chubais insisted that the establishment of a new middle class would create the social basis for democracy. At the height of Yeltsin's rule the state itself engaged in corruption on a grand scale. In the 'loans-for-shares' scandal from November 1995 the state favoured certain 'insider' interests in the privatisation process in return for funds that would ensure that the machinery of government could continue to turn. Insider banks were granted shares in the country's top companies as collateral for loans to a desperate government, but it was understood by all that the government would default on the loans and the oligarchs would get the companies for a song. In this way Vladimir Potanin's Oneksimbank 'purchased' the giant Norilsk Nickel works (the world's largest), the Sidanko oil company, and the Northwest River Shipping Company, while Mikhail Khodorkovsky's Menatep Bank got hold of Yukos, Russia's second largest oil company.

Until 1998 the management of state assets had been 'privatised', with some fifty authorised banks dealing with transfers from the state budget at the central and local levels, allowing unimaginable profits to be made at the state's expense – and above all at the expense of those whose wages were delayed as the banks speculated with funds designated for social purposes. Some ten so-called 'court' banks were at the heart of this system of financial manipulation. The growing budget deficit was exacerbated by various tax exemptions granted to bodies like the Russian Orthodox Church for the import of alcohol and cigarettes, and above all to the National Sports Fund (NFS) established by presidential decree on 1 June 1992. Having been granted generous export quotas on a range of valuable raw materials, out of the billions of roubles that passed through its hands only a tiny proportion contributed to the development of sport, and not a single audit was conducted on the fund throughout its existence until its privileges were revoked in 1995.[33] The system of tax benefits granted to so-called charitable foundations siphoned billions of roubles away from the state budget. In short, the Yeltsin regime allowed the state budget itself to become the object of private speculative manipulation, contributing to the bankruptcy of the state in mid-1998 and the effective default on foreign loans and the moratorium on servicing the domestic debt.

The monopolies and financial groups exerted a disproportionate and direct influence on politics. Bureaucratic, political and economic corruption became entwined as the semi-feudal court politics around Yeltsin allowed a financial-industrial oligarchy to replace formal politics by a system of informal deals. The 'corridors of power' were no longer to be found in government ministries but in the softly carpeted executive suites of the new oligarchs. The very notion of 'lobbying' became pathetically inadequate to describe the way that whole areas of the state were colonised by external interests. Duma deputies allegedly were routinely bribed - in the words of one paper, 'everything can be bought and sold'.[34] The focus of political corruption, however, was the presidency – in a presidential system lobbying will inevitability focus more narrowly on the presidential apparatus than in the more complex multi-layered game typical of parliamentary systems. In Russia the relationship between special interest groups and the presidency was exceptionally close. The presidency was not only the source of 'reform' but was also at the apex of the meta-corruption with which it was accompanied.

The funding of political parties and electoral campaigns is at the sharp edge of political corruption. The best-known example of the latter is the 1996 presidential campaign in which the Yeltsin team (from March 1996 led by the ubiquitous Chubais) spent several dozen (if not thousands) times more money than the law allowed (each candidate could spend 14.5 billion old roubles, or $3.2 million).[35] In February 1996 Russia's leading moguls, inspired by Boris Berezovsky, met at the Davos Forum in Switzerland and created a war chest to bankroll Yeltsin's re-election. The gulf between what the Yeltsin campaign actually spent on the campaign, whose upper estimates reach over $500 million,[36] and the modest sum that he declared is impressive.[37] There was no serious attempt to implement election and campaign laws – except against his opponents. The symbol of the campaign was not the ballot box but a cardboard box containing $538,000 in campaign cash that two of Chubais' aides were caught carrying out of the White House on 19 June, just three days after the first round of voting.[38] One of the two caught with the box was Sergei Lisovsky, one of the masterminds behind the campaign and head of the 'Premier SV' advertising agency, one of Russia's largest adverting companies. There have been allegations that he was somehow involved in List'ev's murder in 1995. List'ev, a television journalist and executive at ORT (Russia's main TV channel), had temporarily frozen all advertising contracts, including that with Premier SV. Yeltsin's victory was due to more than electoral bribery and malpractice, above all arising out of fear of what a victory for the communists would entail, yet the shameless and extravagant promises and their equally brutal repudiation, and the illegal over-spending on the campaign indicated a profound corruption of the political process.

A year after the presidential elections the charges of corruption focused on Chubais' own personal enrichment, with *Izvestiya* alleging that in February 1996, a month after he first left office, the Stolichnyi Savings Bank granted a five-year interest-free $2.9 million loan to his new Centre to Defend Private Property. The funds were allegedly used for his personal speculation in the treasury bills (GKO) market, allowing him to reap lucrative profits which he then pocketed.[39] In a letter to the paper Chubais did not dispute the facts but claimed (quite logically within the framework of what we call meta-corruption) that what he had done was 'absolutely normal' in any democratic country.[40] His action was perhaps not strictly speaking illegal, but using funds donated for charitable purposes for personal speculation is irregular, to say the least. The whole story of Western 'aid' to Russia is similarly beset by a mixture of venality and systemic meta-corruption.[41] There is a similar confusion over the legal status of the use of author's 'advances' in the case of a number of officials in 1997. The story was linked to the intra-elite struggles over the Svyazinvest sale in July 1997, and led to the exposure of a $100,000 advance payment from Servina, a Swiss financial group with links to Potanin's Oneksimbank (the winner of the auction), to Alfred Kokh, head of the state property committee (GKI) responsible for the disbursement of state property, and led to his sacking in August 1997.[42] A similar case was exposed in November 1997 when five high officials, including Chubais, were together found to have received a $450,000 advance. Maksim Boiko, Kokh's successor at GKI, was forced to resign, but Chubais once again weathered the storm. Criminal charges were not filed against the officials on the grounds that there was no evidence that they had embezzled money from the state, although presumably Oneksimbank, in making the excessive payments, expected to receive something in return for its 'investment'.

Corruption in Russia is rooted in the political economy of the transition. Yves Mény has defined corruption 'as a clandestine exchange between two markets – the political and/or administrative market and the economic and social market'.[43] This definition, so pertinent to Russia, is at the core of John Girling's analysis of the issue:

> Corruption is the illegitimate reminder of the values of the market place (everything can be bought and sold) that in the age of capitalism increasingly, even legitimately, permeate formerly autonomous political and social spheres.[44]

For him corruption was more than a 'criminal' problem but a social one, derived in part from the incommensurability of the economic and political spheres that in practice eroded the distinction between public and private matters. Seen in this light, the spread of capitalism to Russia could not but subvert the realisation of the proclaimed democratic ideals together with good governance in its entirety. The close relationship between economic and political elites in a redistribution system devoted to the privatisation of state assets with minimal legal controls and no public oversight fostered not only venality but also meta-corruption. What if Chubais was right, however, and that it did not matter how state property was disbursed as long as it was done quickly and created a substantial class (however narrow its composition) with a vital stake in the preservation of the post-communist order? In these circumstances corruption could be considered a progressive phenomenon. The common good could, it is argued, be achieved by meta-corrupt means, something that is tautologically incoherent but is typical of the paradoxes of post-communism. Mayor Luzhkov's style of managing affairs in Moscow, where the city government took its cut of all deals and reinvested the proceeds in the city itself (like mayor Richard Daley in Chicago in an earlier epoch), suggested that meta-corruption might be the price of to pay to make the transition to capitalism irreversible.

Even more venal forms of corruption, moreover, can be considered functional. While the emergence of meta-corruption has been defended, by Chubais and his allies, as systemically progressive, allowing the rudiments of a capitalist system to be transferred to Russia and a middle class to emerge, a similar argument has been advanced by economists concerning venal corruption. Do its costs always out-weigh its benefits? Might it not encourage economic growth by subverting a stifling bureaucracy and allowing the accumulation of capital?[45] This may be the case in individual cases, but the evidence suggests that corruption deters foreign investment, and in Russia encouraged capital flight totalling at least $100 billion between 1991 and 1998, dwarfing the $6 billion in foreign direct investment and the various painful International Monetary Fund (IMF) loans. If allowed to proliferate corruption ultimately undermines government itself as bureaucrats become more concerned with private profit than public duties. This has certainly been the case in Russia, where the very existence of the state was threatened by corruption, both meta and venal. For Leslie Holmes, indeed, corruption represented a distinctive type of crisis of the state.[46]

According to Berlin-based Transparency International in its Corruption Perception Index (CPI) for 1997, Russia was in 49th place,[47] not a healthy position for a country aspiring to great power status. By 2001 the Index saw Russia in 79th place out of 91 ranked countries, tying with Ecuador and Pakistan, although this was slight improvement over the previous year when Russia was ranked 82nd.[48] By 2005 Russia was ranked one of the most corrupt countries in Europe, and brought the country 30 spots down in its rankings to place it among Albania, Niger and Sierra Leone in 126th place.[49] This finding was confirmed by a survey published by the Indem Foundation in 2005, following an earlier survey in 2001.[50] The surprising finding was the extent of the growth in corruption in the business sphere, with the average size of each bribe growing on average seven-fold, with the gross income of officials growing at least four-fold. As Satarov, put it, 'corruption is a manifestation of the inefficiency of government at all levels', and with Russia's great natural wealth at a time of buoyant prices, it was not surprising that the scale of corruption had increased. He noted that Russia had almost 100,000 dollar millionaires, and several dozen dollar-billionaires.[51] According to the Indem survey, Russians pay $3 billion in bribes a year, with the incidence of corruption of all sorts, including various kickbacks and deals cut with bureaucrats for protection, rising from $33 billion in 2001 to $316 billion by the end of 2005.[52] With so many ways of making extra money, it is not surprising that government service became so popular. Corruption had increased in enlistment offices, education and in land acquisition agencies, with the level of corruption lowest in the pension, employment, housing maintenance and housing registration spheres.[53] In its 2006 report on corruption Indem argued that in 2005 39 million corrupt deals had been carried out, with the average businessperson having to pay a bribe on average twice a year. Seven per cent of a company's turnover on average were devoted to bribes to corrupt officials, with the so-called 'corruption tax' comprising 1.1 per cent of GDP. Only one bribe-taker out of 100,000 was imprisoned.[54]

The 'political economy' approach to corruption is well established.[55] It stresses that political actors will act rationally to advance their (typically material) interests, usually at the expense of the public interest.[56] The approach focuses on the behaviour of agents, which in a situation where property rights are fluid and negative rights not enforced, allowed enormous scope for rent-seeking and corruption. Under Putin the excesses of the 1990s were curbed, but state officials were brought in to monitor the state's economic assets, once again establishing a type of neo-patrimonial system that provided rich scope for corruption of both sorts.

### Anti-corruption measures

We argue that Russia's post-communist system has dual characteristics, both democratising and elite-dominated, venal and meta-corrupt. It is these dual characteristics that made attempts at reform more than cosmetic, and ultimately may allow corruption to be tackled seriously. While anti-corruption campaigns often were little more than an instrument in intra-elite competition, they did at times engage with the problem.

#### The legal definition of corruption

In contrast to Russia's 1960 Criminal Code that made no mention of corruption, the new Code at least recognises the problem. Article 291.1 criminalises the payment of bribes either directly or indirectly to an official whether in a state or private office, while 291.2 outlawed payments to an official to undertake wittingly illegal actions (or inaction). Article 292 defines 'administrative forgery' as an official inserting into official documents known falsehoods or distorting their contents out of mercenary or personal interest. Punishments ranged from a stiff fine to imprisonment. The very definition of the crime represented an important step in combating it, but few prosecutions have yet been brought against officials. In 1995 3,504 charges were brought against corrupt civil servants, the great majority accused of bribery, while according to MVD statistics 700 cases had been found between 1995 and 1998 linking bureaucrats to organised crime, although few prosecutions resulted.[57] A new law on government service came into effect on 1 January 1998 which defined the rights and obligations of civil servants and marked a small step towards overcoming the functional corruption that had defined the Russian state bureaucracy since at least the time of Peter the Great.[58] At the same time, although it is illegal for public servants to work in business, this is only irregularly policed. Under Putin the number of prosecutions rose steeply, and three special prison camps for MVD personnel were built. The enforcement of existing laws began to make a significant contribution to fighting corruption.

### Anti-corruption campaigns and income declarations

Budgetary constraints and problems of low morale inhibit the work of law enforcement agencies. The MVD, responsible for the militia, suffered a haemorrhage of experienced officers and was itself mired in criminality. The anti-corruption campaign waged by the minister of the interior, Kulikov, from mid-1995 revealed awesome depths of venality in the MVD. His high profile campaign, including catching the traffic police red-handed in taking bribes, did little to change the structures that sustained the culture of bribe-taking.

The Yeltsin presidency launched a number of anti-corruption campaigns, but they tended to be a substitute for the kind of changes that would have genuinely tackled the problem.[59] Their primary purpose was symbolic and political. As Valeri Streletsky, the head of the anti-corruption section of the Presidential Security Service in 1995–7, put it, 'We existed on two planes. On the one hand we carried out the war against corruption. On the other, we proceeded out of political interests.'[60] By 1998 Yeltsin had vetoed three Duma anti-corruption laws that might have threatened the interests of his newly enriched allies. A presidential decree of 4 April 1992 was the first official anti-corruption measure, focusing on petty crime in the civil service, and was followed by numerous equally ineffective campaigns. In his annual address to the Federal Assembly on 6 March 1997 Yeltsin acknowledged that corruption had undermined all levels of public service, noting that 'the criminal world has openly challenged the state and launched into open competition with it'.[61] The new anti-corruption campaign encompassed a number of measures, including a decree (drafted by Nemtsov) of 20 May 1997 that forced all government officials, members of parliament, public officials and political appointees to declare their incomes and assets (above all property holdings) in writing on special forms, and one of the sanctions for the first time against officials was the confiscation of personal property. From 1 January 1999 all government officials whose lifestyle exceeded their official incomes had to declare the source of their excess wealth. The actual declarations by leading officials at times verged on the farcical. Chernomyrdin, whose personal wealth in foreign bank accounts was reputed to be in the region of $5 billion, filed earnings of 1.4 million new roubles ($233,000) for 1997, a figure 31 times higher than what he had declared the previous year.[62] Yeltsin himself declared his 1997 income at 1.95 million new roubles ($320,000) derived mainly from his salary, royalties from his memoirs published in 1994 and interest on Russian bank accounts.[63]

As elsewhere, anti-corruption drives are used to punish opponents and to strengthen those politicians who can claim to have 'clean hands'. No campaign is complete without a few sacrificial lambs. The victims in this case were Sergei Stankevich, who had been arrested in April 1997 in Warsaw on an international arrest warrant in connection with an ill-fated Red Square concert, and General Konstantin Kobets, the hero of August 1991 but who in May 1997 was charged with abuse of office, bribery and the illegal possession of firearms. Both had long ago left the top rank of government, and thus their prosecution did not taint the existing authorities. A notable element in any anti-corruption campaign is the use of *kompromat* (evidence of malfeasance) in power struggles among the elite to blacken (compromise) one's opponents. The battle of *kompromat* was waged from the highest to the lowest levels, and not only in Russia.[64] In the run-up to the 2007 parliamentary elections the anti-corruption campaign was intensified and claimed some high-profile victims, including the mayor of Vladivostok, Vladimir Nikolaev, who boasted the underworld nickname of 'Winnie the Pooh'.

*Public supervision and transparency*

From the above it is clear that effective anti-corruption campaigns have to be distanced from executive authorities. In keeping with the dual nature of Russian politics, there were moves in this direction. A General Control Inspectorate (GKU) was established in 1992 to combat corruption, and its first head from March 1992, Yuri Boldyrev, proceeded to do so with gusto, exposing malfeasance in the Moscow mayor's office, GKI and, most notoriously, in the Western Army Group in the former East Germany. For his pains, Boldyrev was forced to resign as Comptroller General in March 1993.[65] Yeltsin had intended the anti-corruption campaign to be directed against his enemies, not his political allies.[66] This case, as we suggested above with other anti-corruption campaigns, was politicised. In 1995 Boldyrev continued his lonely struggle against corruption as the deputy head of the Federal Audit Chamber. His exposure of the 'loans-for-shares' scam helped put an end to the practice, but the fact that the exposure of these cases hardly caused a ripple let alone a scandal indicates that we are dealing here with meta-corruption, not 'simple' corruption. Under Putin the Audit Chamber was headed by Sergei Stepashin and now with presidential backing increased its oversight role over public expenditure, launching numerous investigations, including into the misappropriation of funds in Chechnya. There were plans to increase its powers (with the right to turn directly to the courts and to impose administrative penalties), but accompanied by a change in its status to bring it under presidential control. Instead of the Duma nominating its head, it would be the president (subject to Duma approval); and the president would enjoy the right to order the Audit Chamber to undertake investigations.[67]

In February 2004 Satarov took the lead in establishing a Public Anti-Corruption Council (OSA), bringing together a number of NGOs in the field. OSA organized a network of offices across the country, collecting evidence of alleged corrupt behaviour by regional and local businesspeople, politicians and officials. Only in April 2004, and possibly in response to Satarov's initiative, did the Duma establish its own Anti-Corruption Commission, headed by deputy Mikhail Grishankov.

Public oversight and media campaigns can have only a marginal role. It is not so much that the executive branch is too powerful, but that accountability for its actions is too weak. This is not a counsel for despair, and while what we described above is part of systemic meta-corruption, we also argue that Russia is a dual system where venal forms of corruption can be challenged, and by doing so the legitimacy of meta-corruption is also undermined. Already Yeltsin's March 1997 address to the Federal Assembly recognised the danger that meta-corruption posed to his own power, and promised to abolish the system of authorised banks and replace them with a national treasury, and insisted that future privatisation auctions should be more transparent. Independent watchdog institutions play an important part in reversing the culture of corruption and ensuring that anti-corruption struggles are perceived as more than part of political gamesmanship. The struggle at least sustains an alternative normative system that refuses to accept corruption as 'normal' and upholds a concept of the public good. The abuse of the concept of civil society has led to it being abandoned by some analysts, yet Girling is right to argue that 'the emergence of "civil society" provides the potential for normative counter-claims'.[68] These claims, moreover, as Rutland and Kogan stress, must be rooted in the realities of the country itself. Only Russians, they insist, 'can come up with a formula for a "capitalism with a Russian face" that stands a chance of working in that country', and here legal abstractions should come to terms with the realities of political power: 'Unless one specifies the political conditions conducive to the emergence of a coalition in favor of battling corruption, reforms promoting the rule of law will remain mere castles in the air.'[69] The roots of political corruption lie not in the social psychology of Russians but in specific institutions, structures and practices, and well-formulated and implemented reforms can deal with it at that level.

### Parliamentary and other forms of immunity

Many criminals had run for, and some were elected, to parliament to take advantage of the immunity from criminal prosecution that this conferred on them.[70] In many cases investigations had to be dropped when the suspect successfully ran for office. One of the changes introduced by the new Criminal Procedural Code of July 2002 was that parliamentary deputies lost their blanket immunity from criminal prosecution. A case can now be brought against a deputy without first having to obtain parliament's permission. The Constitutional Court ruled against attempts to grant deputies in regional legislatures immunity, ruling that only a federal law could decide the issue.[71]

### Controlling campaign expenses

National elections have been accompanied by accusations that the CEC had failed to establish clear rules for the financing of electoral campaigns. In the December 1993 campaign there had been confusion over how much a candidate could spend on themselves, allowing (it is claimed) corruption on a grand scale.[72] All candidates have to file financial declarations to the CEC or its equivalents at the local level stating the amount and source of campaign funds. Attempts to smear rivals with the charge that they received support from abroad (which is illegal) or foreign NGOs based in Russia have led to the publication of some of these.[73] Lobbying interests have 'invested' in candidates, hoping for a substantial return on their election. The failure of deputies to perform to expectations in this respect prompted business interests and other groups to participate directly in the December 1995 elections. The CEC has gradually refined the financial rules concerning elections, codified in the 2001 law on parties (see Chapter 7) but the problem, as before, remains inconsistent implementation.

*More market or authoritarianism?*

The economist Anders Aslund has argued that a rapid move to free markets would eliminate corruption.[74] The reduction of state intervention and bureaucratic interference would, in his view, remove some of the sources of distortion that allows corruption to flourish. The analysis is undoubtedly correct in part, but needs to be balanced by an adequate understanding of the role that states play in regulating markets. A strong market requires a strong state. It is at this point that more authoritarian solutions to the problem of corruption became increasingly popular. Alexander Lebed, advancing a distinctive mix of authoritarian populism to resolve the economic crisis and the criminalisation of politics, won the governorship of Krasnoyarsk krai, while Luzhkov advanced a *dirigiste* model to tackle Russia's problems. Putin's response was a combination of market and discipline.

As the 2007–8 succession approached the administration also stepped up its anti-corruption campaign.[75] If Chechnya had been the predominant theme in the 1999–2000 electoral cycle, the struggle against the oligarchs in 2003–4, then the war against corruption became the centrepiece of the elite's struggle to remain in power in 2007–8. In his 10 May 2006 address Putin had called corruption 'one of the greatest obstacles facing our development', and this was followed by a wave of high-profile corruption cases that reached up into the higher echelons of power, and implicated a regional governor and the mayors of two regional capitals. However, the perception that the anti-corruption campaign was no more than a pre-election stunt undermined its legitimacy.[76] As part of the campaign, deputy prosecutor general Aleksandr Buksman announced that Russia's army of bureaucrats were raking in £125 billion annually, not far off the state's total annual revenues. He revealed that in the first eight months of 2006 alone police had discovered 28,000 cases of corruption, a third of which were connected with bribe-taking.[77]

### Continuing problems

The historical and social roots of corruption go deep into Russian and Soviet history, and in the post-communist era threatened the whole democratisation process, undermining the rule of law, democracy, human rights and the very foundations of the emerging civil societies. Mény has argued that the prevalence of corruption undermines the democratic process itself, above all by encouraging a withdrawal from political participation and cynicism.[78] In Russia these features were apparent, with a widespread lack of trust in the new political elite and a grudging participation in the political process. A common attitude to the new leaders was that they were all thieves, but the very definition of what constituted theft was blurred in the context where the transitional regime was built on an '*enrichessez-vous*' programme. Despite the systemic corruption, at the individual level the communist system had been imbued by an ethic of public service, but this was now thrown out with the bath water of communism. The problem was exacerbated by the post-communist bias against idealism of whatever hue and by the dominance of a neo-liberal paradigm that elevated market forces into a new utopia.

Corruption extended not only into many areas of public administration but also into the law enforcement and other security agencies, including in Russia the army. When combined with the increasingly transnational character of organised crime and the vast resources it was able to control, the very bases of state autonomy came under threat. With its roots in the communist period, contrary to expectations the fall of the regimes did not lead to the decline of corruption and organised crime but to their luxuriant growth in the new market conditions. Criminal and bureaucratic forces in Russia combined to form a new and ruthless power.[79]

Corruption undermines the rudimentary systems of financial market regulation, discouraged foreign direct investment and contributed to the currency crises that unrolled out of East Asia from late 1997. Meta-corruption distorted the whole economic system, and indeed a semi-reformed economy trapped between bureaucratic regulation and the market was clearly to the advantage of those who could take advantage of rent-seeking opportunities. While the struggle against corruption could to a degree become a public project, with the mobilisation of the media and social and international organisations (for example, Transparency International) to expose wrong-doing and to act as a watchdog to deter malfeasance by public officials, meta-corruption can only be combated by systematic political action. Corrupt behaviour by public officials can be countered by judicial measures, whereas meta-corruption requires political reform.

## The security apparatus and politics

From the very first days of Soviet power the security apparatus played a major role in the life of the state. As we saw in Chapter 1, barely a few weeks after coming to power Lenin on 20 December 1917 established the Cheka, the forerunner of the KGB. Despite some attempts to curb its powers, the security apparatus, through several changes of name, became the bedrock of Stalin's power and the guarantor of communist rule after his death. The KGB, reorganised in the early 1950s with more limited powers, penetrated society at all levels. In the final stages of *perestroika* the KGB under Kryuchkov worked with the Party elite to save the old system, trying to discredit the Russian leadership and isolating Gorbachev behind a wall of disinformation.[80] The Russian authorities after the coup were faced with the challenge of how to put down this monster.[81] The republican branches of the KGB were transferred to the new states, and on 11 October 1991 the State Council abolished the central KGB (a decision formally ratified by the Supreme Soviet on 3 December) and its functions were divided between five agencies.

### The security agencies

#### Federal Border Service

About half of the KGB's 490,000 employees (some 240,000) were transferred to the Border Protection Committee, which after a number of reorganisations became the independent Federal Border Service in late 1993. Under Putin the Border Service was once again reincorporated into the main domestic security agency (see below).

#### Foreign Intelligence Service (SVR)

In October 1991 the Central Intelligence Service assumed the KGB's spying and counterespionage functions, becoming after the fall of the USSR the Russian Foreign Intelligence Service (SVR). The SVR took over the KGB First Directorate's enormous network of foreign agents, electronic monitoring and communications networks, Space Intelligence Centre and much more. Academician Yevgeny Primakov, its first director, stressed that the SVR would not be under political, individual or corporate control, and its sole purpose would be to protect the state.[82] Its main functions were ensuring the non-proliferation of nuclear weapons, monitoring technology vital for the country, preventing regional conflicts, fighting international crime, and checking business partners of the Russian government. Following Primakov's elevation to the foreign ministry in January 1996, his replacement, Vyacheslav Trubnikov, was a career intelligence officer with a strong record of service to the Soviet regime. The other CIS states lacked sophisticated foreign intelligence operations and were forced to rely on the Russians. The Law on Foreign Intelligence of 8 July 1992 subordinated the SVR to the president, with oversight by parliament and the Prosecutor's Office,[83] while the new law on foreign intelligence of December 1995 unequivocally subordinated the SVR to the president while stressing the importance of human rights. The SVR today employs around 10,000–15,000 personnel, including 300–500 special forces.

### Ministry of Internal Affairs (MVD)

The main successor organisation, at first headed by Vadim Bakatin, was the Inter-republican Security Service (ISS), which by a presidential decree of 19 December 1991 was swallowed up by the Russian Ministry of the Interior (MVD) to form a huge security apparatus called the Ministry of Security and Internal Affairs (MBVD – *Ministerstvo bezopastnosti i vnutrenykh del*), reminiscent of Stalin's monstrous People's Commissariat of Internal Affairs (NKVD). The merger was rejected by the Supreme Soviet and reversed by the Constitutional Court on 14 January 1992, and a separate MVD re-emerged, headed by Victor Yerin, and a new Ministry of Security (MB – *Ministerstvo bezopastnosti*) was created, headed by Yeltsin's ally, Victor Barannikov. The security agencies maintain huge parallel armies separate from the official military establishment. The MVD has some 70,000 Interior Troops (VV), with about half deployed in the defence of government establishments, while the other half, the OMON, was established during *perestroika* as a professional mobile strike force. The MB assumed the KGB's internal role and often appeared to be little different from its predecessor, taking over much of its structures and personnel. The ministry had 135,000 employees, 50,000 of them employed in counter-espionage and the rest, now that its services against dissidents and democrats were no longer required, turned their attention to crime.[84] The pervasive corruption within the MVD accentuated the role of the security apparatus.[85] Today the MVD is concerned not only with traditional police roles but is also responsible for refugees and migration, with the Federal Migration Service (FMS) being incorporated into the MVD in 2001. The MVD also runs an extensive parallel army (VV), which fought alongside the regular army and the FSB in Chechnya. The MVD's estimated strength is 649,000 uniformed personnel, including some 151,000–183,000 internal troops.

### Federal Security Service (FSB)

As the conflict between parliament and the president intensified the MB's position became increasingly difficult, Barannikov was dismissed in July 1993 and replaced by the KGB officer, Nikolai Golushko. His failure to warn the Kremlin of the gathering insurgency by parliamentary forces led to his own dismissal after the October 1993 events. He was replaced by Sergei Stepashin and, following the success of Zhirinovsky's nationalists in the 1993 elections, the MB on 21 December 1993 was reorganised to become the Federal Counter-Intelligence Service (FSK). The decree abolishing the MB argued that it had proved impossible to reform the agency, yet Yeltsin had done little to advance the cause of liberalisation, having used the agency to secure his own power base and foiling attempts by parliament to ensure oversight over state security and intelligence bodies.[86] The president, parliament and the Prosecutor-General now share responsibility for oversight over security agencies.

The security agency soon recovered its confidence and often acted in a manner reminiscent of the KGB, in particular condemning foreign organisations in Russia as front organisations for the CIA. A leaked FSK document, for example, condemned the activities of foreign academic research centres in Russia as part of America's attempts to undermine Russia as a great power.[87] Yeltsin stressed the FSK's role in protecting Russia's economic interests to ensure that the country did not end up 'on the sidelines of the world economy'.[88] The FSK was responsible for the covert war against Djohar Dudaev in Chechnya from the summer of 1994, and it was Stepashin who on 7 December 1994 authorised aircraft to bomb Grozny in direct contravention of a ceasefire brokered by the defence minister, Pavel Grachev.

The creation of the Federal Security Service (FSB) in the heat of the Chechen war,[89] and the appointment on 24 July 1995 of the former *Kommendant* of the Kremlin, Mikhail Barsukov, to replace Stepashin as its head, signalled a new prominence for the agency. The FSB absorbed several other security agencies, with a staff of some 77,640 (both officers and civilian personnel), and although in principle subordinated to the government and president, the body remained dangerously independent and was authorised to conduct operations both at home and abroad (by which CIS states were meant). After several changes of leadership it was this body that propelled Putin to national prominence when he reluctantly took over the directorship in 1998–9. He conducted a thorough reorganisation, including widespread dismissals of its top staff. On being elevated to the premiership in August 1999, Putin arranged for his loyal confidant, Nikolai Patrushev, to take over the FSB.

The FSB is responsible for counter-intelligence, but in addition takes the lead in fighting organised crime and terrorism, as well as overseeing border security. In 2003 the Federal Border Guards Service (FPS) was incorporated into the FSB, and at the same time it absorbed parts of the disbanded Federal Agency for Communications and Information (FAPSI), while other parts went to the SVR. The FSB director also heads the National Antiterrorism Commission, created in 2006 to coordinate the work of the various agencies in this field. The FSB now employs about 66,200 uniformed staff, including about 4,000 special forces, plus about 160,000–200,000 border troops.[90]

The FSB appeared to recreate a monstrous multi-functional agency. Former KGB personnel permeated into many aspects of Russia's post-communist life and the new agencies inexorably extended their influence over Russian life. The Law on Security of March 1992, for example, endowed the MVD, the customs and revenue services, and even the transport sector among others with security functions.[91] The July 1992 Law on the Federal Organs of State Security stated explicitly that the MB was 'a body of executive power', and endowed it with broad prerogatives to combat subversive activity against Russia by foreign agencies and domestic threats to constitutional order, territorial integrity and defence capability.[92] Former KGB censors and Party officials influenced the media, quite apart from using old contacts to line their pockets. In 2001 the FSB was once again given the power to investigate anonymous denunciations by citizens, an aspect of Soviet practices that was abolished with great fanfare in 1988 (and had in any case been limited in 1968), and 90 cities were closed to foreigners and other outsiders for 'security reasons'.[93]

### Federal Guards Service (FSO)

Following the October 1993 events a separate Presidential Security Service (PSB) was carved out of the Main Guard Directorate (GUO) to provide a military force loyal to the president; it was headed by Yeltsin's long-time personal security guard, Alexander Korzhakov. In December 1994 PSB troops marched across Moscow to raid the offices of Vladimir Gusinsky's MOST-bank, which among other things sponsored the independent television station NTV. Korzhakov at this time sought to intervene in crucial policy areas such as arms exports and high technology transfers, and, stepping far beyond his official duties, wrote an intemperate letter to the prime minister warning against the removal of quotas on energy exports. Korzhakov encouraged military intervention in Chechnya, no doubt hoping that a short victorious war would restore his master's fortunes in the presidential elections, while failure would only serve to confirm the need for the PSB and the security services to combat terrorism in Moscow. Korzhakov's role was likened to that of Rasputin in the dying days of the Tsarist regime, and his presence cruelly exposed the factional nature of Yeltsinite politics. Fearing defeat, Korzhakov in March 1996 advocated the cancellation of the forthcoming presidential elections but was overruled; he was fired following Yeltsin's success in the first round of the elections in June 1996.

Transformed into the FSO, the agency is responsible for personal protection of high-ranking officials from the president down, as well protecting strategic buildings. In 2003 parts of FAPSI were transferred to the FSO, including about 50,000 personnel, and a new Service for Special Communications and Information (SSSI) was created. The agency employs between 10,000 and 30,000, including about 3,000 in the Presidential Guard.

### Ministry of Justice

In addition to its legal functions, the ministry took over responsibility for the Federal Penitentiary Service (FSIN) in 1998 from the MVD as one of the conditions of joining the Council of Europe. The FSIN has about 250,000 uniformed prison staff, as well as an unknown number of special forces, some of whom saw action in Chechnya.

### Ministry for Civil Defence, Emergency Situations and Dealing with Natural Disasters (MChS)

This is a civil defence organisation encompassing fire-fighting functions, and is always on hand whenever a natural disaster strikes. It has also provided disaster relief and humanitarian assistance abroad. Since its creation in the early 1990s the ministry has been headed by the charismatic Sergei Shoigu, one of the longest-serving ministers on record. The ministry has about 70,000 personnel, including about 23,000 uniformed civil defence forces, plus another 300,000 in the State Fire Service (GPS).

### Federal Service for the Control of the Drug Trade (FSKN)

As its name implies, this body, created in 2003 on the basis of the disbanded Federal tax Police Service, is responsible for the fight against drug-related crime, as well as narcotic smuggling. It has a staff of about 40,000, including an unknown number of special forces.

### Ministry of Defence (MO)

We shall discuss the MO in Chapter 16, but for the sake of completeness we should note that traditional military personnel in Russia today numbers 960,000, plus about 50,000 Railway Troops (incorporated into the MO in 2004) and about 14,000 former Federal Service for Special Construction (*Spetsstroi*) forces, also absorbed in 2004. The MO is responsible for defending the country against external aggression, although its forces have been used in domestic conflicts (Chechnya).

### Security and politics: the role of the 'siloviki'

The multiplicity of secret services suggested the emergence of a 'security state'. One commentator notes that Russia (and the CIS) is prey to a 'self-perpetuating Chekist culture'[94] that permeates the new social, political, economic and, indeed, criminal structures. Old habits die hard and, despite constitutional guarantees to the contrary, the last years of the Yeltsin presidency were marked by a revival of an autonomous role for the security services. The former head of the government apparatus, Vladimir Kvasov, argued that all telephones and offices in the White House (now the seat of the government) were bugged, and even Sergei Filatov, at the time head of the Presidential Administration, made the astonishing admission that he too might be under surveillance.[95]

The first Chechen war provided further evidence of the consolidation of a traditional security state and revealed the awesome implications of the reconstitution of a reborn security complex. The emergence of what came to be called 'the party of war' suggested that Russian politics were becoming increasingly militarised as the executive came under the influence of a security complex beyond parliamentary control. This militant group included the head of the PSB, Korzhakov, the head of the FSK, Stepashin, and the head of the MVD, Yerin. They were joined by the militant nationalities minister, Nikolai Yegorov, who had urged a forceful resolution of the Chechnya crisis but who became one of the first political casualties of the intervention, being sacked in late January 1995. The unity of the so-called 'power ministries', however, should not be exaggerated. Inter-service rivalries were pronounced and the inadequacies of the war effort brought home to Yeltsin the limits of the security apparatus and the awesome costs in domestic popularity and international isolation that their dominance would entail.

Primakov's appointment as prime minister in September 1998 was taken as a token of 'the resurgence of the KGB in the political life of the country' and a threat to Russian democracy.[96] Primakov's summary dismissal in May 1999, however, rather weakened the argument, although the important role played by people with a security background is significant, accompanied by the rise of the Security Council (see Chapter 6). Above all, Putin's natural political base lies in the security services, having served 16 years in the KGB and then headed the FSB. There is no doubt that Putin drew on his former colleagues to provide muscle and personnel for his policies, although it would be an exaggeration to argue that politics under his leadership was 'securitised'. Contrary to much ill-informed commentary, Putin's KGB past does not automatically make him leader of a newly militant security apparatus thirsting for revenge. Putin had worked in the KGB from 1975 to 1990, and had briefly returned as head of the FSB in 1998–9. Nevertheless, Putin's security background, even though tempered by his work under the liberal mayor of St Petersburg, Anatoly Sobchak, in the early 1990s and then in the presidential administration under Yeltsin, no doubt predisposes him to statist rather than pluralist approaches to public policy issues.

The term *siloviki* is derived from *silovye struktury* (force structures), referring to the armed services, law enforcement bodies, and intelligence agencies. Thus, a *silovik* (plural: *siloviki*) is a former or current member of any of these coercive bodies. Under Putin the influence of these people has grown, to the point even that some have argued that Russian policy is now determined by them. The *siloviki* stress the need to restore the coherence of the state and have strong views about how the economy should be run. The concept of a cohesive 'militocracy' is exaggerated, but the general *silovik* view that the state should take the priority over the anarchy of the market in strategic economic issues and over the unpredictability of the democratic representation of civil society in politics is something that is close to Putin's heart. They were particularly concerned to ensure the consolidation of their power and the perpetuation of their rule even after Putin had left the presidency. Numerous studies have noted the increased role of the *siloviki* under Putin. As a recent work has demonstrated, the federal and regional elite structures now have a significant security component.[97] According to Kryshtanovskaya and White, the proportion of those with a security, military or other law enforcement agencies in leadership positions rose from 4 per cent under Gorbachev to 11 per cent under Yeltsin, and then rose to 25 per cent by the end of Putin's first term as president, with the proportion even higher in national government.[98]

The leading 'securocrats' were well-represented among the 'barons', the senior ministers and Kremlin officials, who worked closely with Putin and regularly attended the unofficial 'kitchen cabinet' held at his country home on Saturday mornings, where they drank tea and discussed the fate of the nation. This group of about eight people includes the heads of the force structures, as well as the prime minister and the head of the presidential administration.[99] It is doubtful whether the prime minister, Mikhail Fradkov, can be considered a fully fledged *silovik*, but he was often considered a protégé of the defence minister Sergei Ivanov and had spent a period in the early 1970s in the KGB academy, where he probably learnt his excellent English.[100] It is not entirely clear whether Ivanov himself can be considered a member of the *silovik* faction since his loyalty was primarily to Putin individually and thus helped Putin constrain factional conflicts. Equally, the head of the Audit Chamber, Sergei Stepashin, was a former head of the FSB yet he kept his distance from the *silovik* faction. Igor Sechin, deputy head of the presidential administration, is usually considered a key representative of the *siloviki*. The *siloviki* group includes another former KGB officer, Viktor Ivanov, also a deputy head of the presidential administration, Patrushev, the head of the FSB, and the former Prosecutor General, Vladimir Ustinov.

The alleged pre-eminent role of the *siloviki* has been challenged by a number of studies. Renz has questioned whether the growth in *silovik* numbers is a conscious strategy by Putin to enhance their influence to create a more authoritarian regime, and she argues that there is no common 'military mindset' among them advocating relatively more authoritarian policies. In her view, they are far from dominant in the policy-making process. Only 9 of 47 leading officials in the presidential administration in 2005 had a security background, and none of the 9 was in the top echelons of power. Only two of 10 presidential advisers were *siloviki*. Putin simply relied on people with whom he had worked in the past, and in her view security officials were just one group of many. Most of Putin's *siloviki* in any case had, like Putin, enjoyed varied careers, and most had worked in other spheres. They certainly did not constitute a coherent clan, she insists, as the concept of 'militocracy' implies.[101] Rivera and Rivera demonstrated that while the number of *siloviki* in responsible government positions had indeed increased, this rise was not as big as Kryshtanovskaya and White had suggested – a three-fold increase since 1998 rather than the reported seven-fold increase.[102] They conclude that claims about 'an emerging "militocracy" are real but overstated'.[103] Above all, they argue that this is balanced by the increased representation of business representatives in all spheres of Russian public life, a nascent bourgeoisie that will in the long-term perhaps have a far greater impact than the temporary assertion of *silovik* authority.

## Human and civil rights

The war in Chechnya and numerous cases where the civil rights of individuals have been abused has tarnished Russian democracy. Ever since the Helsinki Final Act of 1975 introduced a new order of legitimacy for the defence of civil rights the issue has been at the centre of Soviet and Russian politics. The values enshrined by Helsinki, and developed by successive follow-up conferences, provided the normative and ethical basis for *perestroika* and for post-communist democratisation. The Organisation for Security and Cooperation in Europe (OSCE) and the Council of Europe remain the major international bodies ensuring and safeguarding the pan-European human rights regime (see also Chapter 15). There is a human rights element in many of Russia's international agreements: for example, there is a conditionality clause on human rights in the Partnership and Cooperation agreement signed with the EU that came into force in 1997.

The European Convention on Human Rights and Fundamental Freedoms (ECHR), developed by the Council of Europe, became part of Russian law on its ratification on 5 May 1998. This was a revolutionary moment as West European norms were extended to the whole continent, and intensified as part of what is called the 'fourth generation' of rights (social, regional). This new stage in normative development was *conventional* (i.e., based on international conventions) rather than narrowly constitutional. Participation in these conventions is a powerful force, it has been argued, for the 'Europeanisation' of Russia; although others argue that Russia's membership of bodies such as the Council of Europe is premature. Surprisingly, Russia (unlike the UK) has not exercised its right of derogation in time of emergency (Article 15) over Chechnya. Russia has, however, filed its first three 'observations' to the European Court of Human Rights over Chechnya, arguing that domestic remedies still remained to be explored and that criminal prosecutions would follow. The lack of energy in prosecuting abuses in Chechnya was in part a concession to the armed forces fighting against an enemy which itself is guilty of sustained human rights abuses; but this does not absolve Russia of its commitments in this area.

A number of cases have reflected the contradictions in Russia's human rights record, with a number of individuals recognised as political prisoners. In 2006 these included Zara Murtazalieva, a young Chechen citizen arrested in Moscow in 2004 suspected of being a 'black widow' female terrorist, Mikhail Trepashkin, Valentin Danilov, Igor Sutyagin, Mikhail Khodorkovsky, Platon Lebedev, and Svetlana Bakhmina. Alexander Nikitin had faced charges of divulging state secrets in contributing to a report, based on openly available documentation, to the Norwegian environmental group Bellona on the environmental dangers posed by rusting nuclear submarines in the Barents Sea. Acquitted by a St Petersburg court in December 1999, his case was only finally closed in September 2000 by the refusal of the Supreme Court to reverse the acquittal. The military journalist Grigory Pasko was subjected to an equally long drawn-out series of trials and postponements over charges, first made in 1997, that he had committed state treason by disclosing information about the environmental dangers posed by the Pacific Fleet to the Sea of Okhotsk. The treason conviction on Pasko aroused particular controversy. On 25 June 2002 the Supreme Court's military section upheld the conviction, and although soon pardoned Pasko refused to accept that he had been guilty of any crime. The case of Mikhail Trepashkin was particularly disturbing. A lawyer and former FSB colonel, he had tried to discover the truth about the apartment bombings of September 1999. Instead, in May 2004 he was sentenced to a four-year prison term for revealing state secrets and illegally carrying a pistol in his car. Released on parole in September 2005, he was re-incarcerated two weeks later after the state successfully appealed against the parole decision. The academic Igor Sutyagin, an associate of the Institute of the USA and Canada, was arrested in October 1999 and was convicted in April 2004 of revealing state secrets, even though the materials he used were all in the public domain, and sentenced to 15 years in a strict-regime camp. In June 2007 he was refused a pardon. The Krasnoyarsk physicist Valentin Danilov in May 2000 was charged with divulging state secrets to China, and although he was acquitted in December 2003, the verdict was set aside by the Supreme Court and in November 2004 he was sentenced to 14 years in a strict-regime camp. These and other cases added to popular concerns about human rights.[104] It was not clear whether these cases were the exception, with the security services lapsing back into old habits, or whether they were becoming part of the new rules of the game. As in other spheres, were a few exemplary cases intended to act as a warning to the rest?

Putin's assertion about the 'dictatorship of law', although phrased in a neo-Soviet manner, in practice meant the universal application of law. In his comments to a conference of chairs of regional courts on 24 January 2000 Putin gave unqualified support for the principles enshrined in the radical 1992 proposals on judicial reform, and in introducing his reform of the federal system on 17 May he insisted that the 'dictatorship of law' meant the equally strict adherence to federal legislation and observance of the rights of citizens both in Moscow and the most remote region. His repeated avowals, however, did not allay concern and among other responses a conference of 350 human rights organisations in Moscow on 20–1 January 2001 warned, in the words of the veteran human rights activist Sergei Kovalev, of a drift to totalitarianism. A Democratic Conference in Moscow in June 2001 sought to unite 'democrats' in defence of human rights, although the meeting was divided over the degree to which it should move into opposition to the Kremlin.

The Duma has a Human Rights Ombudsman who issues annual reports on the state of human and civil rights in the country. The first appointment to this post was Sergei Kovalev, but his experience in the post was an unhappy one; in March 1995 the Duma dismissed him, partly because of his trenchant criticism of the Chechen war. He was replaced by Oleg Mironov, a former communist who became a vigorous advocate of human rights, issuing hard-hitting reports condemning abuses. Over half of the 25,000 (up from 7,000 in 1998) cases received by his office in 2000 concerned the criminal justice system.[105] His successor, Vladimir Lukin, was a former Yabloko MP, and no less an independent figure. The office employs some two hundred people and includes some specialised departments for investigating complaints. Amendments to the federal constitutional law on the Human Rights Commissioner in October 2006 enhanced their right to initiate parliamentary investigations into human rights abuses. Nearly half of the country's regions also have human rights ombudsmen with responsibilities akin to those of the Duma's. Lukin's annual report for 2006, running to over four hundred pages, noted a sharp jump in the violations of civil liberties, rising by nearly half over the previous year, and the report concluded that Russians did not trust their government: 'They don't believe that authorities work hard to secure their social, economic and political rights.'[106]

The presidential Human Rights Commission, headed under Putin by Vladimir Kartashkin, was sometimes accused of fostering a compliant civil society rather than encouraging autonomy for civic associations. Under Putin the office changed its profile and became the Presidential Council for Promoting Civil Society Institutions and Human Rights. From 2001 inter-regional human rights commissions were established in each of the seven federal districts to ensure that local laws corresponded to federal law in the sphere of human rights. In July 2002 Kartashkin was replaced by another respected activist and Duma deputy, Ella Pamfilova, a vociferous critic of the conduct of the 1994–6 Chechen war. She took a particular interest in protecting Russia's 450,000 NGOs from excessive regulation. On her appointment she insisted that her main aim was to help people 'defend their rights in a civilised manner and to protect them from the caprices of bureaucrats and other people'.[107] This illustrates a point made by a recent study of human rights in Russia, which argues against the stereotype that Russian people neither know nor care about civil rights and human dignity and instead demonstrates that Russia has been instrumental in developing the international human rights regime.[108] The point now, of course, is to ensure its implementation in Russia, and this is a struggle that continues.

# 6    The executive

A constitution is the property of a nation, and not of those who exercise the government.

(Thomas Paine)[1]

The dissolution of the Communist Party and the disintegration of the USSR created a power vacuum that was filled by a hegemonic presidency. The federal presidency in Russia sits at the head of a vast bureaucracy composed of dozens of agencies and thousands of administrators. Russia is technically a semi-presidential system, with the president sharing power with a prime minister and a cabinet of ministers, although the constitution is unequivocal in granting the president priority. This is a bifurcated executive system: on the one hand, the president and his or her apparatus working from the Kremlin and Old Square (previously the headquarters of the Central Committee); and on the other, the prime minister and the government, based primarily in the White House (formerly the Supreme Soviet building).[2] The centre of political gravity returned to the Kremlin, which now adopted many of the institutions and functions of the Politburo of old. The presidency has its own security service, its own Security Council, administrative apparatus and much more. At the same time, out of the rubble of the Soviet regime many traditional features re-emerged, above all in the limited independence of the cabinet and prime minister. The Soviet administrative class only gradually took on the features of a modern civil service. The establishment of a powerful executive overshadowed not only the legislature but also the democratic gains that it claimed to advance. The president is head of government, as well as being the symbolic head of state, and this combination of governmental and symbolic power makes the Russian presidency truly hegemonic.

## The presidency

A presidential system emerged in the last Soviet years to compensate for the decline of the Communist Party, and later the presidential option looked increasingly attractive to overcome the crisis of reform in Russia. Under Yeltsin executive authority became relatively independent from the legislature, a trend given normative form by the 1993 constitution. Many functions of the old legislature, including some of its committees and commissions, were incorporated into the presidential system, providing yet another massive impetus to the inflation of the presidential apparatus. By the same token, some of the conflicts that had formerly taken place between the two institutions were now played out within the presidential system itself. A dual executive system emerged, with the presidency and the government often duplicating each other. The institutional aspects of this have been dubbed the politics of 'institutional redundancy' by Huskey.[3] The Russian presidency began to take on the features of the Tsarist or Soviet systems, with weak prime ministers responsible mainly for economic affairs, a minimal separation of powers and with politics concentrated on the leader. Under Yeltsin an unwieldy concentration of power was achieved, marked by corruption, clientelism and inefficiency. One of the challenges facing Putin was to improve the efficacy of the presidential administration itself.

### Presidential versus parliamentary systems

The debate over the relative merits of parliamentary and presidential systems of government is far from academic in Russia. Advocates of parliamentary government, of the sort practised in Britain or Germany, stress that it encourages democratic forms of conflict resolution; the development of lively party systems; the clear formulation of alternative policy choices; the constant scrutiny of government and public administration; flexibility in the timing of elections if the government loses its majority or the confidence of parliament; and allows mistakes to be corrected and extremes to be tempered. They level three main arguments against presidential systems: over-dependence on the personality of the leader often giving rise to unpredictability; the way that they undermine the development of party systems; and the limits placed on the formulation of clear policy choices and alternative governments.[4] Arend Lijphart stresses the exclusive nature of presidential elections, based on the principle of the 'winner-takes-all'.[5] Juan Linz stresses the problem of 'dual democratic legitimacy', with independent electoral mandates for the executive and legislative branches, creating a situation in which 'a conflict is always latent and sometimes likely to erupt dramatically'.[6]

Presidentialists counter by insisting that parliamentary rule is a luxury afforded only to stable societies. In immature post-communist democracies the attitudes and elites from the past are too strong, the tasks too urgent, the aggregation of interests too fluid, and the social bases for party systems too amorphous to allow parliamentary government. Partisans of presidential rule stress the need for a strong executive (the 'strong hand') to overcome overt and covert resistance in the transition to new forms of political and economic life and to act as an integrative force in a fragmented society and state. In the 1990s the sheer number of parties could not compensate for their organisational weakness, lack of a social base and weak influence in society. The development of parliamentarianism, as a culture of compromise and power sharing, moreover, was hesitant and contradictory. In these circumstances only a strong presidency could provide effective leadership to drive through the necessary reforms. As Yeltsin noted in April 1992, the very unity of the country was at stake and could best be preserved by a strong executive.[7] In his defence of presidentialism in Russia Nichols argues that '*presidentialism is more likely than other arrangements to preserve processes of democratic consolidation in societies that are characterized by a lack of social trust*' (italics in original).[8] These considerations prompted the establishment of presidential systems in all twelve CIS states; Belarus in spring 1994 was the last of the post-Soviet states to establish an executive presidency. Rudimentary party systems, faction-ridden parliaments, and grave economic and social crises appeared to justify the strengthening of executive power, whereas in the

Baltic republics and Central Europe parliamentary systems were established. The experience of Ukraine following the introduction of the constitutional amendment of December 2004, enhancing the power of the Verkhovna Rada through the creation of a government of the parliamentary majority, reinforced the case of those in favour of strong executive leadership in Russia. The constitutional crisis in Ukraine following the March 2006 elections, which gave a parliamentary majority to president Viktor Yushchenko's opponent, Viktor Yanukovich, who became prime minister in August of that year, reminded many of the stand-off between parliament and president in Russia in 1992–3, leading to the bloody events of October 1993. Yushchenko sought to break the stalemate by calling pre-term elections, which after much controversy were held on 30 September 2007, but which once again resulted in a hung parliament. The need for further constitutional reform was agreed by all sides, although the presidentialists sought to bend the stick back in their favour, while Yanukovich talked of transforming Ukraine into a fully fledged parliamentary republic.

Earlier drafts of the Russian constitution had favoured a mixed system along the lines of the semi-presidential system in France, where the president is directly elected by the people and the prime minister has to command a parliamentary majority. The president in France is elected by popular mandate for a five-year (formerly seven-year) term and conventionally enjoys the right to formulate foreign policy and aspects of domestic policy, but the government (since an amendment adopted in 1962, despite De Gaulle's opposition) requires a majority in parliament and thus also enjoys a popular mandate. Such a division of powers within a dual executive is one that was much debated in Yeltsin's final years and into the new presidency, until Putin firmly shut the door on such an innovation. Advocates of constitutional change continue to argue in favour of greater autonomy for the prime minister and the government *vis-à-vis* the president. Events in Ukraine rather weakened this argument.

### The powers of the presidency

Russia's semi-presidential system is modelled on that of France, although with some important differences. The 1993 constitution grants the presidency extensive powers in naming governments, introducing legislation and making policy. The president is the head of state and the 'guarantor' of the constitution (Article 80), elected for a four-year term with a maximum of two consecutive terms (thus allowing a return to the presidency after a break), but without an age limit (Article 81). The powers of the presidency are based on a combination of appointment powers and policy prerogatives. The president nominates the prime minister and can chair cabinet meetings, proposes to the State Duma the director of the Central Bank, nominates to the Federation Council members of the Constitutional, Supreme and Supreme Arbitration Courts, and also nominates the Procurator General. The president is also head of the Security Council, confirms Russia's military and foreign policy doctrines, appoints the commander-in-chief of the Armed Forces, and 'exercises leadership of the foreign policy of the Russian Federation' (Article 86). The president is granted the right to introduce a state of emergency and suspend civil freedoms until new federal laws are adopted. The president reports annually to a joint meeting of the two houses of the Federal Assembly on domestic and foreign policy. The president has the right to issue binding decrees (*ukazy*), which do not have to be approved by parliament, that have the power of law; they must not, however, contradict the constitution; and they are superseded by legislative acts.

Impeachment is extremely difficult, requiring a ruling on a demand by a Duma commission (set up with at least 150 votes) by both the Supreme and Constitutional Courts, to be confirmed by two-thirds of both the State Duma and the Federation Council, and can only be initiated only in the event of 'treason or commission of some other grave crime' (Article 93.1). The president has the right to veto legislation of the Duma and in extreme circumstances to dissolve it (Article 109, and see Chapter 9); if the Duma rejects the president's nomination for the post of prime minister three times, it is deemed to have dissolved itself. Given the sad history of the vice-presidency (Yanaev and Rutskoi), it is not surprising that the December 1993 constitution abolished the post. In the event of the president's incapacity or resignation, power is transferred 'temporarily' to the prime minister and new presidential elections must be scheduled within three months (Article 92.2). The acting president is forbidden 'to dissolve the State Duma, to schedule referendums or to submit proposals on amendments to the Russian constitution or on revising its provisions' (Article 92.3).

The government is subordinated to the president and, formally, does not have to represent the majority party or coalition in parliament (see below). The government is appointed by the president and responsible to him or her. Like the Tsar according to the 1906 constitution, who reserved to himself responsibility for foreign policy, control of the armed forces and the executive, the constitution (Article 80) grants the president control over four key areas: security, defence, home and foreign affairs. Russia's presidency in effect acts as a duplicate government, with the functions of ministries often shadowed by agencies under the presidency. The prime minister therefore exerts only partial control over their own ministers, and is deprived of control over the so-called 'power ministries' responsible for domestic security. The president plays an active role in the policy process, initiating and vetoing legislation. Yeltsin used his decree powers with great gusto, issuing over 1,500 policy-relevant *ukazy* during his term in office while Putin, enjoying a large majority in parliament, relied more on legislation to push through his policy agenda.

The 1993 constitution sought to prevent a repetition of the conflict between executive and legislative authorities that had pushed Russia to the verge of civil war. A strong and largely irremovable president acts as the focus of stability, while the government is largely removed from the control of parliament. As in France, bipolar presidential elections tend to reduce the weight of extremist candidates. The problem of presidential systems, however, is their rigidity – it is almost impossible to change the president in mid-term without bringing down the regime itself; and the lack of effective accountability – parliament can exercise only weak oversight powers over the president and their ministers. Parliamentary systems, on the other hand, allow more flexibility in forming governments and in responding to popular moods. This to a degree is precisely what the advocates of presidential government tried to avoid; only a strong executive, the reformers believed, could drive through the necessary transformation of the country.

### The institutions of the presidency

The presidential system since its inception has been in a process of constant modification. Below we shall look briefly at some of its main institutions and its associated bodies.

*The Presidential Administration (PA)*

This is a constitutional office that is the core of the presidency, consisting today of 18 units, of which 12 are specialised agencies, employing about 2,000 people. Putin's decree of 25 March 2004 was only the last in a long line of reorganisations. It has a number of responsible individuals and departments. The former include the chief of staff and his deputies, helpers and advisers, the press secretary, head of protocol, envoys to the seven federal districts (see Chapter 12), to the Constitutional Court and to both houses of the Federal Assembly. The three largest agencies are the State-Legal Directorate (GPU), formed on 12 December 1991 to prepare the decrees and draft laws of the president,[9] whose functions of the latter are now shared with the Ministry of Justice; the Main Monitoring Administration (GKU), established on 5 August 1991 to oversee regional and republican administration and later becoming the Main Territorial Administration (GTU), responsible for overseeing regional affairs (Putin headed this department in 1997 before going on to lead the FSB); and the Information and Documentation section. Each employs about 150 people. There are also foreign affairs and domestic policy departments. Many of these departments duplicate the work of the government, acting in effect as a shadow administration. A common theme among the many plans for reorganisation is the idea that the government should work exclusively on economic matters, while the presidential administration should focus on political matters, a division of labour that would, it was anticipated, put an end to the competition between the two branches of the executive.[10]

The presidential administration is headed by the chief of staff, one of the most important political positions in Russia since it controls access to the president and helps set the policy agenda. The first head of the PA was Yuri Petrov, formerly Communist Party chief in Sverdlovsk and a typical representative of the so-called 'Sverdlovsk mafia', made up of Yeltsin's former associates from the Sverdlovsk Party Organisation, on whom Yeltsin relied in his early years in power. Petrov was replaced by Sergei Filatov, formerly Khasbulatov's deputy in parliament, who in turn gave way on 15 January 1996 to the former nationalities minister, Nikolai Yegorov, who had been the president's representative in Chechnya from November 1994 to February 1995, during the most intense stage of the fighting. The appointment of the hardline Yegorov indicated the strengthening of Korzhakov's position, long opposed by the liberal Filatov. The emergence of a shadowy half-world focused on the presidential chief of security, Korzhakov, did much to discredit Yeltsin's presidency. He was replaced by Valentin Yumashev, Yeltsin's son-in-law and ghost-writer of his memoirs, who in turn was replaced by Nikolai Bordyuzha on 7 December 1998, at the time considered a potential presidential candidate. He proved not up to the task, and on 19 March 1999 he was replaced by the economist Alexander Voloshin, one of the oligarch Boris Berezovsky's former associates. Voloshin finally gave stability to the administration that continued into the Putin presidency. Voloshin resigned on 30 October 2003 in protest at the arrest of Mikhail Khodorkovsky, the head of the Yukos oil company. He was replaced that day by Putin's confidant from St Petersburg, Dmitry Medvedev, who since 3 June 2000 had been Viktor Chernomyrdin's successor as chair of the board of Gazprom. Medvedev was promoted to first deputy prime minister in the government reshuffle of 14 November 2005, and at the same time was put in charge of the four 'national projects' (health, education, agriculture, housing) and thus given a platform for his bid for the presidency. The new chief of staff, Sergei Sobyanin, had been governor of the energy-producing region of Tyumen since January 2001.

The various deputy heads of the PA are influential figures in their own right, and under Putin represented the factions that reflected alternative policy courses. Vladislav Surkov was responsible for domestic policy, and sponsored the development of the United Russia party and in general oversaw the domestic political scene. He can be characterised as a 'democratic statist', and thus stood outside the *siloviki* (the security lobby) headed by another deputy head of the PA, Igor Sechin. Viktor Ivanov, the gatekeeper for access to Putin, was also someone with a security background and thus also a *silovik*. There were numerous presidential advisers, such as Sergei Prikhod'ko for foreign affairs, Sergei Yastrzhembsky for EU matters and Larissa Brytshcheva for constitutional law.

### The Administration of Affairs

This is, as it were, the Kremlin's 'housekeeping' arm, allocating offices, goods and rewards, and responsible for payment of wage and the like. With its hands on the distribution of resources, this body exercises considerable influence over officials.

### The Kremlin property management department

This notorious agency was established in July 1991 to oversee the vast property empire that fell into the hands of the state with the demise of the Communist Party. In November 1993 it was separated from the PA and on 2 August 1995 it took on the official status of a federal executive body.[11] The department manages the properties of all branches of federal authority, including payment of salaries to parliament members and court justices. It is responsible for the upkeep of 3 million square meters of floor space in office buildings in Moscow, including the Kremlin, the government's White House, the buildings of the State Duma and the Federation Council. It services the 12,000 top Russian officials. In addition, the department owns country houses, workshops, medical establishments, motor vehicle pools, hotels, the Rossiya Air Line that carries top officials of the Russian state, and properties belonging to the Russian state in 78 countries. Its assets are estimated to be worth some $5200 billion, second only to those belonging to the Gazprom monopoly.

Pavel Borodin took over as acting head on 1 April 1993 with a staff of 350, and within five years he had increased the empire ten-fold. He supervised the reconstruction of the government's White House, damaged by the fighting of October 1993, as well as the Senate building in the Moscow Kremlin, where the president's apartments are located. Borodin wielded extraordinary influence as the keeper of presidential favours, and was at the heart of Yeltsin's court. Borodin personally supervised the restoration of the Grand Kremlin Palace, including the Catherine Hall, and it was this that was to provoke his downfall. The work cost perhaps up to $400 million, and was allegedly accompanied by the use of Swiss banks to launder kickbacks in return for reconstruction contracts. It is alleged that Yeltsin's 'family', used in both the figurative and literal sense, received funded credit cards from the Swiss company Mabatex, involved in the refurbishment of the Kremlin. It was Borodin who provided Putin with his entry into national politics by giving him a job in the presidential administration when he found himself jobless following Sobchak's electoral defeat in St Petersburg in 1996. One of

Putin's first acts as president was to move him sideways to become State Secretary of the Union of Russia and Belarus, but in an act of hubris he travelled to America for George W. Bush's inauguration in January 2001, and was promptly arrested in line with a long-standing Swiss arrest warrant in his name.

## The Presidential Council

A State Council (Gossovet), named after the highest consultative body in the Russian empire between 1810 and 1917, was established on 19 July 1991 as a consultative body responsible to the Soviet president to examine presidential decrees, to formulate priorities for government policy and to exercise a degree of control over presidential power.[12] A similar Council was established under the Russian presidency and after a number of name changes following protests from parliament, ended up in February 1993 with a lower status and less autonomy as the Presidential Council. Yeltsin's main councillor, Burbulis, headed the State Council and in the space of 18 months changed his job title five times.[13] Burbulis had taught 'scientific communism' in Sverdlovsk[14] when Yeltsin had been *obkom* first secretary there, and together both negotiated the rough passage through the democratic insurgency to the Kremlin. Having led Yeltsin's personal campaign staff in the presidential election of June 1991, Burbulis remained one of his closest advisers, taking on also the post of first deputy prime minister in late 1991. He was often represented, justifiably, as the *éminence grise* behind the new regime. He was one of the main architects of the first stage of the democratic transformation in Russia: the CIS as we saw in Chapter 2 had been Burbulis' idea, and he was also a strong advocate of Gaidar's shock economic policies. He became the target of bitter hostility, especially from parliament, and was gradually marginalised, until dismissed from all his substantive posts on 26 November 1992. The Presidential Council's 30-odd membership included an eclectic list of the great and the good, but even at its height played a marginal role in policy formation, was rarely convened and was abolished by Putin.

## The Security Council (SC)

A Russian Security Council was established soon after Yeltsin's election as president in June 1991. It was then designed mainly as a consultative body as part of the presidential apparatus and operated in parallel with the government. When he took over direct control of the cabinet in November 1991 Yeltsin dissolved various structures that shadowed the government, including the SC. The Law on Security of 5 March 1992 reconstituted the SC as a body chaired by the president, while a law of 4 April 1992 endowed the Security Council with functions that included the drafting of basic policy guidelines and determining the key issues facing the president. The struggle with parliament prompted Yeltsin to strengthen presidential structures, especially in the field of security and foreign policy. By a decree of 3 June the SC was reformed to draft an annual report as the basic programmatic statement for executive bodies and to draft decisions.[15] The SC's jurisdiction was significantly broadened by a presidential decree of 7 July 1992, allowing it to issue orders to heads of ministries and local governing bodies, as well as controlling the activities of organisations involved in implementing the council's decisions.

Following the October 1993 events the SC was brought under the exclusive control of the president and its membership regularised. According to the 1993 constitution, the president 'forms and heads the Security Council' with its status to be defined by federal law (Article 83.g). Membership is drawn from the heads of the security, law enforcement and judicial agencies, and is part of the Presidential Administration. The amended Law on Security stipulated that the SC was subordinate to the president and chaired by him, and its decisions were to be issued in the form of presidential decrees and instructions. The SC had no independent political standing other than as an instrument of presidential rule. Like the Politburo of old, the SC usually took decisions not by a majority vote but by consensus, thus avoiding individual responsibility by its members.[16] The SC appeared to be the core of that long-sought for 'strong hand', the authoritarian political structure that could manage the system in the transition to a market economy. Opponents accused the SC of replicating Communist Party structures by fusing executive and legislative power, setting the agenda and controlling information to the president.

The SC's job is to prepare presidential policy documents and decisions in the sphere of security, but security soon took on a rather broad definition. During the first Chechen war the SC emerged as an important centre of power, by this time bringing together not only the president, its secretary (Oleg Lobov), but also the prime minister (Chernomyrdin), the foreign minister (Andrei Kozyrev), and the heads of the 'power ministries'. It was the SC that on 29 November 1994 (and confirmed on 7 December) resolved to use force against Chechnya (probably at defence minister Pavel Grachev's instigation), a decision taken by voting rather than by the usual consensual procedure.[17] The appointment of Alexander Lebed, the former head of the Fourteenth Army in Moldova, as secretary of the Security Council on 18 June 1996 was part of an electoral pact but was also a way of giving him an appropriate role in the new administration. In the event Lebed remained stubbornly independent, if not a maverick, and took a very broad view of his duties. Lebed combined the Security Council post with that of national security adviser. He was instrumental in the sacking of the widely despised Grachev, and replaced him with his ally Igor Rodionov.

The scope of the Security Council's work was broadened by a presidential decree of 10 July 1996, charging the council with defending Russia's vital interests in the social, economic, defence, environmental and informational spheres.[18] The Security Council's functions, however, were limited by the establishment on 25 July of a new body, the Defence Council, with a similar membership. The creation of the Defence Council was a classic piece of Yeltsin balancing, designed to counter the growth in the Security Council's status. Lebed sought to transform the Security Council from an advisory into a working body with real power. In his brief tenure Lebed was able to bring the first Chechen war to an end (the Khasavyurt agreement of 31 August 1996), but Lebed's confrontational style within two months led to his own dismissal on 17 October 1996, following which the Security Council went into decline. Putin briefly headed both the FSB and the SC (from 29 March 1999), and on his elevation to the premiership in August 1999 he appointed his long-time associate Sergei Ivanov to take over. When Ivanov became defence minister on 28 March 2001 the SC once again fell into the shade, although its leaders Vladimir Rushailo and Igor Ivanov (the foreign minister until March 2004) regularly convened the body and it devised a number of important policy documents. The periodic rise and fall in the fortunes of the Security Council can be taken as indicative of the hesitant institutionalisation that has taken place in Russia.

The Council is intended as an instrument for devising executive policy and to coordinate the work of other security agencies, but its political influence has reflected the character and status of its successive directors.

## The government

Cabinet government is much more difficult to achieve in a presidential than a parliamentary system. In the USA the post of prime minister is dispensed with altogether and the president chairs cabinet meetings. In France the president has the prerogative to appoint or dismiss the prime minister as long as the latter has the support of parliament, and it was a rudimentary version of this system that emerged in Russia. The prime minister is nominated by the president and then approved or rejected by the Duma, and is consulted in the appointment of ministers, who are responsible both to the president and parliament. Unlike France, however, the Russian prime minister has no independent power base in parliament and thus 'cohabitation' (where the president and prime minister are of different political persuasions) cannot formally exist, although during Primakov's tenure (see below) a weak form of cohabitation did emerge.

The Russian government is a direct descendent of the RSFSR Council of Ministers, but has greatly expanded in size and functions. The prime ministerial apparatus is another of those bureaucratic agencies that has swelled in the post-Soviet years, consisting now of some two dozen departments and over 1,000 full-time officials. The government is responsible both to parliament and to the president, but the precise balance of accountability remains unclear. Government in Russia consists of the chair of the government (the prime minister), a variable number of deputy prime ministers, usually responsible for a bloc of ministers, and federal ministers, generally with portfolios. Bodies like the Presidential Administration and the Security Council, as we suggested above, appears at times to usurp the role of the government. The government's lineage from the past is most visible in the institution of vice-premiers, who simulate the role of the old CPSU Central Committee secretaries, although the presidential administration can also be seen to be the heir of the oversight functions once fulfilled by the Party apparatus.

Russia is not a parliamentary republic but neither is it fully a presidential one in the classical sense. The constitution states that the prime minister is appointed by the president with the consent of the State Duma. The premier forms his or her cabinet, which is then approved by the president, and the two share executive authority. Article 110.1 states that executive power in Russia belongs to the government, but the head of the government is constrained by presidential power. A 'tripartite' system operates in which the government acts as a relatively autonomous centre of political authority in its own sphere, the president sets the overall direction of policy, while the Duma acts in a supervisory capacity and the ultimate source of public accountability by 'keeping the trust of the government', with the power to adopt a vote of no-confidence.

The prime minister is appointed by the president and endorsed by the State Duma and is in principle accountable to both – in principle because parliament's checking power is rather limited. If the president's nomination is three times refused by the Duma it is automatically dissolved and the president's choice is confirmed (Article 111). The Duma's right to veto a nomination has been removed; but it can be assumed that in most circumstances a president would change the candidate after the previous candidate was rejected twice (as happened in September 1998). A prime minister's resignation is tendered to the president rather than to parliament. It is incumbent upon the prime minister to tender his or her resignation following presidential elections, but is not obliged to do so after parliamentary elections.

The office of prime minister, although overshadowed by the presidency in normal times, carries enormous advantages of incumbency, greatly enhanced in the event of a pre-term election. According to the constitution, in the event of the demise or retirement of the incumbent president, the prime minister takes over and new elections are held within three months. Overshadowed by the succession, the campaign for the parliamentary elections of December 1999 began long in advance as potential presidential contenders sought to use them as primaries for the presidential elections that were initially due to have been held on 4 June 2000 but, following Yeltsin's resignation on 31 December 1999, were brought forward to 26 March 2000.

Executive power in Russia is thus exercised by the president and the government, a dual executive system with an unclear relationship between the two. The French constitutional axiom that 'The president presides and the government governs' does not translate easily into Russian practice, since the president does far more than 'preside'. Like its Soviet and Tsarist predecessors, the government is largely restricted to managing the economy and the social sphere, while the president is responsible for foreign, security and administrative issues. The constitution, as we have seen, endows the president with control over foreign and security policy as well as the main direction of domestic policy, and it is this article that provides the juridical basis for presidential rule. While Yeltsin's was an activist presidency, his poor health towards the end opened up the possibility of a new balance of power between the two wings of the executive, a development that Primakov tried to exploit. However, the young and vigorous Putin once again seized the initiative and reasserted the prerogatives of the presidency.

Soviet law since 1988 stipulated that those who take up government posts must resign their parliamentary seats, a principle reaffirmed by the 1993 constitution. Deputies cannot simultaneously be employed in the government or hold paid jobs in any field except teaching, scientific research and culture in general. Once the two-year transitional period ended the principle was rigorously applied and 19 deputies elected from the party-lists in 1995 resigned their seats. Kozyrev, elected to parliament from a single-member constituency in Murmansk, was forced to choose between resigning from the cabinet or giving up his legislative seat. The idea that ministers cannot simultaneously be MPs was designed to maintain the separation of powers, but this mechanical application of the rule (applied also in France) undermines the ability of parties to form a government, weakens the solidarity which binds together the governing party in countries like Britain and Germany, inhibits the Duma's ability to question ministers on a daily basis, and weakens the government's capacity to explain its policies in parliament.

Unlike conventional practice in the West, the ministries themselves are unable to make national decisions but have to prepare the appropriate documentation, which is then adopted as an act of the government as whole. In late 1992 two types of governmental bodies were established: ministries headed by members of the government who resign together with the prime minister; and departments headed by professional bureaucrats who are not members of the government and reporting directly to vice-premiers. A presidential decree of 14 August 1996 defined a ministry as a federal executive agency that enforces government policies and manages all activities in its defined sphere of influence, as well as coordinating the activities of other federal institutions in this sphere. At the sub-ministerial level there are a variety of special bodies, known as state committees, federal services or agencies, whose brief is usually technical and who lack direct access to the government but report through vice-premiers. These include professional bodies like the Patents Agency. Like most other post-Soviet institutions, the government has been subject to endless re-organisation, intended usually to reduce the number of state agencies and the size of the bureaucracy.[19] The plan devised by Dmitry Kozak, at the time cabinet chief of staff, in early 2003 spoke of reducing the number of ministries from 24 to 15–17, while the economic development ministry, on the basis of Kozak's plan, divided the 5,000 functions performed by the state into three categories: setting regulations, applying regulations, and providing state services, with many to be abolished in their entirety.[20] Ministries were to be responsible for the strategic development of policy; agencies were to provide services to public and sector-specific economic activities; while services would be responsible for state oversight and monitoring of implementation. The overall aim was to decrease the number of bureaucrats and to streamline the functioning of government, but in the event neither aim was achieved.

A no-confidence vote in the government can be initiated by a Duma deputy at any time, but the signatures of one-fifth of all Duma members are required for a motion to be placed on the agenda. A no-confidence motion is adopted by a simple majority of total Duma membership (Article 117.3), which then sets in train a complex process of confrontation. The president has two choices: either to accept the motion, dismiss the government and nominate a new prime minister for the Duma's approval; or disagree with the Duma. If within three months the Duma once again expresses its lack of confidence in the government, then the head of state can either sack the government or dissolve parliament by ordering new elections. The threat of dissolution is at the centre of presidential power, protecting the government and restraining the Duma out of fear of provoking pre-term elections. Article 109, however, modifies the dissolution option by stating that article 117 cannot be activated to dissolve the Duma in the year following its election or in the six months before a presidential election. This would imply that in its first year or before a presidential election the Duma can dismiss one government after another with impunity, only having twice to vote a motion of no-confidence and not even having to wait three months between the two votes. The dissolution option can be activated in a second manner, this time on the initiative of the government itself. The prime minister can ask the Duma for a vote of confidence; if the Duma fails to vote in support of the government, the president must either dissolve the Duma or dismiss the government, a decision that must be taken within seven days of the vote.

Despite relatively weak parliamentary powers, governments in a rudimentary way have tended to reflect some of the main concerns of the Duma. Strategic allies have been sought in the chamber to make governance possible, including offering ministerial portfolios to opposition parties when necessary. This did not prevent the Duma holding a vote of no-confidence in the government following 'black Tuesday' (a sudden fall in the value of the rouble on 11 October 1994), and again on 21 June 1995 in protest against the Budennovsk crisis (when hostages were seized by Chechen guerrillas). Chernomyrdin countered by tabling a confidence motion, which if not passed would have led either the Duma or the government falling within a week. Threatened by imminent dissolution, a second vote of no-confidence on 1 July failed (just) to pass, and thereupon Chernomyrdin withdrew his confidence motion. Increasingly exasperated by Putin's neo-liberal economic policies, the communists tabled a no-confidence motion on 17 March 2001, provoking threats of an early dissolution and pre-term elections.

The lack of a direct correlation between the political complexion of the Duma and the composition of the government is probably not sustainable in the long-term, and the most logical resolution of the problem is for the government to be based on a parliamentary majority. In the Yeltsin years there was a fragmented and divided Duma with no stable majority but with a clear predominance of oppositionists, and thus the government of the parliamentary majority was avoided. The architects of the 1993 constitution took precisely this problem into account in drafting the articles on the relationship between government and parliament, deliberately giving the president a relatively free hand in government formation. Having gained a strong pro-presidential majority in parliament, Putin contemplated the step taken early in the French Fifth Republic (despite De Gaulle's opposition) – the creation of a party-based government. In his state of the nation speech in May 2003 Putin noted: 'I believe it possible, taking into account the results of the forthcoming election to the State Duma, to form a professional and efficient government based on the parliamentary majority.'[21] The Kremlin administration had prepared a law to this effect, but at the last minute the plan was scotched.[22]

A powerful group around Putin, bringing together *siloviki* and some liberals, feared that the passage of a constitutional amendment allowing a party or coalition of parties to form the government and nominate the prime minister would deliver the country into the hands of the oligarchs.[23] It was clear that the lobby managed to change Putin's mind on the question, and he did not return to the idea. They feared that if the government was drawn from the parliamentary majority, relations with the president would become even more complicated, as demonstrated in Ukraine in 2006–7. In the United States, as noted, the problem is resolved by abolishing the institution of the prime minister entirely, and subordinating ministers directly to the president. The present Russian system is unsatisfactory from many perspectives, hence the plans for constitutional reform that focus precisely on this issue, but there remains the danger that some of the solutions may well exacerbate the problem of accountability and coherence.

## Prime ministers and their policies

In the nine years of Yeltsin's presidency Russia had six prime ministers and eight governments, three of which were under Viktor Chernomyrdin (see Table 6.1). The rapid turnover of prime ministers in 1998–9 reflected the depth of the crisis that engulfed the country at this time and the search for a suitable successor. Yeltsin feared the emergence of a powerful and independent premier and ensured their subordination to his will. Under Putin stability once again returned to the prime minister's post, with only three serving under him. We will briefly characterise the personalities and policies of the prime ministers.

### *Russia's first 'prime ministers': Silaev and Yeltsin*

Ivan Silaev had been appointed Russian prime minister in June 1990, but on 26 September 1991 resigned to head the new Inter-Republican Economic Commission,

*Table 6.1* Russia's prime ministers

| Name | Period in office | Comments |
| --- | --- | --- |
| Ivan Silaev | June 1990 – 26 September 1991 | The office of premier remained largely 'Soviet' with few powers |
| Boris Yeltsin | November 1991 – June 1992 | Combined the premiership with the presidency |
| Yegor Gaidar | 15 June – 14 December 1992 | 'Acting' PM only since never confirmed by parliament |
| Victor Chernomyrdin | 14 December 1992 – March 1998 | Russia's longest-serving PM, presided over two major changes of government (August 1996, March 1997) |
| Sergei Kirienko | 24 April – 23 August 1998 | Only confirmed by the Duma in May, and thereafter overwhelmed by the financial crisis |
| Yevgeny Primakov | 9 September 1998 – 12 May 1999 | Made an uncomfortable partner to Yeltsin, was dismissed at the first opportunity |
| Sergei Stepashin | 19 May – 9 August 1999 | Very much an interim figure |
| Vladimir Putin | 9 August – 31 December 1999; acting president and PM January – May 2000 | Exercised authority far beyond that typically allowed a PM by Yeltsin |
| Mikhail Kasyanov | May 2000 – 24 February 2004 | Considered at first a holdover from the Yeltsin period but in the event survived far longer than anticipated |
| Mikhail Fradkov | Appointed 1 March 2004 | Appointed as a technocrat to allow Putin to dominate the government and push through reform; like Kasyanov, lasted far longer than anticipated |
| Viktor Zubkov | Appointed 12 September 2007 | Appointed as part of the succession operation |

in effect becoming prime minister of the USSR. This was obviously an unsatisfactory situation, with unclear leadership in both the USSR and Russia. The Russian premiership was left vacant until on 6 November 1991 Yeltsin himself assumed the post, declaring that he would take responsibility for the implementation of reforms while allowing the use of presidential decrees to drive forward the economic transformation. The constitutional status of the Russian government, however, remained ambivalent. As long as Yeltsin had been chairman of the Supreme Soviet there appeared to be no problem with the government's subordination to the Russian parliament. Once a strong presidency emerged, however, and in the absence of a new constitution, conflict was bound to arise as Yeltsin sought to remove the government from legislative control.

In November 1991 the Fifth CPD allowed the president to form a government with only minimal legislative accountability. Yeltsin won the right to appoint his own cabinet, and ministers did not have to gain parliamentary approval.[24] Yeltsin appointed a team of radicals to create a 'government of reforms' whose core was drawn from a group of academics close to Burbulis. Chief among them was Gaidar, 35, the minister for finance and economics who had worked with Yavlinsky and Shatalin, authors of doomed economic reform plans in the Gorbachev era, but who took a more marked neo-liberal free market line. Gaidar had been a Senior Research Fellow at the Institute of Economics, from whence he brought several colleagues into the government, including Alexander Shokhin; a group accused by their opponents of being theoreticians who did not understand how society actually worked. Soon afterwards Russia took over all the USSR ministries and enterprises on its territory, and the scene was set for a radical attempt at social transformation.

Gaidar now launched a radical economic reform programme, promulgated largely by presidential decrees rather than legislative acts. Yeltsin's strategy from late 1991 was directed towards 'a policy of breakthrough', shock therapy in the economy and marginalisation of conservative forces in parliament.[25] A wave of decrees issued by the 'government of reforms' destroyed the old economic administrative-command system. From 2 January 1992 the long-awaited liberalisation of prices at last began, accompanied by enormous prise rises, inflation, and falling living standards (see Chapter 13). The reforms were bitterly criticised by the majority in parliament, Khasbulatov personally, and vice-president Rutskoi. The constitutional situation remained unclear, and as we have seen Khasbulatov's attempts to re-impose parliamentary control over the government provoked a national crisis.

### Yegor Gaidar: 'acting' prime minister

Fearing that popular acceptance of the reforms was reaching breaking point, Yeltsin adjusted the tiller in May–June 1992 when pressure from the conservatives and the industrial lobby forced him to undertake a government reshuffle. Industrialists had criticised Gaidar's government for failing to extend credits to failing enterprises or to soften the social impact of reform.[26] Yeltsin appointed three former state directors to key ministries, including Chernomyrdin, who became a deputy prime minister and took over responsibility for the energy sector. Chernomyrdin had been appointed minister of the Soviet gas industry in 1985, and in 1989 he became chairman of the new state company, Gazprom. As so often with Yeltsin, a compromise in one direction was balanced by a move in the other, in this case Gaidar's appointment on 15 June 1992 as 'acting' prime minister (pending confirmation by parliament, which never came), signalling his determination to continue on the path of radical economic reform. The radical reformer Anatoly Chubais, the head of the State Property Committee (GKI) responsible for privatisation, was promoted to become a deputy prime minister, thus strengthening Gaidar's hand in the cabinet. A 'government of deputy prime ministers' emerged as Yeltsin broadened the political basis for reform policies.

Khasbulatov continued to insist that 'the development of parliamentarianism is the path to democracy'.[27] On 13 November 1992 parliament adopted a modified version of the law giving Congress control over ministerial appointments, granting parliament the sole right to nominate ministers, and subordinating key ministers (like that of foreign affairs) to parliament. This indeed was the basis for a parliamentary republic. The struggle to control the government came to a head at the Seventh Congress in December 1992. The failure of Yeltsin's desperate attempt to take the confrontation between executive and legislative to the country led to Gaidar's fall on 14 December 1992.

### The Chernomyrdin era

The new premier, Chernomyrdin, although committed to more state intervention in the economy, retained the majority of the liberal advocates of 'shock therapy'. Boris Fedorov at this time was given overall responsibility for financial policy, and Chernomyrdin soon retreated from attempts to regulate prices and to save industry by pouring in money, only stimulating inflation. Talk of 'an invisible coup' proved exaggerated.[28] Following the elections of December 1993 Chernomyrdin placed his stamp on the government. Gaidar, Fedorov and some other reformers resigned and Agrarians and others joined, yet the government retained a broadly reformist course. In effect, a 'coalition' government was formed, but of a distinctively Russian type where posts were divided not through discussions between parties but between specific individuals. The constitution does not oblige the president to appoint the prime minister from the parliamentary majority; nevertheless, the president had to be sensitive to the balance of forces in the Duma to avoid his government suffering legislative defeats or votes of no-confidence. Two ministers were from the Agrarian Party, and there were even overtures towards the CPRF to contribute ministers.

The political evolution of Russian government was in full swing even before the Chechen crisis, taking on more of a conservative and nationalist colouring. The democratic internationalism that had been such a marked feature of policy since Gorbachev's time now gave way to a more assertive Russian state nationalism. This tendency was further strengthened following the strong Communist showing in the December 1995 elections. Chernomyrdin remained prime minister even though his 'Russia Our Home' (NDR) party gained only 10 per cent of the vote, but the government further changed its complexion. Kozyrev resigned as foreign minister on 5 January, as did Shakhrai as a deputy prime minister, both preferring to keep their Duma seats. Chubais, the last member of the 'government of reforms' (responsible for the economy) resigned on 16 January 1996. As for the extension of coalition government, Chernomyrdin argued that 'I am in favour of a government that consists of professionals because a government is not a political body.'[29]

In August 1996 Chernomyrdin was re-appointed for a second term, and immediately he was forced to repay in political currency for the financial support that the oligarchs had given Yeltsin in his re-election campaign. The appointment of 35-year-old Vladimir Potanin as first deputy prime minister in charge of economic affairs signalled the regime's close links with the emerging banking sector. In 1993 he had become chairman of Oneksimbank, one of Russia's five largest banks, and helped create the consortium that organised controversial shares for loans auctions with the government. His bank took advantage of these auctions to acquire a 38 per cent stake in the world's largest nickel producer, Norilsk Nickel, and then in July 1997 he was able to take control of the huge telecommunications company, Svyazinvest, in an auction that was widely considered to have been rigged. Potanin's appointment marked recognition of the role that he and other financiers, like Vladimir Gusinsky at the head of the Most Group, had played in bankrolling Yeltsin's re-election. The political economy at the basis of regime politics in post-communist Russia represented a conflation of political and economic resources. For the new elites, the semi-marketised and heavily bureaucratised economy proved rich feeding grounds for rent-seeking. The Russian economy found itself stuck half way between the plan and the market.

The constitution vests supreme power in the president, but during the Chernomyrdin years Yeltsin tended not to interfere in daily politics and thus escaped responsibility for the actions of the government while remaining the supreme political arbiter. This allowed policy drift and indeed, elements of the old Brezhnevite 'stagnation' became apparent. In response to this in March 1997 Yeltsin engineered a major government reshuffle, promoting reformers like Boris Nemtsov (brought in from the governorship of Nizhny Novgorod) and Chubais in an attempt to kick-start the reforms. A continued sense of inertia provoked Chernomyrdin's dismissal in March 1998. Chernomyrdin's increasing self-confidence and view of himself as Yeltsin's successor threatened Yeltsin's ability to control the succession process. Chernomyrdin had become a powerful politician in his own right, building alliances with the communist leadership in the Duma and corporate interests in society; he had not, however, been able to lift the economy out of its prolonged stagnation. His own convoluted words serve as the best epitaph on his period in office: 'We wanted to do things for the best, but it all turned out as usual.'

With Yeltsin's physical decline, the regime thought ever more of the succession. Between March 1998 and December 1999 Russia had five prime ministers. This reflected a structural weakness in the Russian political system, above all in the balance of power between the executive and legislative branches. We can now see that the parade of prime ministers reflected not simply Yeltsin's whims but the search for a way for the regime to perpetuate itself. The idea of a 'succession', of course, is a term more appropriate for a monarchy than a democratic republic, and reflects the pre-eminent role of the presidency. Klyamkin and Shevtsova, indeed, describe the Russian political system as an 'electoral monarchy'.[30] Yeltsin's second term can be considered as devoted mainly to ensuring a succession that would not challenge the system that he had built or threaten the personal security of himself, his family and closest associates. It is this factor that helps explain the rapid turnover of prime ministers following Chernomyrdin's dismissal.

### *Sergei Kirienko: from technocracy to politics*

Yeltsin's nomination of the 35-year-old unknown, Sergei Kirienko, was unexpected. Kirienko had served briefly in the Chernomyrdin government as minister of fuel and energy as Nemtsov's protégé. Kirienko had directed one of the most successful of Nizhny Novgorod's banks. Kirienko's nomination was only accepted by the Duma at the third attempt on 24 April and only after enormous exertions by Yeltsin behind the scenes, together with open attempts to bribe deputies. The appointment of a government of technocrats appeared to signal a new resolve to find long-term economic solutions to fiscal problems. The government made the new state treasury system work more effectively, with some 75,000 budgetary organisations now funded through regular procedures rather than the old *ad hoc* system. It appeared for the first time in some four years that a government had emerged that was serious about structural economic reform focusing, above all on trying to raise federal government revenues by means other than the excessively high interest rate-bearing treasury bonds (GKOs). Moves were taken towards shifting the tax system away from the corporate sector towards individuals and the service sector. However, within weeks of his appointment, on 27 May Kirienko was forced to triple interest rates – to 150 per cent – to defend the rouble. At that time total Russian national debt was 44 per cent of GDP, and government bonds comprised 34 per cent of national expenditure.

With its back to the wall, the government succeeded in getting the Duma to adopt an anti-crisis programme in July whose measures included changing the structure of VAT and personal income tax and introducing a new sales tax of 5 per cent. Kirienko sought to broaden his base of support by inviting the former head of Gosplan, Yuri Maslyukov, to join the government with broad responsibilities for trade and industry. Elected a Communist deputy in December 1995, the leadership of the CPRF denounced his membership of the government and moved to expel him from the party. The Kirienko government was now becoming dominated by the struggle for autonomy: of politics from economics, and of politicians from the dominance of economic oligarchs. By the end of its term in office it became clear that the office of prime minister in Russia was capable of genuine policy initiative. However, lacking a firm parliamentary base, it remained vulnerable to presidential interference.

By August 1998 the Kirienko government began to transform itself from a 'government of professionals' into a more openly political government, in the sense that it began to argue that the solution of some of the country's economic problems lay in politics. Kirienko's brief premiership became dominated by attempts to deal with the financial crisis, above all fears that the government would no longer be able to service its debts. Kirienko struggled to transform oligarchical capitalism into a more open version. His failure to deal with the legacy of nearly a decade of mismanagement led to the partial default of 17 August 1998, and his own dismissal six days later. It was at this time that Nemtsov resigned, leaving the government devoid of liberals.

The recalled Duma met on 21 August, and while sceptical of the government's actions reserved their anger for Yeltsin himself, adopting a vote of censure against him that was adopted by 248 votes to 32. The economic crisis was now extreme, and it was at this time that Yeltsin transformed it into a full-scale political one by dismissing Kirienko and his government on 23 August, and nominating Chernomyrdin to return to his old post. Despite Chernomyrdin's attempts to ingratiate himself with the Communist opposition, his nomination was rejected by the Duma. After being twice rejected, Chernomyrdin's candidature was withdrawn and Primakov, who had served as foreign minister since January 1996, was confirmed as prime minister on 11 September by a vote of 317 to 63. Chernomyrdin was too closely associated with the policies of 1992–8 to win support, and he was the man held responsible for many of Russia's woes. His earlier dismissal no longer made political sense if Yeltsin was willing to re-appoint him prime minister in August. Not only Chernomyrdin's prestige suffered, but what remained of Yeltsin's authority was further eroded in this futile attempt to turn back the clock.

### Yevgeny Primakov: the struggle for consensus

While Yeltsin's regime suffered a severe blow in August 1998, the political system in Russia did not collapse; the political and economic crisis did not become a constitutional one. The appointment of the ex-head of the Foreign Intelligence Service (SVR, 1991–6) Primakov as prime minister revealed, however, just how far the liberal trend had ebbed. Economic stringency under his leadership remained, although it was now more a matter of necessity than conviction, given Russia's indebtedness and inability to collect taxes. In the political field the achievements of earlier years in the spheres of press freedom, human rights and basic liberties were eroded – although not repudiated. The key point, though, was that a new type of coalition politics looked set to emerge, one where government was conducted on the basis of agreement with the majority in parliament. Although the Kirienko government had begun to curb the excesses of the oligarchs, it was only under Primakov that their privileges were openly challenged, especially since they had been much weakened by the partial default of August 1998.

In his early appointments Primakov sought to please the Duma majority. Elements of a genuine coalition government emerged. Maslyukov was appointed first deputy prime minister with overall responsibility for the economy. Victor Gerashchenko, whom Jeffrey Sachs had earlier dubbed 'the world's worst central banker', was reappointed head of the Central Bank. His government, however, was not a formal coalition in the Western sense, and neither was it a party government made up of the group able to command a majority in the Duma. Primakov claimed to represent a government composed of pragmatic professionals, whose party allegiance weighed less than their expertise. Nevertheless, the government did mark a departure from the previous pattern. It was a coalition to the extent that it sought to reflect the distribution of political support in parliament. His government included members of the CPRF and Vladimir Zhirinovsky's Liberal Democratic Party of Russia (LDPR). The finance minister, Mikhail Zadornov, was a former member of the liberal Yabloko faction. The only group now missing was Our Home is Russia (NDR), formerly the party of power: Alexander Shokhin resigned as deputy prime minister ten days after accepting the post. As for regional leaders, only Leningrad *oblast* governor Vadim Gustov was willing to give up his elected post to serve as first deputy prime minister responsible for regional affairs and the CIS.

Many of the country's most prominent politicians refused to have anything to do with Primakov's government, fearing that its failure would blight their electoral prospects. The tone of the government appeared to be retrospective rather than progressive. With Gerashchenko back at the helm of the Central Bank, it appeared that the confusions and hesitancies of the Gorbachev years had returned. Primakov himself had close historical links with the security apparatus and the power ministries (defence, interior as well as foreign affairs), and thus his focus naturally moved away from economic issues towards foreign and internal political affairs. Primakov insisted that his government would not reverse the results of privatisation, thus accepting the property settlement of the Yeltsin years. In the event, it appeared that the best economic policy in Russia was not to have one, and the economy in 1999 staged a modest recovery based on import substitution. The four-fold devaluation of the rouble made imports prohibitively expensive, and encouraged domestic manufacturers and producers to take up the slack. The slogan of the Primakov government, like his period in office as foreign minister, was pragmatism.

Deep structural and institutional changes could only be implemented if the government won credibility, and for that it needed a long-term developmental strategy. The depth of the immediate crisis, however, precluded this. Above all, the political and ideological basis of Primakov's government was unstable. He tried to pursue a right-wing policy with a left-wing orientation. The bankruptcy of his policy of 'pragmatism' was seen in the area that was peculiarly his own, foreign policy. Nato's bombing campaign in Yugoslavia over Kosovo began on 24 March 1999 and lasted 78 days, provoking a rupture in Russia's relations with the West. Primakov isolated Russia in a manner reminiscent of the USSR on the eve of Gorbachev' accession to power in March 1985. The country found itself surrounded by sullen neighbours and few real allies, despite much talk of a 'strategic partnership' between Russia, China and India. The government had been imposed on an unwilling president by an assertive Duma, and Yeltsin disliked Primakov's popularity and independence, and hence sought to replace him with a more loyal and dependent person at the first opportunity. By early 1999 Yeltsin was openly snubbing his own prime minister, and on 12 May 1999 Primakov was dismissed. The response of parliament was remarkably muted, not wanting to provoke early parliamentary elections. Months of preparation for Yeltsin's impeachment collapsed at the first vote.

### Sergei Stepashin: the interim prime minister

Primakov's dismissal reflected an inexorable political logic. He had been forced on Yeltsin by a recalcitrant Duma in September 1999, and Yeltsin never made a secret of his personal distaste for the man. In his place on 19 May 1999 he nominated Sergei Stepashin, the former head of the Federal Counter-Intelligence Service (FSK) in 1994 and one of the hawks in the first Chechen war. He was dismissed from this position in June 1995 as part of the price for his failure to avert the Budennovsk hostage crisis. Stepashin later was one of the few members of the so-called 'party of war', those who had so cavalierly launched the first Chechen war in 1994, to have admitted that it had been a mistake both in conception and implementation. He was returned to office in July 1997 as justice minister, and then as minister of internal affairs (MVD) on 24 April 1998.

Stepashin turned out to be a conscientious prime minister, unwilling to subordinate the government to Yeltsin's electoral campaigning. On his nomination Stepashin hastened to both the Duma and Federation Council to outline his plans and policies. Like Primakov, it was clear that he intended to work with parliament, indicating attempts to institutionalise political support and to move away from the court politics that were so typical of Yeltsin's rule. However, Stepashin's cabinet was fatally divided by the battles between the various clans surrounding the president. Roman Abramovich, one of the favoured oligarchs of the time who had gained control of Sibneft through a number of suspicious deals, threw his weight behind Nikolai Aksenenko, who was made deputy prime minister despite Stepashin's resistance. Stepashin proved unwilling to find an excuse to ban the Communist Party, and thus eliminate one of the main contenders in the December 1999 Duma elections. He also failed to prevent the alliance between the Fatherland (*Otechestvo*) group of Yuri Luzhkov (mayor of Moscow) and the All Russia (*Vsya Rossiya*) alliance of governors to create the Fatherland All Russia (OVR) bloc, especially when the new OVR alliance succeeded in making Primakov their figurehead on 17 August. The new bloc threatened to sweep all before it in the parliamentary elections to propel Primakov to the presidency. Stepashin did not last long, and a more loyal and ruthless man was sought. On 9 August 1999 Stepashin was dismissed.

### Vladimir Putin: the struggle to save Yeltsin

The fifth premier in two years, Vladimir Putin was soon transformed from a reticent official (he had worked 16 years in the security apparatus) into a relatively independent political figure. On nominating him Yeltsin declared Putin a worthy successor, but experience suggested that this was a precarious position. Putin was appointed as a Yeltsin loyalist, and it appeared at first that he would enjoy little more autonomy than his predecessors. Like all of Yeltsin's prime ministers, Putin was not given independence to form his own cabinet and instead had ministers foisted on him by the Presidential

Administration. Above all, Nikolai Aksenenko, as first deputy prime minister, openly pursued his own interests and those of the presidential 'family', and on several occasions (as in the displacement of the head of Transneft), ignored Putin entirely. The influence of Berezovsky and his ally Roman Abramovich, known as the treasurer to Yeltsin's family, remained strong. The energy minister Viktor Kalyuzhny and the interior minister Vladimir Rushailo were part of this group. Putin, however, soon transcended the limitations of his post. On any scale, Putin's metamorphosis was remarkable, and he soon emerged as the leading candidate in the presidential election. The success of his new bloc, Unity, in the December 1999 parliamentary elections opened the way for the unexpected *dénouement* of the succession operation.

At least four factors help explain Putin's remarkable rise. The first is that the Kremlin put its entire weight behind him, attacking his rivals, and providing him with all sorts of open and behind the scenes support. Second, the renewed war in Chechnya turned out to be a genuinely popular war, unlike the first from 1994 to 1996. Putin's image as an 'iron chancellor' was created and sustained by his uncompromising approach to the Chechen problem, with the second war provoked in September 1999 by four bombings of apartment blocks (Buinaksk, two in Moscow, and Volgodonsk) with the loss of over three hundred lives, and the two invasions of Dagestan in August and September by the Chechen insurgent warlord Shamil Basaev. The third factor is that, unlike his predecessors, Putin soon enjoyed unprecedented powers for policy initiation. Although formally he could be sacked by Yeltsin, Putin in the last months of 1999 acted with remarkable confidence and independence. Putin was able to transform the prime ministerial office into a quasi-presidential post, eclipsing Yeltsin personally. Although the Kremlin may have acquiesced in this, the trend with the last few prime ministers had been in this direction anyway. All had seen their popularity ratings soar on appointment to the office. Fourth, Putin appeared able to restore Russia's national dignity, adopting neither an obsequiously subservient nor an impotently assertive attitude towards the West but one based on a measured understanding of Russia's real needs and capacity. In short, Putin's rise was based on a mixture of systemic and personal factors.

### Mikhail Kasyanov: loyalty on the rack

As finance minister in earlier governments, Kasyanov had negotiated the restructuring of the London Club (commercial) debt twice in three years in the late 1990s, Kasyanov was formally appointed premier by Putin in May 2000, but his tenure was accompanied by endless rumours of his imminent dismissal. To be prime minister in Russia's dual executive system is one of the most uncomfortable jobs imaginable, especially when the president is a young and energetic man with ideas of his own and with an eye out for future re-election. In the Soviet era prime ministers had been merely administrative officials, whereas under Yeltsin they had become politicised. Under Putin's activist presidency, the prime minister's office returned to the Soviet pattern. The Yeltsin system continued, however, to the extent that the ministries under Kasyanov remained virtually autonomous baronies, staffed by a vast, formless and poorly trained army of bureaucrats hardly deserving the title of civil servants. The fusion of commercial and political interests reached to the very top of many ministries, with a government appointment seen as a route to personal enrichment. Kasyanov's earlier friendship with the most ruthless of the tycoons, Berezovsky, did not augur well, and he had been known as

'Misha Two Per Cent', allegedly representing his cut of various deals. Unlike Yeltsin, who sacked his prime ministers if they were becoming too popular, Putin found it hard to dismiss officials, and his early period in office in personnel terms was marked by strong continuity with the Yeltsin era. Kasyanov's dismissal on 24 February 2004 on the eve of the presidential election came as a surprise.

### Mikhail Fradkov: the pitfalls of professionalism

Nominated by Putin on 1 March as prime minister, Fradkov was an unexpected choice. An experienced official, he had worked as an economic counsellor in the Soviet embassy in India (1973–5), then between 1975 and 1984 he worked in the heavy industry foreign trade company, in 1985–91 he occupied various positions at the Ministry for Foreign Economic Relations, in 1991–2 he was a senior counsellor of the Russian mission at the UN organisation in Geneva, and was Russia's representative at the General Agreement on Tariffs and Trade), and thereafter mainly worked in various economic posts[31] until in 2001–3 leading the Federal Tax Police before becoming in 2003–4 presidential envoy to the EU. Fradkov was confirmed by the Duma on 5 March, and four days later announced a slimmed-down cabinet of 17 members. The new government reinforced the presence of the economic liberals and brought in some newcomers. Igor Ivanov was replaced as foreign minister by Sergei Lavrov. Fradkov was more of a technocrat and was not openly identified with any of the Kremlin factions, although it was suspected that he sympathised with the *siloviki*. His chief characteristic was loyalty to Putin and for this reason was tipped as a possible interim successor.

## Public administration: from *nomenklatura* to civil service

Administrative weakness was one of the heaviest legacies that the Communist regime bequeathed to the new Russia.[32] Public administration had been subordinated to the Communist Party apparatus and even lacked the basic responsibility of recruiting its own civil servants; this was managed by the Party's *nomenklatura* system. The soviets were primarily political bodies and were never designed to be effective instruments of administration. Their bloated memberships met rarely in plenary session while the actual administrative work was carried out by their executive committees (*ispolkomy*) guided by the local Party organisations, the all-powerful *obkoms* at *oblast* level and *gorkoms* in the cities and towns. Gaidar noted that 'The plenitude of power of the bureaucracy inevitably leads to the complete destruction of the organisation of the work of the state.'[33] The Soviet regime was polymorphous, with little distinction between political, social or economic institutions. T. H. Rigby coined the term 'mono-organisational socialism' to describe this system in which all levels of social activity were controlled by the Party.[34] The weakness of governance was both cause and consequence of the parallel rule of the Communist Party, which gave a semblance of unity and direction to Soviet administration while ensuring that the state (narrowly defined) did not become an autonomous political force in its own right.

Building democratic institutions is at the heart of any democratisation process, but this was relatively neglected in the first post-communist years as attention focused on economic transformation. The state bureaucracy remained one of the least affected institutions in the transition. Compared with the other post-Soviet states, it was both easier and more difficult for Russia to establish the institutions of an independent state. Russia inherited the buildings, staff and networks of the defunct Soviet Union, but this itself caused problems because it inherited the attitudes, bureaucracy and inefficiencies of the old regime whereas the other republics could start with a relatively clean page. Just as Lenin in the early years of Soviet power attributed the defects of the new regime on holdovers from the old system, so too the new government in Russia had a ready object on which to place responsibility for its own inadequacies. The revolution of 1991 destroyed the unity of Soviet power but its elements remained embedded in the Russian body politic. In the mid-1990s over three-quarters of all civil servants were former *nomenklatura* officials.

A law of 31 July 1995 on state service sought to achieve two contradictory purposes: to transform the state apparatus into a modern civil service; while at the same time it sought to defend the corporate interests of the bureaucracy. The former aim was to be achieved by the introduction of examinations, competitive entry, and better training. The second was achieved by inertia, with a lack of turnover leading to nearly half the personnel of some ministries being of pension age, while the whole system was marked by the growth in corruption. With wages in the public sector falling relative to what could be earned in business, the administrative system either 'commercialised' its own activities through corruption, or its most active members left. Civil servants were forbidden to participate in business by a law of 22 March 1991, yet many continued their economic activities.[35] The establishment in 1997 of a Commission for Administrative Reform helped formulate the tasks, and some of their ideas were reflected in Yeltsin's annual address to the Federal Assembly in 1998. The Presidential Administration, however, jealous of its personnel appointment rights, proved an obstacle in the way of the fulfilment of the president's own programme.[36]

Although Russia has only half the population of the former USSR, its government bureaucracy is no smaller. Already by September 1992 Russia had 137 central ministries and departments, compared to 85 in the former USSR. By 1 October 1995 the 73 federal ministries, state committees, committees and services employed some 30,000 people; 5,000 officials (excluding technical staff) were employed by the president's office and 2,000 by the cabinet secretariat; while federal agencies in the regions employed an astonishing 364,000, double the 187,000 for the whole USSR in 1990.[37] In the post-communist era the state bureaucracy grew enormously and became one of the most rigid and reactionary forces in the country. In 1990 the whole Soviet administrative apparatus, including central, regional and local government and the ministries, numbered 662,700, but by 2000 the bureaucracy in Russia alone numbered over a million *chinovniks*. If all administrative personnel at the federal and regional levels are included, the total rises to 1.2 million,[38] and despite attempts at reform this had risen to 1.5 million by 2006. In 2005 alone another 150,000 public servants were appointed. A relatively small proportion was federal, numbering 41,100 in 2005 (up from 25,000 in 2000), whereas in the regions the bureaucracy swelled to 1,420,900 in 2005.[39]

Bogged down in elite conflicts and institutional turf wars and lacking a solid professional core of modern administrators, reform in this sphere proceeded as contradictorily as in most other areas. A professional civil service reflecting civil society rather than acting as an administrative instrument of executive authority only slowly emerged. A General Directorate to train senior *cadres* for the civil service (known as Roskadry) was established by a decree of 28 November 1991, accompanied by plans to introduce competitive entrance exams and the like. The Institute of Management in Moscow was transformed into a new Civil Service Academy, designed to train a new generation of professional government employees. At the same time, the material incentives for senior government service were greatly improved from 1997, including free housing allocation and seniority pay. The presidency itself became ever more active in appointments, with any personnel appointments of any significance having to be cleared first not only with the presidential administration but also, increasingly, with the security services as well, justified by the need to combat crime and corruption.

# 7 Party development

> A Party is not, as classical doctrine (or Edmund Burke) would have us believe, a group of men who intend to promote public welfare 'upon some principles on which they are all agreed' ... A party is a group whose members propose to act in concert in the competitive struggle for political power.
>
> (Joseph A. Schumpeter)[1]

Political parties play a fundamental role in modern representative democracy. They connect civil and political society, advance the perceived interests of individuals, groups and social strata while aiming consciously to develop these constituencies, and provide a link between civil society and the state, espousing the claims of the one and enforcing the rules of the other.[2] In post-communist Russia parties only marginally fulfilled these functions. The relative independence of government from both parliamentary oversight and party control, and the emergence of a powerful presidential system based on the apparatus of the state, marginalised the political role of organised social interests. Trapped between an ill-formed state system and rudimentary civil society, the nascent representative system was over-shadowed by other forms of social aggregation like the military and security apparatus, oligarchical financial and commercial interests, regional governors, and above all by the regime and its apparatus. Rather than parties generating the political dynamism that formed government, the regime itself tended to take the initiative in party formation. This chapter will examine the tortuous process of party development in Russia, noting that a multiplicity of parties does not of itself demonstrate the existence of a functioning party *system*. As we will see in Chapter 8, Russia's electoral politics focuses on parties, and they structure politics in the Duma (Chapter 9). Parties have become an essential element in the Russian political scene, but they remained a subaltern social form.

## Stages of party development

Party development in Russia evolved through four main phases. The first was the insurgency stage of movements and *neformaly* (informal) organisations accompanying the dissolution of the power of the Communist Party of the Soviet Union (CPSU) during *perestroika* (1985–91). The second stage was the period of constitutional crisis between August 1991 and October 1993, when the presidency and parliament struggled for supremacy. In the absence of elections and the fight for political power between rival elite factions, we have characterised this period as a peculiar sort of 'phoney democracy'.

The third stage was inaugurated by the dissolution of the old Russian legislature and the events of 3–4 October 1993. This period, lasting up to Yeltsin's resignation in December 1999, was characterised by a contradictory dual adaptation. Political leaders and organised interests adapted themselves to constitutional and democratic mass politics, largely renouncing the street politics of the insurgency and 'phoney democracy' phases. Democratic forms and constitutional norms, however, were adapted to the needs of the political leadership (the regime), thus undermining the real impact that organised political interests could have on the conduct of government and the shaping of policy. In the fourth phase, accompanying Putin's presidency from 2000, the role of political parties was formalised and the policy process broadened, but popular representation was constrained by statist-governmentalism. The hybrid nature of the regime, drawing its legitimacy from pluralist democracy while suborning the electoral process, endowed the system with numerous contradictions and allowed conflicting evaluations of the nature of the new system. We will examine all four phases – insurgency, 'phoney democracy', dual adaptation and formalisation – in more detail below.

### *The insurgency phase*

The dissolution of communist power was accompanied by the emergence of movements covering social, environmental, gender and other issues, as well as the formation of the first political popular fronts and proto-parties.[3] The tumultuous proliferation of *neformaly* and an independent press reflected a distinctive type of negative popular mobilisation against the old regime that proved very difficult to channel into positive civic endeavour. The politics spawned by the insurgency phase was untidy and anarchic yet they undermined political cultural theories stressing Russian passivity and innate authoritarianism.[4] The integration of this upsurge of civic activism into a new polity, however, remained problematical.[5] Much of this activity was united by little other than its anti-systemic character, devoted to overcoming the dominance of the CPSU. When it came to a positive programme, Russian political society proved deeply fragmented, quite apart from its inability to impose accountability on the authorities and even on its own leaders.

The Leninist-Stalinist terror and decades of stifling one-party rule ruptured continuity with the past. Pre-revolutionary Russia was characterised by hundreds of societies and clubs, and this rich associational life continued into the early Soviet period but thereafter dried up to the degree that only three social organisations were created in the Brezhnev years.[6] Early studies of the *neformaly* blurred the distinction between political and social activities – and for good reason: *any* autonomous social activity represented a repudiation of the old 'administrative-command' system (to use the term of Gavriil Popov, mayor of Moscow between June 1991 and June 1992). Gorbachev's model of reform communism, which he called *perestroika*, broadened the scope for independent initiative as long as it endorsed his model of development.[7]

The establishment of the Democratic Union (DS: *Demokraticheskii soyuz*) on 9 May 1988 marked the beginning of the renewed era of multi-party politics in Russia. Rejecting Gorbachev's attempts to expand the base of the Party regime by incorporating new social forces, the party declared its outright opposition to Soviet power and its allegiance to a 'peaceful democratic revolution'.[8] The party adopted a strongly anti-communist line, favouring the introduction of Western-style liberal democracy and market economy. Many of the DS's campaigns at first appeared blasphemous but soon entered the vocabulary of the public and then became official policy. It was the DS which first raised the Russian tricolour at the Kazan Cathedral in St Petersburg and Pushkin Square in Moscow, and indeed which first launched the campaign to rename Leningrad. After the August coup the DS insisted that the revolution was still to come, that a change of symbols had taken place but not the revolution of democracy itself. They insisted that popular consciousness was permeated by a totalitarian mentality and had simply transferred its loyalty from the Bolsheviks to the 'good Tsar' Yeltsin and had still not attained a sense of civic responsibility.[9] The problems attending the development of the party, like poor organisation, abstract theorising, leadership splits and low membership, were to be mirrored by countless other parties later.

In some non-Russian republics the informal movement took the form of popular fronts, with Sajudis in Lithuania one of the largest representing aspirations for national autonomy and, later, independence. These popular fronts were catch-all single-issue movements and acted as the substitute for political parties. In Russia the absence of an all-encompassing national issue meant that popular fronts were weak and no single movement for the whole nation emerged. Democracy took the place of nationality politics as a mobilising force, and as mass electoral politics emerged Democratic Russia (*Demrossiya*) came the closest to becoming a national movement. *Demrossiya* was formally established in January 1990 as an umbrella organisation to fight the March elections, and at its formal inaugural congress on 20–1 October some 18 social movements and 9 political parties came together. *Demrossiya* played a leading part in maintaining the pressure on Gorbachev in the year before the coup and its candidate, Yeltsin, emerged triumphant in the presidential elections of June 1991. After the coup, however, Burbulis was the only major figure from *Demrossiya* offered an important political post, and the rest had to be satisfied with jobs in the localities or in administration. Yeltsin refused to subordinate himself to the social movement that helped bring him to power.

The insurgency phase in Russia was both shorter in time and more anarchic than in most of Eastern Europe.[10] The ending of the CPSU's guaranteed monopoly on power in March 1990 was followed by a wave of new parties, formalised by the Soviet Law on Public Associations passed on 9 October 1990, which placed political parties and independent trade unions on a legal footing. By late 1990 there were at least 457 political or politicised organisations in Russia, confronting analysts with major problems of classification.[11] Many of the new parties were barely distinguishable from the burgeoning mass of *neformaly*, but by early 1991 some 100 organisations could be recognised as political parties, of which only about 20 recruited in other republics.[12] The problem soon became one not of the lack of parties but one of 'over-partification', hundreds of small groups covering every known, and some newly discovered, nook and cranny of the political and social spectrum, and some several times over. Broadly speaking, up to August 1991 Russian politics were characterised by a bipolar struggle between communist and 'democratic' movements, with the embryonic national and patriotic movements torn between the two.

The end of the CPSU's monopoly allowed informal movements to take on more structured forms, but they remained stamped by the politics of insurgency. Elections before August 1991, and in particular those of March 1990, were not fought between different social and political groups on the basis of alternative platforms and social groups defending their interests, but rather as voting alliances against a discredited regime (see Chapter 7).[13] The onset of electoral politics *preceded* the emergence of a multi-party system, something that distorted the whole process of party formation. Elections were dominated by the anti-politics of opposition to the communist regime, and movements were largely unable to make the transition from mobilisational to representational politics.[14] Practically, all respondents in a survey of middle-level *Demrossiya* activists stressed that the movement prospered because of its commitment to the removal of the CPSU from power and the transition to a new social order.[15] Thus unity in the insurgency phase was forged by the negative programme of opposition to the communist regime, in favour of greater civic freedom and a looser form of federation, but failed to define positive political and social programmes.

The informal movement was only one route of party formation in this period, with others emerging from within the CPSU itself, together with openly anti-communist alliances and the 'revolutionary movement' represented by DS and Democratic Russia.[16] All reflected a rather simplistic bipolarity, and the struggle against the CPSU (from within and beyond) promoted the proliferation of pseudo-parties. While the term proto-parties suggests a natural evolution to full-blooded party status, pseudo-parties were caricatures of the conditions in which multi-party politics came to Russia. Dozens of parties emerged and scored easy victories with the minimum of organisational or intellectual resources against the debilitated CPSU and the decaying Soviet order. Who needed a defined programme when the old system provided such a vulnerable target? The new parties were marked by

> numerical weakness, weak and amorphous organisational structures (particularly at the local level), regionalism, ideological vagueness and a negativism bordering on populism, and low-calibre leaders who, for the sake of self-affirmation, actively set themselves up against other parties, even ones that were ideologically close to them.[17]

The emerging multi-party system was highly fragmented. If the process within the CPSU can be described as from party to faction, then the larger process can be described as from faction to party, a transformation that very few groups actually achieved. There remained a gulf between insurgent elites and the political system. This gulf was reproduced once a section of the insurgent elite, headed by Yeltsin, came to power in August 1991 in an independent Russia.

### 'Phoney democracy': August 1991–October 1993

Parties and the structure of party politics depend on the timing of elections and type of electoral system. The electoral process is a major stimulus for the development of parties and a party system, and hence the absence of a general election up to December 1993 inhibited further democratisation. Parties in this period, quite simply, had nothing to do. In the absence of elections most political associations barely qualified to be termed parties, failing to meet Sartori's basic definition of a political party as 'any political group that presents at elections, and is capable of placing through elections, candidates for public office'.[18] In the absence of elections a peculiar sort of 'phoney democracy' emerged as the regime born of the August coup consolidated itself.

By 20 February 1992, 38 political organisations had been registered with the Russian Ministry of Justice,[19] and by April of that year, according to Sergei Stankevich, there were 820 registered public associations, including 25 political parties, encompassing over 300,000 people.[20] By May 1993 the number of registered organisations had risen to 1,800.[21] The new parties, however, palpably failed to become the basis of the new political system, and Russia moved from being a one-party state to a non-party state, albeit accompanied by numerous pseudo-parties. The onset of pluralism in Russia was not the same thing as the establishment of a multi-party system, and, instead, politics focused on the struggle between institutions (above all between parliament and the president) rather than between parties in parliament. The period was characterised by a distinctive type of dual power in which a presidential apparatus was superimposed on the nascent parliamentary system, with little coordination between the two. Parties were left hanging in the air with little constructive purpose.

Maurice Duverger stresses the electoral and parliamentary origins of modern political parties;[22] and in the absence of either the development of a multi-party system stagnated. The elimination of the CPSU and the ensuing vacuum opened up new political spaces but failed to trigger political mobilisation. Highly fragmented political parties divided over political, economic and nationality policy. Against the background of the kaleidoscopic formation, division and reformation of *groupuscules* calling themselves parties, a broadly bipolar system emerged in which 'democrats' stood against various nationalist, patriotic and communist splinter organisations dubbed 'red-browns', the alliance of communist rejectionists and nationalist reactionaries. The ideological homogeneity of the insurgency phase now gave way to programmatic divergence over such issues as the powers of the presidency, relations with the 'near abroad and, above all, economic reform. Programmes began to reflect the realities of contemporary Russian politics rather than idealised versions of abstract transitional processes to 'the market' or of 'rejoining world civilisation'.[23] Anti-communist unity now gave way to polarisation not only in the content of programmes, as the umbrella 'democratic' movement ceded ground to patriotic and nationalist organisations, but also in the 'irreconcilable' style of politics that came to predominate at this time.

The pseudo-parties had been sustained by the circumstances attending the dissolution of communist power and not by their popular appeal, leadership qualities or organisational resources. The social base of the 'democratic' movement was extremely heterogeneous, including intellectuals, security officials and miners, united only, according to Popov, by their 'hatred for the bankrupt CPSU regime'.[24] The failure of social movements to 'particise' themselves, notably in the case of *Demrossiya* and also the Civic Union later (see below), is one of the distinctive features of the transition in Russia.[25] The disappearance of the CPSU removed the incentive for the 'opposition' to unite, while much of the old CPSU elite made a smooth transition and became part of the new establishment. A gulf remained between the parties emerging from below and official representation in the legislature, with parliamentary and popular organisations operating on separate levels, inhibiting the development of distinct party identities and organisations. Four ideological trends predominated in this period (for an overview of electoral performance, see Table 7.1).

The first is the so-called 'democratic' wing. Attempts to create a political bloc in support of Yeltsin and his reforms repeatedly failed. A number of parties were established in 1993 in anticipation of general elections, notably Gaidar's Russia's Choice, representing the 'party of power', Sergei Shakhrai's Party of Russian Unity and Concord (PRES), which adopted a moderately critical stance even though some of its leaders

*Table 7.1* Vote distribution between major parties (PR vote), 1993–2007

| | 1993 | 1995 | 1999 | 2003 | 2007 |
|---|---|---|---|---|---|
| **Turnout**(percent) | 54.8 | 64.4 | 61.7 | 55.7 | 64.1 |
| **The 'against all' vote** | 4.22 | 2.77 | 3.30 | 4.70 | n.a |
| *Five elections* | | | | | |
| Communist Party (CPRF) | 11.6 | 22.3 | 24.3 | 12.6 | 11.6 |
| Liberal Democratic Party (LDPR) | 21.4 | 11.2 | 6.0 | 11.5 | 8.1 |
| Yabloko | 7.3 | 6.9 | 5.9 | 4.3 | 1.59 |
| *Four elections* | | | | | |
| Agrarian Party | 7.4 | 3.8 | n.a | 3.6 | 2.3 |
| *Three elections* | | | | | |
| Women of Russia | 7.6 | 4.6 | 2.0 | n.a | n.a |
| Union of Right Forces (SPS) | n.a | n.a | 8.5 | 4.0 | 0.96 |
| *Two elections* | | | | | |
| Russia's Choice | 14.5 | 3.9 | n.a | n.a | n.a |
| Russian Unity and Concord (PRES) | 6.3 | 0.4 | n.a | n.a | n.a |
| Cedar | 0.7 | 1.4 | n.a | n.a | n.a |
| Our Home Is Russia | n.a | 10.1 | 1.2 | n.a | n.a |
| Communist Workers for Russia | n.a | 4.5 | 2.2 | n.a | n.a |
| Congress of Russian Communities (KRO) | n.a | 4.3 | 0.6 | (see Rodina) | n.a |
| United Russia (Unity + OVR) | n.a | n.a | (see Edinstvo) | 37.6 | 64.3 |
| *One election* | | | | | |
| Democratic Party of Russia (DPR) | 5.1 | n.a | n.a | n.a | n.a |
| Edinstvo (Unity) | n.a | n.a | 23.3 | n.a | (see UR) |
| Fatherland – All Russia (OVR) | n.a | n.a | 13.3 | (see UR) | (see UR) |
| Rodina (Motherland) | n.a | n.a | n.a | 9.0 | (see JR) |
| Social Justice Party | n.a | n.a | n.a | 3.1 | n.a |
| Party of Russia's Rebirth | n.a | n.a | n.a | 1.9 | (see Patriots of Russia) |
| People's Party | n.a | n.a | n.a | 1.2 | n.a |
| Just Russia (JR) | n.a | n.a | n.a | n.a | 7.74 |
| Civic Force | n.a | n.a | n.a | n.a | 1.05 |
| Patriots of Russia | n.a | n.a | n.a | n.a | 0.89 |
| Party of Social Justice | n.a | n.a | n.a | n.a | 0.22 |
| Democratic Party | n.a | n.a | n.a | n.a | 0.13 |
| *Other parties/against all/invalid* | 18.1 | 26.6 | 12.7 | 11.2 | n.a |
| TOTAL (%) | 100 | 100 | 100 | 100 | 100 |

*Sources*: Adapted from Richard Rose, Neil Munro and Stephen White, 'Voting in a Floating Party System: the 1999 Duma Election', *Europe-Asia Studies*, Vol. 53, No. 3, May 2001, pp. 419–43, at p. 424; with 2003 data from *Vybory deputatov gosudarstvennoi dumy federal'nogo sobraniya Rossiiskoi Federatsii 2003: elektoral'naya statistika*, Central Electoral Commission (Moscow, Ves' Mir, 2004), pp. 29, 141, 192; and 2007 data from www.cikrf.ru.

were in government, and a bloc bringing together 'oppositional democrats' headed by Yavlinsky, Yuri Boldyrev and Vladimir Lukin, the Russian ambassador to America, to form a group based on their initials, Yabloko (Apple).

Second, in the centre the All-Russian Union for Renewal (*Obnovlenie*) was formed in June 1992 by Arkady Vol'sky, the chairman of the Russian Union of Industrialists and Entrepreneurs (RUIE, formerly the Scientific Industrial Union), and was soon dubbed the 'party of managers'. Renewal sought to act as a coalition of the managers of state enterprises, the new private entrepreneurs, and the chief executives of local government. On 21 June 1992 Vol'sky's Renewal joined with Alexander Rutskoi's People's Party of Free Russia (PPFR), formerly the Communists for Democracy faction formed in March 1991, and Nikolai Travkin's Democratic Party of Russia (DPR) to establish the Civic Union, a 'constructive' and 'loyal opposition' bloc against not Yeltsin but Gaidar's economics team whose policies, they insisted, could provoke a social explosion.[26] The Civic Union favoured a slower and more socially oriented approach to economic reform.[27] The group was wary of the West, favoured greater integration within the CIS and adopted what they called a broadly Eurasianist perspective.[28] The Civic Union was not an ideological alliance but a pragmatic attempt to rally the opposition of the centre. Vol'sky hoped to convert the RUIE into a fully fledged Industrial Party, but hesitated out of fear of creating 'yet another flash-in-the-pan party formed "from the top"'.[29] In the event, following a disappointing performance at the Seventh Congress of People's Deputies in December 1992, the Civic Union withered away, although the RUIE remains one of the most important interest groups in Russian politics.

Third, the national-patriot movement covered a wide spectrum, from national-socialists at one extreme to democratically minded Russian 'statists' at the other. A percipient article at the time argued, 'We should not fool ourselves: this movement will inevitably come to power, if only because it is the only political force which played no part in the crimes, mistakes and oversights of recent years.' Just as Yeltsin defeated Gorbachev because of his intuitive understanding of the mood of Russia, so the national-patriotic forces would triumph because of their understanding that Russia was tired of humiliation and of experiments, whether of the communist sort or those copied from Western models.[30] The analysis was accurate but premature: Putin's programme of national democracy was precisely a response to these concerns.

The national-patriots weakened their own position by emphasising one strand of Russian statism at the expense of the other. Their stress on a greater Russia, encompassing other Slavic areas, appeared not only futile but dangerous as well, carrying within it the potential for war with Ukraine, Kazakhstan and others. The slaughter that accompanied Serbia's claims to defend the rights of Serbs in Croatia and Bosnia by incorporating them into a 'greater Serbia' stood as an awful warning of what could happen in the former USSR. From December 1991 Yeltsin began to talk of a 'red-brown' coalition between rejectionist communists and revanchist Russian nationalists. Such an anti-Yeltsin coalition did indeed take shape and presented a radical challenge to the August settlement. They had a cause, the rights of Russians 'abroad', the bowing to the West, and the alleged economic incompetence of Gaidar's government accompanied by the catastrophic fall in living standards and a deep economic recession.

They were weakened, however, by the tendency to drift towards irreconcilable extremism.[31] The leader of the Russian National Assembly (*Russkii obshchenatsion-alnyi sobor*, RONS), the former KGB general Alexander Sterligov, for example argued that the 7 years of *perestroika* had completed the 70-year process of the 'total destruction of the life of the Russian people and its statehood', and sought 'by constitutional means to overthrow the present government of national betrayal'.[32] The nationalists adopted ever more extreme positions, calling not only for the overthrow of the government but by mid-1992 challenged the president himself. The creation of the National Salvation Front (NSF) signalled a deepening of political polarisation. Established at a founding congress of some three thousand communists and nationalists on 24 October 1992, the NSF brought together some of the more irreconcilable nationalists.[33] The NSF was declared unconstitutional by Yeltsin on 28 October 1992, the first political movement to be banned in Russia since the coup. On 12 February 1993 the Constitutional Court lifted the ban and the NSF went on to lead the military resistance to the dissolution of parliament in September-October 1993.

A distinctive mix of great Soviet patriotism, populism and Russian nationalism was propounded by Zhirinovsky, leader of the clearly misnamed Liberal Democratic Party of Russia (LDPR). At its founding congress on 31 March 1990 Zhirinovsky, a 44-year-old lawyer working in a publishing house, was elected leader. Born in Almaty (then called Verny), of a Jewish father and Russian mother, like many from the periphery he was more of a nationalist than those living in the metropolis. Zhirinovsky made much of the fact that he was one of the few Russian leaders who had never been a member of the Communist Party, though he apparently worked closely with the security establishment. His programme in the presidential elections of June 1991 was a simple one: to cut the price of vodka, to restore Russia's greatness by renaming the USSR (including the Baltic republics) Russia, and to keep Soviet troops in Eastern Europe until 'Russia' was ready for their return. This programme attracted six million voters, some 7.8 per cent of the electorate. He went on to attack Yeltsin for pursuing an 'anti-national, anti-Russian policy', and averred that the majority of Russians were in favour of dictatorship and called for the restoration of the Russian empire, first, within the borders of the former USSR and later to encompass the former Tsarist empire, including Poland, Finland and Alaska.[34] Zhirinovsky directed his appeal to disaffected sections of society threatened by the market, and part of the business community who valued stability above democracy. The LDPR kept its distance from the maelstrom of nationalist movements and was able to take advantage of the political vacuum created by the destruction of many militant nationalist movements in October 1993 to triumph in the December elections.

Communists represented the fourth main tendency. The fall of communist power was followed by a debate over whether the CPSU had been a party at all or a 'quasi-state organisation that concentrated all the basic functions of power in its hands'?[35] A group of 36 Russian MPs appealed to the Constitutional Court to adjudicate the legality of Yeltsin's three decrees issued between 23 August and 6 November 1991, banning the CPSU in Russia and confiscating its property.[36] A counter-petition by a group of Russian MPs led by Oleg Rumyantsev claimed that the Party's activities had been subversive and illegal, 'usurping state power and undermining state sovereignty that belongs exclusively to the people', and thus that the ban had been constitutional.[37] The Court on 26 May 1992 ruled that the two petitions would be considered together, and the hearings on the legality of the three decrees opened on 7 July 1992 and soon turned into a trial of the Party's activities since October 1917. The presidential team argued that the CPSU had not been a party but a state organisation, and therefore not the courts but the president had the right to decide its fate.[38] On 30 November 1992 the Court ruled that Yeltsin had acted lawfully in banning the CPSU's ruling bodies, but not its local branches. In effect, the Party was divided into two: the local membership and the governing bodies dominated by *apparatchiki*. The latter, as Yeltsin asserted, had become entwined with the state and were illegal; but the mass of the rank-and-file membership had been perfectly legitimate members of a political organisation and were entitled to renew their activities.[39]

Following the Court's ambivalent ruling Valeri Kuptsov, the last leader of the CP RSFSR, insisted that the Party would start reorganising and called for Yeltsin's impeachment. The Communist Party of the Russian Federation (CPRF) came back to life on 13–14 February 1993 at a conference in the Moscow region. Four of the successor parties attended, including Roy Medvedev's Socialist Party of Working People (SPWP) and Alexei Prigarin's Union of Communists, and the whole session was presided over by Ivan Rybkin, organiser of the Communists of Russia parliamentary fraction. Old-style Stalinists and pensioners were well represented, but the words 'of the Russian Federation' in the party's name signalled its recognition of existing borders. Gennady Zyuganov, long associated with the Russian nationalist wing of the movement and formerly leader of the so-called 'Committee of the National-Patriotic Forces of Russia' and author of 'A Word to the People' (the manifesto of the coup), was elected leader. Viktor Anpilov's militant Russian Communist Workers' Party (RCWP) refused to join, and Nina Andreeva's Stalinist All-Union Communist Party of Bolsheviks (VKPB) also kept its distance, but even without them the CPRF soon eclipsed all other parties. The CPRF transcended the politics of insurgency and drew on reserves of organisational and political experience matched by no other. It claimed to be the official successor to the CPSU, and thus hoped to have some of its property restored by the courts. Rejecting the calls of some of irreconcilable oppositionists to boycott the December 1993 elections, Zyuganov led the party to a respectable third place (see Table 7.1). The CPRF became Russia's largest party, with a membership peaking at over half a million, and acted as the main opposition party.

In the phoney democracy phase parties neither guided the president nor formed the government, and parliament and the parties in it were marginalised. Parties fulfilled the communicative and link functions between the political elite and the people only fitfully. The failure to integrate parties into the operation of the political system undermined the stability of the new democratic institutions and forced reliance on a supra-party technocratic ideology of democratic and market reforms from above. The administrative regime, consisting of the president and the administration, could not be held accountable to parties or parliament. The absence of a multi-party *system* impeded the development of serious parties, but at the same time the absence of serious *parties* inhibited the development of a multi-party system. Elements of phoney democracy were to become an enduring feature of the Russian political system.

### Dual adaptation, December 1993–December 1999

The adaptation stage was marked by the adoption of a new constitution and the first genuine national multi-party elections of 12 December 1993. The electoral system (Chapter 8) was designed to encourage the development of a multi-party system, but did so only partially. The pseudo-parties of the earlier periods were now faced with the hard school of an election in which their inflated claims of support were finally put to the test; few withstood the challenge and most faded into the obscurity whence they had come. The adoption of the hybrid electoral system only revealed more starkly the fault lines in Russian society. Thirteen parties and electoral blocs negotiated the hurdles to stand in the election, and of these only eight cleared the 5 per cent threshold. The election contributed to the development of parties by forcing the development of organisations and alliances, while the adoption of the constitution finally provided a stable institutional framework in which parties could operate. The hasty formation of *impromptu* and often unprincipled electoral associations, however, can also be seen as disruptive of the process of party organisation and consolidation. The LDPR registered notable success in gaining 59 of the 225 party list seats, yet the organisation was less a party (with 40 per cent of its deputies not even members of the party) than a vehicle for Zhirinovsky's charismatic leadership.

A new generation of parties emerged, most of which drew their provenance from earlier stages but adapted to the dramatically changed political climate. The consolidation of the party system as an integral part of Russian government proved problematical, but the characteristic feature of this period was the adaptation of political parties to the conventions of democratic electoral and parliamentary politics. The extremes of left and right were marginalised. However, the second aspect of this adaptation was less positive: to the exigencies of regime politics and the structures of power themselves.

The attempt to 'parliamentarianise' the opposition by taking them off the street was only partially fulfilled.[40] The establishment of a viable parliamentary system created a forum in which party politics could flourish, but hopes that elections would kick-start the party system, however, were only disappointed. The presence of relatively small factions and groups in the First Duma prevented the establishment of a stable majority, inhibited the development of parliamentary government, and perpetuated the supra-party system of regime politics. Party factions were once again relatively fluid and deputies were marked by a lack of discipline. Many deputies elected on the party lists, moreover, were not even members of the parties they officially represented, notably in Zhirinovsky's LDPR, whose Duma caucus frequently split. The lack of correspondence between the composition of parliament and the formation of the government, moreover, accentuated the fragmentation of the Russian party system. The major centres of power were based on personalities, many of whom were outside the parliamentary and party system, and within parties links between the leadership and membership were tenuous. Parties were trapped between strong executive authority and an amorphous civil society.

To heal the wounds inflicted by the October events and to stabilise the political situation, Yeltsin sponsored a Charter for Civic Accord, signed by 148 political, trade union, religious and public figures on 28 April 1994.[41] The president promised not to launch early parliamentary elections, while the signatories in return promised not to demand early presidential elections, and a ban on strikes was to be observed. Zhirinovsky signed up, but the opposition was notable by its absence, with the CPRF and its close ally, the Agrarian Party, refusing to sign, while Yavlinsky did not even attend the ceremony, regarding the whole exercise as pointless, 'imposing no obligations on anyone'.[42] The opposition, meanwhile, had organised its own 'Accord for Russia', including the CPRF, the APR, Rutskoi, and the former head of the Constitutional Court, Zor'kin. Both the oppositional Accord for Russia and Civic Accord reflected the traditional pattern of 'supra-party' bloc politics and harked back to the inclusive 'popular front' politics of the insurgency phase; both were 'anti-party' in their very essence by seeking to replace competitive multi-party politics by para-constitutional corporatist deals. By the end of the year, in any case, Yeltsin quietly repudiated his Accord.

In the run-up to the parliamentary elections of December 1995 Russia's already fragmented party system atomised even further. By May 1995, 79 parties had registered an interest in fighting the elections, and by the time the process was complete in late November 43 groups were allowed to stand, making the ballot paper an extraordinarily thick document. All the familiar features of post-communist party building were taken to new extremes: the emphasis on personalities, amorphous and poorly drafted programmes, the deinstitutionalising influence of regional politics, the constant splitting and sub-dividing of parties and factions, and the absence of party discipline. Although the major players came from above, there was an enormous ferment of primary activity in the wards and the degree of grassroots democracy should not be minimised. The campaign was marked by a novel professionalism, with numerous image-making agencies at work and vigorous fund-raising activities. PR (in Russian *piar!*), indeed, became one of the major growth industries and allowed many a social scientist to prosper as they advised candidates and electoral blocs on what they liked to call 'political technologies' and 'image making'.

It is against the background of a fragmented party scene that an attempt was made to impose an ordered two-party system from above. The plan was to unite the centre-right parties around a political bloc to be led by Chernomyrdin, while the centre-left would be anchored around a movement led by Rybkin, the speaker of the Duma. It soon became clear that Rybkin's bloc would not be much more than a loose alliance of parties, losing even the support of his own APR, and it failed to enter the Second Duma. Chernomyrdin's bloc fared rather better. At its founding congress on 11 May 1995 the new party adopted the grand name of 'Russia Our Home' (*Nash dom Rossii*, NDR), dedicated to 'progress without shocks' and promising to lead Russia into an era of stability and strength. The energy lobby, and in particular Chernomyrdin's old fiefdom Gazprom, supported the new venture. Its key slogan was 'pragmatism', but the way the party was conceived and built suggested a new attempt at '*nomenklatura* democracy', a top-down attempt to secure the existing order.

The adaptation phase began to bring ideology, social interests and party structures into alignment. Russia remained distant from a real multi-party system, however, and as the dust settled on frenetic party formation and reformation the country was left with only one genuine party – the Communist Party, inherited from the previous age. The CPRF under Zyuganov became one of the few genuine mass parties, with a membership of some 550,000, a strong if contradictory programme and a serious national organisation. This was reflected in its triumph in the December 1995 elections, coming top in the proportional part of the elections with 22.3 per cent of the vote, giving it 99 seats in the Duma plus another 58 single-member seats (see Table 7.2). The results came as a surprise to many, above all the strength of the combined rejectionist vote (CPRF and LDPR). It was not clear whether the return of communists to influence in Russia was an indication of the failure of the democratic transition or evidence of its success. The 'centre' was anchored in the relatively disappointing vote for Russia Our Home, while Yabloko was the only 'democratic' party to enter the Duma.

Yavlinsky considered the victory of only four parties in the party list contest in the December 1995 elections a sign that Russia had outgrown the 'infantile stage of multi-partyism'.[43] Popov noted that the general-democratic stage of the transformation was

*Table 7.2* Secular trends in party list voting

| | 1993 | 1995 | | 1999 | | 2003 | | 2007 | |
|---|---|---|---|---|---|---|---|---|---|
| | *% total* | *% total* | *Change on previous election* | *% total* | *Change on previous election* | *% total* | *Change on previous election* | *% total* | *Change on previous election* |
| Communists | 20.3 | 30.6 | +10.3 | 28.1 | −2.5 | 19.3 | −8.8 | 11.57 | −7.73 |
| (parties) | (2) | (3) | (+1) | (5) | (+2) | (3) | (−2) | (1) | (−2) |
| Centrists | 23.1 | 24.8 | −1.7 | 41.9 | +17.1 | 41.1 | −0.8 | 74.47 | +33.37 |
| (parties) | (5) | (13) | (+8) | (9) | (−4) | (5) | (−4) | (4) | (+4) |
| Democrats Reformers (parties) | 27.3 | 16.1 | −11.2 | 15.0 | −1.1 | 8.5 | −6.5 | 3.6 | −4.9 |
| | (3) | (11) | (+8) | (3) | (−8) | (3) | (no change) | (3) | (no change) |
| National Patriots | 22.8 | 21.8 | −1.0 | 7.4 | −14.4 | 23.0 | +15.8 | 9.25 | −13.75 |
| (parties) | (1) | (9) | (+8) | (5) | (−4) | (8) | (+3) | (3) | (−5) |
| Against all | 4.2 | 2.8 | −1.4 | 3.3 | +0.5 | 4.7 | +1.4 | n.a | n.a |
| Turnout | 54.8 | 64.4 | +9.6 | 61.9 | −2.5 | 55.7 | −6.2 | 64.1 | +8.4 |

*Sources*: Yitzhak Brudny, 'Continuity or Change in Russian Electoral Patterns? The December 1999 – March 2000 Election Cycle', in Archie Brown (ed.), *Contemporary Russian Politics: A Reader* (Oxford, Oxford University Press, 2001), p. 164; Viktor Sheinis, 'Vybory i politicheskoe razvitie', in M. McFaul, N. Petrov and A. Ryabov (eds), *Rossiya v izbiratel'nom tsikle 1999–2000 godov* (Moscow, Gendal'f and Moscow Carnegie Center, 2000), pp. 385–6; Yusup Abdurakhmanov, 'Ideological Orientations of the Russian Electorate in Duma Elections', *Perspectives on European Politics and Society*, Vol. 6, No. 2, 2004, pp. 209–37, at p. 220; materials from Central Election Commission 2003 and 2007.

*Note*: The ideological groups are collated as follows (main parties only):
**Communists:** Communist Party of the Russian Federation (CPRF); Agrarian Party of Russia (APR) until 2003; Communists – Toiling Russia – For the Soviet Union!; Russian Party of Pensioners and Party of Social Justice.
**Centrists:** Women of Russia; Party of Russian Unity and Concord (PRES); Democratic Party of Russia (DPR); Party of Workers' Self-Management; Our Home is Russia (NDR); Unity/Medved ; Fatherland – All Russia (OVR); United Russia; Just Russia; Agrarian Party (in 2007); Democratic Party.
**Democrats Reformers:** Russia's Choice; Democratic Choice of Russia (DVR); Russian Movement for Democratic Reforms; Russian Constitutional Democratic Party; Union of Right Forces (SPS); Yabloko; Civic Force.
**National Patriots:** Liberal Democratic Party of Russia (LDPR); Congress of Russian Communities (KRO); Rodina (Popular Patriotic Union); Patriots of Russia; Party of Social Justice.

complete, the fundamentals of democracy had been introduced, and the first phase of privatisation was complete. More importantly, Russia's political configuration changed. The transition was based on an alliance between reformist sections of the Soviet bureaucracy and a programme drawn from liberal Westernisers, marginalising the democratic movements born during the insurgency against communism. A new model began to emerge in which political space became rather more structured, but the gulf between this and the conduct of government remained.

One way of bridging this gulf would be to create a presidential party, an idea mooted by Yeltsin on several occasions, but every time he fought shy of undertaking the organisational work required for such a venture. Instead he repeated the mantra that he was 'president of all Russians'. Attempts to unite the 'democratic' forces behind a single presidential candidate came to nothing, and instead in the 1996 presidential elections the organisational and financial resources of the presidency itself, allied with powerful 'oligarchs' to which the presidency then became indebted, were the key resource that ensured Yeltsin's re-election.

By the time of the December 1999 election the situation had somewhat stabilised with 26 blocs standing and six entering parliament, including the newly formed Unity (*Edinstvo*) organisation supporting Putin's presidential ambitions. Although the centre of Russian politics, rooted in market reforms, international integration and representative democracy, lacked convincing political representation, the adaptation phase had to a large degree universalised these policies, albeit without some of the liberal rhetoric of the earlier era. The frantic regrouping of parties in the adaptation phase, however, could not disguise the weakness of the party system and all forms of social representation.

### Formalisation stage, 2000–8

Against this broad characterisation of the contemporary Russian party scene there were discernible tendencies transforming the fragmented and amorphous party scene into something approaching the emergence of a party system with effective parties, differentiated programmes and stable electorates. The formalisation phase, in which Putin sought to transcend Russia's historical contradictions and its contemporary political divisions, in the sphere of party politics was marked by differentiation, which took place in three ways.

- Frenetic party formation and reformation continued, but the 1995 and 1999 elections distinguished a small group with representation in the Duma from the mass of pseudo-parties.
- The programmes and policies of this small group were now far more clearly differentiated along the classical political spectrum – the CPRF on the left, Unity and Luzhkov's Fatherland in the centre, Yabloko and the SPS on the centre right, and the LDPR on the nationalist right, although cross-cutting issues allowed alliances across the spectrum.
- Russian society itself began to develop a contoured political structure as class, societal and institutional interests, which in the Soviet era related to each other in non-political ways, now asserted their positions by employing the classical gamut of democratic instruments, above all parties.

Differentiation in the Russian population was reflected in more stable party alignment between demographic and economic groups. Yabloko, SPS, Women of Russia, Russia's Democratic Choice and the LDPR attracted younger people, while the Communists and Agrarians appealed to the older generation and the poor. People with little education preferred the Agrarians, LDPR, and Communists, while SPS and Yabloko attracted the more highly educated. Yabloko appealed to the old intelligentsia, while SPS to the market-oriented new middle class. Reformist parties were more strongly represented in the capitals of Moscow and St Petersburg, while the APR dominated the villages, although the Communists had growing support, while liberals were rarely supported here. Many of the new generation of parties were now better funded and began to sink local roots, drawing on a well of consistent support with name and programme recognition. Parties began to mobilise their resources more effectively and to devise programmes that reflected Russia's genuine problems.

Although Putin's rise had been sponsored by Yeltsin, his policies and political style in many respects represented a repudiation of Yeltsinism as elitist-oligarchical rule gave way to statist-governmentalism. This was evident in the sphere of party development.

Putin came to power proclaiming the need for his government to have proper social support reflected in political organisation. On several occasions Putin argued that 'Russia needs a real multi-party system', not parties 'that represent only themselves, but rather ... reflect the interests of large groups of society', which could 'shape the policies of the state'.[44] It appeared that this would take the form of a two- or three-party system, with Unity (a party that did not hide its aspiration to become the 'ruling party') becoming the core of a presidential party. The merger of Fatherland and Unity in 2001 to create United Russia appeared to be the first step in this direction. By contrast with Yeltsin, Putin identified himself with the pro-Kremlin party of power, but like Yeltsin, he balked at formally establishing a presidential party. Putin appealed to voters across the political spectrum, but attempts to create a party system from above, however, was in danger of reducing all parties to little more than shades of a single 'party of power'. The creation of Just Russia (*Spravedlivaya Rossiya*) in 2006 (see below) undermined the development of United Russia into a hegemonic party, and introduced a party-political aspect to the competitive factionalism within the elite in the centre and regions.

A number of questions emerged as Putin reorganised Russian governance: would his support for a more structured party system recognise and incorporate the pluralism that had emerged since the late 1980s, or would he try to reduce parties to little more than departments of state responsible for organising public politics; to what extent would a genuine system of governmental accountability to society emerge; and would the environment (above all, a free media, free and fair elections, an independent judiciary and a transparent funding regime) allow parties and other social organisations effectively to participate in Russian public life as independent actors? Above all, as Putin used the presidency as an instrument of political change, would the presidency itself become responsible to public and parliamentary accountability? From Putin's public utterances in his first period in power, it was clear that he himself did not know the answer to these questions. We outline the features of party formalisation below.

## Normative framework of party development

There is no mention in the constitution concerning the adoption of a law on political parties. Throughout the 1990s there were attempts to adopt a law to supersede the 1990 Soviet law on public associations, but up to 2001 no overall legislation had been adopted to regulate the sphere of social organisations. The lack of rules concerning the financing of political organisations meant that commercial organisations were given a free hand, and sought to ensure the maximum benefit from their 'investment'. In the absence of structured party politics lobbies formed their own parties, as with the Agrarian Party. At the same time, the presidency relied on quasi-political 'parties of power', combining the organisational and financial resources of the executive branch with access to the media.

The first major attempt to adopt a law on political parties came in December 1995, when the Duma discussed a draft that sought to regulate the types of parties that could be formed, procedures for creating and registering them, their rights and responsibilities, and ways of monitoring their activity. Three types of political parties were envisaged: national, with regional organisations in at least 45 components of the Russian Federation; interregional, with membership from at least two components; and regional. Party groups were prohibited from forming in executive agencies or local government, the armed forces, law enforcement agencies, or in the staffs of state or local legislative authorities. Funding for the election campaigns of national parties was to come from federal resources, although they could engage in economic activity of their own and accept donations.[45] Some of these ideas were incorporated into the law adopted in 2001, although the idea of different types of party was dropped.

The law on political parties became part of the larger package of changes to the electoral system, discussed with great energy after every election. Moser notes the effects of Russia's dual electoral system, favouring parties which can combine high name recognition with local organisation.[46] The main party that fitted this bill was the CPRF, allowing it to maintain strong parliamentary representation. In a situation of party and candidate proliferation (in December 1995 an average of 12 candidates fought for every single-mandate seat) the more disciplined and organised CPRF was able to win in single-mandate seats with a small proportion of the total vote. Governors themselves favoured a revision of Russia's electoral law to increase the number of deputies elected directly from local constituencies, something that would allow them greater leverage than the party-list system.

Following the 1999 election discussion was resumed with unusual urgency. Alexander Veshnyakov, the chair of the Central Electoral Commission, argued that a law on political parties was required to make their financing and organisation more transparent, and in return only genuine political parties would be allowed to participate in parliamentary elections. Such a reform would at a stroke eliminate the pseudo-party electoral associations. Already in the 1998 Ukrainian election only parties were allowed to stand on the party list. Consolidation would also be achieved by Unity's proposal to raise the PR threshold from 5 to 7 per cent. Not surprisingly Yabloko, which barely crossed the 5 per cent threshold in the 1999 election, sought to retain the existing level.[47] Attention also focused on campaign financing, the role of the media in elections and the structure of political parties.

The new law on parties, after much debate and over a thousand amendments to the draft proposed by Putin in December 2000, was finally signed into law on 11 July 2001.[48] Its main stipulations, which came into effect after a two-year transition period, were as follows (note that some of these points were superseded by later legislation, discussed below):

- Parties had to have a membership of at least 10,000 nation wide; with no fewer than 100 members in at least half (that is, in no fewer than 45) of Russia's regions; and branches of at least 50 members in the others. Groups that failed to meet these conditions could be disbanded by a decision of the Supreme Court.
- Only registered political parties are allowed to participate in national polls, thus effectively excluding the various movements and regional parties. The idea was to undermine various substitute regional parties.
- Parties must regularly advance candidates in elections.
- Parties are not allowed to appeal to sectional interests, and those advancing religious, racial, ethnic and professional causes are forbidden.
- No one can be a member of more than one party.
- To secure state financing, a party has to win more than 3 per cent of the PR vote in Duma elections, win 12 single-mandate seats in parliamentary elections, or three per cent of the vote in presidential elections.

- Federal assistance no longer comes before elections but is paid afterwards in proportion to the number of votes won. Parties that fail to gather 2 per cent of the vote have to return the money for the free airtime on state radio and television stations that they received during the campaign. Failure to pay will mean disqualification in the next election.
- Parties have to present an annual financial account reporting the amount received from donors and be open to auditors to examine their financial activities.
- Private contributions to political parties are limited, as are corporate contributions, and have to be made by bank transfer. Foreigners and international organisations, as well as enterprises that are 30 per cent state owned, are banned from making financial contributions. A limit was set to the amount a party can collect in private campaign contributions.
- Changes to the role of the media tried to draw a clearer line between information and commentary in an election campaign.
- Compliance with the law is the responsibility of the justice ministry, not the Prosecutor General's office as originally intended, with the decision on banning to be made by the Supreme Court.

The key point was to reduce the number of parties by several orders of magnitude, something that was swiftly achieved. About three-quarters of Russia's 197 parties were de-registered, leaving only about 50 to fight national and regional elections, and even this number was later reduced. Critics argue that regional membership requirements ignore variations in the population between regions, and thus preclude party registration for many groups. The law essentially destroyed regional political parties. The provisions of the law enunciating general principles and forbidding ideologies of supremacy based on racial, ethnic, social, religious or other grounds were considered weak. Above all, the law was criticised for the vague wording of clauses allowing parties to be 'disbanded'.[49]

The law on parties was reinforced by a federal law of May 2002 that stipulated a mixed-member parliamentary electoral system in all of Russia's regions. The law, which came into effect on 15 July 2003, stated that regional parliaments were to be formed on the party principle, with half to be elected by proportional representation. The measure reinforced the administration's desire to ensure that parties played a greater representative and political role across the country, as well as to undermine 'regional fiefdoms' (see Chapter 12). Modifications to the law regulating presidential elections of 27 December 2002 permitted parties to nominate candidates for presidential elections without having to collect signatures, thus reinforcing the primacy of parties in elections.

In October 2004 the law on parties was modified to restrict further the scope for smaller parties. From 1 January 2006 parties require a minimum of 50,000 members and regional branches with no fewer than 500 members each in more than half of Russia's regions where the population exceeds 500,000, and branches with no fewer than 250 people in the others. The financial rules became even more burdensome, including quarterly financial reports. Parties not only have the right but *must* contest elections, and not only at the national level (parliamentary and presidential) but also at the regional (gubernatorial and legislative) and municipal levels. At the same time, parties are the *only* organisations allowed to contest elections. Civic associations may join an electoral bloc with parties, but cannot advance their own candidates.

The registration process is now managed by a Federal Registration Service (FRS), created in 2005 under the Ministry of Justice. All parties, including long-standing ones, had to go through the registration process, including a congress to adopt the party's statutes and the re-registration of regional branches to ensure that the party has the requisite number. The founding congress, with a minimum of 150 delegates from at least 45 regions, elects the party's leading bodies and adopts a programme. The party is then registered nationally, followed by the registration of its regional branches with local divisions of the justice ministry, and finally the central ministry validates the completion of the process. After registration the ministry continues to monitor observance, and has the right to suspend a party found to be contravening the rules. Suspension cannot take place during an election, and parties that enter the Duma on party lists cannot be suspended within five years of their election. Parties have the right to appeal to the courts against suspension, and the final ruling on dissolving a party is taken by the Supreme Court. Parties that fail to meet the new conditions lose the status of a political party and are either transformed into a social organisation or disbanded. The deadline to be reregistered was 1 January 2006, by which time 35 parties had been registered, with some 20 organisations having fallen by the wayside. In January 2007 the FRS announced that only 17 parties had been granted the right to take part in the December 2007 parliamentary elections, with the rest of the 35 having failed to comply with the rules on numerical membership or the number of regional branches. They faced the choice of either dissolving themselves or becoming an NGO.

The Putinite attempt to create a party system national in scope and representing specific interests, values and programmes that could be put before the electorate was a rational response to political fragmentation and 'floating' party development (see below). Equally, the attempt to forge a national party system as an integrative force for the country as a whole makes a lot of sense, especially when faced with regional segmentation on a massive scale in the 1990s. However, excessive intervention by the regime and its manual attempts to mould a party system raised questions about the long-term sustainability of Putin's plans.

## The party system today

In their study of post-communist party systems Kitschelt *et al.* argue that

> In the final analysis, whether democracy becomes the 'only game in town' depends on the *quality of democratic interactions and policy processes* [italics in original] the consequences of which affect the legitimacy of democracy in the eyes of citizens and political elites alike.[50]

The quality of democratic procedures determines democratic consolidation and not only the durability of the system. This is particularly pertinent for Russia, where the formal institutions of democracy often mask quite undemocratic practises. Already in 1911 Robert Michels had argued that political parties, whatever their programmatic aspirations, tend to succumb to the oligarchic tendencies inherent in modern social organisation.[51] Russia appears to have fallen victim to this 'iron law of oligarchy' even before party life has become routinised. Most large social organisations, including parties and trade unions, tend to be top-heavy bureaucratic organisations with weak links with the mass of their membership.

### Party saturation and continuity

Until Putin's reforms there were few institutional barriers to the entry of new parties, transforming Russia from a one-party state in the Soviet period to one with hundreds of parties. By early 2001 Russia had 56 registered parties and 150 political associations,[52] but party saturation (as in most post-communist countries) remained remarkably low. The post-communist model of parties as electoral organisations focused on parliamentary life and party-list elections undermined the need for large constituency organisations. The large numbers involved in the demonstrations, marches and so on during the insurgent 'movement' phase of party formation was not translated into party membership, especially since mobilisation declined dramatically in the 1990s. Most parties were marked by limited recruitment to create a mass of 'divan' parties. In 1994 only 3 per cent of adults were members of any of the parties, movements and associations,[53] and this figure thereafter fell to some 1 per cent by 2003, but rose thereafter to approach 3 per cent once again by 2007. Until the emergence of United Russia and Just Russia only the CPRF was the only real mass party, with its half million members until 2003 double the membership of all other parties taken together. Disillusioned by cross-ideological alliances, reflecting too often opportunism rather than principle, society was depoliticised. This was not so much disengagement as demobilisation, since the persistently high turnout in elections (see Table 8.8) suggests that withdrawal was from party politics, narrowly defined, rather than from politics in general. Party membership as a proportion of the adult population remained very low, until the 'parties of power' began mass recruitment campaigns from 2004. Already in 2001 Unity claimed a membership of 350,000, rising to a million and a half by June 2007. This represented a peculiar form of repoliticisation, managed by the regime itself.

According to Richard Rose and colleagues, Russia had a 'floating party system', where parties came and went and thus inhibited stable party identification as electors were forced to become 'floating voters'.[54] Party affiliation was rendered difficult by changes in party labels, accompanied by a gradual shift in general political orientation towards the centre (see Table 8.10). Only three parties fought all four Duma elections up to 2003, while a whole slew of parties appeared once and then faded away (Table 7.1). The proportional part of the 1993 Duma election was contested by 13 associations, of which 8 crossed the 5 per cent threshold; in 1995, 43 groups entered the fray, but only 4 entered parliament; in 1999, 26 party lists were registered and 6 parties crossed the 5 per cent threshold; in 2003 23 groups competed but only 4 won seats; and in 2007 only four of the eleven parties contesting the election entered parliament. Only 3 of the 8 blocs elected in 1993 made it into the 1995 assembly, joined by 3 new parties in 1999. Of the 6 parties that crossed the threshold in 1999, 3 were new: Unity as the reconstituted 'party of power'; the centre-left grouping Fatherland-All Russia (OVR), and the liberal Union of Rightist Forces (SPS). Of the 4 that made it into the 2003 Duma, 2 had enjoyed a continuous presence since 1993 (the CPRF and the LDPR), one since 1999 (United Russia), joined by the new party Rodina (replaced by JR in 2007). The secular trend in party list voting is graphically illustrated in Table 7.2, illustrating the shifts in the number of parties fighting in each major ideological family and the overall trend of support for each family. The overall picture is of core continuity in parliamentary representation, accompanied by some radical changes, although the overall tendency is towards less 'floating' and more consolidation.

### *Types of party*

Russia's party system is characterised by three broad types of party. We have examined ideological orientations above, but here we focus on their relations with the regime. In broad terms, three types can be identified. The first can be described as *programme* parties, those with a clear platform adopted by some sort of process of inner-party democracy and pursued by the leadership and consistently presented to the public. The second in one way or another are *project* parties, created typically not long before elections as part of an ulterior strategy of competing elite groups. A classic project party was Rodina in the 2003 election, designed to draw votes away from the Communist Party. The third type is various government-sponsored groupings to represent the system itself. This type can described as *regime* parties, when they are sponsored by the ruling group, established to manipulate and shape political space and in some cases to act as what is called 'the party of power'. A 'party of power' can be defined as a political organisation created with the assistance of the executive to participate in elections and the legislative process.

### *Programme parties*

The organisation that most properly deserves the title of 'party' was the CPRF. With a network of regional organisations covering the entire country, some 20,000 primary cells and a membership of about half a million, and a large deputy faction in all three post-communist State Dumas, the CPRF was an important political force. The CPRF became one of the cornerstones of Russian parliamentary life and although somewhat eclipsed in December 1999 by Unity, the CPRF remained the largest group in parliament before declining dramatically in 2003. The party was unable to realise its potential and its leader, Zyuganov, appeared forever to be the runner-up and never the victor, as in the 1996 and 2000 presidential elections. The CPRF's ideology was a potent and largely incompatible mix of nationalist, imperialistic (in the Soviet sense) and communist principles; its policies were incoherent in that elements of the market were accepted as long as market *forces* were to be constrained; and its politics appeared to place its own institutional comfort (above all in the Duma) above principle. The party was the main oppositional force in the Duma, yet its policy stances too often appeared opportunistic and contradictory.

The CPRF remained torn by problems of political identity. Was it a revolutionary party intending to overthrow Russia's nascent capitalist institutions, or was it more of a social democratic party seeking to humanise the workings of the capitalist market? What would be the balance between nationalism and socialism? These questions, faced by the whole social democratic movement in the early part of the century and by the West European communist parties in the post-war era, was one that confronted post-communist communist parties in a particularly stark form. These ideological questions were far from abstract since on them hinged questions of organisation and strategy. To what degree would the party support strikes and street demonstrations; would the emphasis be on the working class or the intelligentsia; what would be the party's economic policy;

how would the party relate to the other former Soviet republics? On all these questions the CPRF equivocated. The absence of a clear-cut ideology and the aged profile of its membership inhibited the mobilisation of the party's resources. Above all, its nationalist ambitions, socialist aspirations and its democratic commitments were far from integrated. Russia's largest party for so long, by 2006 the CPRF's membership had fallen to no more than 180,000. Following the December 1999 election some of the tension in the CPRF came out into the open. A new political movement of the moderate left, headed by the Speaker of the State Duma, Seleznev, was formally established in September 2000. Called *Rossiya*, the new movement remained allied to the CPRF but the relationship was strained, especially since it was suspected that the movement had been inspired by the Kremlin. These strains were even sharper after the 2003 election, with an attempt to oust Zyuganov in 2004. He fought off the challenge, but the party became even more of a bureaucratic husk and would no doubt continue to decline.[55]

Yavlinsky's Yabloko party had since its foundation in 1993 represented the anti-Yeltsin wing of the 'democratic' movement. It too, like the CPRF, lacked a clear ideological orientation: it was clearly a liberal party, but opposed some of the neo-liberal policies pursued by the reformers; but it was also a social democratic party, although one with few links to the working class. The party seemed locked in a trajectory of gentle decline, hence following the 1999 election it discussed some form of alliance with the Union of Rightist Forces, although in both the 2003 and 2007 elections the parties fought separately. This had a disastrous effect in 2003, and neither party in 2003 and 2007 crossed the PR threshold to enter parliament. Of the other groups, only a limited number could be considered parties as such. One of these was the Liberal Democratic Party of Russia (LDPR), headed by the flamboyant Zhirinovsky. In the early 1990s the party was rampantly nationalist and imperialist, in the sense that it sought to recreate the USSR, but by the end of the decade it had lost some of its fire and, indeed, had become a steady supporter of the government in the Duma, a feature which continued under Putin.

*Project parties*

Rodina was established only four months before the 2003 election as a project party with the intention of stealing votes from the communists. It brought together the economist and former communist deputy Sergei Glaz'ev and Dmitry Rogozin, the founder of the Congress of Russian Communities (KRO) in the early 1990s. Rogozin had taken over as head of the international affairs committee of the Third Duma, and acted as the presidential representative on the Kaliningrad issue in negotiations over the transit regime with the enlarging EU. Rogozin was a vigorous defender of the rights of 'Russians abroad', above all in the former Soviet states. Glaz'ev's main innovation in the 2003 campaign was a distinctive brand of anti-oligarch populism, and in particular the idea for a 'natural rent' tax on energy producers, something along the lines of New Labour's 'windfall tax' of 1997. The Kremlin's divide and rule policy was more effective than anticipated, and Rodina was able to steal away a significant part of the communist electorate, winning 9.1 per cent of the vote. Positioned as a party of the 'patriotic left', Rodina appealed to the two core elements in the communist position: its leftism and its nationalism. Rodina's programme was based on 'social justice and economic growth'.[56] Fearful of its increased independence, in 2004 the Kremlin provoked various splits until it finally became part of Just Russia in October 2006.

*Regime parties*

Party forms of representation have traditionally been over-shadowed in Russia by the predominance of conglomerate pseudo-parties like Our Home is Russia (NDR) in 1995 and Unity in 1999. These were typical regime parties, known as 'parties of power'. Unity was neither a modern political party nor a mass movement but was instead a political association made to order by power elites to advance their interests. United Russia combined the administrative resources of the state with an ideology of liberal patriotism, and occupied the centre-right niche in the political spectrum. The initial base of United Russia (Unity) was regional officialdom, with the 39 founding governors (mostly not of the first rank) in autumn 1999 swelled by new cohorts once the success of the body became clear. In December 2001 the merger of Unity with Fatherland-All Russia and some other groups gave birth to United Russia, and by March 2006 the party had registered its one millionth member and boasted of recruiting its second million in time for the elections of December 2007. United Russia cannot be characterised as the ruling party under Putin, since in Russia the parliamentary majority does not form the government. It was the party *of* power, but not a party *in* power. The party dominated parliament and pushed through the regime's legislative agenda. United Russia's dominance meant that membership became essential not only for a political career but also for a bureaucratic one.

The experience of earlier 'parties of power' in the 1990s was not encouraging for the long-term viability of UR. Earlier incarnations, notably 'Democratic Choice' (although it was less a 'party of power' and more a programme party since it had a clear ideology and an independent status) and 'Our Home is Russia', rapidly faded away once their sponsors lost political office. Fearing that UR would share the fate of earlier dominant parties once Putin stepped down in 2008, the deputy head of the PA responsible for party development, Vladislav Surkov, warned its party activists on 7 February 2006 that 'United Russia's task is not just to win in 2007 but to think how to achieve the party's dominance over the next 10–15 years'. Surkov warned the party that it would have to 'reduce its dependence on administrative resources' and would have to 'master the habits of ideological battle'.[57] The party would have to find new ways of ensuring that it remained meaningful for its membership, united on little else other than loyalty to Putin, and attractive to voters in the country. If the door to dominant regime party status was closed, then it would have to transform itself into a full-scale programme party.

Until the creation of Just Russia it looked as if Unity (or its equivalent) would become the core of a new type of hegemonic party system in which patronage and preference would be disbursed by a neo-*nomenklatura* class of state officials loyal to Putin. The party of power was becoming the party of patronage as well. It appeared to be treading the well-worn path towards becoming a dominant regime-party, like the PRI in Mexico between 1929 and 2000, or even in Japan after 1955 and Italy during the period of Christian Democratic predominance up to 1992. United Russia looked like becoming the core of a patronage system of the type that in July 2000 was voted out of office in Mexico after 71 years. From 2003, moreover, United Russia began to take on more competitive qualities as it sought to broaden its political base and enhance it popular legitimacy. As it becomes ever more a hybrid *programme-regime* party it may just gain sufficient staying power to survive Putin's departure from office. The creation of

Just Russia was designed to balance UR from a centre-left perspective, and thus moved straight into the programme-regime stage of development. The creation of JR constrained the development of UR into a dominant party.

For some in the Kremlin, an excessively strong UR was to be feared as much as a weak UR was for others, and this was one factor behind the creation of yet another regime party, this time intended to represent the centre-left part of the political spectrum. If Surkov was behind the development of UR, the new grouping was apparently sponsored by the *siloviki*. The formal merger of Rodina (Motherland) with the Party of Life and the Party of Pensioners took place at a congress on 28 October 2006 to create the new party, Just Russia. The number of parties eligible to fight the 2007 elections was reduced to 17. The new party was headed by the speaker of the Federation Council and the former head of the Party of Life, Sergei Mironov, while Alexander Babakov, the former chairman of Rodina, became secretary of the new party's central council presidium. Mironov spoke of the party winning half a million members by the 2007 elections, although the experience of his leadership of the Party of Life did not inspire confidence that this could be achieved. Like Rodina in 2003, the aim was to wean away part of the membership and electorate from the Communists and Zhirinovsky's Liberal Democrats, and thus there was a project party facet to the new organisation. Just Russia declared its support for Putin, but advanced a socialist programme in contrast to UR's centre-right programme, and thus tried to identify itself more as a 'party of the people' than a party of power.

The creation of the new party had the potential to create a more competitive party environment, one taking on aspects of a classic two-party system. Although built from the top down, regional and national elections became ever more structured by the tension between these two regime parties. By dint of the need to develop popular support, with the threat of administrative resources being withdrawn following Putin's departure, these two parties became ever more programme-regime parties.

## Problems of social representation

The political and social environment attending the emergence of a party system in Russia is reminiscent of the early US experience. The American constitution from the beginning was explicitly biased against parties, termed factions by James Madison. To the present day the two major US parties act as loose coalitions rather than as the disciplined and structured parliamentary parties of the classic West European sort. Emerging from the suffocating tutelage of the Communist Party, such anti-party views fell on fertile ground in Russia. Years of communist dominance had 'discredited the very concept of "party"'.[58] In his book *Rebuilding Russia* Solzhenitsyn argued against party politics, to allow the organic fabric of community to develop. He noted that

> Party rivalry distorts the national will. The principle of party-mindedness necessarily involves the suppression of individuality, and every party reduces and coarsens the personal element. An individual will have views, while a party offers an ideology.[59]

In the event, associational life and representative institutions developed rapidly, but of a distinctive type. The representative system and the regime operated largely independently; Putin sought to close the gap, but the basic result was simply the establishment of a new type of regime hegemony that incorporated parties into an expanded and revived governmental process.

Democratic theory speaks of representative democracy but it is party democracy that is most commonly meant, focusing above all on competition between parties to win votes and form governments. While the age of mass parties may everywhere be in decline, the political party as a representative institution remains central to any model of democratic institutionalisation. Classical analyses, notably that of Stein Rokkan, attribute the features of emerging party systems to the cleavage lines generated by the great processes of nation and state-building: workers and capitalists, church and state, centre and periphery, giving rise to certain categories of parties (socialist, Christian, conservative, liberal and so on), although the correspondence between the cleavage and a particular party may be based on any number of independent variables.[60] In post-communist Russia the lines of such a cleavage structure are blurred to the point of illegibility. Instead, identity, ideological and interest conflicts interact in unpredictable ways and mostly do not line up to reinforce each other. In fact, the very opposite appears to be the case, with political affiliations torn by cross-cutting concerns. Identity conflicts, for example, are particularly pronounced in the ethnic republics, but they are reinforced neither by economic interests nor by ideological concerns and hence remain relatively marginal. In addition, mechanisms of patronage and political clientelism are divorced from the party system,[61] and thus one of the main factors that promotes party development elsewhere is largely absent in Russia.

According to Rokkan, there is an extraordinary continuity in the political alignments and party systems in Europe between those of the 1920s and the 1960s, suggesting that parties first in the game capture most of the resources available for support (voter loyalty, programmes and so on) leaving the system 'frozen' and making it very difficult for new parties to break in, irrespective of the changes that may have transformed society.[62] Rokkan suggested differing processes of political mobilisation between the establishment phase of party alignment and the continuity phase, with changes later tending to be channelled through existing parties rather than through the establishment of new ones. Russia is still far from this, and rather than being 'frozen' Russia's party scene remains fluid.

The type of resources available for party formation has shaped the party system. In the insurgency phase mobilisation took place largely on ideological grounds, whereas later this shifted to a variety of forms but was marked by the weakness of organised social groups in civil society coming together to seek political representation. Instead, parties drew on the organisational resources of the state itself, with various ministries providing the organisational resources for a number of parties. Attempts to seek independent support raised the profile of a number of 'oligarchs', but following the assault on Khodorkovsky and the Yukos oil company in 2003, this source of support (at least openly), dried up. The Kremlin strictly controlled the resources available for party development, apart from that coming in clandestinely from exiled oligarchs such as Berezovsky. Those groups fortunate enough to enter the Duma were able to draw on the administrative and technical resources allowed deputies (up to five advisers paid by the state, plus secretarial and other help) to promote the development of the associations to which they belonged. Insiders carved out areas of concern and resources to further their own political ends. The role of prominent personalities, often with access to sources of financial support, is striking. Although most parties had adapted to the conventions of parliamentary politics, they had also succumbed to intrigue-ridden regime-dominated politics. This dual adaptation under Putin began to give way to a rather more formalised, although some feared not necessarily more democratic, system.

Party development in Russia reflects, in an exaggerated form, processes common to most post-communist countries.[63] How can we explain the under-developed character of Russian party development? Is there something specifically post-totalitarian inhibiting the development of an effective party system, or is the problem broader, reflecting a general crisis of party systems in mature industrial democracies? We can identify eleven factors that inhibit the development of an effective party and representative system in Russia: Russian history and political culture; the provenance of parties as part of the insurgency against the decaying communist regime; the character of the state; presidential patterns of politics and governance; the existence of party substitutes; the electoral system; parliamentary politics and government formation; the regionalisation of politics; the post-totalitarian legacy of a fragmented society; the social bases of partisan alignment; and the general crisis of parties and organised interests in modern societies. Having said this, we should immediately add the caveat that the role of parties and organised interests in post-communist Russia has been far from negligible: they remain important actors in parliamentary and presidential elections.

### *History and political culture*

Post-communist party formation has much in common with Russia's first attempt to establish a multi-party system between 1905 and 1917. The dominance of individuals, the relative lack of influence on government, shifting leadership alliances, poor ties with the mass membership, wild sloganeering and the tendency for abstract ideological demands to take the place of immediate political programmes, are all comparable with the earlier period.[64] In addition, the upsurge of party formation and hopes for the constitutional development of politics between 1904 and 1907 was ultimately inhibited by the reconstitution of imperial power;[65] and likewise the insurgency phase of party formation up to 1991 was eventually constrained by the emergence of regime politics. The way that the Bolsheviks, being only one among many political parties, were able to come to power and establish a one-party system, remains a warning of what might come of Russia's bacchanalia of party formation and mutation.[66] According to a survey from 1917 to 1990, the central feature of Russian party formation has been the absence of a broad social basis and the effect of an archaic unity (in both Tsarist and Bolshevik guises), combined with state dominated forms of industrial development.[67]

It is often asserted that Russian political culture is hostile to the emergence of political parties because of a popular commitment to collective values and a predilection for a single authoritative source of political authority.[68] As Stephen Welch has pointed out, however, political culture is far more malleable than sometimes suggested, and in place of the traditional static approach suggests a dynamic model stressing the evolutionary dynamics of political culture.[69] This is illustrated by the case of America where, as noted, the political culture was originally hostile to parties but gradually a party system became accepted.[70] In Russia, too, traditional appeals to collectivism, both of the traditional Russian sort (*sobornost*) or of the Soviet communist variety, do not necessarily undermine ideological cleavages and policy preferences taking the form of partisan alignment. The experience of over a decade of free multi-party elections suggests that the Russian voter is as sensitive to party affiliations as electors in any other country even though, as we have suggested above, this may not take the form of voting for the same party from one election to the next. The extraordinary stability of electoral preferences, with roughly a third of the vote from one election to the next supporting the left nationalist opposition, and a fifth the liberal democrats, suggests the presence of the political base for a two-party system.

### The legacy of insurgency

The formative phase of a social formation is crucial, and never more so than in the case of Russia's transition from communism. As Golosov notes, the roots of the fragmented and undeveloped party system lie in its genesis.[71] Insurgency politics left its mark on Russian party formation. The manner in which the old regime dissolved gave rise to a distinctive establishment phase. The legacy of the unprecedented concentration of political power and claims to ideological predominance by the CPSU provided an inauspicious terrain for parties to claim a share in power. Post-communist Russian politics does not operate on a *tabula rasa* but where traditional social institutions and groups try to preserve their position while challenged by new social actors. The deceptive ease and the incomplete way in which the old regime finally fell masked the resilience of the former structures, both formal (e.g. the *nomenklatura* elite) and informal (mafia-type structures).

During *perestroika* the negative connotations of the concept of 'party' led many groups to call themselves 'unions', 'movements' or 'associations'. The fluid politics associated with the insurgency phase continued into later years, with few associations imposing rigorous membership criteria, or even maintaining membership registers. Insurgency politics were characterised by the weakness of the link between parties and political representation in legislative bodies. A great mass of deputies were swept into the soviets as part of the democratic tide of 1989–90, yet once elected they lacked a structured political identity and as a mass reflected the amorphous character of the party system in its entirety. Insurgency politics were marked by the ability of small groups and leaders to achieve victories and prestige with relatively small organisational, membership and, indeed, financial, resources. Parties until well into the post-communist era remained stamped by the formative stage and largely remained elitist organisation with a fairly small mass base and fluid organisational structures. The major legacy of the politics of insurgency is the gulf between the elite (above all those elected to legislative bodies) and the mass membership.

### The character of the state: institutional design

The character of state formation following communism was crucial in establishing the context for party development. As M. Steven Fish notes of the *perestroika* period, the nature of political groups was determined largely by 'the character of state power'. Ideas and the convictions of individual politicians played a minimal role, while the critical legacy of a society thoroughly permeated by an activist state was determining.[72] Post-communist Russian state-building proved inimical to the conversion of the insurgent political formations into genuine political parties. The state did little to assist the development of parties or a party system, and little came of Yeltsin's promise to provide assistance at a meeting with the leaders of 15 of the largest parties on 12 December

1991.[73] The institutional framework of post-communist politics, moreover, inhibited the development of a functioning party system, with the government chosen, as we have seen, on a non-party basis. Above all, the gulf between the representative system and the regime and the thorough bureaucratisation of social relations inhibited the political organisation of sectional interests. According to Kulik, issues of institutional design, above all the separation of powers, party legislation and the electoral system, inhibited the 'programmisation' of parties, and thus even the so-called 'parties of power' remained 'under power' rather than allowing them to be 'in power'.[74]

### Presidential politics

Presidential systems in the best of circumstances tend to inhibit the emergence of party government, while Yeltsin's insistence on the non-party essence of presidential rule further reduced its potential. Yeltsin's first act on being elected chairman of the Russian Congress on 29 May 1990 was to suspend his membership of *Demrossiya*, insisting that he would defend 'the interests not of separate groups or parties or organisations but the interests of the peoples of the Russian Federation'.[75] On resigning his CPSU membership on the last day of the Twenty-eighth Congress in July 1990 Yeltsin declared that he would join no party and declared himself to be above party politics. *Demrossiya* had provided crucial support for Yeltsin's presidential victory in June 1991, yet his victory did not lead to its consolidation as the 'party of power', or indeed, to its consolidation as a party at all. Yeltsin clearly felt more at ease working through his own 'team' free of political or social control, and his claim to be president of all Russians only strengthened the tendency towards charismatic above-party leadership. In the presidential elections of 1996 Yeltsin ran as an independent, as did Putin in 2000 and 2004 and Medvedev in 2008.

The development of a hegemonic presidency undermined party development. The representative system, epitomised by parties, is largely divorced from the process of forming governments. The very structure of government is inimical to the development of a party system, with the premier and cabinet chosen on a non-party basis and forced to resign their seats as deputies on appointment. The idea was to maintain the separation of powers, but this rather crude principle, typical of presidential systems, only divorced the power and representative systems from each other, and weakened the accountability and responsibility of both.

### Party substitutes

Despite numerous political parties, none have become fully institutionalised as part of the operation of the polity. Quite why this is the case is explained by Henry Hale's ingenious theory of party substitutes. He takes a market approach, arguing that the political capital enjoyed by parties can be divided into two, 'administrative' and 'ideational', and on that basis identifies four types of party: programmatic, clientelistic, ideational and minor. The supply and demand of political parties is examined in that framework, but he adds another crucial variable – the existence of party substitutes that can act as alternative electoral actors. Thus the prerogatives usually ascribed to parties, above all formulating and channelling political demands, in Russia was undertaken by party substitutes, notably regional parties and business bosses. In this light, Putin's reform of the party system is interpreted as a way of destroying the party substitutes that came so close to taking power in 1999 (which rather 'spooked' the Kremlin) and not as an end in itself, to strengthen parties as autonomous actors.[76] Hale argues that parties have played a larger role in Russian politics than is sometimes allowed, in particular in electoral politics, although some of the dynamism had stalled by the end of the 1990s, only to pick up again from 2003 once party substitutes had been undermined. While Putin was careful to ensure that the presidency remained in control of the policy agenda, a terrain in which party substitutes have been weakened may allow the law of unintended consequences to come into play, and parties may in due course be able to assert themselves against the executive to claim an independent role in the polity.

### The electoral system

The institutional design of an electoral system lies at the heart of a new democratic system.[77] The attempt to manipulate the electoral system to encourage the consolidation of effective electoral parties proved only partially successful. The version of the electoral law presented to the Constitutional Assembly in June 1993 by a group of experts led by the deputy Victor Sheinis proposed a mixed system on the German model of direct constituency elections and party lists, intended precisely to encourage the development of a party system.[78] The introduction of the party-list system for the election of half the deputies to the State Duma, although designed to stimulate the creation of solid political parties, in practice accelerated the fragmentation of the party system. The 1995 electoral rules, for example, allowed only twelve Moscow politicians on the party list, encouraging those lower down the list to form their own electoral blocs.

The mixed plurality and proportional electoral system used in Russia up to 2003 has certain political consequences, some of which have been noted above. It has been argued that 'a proportional system in a country with an undeveloped civil society only impedes the growth of genuine multi-partyness'.[79] The establishment of electoral blocs allowed numerous small parties, which independently would not have been able to cross the 5 per cent threshold, to gain seats in the new Duma. The formation of associations to fight elections was governed by one logic – the attraction of star leaders, the search for campaign sponsors and the like – which does not correspond to the logic of genuine party formation: the patient consolidation of regional organisations, the honing of a programme and the establishment of a permanent central staff. Electoral pacts undermined the development of a normal parliamentary party system. In response to this the new electoral and party laws of 2001 allow only registered parties to fight elections. As for the single-member districts, parties did not fight the majority of seats in the constituencies, and party affiliation made little difference to the vote. In all three Duma elections in the 1990s a large proportion of all constituency deputies were elected as independent deputies rather than by party affiliation, and this was then reflected in the relative fluidity of factions in the Duma. This fluidity was exacerbated by the lack of continuity in the choice of parties offering themselves up for votes from one election to the next. Instead of parties in search of an electorate, an electorate in search of parties emerged. The shift to a wholly proportional electoral system and the seven per cent representation threshold in the 2007 election, combined with other innovations in the norms of party development, may well consolidate the role of a small number of parties.

### Parliamentary politics and government formation

Just as the engineers of democracy sought to mould the electoral system to promote party development, so, too, there were attempts to shape the working arrangements of the State Duma to create cohesive party groups. The weakness of party factions in the Congress of People's Deputies was widely considered to be one reason for it having been captured by radicals in the phoney democracy period. In the Duma there are strict rules about the minimum number of deputies required to form a group (35 at first, later 55), and only those parties crossing the 5 (7) per cent threshold have the right to call themselves party factions. Parliamentary committees are formed on the party principle, although there was a shift from a proportional to a majoritarian system. The rules governing Duma organisation are designed to support party politics, but these attempts were undermined by the nature of Russia's political system. The upper house of the Federal Assembly, the Federation Council, in the form in which it existed up to 2001, was based not on party but on regional representation.

Parties fight elections, but in Russia they do not fight elections to form the government. As we have seen, there is no direct correlation between representation in parliament and the colour of the government. Instead, a syncretic political process predominated. Extensive individual cooptation, personalised ties and a relatively fluid party system, mean that the distinction between parties in government and those in opposition was unclear. Russia's Choice was established as the party of government, yet ministers in that very same government were members of opposition parties. In the 1995 elections Russia Our Home managed the remarkable feat of presenting itself as the party of government while at the same time criticising the shortcomings of that very same government. The CPRF had tacitly supported Chernomyrdin's government on several occasions, and during Primakov's premiership in effect became part of the governing coalition. Voters, understandably were often confused by the 'choice' offered to them, and even more so since the relationship between parties and the government, let alone the government and the presidency, was not always clear. Various extra-constitutional accords and fora were established as part of Yeltsin's attempts to incorporate active political forces into a dynamic and mobile form of consensus politics run firmly from the top. It appeared that Yeltsin, quite simply, did not understand the principles on which a multi-party system operates. Under Putin the Duma and Federation Council were joined by para-constitutional bodies like the State Council and Public Chamber (see below), reducing the primacy of parliament. Neither of the two innovations featured parties.

### Regionalism and party politics

The Russian party system is highly fragmented and its reach is partial. Historically, parties have emerged as the coalition of local or sectional interests that have only later been aggregated at the national level. In post-communist Russia regionally based parties were weak and had minimal impact on national politics, until they were effectively phased out by Putin. Parties based on ethnic politics are wholly delegitimated. Most party formation in Russia has been top down, only reinforcing the tendency for much of politics to be conducted outside the framework of party politics, whether national or local. One of the reasons for this is the fragmentation of political space itself. Under Yeltsin a rich variety of regional political systems and regimes emerged, ranging from the democratic to the outright authoritarian, and national parties had to accommodate themselves to local circumstances. Local name recognition and political capital derived from non-partisan sources are often as important as organisation in regional elections.

One and the same party label could mean very different things to people in various parts of the country until Putin's reforms forced the creation of more genuinely national party organisations. Nevertheless, even the national parties have distinctive regional identities. No single party could hope to encompass the regional, national, ethnic, class, group, elite and other cleavages in society, and nor could a single party mediate the multiple social forces, processes and ideologies that buffeted intellectual life. The sheer size of the country made it difficult to constitute a genuinely national party penetrating not only the major cities but also provincial towns, rural areas and the national republics. Regional elites had incentives to exploit personal connections and to cultivate local sponsors than to devote their energies to the long-term strategy of building up party organisations. Putin's attempts to homogenise Russia's political and legal space created a more auspicious environment for the development of a national party system. The stipulation that half the members of regional assemblies have to be elected by PR galvanised party life in the regions. The emergence of United Russia as the putative hegemonic national party has the potential to transform the Russian party scene by bringing together power and electoral maximisation strategies of governing elites while provoking the counter-mobilisation of oppositional parties on a national scale even if kick-started from above, as was the case with Just Russia. A classic two-party system may yet emerge.

### The post-totalitarian society

Whereas in most post-communist Central European and Baltic countries functioning national party systems based on the classic left-right division have become consolidated, in Russia, where communism lasted much longer and with greater intensity, only a glimmer of such a consolidation is evident. The legacy of the unprecedented concentration of political power and claims to ideological predominance by the CPSU provided an inauspicious terrain for parties to claim a share in power. We have noted the popular 'anti-party' mood, but the problem was deeper. Traditional social institutions, groups and practices are deeply embedded despite the formal change of political regime, and new social forces and democratic social institutions (above all political parties) remain superficial. In post-communist countries political and social structuration takes distinctive forms. Classic theories of party development connected particular interests with party alignment, but Russia's post-totalitarian social structure blurred the link between party choice and socio-economic structure. However, the correlation existed, as evidenced for example by the consistent support of the agrarian sector for the CPRF (until 2007) and of young upwardly mobile urbanites for Yabloko and other liberal parties. In general, though, Kulik accurately identified the emergence of a vicious circle in which parties developed but were weak because of the 'post-totalitarian condition of Russia', while society could not be democratically integrated into the state without powerful parties.[80]

The weakness of the state and the regime's personalised style of rule, moreover, encouraged the development of a type of mimetic pluralism where political bargaining takes informal forms, above all within relatively narrow elite circles, and subverts institutionalised patterns of interest aggregation. Political integration tends to bypass political parties, and mechanisms whereby parties can be integrated into the governmental process remain undeveloped. The mass mobilisation that does take place is derived not from social cleavages but from the organisational capacity of 'political machines'.[81] In short, the post-communist psychological atmosphere, social structure and political processes inhibit party development. Socio-economic and other social interests acted directly on the state without the mediation of traditional 'gatekeeper' organisations like parties. In these circumstances the running of 'party' elections in an atomised and essentially 'non-party' country could not but have perverse consequences. Few parties represented the interests of specific social groups, although gradually programmatic crystallisation has taken place and the outlines of a traditional political spectrum along which parties align is beginning to emerge.

### Social interests and partisan representation

Schmitter argues that substantial changes have taken place in the role and nature of parties in established Western democracies, and that it would be anachronistic to assume 'that parties in today's neodemocracies will have to go through all the stages and perform all the functions of their predecessors'.[82] The secular-religious divide appears in a new light in post-communist conditions, although in the West, too, party alignments derived from this cleavage are waning. In Russia the Orthodox Church had acquiesced in its own subservience to the regime, and this ambiguity tended to undermine its political and moral authority in the post-communist period. Even in Poland where the Catholic Church had been unambiguous in its call for political openness, the advanced secularisation of society prevented the emergence of a serious religiously based party in the aftermath of Solidarity.

Socialist movements of the classical sort have also had their day; they appear a phenomenon of the late nineteenth to the late twentieth century and inappropriate for the challenges facing the world in the twenty-first century. A response to modernisation, industrialisation and the onset of mass society and a reflection of resistance to the market economy and the secularisation and individualisation of social life, the apparent triumph of liberalism has left the distinctive features of alternative politics without an anchor. Attitudes do not line up with partisan alignment, as the various attempts to establish a mass social democratic party demonstrate. As Fyodor Gavrilov put it:

> The average Russia voter is a textbook social democrat. He's in favor of the market, but with broad social guarantees. He's for civil rights, but as long as they're vigorously enforced by the state. He supports the family, but he's for the right to abortion and divorce.[83]

But the average Russian elector does not vote for the various social democratic parties on offer. Both Christian and social democracy were responses to the traumas accompanying the rise of market capitalism but have found it difficult to sustain alternative policies in mature industrial societies. The Russian voter was offered a number of social democratic parties, including Gorbachev's United Social Democratic Party, but few voted for them.

In Russia, of course, the capitalist social formation is only now emerging and the problem is inverted: if in the West capitalism has matured and, on the whole, delivers the goods, in Russia it is difficult to organise against a capitalism which is struggling to be born and that may one day deliver Western standards of prosperity. This 'ideological' inhibition against militant anti-capitalist politics (shared in part even by the CPRF) is reinforced by the numerous structural and institutional constraints discussed above. Regime autonomy was sustained by its self-proclaimed modernising mission; allegedly fulfilling tasks that were too important to be threatened by the vagaries of electoral politics. The monolithic character of the CPSU was reproduced in an inverted form by the emerging opposition movements, united only in their desire to destroy the communist monopoly. This negative unity was perpetuated after the fall of the regime by a commitment to the broad principle of creating a market system in Russia, and even those movements which criticised capitalism were unable to sustain an effective alternative programme. Post-communist party formation was inhibited by the 'post-historical' period in which it was born, where the great ideologies associated with modernity have given way to an individualised politics of identity, self-satisfaction and, in the case of the CPRF, by a retrogressive vision of Russian nationalism.

The absence of a recognisable social base to the new political parties was perhaps the single most important factor inhibiting the development of party politics.[84] Parties in Russia suffer a two-fold estrangement: from the social and political interests that they claim to represent; and from the coherent formulation of a forward-looking policy taking into account actually existing realities rather than an ideologised version of what should be. This double disassociation inhibits the consolidation of a coherent governing coalition or an effective opposition. The disjuncture between marrying an ideology to an organisation and a social group was stark, weakening the institutions of political society. The absence of social subjects able to express their interests reinforced the role of leadership and personalities. Ludmilla Alekseeva, for example, notes that 'The role of political parties among workers is extremely small'.[85] In an ironic version of 'catching up and overtaking', and indeed of 'combined and uneven development', post-communist Russia displayed the symptoms of an advanced 'postmodern' social structure in a society whose 'modernity' remained archaic. It is this 'modernisation without modernity' that we label mismodernisation (see Chapter 19).

The actual structure of the Russian social terrain, however, is extraordinarily complex. Post-communist political life is even more fractured than the 'postmodern' and 'post-industrial' societies of the West. The extreme pluralism that emerged in these conditions gave rise to a permanently fragmented party system and an unstable democratic politics.[86] While numerous groups existed, it is probably premature to talk of interest group politics: few generated a homogeneous 'interest' and party politics was not as yet 'sub-system dominant'. The weakness of the state did not necessarily mean the strength of society but indicated a general crisis of political institutions and civil associations in post-communist Russia.

### The general crisis of parties and partisan representation

Party development in Russia reflects only in more extreme form what some have identified as the 'unfreezing', if not general crisis, of parties in European politics.[87] The shift from materialist to post-materialist preferences in the value system of voters and the apparent decline in the role of parties as such, eclipsed by new forms of participation such as social movements and alternative forms of political communication (such as television), have given rise to a new volatility in established party systems.[88] Although there is much evidence to suggest overall stability in party systems,[89] the end of the Cold War has promoted increased fluidity in some party systems. The 'end of ideology', the thesis advanced by Daniel Bell in the late 1950s[90] and taken up by Francis Fukuyama in the form of the 'end of history',[91] promoted a more managerial approach to social development, while ideology itself, as reflected in party programmes and manifestos, became more symbolic rather than a guide to action.

Everywhere the old cleavage between left and right is blurred, the left itself has taken on new forms, and the era of ideological mass parties appears over.[92] The fusion of information and communications technology has accelerated the creation of 'virtual' communities in which politics has become even more spectral, reduced to the level of images and attractions that have little relation to the realities of public life.[93] Jacques Derrida argues that the media has rendered the professional politician 'structurally incompetent' by generating a set of demands associated with performance on air and image projection that displaces parties and parliaments.[94] Parties in general, from this perspective, appear obsolete as vehicles of popular mobilisation, regional and national identity formation, individual development, and, in the Russian context, even as instruments of power. In contrast to the 'golden age' of parties from the late nineteenth century to the 1970s, the contemporary era is marked by a plurality of competing forms of political representation (in particular, single-issue pressure groups), and the space in which parties operate has changed dramatically. The electronic media acts as the functional equivalent of political parties, able to mobilise an electorate and substitute for a network of party committees. The traditional baggage of political organisation and nationally organised political parties appears dispensable when an effective performance and advertisements on the silver screen count for so much – as American politicians long ago realised.

# 8    Electoral politics

Divide the electorate, unite the nation.

(Vladislav Surkov)[1]

Elections play a necessary part in the development of a democratic society, but they are not sufficient to denote the achievement of democracy, defined as popular control over the executive through effective representation in a legislature. Between 1989 and 2008 Russia saw fourteen competitive national elections and three national referendums. In that time the institutional framework for elections has changed considerably, with electoral legislation constantly changing, while there has been only limited continuity in the choice of parties facing the voter. However, certain behavioural patterns have emerged that are repeated from one electoral cycle to the next. At the same time, despite all the vicissitudes of electoralism, the legitimacy of the new political order is firmly rooted in the popular validation achieved through the ballot box. Russia's electoral politics, however, are constrained and relatively isolated from power relations. In terms of *succession*, changes of government and even the presidency appear disconnected from the outcome of elections in anything other than formal terms. In terms of *accountability*, both at the federal and regional level, elections have been rather more free than fair, with the electoral process often distorted by asymmetries in financial, administrative and power resources.

## Founding elections and electoral management

Although results have more or less accurately reflected electoral preferences, elections have been marred by numerous abuses. Elections in Russia reflect the hybrid nature of the political system. Democratic processes in the centre co-exist uncomfortably with a presidential regime that is to a degree self-perpetuating and in the regions with a variety of regime types that try to subordinate electoral processes to administrative control. Dual adaptation meant that the regime was to a degree constrained by electoralism but at the same time was able to restrict the free operation of electoral uncertainty.

### Founding elections

Competitive, if not yet multi-party, elections were the centrepiece of Gorbachev's liberal-isation programme. Rather than relegitimising the Soviet system, however, they acted as a powerful vector contributing to its dissolution. The first attempt at competitive elections was in the local soviet elections of 1987, where some 5 per cent of seats were fought in multi-candidate contests.[2] The elections in spring 1989 to the new USSR Congress of People's Deputies marked an important new stage in competitive elections, but the choices were limited (see Table 1.1). The spring 1990 elections to the new Russian CPD (Chapter 1) revealed the depth of popular hostility to the old regime. The actual operation of the new 'parliaments', moreover, revealed the limitations of '*perestroika* democracy', a legacy that also impeded the development of genuine parliamentarianism in Russia later. Gorbachev, moreover, did *not* place himself before the people in March 1990, and instead was selected as president by the Soviet Congress. The 'disconnect' between electoral cycles and executive power was already evident.

The Russian parliamentary election of 4 March 1990 (with the second round on 18 March) marked an important moment in the 'insurgency phase' of the democratic opposition and, of greater long-term importance, the shaping of a distinctively Russian political identity. The vessel of democratic politics was no longer the USSR but 'Russia', or as the democrats tended to put it at the time, 'the country'. Only Russia retained the two-tier legislature, and the election was to a 1,068-member CPD, which in turn selected a smaller Supreme Soviet responsible for current parliamentary matters. Constitutional and other high policy matters were the prerogative of the full Congress.

Following widespread criticism of the 1989 elections, the electoral system was modified to remove some of the filters on the nomination of candidates, abolishing the pre-electoral district meetings and the bloc of seats reserved for 'social organisations'.[3] This allowed a wave of independent candidates to be nominated, supported by numerous voters' associations established in the wake of the disappointments of the previous year. This did not prevent numerous violations, with nominated independent candidates arbitrarily being refused registration, their names being deleted from the ballots, and with fraudulent counting in areas beyond the supervision of independent observers. The democrats' strength lay in industrial regions and cities, whereas in rural areas, where neo-feudal relations had emerged, local Party and collective farm (*kolkhoz*) officials were able to deliver the vote for their candidates.[4] There is little evidence, however, of widespread fraud, especially since the electorate had become more politicised since the previous year, partly by the spectacle of the televised Soviet CPD debates. A dual adaptation took place: of communist elites to democratic procedures; and democratic procedures to the constraints of regime politics. This is a characteristic feature of the transition in Russia, a theme to which we have already alluded.

The notion of a founding election figures prominently in the literature on transition,[5] but in Russia the issue is by no means clear cut. The elections of 1989 to the Soviet CPD represented an enormous step towards the introduction of competitive politics, but the absence of party choices and the limits to campaigning hardly allow this to be reckoned Russia's 'founding' election. Much the same can be said about the Russian republican elections in March 1990, although the subject now at least was Russia proper. The absence, indeed, of a founding election in the 'phoney democracy' period immediately following the change of regime in August 1991 and the disintegration of the USSR later that year had a deep impact on the shape of Russia's struggling democracy, retarding party development and allowing a state system to consolidate itself relatively insulated from popular control. The Russian election of December 1993 was in effect the founding election; but it did not entail a change of government and was held in an atmosphere of extreme polarisation; the electoral law was imposed by decree rather than legislative consultation.

Rather than identifying any single event as the founding election, it may be best to consider all of the elections held so far as part of an extended process of democratic habituation and adaptation. The hybrid nature of Russian democracy is reflected in the absence of a founding election, and each electoral cycle has reinforced electoralism as the preferred mode of legitimating authority. Electoral politics have limited the choices of the regime and, however imperfect the procedures, determined the nature of Russia's emergence from communism. While the elections may have been flawed, the commitment to electoral politics precluded some of the harsher options. Chinese-type authoritarian modernisation was excluded once *perestroika* legalised political contestation. Gorbachev's own attempts to control the transition within the framework of 'managed democracy', retaining a leading although modified role for the Communist Party, shattered under the impact of electoral defeats and the emergence of parliamentary assemblies legitimised by the popular vote. Gorbachev's own refusal to accept the electoral challenge when taking on the post of Soviet president weakened his legitimacy, whereas Yeltsin's clear victory in the Russian presidential elections of June 1991 gave him the popular mandate to face down the coup attempt and ultimately to challenge Gorbachev himself.

### *Central Electoral Commission (CEC)*

The Central Electoral Commission (CEC) was established to regulate the 1993 election, and afterwards it became a permanent agency. Dubbed 'the ministry of elections', the CEC monitors the whole electoral process.[6] The CEC consists of 15 members: 5 chosen by the president, 5 by the State Duma, and 5 by the Federation Council. Elections from 1993 were supervised by CEC head Nikolai Ryabov, whose watch was accompanied by persistent allegations of electoral fraud. His replacement following the 1996 presidential elections, Alexander Ivanchenko, was considered a more independent figure, but presided over numerous regional electoral scandals. He was replaced in turn in March 1999 by Alexander Veshnyakov, who presided over major changes to the electoral system until the endless tinkering with the system became even too much for him, and he was replaced as head of the CEC in March 2007 by Vladimir Churov. Churov is a former member of the LDPR and a physicist by training with no legal background. It appears that his main recommendation for the post is that he hails from St Petersburg and was Putin's former classmate. He made no secret of his view that 'Putin is always right', a rather disturbing echo of Boxer's slogan in Orwell's *Animal Farm*.

## The electoral system and its reform

Russia's electoral system has been subject to frequent changes, with the electoral legislation modified following every electoral cycle and becoming ever more detailed. If the first election law in 1994 was 29 pages long, the 2005 law now runs to 325. This has inhibited the routinisation of electoral conduct and voter expectations, with the terms of political trade in a state of constant flux. The parties chasing the votes of the citizen have also changed considerably between electoral cycles, the characteristic feature of a floating party system,[7] although continuity has strengthened over time. Already in 1995 Yeltsin had proposed that only a third of deputies should be elected from party lists, as part of his attempt to reduce communist representation. In 1997 he proposed that the Duma should be elected entirely from SMDs in two rounds, a motion defeated by the massed ranks of the existing Duma parties. In May 1999 Chernomyrdin suggested that the Duma should be dissolved and that the next Duma should be elected from SMDs alone. In the event, precisely the opposite system was introduced in 2004 and from 2007 a wholly proportional system was applied.

### Electoral engineering

Electoral systems are not neutral institutions but reflect society and the aspirations of the political elite. A fully proportional system is usually designed to ensure the sovereignty of parliamentary representation and its pre-eminence over the power of the executive. A majoritarian system, on the other hand, prioritises governmental stability and the relative autonomy of the executive. While proportional representation tries to *represent* the plurality of needs, demands and interests in society, a first-past-the-post electoral system seeks to *constrain* them in the name of governmental stability.[8] Russia tried to achieve both in one fell swoop, but failed effectively to achieve either. A majoritarian system is intended to achieve a parliamentary majority, but in Russia such a majority is to a degree irrelevant since the government, appointed by the president, is not directly accountable to parliament and is not based on the ability to muster a stable majority in parliament. Other than confirming the president's nomination for prime minister, the Duma's role is limited to legislative activity and the adoption of the budget. Proportional systems tend to lead to the fragmentation of parliamentary representation, and it is for this reason that the 5 (later 7) per cent representation threshold was introduced.

In the mixed system introduced in 1993, half the seats to the new 450-member State Duma were elected by the traditional first-past-the-post single-member districts (SMDs), but the other half were elected from party lists (PL) according to a weighted system of proportional representation. In order to be eligible to stand, a party or bloc required at least 100,000 nominations, with no more than 15,000 signatures drawn from any one of Russia's 89 regions and republics; the bloc or party had to have demonstrable support in at least 7 regions or republics. This provision was designed to stimulate the creation of a national party system, to overcome the proliferation of small parties, and to avoid the dominance of Moscow. To enter parliament on the PL system a party had to take at least 5 per cent of the national vote, with the whole country considered one giant constituency.

The electoral system for the State Duma differed from Soviet practices in three main ways. First, instead of a simple first-past-the-post system, a mixed proportional and majoritarian system was adopted, with half the seats to the 450-member Duma to be elected from single-member districts (SMDs) and the rest to be chosen on a proportional basis from federal party-lists (PL). This drew on German experience but was adapted to Russian conditions. The old majority electoral system used in Russia up to that time was unusual, with most other post-communist countries having reverted to the proportional systems prevalent before communism, and indeed the elections in November 1917 to the Russian Constituent Assembly had been proportional. Second, the method of nominating candidates was changed from the Soviet emphasis on labour collectives and gatherings of electors to a uniform system of collecting signatures. Candidates simply had to get enough signed support to be registered. Third, the subject of the electoral process changed from amorphous labour collectives to electoral associations and blocs. All three changes were intended to promote the development of a party-political system in Russia. The abolition of the second round in single-member districts was particularly criticised, but according to a study by Alexander Sobyanin it is unlikely that its retention would have made much difference to the results in December 1993.[9]

The electoral system was manipulated by reformers to promote specific goals, above all to encourage the development of a multi-party system.[10] The mixed proportional and constituency system, according to Victor Sheinis, one of its main architects, would not only foster a party system but also avoid 'an atomised parliament with factions like those we have today, representing no more than interest clubs'.[11] According to Ryabov, the proportional elections played a positive role 'in the development of the parties and movements themselves, assisting the development of multi-partyism in Russia'.[12] Others, however, argue that the electoral system worked more to strengthen parliamentary factions than parties.[13] As we have seen (Chapter 7), while voter alignment may have remained relatively stable, the fluidity in the parties available to express their preferences forced voters to choose anew in each electoral cycle.[14]

Although in the run-up to the 1999 election there was much talk of changing the electoral system, above all by abolishing the PL system and replacing it with all 450 deputies being elected from SMDs, a reform favoured by the presidency, only relatively minor changes were made to the electoral law.[15] The main change was to ensure on a sliding scale that at least 50 per cent of the votes cast in the PL part of the ballot is represented in the Duma. Scrutiny of candidates and signatures for party lists were more rigorous. Blocs could opt to lodge a deposit with the CEC rather than collecting the requisite 200,000 signatures, no more than 14,000 of which were permitted from any one region. Some two-thirds of parties and electoral associations, and a significant number of candidates in single-mandate constituencies, opted to pay a deposit rather than collect signatures.[16] The personal finances of candidates were to be examined in greater detail than ever before.[17] The 18 blocs that fell below the 2 per cent PL threshold had to repay the Central Electoral Commission funds allocated during the campaign and compensate the print and state and private electronic media for the free media exposure granted to all blocs on the ballot. In the event of non-payment they were barred from future elections. The 17 blocs that chose to place a monetary deposit to register for the ballot instead of collecting signatures and gained less than 3 per cent lost their deposits.

### Putin's reforms: first phase

The law on political parties adopted in 2001 had a profound impact on the electoral process, allowing only registered parties to stand and changing electoral finances (see Chapter 7). A new framework law on elections for parliament and the presidency was adopted on 12 June 2002, with specific laws for each, respectively, being signed into law by Putin in December 2002 and January 2003, and the whole package came into effect on 14 July 2003. Putin also signed into law the use of the automated vote counting system 'Vybory'. In keeping with the aim of raising the status of parties, only national parties now had the right to nominate candidates in federal and regional elections. The 2001 law still allowed the creation of political blocs, but these are now limited to three members, of which at least one had to be a political party. The amended party law of 2004 banned the creation of electoral blocs in their entirety, with the intention of forcing parties to merge to create more permanent viable electoral organisations. Individual citizens can still nominate themselves for office, but groups of voters are now deprived of this right, although in local elections non-political groups can still nominate candidates. Thus (starting with the 2007 parliamentary election) voter groups can no longer nominate candidates, and instead only candidates proposed by parties and individuals are allowed. The others have to collect two million signatures, with no more than 50,000 from any one region, a tough task for any party. There are much stricter rules requiring the full disclosure of a candidate's sources of financial support, a measure that will discourage independent candidates (those not belonging to a political party), while at the same time deterring candidates sponsored by criminal or other shady networks.

Parties entering parliament from 2003 enjoyed a number of new benefits. They are financed from the state budget according to the number of votes that they receive, and their candidates in later elections do not have to gather signatures or provide a deposit to participate. The law stipulated that at least three party list groups had to enter the 2003 Duma (up from the minimum of two earlier), leading to only 30 per cent of the electorate in the 2003 election not being represented in parliament. A 7 per cent representation threshold was put in place for the 2007 elections, approaching the Turkish level of 10 per cent. In the December 1995 elections 49.5 per cent of Russian voters failed to get the group they voted for elected. For this reason the new law stipulates that irrespective of the number of votes they obtain, a minimum of two parties have to enter parliament, but parties elected to the Duma must collect over 60 per cent of the vote between them. In regional elections, too, since December 2003 at least half of the seats in regional legislatures have to be elected through party lists, a move also intended to help structure public organisations.

Parties crossing the threshold to enter the Duma have the right to nominate a presidential candidate directly. Nominating parties and blocs gain extra free newspaper space and airtime, in addition to that granted to all candidates. Half of this goes to candidates and half to the nominating parties, thus giving an advantage to party-nominated candidates. The aim clearly is to focus political competition on probably no more than five major parties. These parties are intended to act as a counter-weight to regional executives if they are able to establish a powerful presence in regional legislatures, and at the national level they will counteract the influence of the oligarchs. One of them could sooner or later become the presidential party. The ability of electoral commissions and the courts to interfere in the electoral process by refusing to register or disqualifying candidates has been restricted. The causes that could provoke such actions have been pared down, and the right to cancel a candidate's registration for violating electoral legislation has been granted exclusively to the courts. This prerogative is itself limited and has to be done by a lower court at least five days before the election. Regional and local government authorities no longer form electoral commissions, and instead higher level electoral commissions form the district, territorial and ward electoral commissions as well as nominating their chairs (in the past the commissions had elected their own chairs). Regional and local government administrations establish the respective regional and local commissions as in the past, but these commissions now have two members appointed by the higher commission and the chairs of these commissions are chosen on the recommendation of the higher commission. The aim was to reduce the influence of regional and local governments on electoral commissions. As in other spheres, centralisation was intended to promote rather than to undermine democracy, although the outcome tended to be more centralisation and less democracy.

### Putin's reforms: second phase

In the wake of the massacre of schoolchildren at Beslan on 1–3 September 2004, Putin on 13 September announced a major electoral reform. He proposed that the whole Duma should be elected wholly through proportional representation (PR), thus abolishing representation from the 225 SMDs. He argued that a purely proportional electoral system would help achieve his long-term goal of reducing the number of small parties. It would also remove the bloc of independent deputies, elected from SMDs, who tended to be dependent on the governors. The great majority of the 67 'independent' deputies elected in 2003 joined United Russia. The mixed electoral system, and above all the SMDs, provided access to parliament for individuals and small parties and thus weakened the incentives for party consolidation. The measure was one of the ideas advanced by the CEC in earlier discussions, which included the idea that regional elections should be held twice a year (March and October) on the same day.[18] The new fully PR system threatened to weaken the predominance of United Russia, now deprived of the additional independent deputies. The Moscow Duma elections of December 2005 demonstrated the process at work: the 20 deputies elected by PR were shared between 3 parties, whereas United Russia took all 15 single-member seats.

The new electoral law passed its first reading on 24 December 2004, and after considerable debate was adopted on 18 May 2005.[19] Deputies balked at the idea that penalties should be imposed on parties whose top three national or leading regional candidates gave up their mandates. In response to OSCE criticisms of the 2003 election, the original plan was that candidates who had no intention of taking up their seat would not only lose their mandate, but the party would lose the seat as well, but the idea was defeated. The federal list was now reduced from 18 to three people, who would act as the face of the party, while there were to be a minimum of 100 regional lists, with a prioritised order of names. The ballot paper has the name of the party and the names of the three federal candidates. The ballot in the regions would also have the name of the person representing the party in that region. The proposals reduced the permitted share of discarded signatures on nomination forms from the earlier 25 to 10 per cent, thus giving greater scope for lists to be rejected. The idea of a biannual common voting day was adopted.

The premium is now on the creation of durable parties. The creation of party blocs is prohibited, so each individual party has to clear the 7 per cent threshold to enter parliament. Blocs had been created to attract voters, but had then dissolved although deputies elected on its ticket had retained their seats. As we see below, an 'imperative mandate' now operates whereby a seat is lost if a deputy changes party. The higher representation threshold of 7 per cent was designed to force consolidation, and the new parties would now be forced to present voters with a defined political platform with national appeal. The 7 per cent barrier is complemented by a floating threshold to ensure that 60 per cent of the votes cast are represented; and that at least two parties enter the Duma. All those winning over 7 per cent automatically enter the assembly, and the next largest parties are allowed in until the 60 per cent threshold is reached. For those meeting these conditions, mandates would be distributed in the following way: the three on the federal lists, and then the people at the head of the regional lists in proportion to the votes cast in that region. There was thus a strong incentive for those on regional lists to work with the voters of that region. There would be tough competition not only between parties, but also within parties, above all in the selection process to ensure that attractive candidates were chosen, to ensure that they did well in specific regions.

Seats in the Duma are allocated on the basis of the size of a party's vote in each region. Large cities get fewer seats and smaller regions gain increased representation. In keeping with the constitutional principle that people can stand for election without restrictions, independent candidates are able to fight elections, but they have to pit themselves individually against parties. If they win more votes than the regional lists put forward by parties, they are elected. This is unlikely, and even if they do win it is not clear what they will be able to achieve on their own in a party-dominated parliament. Effectively, there will no longer be independent deputies but only deputies from specific party lists, and they will be responsible to that party for their work. If a deputy leaves the party from which they have been elected, perhaps to join a rival party or to become an independent, then that mandate is terminated – the imperative mandate.[20] A deputy loses their seat if they switch parties, but not if they are expelled from a party faction – in which case their mandate continues. If someone leaves voluntarily, then the party passes the seat to the next person on the list. The logic of the new system is to allow winning parties to form the federal government and the executive bodies in Russia's regions, a fundamental change that Putin favoured but hesitated to implement. Other aspects included allowing only observers from parties participating in the elections to scrutinise the polls; thus the role of independent observers was eliminated. Once again there were attempts to restrict media coverage of elections and referendums. Media outlets would be liable to prosecution if they broadcast or printed false or erroneous reports during an election campaign.

The great majority of deputies will be wholly dependent on party structures at every stage of the process, from candidate selection through to Duma membership. On the positive side, the CEC argued that dependence on the administrative resources of regional leaders would diminish, and stressed that even in the old system independent candidates were forced to join a party faction in parliament, thus losing their independence. The new system was unlikely to see a reduction in the use of administrative resources. Ukraine at this time also moved to a fully proportional system, introduced as a result of the constitutional amendments adopted by the Verkhovna Rada at the time of the Orange revolution on 8 December 2004. In Ukraine's parliamentary election of 26 March 2006 over 40 parties and blocs participated and the outcome precipitated the crisis to which we have already referred.

The tinkering with the electoral system did not stop there, and on 12 July 2006 the UR-sponsored law that abolished the 'against all' option in elections was signed into law.[21] This was despite a decision of the Constitutional Court in November 2005 that not only recognised the legitimacy of the 'against all' category, but also recognised the right of electoral agitation in favour of this option.[22] Since the introduction of this box on ballot papers in 1993 (to replace the old Soviet system of crossing out names), some 5 per cent of voters used this category in national elections to register their dissatisfaction, and in some regional elections the total has risen to about 15 per cent. In the 2003 election the 'against all' category nearly entered parliament as an independent group, while in three single-mandate districts the 'against all' vote was the largest and forced

*Table 8.1* The 'against all' vote, 1991–2004

| Election | Votes cast 'against all' | % |
|----------|--------------------------|---|
| 1991 – presidential | 1,525,410 | 1.92 |
| 1993 – parliamentary | 2,267,964 | 4.22 |
| 1995 – parliamentary | 1,918,151 | 2.77 |
| 1996 – presidential I | 1,163,921 | 1.54 |
| 1996 – presidential II | 3,603,760 | 4.82 |
| 1999 – parliamentary | 2,198,702 | 3.30 |
| 2000 – presidential | 1,414,673 | 1.88 |
| 2003 – parliamentary | 2,851,600 | 4.70 |
| 2004 – presidential | 2,396,809 | 3.45 |

a re-rerun (see Table 8.1). The option encouraged turnout, but meant that the protest vote was amorphous. The original idea in 1993 was to ensure that some of the protest vote was siphoned away from communists and others, and clearly by 2006 the regime felt confident enough to do away with this safety valve. It also ensured that there would be no campaign encouraging people to vote 'against all' in the March 2008 presidential election, which could potentially render the result invalid. The report of the OSCE's Election Observation Mission on the December 2003 Duma election had specifically recommended the abolition of the 'against all' option,[23] but its abolition was nevertheless condemned by all opposition parties as further restricting the choices available to voters and by much of the Western media as a further sign of Russia's democratic backsliding.

The abolition in November 2006 of minimum turnout thresholds, which had been 50 per cent in national elections, 25 per cent minimum in regional and 20 per cent in municipal elections, further undermined the legitimacy of the electoral process. Veshnyakov argued that the move was 'premature', noting that there had been no problem with voter turnout in national elections, and that the step lacked popular legitimacy and was perceived to benefit only the authorities.[24] The change was accompanied by a range of restrictions being placed on canvassing, including a ban on criticising a rival candidate on television and in agitation materials, although the prohibition did not apply to printed publications or radio. Yet more reasons, including the ban on loosely defined 'extremism', were now available to the authorities to refuse to register or to remove a candidate. The June 2002 law against political extremism was amended in 2006 to bar parties from contesting elections if one or more of their members were convicted of extremism. The cumulative effect of these changes, which came into effect on 7 December 2006, could be a fall in turnout as citizens turn their backs on an ever-more manipulated electoral process.

Under Putin the Russian electoral system became ever more regulated, and the competitiveness of the whole process became ever narrower. If in the 1995 Duma elections 285 parties and movements were eligible to compete with a 5 per cent representation threshold, in 2003 movements were excluded and only parties that had met stringent registration requirements and had a membership of 10,000 could participate, reducing the number to 64. For the 2007 elections minimal membership was raised to 50,000; the threshold was raised to 7 per cent; single-mandate seats were abolished, thus inhibiting individuals nominating themselves as independents; electoral blocs were banned, preventing parties agglomerating into more powerful electoral blocs; the 'against all' option was no longer available; the minimum turnout threshold had been abolished; and only political parties and state bodies had the right to send observers to polling stations. The number of parties fighting the 2007 election shrank to 11. To cap it all, elections for regional executives had been abolished (see Chapter 12). As Gel'man notes, 'Hyper-fragmentation and high competitiveness in Russia's electoral market were replaced by trends towards a monopoly of the ruling elite.'[25]

## The experience of elections

Despite flaws in their conception and implementation, elections have nevertheless played an important part in the development of Russian democracy. Unlike most other post-communist countries, relatively free elections were held in Russia some two years *before* the fall of communism. This gave rise to a peculiar amalgamation of the structures and elites of the old regime with a novel legitimacy derived from their partial adaptation to democratic electoral politics. This hybrid system, in which change was led largely from within the system itself, marginalised the democratic insurgency and helped insulate the regime from the usual effects of electoral politics. Afanas'ev has called this an 'authoritarian adaptation'.[26] The issue, however, is not so much the nature of the regime (authoritarian or democratic, or something in between), but the fact that the power system, of whatever stripe, has been able to achieve an unwarranted ability to manipulate the electoral system and elections, although it has not been able entirely to subordinate electoral outcomes to its will. A degree of uncertainty remains in the electoral process. Only when that has gone can we talk of wholesale 'authoritarian adaptation'.

### *State Duma elections, 12 December 1993*

Only after the October 1993 events did Russia embark on its first genuine multi-party electoral campaign, but the circumstances were hardly propitious for a fair and honest election.[27] The referendum, as we have seen (Chapter 4), provided Russia with a consti-tution that, despite its many flaws, established the ground rules for a democratic political process. The results of the parliamentary election, however, revealed the profound divi-sions in Russian society: no clear winner emerged and the new parliament was deeply fragmented. Elections were held at the same time for the upper house, the Federation Council (Chapter 9).

The party-list system in the Duma election incorporated a 5 per cent threshold to prevent the proliferation of small parties. To enter parliament a party had to take at least 5 per cent of the national vote, with the whole country considered one giant constituency. It was assumed that this would give reformist candidates an advantage since their natural strength in the big cities, above all in Moscow and St Petersburg, would counteract the conservatism of rural areas. In contrast to earlier practice the elections were to be held in one round, thus abolishing run-off contests, and the old minimum turnout requirement of 50 per cent was reduced to 25 per cent. Candidates required a minimum of 1 per cent nominations to enter the contest in single-member districts unless they had been nominated officially by one of the party blocs, in which case the necessity of obtaining what on average was 4–5,000 signatures was waived. Coming soon after the October events, the requirement that the passport number had to be included alarmed many potential signatories and made canvassing by opposition groups difficult. In the event,

1,586 candidates contested the elections in Russia's 225 single-member constituencies.[28] The other 225 seats in the State Duma were distributed to the parties on a proportional basis as long as they cleared the 5 per cent threshold.

If during the April 1993 referendum some 60 per cent of voters supported Yeltsin and some 40 per cent the opposition, by December 1993 the picture had changed (see Table 8.2). The two explicitly pro-government parties, Russia's Democratic Choice and the Party of Russian Unity and Consensus (PRES), jointly polled 22.2 per cent of the vote, less than the LDPR alone. The total opposition vote now reached 43.2 per cent (22.9 per cent LDPR, 12.4 per cent, CPRF, and 7.9 per cent APR); whereas the proportion voting for the 'democrats' (both in power and in opposition) had fallen to 33.2 per cent (15.5 per cent Russia's Choice, 7 per cent Yabloko, 6.7 per cent PRES and 4 per cent Sobchak); while the Women of Russia bloc (8 per cent) inclined towards the communists, and Travkin's DPR (5.5 per cent) and the Civic Union (1.9 per cent) sought to occupy what appeared to be a disappearing centre. Another interpretation, of course, for the weak

*Table 8.2* State Duma election, 12 December 1993

*Turnout and validity*

- Out of a total electorate of 106,170,835, 53,751,696 valid ballot papers were cast.
- Of which 46,799,532 were for the eight groups passing the 5% barrier.
- The official turnout figure (58,187,755) represented 54.8% of registered voters.
- Only 25% needed to vote for the Federal Assembly elections to be valid.

*Result*

| Party/bloc | Party list | | Single-member seats | Total seats | |
|---|---|---|---|---|---|
| | % | Seats | | No. | % |
| Russia's Choice | 15.51 | 40 | 30 | 70 | 15.6 |
| LDPR (Zhirinovskii) | 22.92 | 59 | 5 | 64 | 14.2 |
| Communist Party | 12.40 | 32 | 16 | 48 | 10.7 |
| Agarian Party | 7.99 | 21 | 12 | 33 | 7.3 |
| Yabloko (Yavlinskii) | 7.86 | 20 | 3 | 23 | 5.1 |
| Women of Russia | 8.13 | 21 | 2 | 23 | 5.1 |
| PRES (Shakhrai) | 6.76 | 18 | 1 | 18 | 4.0 |
| DPR (Travkin) | 5.52 | 14 | 1 | 15 | 3.3 |
| 5% representation threshold in the party-list vote | | | | | |
| Civic Union | 1.93 | 0 | 1 | 1 | 0.2 |
| RDDR (Sobchak) | 4.08 | 0 | 4 | 4 | 0.9 |
| Dignity & Charity | 0.70 | 0 | 2 | 2 | 0.4 |
| New Names | 1.25 | 0 | 1 | 1 | 0.2 |
| Cedar | 0.76 | 0 | — | — | — |
| Against all | 4.36 | 0 | — | — | — |
| Spoiled ballots | 3.10 | — | — | — | — |
| Independents | — | — | — | 141 | 31.3 |
| Postponed | — | — | 6 | 6 | — |
| Total | — | 225 | 225 | 450 | 100 |

*Sources*: *Rossiiskaya gazeta*, 28 December 1993, p. 1; *Byulleten' Tsentral'noi izbiratel'noi kommissii Rossiiskoi Federatsii*, No. 1 (12), 1994, p. 67.

*Note*: The top 8 percentages in column 1 refer to the latter figure; the rest to the former, hence the column exceeds 100%.

performance of the openly centrist parties is that all the others now moved to occupy 'centrist' positions - all, that is, with the exception of Zhirinovsky's LDPR.

Any judgment on the political culture of Russia based on these elections must be tempered by the relative arbitrariness of the results. If the elections had been held only on a proportional system, the LDPR would have been the single largest group; but if the old two-stage single-member system had been retained, the LDPR would hardly have figured. While support for reformist candidates remained strong in Moscow, St Petersburg and some other places, in the provinces their support fell sharply: by 15 per cent in Vologda *oblast*, in Vladimir *oblast* by 10 per cent, and so on. Lyubarsky argues that the riddle is easily resolved: widespread fraud by the old Soviet apparatus. He insists that support for reformist forces had not declined but had probably increased.[29] The results of the referendum adopting the constitution held at the same time have also been questioned, and the charge of vote-rigging still hangs over the December 1993 elections.[30]

### State Duma elections, 17 December 1995

The president's draft electoral law of November 1994 exempted groups already represented in the Duma from having to collect signatures to support their candidacy, a provision that was dropped later, as was the prohibition on candidates standing simultaneously in party-list and single-member elections. The presidential draft proposed reducing the proportion of those elected from party-lists from half to a third, returning to the original proposal of 1993. The electoral law adopted in June 1995 forced party leaders to prune the number of Moscow-based politicians on the party-list to 12, with the rest to be chosen from the regions. Only parties or movements registered six months before parliamentary elections could enter the campaign, thus drawing a clear cut-off point beyond which party formation would be pointless. The number of parties nevertheless proliferated to reach some 300 and engaged in frenetic bloc-making to collect signatures. The number of signatures now required for the registration of electoral associations doubled to 200,000, with no more than 7 per cent from any one of Russia's 89 component units. To stand in a single-member district a candidate had to collect signatures from 1 per cent of the voters (which could count towards the 200,000 if the candidate was officially part of a bloc), and the candidate who gained a simple plurality of votes won.

The retention of the 225 : 225 split in the election and the unchanged minimum voter turnout threshold at 25 per cent signalled not only the strength of vested interests of the factions already in parliament but a continued commitment to the belief that a proportional system stimulates the development of parties. The retention of the 5 per cent threshold for party-list candidates to enter parliament, however, was bitterly contested on the grounds that a significant proportion of the vote might end up unrepresented; instead, a 'representation threshold' was suggested by presidential aide Georgy Satarov whereby the threshold percentage would be gradually lowered until 75 per cent of votes cast were represented.[31] Victor Sheinis defended the law on the grounds that tiny parties 'do not have the right to exist' and that it should encourage the creation of strong parties. He admitted that the lack of a second round in single-member districts was the electoral law's greatest flaw.[32]

The two-party system envisaged by Yeltsin in April 1995 had not materialised. He had sought a centre right dominated by Chernomyrdin's NDR, while the centre left slot was to be taken by Ivan Rybkin's Electoral Bloc; the latter went through several permutations and was challenged by a number of social democratic, trade union, and manufacturers' associations, as well as the Women of Russia bloc running with a federal list of 80 women.[33] Even more than in 1993, the 'democratic' part of the political spectrum fragmented into small groups. Party leaders calculated that by gaining access to free air time by heading a party-list group their chances in single-member districts would be enhanced; they thus placed their individual interests above those of the movement, something not restricted to the democratic camp.[34] The tactic worked for Irina Khakamada of Common Cause, returning to the Duma from a single-member district although her party failed to cross the threshold, as it did for Boris Fedorov from Forward Russia! (which sought to attract the patriotic as well as the democratic vote), for Vladimir Lysenko from the Pamfilova-Gurov-Lysenko bloc (established in Summer 1995 on the basis of the Republican Party of Russia which had earlier been part of Yabloko), and for Konstantin Borovoi from the Party of Economic Freedom. Gaidar's Russia's Democratic Choice – United Democrats failed to reach agreement with Yabloko, although they tried to avoid candidates in single-member districts standing against each other.

The left was dominated by the CPRF, the Agrarian Party of Russia headed by Mikhail Lapshin, and a number of extremist parties, above all Victor Tyulkin's and Victor Anpilov's bloc Communists-Working Russia-For the Soviet Union. Zyuganov's CPRF came into the elections the beneficiary of the widespread discontent with the course of reforms and the victor in numerous regional elections. The CPRF's electoral manifesto was more a blend of patriotic populism than communism, avoiding a commitment to specific Soviet policies while stressing the reintegration of the USSR. Zyuganov sought to reassure Western business that the CPRF would not destroy the private sector if it came to power, something he once again promised at the World Economic Forum at Davos in March 1996, although his campaign documents spoke of the opposite.

The nationalist wing was once again dominated by Zhirinovsky's LDPR. It had won almost a quarter of the vote in 1993 but was now forced to share the national-patriotic vote with numerous other groups. Patriotic centrists were represented by the Congress of Russian Communities (*Kongress Russkikh Obshchin*, KRO), whose leader was the former secretary of the Security Council, Yuri Skokov. Second on the list was General Lebed (retired), formerly commander of the Twelfth Army in Moldova, who made clear his presidential ambitions. The KRO had been established by Dmitry Rogozin in 1993 but he had ceded first place later to Skokov. Lebed announced his entrance into active politics in April 1995, when he joined forces with Skokov, and he resigned his commission in May. There were tensions within the KRO, and in particular between Lebed and Skokov, who also nurtured presidential ambitions and allegedly noted that Lebed's 'education is inadequate. He is not ready yet to be president'.[35]

As in 1993, the electoral system amplified the representation of the parties making it over the threshold (four in this case), and voters supporting the other 39 blocs were in effect disenfranchised (see Table 8.3). With some 34 million votes in 1995 'wasted', the political preferences of a large segment of the electorate were not reflected in parliament. All of this once again raised the question of changing the electoral system; lowering the 5 per cent threshold; reducing the proportion of MPs elected from party-lists or abolishing the proportional part of the election entirely; and reintroducing a second round in single-member districts.

*Table 8.3* State Duma election, 17 December 1995

*Turnout and scope*

- Out of a total electorate of 107,496,558 million registered voters, 69,204,820 million (64.44%) participated.
- A total of 1,320,620 ballots were declared invalid, leaving 67,884,200 valid ballots.
- Only 25% needed to vote for the elections to be valid.
- Gubernatorial elections were also held in twelve regions in which 25% of the population live, something that helped inflate turnout figures.
- Twenty-five electoral associations received less than 1% of the vote and seven received between 1 and 2%.

*Result*

| Party/bloc | Party list | | Single-member seats | Total seats | 1993 seats |
|---|---|---|---|---|---|
| | % | Seats | | | |
| CPRF | 22.30 | 99 | 58 | 157 | 45 |
| LDPR | 11.18 | 50 | 1 | 51 | 64 |
| Russia Our Home | 10.13 | 45 | 10 | 55 | N/A |
| Yabloko | 6.89 | 31 | 14 | 45 | 25 |
| 5% representation threshold in the party-list vote | | | | | |
| Women of Russia | 4.60 | 0 | 3 | 3 | 23 |
| Working Russia | 4.53 | 0 | 0 | 0 | 0 |
| KRO | 4.31 | 0 | 5 | 5 | N/A |
| PST | 4.01 | 0 | 1 | 1 | N/A |
| DVR | 3.86 | 0 | 9 | 9 | 76 |
| APR | 3.78 | 0 | 20 | 20 | 55 |
| Derzhava | 2.59 | 0 | 0 | 0 | N/A |
| Forward Russia! | 1.94 | 0 | 3 | 3 | N/A |
| VN | 1.61 | 0 | 9 | 9 | N/A |
| Pamfilova *et al.* | 1.61 | 0 | 2 | 2 | N/A |
| Rybkin bloc | 1.12 | 0 | 3 | 3 | N/A |
| Blocs with 1 MP | — | 0 | 10 | 10 | N/A |
| Independents | — | — | 77 | 77 | 162 |
| *Total* | 100 | 225 | 225 | 450 | 450 |

*Sources*: *Segodnya*, 27 December 1995, p. 2; *Moscow News*, No. 51, 29 December 1995, p. 2; *Segodnya*, 30 December 1995, p. 1; *OMRI Daily Digest*, No. 1, Part 1, 2 January 1996.

*Note:* Although 1.3 million ballots were declared invalid the 5% party list threshold was calculated using the total number of ballots cast, not only valid ballots.

*Abbreviations*: CPRF – Communist Party of the Russian Federation; LDPR – Liberal Democratic Party of Russia; Working Russia (KTR) – Communists-Working Russia-For the Soviet Union; KRO – Congress of Russian Communities; PST – Party of Workers' Self-Management; DVR – Russia's Democratic Choice; APR – Agrarian Party of Russia; VN – Power to the People.

While the vote in 1993 for the LDPR represented the 'soft' backlash against the government's policies,[36] the vote for the CPRF in 1995 was the 'hard' backlash. The strong showing for the CPRF not only reflected anger at the painful economic reforms, but also a broader disenchantment with the post-August 1991 political order. However, the CPRF's 22 per cent represented only 15.2 million votes: the total opposition vote of some 37 per cent was less than in 1993, while the vote for pro-reform parties fell to 22 per cent. The LDPR's vote halved from that in 1993, yet successfully crossed the party-list threshold but won only one single-member seat. The failure of patriotic organisations like KRO to enter parliament was the greatest surprise. In contrast to 1993, the 1995 electoral law set specific limits on campaign spending for parties and candidates, although these were clearly exceeded by some of the blocs.

### Presidential election, June–July 1996

In 1996 the first-ever elections for the head of state of a sovereign and independent Russia were held. No candidate obtained more than 50 per cent of the vote in the first ballot (held on 16 June 1996) so the two front-runners entered a run-off poll a fortnight later on 3 July (see Table 8.4). Yeltsin's own chances of re-election were reduced by the horrors of the Chechen war and his own ill-health. His popularity had fallen dramatically, from 37 per cent in December 1992 to 6 per cent in June 1995.[37] The December 1995 Duma election acted as a primary for the presidential election, identifying the strongest candidates and eliminating the weakest. Several contenders announced their candidacy, including Zyuganov, Lebed, Yavlinsky, Gorbachev and, of course, Zhirinovsky, without whom no election would be complete. Yeltsin's critics could not agree on a single convincing candidate, hence he remained in with a chance. It did not look like this in early 1996, however, and the hardliners in Yeltsin's entourage, known as the 'party of war' for their advocacy of the first Chechen war in December 1994, urged Yeltsin to cancel the elections and declare a state of emergency to thwart what they insisted was the threat of a communist victory, and all that this entailed. Leading the call for the postponement of the elections was the head of Yeltsin's presidential security service, Alexander Korzhakov, but his views were defeated by an alternative group headed by Chubais. The latter, with his typical decisiveness, was able to draw on the resources of the 'oligarchs' to organise Yeltsin's successful electoral resurrection. In a notorious letter, the 'Appeal of the 13',[38] a number of the top oligarchs pledged their support for Yeltsin, and made unquantifiable sums available to his campaign.

The first round largely confirmed Russia's traditional electoral geography, with Zyuganov gaining strong support on the southern fringe and the 'red-belt' to the south-west of Moscow, although Yeltsin unexpectedly defeated the opposition in the Far East. Yeltsin fought a surprisingly effective campaign, looking fitter than before and focusing on the threat posed by the communists. The media (notably Gusinsky's NTV) fell in behind his candidacy, fearing the consequences of a communist victory, as did a large proportion of the electorate. Lebed's strong showing owed something to the covert support of Yeltsin's team, but much more to his own charisma: if in December 1995 he had been an 'iron-fisted populist', by June 1996 he appeared to have become an iron-fisted democrat.

Between rounds Yeltsin sacked some of his more unpopular officials (including defence minister Pavel Grachev and Korzhakov) and appointed Lebed secretary of the Security Council and presidential national security adviser with the brief to root out corruption and crime. Yavlinsky fought a typically poor campaign, failing to become the candidate of a united 'third force', while Zhirinovsky was pushed into fifth place. Yeltsin secured a convincing victory in the second round from an electorate afraid that a change of president would entail a change of regime. The 30 million votes cast for Zyuganov represented a large constituency of dissatisfied citizens, but he failed to broaden his support beyond the communist and national-patriotic opposition. Despite continuing fears over his health, Yeltsin successfully exploited the slogans of continuity, stability and reform.

*Table 8.4* Presidential election, June–July 1996

*Electoral system*

- Direct elections without electoral districts
- No candidate obtained over 50% of the vote in the first round so the two top candidates went on to a second round held two weeks after the announcement of the results of the first (3 July).

*First round, 16 June 1996*

*Turnout*

| Registered voters | 108,495,023 | |
|---|---|---|
| Turnout: | 75,587,139 | (69.81 %) |
| Total valid ballots: | 74,515,019 | |
| Total invalid ballots: | 1,072,120 | |

*Results*

| Candidate | % | Number of votes |
|---|---|---|
| 1 Boris Yeltsin | 35.28 | 26,665,495 |
| 2 Gennadii Zyuganov | 32.03 | 24,211,686 |
| 3 Alexander Lebed | 14.52 | 10,974,736 |
| 4 Grigorii Yavlinsky | 7.34 | 5,550,752 |
| 5 Vladimir Zhirinovsky | 5.70 | 4,311,479 |
| 6 Svyatoslav Fedorov | 0.92 | 699,158 |
| 7 Mikhail Gorbachev | 0.51 | 386,069 |
| 8 Martin Shakkum | 0.37 | 277,068 |
| 9 Yurii Vlasov | 0.20 | 151,282 |
| 10 Vladimir Bryntsalov | 0.16 | 123,065 |

*Sources*: *Rossiiskaya gazeta*, 22 June 1996, p. 1; *Vestnik Tsentral'noi izbiratel'noi komissii Rossiiskoi Federatsii*, No. 14 (34), 1996.

*Note*: The percentages are calculated from the total vote.

*Second round, 3 July 1996*

*Turnout*

- To avoid a fall in the turnout between the two rounds the day of the election was shifted from the usual Sunday to a Wednesday, which was declared a holiday. The tactic worked and turnout fell only marginally.

| Registered voters | 108,600,730 | |
|---|---|---|
| Turnout: | 74,815,898 | (68.87%) |
| Total valid ballots: | 73,926,240 | |
| Total invalid ballots: | 780,405 | |

*Results*

| Candidate | % | Number of votes |
|---|---|---|
| 1 Boris Yeltsin | 53.82 | 40,208,384 |
| 2 Gennadii Zyuganov | 40.31 | 30,113,306 |
| Against both candidates | 4.83 | 3,604,550 |

*Sources*: *Rossiiskaya gazeta*, 10 July 1996, p. 1; *Vestnik Tsentral'noi izbiratel'noi komissii Rossiiskoi Federatsii*, No. 16 (36), 1996.

The executive's ability to impose a crude bipolarity on the electoral process reflected the weakness of the emerging party system.

### Duma election, 19 December 1999

The parliamentary elections of 1999 once again, as in December 1995, acted as a 'primary' for the presidential elections. Those who did well in the parliamentary elections emerged as favourites, while the credibility of candidates whose electoral blocs did badly was undermined. The inter-weaving of parliamentary and presidential considerations is one of the most fascinating aspects of the whole process. It affected the whole development of the party system, and added multiple complications in the calculations of political leaders.

By 1999 the attempt to impose the old bipolarity on the electoral process was no longer credible. The CPRF suffered from defections in the run-up to the December 1999 elections, above all with the majority of the Agrarian Party of Russia (APR) allying itself with the powerful new grouping headed by the former prime minister, Yevgeny Primakov. This electoral association (OVR) was made up of the *Otechestvo* (Fatherland) organisation, led by the mayor of Moscow, Yuri Luzhkov, and *Vsya Rossiya* (All Russia), comprised of some of the leading regional leaders like Vladimir Yakovlev of St Petersburg and President Mintimir Shaimiev of Tatarstan. The regions and their increasingly independent leaders emerged as a crucial new force in Russian elections. The spate of regional party formation in the run-up to December 1999 demonstrated just how fragmented the political field was. The fact that no single 'party of the regions' emerged, however, once again testified to the political and economic fissures within the regional 'lobby'.

In previous elections the regime had always put forward a single quasi-presidential 'party of power' (Gaidar's Russia's Choice in 1993 and Chernomyrdin's Our Home is Russia in 1995). The emergence of a reconfigured but oppositional 'party of power', focused on Primakov, the national security establishment, regional elites, and industrial and financial groups, was nipped in the bud by Primakov's dismissal as prime minister in May 1999. It was to counter the destabilising threat to the succession that in September 1999 the Kremlin sponsored the creation of the Unity (*Edinstvo*) governors' bloc to act as the official 'party of power'. It was headed by the popular Sergei Shoigu, the long-time head of the Ministry of Emergency Situations (MChS). Unity was certainly not a modern political party, but neither was it a mass movement. It was perhaps the best example of a political association made to order by power elites, to act as the simulacrum of a competitive political organisation and to occupy the space where genuine political parties should belong. Discussion of the serious issues facing the country was overshadowed by the struggle between powerful elite coalitions made up of politicians, oligarchs and regional leaders, reflected above all by the struggle between OVR and Edinstvo. The genuine political parties, like the CPRF and Yabloko, were marginalised as programmatic debate was subsumed into the struggle for the succession. The creation of a highly presidential system meant that the stakes had become extraordinarily high, since the presidency meant access to the vast financial resources of the state and its patronage. At stake was the very survival of the Yeltsinite regime system where political power and economic advantage had become almost indistinguishable.

The results (see Table 8.5) indicated that Russian electors had learnt to cast their votes strategically.[39] If in 1995 49.5 per cent of the vote was cast for the 39 parties failing to cross the 5 per cent threshold, in 1999 this fell to 18.9 per cent of the vote being 'wasted' on the 20 blocs failing to make the threshold. With the consolidation of the vote around 'mainstream' parties, there was less of a 'multiplier' effect and only 18 per cent of the party list seats were redistributed as a 'bonus' to the six successful parties. The CPRF won 22 per cent of the PL vote in 1995, and noted a slight increase in 1999, although they did far worse in SMDs. The Zhirinovsky bloc saw its base further eroded (down from its 11 per cent in 1995), but contrary to most predictions overcame the 5 per cent representation barrier. The success of Unity reflected the continuing presence of a large floating centrist and power-oriented vote, given partially to Our Home is Russia (NDR) in 1995. Unity almost entirely lacked an ideology other than state consolidation around the presidency, and no new ideologically based party has been able to emerge since the founding election of the present system in December 1993. Yabloko remained true to its tradition of losing about a percentage point in each parliamentary election, but overall the position of the liberals was consolidated by the success of the SPS. In earlier elections the 'democratic' vote was split among rival groups, but this time the SPS brought the majority together to register a significant improvement in representation, although some might argue (given their support for Putin and the Chechen war) that this was at the price of giving up their liberalism.

### Presidential election, 26 March 2000

The 1999 Duma election weakened the presidential pretensions of all main opposition candidates – Luzhkov, Yavlinsky, Primakov and Zyuganov. Russia's hybrid electoral system encouraged the development of hybrid political parties: parliamentary parties concerned with winning seats in the Duma; and presidential catch-all groupings concerned to maximise support for potential contenders. The system inhibited parties from developing effectively in either direction. The overwhelming winner of the parliamentary election was someone who was not even a candidate – Vladimir Putin. The election provided the presidency with a strong base in the Duma, it drew the teeth of the main opposition figures, and it boosted the prestige of Putin. Seizing the opportunity, on 31 December 1999 Yeltsin resigned and Putin became acting president, giving him the powerful advantage of incumbency in the presidential election rescheduled for March 2000. Yeltsin saw in Putin the fulfilment of his long-term desire to ensure a smooth transition to someone who would ensure his personal security and elite continuity. The Duma elections cleared the way for the coronation of the presidential heir apparent, Putin, and thus were only the first stage in a single electoral cycle.

The political regime associated with Yeltsin proved able to reproduce itself; although the change of leader provoked modifications, the essentials of the political system established in the 1990s survived the succession. Beneath the cycle of political crises, sackings, resignations and dramatic démarches since 1995 there lay a more profound struggle for the succession. In his televised resignation speech on 31 December 1999 Yeltsin spoke of his desire to have set the precedent of the 'civilised voluntary transfer of power' after the elections originally timetabled for June 2000, but 'Nevertheless, I have taken another decision. I am resigning.' There was no danger of Russia returning to the past, and thus, Yeltsin argued, 'I have achieved the main task of my life' and thus he did not want to

*Table 8.5* State Duma election, 19 December 1999

*Turnout*

- Out of some 108 million Russian electors, over sixty million voted, a turnout rate of 61.7%, comfortably exceeding the minimum 25% requirement.
- An additional 1.2% of the electorate cast invalid votes.

*Result*

| Election association or bloc | Party list (PL) vote (%) | PL seats | Single-member districts (SMD) | Total (%) |
|---|---|---|---|---|
| Communist Party of the Russian Federation (KPRF) | 24.29 | 67 | 47 | 114 (25.9%) |
| Unity (Edinstvo) or Medved (Bear) | 23.32 | 64 | 9 | 73 (16.6%) |
| Fatherland (Otechestvo)/All Russia (OVR) | 13.33 | 37 | 29 | 66 (15.0%) |
| Union of Right Forces (SPS) | 8.52 | 24 | 5 | 29 (6.6%) |
| Zhirinovsky Bloc | 5.98 | 17 | 0 | 17 (3.9%) |
| Yabloko | 5.93 | 16 | 4 | 22 (4.5%) |
| *5% threshold* | | | | |
| Communists, Toilers of Russia-for the Soviet Union | 2.22 | — | — | — |
| Women of Russia | 2.04 | — | — | — |
| Party of Pensioners | 1.98 | — | 1 | — |
| Our Home is Russia (NDR) | 1.20 | — | 8 | — |
| Party in Defence of Women | 0.81 | — | — | — |
| Bloc of Congress of Russian Communities (KRO) and the Movement of Yurii Bodyrev | 0.62 | — | 1 | — |
| Movement for Civil Dignity | 0.62 | — | — | — |
| Stalinist Bloc – for the USSR | 0.61 | — | — | — |
| Movement in Support of the Army (DPA) | 0.59 | — | 2 | — |
| Peace, Labour, May | 0.57 | — | — | — |
| Bloc of General Andrei Nikolayev and Academician Svyatoslav Fyodorov | 0.56 | — | 1 | — |
| Russian All-People Union (ROS) | 0.37 | — | 2 | — |
| Party of Peace and Unity | 0.37 | — | — | — |
| Russian Socialist Party (V Bryntsalov) | 0.24 | — | 1 | — |
| Movement of Patriotic Forces 'Russian Cause' | 0.17 | — | — | — |
| Conservative Movement of Russia | 0.13 | — | — | — |
| All-Russian Political Party of the People | 0.11 | — | — | — |
| Spiritual Heritage | 0.10 | — | 1 | — |
| Socialist Party of Russia (I Rybkin) | 0.09 | — | — | — |
| Social Democrats | 0.08 | — | — | — |
| Against all | 3.36 | — | — | — |
| Independents | — | — | 105 (23.8%) | — |
| *Total* | 100 | 225 | 216 | |

*Sources*: *Vestnik Tsentral'noi izbiratel'noi komissii Rossiiskoi Federatsii*, No. 1 (91), 2000, p. 231; *Nezavisimaya gazeta*, 30 December 1999, p. 1; The results can also be found at the Central Electoral Commission's website: http:/www.fci.ru/gd99/vb99_int/pif_r00.htm

impede the smooth transition to a new generation of politicians. There was 'no reason to hang on to power when the country had a strong person worthy of becoming president'. As Yeltsin himself admitted, his premature exit meant that Russia would not see one democratically elected leader transfer power to another in direct accordance with the expectations laid down in the constitution. Instead, there was an attempt to pre-empt the choice of the voters by transferring power to a designated successor for whom the most benign electoral environment had been established.

Putin presented himself as a symbol of confidence and stability, promising to maintain Russia's system of power and property while radically renovating the state system and developing political and legal reform. Putin committed himself to the maintenance of the existing constitution, although he argued that some institutional innovation could take place within its framework. As acting president Putin could set the terms of the debate, and present himself as a statesman while his opponents scrabbled for votes. Putin enjoyed the advantages of incumbency of not only one post but two, as acting president and prime minister, and thus he was far from an ordinary candidate. Putin's programme, in so far as there was one, encompassed almost every conceivable shade of opinion and thus allowed no space for a coherent alternative. An open letter to the electors in late February contained no more than generalities.[40] While the overall result (see Table 8.6) may have been a foregone conclusion, Putin's first round victory (although by a relatively narrow margin) emulated Yeltsin's triumph in the 1991 presidential election and endowed Putin's presidency with extra legitimacy. Like Yeltsin's 1996 election,

*Table 8.6* Presidential election, 26 March 2000

*Turnout*

| | | |
|---|---|---|
| Registered voters: | 109,372,046 | |
| Turnout: | 75,181,071 | (68.74%) |
| Total valid ballots: | 75,070,776 | |

*Result*

| Candidate | % | Number of votes |
|---|---|---|
| 1  Vladimir Putin | 52.94 | 39,740,434 |
| 2  Gennadii Zyuganov | 29.21 | 21,928,471 |
| 3  Grigorii Yavlinsky | 5.80 | 4,351,452 |
| 4  Aman Tuleev | 2.95 | 2,217,361 |
| 5  Vladimir Zhirinovsky | 2.70 | 2,026,513 |
| 6  Konstantin Titov | 1.47 | 1,107,269 |
| 7  Ella Pamfilova | 1.01 | 758,966 |
| 8  Stanislav Govorukhin | 0.44 | 328,723 |
| 9  Yurii Skuratov | 0.42 | 319,263 |
| 10  Aleksei Pokberezkin | 0.13 | 98,175 |
| 11  Umar Dzhabrailov | 0.10 | 78,498 |
| Against all candidates | 1.88 | 1,414,648 |

*Sources*: *Vestnik Tsentral'noi izbiratel'noi kommissii Rossiiskoi Federatsii*, No. 13 (103), 2000, pp. 63–5; *Rossiiskaya gazeta*, 7 April 2000, p. 3; The full results are in *Vestnik Tsentral'noi izbiratel'noi kommissii Rossiiskoi Federatsii*, No. 16 (106), 2000.

*Note*: The percentages are calculated from the total vote.

moreover, the result was tainted by accusations of malpractice, above all in places like Dagestan where straightforward ballot-stuffing allegedly took place, and elsewhere the use of administrative pressure by officials has been documented.[41]

### Duma election, 7 December 2003

A total of 18 political parties and 5 blocs fought the election.[42] Turnout at 54.7 per cent represented a return to the level of December 1993 (54.8 per cent), compared to the 61.7 per cent of December 1999 and 64.4 per cent in December 1995. The 'against all' category just missed reaching its own independent representation with 4.7 per cent of the vote (see Table 8.7), indicating voter protest against the choices on offer. The average 'against all' vote in single-mandate districts was 12.9 per cent, for which 7.7 million votes were cast, forcing a re-run in three where this category gained the most votes.[43] The greatest winner in the election undoubtedly was United Russia, taking 37.4 per cent of the PR vote and some 120 single-mandate seats, joined soon after by another 60 independents, giving them a two-thirds majority in the Duma.

Liberal parties were effectively squeezed out of the Duma. The social democratic Yabloko won only 4.3 per cent of the vote, and thus failed to cross the 5 per cent representation threshold. The more neo-liberal SPS fared even worse, winning a mere 4 per cent. Together they won only 7 constituency seats, down from the 49 in the previous Duma. The CPRF fought a confused and passionless campaign. Conservative traditionalists flocked away from the CPRF to UR and Rodina, a party established not long before the election to draw votes away from the Communists (see Chapter 7), leaving the CPRF with a rump marginalised electorate. The CPRF vote collapsed, gaining less than half as many seats in parliament, 52 instead of 125, with only 12.7 per cent of the vote compared to 24.3 per cent in 1999. The authorities sought to link the communists to the oligarchs, from which the CPRF had received considerable support. The elections signalled that the CPRF, like its French counterpart a generation earlier, was gradually withering away.

### Presidential election, 14 March 2004

Putin's enduring popularity was confirmed by his re-election for a second term (Table 8.8). However, his victory was tarnished by a number of factors, including the withdrawal of some of the leading candidates and attempts to boycott the election. In the interval between the Duma elections and the presidential ballot in March 2004 a group of radical critics of Putin's administration created 'Committee 2008', headed by the chess grandmaster Gari Kasparov. The strategy was to establish a democratic alternative to Putin's regime. Committee 2008 and other liberals called for a boycott of the election.[44] A turnout below 50 per cent would render them invalid. According to Yavlinsky, 'free, equal, and politically competitive elections are impossible' since the country lacked the three essential ingredients for a free election: independent courts, free mass media and sources of finance free from Kremlin influence.[45] Others suggested that the party in any case lacked the resources to collect the required two million signatures. Putin was infuriated by the idea of a boycott, arguing that those advocating abstention were 'cowards' and that the idea was 'stupid and harmful' and proposed by 'losers'.[46] Divisions in the liberal camp, and within the SPS itself, were revealed in the inability to agree on a common candidate for the presidency. The only other serious candidate was Glaz'ev,

*Table 8.7* State Duma election, 7 December 2003

*Turnout*

- Out of 108,906,250 million Russian electors, 60,712,300 votes were cast (55.75%), of which 59,297,970 valid votes were cast (54.73%), comfortably exceeding the minimum 25% requirement.
- An additional 948,409 (1.56%) cast invalid votes.
- Votes needed to cross the 5% barrier: 3,031,659.
- 42,838,865 votes (70.65%) were cast for the four groups exceeding the representation threshold.

*Result*

| Party | Votes (PR) | % of turnout | Seats | | |
|---|---|---|---|---|---|
| | | | *From PR list* | *From SMD* | *Total* |
| United Russia | 22,779,279 | 37.57 | 120 | 103 | 223 |
| Communist Party (CPRF) | 7,647,820 | 12.61 | 40 | 12 | 52 |
| Liberal Democratic Party (LDPR) | 6,943,885 | 11.45 | 36 | 0 | 36 |
| Motherland (Rodina) | 5,469,556 | 9.02 | 29 | 8 | 37 |
| *Representation threshold (5%)* | | | | | |
| Yabloko | 2,609,823 | 4.30 | 0 | 4 | 4 |
| Union of Right Forces (SPS) | 2,408,356 | 3.97 | 0 | 3 | 3 |
| Agrarian Party (APR) | 2,205,704 | 3.64 | 0 | 2 | 2 |
| Russian Party of Pensioners and Party of Social Justice | 1,874,739 | 3.09 | 0 | — | — |
| Party of Russian Revival – Russian Party of Life | 1,140,333 | 1.88 | 0 | 3 | 3 |
| People's Party | 714,652 | 1.18 | 0 | 17 | 17 |
| Yedenenie (Unification) | 710,538 | 1.17 | 0 | | |
| New Course – Automobile Russia | 509,241 | 0.84 | 0 | 1 | 1 |
| For Holy Russia | 298,795 | 0.49 | 0 | — | — |
| Russian Ecological Party 'Greens' | 253,983 | 0.42 | 0 | — | — |
| Development of Entrepreneurship | 212,825 | 0.35 | 0 | 1 | 1 |
| Great Russia – Eurasian Union | 170,786 | 0.28 | 0 | 1 | 1 |
| True Patriots of Russia | 149,144 | 0.25 | 0 | — | — |
| United Russian Party 'Rus' | 148,948 | 0.25 | 0 | — | — |
| Party of Peace and Unity (NME) | 148,208 | 0.25 | 0 | — | — |
| Democratic Party of Russia | 135,294 | 0.22 | 0 | — | — |
| Russian Constitutional Democratic Party | 113,184 | 0.19 | 0 | — | — |
| Party SLON | 107,444 | 0.18 | 0 | — | — |
| People's–Republican Party of Russia | 80,416 | 0.13 | 0 | — | — |
| Other parties | | | 0 | 0 | 0 |
| Against all | 2,851,600 | 4.70 | — | | |
| Independents | | | | 67 | 67 |
| Total | 59,684,768 | | 225 | 222* | 450 |

*Source*: *Vybory deputatov gosudarstvennoi dumy federal'nogo sobraniya Rossiiskoi Federatsii 2003: elektoral'naya statistika*, Central Electoral Commission (Moscow, Ves' Mir, 2004), pp. 29, 141, 192; http:/www.izbirkom.ru/way/1269570/viboryrefer_obj/. Accessed 13 January 2004.

*Note*:* In single-mandate districts in Ulyanovsk, Sverdlovsk and St Petersburg 'against all' gained most votes on 7 December. In repeat State Duma elections United Russia, LDPR and Rodina won one seat each.

*Table 8.8* Presidential election, 14 March 2004

*Turnout*

- Out of 107,727,274 million Russian electors, 69,292,875 (64.32%) took part, comfortably exceeding the minimum 50 % requirement.
- 578,824 (0.53%) cast invalid votes.

*Result*

| Candidate | Vote | % |
|---|---|---|
| Putin, Vladimir | 49,565,238 | 71.31 |
| Kharitonov, Nikolai (CPRF) | 9,513,313 | 13.69 |
| Glazev, Sergei | 2,850,063 | 4.10 |
| Khakamada, Irina | 2,671,313 | 3.84 |
| Malyshkin, Oleg (LDPR) | 1,405,315 | 2.02 |
| Mironov, Sergei | 524,324 | 0.75 |
| Against all | 2,396,219 | 3.45 |

*Source*: *Vybory prezidenta Rossiiskoi Federatsii 2004:elektoral'naya statistika*, Central Electoral Commission (Moscow, Ves' Mir, 2004), p. 106; Central Electoral Commission: http:/www.pr2004.cikrf.ru/index.html. Accessed 25 March 2004.

formerly a co-leader of Rodina with Rogozin, but the two had fallen out following the parliamentary elections. Glaz'ev sought to present himself as an independent politician who would be a credible successor to Putin in 2008. Glaz'ev's ambition turned the Kremlin from an ally into an enemy.[47] The Kremlin encouraged Rogozin to become sole leader of Rodina and he replaced Glaz'ev as head of its Duma fraction. Glaz'ev emerged much weakened as a result of the bruising campaign, despite his 4 per cent.[48] Zyuganov, leader of the CPRF, refused to participate in the elections and instead the communists were represented by the second rank figure, Nikolai Kharitonov, who in the event did remarkably well, having been given significant media coverage in return for not pulling out of the race. The former speaker of the Duma, Ivan Rybkin, was backed by Berezovsky from London, but turned out to be tragicomic figure. His withdrawal in mysterious circumstances, following a five-day disappearance in Kiev, gave rise to the term 'rybkinisation' of the opposition: incoherent, incompetent and insubstantial.

As in 2000, Putin fought a non-campaign, although his strategy was extremely effective. Serious opposition had already been weakened by the withdrawal of experienced candidates such as Yavlinsky and Zyuganov, while Zhirinovsky appointed his bodyguard, the former boxer Oleg Malyshkin, to run in his place. Putin fought on his record, and also on a forward-looking programme of continued state and economic reform.[49] The dismissal of Mikhail Kasyanov as prime minister *before* the election, and the appointment of the technocrat Mikhail Fradkov at the head of a reduced cabinet of an overwhelmingly liberal and modernising orientation, was a clear signal of Putin's intentions in his second term. It indicated that he was at last conclusively distancing himself from the remnants of Yeltsin's 'family'. In voting for Putin on 14 March, the electorate was supporting not only an individual but the consolidation of a system and the development of a programme. Although Putin's victory was far from unexpected, the scale of his triumph should not be under-estimated and marked a significant improvement over the 53 per cent won in 2000. In Tatartsan and elsewhere there were reliable reports of ballot box stuffing, while the extraordinarily high turnout in some regions undoubtedly suggests the enthusiastic use of 'administrative resources'.[50] However, the general conclusion that Putin gained the overwhelming endorsement of the Russian electorate cannot be gainsaid, winning in every single region.[51] He remained the symbol of national unity and of aspirations for a better life.

## Direct democracy: referendums

The direct appeal to the people is a two-edged sword. While on the one hand a referendum may be seen as a useful supplementary tool to promote popular participation and democratic accountability, the use of the plebiscite is also the traditional instrument used by authoritarian leaders to enhance their powers, defeat their enemies and to legitimate their rule. The referendum is often used to achieve popular support for a new constitutional order, but in the post-Soviet world it has also been used to establish authoritarian presidencies. The referendum has been employed as an instrument of simple majoritarianism in the name of 'the people', prioritising the majority at a particular moment over the enduring values of the 'conceptual' people whose sovereignty is embedded in democratic constitutions. Plebiscites have a powerful authoritarian potential and have been used by dictators throughout the twentieth century, notably by Hitler. The referendum was also used by Charles de Gaulle to legitimise the adoption of a new French constitution in 1958, and then once again in October 1962 on the direct election of the president in an act that was technically unconstitutional.

The use of sovereignty referendums provided a legal and democratic means for the right of self-determination to be exercised in the disintegrating communist federations. A number of post-communist countries conducted 'sovereignty referendums' (*'pouvoir constituant'*) on the core issue of independence: 9 out of 15 Union Republics held these before the disintegration of the USSR in December 1991, and 4 of the seceding republics in Yugoslavia. In the USSR these were balanced by Gorbachev's 'anti-secession' referendum of 17 March 1991, boycotted by 6 of the most eager secessionists: Estonia, Latvia, Lithuania, Moldova, Armenia and Georgia (without Abkhazia). Like Tatarstan, Chechnya lacked union republic status and was thus not considered an appropriate vessel in which to conduct a sovereignty referendum. In a referendum in 1995, 80 per cent of the Transniestrian population voted for the region to become an independent member of the CIS, a result repeated in 2006. No such right exists in the Russian Federation today and thus could not be applied to regulate the Chechen crisis.

The options for Chechnya, moreover, were further limited by the process of adopting the Russian constitution and then the great difficulty in introducing changes to that document. As we have seen, Russia's 'constituent referendum' on the adoption of its constitution took place on 12 December 1993 in the wake of the violent struggle between the president and parliament. In Russia modifications to the constitution are exceptionally difficult and cannot be achieved by the relatively simple mechanism of a modifying referendum. As noted, its core chapters (1, 2 and 9) require the convocation of a Constitutional Assembly, while the rest have to be approved by a super-majority of each house of the Federal Assembly and the legislatures of at least two-thirds of the regions of Russia. Special provisions govern amendments to Article 65, dealing with the composition of the Russian Federation; this is covered by a federal constitutional law.

Historical experience suggests that the sovereignty referendum is a poor instrument for determining the fate of a state.[52] What is the relevant people who should be asked their opinion of the matter? A vote in the larger state on whether a small area should be allowed to secede is as problematic as a vote held only in that small area. Just as in Canada, where the question of who should decide the fate of Quebec remains unresolved, so too in Russia and other post-Soviet states the *pouvoir constituant* is precisely what is at issue. The vote in the two Estonian cities of Narva and Sillamse in 1993, dominated by Russians, for autonomy was declared invalid by the Estonian parliament. Thus the referendum is an inadequate means for determining whether a people are entitled to self-determination. The problem, however, is that no other methods, such as adjudication by an international agency or representative body, is any better. This is indeed a circle that cannot be squared by formal normative methods but is usually resolved by political luck or force.

Russia's first experience of the referendum was in the dying days of the Soviet Union. In a desperate attempt to save the crumbling USSR, on 17 March 1991 Gorbachev appealed above the heads of the warring elites and national groupings to the people. The result of the referendum, the first and last ever held in the USSR, demonstrated strong support for the continuation of the union (see Table 1.2), but it also revealed just how vertically segmented this support was: as we have seen, six republics refused to take part. In the post-Soviet world the referendum has repeatedly been used by incumbent presidents against hostile legislatures. The first attempts in this direction were by Yeltsin, who in the referendum of 25 March 1993 sought to go over the head of the recalcitrant CPD to the people. Although he gained renewed legitimacy, the institutional context did not allow the crisis to be resolved in this way. Following the forced dissolution of the Congress in September–October 1993, Yeltsin called a referendum on the adoption of a new constitution and achieved a contested majority for the founding document of the new state.

Other presidents have been more successful. Aleksandr Lukashenko in Belarus achieved his populist presidentialism by plebiscites on 14 May 1995 and 24 November 1996, and then again to allow him to run for more than two terms in a referendum in October 2004. In Kazakhstan president Nursultan Nazarbaev undermined the fragile independence of parliament by adopting a new constitution on 30 August 1995. In Moldova a referendum on 23 May 1999 called by President Lucinschi sought to transform a mixed parliamentary-presidential system into a fully presidential one. In response, parliament voted to downgrade drastically the role of the presidency, and now Moldova is effectively a parliamentary republic. President Leonid Kuchma in Ukraine referred six questions to the people on 16 April 2000 to weaken what he considered an obstructive parliament (the *Verkhovna Rada*) and transform Ukraine into a presidential republic. Thus the referendum is a powerful instrument in the hands of presidents seeking enhanced powers, but occasionally their plans are thwarted or reversed. It should also be noted that in a number of countries (Belarus, Kazakhstan, Turkmenistan, Tajikistan and Uzbekistan) the referendum has been used to prolong the term in office of incumbent presidents, especially when there are constitutional prohibitions on being re-elected twice. For example, on 27 January 2002 voters in Uzbekistan approved an amendment to the constitution that extended the presidential term from five to seven years, allowing president Islam Karimov to remain in office beyond 2005, as when originally elected, to 2007. In 1995 another referendum had extended his first five-year term, starting when he had been elected president in 1991, a further five years. On 23 December 2007 he was re-elected for a further seven-year term. Putin refused to take this path in Russia, and left office at the end of his mandated two terms in 2008.

In Russia the Federal Constitutional Law on the Referendum came into force on 10 November 1995, stipulating that at least half of registered voters must participate for the referendum to be valid.[53] To initiate a referendum two million votes must be collected, to be verified by the CEC. In 2000 environmental groups collected 2.5 million signatures on a petition to hold a national referendum on Putin's decision to import spent nuclear fuel, but the CEC disallowed over 600,000 signatures thus leaving the total just short of what was required. A new law on referendums of 27 September 2002 prohibited them in the last year of a parliament or that of the president, while yet another law on referendums of 28 June 2004 severely limited the scope for independent initiatives in this sphere, reinforcing the ban on referendums on constitutional issues in the year before parliamentary elections and requiring two million signatures and an extensive initiative group (no fewer than 100 people in no fewer than 40 regions, whose signatures had to be witnessed by a notary). The law allows constitutional amendments to be decided by referendum. The president determines whether a referendum can take place, and one can only take place 60 days after first notification.

## Electoral engagement

Numerous theories seek to understand elections, in post-communist societies and elsewhere.[54] The classic approach is to suggest that voting behaviour is associated with socio-economic divisions and interests, but this can hardly be applied (yet) to Russian society.[55] Simplistic rational choice theory would suggest that governments that deliver the goods get rewarded, whereas those held responsible for poor economic performance (on a national or personal level) are punished. Rising standards of living in the early 2000s were reflected in popular support for Putin. More nuanced approaches seek to incorporate belief systems and political commitments into voting behaviour, the role of negative or 'protest' voting, as well as the problem of 'tactical' voting.

This did not prevent a relatively high turnout over the years (see Table 8.9), suggesting a popular commitment to the democratic process. After a decline in turnout between 1989 and 1993, turnout rose to 64.5 per cent in the December 1995 parliamentary elections and then averaged 68 per cent in the 1996 presidential elections before falling to 61 per cent in 1999. Changes in turnout are not spread equally across the political spectrum. Communist voters, who tend to be older, are the most committed voters (it having been compulsory in the Soviet period), thus a low turnout works to the advantage of the left. By contrast, the higher the turnout, the better the liberals do since the vote for the communists is relatively stable.

Post-communist elections in Russia might well reflect the immaturity of the Russian electorate and its susceptibility to demagogic promises, but they also reflect a growing stabilisation of the system focused on a centrist ideology of consolidation and stability. The party system is beginning to stabilise, and some long-term trends in voter alignment are beginning to emerge (Table 8.10, and see Tables 7.1 and 7.2). The institutional immaturity of the democratic system is giving way to a system that begins to reflect broader political and social processes. However, crisis elements have not disappeared, and extensive institutional reorganisation of the electoral system remains typical of the system.

*Table 8.9* Electoral turnout

| Election or referendum | Turnout (%) |
|---|---|
| Soviet parliamentary election, 26 March 1989 | 89 |
| Russian parliamentary elections, 4/18 March 1990 | — |
| Referendum on renewed union, 17 March 1991 | 75.4 |
| Presidential election, 12 June 1991 | 74.7 |
| Referendum of 25 April 1993 | 64.5 |
| Duma election and referendum, 12 December 1993 | 54.8 |
| Duma election, 17 December 1995 | 64.4 |
| Presidential election: 16 June 1996 (1st round) | 69.8 |
| 3 July 1996 (2nd round) | 68.9 |
| Duma election, 19 December 1999 | 61.7 |
| Presidential election, 26 March 2000 | 68.7 |
| Duma election, 7 December 2003 | 55.7 |
| Presidential election, 14 March 2004 | 64.3 |
| Duma election, 2 December 2007 | 64.1 |

*Table 8.10* Political preferences in federal elections, 1991–2004 (% of those voting)

| Year | Communists | National-patriots | Centrists | Liberals |
|---|---|---|---|---|
| 1991 | 28.0 | 8.0 | 3.5 | 58.6 |
| 1993 | 21.3 | 23.9 | 26.1 | 28.7 |
| 1995 | 32.8 | 21.1 | 22.6 | 20.6 |
| 1996 | 32.5 | 20.7 | 36.8 | 8.4 |
| 1999 | 28.2 | 7.1 | 44.3 | 15.1 |
| 2000 | 32.2 | 2.8 | 53.9 | 8.3 |
| 2003 | 16.5 | 21.6 | 45.8 | 9.8 |
| 2004 | 13.7 | 6.1 | 72.1 | 3.8 |
| 2007 | 11.6 | 9.2 | 74.5 | 3.6 |

*Source: Vybory prezidenta Rossiiskoi Federatsii 2004: elektoral'naya statistika*, Central Electoral Commission (Moscow, Ves' Mir, 2004), p. 128; updated.

The revolutionary implications of the fall of communist power and the change in property relations has not yet given birth to a stable new class or ordered hierarchy of elite privileges and societal values. The whole concept of 'support' appears friable and susceptible to rapid changes; and by the same token, 'opposition' to a large degree cannot be taken as a stable political position but a reflection of temporary antipathies. Elections, nevertheless, have stabilised the political system, providing peaceful forms for ideological contestation.

Early votes, however, were constrained by external factors: in 1989 by the Party apparatus; in 1990 the elections were partial in that the Russian parliament was far from sovereign; in June 1991 the Russian president was formally subordinated to all-union structures; and the December 1993 elections were held in the wake of a political cataclysm with a large swathe of the political spectrum excluded. Only in December 1995 were all the elements of a free election in place, governed by an electoral law passed by parliament and within the framework of a stable constitutional order. But by that time the ability of elections to change the political order was constrained by the consolidation of dual adaptation. The 1996 presidential election confirmed not choice *within* the system but once again the polarised nature of the contest forced a choice *between* systems; in the context, this struggle between two versions of the polity meant the absence of choice in terms of policy options. The 1999–2000 electoral cycle was dominated by the problem of the succession to Yeltsin, and although once again although apparently about choice between candidates, was subsumed into the struggle of the Yeltsin regime to perpetuate itself. In 2003–4 the elections were used to consolidate Putin's regime, and were marked by the strengthening of the centre in the form of the United Russia party and the weakening of both left and right. The lack of competitiveness of the 2004 presidential election confirmed the dominance of Putin's hegemonic regime. This was confirmed by the 2007 Duma election, which saw the vote for VR rise to 64 per cent, while the CPRF vote fell to 11.6 per cent, the LDPR received 8.1 per cent and JR 7.7 per cent.

Electoral politics in Russia have been a distinctive mix of quasi-elections and referendums. Votes have had a plebiscitary character in that they have focused as much on the nature of the political order as on the renewal of the personnel of an existing system; constitutional politics have not yet given way to 'normal' politics and the rotation of administrations. Incumbent elites have been able to perpetuate their rule by exerting dominance over the central media and the use of 'administrative resources'. The plebiscitary nature of Russian democracy became entrenched as public opinion was shaped to consolidate the rule of the existing power system. Rather than providing a mechanism for governmental renewal, elections underwent an 'authoritarian adaptation'.[56] Representative democracy, in which elections lead to the transfer of power from one group or another, was thereby undermined. The institutional basis for this type of electoralism was the powerful presidency, which discounted strong parties and weakened the role of parliament.

Despite the flaws, electoral politics have had a tangible effect by becoming the main form of social contestation, reducing the typically Russian contest of ideological absolutes. In the 1990s the old struggle between 'Westernisers' and 'Slavophiles' was echoed in the tension between 'Atlanticists' and 'Eurasianists', while the binary structure of politics was reflected at first in the struggle between 'democrats' and 'partocrats', and later between 'democrats' and 'red-browns'. Elections became one channel of political mobility, although by no means the primary one, bringing new people into political life; people who in one form or another reflected real social interests.[57] This was over-shadowed, however, by the ability of the presidential regime to coopt personnel and resources in ways that by-passed the electoral process.

# 9    The legislature

Men are in public life as in private, some good, some evil. The elevation of the one, and the depression of the other, are the first objects of all true policy.

(Edmund Burke)[1]

The birth of parliamentarianism in Russia has been tortuous. Three times in Russian history a legislature has been dissolved by force: on 9 July 1906 Nicholas II used troops to dissolve the First State Duma, only two months after its convocation; the long-awaited Constituent Assembly met for only one day on 5 January 1918 and was forcibly prevented by the Bolsheviks from reconvening the next day; and on 21 September 1993 Yeltsin ordered the dissolution of the Russian Congress of People's Deputies (CPD) and the Supreme Soviet. In addition, the Soviet CPD, established amidst so many high hopes by Gorbachev in 1988–9, was prematurely terminated in September 1991, and its Supreme Soviet followed into the dustbin of history by the end of the year. The first two pre-revolutionary State Dumas were dissolved prematurely (the First, as noted, by force, and the Second lasted only three months from February to June 1907), the Third (1907–12) lasted its full term, the Fourth was brought to a sudden end in February 1917, and none were marked by conspicuous success in bringing executive authority under effective control. After 1993 Russia tried once again to establish a viable parliamentary system.

## Elections to the State Duma

The 1993 constitution abolished the two-tier system of Congress and Supreme Soviet and created a bicameral Federal Assembly: the upper house, the Federation Council (FC), made up (at the time) of 178 representatives, two each from Russia's 89 federal components; and the lower house, the State Duma, with 450 deputies elected for a four-year term. The establishment of the Federal Assembly marked a decisive break with Soviet traditions. The constitution outlined the functions of the two chambers of parliament, with the powers granted to the Assembly balanced by countervailing powers of the executive. Although the powers granted the Federal Assembly are relatively weak, they are far from negligible. The First State Duma elected in December 1993 was an interim one and lasted only two years. A mixed electoral system was adopted for the first four dumas, with half the deputies elected by a proportional party-list system and half from single-member constituencies; whereas the elections to the Fifth in 2007 were entirely proportional (Chapter 8). As we can see from Table 9.1, the composition of the

*Table 9.1* Membership of the State Duma

| | Seats in First Duma (%), elected Dec. 1993 | Seats in Second Duma (%), elected Dec. 1995 | Seats in Third Duma (%), elected Dec. 1999 | Seats in Fourth Duma (%), elected Dec. 2003 |
|---|---|---|---|---|
| Communist Party of the Russian Federation (CPRF) | 46 (10.3%) | 149 (33.1%) | 89 (20.2%) | 52 (11.6%) |
| Liberal Democratic Party of Russia (LDPR) | 64 (14.3%) | 51 (11.3%) | 17 (3.9%) | 36 (8.05%) |
| Yabloko | 29 (6.5%) | 46 (10.2%) | 21 (4.8%) | — |
| Russia's Choice | 72 (16.1%) | — | — | — |
| New Regional Policy | 65 (14.6%) | | — | |
| Agrarian Party (APR) | 56 (12.65) | — | — | — |
| Party of Russian Unity and Consensus (PRES) | 29 (6.5%) | — | — | — |
| Women of Russia | 23 (5.2%) | — | — | — |
| Liberal Democratic Union of 12 December | 23 (5.2%) | — | — | — |
| Democratic Party of Russia (DPR, Travkin) | 15 (3.4%) | — | — | — |
| Russia's Way | 11 (2.5%) | — | — | |
| Our Home is Russia (NDR) | — | 65 (14.4%) | — | — |
| Russia's Regions | — | 41 (9.1%) | 38 (8.6%) | — |
| People's Power | — | 37 (8.2%) | — | — |
| Agrarian Bloc | — | 35 (7.8%) | — | — |
| Unity (1999); later United Russia (UR) | — | — | 81(18.4%) | 306 (68.5%) |
| People's Deputy | — | — | 58 (13.2%) | — |
| Fatherland — All Russia (OVR) | — | — | 45 (10.2%) | (part of UR) |
| Agro-Industrial Group | — | — | 41 (9.3%) | — |
| Union of Right Forces (SPS) | — | — | 32 (7.3%) | — |
| Rodina (Motherland) | — | — | — | 39 (8.72%) |
| Unaffiliated | 13 (2.9%) | 26 (5.8%) | 18 (4.1%) | 14 (3.1%) |
| *Total* | *446 (100%)* | *450 (100%)* | *440 (100%)* | *447 (100%)* |
| Independents (at the time of election; many later joined deputy groups) | 141 (31.3%) | 77 (17%) | 105 (23.3%) | 67 (14.9%) |

*Source*: Thomas F. Remington, 'The Russian Federal Assembly, 1994–2004', *Journal of Legislative Studies*, Vol. 13, No. 1, March 2007, pp. 121–41, at p. 127; modified.

*Note*: Parties crossing the 5% threshold (7 per cent from Dec. 2007) are automatically entitled to create a parliamentary 'faction', consisting of those elected on its list and those joining it, many of whom were elected as independents. In addition, a deputy group can be established with the same rights and privileges as a faction if it had a minimum of 35 affiliated deputies (55 from January 2004). Some deputy groups were 'lent' deputies from factions that crossed the 5% threshold, hence their totals (for example, of the CPRF) are lower than presented in the tables showing the election results.

*Table 9.2* Gender balance in the State Duma

| Duma | Women | | Men |
|---|---|---|---|
| | Total | As % of total 450 deputies | |
| 1st – 1993–5 | 63 | 14.0 | 387 |
| 2nd – 1995–9 | 49 | 10.9 | 401 |
| 3rd – 1999–2003 | 36 | 8.0 | 414 |
| 4th – 2003–7 | 44 | 9.8 | 406 |
| 5th – 2007–11 | 63 | 14.0 | 387 |

*Note*: Totals take into account by-elections and replacements.

Duma reflects a combination of a stable core membership and a fluid periphery. Table 9.2 demonstrates that with the collapse of the Women of Russia bloc, the predominance of men in the Duma increased.

### The First Duma (1994–5)

Elected for a two-year transitional period, this convocation was fragmented and torn between a large nationalist bloc in the form of Zhirinovsky's LDPR, a liberal group focused in Gaidar's Russia's Choice, and a communist bloc.

### The Second Duma (1996–9)

The Second Duma was less fragmented than its predecessor, and the presence of only four factions dramatically altered its voting dynamics, with fewer smaller factions to mediate and moderate policy-making. The more radical deputies elected from the party lists were diluted by members elected from the constituencies, often without any clear political affiliation, but the cost was a lack of clear political orientation in the Duma itself.[2] The Duma contained 157 members of the old Duma (35 per cent), 49 per cent of the new convocation had been legislators at various levels before, 52 had worked in various executive branches, 15 had previously been members of the Federation Council, and 29 per cent came from Moscow.[3] Although the CPRF did remarkably well, winning 149 seats, the pro-communist bloc with 45 per cent of the seats failed to obtain the two-thirds required to overturn a presidential veto. The CPRF faction reflected the age profile of the party as a whole, with over one-third over 50, and another 6.5 per cent over 60; workers accounted for no more than 7 per cent.[4] Communist dominance did not entail constitutional paralysis, although the Belovezh Accords were denounced and there were attempts to put Yeltsin on trial, but forced the president to rely on his decree powers to push through his reform agenda.

### The Third Duma (2000–3)

For the first time a president commanded a stable majority in the Duma, even though its political composition was more fragmented than it had been in the previous Duma. The Third Duma could muster some 280 votes as part of a broad non-communist coalition, a healthy majority in support of Putin's government. Unity, which received Putin's 'unofficial' blessing, became the core of a pro-government alliance. About a third (166) of the deputies from the previous convocation were re-elected to the new Duma.[5] The CPRF won 24.29 per cent of the party list vote, giving it 67 seats, and 47 SMD seats.[6] In the Duma a CPRF faction with 90 members was formed, together with an allied 'Agro-Industrial' faction of 39. The loss of its former allied Agrarian and Popular Power groups reduced the left's share of the Duma from 211 (47 per cent) to 127 (28 per cent). The relatively poor showing of OVR rebounded to the benefit of the CPRF, now no longer seen as the main enemy, and indeed the communists had long proved a useful foil to the Kremlin. There was in any case a large area of agreement between the government and the left, including most security issues (above all Chechnya) and support for the military-industrial complex. The situation in the Third Duma was more like that of the First (1993–5), with a greater number of factions and with no hegemonic bloc like the one represented by the Communists, Agrarians and Popular Power in the Second Duma.[7] In the spring of 2001 the creation of a presidential coalition under the name of United Russia of four parties (Unity, OVR, People's deputy and Russia's Regions) formed a majority that voted together and increased party discipline. For the first time parliament and the government were able to work together to adopt necessary legislation. The regime itself under Putin sought to maintain control over parliament, calling on it to focus on legislative work and not to pick quarrels with the government.

### The Fourth Duma (2004–7)

The December 2003 elections gave the presidency a constitutional majority (two-thirds) in the Duma. United Russia alone had over 300 seats, and it towered over the remnants of the opposition and gave the president a partisan majority that allowed him to dominate the legislature. The two main liberal parties, Yabloko and SPS, failed to cross the 5 per cent threshold, leaving the CPRF as the main representation of the 'independent opposition'. There was a high turnover, with 54 per cent of those seeking re-election losing their seats. In effect a change of political generations took place. Those who had come to prominence in the late *perestroika* period and been active in the early years of the Russian parliament were swept away, and in their place a new class of 'parliamentarian-functionary' emerged. This was most notable in the case of UR. In addition to functionaries, a sizeable group of nationalists, encompassing nearly 30 per cent of deputies, took their seats in the new assembly, many of them swept in on the Rodina groundswell.[8] The Rodina faction, contrary to the expectations of its Kremlin sponsors, became the voice of the nationalist opposition. The party's aggressive nationalism turned out not to be not to the Kremlin's taste, and in March 2006 they engineered leadership change to install a more sympathetic head.[9] Rodina later became part of the new left-leaning but pro-Kremlin Just Russia party.

With the solid bloc of UR and allied votes, combined with the fact that centrists now enjoyed the chairmanship of all significant committees and domination of the Duma's administrative apparatus, one could fairly say that Putin had tamed parliament. The Kremlin had majority support from a single party, reducing the winning coalition to one relatively disciplined group. Parliamentary politics became less inclusive, more executive dominated and with a greater concentration of power within the Duma.

### The Fifth Duma (2008)

These features were accentuated in the Fifth Duma, in which VR had 315 seats, the CPRF 57, the LDPR 40 and JR 38.

## Organisation

After October 1993 some of the structural sources of conflict between parliament and the presidency were eliminated. The creation of a bicameral assembly represented a major advance towards democracy in Russia. The abolition of the Supreme Soviet's Presidium, which had in effect become an alternative government, now gave the concept of the separation of powers institutional form. Whereas deputies in the old Supreme Soviet veered towards irreconcilable opposition, politics in the new Duma tends towards the political centre. The redistribution of powers between the branches of government established a viable political system and eliminated the source of some of the earlier conflicts.

The first task facing the First Duma was to establish its own working practices. It adopted a law on the status of deputies, the Duma's budget, regulations (*reglament*) on its work and on secretarial and other support for deputies. Article 97.3 of the new constitution insists that 'Deputies to the State Duma work on a professional permanent basis' unless engaged in teaching, scientific research or work related to the arts; the transitional arrangements for the First Duma, however, allowed ministers to remain MPs.

The Duma meets in plenary session for only two days a week, and the other three are devoted to work in the committees. Parliamentary committees were created on the party principle in an attempt to kick-start the party system, as was the rule that a party group required a minimum of 35 deputies to be registered. According to Mikhail Mityukov, the chair of the presidential commission on legislative proposals and the main author of the regulations governing the work of the new assembly, the rules prevented the emergence of a new Khasbulatov, and by focusing on party factions promoted the development of a party system. The chair of the Duma and the vice-chairs were to belong to different factions, and instead of a Presidium there was a Conference consisting of the chairs and delegates from factions and groups with voting power in proportion to their size. The Conference's role was to be purely organisational. The rules, moreover, allowed a faction or bloc to recall a deputy and replace him or her with one further down the party list.[10] The distinction between factions and groups is important: a faction is formed by parties crossing the 5(7) per cent threshold (8 in the 1993 elections, 4 in 1995, 6 in 1999 and once again 4 in 2003 and 2007); whereas deputy groups, enjoying the same rights as factions, can be formed on an *ad hoc* basis as long as (according to rules adopted in January 1994) a minimum of 35 deputies join. This allowed the large number of deputies elected as independents in single-member constituencies to combine, although some joined the established factions (see Table 9.1). In January 2004 the number required to create a group or a faction was increased to 55, and as a result no independent group was formed in the Fourth Duma, further marginalising independent deputies.

Learning from bitter experience, the Duma no longer has a presidium and instead the Duma Council sets the legislative agenda and manages general organisational affairs. It consists of all the party leaders with equal voting rights, irrespective of the size of the party group. The Council (and the committees) are subject to votes on the floor of the house, and thus rank-and-file deputies are able residually to influence the legislative process. Equally, the powers of the speaker have been much reduced to prevent the emergence of another Khasbulatov. The speaker is supported by a first deputy speaker and a number of other deputy speakers, representing various political currents in the Duma. The candidate from the Agrarians, Ivan Rybkin, was elected chair of the First Duma, with the support of communists and the LDPR, but in contrast to his predecessor, Khasbulatov, he turned out to be a fair and non-partisan speaker. Rybkin's supple leadership played an important part in facilitating cooperation with the executive and thus restored the credibility and authority of parliament.[11] His successor in the Second and Third Dumas was Gennady Seleznev, a deputy speaker in the First Duma and from January 1995 a secretary of the CPRF's Central Committee. Like Rybkin, once in the job of speaker his political identity was largely subsumed into that derived from the post. Although at first he refused to suspend his Communist Party membership, he claimed he would work on behalf of the Duma as a whole and concentrate on improving the Duma's functioning.[12] From the moderate wing of the CPRF, Seleznev went on to establish the social democratically oriented 'Rossiya' group within the CPRF until leaving the CPRF in 2002. The Putin loyalist Boris Gryzlov, simultaneously the head of the United Russia party, was selected speaker of the Fourth and Fifth Dumas.

It is in the committees that acts are discussed and amendments proposed, work that is invisible to the general public until it bears fruit in legislation. While much legislation passes through on the nod in Western parliaments, in Russia each paragraph tends to be the subject of heated debate by the Duma as whole. Duma committees (there were 23 in the First and 28–32 thereafter) were at first divided among factions according to what is known as portfolio agreements. Chairships are highly prized, divided not only between the factions crossing the 5 per cent threshold but also the groups formed in the new Duma. Elections are followed by an unholy scramble to gain the chairmanship of the committees, usually leaving some of the parties bruised and alienated. Following the 1995 elections, for example, the CPRF headed nine committees, the three other factions four apiece, and the rest divided among the three other groups. Although the 1999 elections delivered a solid block of pro-presidential legislators, no party or group enjoyed an absolute majority (over half of the 450 seats), let alone a two-thirds constitutional majority. This had been the case in the first two Dumas as well, and this explains the non-majoritarian features of the Duma's internal organisation at that time. Posts in the Duma's two-dozen odd committees were divided between the parties on a proportional basis. However, in the deal struck on 18 January 2000 between the Communists and Unity for the division of committee chairs and vice-speaker posts the old principle of proportionality was abandoned. The seizure of the majority of committee chairs by the CPRF and Unity factions aroused particular bitterness (the CPRF kept 9 and Unity took 12, while 5 went to the allied People's Deputy faction), provoking a walk-out and protests by the other groups. Later the CPRF became highly critical of Putin's leadership, and as a result on 4 April 2002 a reshuffle (probably Kremlin-inspired) saw the Communists losing the leadership of seven of its committees, and their resignation from the others as they went into open opposition to the presidency.

The majoritarian nature of parliament intensified in the Fourth Duma in 2004. Instead of the traditional proportional sharing of committee chairships, however unfairly they may have been distributed following the 1999 election, a majoritarian winner takes all system was now applied, with United Russia taking the leadership of all 29 committees. There had initially been plans to apply the quota principle, which would have allowed the other parties two or three chairs, but according to UR, the various statements by the opposition showed that they were not ready to assume an adequate level of responsibility. Party leaders are now able to assume leadership positions, and for the first time the head of a political association could also assume the chairship of a committee, reducing the number of leading posts in the assembly. The Duma Council, the body that manages the Duma's agenda, is no longer formed from representatives of each party but by the Duma speaker and their deputies. As a result, United Russia took 8 out of 11 seats on the Duma Council, as well as 7 out of 10 deputy speaker posts. The role of the deputy speakers in the legislative process increased, while that of the heads of party factions was diminished.[13] In the past parliamentary leaders had been able to operate at one remove from party bosses, and this practice now disappeared, as seen in Gryzlov simultaneously becoming speaker and remaining head of UR. As a result, there was much talk of the institutional degradation of the Duma.

In institutional terms, power in the Duma increasingly focused on the party factions rather than the parliamentary committees. The introduction of the imperative mandate in 2006, whereby deputies are not allowed to leave the parties from whose lists they are elected, greatly strengthened the hand of faction leaders. The predominance of a small number of large groupings enhanced the power of the caucus leaders, and in particular that of the leadership of United Russia. Considered a pedestal party for the Putin administration, there is no doubt that the group acted as the transmission belt of Kremlin concerns into the legislative process. At the same time, the diversity of views within UR meant that it acted as a sounding board for parliamentary and social concerns back to the presidency, and sometimes it even sought to introduce legislation that met with only equivocal support in the Kremlin.

## Role

The adoption of the constitution inaugurated a new period in the development of parliamentarianism in Russia. Yeltsin's alleged strategy for a 'controllable democracy' in Russia was only partially successful. The new legislature, in contrast to the old Supreme Soviet, is clearly now the junior partner, but fears that the new legislature would be a 'pocket' parliament proved exaggerated. The legislature has not been converted into a branch of the executive; nor can it claim the prerogatives of the executive. The Duma was able to carve out an important role for itself *despite* the formal provisions of the constitution but *within* the constitution's framework. The constitution, moreover, does not regulate in detail the relations between the executive and the legislative branches of government, and it is these very ambiguities that potentially allow the development of a viable parliamentarianism in Russia. Arguments remain in favour of increasing the powers of the legislature and the creation of a government based on the 'parliamentary majority' while simultaneously increasing the powers of the government and, commensurately, decreasing those of the president. These views gained significant support in late 1998–9, but were marginalised by Putin's personal predominance of the political scene and the apparent moratorium placed on constitutional change, but they have certainly not gone away.

Although there is a tendency to denigrate the role of the Russian parliament, the Duma plays a critical role in Russian politics. Its political composition matters a lot, hence the intensity of the competition in parliamentary elections. Voting patterns are not always predictable. For example, Zhirinovsky's LDPR usually votes in support of the government and in the Second Duma supported economic austerity measures with greater enthusiasm than the supposedly liberal Yabloko party. The dominance of the left in the 1990s impeded the adoption of important legislation, especially on economic issues like foreign direct investment and the land code. The law on production sharing agreements (PSAs) in the oil industry was held up for three years and even then probably did not go far enough, the liberalisation of land ownership and sales remained a permanently vexed issue, and the rejection of important parts of the anti-crisis package in July 1998 gutted them of whatever coherence they may have had.

The Duma is at the heart of the legislative process, drafting and endorsing laws and issuing directives (*postanovleniya*). A number of bodies are granted the right to initiate legislation, including the government, the Federation Council and the president (Article 104.1), who was also granted, as we have seen, the right to issue laws by decree as long as they do not contravene the constitution. Legislative acts take priority over presidential decrees; if discrepancies persist the Constitutional Court adjudicates contradictions between parliamentary legislation and presidential decrees. The Duma and the Federation Council can override a presidential veto or decree if both houses can gather a two-thirds majority. A simple majority of the Duma and then of the FC is required for a bill to become law; although; budgetary and taxation laws also require the approval of the government. Bills are then passed to the president and if within 14 days he or she vetoes it, it is then sent back to parliament and can only become law if passed by two-thirds of the deputies in both chambers. In its 2-year convocation the First Duma passed 461 draft laws, 282 of which were signed into law by president Yeltsin. Three out of the 12 constitutional laws were adopted (On Referendums, on the Constitutional Court, and on the Supreme Arbitration Court). During the Second Duma (1996–9) over 500 bills were passed and signed into law by the president, and much of this (some 122 laws) was significant legislation of enduring importance.[14] The productivity of the Third Duma (2000–3) and the Fourth (2004–7) was if anything higher, providing the legislative basis for Putin's reforms. Legislation in the early Putin presidency was largely initiated by the executive; some 72 per cent of all bills in spring 2000, for example.[15] The introduction of the so-called 'zero reading' under Putin streamlined the legislative process, but at the expense of debate, and there is a general perception that the quality of legislation during his presidency declined.

Formally, the Duma lacks the right of interpellation (the calling of ministers to account in writing) but the work of ministers has been monitored through the committee system, and the Duma devotes the last hour of every Friday to examine the work of ministries. The Duma also lacks sufficient powers to monitor the implementation and observance of the laws it passes, without which legislative activity becomes meaningless. The Duma does, however, hold parliamentary hearings, and many of the resulting recommendations have been adopted by the ministries concerned or incorporated into decrees and laws. Despite the limited rights formally granted by the constitution, parliament's oversight functions have grown. The constitution provides an effective environment for political stabilisation, marginalising extremism and facilitating compromise and consensus, although the unbalanced separation of powers means that it provides a poor forum to ensure presidential accountability.

The Duma's prerogatives include the initiation of impeachment proceedings against the president, endorsing the president's choice of the prime minister, declaring an amnesty (the president retains the right to issue pardons), and calling for a vote of confidence in the government as a result of which the president can either change the government or dissolve the Duma (Article 103, and see Chapter 5). A parliamentary amendment of 14 April 1995 requires a faction to collect a minimum of 90 votes before tabling a no-confidence motion in the government. The Duma's oversight functions over the budgetary process are relatively limited, simply adopting the budget as a whole. This does prevent the adoption of the budget in the autumn session becoming traumatic. Only in December 1995 was a budget adopted before it was actually due to come into effect; and for the first time in 2000 was a budget adopted that balanced income and expenditure. By 2007 the new three-year budgetary system was being discussed as early as June.

The most controversial issue is the relationship between parliament and the choice of prime minister and the cabinet. In parliamentary systems the government is chosen by parliament and held accountable to it, but other than endorsing the president's choice of prime minister the Duma has little to say in the formation of the government and cannot dismiss specific ministers, let alone the prime minister. The State Duma has the right to reject two presidential nominees for prime minister, but if it rejects them a third time then the president can dissolve the Duma, a right that cannot be exercised in the first year after parliamentary elections (Article 109.3) or in the six months prior to presidential elections (Article 109.5). Despite the constitution's stipulation that the head of the government is nominated by the president, the State Duma must give its consent and normal parliamentary practice, albeit in an attenuated form, has asserted itself to ensure some correspondence between the composition of the government and the political complexion of the Duma. The debate over changing the constitution to enhance the Duma's powers in the appointment of the prime minister and cabinet ministers was particularly active during Primakov's premiership, and was a live issue in 2003. In addition, there is discussion over the need of constitutional amendments to increase the Duma's control over the budgetary process and its general oversight over the executive.

After 1993 Russia for the first time was able to create a genuine parliament. Virtually all deputies have completed higher education and work in parliament on a full-time basis. The new legislature has become an effective professional parliament and not simply a decorative adjunct to presidential politics and party struggles. The Duma proved capable of independent initiatives, but its powers were limited. In February 1994 the Duma exercised its questionable right to pardon those involved in the events of 3–4 October 1993 and in the 1991 coup. Despite Yeltsin's protests, Rutskoi, Khasbulatov and others were released from gaol, and an end was put to the affair. The first Chechen war (1994–6) revealed the limits of the Duma's powers, with unsuccessful attempts to bolster the legislature's control over military action within Russia, and at the same time exposed its divisions; factional differences prevented the passage of a no-confidence vote on the government. The crisis starkly revealed the changed balance of power between the executive and the legislative. For Putin the Duma was an effective ally to push through the reforms he wanted. The presidential veto on legislation now rarely needed to be used. The proportion of bills signed into law by the president increased from 61 per cent in the First Duma (1994–5), 74 per cent in the Second (1996–9) and rose to over 95 per cent in the Third (2000–3),[16] and remained at that level in the Fourth. As time passed, of course, there were fewer items of landmark legislation. Critical voices with some justice argued that much of this legislative activity lacked sufficient time to be improved by parliamentary debate, and indeed that the Duma had become little more than an extension of the Kremlin, a 'transmission belt' rubber-stamping its initiatives and thus confirming the views of those who argued that Russia had become a 'managed democracy'.

Estimates in mid-2003 found that some 57 per cent of Putin's coalition in the Third Duma was made up of constituency deputies, and according to Hale and Orrtung they were 'the key to Putin's first-term legislative juggernaut'.[17] This was intensified in the Fourth Duma, and enhanced by the strong showing for UR. Although Putin now enjoyed a constitutional majority in the Duma, he refused to consider amending the constitution.[18] At the same time, there were limits to Putin's ability to get his way. As he noted in his 7 February 2006 Spanish interview, 'My influence on the Duma is naturally substantial but it is overly exaggerated because parliamentarians have their own opinion on some issues.' He used the example of the abolition of the death penalty, which he personally favoured but which would not find a parliamentary majority. 'I do not raise issues that would arouse a negative reaction or rejection', he stated, in a comment typical of his cautious style in routine politics.[19] In December 2006 only 27 deputies voted to ratify a protocol designed to streamline the workings of the European Court of Human Rights, despite Putin's strong endorsement of the measure. As noted, a fifth of all cases before the Court at that time came from Russia, indicating the lack of efficacy of the Russian court system. The status of parliament in popular opinion, never very high, was not improved, while the quality of the laws passed declined as the obedient majority pushed through the regime's agenda. Even worse, with its enormous majority United Russia shaped the rules of the political arena to suit its purposes.

Yeltsin had little respect for his parliaments, being irritated by what he considered its unconstructive approach. Relations between the two branches of power were adversarial, but in the new institutional framework, rarely confrontational. The relationship changed as a result of the 1999 election and the change of the presidency. Instead of the Duma being dominated by an anti-presidential majority of communists and independent deputies, the Kremlin regime gained one in which no single orientation could dominate. The dynamics of presidential-parliamentary relations changed radically. The presence of the pro-presidential Unity bloc provided the Kremlin with a compliant bloc of deputies. For many this represented a decline in the Duma's role. One commentator argued that 'today the Duma plays a significantly smaller role than under Yeltsin or Nicholas II'.[20] The Duma's role as the initiator of legislation had certainly declined, and instead the Duma tended to act on bills proposed by the Kremlin.[21] The creation of a stable parliamentary majority under Putin had the positive effect of streamlining the legislative process, but at the same time it removed much of the need for bargaining and consensus and created a more majoritarian and exclusive political environment. The Duma became less of a veto player in Russian politics, while at the same time the other leg of Russia's bicameral system, the Federation Council, was also weakened.

## The Federation Council (FC)

The 1936 'Stalin' constitution made the two chambers of the Supreme Soviet, the Council of the Republic and the Council of the Nationalities, in effect two parts of a single unit, often meeting together and with a single presidium, whereas the Federal Assembly today is a genuinely bicameral body. The State Duma and the Federation Council are located in different buildings and meet separately, except for ceremonial occasions such as the president's annual spring address to both houses. The FC allows the direct representation of the components of the federation in the parliamentary system and acts like the Senate in the USA, with two representatives apiece from Russia's components, representing the executive and legislative branches (Article 95.2). It is a body responsible for a range of national issues, but is especially concerned with ethnic issues (the 'nationalities question', in Soviet parlance), the prerogative of the old Council of Nationalities, and bears special responsibility for the monitoring of regional issues.

### Forming the Federation Council

While the constitution stipulates that the Duma is to 'elected', it does not specify a mechanism for the 'formation' of the Council. According to the constitution (Article 95.2), the FC 'consists of two representatives from each member of the Russian Federation; one each from the representative and executive bodies of state power', but the detailed procedure for 'forming' the FC was to be regulated by federal law (Article 96.2). The notion of 'forming' (*formirovanie*) allows varying interpretations, including election, delegation or appointment.[22] The upper house in Germany, the Bundesrat, is appointed, but the Duma argued that this was unsuitable for Russian conditions and insisted that the Federation Council should remain an elected body. But should the elections be direct or indirect; if the latter, should the heads of administration and the legislatures be elected and then automatically made members of the FC? The majority of heads of administration at that time were not elected but appointed by the president, while about half of the local legislatures were filled by appointees of the executive authorities. From 1996 the heads of the executive and legislature in the regions were elected, but this only raised more sharply issues of conflict of interest and more practical questions of how 'senators' could manage simultaneously to be effective regional and national politicians. The problem of how to form the upper chamber rumbled on throughout the Yeltsin years and was then a nettle grasped firmly by Putin, although there are major reservations over whether his solution is the optimal one and thus the issue remains firmly on the agenda.

### Phase one, 1993–5

Yeltsin's plan to convert the unelected Federation Council created in August 1993 into the upper chamber of parliament was opposed even by his own supporters, and soon after the October events he announced simultaneous elections to both houses of the Federal Assembly.[23] Two seats were available in each of Russia's 89 republics, regions, federal cities and other federal areas. A total of 494 candidates fought directly for seats in the 178-seat upper house. Some 40 per cent of candidates to the Federation Council were leaders of executive authorities and 16 per cent were heads of legislatures.[24] Electoral associations were largely irrelevant and the great majority of members elected (108) were independents. Dominated by elites from the regions and republics, the FC brought together many experienced and serious politicians, including presidents of the republics and regional governors. The first convocation of the FC by and large supported the Yeltsin administration, voting for the Social Accord Treaty in April 1994 and gave critical support on other issues. The selection of Vladimir Shumeiko, a close presidential ally and a member of Russia's Choice, as speaker helped moderate conflicts between the Council and the president. Since the majority of members were employed elsewhere, however, absenteeism was high and it was often difficult to gather a quorum. While Duma deputies customarily spend three weeks in four in parliament and a week in their constituencies (if elected from constituencies), it was the other way round for members of the FC who usually had major responsibilities in their regions.

*Phase two, 1995–2000*

It took two years to establish what was anticipated would be long-term rules for selecting members of the FC. The delay in adopting a law threatened to undermine the validity of the 1995 Duma elections, since one house on its own cannot pass legislation. The legislative committees of both houses supported the electoral variant, which would have created a popularly elected, full-time Council, and a law to this effect was passed on 27 July 1995 but was vetoed by the president. Yeltsin wanted regional leaders, most of whom he had appointed, to become Council members automatically. At that time 66 out of 89 regional governors and presidents of republics were presidential appointees. According to a second version adopted on 11 October, taking into account Yeltsin's objections, the administrative and legislative heads of each region would become Council members *ex officio*, but the governors would be popularly elected as well. Governors who were presidential appointees would have to face the voters before the presidential election scheduled for June 1996. Yeltsin, who wanted the governors he had appointed to remain in place so that they would support him during the presidential campaign, once again vetoed the law.[25]

In concession to this the final law adopted by the Duma on 5 December 1995 allowed the postponement of gubernatorial elections for up to one year (to be held no later than December 1996, although twelve exceptions were made allowing elections in December 1995). According to the law the FC was formed from the governors (heads of administration) and legislative heads from each of Russia's 89 components. Those republics with bicameral assemblies (like Karelia and Yakutia) were forced to choose between their two speakers. A candidate won if they gained 50 per cent plus one of the vote; if not, the contest went to a second round between the two leading candidates.[26] The Duma had been forced to use a two-thirds majority to over-ride the objections of the Council, since most of the members elected in 1993 were neither heads of regional executives nor chairs of regional legislatures. The new Federation Council took office in January 1996.

The stakes in regional elections were now doubled since each of the executives elected became, *ex officio*, a member of the FC, while the chairs chosen by the legislatures also joined the Council automatically. Only one-third of the second convocation of the FC had sat in the first, with the heads of the Moscow, Petersburg and Chechnya power bodies joining for the first time.[27] The new FC elected the former Politburo member Yegor Stroev as its chair on 23 January 1996. He sought to strengthen Russia's federal system, above all through budgetary devolution, while improving the work of the FC, in particular by addressing the problem of poor attendance. Stroev had been elected governor of Orël *oblast* on 11 April 1993 and won a seat in the FC in December 1993 with 80 per cent of the vote. The Council was now in a state of permanent renewal as the regional elections took place at various times.

The system adopted in 1995 for forming the Council was clearly unsatisfactory. Direct popular elections (as applied in 1993), would have created an upper house of professional legislators who could devote their full attention to the legislation under consideration.

Instead, a Council of part-time members was created, who simultaneously held high office in their home regions. The principle of separation of powers was clearly violated, since regional executives sat in the national legislature. Their focus, moreover, was on striking deals with the federal government to benefit their own region rather than working for the national good and fighting for an independent stance by the FC. As a powerful regional lobby, they were able to block legislation that threatened their interests. The Council was rarely in session and was easily dominated by its own officialdom and the federal authorities.

### Phase three, 2001–8

It was for this reason that one of Putin's first acts on coming to power was to change the way that the FC was formed. The idea at first was to return to an electoral variant, to allow executive and legislative leaders to concentrate on managing their regions. In the event, to appease the regional lobby, a system of delegation was adopted. The new 'senators' would be full-time delegates of the regional authorities, nominated by regional leaders and legislative bodies. The problem of the 'separation of powers' remained unresolved. The existing members of the FC lost immunity from criminal prosecution, but in compensation they controlled the nominees; their influence on national affairs was little diminished.[28] The passage into law of even this rather half-boiled measure was subject to extensive bargaining, with three Duma votes in support of Putin's measure being over-turned by the Council, leading to the formation of a Conciliatory Commission. The governors managed to achieve a 'soft turnover' of the membership of the Council, striving to stay until the end of their terms and only then giving way to their nominated successors. The original plan was for the new composition of the Federation Council to be in place by 1 February 2001. The governors in addition tried to maintain sole control over the nomination of the new representatives, without their nominations having to be ratified by the regional assembly. The governors, moreover, demanded the right to recall the regional representatives from the upper chamber.[29]

The measures voted on 19 July 2000 agreed that a governor's appointment of a representative could be blocked by a two-thirds majority in the regional legislative assembly within two weeks. Dismissal was also to be approved by a two-thirds majority of the local legislature. Agreement was also reached over a 'soft turnover' of Federation Council members, with governors leaving the Federation Council as their terms expired or by 1 January 2002 at the latest. A large number of governors faced election in autumn 2000, and were not able to return to the upper chamber. In all, thirteen amendments were approved. Although Putin had made some concessions, the overall package was in line with his aspiration to create a full-time working upper chamber. On 19 July 2000 the compromise bill was approved by the Duma and on 26 July it was adopted by the upper house by the surprisingly large majority of 119 votes in favour and 18 against, with four abstentions. The vote did not so much reflect the senator's enthusiasm for the reform as resignation that any contrary vote would simply be over-ridden by the Duma.

The Federation Council is now formed by two permanent representatives, one nominated by each region's executive branch and one by the legislature. The new representatives can be dismissed in the same way as they are selected. Current members of the Federation Council who were not members of local legislatures lost immunity from criminal prosecution after 1 January 2002. Regional leaders won the right to recall their representatives, thus reducing the latter to little more than puppets. The new composition of the Federation Council was highly heterogeneous. For example, the newly elected governor of Krasnodar krai, Aleksandr Tkachev, in late 2000 appointed his predecessor Nikolai Kondratenko, who had become notorious for his anti-semitic comments. Up to a third of the new senators had no ties with their nominating region, appointed typically because of their lobbying powers in Moscow. A large number were businesspeople and others who combined duties in the FC with other activities. A law in 2007 introduced a 10-year residence qualification in the regions to be represented by senators, although the changes would be introduced gradually to allow existing members to serve out their terms. The 10 years would start from when a person turned 18, but would not have to be continuous, and would apply primarily to FC members nominated by regional legislatures.

The chairman of the Federation Council, Yegor Stroev, had long argued in favour of constitutional reform, but Putin's plans were not to his liking. He insisted that neither parliamentary house quarrelled with Putin's main argument that a system of power had to be built: 'Russia must be a federal, democratic, unified country where all laws are the same for all citizens, whether they live in Chechnya, Tatariya, or Orël *Oblast*.'[30] Indeed, at this time Fedorov, together with some like-minded senators, sought to appeal against the reforms of the Federation Council to the Constitutional Court, insisting that the changes entailed a 'revision of the existing constitutional structure of the Russian Federation'.[31] With the replacement on 6 December 2001 of Stroev by the Petersburger and Putin ally Sergei Mironov as speaker of the upper house, the Federation Council was brought firmly within the ambit of the presidential bloc. Yet another link in the chain of the 'vertical of power' had been forged.

This was reinforced by the shift to the appointment of governors in 2004 (see below). The term of a governor's representative in the FC is the same as that of the nominating governor, so if a governor's term ends prematurely, so does that of the representative. The abolition of gubernatorial elections clearly undermined the separation of powers at the federal level. Important questions about the constitutional status of the new-style Federation Council remain. The upper chamber according to the 1993 constitution has the right to declare a state of emergency, to authorise the use of the military abroad, to appoint and remove the Prosecutor- General, and many other important functions. With the new assembly made up of nominated figures, is it appropriate for these tasks to remain with the assembly; would it not be better for them to be fulfilled by the Duma? A constitutional amendment would be required to make the change, yet Putin consistently avoided talk of amending the constitution. The reform raised important institutional questions, as well as equally important political ones. As the president of Chuvashia, Nikolai Fedorov, noted at the time, 'the bill causes a destruction of the system of checks and balances, and is very dangerous for democracy.'[32] This state of affairs was unsustainable, and hence discussion during Putin's second term of returning to a directly elected upper chamber became even more intense.[33] This was an issue that Putin's successor would have to deal with as a matter of urgency.

### State Council and Legislative Council

The creation by presidential decree on 1 September 2000 of a para-constitutional consultative body known as the State Council under the president further undermined the

Federation Council. Stroev in particular opposed the establishment of the new body, whose relationship with the existing two houses of parliament is unclear.[34] The head of regional affairs in the Presidential Administration, Sergei Samoilov, suggested that the new State Council would fulfil important functions, such as key appointments and the declaration of war and states of emergency, but conceded that such a drastic shift of responsibilities away from the Federation Council would 'require some legislative changes or amendments to the constitution'. However, he was in no hurry to see the constitution amended, insisting that 'the constitution has sufficient political and legal flexibility.'[35] The creation of the State Council is a classic example of Putin's para-constitutionalism, by-passing the constitution rather than changing it.

The State Council is made up of regional leaders, allowing them to retain direct access to the national leadership. Since the body is consultative, its creation did not require amending the constitution. The State Council appeared a sop to the regional leaders displaced from membership in the Federation Council. Its presidium consists of seven regional leaders serving for six months each, one from each federal district. It meets in plenary session once every three months to discuss two main topics, usually prepared by one of the commissions headed by a presidium member, which in turn supervise the 22 working groups. The State Council took on functions that were the prerogative of parliament, including discussing regional and federal reform, but its views lacked legislative force. A decree signed by Putin on 24 February 2007 modified the Council's structure. It now has an Advisory Commission, made up of between 10–15 academics and former regional leaders to be selected by the president.[36] Thus the restrictions on former regional leaders participating in the Council's work was lifted; the decree of 1 September 2000 had allowed only those who had served two terms on the Council to continue their membership.[37] The State Council thus became rather more similar to the Yeltsin-era Presidential Council, which quite apart from anything else was intended to improve the quality of information received by the executive.

To balance the State Council, a Legislative Council was created on 21 May 2002 to allow the heads of legislative assemblies to take part in the discussion of national policies. It meets in plenary session twice a year, but its presidium, comprising the heads of certain regional assemblies, leading figures of the FC, and the seven *polpredy*, meets quarterly. The president and federal ministers also occasionally attend plenary sessions.

### Role of the Federation Council

The constitution requires an upper house for the Duma to be able to act as a law-making body. The FC shares the legislative role with the Duma, with a majority in both houses required for most bills to become law. If the president vetoes a bill, a two-thirds majority is required to override the veto. Certain legislative functions are exclusively the preserve of the upper house (Article 102.1), above all matters affecting the republics and regions, approval of internal border changes, confirming presidential decrees, imposing a state of emergency or martial law, the use of armed forces outside the Russian Federation, scheduling presidential elections, impeachment of the president (following a complicated procedure), and certain judicial functions including (on the president's initiative) ratifying and removing from office the Procurator-General, appointing judges of the Constitutional, Supreme and Supreme Arbitration Courts, and overseeing federal laws adopted by the State Duma.

Bills are usually drafted by committees of the Duma and then, if passed by a simple majority, are sent to the FC where, if supported by half of the FC, become law when signed by the president. In case of disagreement a reconciliation committee is established. Most laws passed by the Duma are automatically forwarded to the president if the Council does not consider them within 14 days. Certain categories of laws, however, must be approved by the Council before they are sent to the president. These include laws concerning the federal budget; federal taxes and collections; financial, currency, credit, or customs regulations, as well as monetary emissions; the ratification or denunciation of international treaties; the status and defence of Russian Federation borders; and declarations of war and peace. The question of equality of rights between the two houses does not arise since the two bodies have different functions, a major advance in the development of constitutional order in Russia. However, certain functions that might properly be considered the prerogative of the Duma, like the right to introduce a state of emergency or the decision to send troops abroad, are granted by the constitution (Article 102) to the FC rather than to the Duma as a result of the convulsions of 1991–3.[38]

Since members of the FC between 1996 and 2001 were full-time regional officials, they had little time to devote to Federation Council matters, usually no more than three days a month. To compensate, the FC's apparatus was strengthened to increase the throughput of legislation. Indeed, the work of the FC's specialist committees at this time was exemplary, drawing on a large pool of expertise. The FC acts as a counterweight to the Duma and has been able to moderate conflict between the president and the lower house, especially when the latter (like the Second Duma between 1996 and 1999) was dominated by communists. The Council rejected draft laws (for example, on social benefits or restrictive land codes) that would have been vetoed by Yeltsin, thus lowering the political temperature. The work of the upper house demonstrated the irrelevance of party labels, and appeals for support had to be couched in the language of regional interests. As the membership of the Council changed in 2001, however, a group called 'Federatsiya' was formed in support of Putin encompassing some hundred members. The Council today is loosely affiliated along party lines, with United Russia predominant in the Putin era, as in the lower house.

# Part III

# Nationalism, federalism and regionalism

The disintegration of the USSR posed ever more sharply the question of how an independent Russia would organise its territorial space and the multinational community of which it was composed. Many in Russia feared that the centrifugal forces that had torn the Soviet Union apart would not stop there and threatened the very existence of Russia as a state. The secessionist challenge posed by Chechnya was only the most extreme form of a general spirit of the period that sought to enhance the powers of Russia's sub-national units. For a number of republics, and indeed some regions, within Russia, sovereignty came to be equated with federal non-interference in their internal affairs and economic autarchy. Instead of developing a sustained legal framework for federalism, under Yeltsin a segmented regionalism emerged reflecting not so much the spatial separation of powers but the fragmentation of political authority. Sovereignty claims by regional leaders, including in the republics, gained little support among the non-titular peoples, and even titular groups were divided. Putin sought to achieve the reconstitution of the citizen as the subject of Russian political space by giving substance to the idea of *Rossiiskii* citizenship – an aim that has been explicit effectively since the end of the nineteenth century. The degree to which the Russian state can serve as a framework for articulating multinational aspirations is as unclear now as it was then. The First World War 'revealed the incapacity of the weakly integrated and underinstitutionalized Tsarist state to stretch – in Benedict Anderson's neat formulation – "the short, tight skin of the nation over the gigantic body of the empire" (p. 84)'.[1]

The existence of Russia in its present borders is disputed. Gorbachev questioned the viability of Russia on its own. As he put it:

> increasingly, the Russian people understand they were deceived...the press and television in Russia try to convince people that what is needed today, above all, is to think about 'how to live in Russia'. *But in fact the very question of 'how to live in Russia' involves the question of what to do about integration, how to arrange relations with other member states of the CIS* [italics in original].[2]

All three federal communist systems had disintegrated: the USSR, Yugoslavia and Czechoslovakia, and in the early 1990s many expected the Russian Federation to go the same way. In the event new ways were found of binding together the new state. The comparison with the USSR is misleading because the dynamics of Russian politics are very different; there are powerful centripetal trends that check the tendency towards disintegration. Fear of disintegration, however, permeated the politics of the post-communist era.

# 10   National identity and state-building

> States are not given by some supranatural dispensation. They are the result of purposeful activities exercised through forced projects or political contracts. States are not eternal – especially not as to size and shape – and they are perceived differently by members of the society, designated by state borders as well as by the outside world. States are constituted not only by territories, by citizenship, and by a legal-constitutional framework ... Only shared values, symbols, and a mutually accepted legal-political order can provide the necessary broad popular legitimization: top-level agreements and even international recognition are insufficient to build or uphold a state.
>
> (Valeri Tishkov)[1]

One of the unique features of West European development was the emergence fairly early on of territorially sovereign states whose relations were regulated, at least since the Treaty of Westphalia in 1648, by a rudimentary system of international law. These sovereign states in time evolved into nations based on principles of popular sovereignty in which the nation was considered to consist of a broad political community expressing the political will of all the people. In the eastern half of the continent, however, dominated by empires until the First World War, the concept of nation retained a primordial ethnicised content whereby an individual was a member of an ethnic community irrespective of their will. The nation was a community relatively independent of politics, allowing several culturally based nations to coexist within a multinational state. Kohn drew the famous distinction between the alleged 'Western' form of nationalism, which was 'civic' and 'rational', and the 'Eastern' type that was 'organic'.[2] Such a distinction is inappropriate for contemporary Russia, although the distinction does help structure debate. Russia offers a third approach to the idea of nationhood where ethnicity and democratic inclusion is entwined with the ethics of state survival itself. It is the tension between these three currents – national (ethnic) self-affirmation; civic participation (building a democratic political community) and (imperial) statism – that have shaped post-communist Russian national identity and state building.

## From empire to state

The natural corollary of the question 'what is Russia?' is the question 'who are the Russians?' The population of Russia at the time of the 1989 census was 147.02 million, 51.4 per cent of the USSR's population of 286.72 million. The proportion of ethnic Russians in the Soviet population had fallen to just over half, 50.78 per cent, but in

Russia itself they represented 81.5 per cent (119.86 million).[3] Thus 18.5 per cent of the population of the Russian Federation (some 27 million people) at the time of independence were ethnically non-Russian (*Rossiiskie* rather than ethnically *Russkie*). Slightly fewer, some 25 million, ethnic Russians in 1989 lived beyond its borders. The fundamental ambiguity over the definition and status of Russians abroad, described by terms such as 'compatriots' (*sootechestvenniki*) or 'Russian speakers' (*russkoyazychnye*), reflects ambiguity over the identity of Russia itself. Sovietisation was no less intense in Russia than in the other republics, but the largely Russian face to the Soviet regime masked the devastation that Russian culture and society had also suffered during the communist period. While political representation was denied Russia, the opportunities for social advancement in the Soviet regime were enhanced and the cultural prestige of Russia was augmented. It is for this reason that Russian nationalism was to stand in a far more complex relationship to the communist regime and democratic revolution than elsewhere.

### Empire and nation

Neither the Russian empire before 1917 nor the USSR had been nation-states in the conventional sense, but neither were they, according to patriots and others, empires in the colonialist sense. Beissinger stresses the ambiguity in the distinction between states and empires, with the Tsarist empire in particular representing 'a confused mix of empire and state-building'.[4]

Russia did not have an empire; it was an empire. For much of its history Russia did not have a nation as such.[5] In 1721 Peter the Great had declared Russia an empire, a move designed to elevate the grandeur of the country and his throne, but even before that the country had not had stable institutions of nationhood. The very existence of Muscovy was bound up with dynastic politics and its sense of nationhood was only embryonic. Occupied by the Mongols from 1240 to 1480 and with the various Russian principalities forced to pay tribute to this alien power, Russia had been torn away from Europe and its developmental pattern ever since had been at odds with mainstream European patterns. The Muscovite state had been the central force in the struggle against the Mongols, and ever since Russian national identity has been preoccupied with national defence. On the great Eurasian plain, with few natural boundaries other than major rivers but no mountains other than the severely eroded Urals chain, defence took the form of expansion, and from the sixteenth century the drive to 'gather the Russian lands' around Muscovy accelerated. Migration, colonisation and state expansion were the rhyme, if not the reason, of Russian history. Russian identity and the Russian state became bound up with the idea of territorial expansion of the empire. In the words of Sergei Witte, Russia's great statesman at the turn of the twentieth century, 'ever since the time of Peter the Great and Catherine the Great there has been no such thing as Russia; only a Russian empire'.[6]

Russia entered the modern era as an empire, but a distinctive one since it lacked the characteristic division between a metropolis and a periphery. The development of the Russian state thoroughly confused the concepts of empire and nation, although the encounter with the stubborn resistance of the North Caucasian peoples in the nineteenth century saw Russia's expansion assume more classically colonial features. On the whole, the pattern of Russian expansion was absorptive rather than simply destructive, and ever more nations lived together within the framework of imperial institutions and law. It was far from being the 'prison-house of peoples', as Marx had inadequately dubbed the Russian multinational empire, although for Poles and Chechens, the two nations who most stubbornly resisted subordination, Marx's designation was accurate. Only under Alexander III in the 1880s had there begun a general retreat from imperial supranational policies to build a Russian nation through the Russification and assimilation of peoples. Russia at this time moved away from being an 'empire-state' based, like the Habsburg empire, not on the colonial model of the subjugation of peoples but a system in which all came under the tutelage of an abstract supra-ethnic ruler (the emperor).

The USSR, too, had been an empire-state, incarnated no longer in the form of an individual but in the guise of the collective emperor, the Communist Party. Lenin had been hostile to Russian nationalism, considering it almost by definition as chauvinistic. Within months of the Bolshevik revolution, Lenin began a ruthless attack on the cradle of Russian national identity, the Russian Orthodox Church, expropriating its wealth and launching a virulent campaign of atheism. Lenin was well aware that the Orthodox Church represented a bastion of civil society and thus an island of resistance to Bolshevik values and political dominance. He was intent on not allowing Russian Orthodoxy to assume the role that the Roman Catholic church played in Poland, as the symbol of resistance to Russian imperial power; and later, in the post-war communist years, as the bastion of national culture that ultimately contributed to the fall of Polish communism. In Russia by the late 1920s the official church had compromised with the atheist state in what was called Sergianism, after the capitulation of Patriarch Sergei to the secular authorities in 1927. The policy of indigenisation (*korenizatsiya*) during the 1920s, which sought to redress some of the imbalances of Tsarist nationality policy by advancing national elites to positions of power in the non-Russian areas, was inherently anti-Russian. This was a golden period for most non-Russian nationalities, advancing national languages and cultures, before the policy was largely reversed by Stalin in the 1930s, although native language teaching remained.[7] Stalin's collectivisation from 1929 destroyed the peasantry, the backbone of the Russian nation and the source of its most profound spiritual and cultural traditions; and the purges in 1937–8 destroyed the old intelligentsia, the source of the brilliant age of cultural achievement from the middle of the nineteenth century.

A new Soviet intelligentsia was born, and at the same time concessions were made to the form if not the content of Russian identity and history. Stalin increasingly used Russian nationalism as a way of relegitimising the Soviet system, especially during the Second World War (known as the Great Patriotic War, to distinguish it from the Patriotic War of 1812 against Napoleon) but at the same time gutted it of any cultural or historical dynamism. The complaints of the other republics against the union centre were often directed against Russia, with whom the union was understandably and often deliberately confused. To the other republics (and to a certain extent to Russians as well), Soviet power was synonymous with Russian power. Russians predominated in positions of authority, especially in the central apparatus of government and party, and the Russian language and culture buttressed their position. The USSR appeared a 'Russian' empire in a new guise.[8]

Russia's identity was dissolved in that of the USSR, and not only the peripheral republics but Russia also was ruled by Soviet Moscow in a neo-colonialist manner. The development of Russian national consciousness and statehood was inhibited. Russia itself was less shielded against central policies than perhaps any of the other republics, and its social and economic welfare was neglected. Its educational level was among the worst of any of the republics, and its standard of living was in the middle range. The physical decay of Russia's towns and countryside was vividly described by Russia's 'village writers', such as Valentin Rasputin and Vasily Shukshin, and demonstrated for them Russia's lack of economic and social privileges in the Soviet system. What was to be done about it was another question, since Russia was the core of the Soviet 'empire', even though Russia may not have been particularly privileged in that system. Unlike the 'national liberation' movements in the other republics of the USSR, Russian anti-communist movements were not necessarily anti-imperialist or ethnically based. Russia had never achieved a developed sense of itself as a nation-state and no distinction between empire and nation was considered necessary in Russian thought, since Russia by destiny was considered to be an imperial nation. Even the Slavophiles of the nineteenth century did not advocate a retreat from empire, although they recognised the burden that it imposed. This fragmented response to the Soviet system's simultaneous exploitation and elevation of Russia continued into the independence period and beyond. The democratic movement in Russia, unlike in the Baltic republics and elsewhere, could not simply jettison Soviet 'imperialism', since this meant the rejection of much of what had made Russian history meaningful to many generations. The full implications of this dilemma have still not been fully worked out in contemporary Russia.

Only from the 1960s, as part of so-called dissent, did a rediscovered sense of anti-Soviet and anti-imperial Russian national identity and consciousness begin to take shape.[9] The new Russian nationalists were sustained by a profound sense of the crisis in which the Russian nation found itself, a crisis marked by the weakening sense of Russian identity, the loss of Russian national traditions, the destruction of the countryside and social coherence, and Russia's lack of status within the USSR. Solzhenitsyn was one of the first to argue that Russia was paying too high a price for empire, an empire moreover that was only pseudo-Russian, insisting that Russia was squandering the resources it needed for its own regeneration. He stressed that the heart of the Soviet system was an ideology based not on a people but on an abstract utopianism interpreted by a political party, and warned against the destruction of the Russian people while arguing that minority groups should be allowed to secede from the USSR.[10] He urged the regime to abandon communist ideology, insisting that only if it did so could it save the people, and probably itself too. For his pains, in 1974 he was sent into exile. Igor Shafarevich argued that in their attempts to undermine so-called 'great Russian chauvinism', the old regime had generated and sustained an innate Russophobia.[11]

During the 'stagnation' period under Brezhnev an *official* Russian nationalism flourished to buttress the decaying regime, but this nationalism was used to support Soviet colonialist imperialism both in relation to the non-Russian Soviet republics and abroad. Early on in Brezhnev's regime two members of the Politburo, Dmitry Polyansky and Alexander Shelepin, were dismissed for allegedly promoting the Russian nationalist cause and defending Russian national interests. Only a few years later, however, Alexander Yakovlev, later to be one of the architects of *perestroika,* was punished for his denunciation of renascent Russian nationalism. In a long article in the November 1971 issue of *Literaturnaya gazeta* Yakovlev, then acting head of the Propaganda Department of the CPSU's Central Committee, condemned the anti-Leninist stance adopted by various nationalists and neo-Stalinists in some official publications. In response, he was dismissed from his post and sent into 'exile' in Canada to serve as Soviet ambassador until recalled by Gorbachev. The incident revealed the extent to which communist ideology was being eroded by an incipient Russian nationalism long before the fall of the USSR. The regime tolerated a Sovietified Russian nationalism to compensate for the declining appeal of Marxism-Leninism, but repressed all manifestations of an independent anti-communist Russian national ideal.

### From Soviet to Russian

When the long-awaited revolt of the nationalities against the Soviet state came, it was led by Russia, something few had anticipated. The disintegration of the USSR was accompanied by some unanticipated political dynamics. Who could have predicted, for example, that in the final period of the Soviet Union an alliance would form between Russian radicals and nationalists in the other republics;[12] or between Russian nationalists and communist hardliners? Communist internationalism now gave way to a 'renationalisation' of politics, and some strange patterns emerged. Russian radicals after the coup were astonished to find themselves denounced as 'democratic imperialists' by newly mobilised nationalists in the other republics, a large proportion of whom had until recently been loyal Soviet officials. Although in the Soviet system power relations to some extent coincided with ethnicity, with Slavs (rather than Russians narrowly defined) predominant, the struggle against communism was only tangentially a struggle against the dominance of ethnic Russian, especially since under Brezhnev national elites had thoroughly consolidated their positions in the ethno-federal republics.

Already towards the end of the Soviet regime the distinctive features of patriotic and nationalist tendencies in Russian national thought had emerged. The *patriotic* trend stressed Russia's spiritual traditions, the revival of Orthodoxy, and the need to act as stewards of Russia's environment in harmony with the many peoples who share the Eurasian land mass. The *nationalists* espoused a far more aggressive view, stressing Russia's imperial role as the 'gatherer of the lands' and drew on the national Bolshevik tradition of Nikolai Ustryalov in the 1920s and the *Eurasianist* thinking of the time to proclaim Russia's separateness from the West and its destiny to dominate the Eurasian landmass. They emphasised the need for military power, rule over the non-Russian peoples and contempt for the decadent West.[13] The Soviet regime could make common cause with the second but was profoundly at odds with the first.

In the union republics the awakening of political consciousness during *perestroika* took on national forms: the struggle against Sovietisation was accompanied by the attempt to separate from the 'centre' in Moscow, thus implicitly taking on an anti-Russian hue. The rebirth of Russia, however, was a struggle not only against the communist centre but also against elements of Russia's own history. Here it was not only the story of the imposition of a foreign ideology borne by an alien culture, but of destroying a system that in a peculiar form had made Russia great. Rejecting the Soviet and communist past meant rejecting not only the tragedies but also the triumphs of the past: the gleaming hydro-electric installation on the Dnieper, Stalingrad, the Soviet flag over Berlin in May 1945, the first sputnik in space in 1957 followed soon after by the first cosmonaut (Yuri Gagarin in 1961), and the achievement of superpower parity in 1976. While nationalism and anti-communism marched hand in hand in the non-Russian republics, in Russia there could be no such simple equation. Russian nationalists allied with hardline communists to save the (imperial) state.

The contradiction between the *nationalist* and *patriotic* faces of Russian national thinking (the term nationalism here is misleading) became evident during *perestroika*. The regime sought to use the nationalists against patriots and democrats, who were irreconcilable opponents of the communist (if not Soviet) regime. Russia's patriotic rebirth was perceived as one of the main enemies of communism and thus the authorities tried to discredit it. The extremist Pamyat' nationalist organisation, peddling a hysterical anti-semitism accompanied by the denunciation of freemasons, foreigners and democrats, was probably sponsored (and certainly tolerated) by the KGB to discredit the independent movement in general and Russian patriotism in particular. The influence of Pamyat', however, was greatly over-rated, in particular by those who sought to discredit any manifestation of Russian national identity, and the group never gained more than a handful of votes in any of the elections in which they stood. In a typically ambiguous way Gorbachev sought to co-opt some elements of Russian national rebirth to buttress the regime. The Orthodox Church in 1988 was allowed to celebrate the millennium of Christianity in Russia with great pomp, the representation of non-Russians in the Politburo was decreased to one (Shevardnadze), republican Party leaderships were purged to eliminate some of the corruption, and Russians given a greater role in Kazakhstan, Turkmenistan and Uzbekistan, and the 'project of the century', the scheme (opposed by Russian patriots) to divert Siberian rivers to Central Asia was cancelled.

Following the elections in March 1989 the struggle intensified for Russia to become a fully fledged republic within the USSR, with the full range of republican institutions and social organisations. Between the patriots and the nationalists the democrats now emerged as advocates of a distinctive form of denationalised (civic) political community in an independent Russian state. These 'democratic statists' sought to reassert Russia's political institutions and sovereignty in the struggle against the communist regime and the Soviet centre. The Russian nationalists now became alarmed, since while they supported the rebirth of Russia they considered that this should take place only within the framework of a (non-communist) union, insisting that Russia was the historic core of a multinational community. The nationalists, and indeed some of the patriots, soon realised that the struggle for state sovereignty by the many peoples that made up the USSR threatened the existence not only of communism and the Soviet Union but also of Russia itself.

A tacit alliance between Russian nationalists and conservatives within the communist regime itself was forged to preserve the union. The nationalists condemned the Union Treaty on the eve of the coup, as in Zyuganov's 'A Word to the People', the manifesto of the coup, and fought the hardest for a renewed union afterwards. Zyuganov's brand of communist nationalism later became the dominant trend in the CPRF.

### Russia after the empire

From the perspective of power politics, Russia was the greatest loser at the end of the Cold War. The fall of the USSR undermined the principles on which Russians had defined themselves as a state for centuries. The Bolshevik experience had lasted a mere 74 years, but its fall shattered the statehood (*gosudarstvennost'*) that had emerged in the course of a millennium. Russia had lost territory before when in 1918 Poland and Finland gained their independence, although some of their territory was regained by Stalin during the Second World War. The separation of the Central Asian republics also did not affect Russia's core perception of itself, having only been incorporated in the late nineteenth century and then bound loosely to Russia. But the alienation of Ukraine, and to a lesser degree Belarus, struck at the very heart of Russian self-identity. It was in Ukraine that the Russian state emerged and here were born many of Russia's greatest writers: Nikolai Gogol in Poltava, Anna Akhmatova in Odessa and Mikhail Bulgakov in Kiev. The former editor of *Moscow News*, Len Karpinsky, observed that 'Millions of Russians are convinced that, without Ukraine, it is impossible to speak not only of a great Russia but of any kind of Russia at all.'[14] It came as a shock for Russians to have to start thinking about Ukraine as a separate country: a shock that the English survived when most of Ireland and the homeland of some of the greatest 'English' writers such as Jonathan Swift and George Bernard Shaw achieved independence.

Ukrainians, however, argue that the contemporary Russian state draws its provenance not from Kiev but had developed as a new state separate and distinct from the earlier Kievan Rus' following the Mongol conquest.[15] As the French discovered during the decolonisation of Algeria, it is not always easy to distinguish between core and periphery. On the Eurasian landmass, with weak natural frontiers, historically shifting borders and centuries of migration and intermarriage, this is an even more intractable problem. The separation of Algeria or Ireland did not strike to the very heart of the identities of France or Britain, but Russia appeared to lose part of its soul. Those on the wrong side of borders after 1991 were liable to develop a form of *pieds noirs* nationalism, and those on the 'right' side could become prey to revanchism and neo-imperialism.

After the Soviet collapse Russia lost access to nearly half of its traditional ports, retaining only 600 kilometres of the Black Sea coast and the same length of the Caspian shore. Half the merchant fleet went to Russia while the Black Sea Fleet became the subject of acrimonious disputes with Ukraine. Sentiments of defeat, retreat, loss and humiliation placed enormous strains on the fragile democratic institutions. Democracy and the attempts to rejoin Western civilisation in the popular mind began to be equated not only with economic hardship but the destruction of the state itself. The writer Alexander Zinoviev had already argued that *perestroika* was an unmitigated disaster, dubbing it *katastroika*.[16] Now others began to argue that democracy itself was a comparable disaster for Russia.[17] The USSR had reformed itself out of existence, and now there was a danger that Russia would go the same way.

## Russian nationalism and national identity

The fall of the USSR forced a redefinition of Russian identity: Russia had never been a nation-state, and it was now not a question of appealing to tradition but of creating a new national identity. One of the issues dividing patriots, nationalists and democrats was the question of how much of the Russian past was 'usable' in the present. Tsipko asked 'if the formation of a new Russian statehood is unavoidable, on which historical foundations should it be built?'.[18] The choice between 'empire' and 'nation' was far from clear cut, since by its very nature there would be imperial elements in Russian national identity derived not necessarily from any aggressive tendencies but from its sheer size, history and demography. The patriots sought to maintain the union (by democratic means), and even sections of the reborn democracy could not reconcile themselves to the smaller nation-state form of Russia, while the nationalists openly espoused the reintegration of the former Soviet Union, denouncing the creation of the CIS.

### Nationalism and patriotism

Russia's 'nationalism' is of a peculiar sort. The country's struggle for sovereignty in the late Soviet years was both national *and* democratic; Russia's rebirth as an independent state took a national form but did not adopt the classic exclusive forms of nationalism. 'Nationalism' as such is something largely alien to the Russian tradition, where the focus has historically been on maintaining the state or empire. Russian ethnic nationalism has traditionally been rather weak, and instead the main identifiers of political identity have been more statist and civilisational. Klyamkin noted that 'Nationalism has not taken root in the Russian mentality, and contrary to the West, is perceived by Russians with suspicion.'[19] Patriots in the Slavophile tradition consider nationalism yet another Western invention, like Marxism, imposed on the long-suffering Russian people from outside.

The distinction between patriots and nationalists is one drawn by patriots themselves. Patriots draw on the 'soil-bound' (*pochvennik*) tradition of Slavophilism and stress the existence of a historically constituted supranational community on the Eurasian land-mass in which all the various peoples were broadly able to pursue their own destinies, even when incorporated into the Russian empire. While Russians might be an 'elder brother' to some of the peoples, with a particularly rich culture and destiny, all the various cultures had an equal right to their development. This 'imperial' approach is supranational and stresses the rights of individuals and communities rather than nations. The Eurasianist Elgiz Pozdnyakov insists that patriotism, love of the motherland and one's people, has nothing common with nationalism.[20] In his view 'Nationalism is the last stage of communism, the last attempt of an outdated ideology to find in society support for dictatorship'.[21] We have seen that this was indeed the case in 1989–91, when hardline communists forged an alliance with conservative Russian nationalists. The nationalists stress precisely the development of state structures exalting the ethnic Russian nation and defend a type of colonialist relationship with other peoples and its neighbours. Nationalists consider the Soviet regime, with its crude 'Russification' poli-cies and its power politics, in a more favourable light than the patriots, and hence were willing to ally with old-style Soviet communists.

The tension that was apparent throughout the Soviet era, and which divided the 'dis-sident' Russian national movement in the Brezhnev years, continues to this day. On the one hand, the *gosudarstvenniki* (statists or state-builders) argue that a strong Russian state is the central feature of the very existence of the Russian people, and thus draw on the tradition of the 'national Bolsheviks' who from the 1920s made their peace with the Soviet system, which had re-assembled most of the Russian empire. Today this tra-dition is reflected most vigorously in the pages of Alexander Prokhanov's paper *Zavtra* (before October 1993 *Den'*), arguing that for centuries the Russian multinational state had been engaged in a struggle to defend 'the Russian idea' against cosmopolitanism, freemasonry and Zionism. As Dostoevsky had suggested earlier, Russia should turn its back on the decadent and insidious West and seek its destiny in the East (the Eurasian option). On the other hand, the *vozrozhdentsy* (a term that can loosely be translated as 'revivalists') condemned the Soviet state and Marxist ideology for having subverted the true nature of Russian statehood and culture, and insist that only the cultural and moral revival of the Russian people, based on the values of Orthodoxy, can save Russia. Solzhenitsyn is firmly in this tradition, insisting unequivocally: 'The time has come for an uncompromising *choice* between an empire of which we ourselves are the primary victims, and the spiritual and physical salvation of our own people.'[22]

Yeltsin's own approach was unabashedly that of a civic nationalist. He exploited the power of Russian patriotism in the struggle against communism, and later sought to find a way of incorporating patriotic demands within the democratic political order, a balancing act that was not always successful and appeared at times to concede too much to nationalists. Ultimately, however, he did not compromise in his struggle to advance an inclusive form of Russian citizenship, and rejected all forms of exclusive ethnicised nationalism, a policy continued by Putin later. Neither Yeltsin nor Putin tried to take advantage of the grievances of Russians abroad to broaden their political base. While Hitler had exploited the grievances of the *Volksdeutsche* (Germans after the First World War who ended up as minorities in the newly independent national states), the Russian leaders refused to make capital out of the concerns of a comparable group of '*Volksrussen*' in the former USSR. Excoriated by the national-patriots for allegedly betraying their compatriots, Yeltsin remained the president of all citizens in Russia and refused to proclaim himself the militant defender of Russians abroad, as Slobodan Milošević had done in Serbia.

In the post-communist world Milošević was an extreme form of a general type: the *nomenklatura* nationalist. In the Russian republics there was no shortage of this type of leader, in particular in the North Caucasus and the Volga. Numerous studies have demonstrated how the political establishments existing at the end of communism successfully maintained themselves in power, typically by placing themselves at the head of national movements. Instead of taking a virulently expansionist form, as in the quest to create a 'greater Serbia', *nomenklatura* nationalists in post-communist Russia precisely focused on drawing the sting from ethnic mobilisation. In Tatarstan, for example, Shaimiev exploited the power of Tatar national feelings but managed to incorporate the large non-Tatar communities into the expanded definition of Tatarstani sovereignty.[23] However, where the fall of communism was accompanied by a revolution against the *nomenklatura*, as in Chechnya, events took a more violent turn. In Chechnya radical decommunisation was accompanied by the coming to power of radical nationalists. This was the case also in Georgia under Zviad Gamsakhurdia, provoking secessionist movements in South Ossetia and Abkhazia. In Central Asia, however, *nomenklatura* nationalists firmly held on to power. In Turkmenistan the old party boss Saparmurad Niyazov transformed himself into a post-communist nationalist leader, as did Nazarbaev in Kazakhstan and Islam Karimov in Uzbekistan. In Tajikistan the forces of radical nationalism and *nomenklatura* officialdom were more evenly ranged, resulting in a bitter civil war in which the latter finally triumphed. The most spectacular transformation was of Leonid Kravchuk in Ukraine, who changed from being the persecutor of national aspirations in the communist era to the proponent of nationalist state-building.

Although Yeltsin was a scion of the *nomenklatura* himself, retaining many of the habits of mind of that class, he personified all the contradictions of Russian national rebirth. He was able to transform himself from Party boss into national leader, but it was never clear whether he was able genuinely to make himself a democrat. He remained loyal to a post-imperial civic identity, but it was challenged by those who argued that he failed adequately to defend Russia's national interests. The civic approach was found wanting because of its failure effectively to incorporate patriotic concerns about the loss of Russia's status, the failure to defend Russians abroad or the integrity of the country at home. The strong vote given to the 'neo-imperial' part of the political spectrum (the communists and nationalists) reflected aspirations for the restoration of empire, territory, prestige and order. The weakness of organised liberal blocs left a profound political vacuum that various nationalist and patriotic groups sought to fill. The anti-Soviet democrats believed that the destruction of the old system would allow a new democratic system to be created, but they lacked a convincing programme of political and economic reforms for Russian conditions. The patriots advanced a set of alternative conservative values that were perhaps more in keeping with Russian traditions: nationality (*narodnost'*), fairness (*spravedlivost'*), patriotism and statehood (*gosudarstvennost'*), accompanied by such notions as spirituality (*dukhovnost'*) and morality (*nravstvennost'*) as part of the reinterpretation of the 'Russian idea' which rejected the liberal emphasis on materialism, the democratic emphasis on individualism and the reformers' emphasis on Westernisation. Post-communist Russian patriotic movements, however, found themselves locked into a dialectics of extremism. The excesses and hysteria that marked much of the thinking of the national-patriots during the transition period inhibited the development of a constitutional patriotic conservatism – until Putin gave voice to this constituency.

A distinctive liberal 'national democratic' tendency began to take shape in the early 1990s, joined in the early period by such figures as Rumyantsev, Lukin, Stankevich, Boris Fedorov and many more. The new national democrats insisted that they could provide an alternative to the 'vulgarised version of the "Russian idea"', which stressed the cult of the state and of Russia as a great power, and which associated the idea of empire and state. They insisted that 'only a democratic Russia could be great', a greatness which lay 'not in force but in truth, not in material power but in nobility of spirit'. The growth of chauvinism would only provoke the persecution of Russians in other CIS states, and then turn back on Russia itself in the form of refugees and migration.[24] National democrats tried to demonstrate that not all manifestations of Russian identity were right-wing and sought to retrieve the national idea from the domination of the nationalists, including the national communist in the CPRF, with their inability to understand the aspirations of the peoples of Russia for sovereignty, their crude threats to the other former Soviet republics and their hankering for the restoration of the old USSR. This national democratic tendency came into its own under Putin, combining liberal market principles, democratic legitimacy, resigned acceptance that the Soviet Union was gone forever, and the need for international economic integration, but fiercely defending what they perceived to be Russia's national interests.

### Defining the national community

Russia had never been (and still is not) a classical nation-state focused on a single titular nationality but remains a 'state-nation' – a multinational entity focused on the institutions of the state.[25] The 2002 census identified 182 distinct nationalities living in Russia, although ethnic Russians made up 79.8 per cent of the population, down from the 81.5 per cent in 1989 (Table 10.1). We can take the argument a little further and argue that in state-nations the concept of multiculturalism is inadequate, since it suggests toleration by a hegemonic nation of the values of other, more recent, additions to the community. Instead, we can tentatively advance the notion of *pluriculturalism*, where

Table 10.1 National composition of Russian Federation, 1989 and 2002

| Ethnic group | 1989 | | Living on the territory of their own ethno-federal unit, 1989 | | 2002 |
|---|---|---|---|---|---|
| | Total | % of RF population | Number | % of the national group | |
| Total population | 147,021,869 | 100 | – | – | 145,166,731 |
| Of whom: | – | – | – | – | |
| Russians: | 119,865,946 | 81.53 | – | – | 115,889,107 |
| living outside ethno-federal areas | 108,063,409 | 73.50 | – | – | |
| living in others' ethno-federal areas | 11,802,537 | 8.03 | – | – | |
| Tatars | 5,521,096 | 3.75 | 1,765,404 | 31.97 | 5,554,601 |
| Ukrainians | 4,362,872 | 2.96 | – | – | 2,942,961 |
| Chuvash | 1,773,645 | 1.21 | 906,922 | 51.10 | 1,637,094 |
| Bashkirs | 1,345,273 | 0.91 | 863,808 | 64.21 | 1,673,389 |
| Belarusians | 1,206,222 | 0.82 | – | – | 807,870 |
| Mordvinians | 1,072,939 | 0.72 | 313,420 | 29.21 | 843,350 |
| Chechens | 898,999 | 0.61 | 734,501 | 81.71 | 1,360,253 |
| Germans | 842,000 | 0.57 | – | – | 597,212 |
| Udmurts | 714,833 | 0.49 | 496,522 | 69.46 | 636,906 |
| Maris | 643,698 | 0.44 | 324,349 | 50.39 | 604,298 |
| Kazakhs | 635,865 | 0.43 | – | – | 653,962 |
| Avars | 544,016 | 0.37 | 496,077 | 91.19 | 814,473 |
| Jews | 536,846 | 0.36 | 8,886 | 1.65 | 229,938 |
| Armenians | 532,390 | 0.36 | – | – | 1,130,491 |
| Buryats | 417,425 | 0.28 | 341,185 | 81.74 | 445,175 |
| Ossets | 402,275 | 0.27 | 334,876 | 83.24 | 514,875 |
| Kabards | 386,055 | 0.26 | 363,492 | 94.15 | 653,962 |
| Yakuts | 380,242 | 0.26 | 365,236 | 96.05 | 443,852 |
| Dargins | 353,348 | 0.24 | 280,431 | 79.36 | 510,156 |
| Azerbaijanis | 335,889 | 0.23 | – | – | 621,840 |
| Komis | 336,309 | 0.23 | 291,541 | 86.69 | 293,406 |
| Kumyks | 277,163 | 0.19 | 231,805 | 83.63 | 422,409 |
| Lezgins | 257,270 | 0.17 | 204,370 | 79.43 | 411,535 |
| Ingush | 215,068 | 0.15 | 163,762 | 76.14 | 413,016 |
| Tuvans | 206,160 | 0.14 | 198,448 | 96.26 | 243,442 |
| Peoples of the North | 182,000 | 0.12 | – | – | – |
| Moldovans | 172,671 | 0.12 | – | – | 172,330 |
| Kalmyks | 165,821 | 0.11 | 146,316 | 88.28 | 173,996 |
| Gypsies | 153,000 | 0.10 | – | – | 182,766 |
| Karachais | 150,332 | 0.10 | 129,449 | 86.11 | 192,182 |
| Komi-Permyaks | 147,269 | 0.09 | 95,215 | 64.65 | 125,235 |
| Georgians | 130,688 | 0.09 | – | – | 197,934 |
| Uzbeks | 126,899 | 0.09 | – | – | 122,916 |
| Karelians | 124,921 | 0.08 | 78,928 | 63.18 | 93,344 |
| Adygeis | 122,908 | 0.08 | 95,439 | 77.65 | 128,528 |
| Koreans | 107,000 | 0.07 | – | – | 148,556 |
| Laks | 106,245 | 0.07 | 91,682 | 86.29 | 156,545 |
| Poles | 95,000 | 0.06 | – | – | 73,001 |

(Continued)

*Table 10.1* cont'd

| Ethnic group | 1989 | | Living on the territory of their own ethno-federal unit, 1989 | | 2002 |
|---|---|---|---|---|---|
| | Total | % of RF population | Number | % of the national group | |
| Tabasarans | 93,587 | 0.06 | 78,196 | 83.55 | 131,785 |
| Greeks | 92,000 | 0.05 | – | – | 97,827 |
| Balkars | 78,341 | 0.05 | 70,793 | 90.36 | 108,426 |
| Khakas | 78,500 | 0.05 | 62,859 | 80.07 | 75,622 |
| Nogais | 73,703 | 0.05 | 28,294 | 38.39 | 90,666 |
| Lithuanians | 70,000 | – | – | – | 45,569 |
| Altaians | 69,409 | 0.05 | 59,130 | 85.19 | 67,239 |
| Cherkess | 50,764 | 0.03 | 40,241 | 79.27 | 60,517 |
| Nenets | 34,190 | 0.02 | 29,786 | 87.12 | 41,302 |
| Evenks | 29,901 | 0.02 | 3,480 | 11.64 | 35,527 |
| Khants | 22,283 | 0.01 | 11,892 | 53.37 | 28,678 |
| Rutuls | 19,503 | 0.01 | 14,955 | 76.68 | 29,929 |
| Aguls | 17,728 | 0.01 | 13,791 | 77.79 | 28,297 |
| Chukchis | 15,107 | 0.01 | 11,914 | 78.86 | 15,767 |
| Koryaks | 8,942 | – | 6,572 | 73.49 | 8,743 |
| Mansis | 8,279 | – | 6,562 | 79.26 | 11,432 |
| Dolgans | 6,584 | – | 4,939 | 75.01 | 7,261 |
| Tsakhurs | 6,492 | – | 5,194 | 80.00 | 10,366 |

*Sources*: *RSFSR v tsifrakh v 1989g.* (Moscow, Financy i statistika, 1990), pp. 23–5, modified; for 2002 data, *Svodnye itogi Vserossiiskoi perepis' naseleniya 2002 goda: itogi vesrossiiskoi perepisi naseleniya 2002 goda*, Vol. 14 (Moscow, Federal'naya sluzhba gosudarstvennoi statistiki), Table 4.1, pp. 272–5.

the community is comprised of a number of autochthonous peoples, each of whom can be considered native to the country and with equal rights to be considered the founding peoples of the state. This certainly would be the view of the Tatars, who have lived on the Volga for as long as Russians have inhabited their principalities on the Moscow and upper Volga rivers.

In this context, where historical and territorial narratives are contested, it is not surprising to find that Russian national identity is fluid and multi-layered. This is reflected in the rich but confusing language used to define Russians living in the RF and in the former Soviet states. Russians can define themselves in many different ways.

- To call oneself an ethnic *Russkii* signifies membership of the Russian people and a proprietary right of access to the Russian state, including protection by the Russian Federation.
- To be a *Rossiyanin*, on the other hand, emphasises membership of a non-ethnically defined community of citizens of many different ethnicities in the Russian Federation and beyond. Yeltsin was particularly keen on developing the notion of a supra-ethnic Russian identity, whereas Putin has advanced a rather more rooted pluriculturalist perspective, where each nationality can affirm its own identity as long as they are firmly subordinated as citizens to the Russian state. In Turkey an analogous term was introduced in the early 2000s, with the word *Turkiyelilik* denoting 'citizen

of Turkey', and already within four years an astonishing half of the population designated themselves as such.[26]

- A third definition is *Russkoyazychnye*, Russian-speakers. This suggests a broader community than that encompassed by the RF and includes Russian-speaking titular nationalities and minority groups. In Ukraine this would broaden the 11-million ethnic Russians to some 20 million, encompassing some 7 million Russian-speaking Ukrainians. Russian nationalist politicians have sought to gain political weight by exploiting the alleged grievances of this group, and the one below. However, the decline of Russian-language use reflects the long-term numerical decline of the community. In 2006 Russian was still the world's fourth most-spoken language, after English, Chinese and Spanish. The 130 million native speakers in Russia (excluding infants) were joined by another 26.4 million citizens of the former Soviet states whose native language was Russian, with another 7.5 million Russian-speakers scattered across the world.[27]

- A rather weaker category are *sootechestvenniki*, or compatriots, encompassing former citizens of the Soviet Union who seek to affiliate themselves in one way or another with the RF, but towards whom the RF itself bears no legal responsibility and towards whom political obligations are usually instrumental and mostly ignored unless suiting some broader purpose of the Russian political elite.[28] Under Putin this group was targeted as the source of labour migration and in-migration to compensate for population decline in the RF.[29] A number of pan-Eurasian associations have been established to represent the alleged interests of this diaspora community, beginning in 1994 with the Council of Compatriots, but the very term 'compatriot' remains contested.[30]

- The notion of citizen (*grazhdanin*) has gained in weight, and for Putin entailed an individual relationship to constitutional obligations that transcends ascriptive identities. The notion has gained in legal and political definition and suggests Russian diplomatic and political protection. The concept is at the core of the civic definition of nationhood.

- By analogy with the large Polish diaspora community sometimes known as 'Polonia', we can identify a nascent 'Russonia', a virtual community united by language and culture. Ethnic Russians now make up the second-largest minority within the European Union, with large settled communities in the Baltic republics and newly established groups in capitals such as London, where over a quarter of a million can now be found. New Russian-language newspapers and television stations cater for Russian diasporic settlements. Members of Russonia, although living elsewhere, are still oriented towards Russian values and culture. The concept of Russonia indicates the presence of a transnational community that resists full integration into the nation in which it finds itself, but which has few direct political links with the Russian state. It is a virtual community with little formal institutional identity, but which has an enormous cultural resonance in both its host state and with its putative 'mother' country. When one part of Russonia is attacked, as in Turkmenistan under Niyazov, the whole community endures a collective chill. The story of Russonia is far from over.

- Notions of pan-Slavic unity circulate at the borders of structure and ideology. Pan-Slavism has always been a very selective idea, with the Poles consistently resisting the view that they form a community of fate with their East Slavic brothers, or even with their West Slavic neighbours such as the Czechs and the Slovaks. In post-Soviet Eurasia Ukraine has now taken the role traditionally occupied by the Poles, refusing to entertain the idea that its membership of a broader community should be taken for granted; although in contrast with the Poles, there is a deeper popular sentiment in favour of various forms of solidarity with the East Slav community. The core Slavic axis today is between Russia and Belarus, but even here plans for the creation of a common state have proceeded in fits and starts since the 1990s, and are unlikely to result in full union in the foreseeable future. The presence of Kazakhstan as the great motor of integration, with its president, Nazarbaev, proposing various forms of Eurasian Union almost from the day after the disintegration of the Soviet Union, is clearly anomalous. Although hosting a large part of Russonia, Nazarbaev's plans clearly focus more on political and economic unity rather than trying to constitute some sort of Slavic entity.

Brubaker stresses that the three corners in his triadic relationship between the nationalising *state*, the national *minority* and the external *homeland* are fundamentally dynamic and relational concepts.[31] This is reflected in the debate over terms to be used to describe groups in the republics within the RF and beyond: indigenous population, titular nationality or premier groups. The idea of a 'titular nationality' is a very Soviet term and overshadows the rights of titularity that can be endowed by civic mechanisms. It is clear, moreover, that Russians outside the RF lack a single identity and are far from comprising a single category. Many non-Russian minorities who speak Russian consider themselves 'Russians'; while about 40 per cent of Russians 'abroad' were born in their republic of residence,[32] and many feel that they belong in that republic.

So, what is the Russian nation and how can it be identified?

- It can be associated with the Russian language and therefore with Russian speakers (*Russkoyazychnye* or *Russofony*). This immediately raises a number of problems. What about the large number of Russian-speakers (many of whom are ethnically non-Russian) in the former Soviet republics outside Russia? Are they part of the Russian nation; and if so, what relationship should they have with the Russian state?

- Alternatively, the Russian nation could be determined by ethnicity, with only ethnic Russians (*Russkie*) considered part of the Russian nation. But what about the 19 per cent of the inhabitants of the Russian Federation who are not ethnic Russians; and how is one to establish the difference, for example, between an ethnic Russian and an ethnic Belarusian? How does one define ethnicity? Is the Soviet definition of ethnic Russians as 'having Russian parents' acceptable? What about those of mixed parentage?

- The Russian nation can be identified through religion. For some scholars, like Edward Keenan, the Orthodox church stands as the 'only authentically Russian national institution'.[33] But Russia since the sixteenth century has contained significant numbers of Muslims, and today a number of the Federation's republics (in particular on the middle Volga and the North Caucasus) are reviving Islamic culture and institutions. What about the Buddhists, Jews and pagans; what is their nationality? In addition, in a secular society, how many Russians today are practising Orthodox Christians?

- The Russian nation can be identified more broadly with its culture, but this again raises a number of problems. For example, Gogol is quintessentially part of Russian culture yet he was, as mentioned, of Ukrainian provenance.
- Finally, the Russian nation can be defined through its common history. This is the path taken by the Eurasianists who argue that 'the peoples of the old empire possess a common past that preceded both Tsarism and Soviet communism'. For them the Russian nation encompasses 'that vast stretch of continental land from the Carpathians to the Pacific'.[34] This is probably too broad a category to be of much operational significance since reliance on a single definition blurs precisely the problems in establishing the contours of the national community.

The conflicting interpretations of Russian national identity are paralleled in the recent upsurge of discussion over what it means to be British or English. This fragmented character of modern identity is characteristic of our era, and is certainly not something to be deplored. Indeed, recent debates about multiculturalism and the possibility of multiple identities suggest a freedom from ascriptive roles that is the essential accompaniment of a democratic society. However, under pressure of real and constructed terror threats, states have turned inwards and have repudiated some of this freedom. In the Russian context, fears of migrants and loss of status have provoked a xenophobic backlash and a rising nationalism that may in the end repudiate the pluriculturalism that is at the very heart of Russian national development.

### The contours of national identity

While it is hard enough to define the Russian nation, the associated question of national identity is even more intractable.[35] The new identity is torn between four distinct approaches, which, while not exclusive, define the nature of the new polity.

#### Return to empire

The first is the restoration of an imperial role and the recreation of some sort of union. The debate over Russian national identity is overlain and complicated by the problem of Tsarist imperialism and the Soviet Union. While most neo-communist movements (like the CPRF) use the language of militant Russian nationalism, their relationship with 'genuine' Russian national thinking is ambivalent: Russian statism is not necessarily the same as neo-Soviet imperialism. Movements like Zhirinovsky's LDPR are essentially imperialist and openly display their irredentism, adopting an avowedly 'imperial' stance on the disintegration of the old union. The solid vote for the LDPR in parliamentary elections, and in the 2003 election for the Rodina bloc, reflects the disenchantment of those who equate democracy with disintegration and loss of national prestige. Henry Kissinger has repeatedly warned that Russian nationalism could be translated into a desire to return to a position of dominance over the other republics.[36]

#### Ethnicity and state

Another focuses on ethnicity, on loyalty to ties of blood and kinship. The nation (defined here as an ethnic community) is not necessarily coterminous with state: the Russian (like the Hungarian) state today is smaller than the Russian nation, whereas in most of the other fourteen post-Soviet republics the state is larger than the nation. The ethnic definition is opposed by democrats, patriots and nationalists alike (the latter appealing to imperial supranational traditions), although claims to defend Russians 'abroad' contains elements of ethnicised nationalism. The Slavic identity has rather more resonance, focusing on Russia as a nation of the Eastern Slavs (Russia, Belarus and Ukraine). The *nomenklatura* nationalists in places like Tatarstan or South Ossetia are careful to check claims to ethnic exclusivity made by the titular nationality. Thus the dynamics of post-communist Russian politics differ from those in Yugoslavia, but there remains a devastating potential for ethnic conflict.

### Culture and state

The third approach stresses the development of a cultural community, the view that the core of Russian national identity is found not so much in its imperial traditions but in religio-cultural features. One of the most sophisticated exponents of this view is Dmitry Likhachev. Born in 1906, Likhachev was a witness to the revolution and its sufferings. Arrested in 1928, he spent six years in the notorious Solovetsky camp, a former monastery on an island in the White Sea which Lenin in 1920 converted into a prison.[37] Likhachev survived and pursued a life of scholarship in his chosen field of philology until his death in 1999. He traced the interaction between Russia and Europe and stressed that Russian culture was part of European culture in general. He opposed the myth of Russian exceptionalism and supported the view that Russia was fully part of pan-European development. At the same time, Likhachev extolled the elements that made Russia Russia, above all the Orthodox Church and its liturgy, though he opposed theocratic versions of Russian destiny. Contrary to much writing in the political culture vein, he insisted that an ethos of individualism had been growing since at least the seventeenth century to temper the traditional collectivism of Russian society. Respect for tradition, he insisted, should not entail the 'mechanical imitation of what has ceased to exist'. Praising patriotism, he condemned nationalism as a pathology parasitic on genuine love of one's motherland, and in particular he denounced Great Russian nationalism and anti-Semitism.[38]

The cultural definition of Russian statehood is also fraught with dangers; it is not clear how any version of cultural homogeneity, defined even in weak terms of a dominant tradition, is possible in a country marked by such ethnic diversity. In relation to other groups the old messianism about Russia's leading role and the cultural mission of Orthodoxy, formulated at the end of the last century by V. Solovyev and others, can appear threatening. An inverted form of this messianism was used by the Bolsheviks to sustain the idea of the universal proletarian revolution emerging out of Russia, and the struggle for democracy on occasion became a new form of traditional messianism.

### 'Civis Rusanis sum'

The fourth approach argues precisely that the loss of Russia's imperial role and the fragmented sense of Russian nationality can be compensated by the establishment of a new identity based on the civic institutions of revived statehood. The major obstacle to the development of a civic national identity is the emergence and consolidation of national elites in the autonomous republics and regions of Russia, and the persistence of the 'greater Russia' idea. Nevertheless, Russia has a unique chance of forging a new national identity not despite but because of the catastrophic failure of the old system; there appears to be no choice but to start again. The civic approach to Russian national identity and the democratic statist approach to rebuilding the country became the dominant ideology of the government after August 1991. This stresses civic responsibility, the rebirth of Russian statehood governed by law, a democratic and inclusive form of nationalism, and good relations with all the other resurgent nationalisms both within and beyond Russia.

The rediscovery of national identities, language and culture is an essential element of democratic state-building. Often the discovery of one's own culture only enhances respect for others; as Friedrich Engels long ago observed, 'The Poles are never more internationalist than when they are at their most national'. Nationalism in the anti-communist revolution therefore has a dual character; both integrative and supportive of state-building and political order (with or without democracy); and divisive, when ethnicised or exclusive nationalism is used by elites or oppositional forces to gain power and to preserve what they see as threatened national identities.

## The symbols of statehood and power

A nation only exists when it shares a set of symbols and orientations towards its own history. In the 1990s Russia had remained bitterly divided in this respect, with national communists arguing that the Soviet Union had reflected Russia's national greatness, while liberals pointed out the enormous costs in human lives and ultimately in relative economic backwardness. These divisions were reflected in the struggle to adopt the various symbols of the new state and its commemorative calendar. In the 1990s Russia had muddled through with a number of temporary arrangements, and only under Putin were a number of decisions taken that sought to put an end to the 'provisional' character of the post-communist order. The 'Provisional Government' that ruled for the few months following the fall of Tsarism in February 1917 had also not been able formally to adopt the symbols of the state, and this had been one of the defining aspects of its 'provisional' character. The nationalist opposition in the 1990s considered Yeltsin's government another set of *vremenshchiki* (provisionals), destined to be swept away by the patriotic and nationalist-communist tide. Although Putin forced through a set of fundamental decisions, an element of uncertainty remained, especially over national holidays, revealing that Russian society remained fundamentally 'torn' over its value orientations.

- Peter the Great had established the tricolour as the national standard in 1699, preferring what had been the banner of the merchant marine over dozens of other flags since it represented peace and friendship. The red, blue and white of the Tsarist tricolour represented the unity of the army, civilians and the Church, but it was only one of numerous flags. The tricolour was used by the Provisional Government in 1917 and in 1990 was adopted by the democratic movement, and symbolised the defeat of the coup in August 1991. No law, however, could be passed under Yeltsin making this the state flag because of opposition in parliament. On 8 December 2000 the tricolour was confirmed as the Russian flag.

- The Tsarist state emblem was the two-headed eagle, looking both East and West, and this had been used in the 1990s but no law had been adopted. On 25 December 2000 the two-headed Tsarist eagle, stripped off the shields denoting Muscovy's victory over the former Russian principalities, but with the addition of two small crowns flanking a large one intended to symbolise the sovereignty of the Russian Federation and its republics, became the state emblem.
- With the fall of communism a new anthem had been devised drawing on the work of Mikhail Glinka, but this wordless melody had never struck a popular response. Indeed, Russia's sports team returning from the Sydney Olympics in 2000 complained how bewildered they had been when the anthem was played. The 'new' national anthem adopted on 25 December 2000 was the old anthem composed in 1943 by Alexander Alexandrov, with new words written by the author of the original lyrics, Sergei Mikhalkov (the father of film director Nikita Mikhalkov).[39] It thus appeared that all three periods of Russian twentieth-century history had been reconciled: the Tsarist, Russia's brief experiment with democracy in 1917, and the Soviet. For many, however, the restoration of a version of the Soviet anthem reflected the validation of the Soviet experience. For them the old Soviet anthem represented not wartime victories or Yuri Gagarin's space flight, but the Gulag and repression. One of the harshest critics was Yeltsin, who implied that the change was symbolic of a broader rejection of post-communist reform.

There were other arenas of symbolic contestation. One of the most controversial was over what to do with Lenin's embalmed remains in the shrine built on Stalin's orders on Red Square following Lenin's death in January 1924. Putin repeatedly stressed the need to maintain the stability of society and consensus, and he was well aware of just how explosive this issue could become for the country. At his press conference on 18 July 2001 Putin stated that he opposed the removal of Lenin's body from the mausoleum because many Russians still 'associate the name of Lenin with their own lives'. The reburial of the leader of the Bolsheviks and founder of the Soviet state would send a signal to people that 'they had worshipped false values' and would threaten the existing political and social balance.[40] It need hardly be added that Putin was one of those who had grown up under Lenin's shadow, and an attack on the first Soviet leader would cast a shadow over his own life experience. In addition, up and down the land statues of Lenin still adorn the central squares of countless towns, and the main street is often still a Lenin Prospect. An attack on Lenin in Moscow would provoke bitter controversies everywhere else. Putin's policy acknowledged the sensitivities of the older generation, but failed to take into account the need for a more open public acknowledgement of the monstrous crimes committed by the Bolshevik leader. The wounds of the past failed to heal, and no new narrative of reconciliation, recognition and atonement emerged.

This applies in particular to the appreciation of Joseph Stalin, Lenin's successor and the man who led the Soviet Union to victory over Nazi Germany in 1945 and built the country into an industrial and military superpower, but who in the process murdered millions of his own citizens and ruled through terror and suppression. We shall return to the problem of history in Chapter 19, but here let us note that the problem of coming to terms with the Lenin-Stalin dictatorship remains one of the great pieces of unfinished business in post-communist Russia. It may simply be too soon for the country to grapple with this divisive issue. After all, it was only after 1968 that Germany really came to terms with its past, and in some ways France is only now beginning to understand the nature of the Vichy regime and the depth of collaboration of the ruling class of the time. In Russia the struggle at the symbolic level focused on naming. There has been a long drawn-out struggle to restore the name of 'Stalingrad' to the city on the Volga that had been the site of one of the world's greatest battles from November 1942 to February 1943, with some two million dead, and which marked the turning point in the Second World War as the German advance was halted. After Stalin's death Khrushchev had renamed the city Volgograd, and many democrats after 1991 wished to see the pre-revolutionary name of Tsaritsyn restored (derived from a Tatar word and nothing to do with the Tsar). Already Leningrad had become St Petersburg, Kalinin had gone back to Tver, Molotov to Perm, Kuibyshev to Samara, although Lenin's birthplace (officially) remained Ulyanovsk and not Simbirsk. Putin argued that 'the return of the name of the city in our country at present would, I am simply convinced of this, generate some sort of suspicions that we are returning to the times of Stalinism'.[41] Putin's caution on this question was fully justified. On the sixtieth anniversary of the end of the battle in 2003 the plaque next to the eternal flame by the Kremlin wall was changed from Volgograd to Stalingrad, and it soon became a shrine not only to the memory of those who died there but also to the man whose name it bore.

The celebration of Russia's commemorative holidays was no less controversial.

- The celebration of victory day (9 May) in the Great Fatherland War remains the centrepiece of Russia's festive calendar, as it was in the Soviet Union. The sixtieth anniversary of the end of the war in 2005 was marked by major events in Moscow, to which world leaders were invited. However, rather than celebrating a common victory the commemoration demonstrated the lack of common purpose, and revealed the degree to which post-communist Russia remained isolated not only from its former great power allies and but also from former members of the communist bloc. Putin's decision to restore the red flag as the symbol of the Russian Army, and then in 2002 to return the red star as the emblem of Russia's armed forces, were taken by many to be sign of a continuing 'velvet restoration' of the old order in Russia. This was not the case, and from 2007 regimental banners dropped communist-era symbols and returned to eagles and crowns.
- The anniversary of the October revolution (7 November) since 1996 had been cel-ebrated as a day of Concord and Reconciliation, but Yeltsin had hesitated to fill the event with concrete meaning (peace was notable by its absence, and it was never clear who or what was to be reconciled). In 2005 the holiday was shifted to 4 November to commemorate the defeat by a civil militia of the Poles occupying the Kremlin in 1612 during the 'time of troubles' (*smuta*), and it was henceforth known as the Day of National Unity. The new holiday was designed to foster the patriotic spirit and thus to help heal the wounds of Russia's terrible twentieth century, but by giving the event an overtly nationalist flavour the authorities allowed the day to be appropriated by xenophobes and racists. In 2005 various hardline nationalists, including the Movement Against Illegal Immigration (DPNI), banded together to stage a public rally called the Russian March demanding the expulsion of foreign nationals and the like.
- In 2005 the national day, 12 June, was no longer celebrated as Independence Day, since that was considered to stress rather too much the break-up of the Soviet Union,

and instead it became Russia Day, emphasising, as Putin put it on 12 June 2006, that it was 'a day of tribute to Russian statehood, the country, and the historical choice' the people of Russia made in the early 1990s.[42] Independence Day was always an anomaly, since Russia had never been a colony. None of the former empires such as Britain, France and Spain have such a holiday for obvious reasons, whereas for former colonies like the United States, Argentina and India they are the centrepiece of national identity.

- Putin was even less comfortable with celebration of the defeat of the 19–21 August 1991 putsch, and deeply ambivalent about Russia's emergence as an independent state in December of that year. These formative moments in Russia's state development had a strong negative element – the dissolution of the Soviet alternative in August, and the disintegration of the Soviet state in December – and hence celebration was coloured by regret. On the tenth anniversary of the August coup, for example, Putin travelled to the White Sea monastery of Solovetsky, formerly the prison camp where Likhachev had been incarcerated, and thus he avoided having to take a stand one way or another on the significance of the event. The pattern was repeated in later years, and the fifteenth anniversary of the coup and Soviet disintegration passed almost unnoticed.

- The celebration of the adoption of the constitution on 12 December 1993 could have been used as the symbolic founding of a new democratic Russia, but under Putin from 2005 the day was removed from the list of national holidays. Russia's constitution is an almost classically liberal document, yet a mere three years later in 1996 Yeltsin was already looking for a new 'national idea', suggesting that the constitution was somehow an inadequate document to encapsulate the aspirations of the people, and less than a decade after its adoption 12 December was no longer a national holiday. This undermined the legitimacy of the constitution and weakened its role as the moral as well as legal compass for society, and indeed eroded the liberal idea as a whole.

## State-building: borders and citizenship

Post-communist Russia embarked on a distinctive type of nation-building on the foundations of a fragmented sense of the political community and an unclear definition of national identity. Nation-building in Russia faces some of the problems that had brought down the USSR. The aspirations of some of Russia's republics (Chechnya and Tatarstan in particular) replicated those of the Baltic and South Caucasian republics earlier, threatening to tear the federation apart. There are major differences, however, and these will be examined below.

### Building the political community

Soviet policy had simultaneously maintained separate national identities, above all through the notorious point 5 of Soviet passports where individuals had to state their ethnic identity (chosen from either the maternal or paternal line, but once entered largely irrevocable), and crushed any but the most formal political expression of that identity. The Soviet regime had been shockingly careless about generating a substantive sense of *Soviet* nationality, limiting itself to abstractions about 'eternal friendship' between peoples united in an 'indivisible union'.[43] Like the USSR, the Russian Federation is also a multinational state, with some 27 million non-ethnic Russians living in a state consisting of 182 recognised nationalities. In three crucial respects, however, Russia is a very different multinational state than the USSR: the absolute predominance of ethnic Russians (81 per cent in the RF compared to about half in the USSR); the very large proportion of ethnic Russians in the potential secessionist states, comprising 10.4 million (45.1 per cent) out of a total population of 23.1 million people living in the republics, and in 9 of the 21 republics Russians are a majority (see Table 10.2); and Russian cultural identity as the relatively unmediated core of the new state.

*Table 10.2* The republics of Russia

| Name of republic | Capital | Population, 1 Jan. 2006 | Population, 1 Jan. 1994 | Titular nationality (%) | Russians % | Russians Number |
|---|---|---|---|---|---|---|
| Adygeya | Maikop | 442,700 | 446,800 | 22.0 | 68.0 | 303,825 |
| Altai | Gorno-Altaisk | 204,500 | 196,700 | 31.0 | 60.4 | 118,807 |
| Bashktostan | Ufa | 4,063,400 | 4,042,000 | 22.0 | 40.0 | 1,616,800 |
| Buryatia | Ulan-Ude | 963,300 | 1,056,600 | 24.0 | 69.0 | 729,054 |
| Chechen-Ingush | Grozny | – | 1,235,000 | 70.7 (1) | 23.1 | 306,075 |
| Chechnya | Grozny | 894,000 | – | – | – | – |
| Chuvashia | Cheboksary | 1,292,200 | 1,359,000 | 67.8 | 26.7 | 362,853 |
| Dagestan | Makhachkala | 2,641,000 | 1,925,000 | 80.2 (2) | 12.0 | 231,000 |
| Ingushetia | Magas | 487,000 | – | – | – | – |
| Kabardino-Balaria | Nal'chik | 288,700 | 785,900 | 58.6 (3) | 32.0 | 251,488 |
| Kalmykia | Elista | 431,500 | 321,700 | 45.4 | 37.7 | 121,281 |
| Karachai-Cherkessia | Cherkessk | 702,300 | 434,000 | 41.0 (4) | 42.0 | 182,280 |
| Karelia | Petrozavodsk | 697,500 | 799,600 | 11.0 | 72.0 | 575,712 |
| Khakassia | Abakan | 538,200 | 583,000 | 11.5 | 80.0 | 466,400 |
| Komi | Syktyvkar | 985,000 | 1,246,000 | 23.3 | 57.5 | 716,450 |
| Marii-El | Ioshkar-Ola | 711,600 | 764,000 | 43.0 | 48.0 | 366,720 |
| Mordovia | Saransk | 856,800 | 963,800 | 32.5 | 60.8 | 585,990 |
| North Ossetia – Alania | Vladikavkaz | 1,162,800 | 651,000 | 53.0 | 29.9 | 194,649 |
| Sakha (Yakutia) | Yakutsk | 949,900 | 1,074,000 | 33.4 | 50.3 | 537,000 |
| Tatarstan | Kazan | 3,761,500 | 3,723,000 | 48.5 | 43.3 | 1,612,059 |
| Tyva | Kyzyl | 308,500 | 306,000 | 64.3 | 32.0 | 97,920 |
| Udmurtia | Izhevsk | 1,544,400 | 1,642,800 | 30.9 | 58.9 | 967,609 |
| **Total** | | | **21,161,000** | **48.7** | **51.3** | **10,864,073** |

*Sources*: *Novaya Rossiya: Informatsionno-statisticheskii al'manakh* (Moscow, Mezhdunarodnaya akademiya informatizatsii, 1994), pp. 137–45, modified; *Russia in Figures: 2006* (Moscow, Rosstat, 2006), pp. 40–7.

*Notes:* 1 Chechens comprised 57.8% and Ingush 12.9% of the total population.

2 This percentage represents the sum for all the indigenous peoples of Dagestan made up of the following peoples: Agul 0.8%; Avar 27.5; Dargin 15.6; Kumyk 12.9; Lak 5.1; Lezgin 11.3; Nogai 1.6; Rutul 0.8; Tabasaran 4.3; Tsakhur 0.3.

3 Kabards 49% and Balkars 9.6% of the population.

4 Karachai 31% and Cherkess 10% of the population.

The place of ethnic Russians themselves in the new order, and the juridical form that the cultural and historical differences of other ethnic groups should take, however, remains contested. The great majority of peoples and federal units were agreed that a distinctively *Russian* political community should emerge, but this was contested by a few. One group that did contest this proposition was the Chechens, launching what ended up becoming a violent bid for secession because of the failure (one shared to different degrees by both sides) to exploit the new political opportunities opened up by Russia's democratisation to renegotiate the relationship (up to a politically negotiated separation). Tatarstan also questioned its relationship with the nascent Russian political community, but did so politically – taking skilful advantage of the new circumstances to extend the boundaries of its own sovereignty. In international affairs sovereignty is an absolute (either a state is recognised as autonomously empowered to enter foreign relations or it is not); whereas in domestic politics sovereignty is a far more malleable notion, with federalism the political form of shared sovereignty.

While federalism is one way of sharing sovereignty, the 'asymmetry' in Russia's federal relations reflected the painful attempt to devise appropriate forms of power-sharing. Too often a zero-sum logic operated, with a gain for one side considered a defeat for the other, ramping up exclusive advantages that in the event led to unsustainable imbalances in state development. In his attempt to iron out the asymmetries in Russian federalism Putin was in danger of blocking one of the sources of innovation that had allowed a relative equilibrium to emerge in inter-regional relations in Russia. At the same time, however, Putin's aim – to ensure equality of citizenship rights across Russia – represented a vision of the political community that found considerable support, not only among ethnic Russians but others as well. Universal citizenship sought to undermine not only segmented regionalism but also challenged the emergence of ethnocratic states in some of the republics, where the titular populations were privileged over the rest (see Table 10.2).

We suggested above that Russian nation-building is torn between three forms: ethnic self-affirmation; supranational statism, and the attempt to establish a democratic *political* community. In practice, the three are not mutually exclusive and Russian nation-building contains elements of all three. However, the three represent quite different visions of what Russia should be like.

### Borders and secessionism

The borders of the USSR were predicated on an expanding communist world system and in a sense, as Strada points out, they only formally ran across space: essentially, they ran across time.[44] Under Stalin, however, border policy took on a far more instrumental role, and while often formally arbitrary they were part of a conscious design to foster ethnic conflict as part of his *divide et imperare* policy, to make all nationalities dependent on Moscow. The current borders established by the communist regime reflect neither the historical legacy nor demographic realities (see Table 10.3); but neither would any others – hence the Russian national-patriotic argument that there should be no borders at all. The Russian government rejected the ethnic principle of state-building and sought to find a balance between collective and individual rights while trying to ensure through the CIS that the administrative borders that had now become state frontiers should be 'transparent', allowing free passage for citizens of CIS states. Ukraine, however, objected

*Table 10.3* Nationalities in the republics, 1989 (%)

| Republic | Pop. (000) | Titular nationality in republic | Russians (%) | Minor nationalities | (%) | Other (%) |
|---|---|---|---|---|---|---|
| Russia | 147,386 | – | 82.5 | Tatar | 3.8 | 15 |
| Estonia | 1,573 | 61.5 | 30.3 | Ukrainian | 3.1 | 5 |
| Latvia | 2,681 | 52.0 | 34.0 | Belarusian | 4.5 | 9 |
| Lithuania | 3,690 | 79.6 | 9.4 | Polish | 7.0 | 4 |
| Moldova | 4,341 | 64.5 | 13.0 | Ukrainian | 13.8 | 9 |
| Belarus | 10,200 | 77.9 | 13.2 | Polish | 4.0 | 5 |
| Ukraine | 51,704 | 72.7 | 22.1 | Jewish | 0.9 | 4 |
| Armenia | 3,283 | 93.3 | 1.6 | Azeri | 2.6 | 2 |
| Azerbaijan | 7,029 | 82.7 | 5.6 | Armenian | 5.6 | 5 |
| Georgia | 5,449 | 70.1 | 6.3 | Armenian | 8.1 | 16 |
| Kazakhstan | 16,538 | 39.7 | 37.8 | German | 5.8 | 16 |
| Kyrgyzstan | 4,291 | 52.4 | 21.5 | Uzbek | 12.9 | 14 |
| Tajikistan | 5,112 | 62.3 | 7.6 | Uzbek | 23.5 | 6 |
| Turkmenistan | 3,534 | 72.0 | 9.5 | Uzbek | 9.0 | 10 |
| Uzbekistan | 19,906 | 71.4 | 8.3 | Tajik | 4.7 | 16 |
| **Total** | **286,717** | | | | | |

*Sources: USSR: Facts and Figures Annual*, edited by Alan P. Pollard, Vol. 15, 1991 (Gulf Breeze, FL, Academic International Press, 1991), pp. 499–502.

to the distinction between 'internal' and 'external' borders, and insisted that they all should be considered state borders. There was a gradual hardening of these frontiers, exacerbating problems of citizenship.

There appeared no logical reason why the 15 union republics should be the best state form for the emerging post-communist national communities, and the fall of the old regime was followed by tension as territories sought to make adjustments to the Soviet legacy. There were conflicts in the Transnistria and the Gagauz area of Moldova, the Crimea and Transcarpathia in Ukraine, Abkhazia and South Ossetia in Georgia, civil war in Tajikistan, and many more. The disintegration of the USSR and Yugoslavia revealed the contradiction between the two central principles of the OSCE: the immutability of borders and individual human rights. What if a group of people wished to change the borders and live in a different state? There are no mechanisms available to facilitate the transfer of territory, and history would suggest that border changes are almost always the result of *force majeure*. This was certainly the case with the advance of Kosovo towards full statehood, facilitated by Nato's intervention in 1999. However, when it came to Chechnya, the insurgency did not gain full-scale international support and was crushed by Russian military force. Throughout Russia there was no clear answer to the problem of reconciling individual rights with the rights of minority groups, the struggle between civic and ethnic identities.[45] The border question became perhaps the single most important symbolic issue in the former Soviet Union. The question acted as a mirror to post-communist politics, testing the readiness of states for democratic and peaceful solutions to intractable problems involving not only territory but questions of national identity and competing truths, if not myths, about the past and present. The border question in Eurasia interrogated the

*Table 10.4* Ethnic Russians and Russian-speakers in Soviet Republics outside Russia, 1989

| Republic | Ethnic Russians | | Russian-speaking | |
|---|---|---|---|---|
| | *Estimated* | *As % of population* | *Estimated total* | *As % of population* |
| Estonia | 474,000 | 30.3 | 544,000 | 34.8 |
| Latvia | 905,000 | 34.0 | 1,122,000 | 42.1 |
| Lithuania | 344,000 | 9.4 | 429,000 | 11.7 |
| Moldova | 562,000 | 13.0 | 1,003,000 | 23.1 |
| Belarus | 1,342,000 | 13.2 | 3,243,000 | 31.9 |
| Ukraine | 11,355,000 | 22.1 | 16,898,000 | 32.8 |
| Azerbaijan | 391,000 | 5.6 | 528,000 | 7.5 |
| Armenia | 51,000 | 1.6 | 66,000 | 2.0 |
| Georgia | 341,000 | 6.3 | 479,000 | 8.9 |
| Kazakhstan | 6,227,000 | 37.8 | 7,797,000 | 47.4 |
| Kyrgyzstan | 916,000 | 21.5 | 1,090,000 | 25.6 |
| Tajikistan | 388,000 | 7.6 | 495,000 | 9.7 |
| Turkmenistan | 333,000 | 9.5 | 421,000 | 12.0 |
| Uzbekistan | 1,653,000 | 8.3 | 2,151,000 | 10.9 |

*Sources*: *Naselenie Rossii: ezhegodnyi demograficheskii doklad* (Moscow, Centre for the Demography and Ecology of Man, 1993), p. 15.
*Note:* The category of Russian-speakers includes non-ethnic Russians regarding Russian as their native language. Since 1989 there has been considerable out-migration of Russians from these republics and thus the figures given above are likely now to have decreased.

very essence of the modern nation-state form of political-territorial organisation (see Table 10.4).

Soviet borders were intended to be purely administrative divisions and not state frontiers. For this reason, among others, the regime could move the borders arbitrarily and take little account of ethnic and other factors. In Central Asia borders were artificial and designed to cut across ethnic groups. In 1954 Khrushchev had been able to transfer the Crimea from Russia to Ukraine with barely a whisper of protest in Russia. When in 1991 these arbitrary lines became state borders, the scene was set for ever more conflicts. By late 1991 there were some 168 territorial-ethnic disputes in the former USSR, four times as many as in 1990, and of that figure 73 directly concerned Russia.[46] Nearly a quarter of Russia's 61,000 km of border was not 'formally recognized and specified in any international legal acts'.[47] Rutskoi insisted that the real Russia could not be contained within the borders of the artificial Russian Federation, though he failed to specify where precisely they should lie or how they could be changed.[48] At the same time, the separation of the peripheral republics exposed what had been the Russian heartlands, and now only 30 rather than the earlier 47 of Russia's 76 primary components lacked external borders. Attempts to strengthen borders, moreover, were fraught with problems. The Russo-Azerbaijani frontier, for example, is straddled by the Lezgin people living in both republics, and for long it did not become a policed state border. With its millions of compatriots abroad, Russia favoured the transparency of borders, though was concerned about the security risk posed by its open frontiers to the South. Drugs and arms smugglers and other criminals took advantage of weak frontier controls. Russia assisted the CIS republics to police their external frontiers rather than establishing stronger controls on its 'internal' borders, but this could at best be an interim strategy.

As soon as a line is drawn on a map the question of secession arises focusing on four main problems: borders and the allocation of territories; the rights of minorities (and in some cases majorities) in the territory that has seceded; the rights of secessionist nationals in the country from which the territory has seceded; and the problem of procedures – how do we know that the leadership of the secessionist territory genuinely reflects the stable wishes of the majority of the population in the territory concerned? All these issues were manifestly present in the case of Chechnya's bid to secede from Russia, but to a lesser extent in some other regions.

Unlike the Soviet constitutions, the Russian constitution does not grant the right of secession. One of the few guarantees of stability in Africa had been the declaration by the Organisation of African Unity in 1964 that the colonial borders, however unfair and divisive of 'tribes', should be retained. This principle, despite all the wars, has held to this day, and a similar statute was enacted in Latin America. One of the basic principles of the OSCE is the recognition by member states of the inviolability of each others' borders, a stance which did not help attempts to resolve the Nagorno-Karabakh crisis. During *perestroika* the principle was extended to the USSR in the affirmation that internal borders were unchangeable, a stance that strengthened the legitimacy of the union and autonomous republics, even though Article 78 of the USSR constitution made provision for changes. It was perhaps less Helsinki and more Karabakh that confirmed the sanctity of intra-Soviet borders.

But the border question would not go away. The announcement by Yeltsin's press secretary, Pavel Voshchanov, following the August 1991 coup that borders were negotiable if republics became independent drew accusations of Russian chauvinism. Nazarbaev condemned the raising of the question on the grounds that it would make keeping the USSR together much more difficult, but both the border incident, and the earlier threat of sharply raising the price of Russia's energy, were raised out of a 'unifying' impulse, to warn of the consequences of secession. But the means had undermined the goal, not for the last time, and set alarm bells ringing in the capitals of the other republics. Yeltsin had hoped to make the other republics aware of the price and dangers of seeking full independence, but the plan backfired and accelerated the disintegration of the USSR. A similar process was at work in Putin's attempt to impose market prices on Russian energy exports to its neighbours, accelerating the centrifugal tendencies in the CIS. In the earlier case the perceived threat of Russian neo-imperialism was greatly increased, and this helps explain the overwhelming vote for Ukrainian independence on 1 December 1991. Instead of a clear principle becoming the 'guarantor of stability',[49] it became the source of destabilisation. Putin does not appear to have learned this lesson when he raised energy prices to Ukraine and Belarus in 2006.

The Russo-Japanese frontier between the Kurile Islands is the only Russian border not to be recognised in international law, although a number of others have not yet been formally ratified, including that with Estonia (the border with Latvia was ratified in 2007). The majority of the 20 frontier disputes, however, were gradually resolved, notably with China, but some proved more intractable. Japan made territorial claims on Russia over the Kurile islands, while some revanchist groups in Germany sought the return of the Kaliningrad region. Areas of Karelia and Pechenga were forcibly incorporated into the USSR during the war, but Finland agreed that the borders would only be changed through legal processes and according to OSCE principles. The major border dispute was with Estonia over lands that had been granted to it by the Treaty of Tartu of 1920, but which had been excluded from Estonia by the Molotov-Ribbentrop Pact of 1939 and after the war incorporated into the Pskov and Leningrad regions of Russia. To many

Russians it seemed illogical for Estonia to deny the validity of any Soviet acts, and yet to lay claim to territory on the basis of an act of the discredited Soviet regime, whose arbitrariness in drawing boundaries was well-known. The disputed territory covered only a total of 1,924 sq km (750 sq miles) and contained no major towns and was populated by Russians. Russia was fearful of establishing a precedent, itself having renounced any territorial claims against any of its neighbours. It was not clear why nationalists in Estonia wished to incorporate a Russian area when the country already had problems with the Narva region, the great majority of whose population were Russians. In 1995 the conflict was regularised and Estonia officially renounced claims to the area. A border treaty with Estonia was initialled in 2005 and moved towards ratification on the condition that nothing was added or subtracted from the text, but nationalists in the Estonian parliament simply could not resist adding an appeal to the Treaty of Tartu in the text, something that was obviously unacceptable to Russia.

In Russia the possibility of border changes was much debated. Travkin noted that 'The frontier problem has always been at its most acute when an empire falls apart'.[50] He opposed the revision of borders, and denied that Russia was interested in grabbing land but was 'struggling for national and state survival'. In particular, he insisted that Russia had a duty to defend its nationals living outside its borders, such as in Transnistria, though in democratic ways. Other patriotic groups, like Popular Accord and the Russian National Union, argued that borders could be changed, and recommended a version of the system used to demarcate the border between Poland and Germany in Upper Silesia in 1920–1, where plebiscites were held district by district. The precedent did not augur well since in Silesia most districts voted to return to Germany, yet the region remained with Poland.[51] Hardliners insisted that 'At the present time, relations between CIS states do not lend themselves to regulation by diplomatic means alone.'[52] Kozyrev warned that the demands by the national-patriots to resolve border conflicts by imperial methods, including the use of armed force, would lead to the collapse of the CIS and the emergence of a ring of hostile states around Russia.[53]

Solzhenitsyn in 1991 recommended the retreat of Russian power to defensible borders around the Slavic heartlands (Russia, Ukraine, Belarus and North Kazakhstan). He insisted:

> *We don't have the strength* for the peripheries either economically or morally. *We don't have the strength* for sustaining an empire – and it is just as well. Let this burden fall from our shoulders: it is crushing us, sapping our energy, and hastening our demise.[54]

He noted 'with alarm that the awakening Russian self-awareness has to a large extent been unable to free itself of great-power thinking and of imperial delusions'.[55] The USSR had disintegrated along lines of fracture which did not correspond to those that would be recognised by Solzhenitsyn and others as somehow 'natural', reflecting the ethnic and historical core of a post-imperial Russian state. Solzhenitsyn's belief that the 'irresponsible' and 'haphazard' Soviet borders could be corrected by 'panels of experts' and local plebiscites was impractical.[56] The view that Russia could become a genuinely post-imperial state following the adjustment of borders was considered by its neighbours as a typically Russian imperialist approach.

However much borders are moved, there cannot be an exact fit between state and nation. Furman notes that the right of states to inviolable borders contradicts the rights of nations to self-determination. The present borders of Russia and the other republics are absurd, yet, he warned, referring to the tragic precedents of Versailles Germany and 1990s Serbia, while accepting the present line of the borders means acquiescing in the repugnant decisions that had led to the present demarcation, democrats had no choice but to accept them. Russia found itself in the position of inter-war Germany:

> A large country surrounded by weaker countries with national minorities represent-ing the large country, especially if these national minorities are oppressed (and any national minority may well be oppressed, to a certain extent), is virtually unable to withstand the temptation to use its strength.

He urged that Russia, as the most powerful country in the CIS, should set an example of a peaceful and humane resolution of border and national issues, up to and including legal provision for the secession of the Tatars and Chechens, which would then give it the moral right to back minorities in other republics.[57] The rights of minorities in secessionist territories were forgotten. Borders demarcate not only territories but competing truths: they cut across both time and morality.

### Citizenship and nationality

Up to December 1991 almost all the inhabitants of the USSR had been Soviet citizens; with the demise of the USSR in theory they all became stateless until each republic adopted its own citizenship laws. Russia's first citizenship law of 28 November 1991 granted citizenship to all resident in Russia or the USSR as long as they registered with the Russian authorities and did not take the citizenship of another state. Citizenship was granted to all those legally resident in the country on 6 February 1992. Dual citizenship was allowed only to those who opted to keep Soviet citizenship. The Russian government declared itself the protector of Russian citizens at home and abroad and banned the typically Soviet practice of depriving people of their citizenship. With the collapse of the USSR a modified version of the law on 6 February 1992 removed the reference to dual Soviet citizenship and allowed any Soviet citizen resident in the USSR on 1 September 1991 to take out Russian citizenship within three years, as long as they had not adopted the citizenship of the republic in which they were residing.[58] A further amendment of 17 June 1993 removed the ambiguities surrounding the Baltic republics and Georgia that had declared independence before 1 September 1991, and allowed residents in other republics to keep their local citizenship while taking out Russian citizenship.[59] From 1 January 2001 the old simplified system for Soviet passport holders to gain citizenship through simple registration procedures was abolished, and instead a complex set of documentation and residence permits had to be provided. This built on Putin's decree of 17 May 2000 that made it harder for residents in the CIS and the Baltic states to gain a Russian passport.[60] The president had spoken of encouraging labour migration from the CIS, and these moves were hardly likely to encourage this. In 2006 there were still 1.5 million people who had not yet become naturalised. On 5 January 2006 Putin extended the deadline for former Soviet citizens to gain Russian citizenship to 1 January 2008, and simplified some of the earlier requirements, and new provisions made it easier for those who obtained a residence permit after 1 January 2002 to gain citizenship.

Thus Russia adopted an inclusive citizenship policy (although becoming slightly more restrictive), recognising Russian citizenship for millions living outside its borders. The main desired political status for those living outside the RF is dual citizenship. Russia sought through bilateral treaties to ensure that other states granted the right to dual citizenship, but this is something that none of the other republics have been willing to grant. Russia, fearing a flood of refugees, reasoned that its compatriots would be more likely to stay in the other republic if they knew that they could move to Russia at any time. The Russian government, however, did not consistently pursue the idea of dual citizenship in the other Soviet republics.[61] For the other republics the adoption of citizenship laws was a crucial element in state-building, but at the same time proved bitterly divisive. All the republics, with the exception of Estonia and Latvia (who adopted exclusive citizenship laws) offered citizenship to all resident on their territory on the day the citizenship law came into effect. Russia's attempt to convince the other republics to allow dual citizenship was resisted on the reasonable ground that divided loyalties would inhibit the develop of loyalty to their new home state. In Ukraine dual citizenship was regarded as the first step towards renewed union with Russia, and even republics like Kazakhstan and Kyrgyzstan, which favoured closer relations with Russia, feared that it would undermine new national and civic identities.

There is a similar battle within Russia itself. The 1996 law on 'National Cultural Autonomy' gave ethnic groups either lacking a defined territory, or living outside the area in which they were nominally titular, the right to create cultural institutions such as schools or social support institutions. This law marked a radical departure from Stalinist practices, which had tied national development very much to a specific territory, and with few opportunities for those living elsewhere to express their cultural identity. This particularly affected the Tatars, three-quarters of whom, as we have seen, live outside Tatarstan. They have been among the most active groups taking advantage of the opportunities offered by the 1996 act. The law sets strict registration procedures, and forbids ethnic communities established in this way from engaging in politics.[62] Although transcending Soviet practices, the law reflected Soviet thinking in still talking of 'nationality', rather than the Western concept of ethnic group, and suggesting, for example, that Tatars were part of a 'diaspora' even though they had been living in Moscow and across the Volga region (outside what is now Tatarstan) for as long as Russians had. The legal restrictions placed on their activities and the traditional concepts used to describe the process indicated the distance that Russia still had to go to achieve an autonomous civil society.[63]

Putin sought to undermine the emerging elements of an 'inner abroad' by claiming to assert the undisputed priority of Russian law. Russian citizenship was to become universal throughout the country, undermining attempts to impose various types of 'quasi-citizenship' in some of the republics. In particular, in Tatarstan and Bashkortostan the Russian passport was to be introduced even though, against the objections of the local authorities, it did not specify the holder's nationality or use the local languages. A government order of 8 July 1997 had ordered all Soviet passports to be replaced with the new ones, but instead local identity documents had been issued. This made it difficult for their citizens to enter universities elsewhere in Russia or to travel abroad. The distribution of the new Russian passports provoked protests in Kazan and elsewhere. The Tatar Public

Centre, for example, on 2 January 2001 condemned Moscow's 'colonialist' policy that sought to restrict the rights of Russia's national republics. They condemned in particular the new passports, that allegedly contained numerous Orthodox symbols and which failed to specify the holder's ethnicity.[64] In the event, the passports were issued with an insert in the native language. It was at this time that Tatarstan planned to switch back to using the Latin alphabet, a move blocked by the Russian parliament.

Much of the discussion over citizenship focuses on the tension between ethnic and civic definitions. An ethnic definition of citizenship bestows citizenship rights only to titulars; a civic definition grants all those born in a given territory or permanent resident there for a certain period of time the same civil rights as citizens. The situation is far from straightforward, however. For example, laws making the language of the titular nationality the state language privileges native speakers, fluent in job applications and favoured in appointments to administrative posts. More broadly, the Russian nationalist cry of 'Russia for Russians' is, as Kapuscinski notes, torn by an irreconcilable contradiction

> between the criterion of blood and the criterion of land ... According to the criterion of blood, the point is to maintain the ethnic purity of the Russian nation. But such an ethnically pure Russia is only part of today's Imperium. And what about the rest? According to the criterion of land, the point is to maintain the full extent of the Imperium. But then there can be no hope of maintaining the ethnic purity of the Russians.[65]

The tension between blood and land, the ethnic and the imperial agendas, is here vividly portrayed, but it leaves out of account the third option, the democratic political community based on inclusive civic principles.

# 11 Federalism and the new state

> A multitude is strong while it holds together, but so soon as each of those who compose it begins to think of his own private danger, it becomes weak and contemptible.
>
> (Niccolo Machiavelli)[1]

The Russian empire grew through a process of overland expansion. Rather like the United States, it occupied territories across a vast continental mass, a type of colonisation that is largely irreversible. The emergence of these two continental states overshadowed the traditional nation-state and each, as Alexis De Tocqueville foresaw, seemed 'called by some secret design of Providence one day to hold in its hands the destinies of half the world'.[2] The major difference, however, between the two is that whereas America some two hundred years ago devised an effective political system and a sturdy relationship between individual states and the federal authorities, Russia is still in the process of building a viable relationship between the centre and the regions. Although the 1993 constitution establishes the framework of Russian federalism, its ambiguous formulations and provision for further laws delimiting powers between the centre and the regions stimulated a repeated although more muted version of the 'war of the laws' that had brought down the USSR.

## Ethno-federalism and its legacy

The concept of path dependency argues that earlier institutional choices foreclose options later. This is nowhere truer than in the development of Russia's federal relations. The Soviet state had been federal-unitary; federal in form, but in effect unitary. The heart of the old state system, the CPSU, had never pretended to be federal and instead had been a centralised body governed by its Central Committee and Politburo in Moscow. The 14 Party organisations in the union republics had been no more than a single unit governed by the principles of democratic centralism. Within Russia only certain autonomous areas populated by national minorities were the subjects of ethno-federalism, whereas regions inhabited by the titular nationality (Russians) were effectively part of a unitary and centralised state. Russia was bequeathed a complex ethno-federal system in which what were to become its 89 regions were divided into a number of status groups, each jealously defended by its local elites.

### The Soviet ethno-federal system

Defeat in war and the fall of Tsarism in 1917 allowed several nations to leave the Russian empire. The aspirations of Poland and Finland to independence went largely unopposed; whereas Ukrainian independence was precarious and was undermined as soon as the Bolsheviks won the Civil War of 1918–20. Earlier declarations in favour of 'the right of nations to self-determination', notably in Lenin's 1916 pamphlet of that name, was modified in January 1918 by Stalin, the people's commissar of nationalities, to be 'a right not of the bourgeoisie, but of the working masses of the given nation'.[3] National liberation was subordinated to the class struggle. The Bolsheviks once again 'gathered the lands' of the historical Russian state, but based on the new principle of 'socialist internationalism'. Autonomous national independence movements were crushed, as were varieties of 'national communism'. Ultimately a state was recreated that reflected Lenin's views of national self-determination, enshrining the principle of territorial autonomy for specified ethnic groups with the formal right to 'self-determination up to and including secession'. In practice, of course, in keeping with the Marxist view that economic modernisation would make national differences redundant, national aspirations were firmly subordinated to the imperatives of socialist construction, as defined by the Bolsheviks themselves.

The principle of federalism was only grudgingly acknowledged, and then only partially implemented. While Lenin in his 'Declaration of the Rights of the Toiling and Exploited People', prepared for the Constituent Assembly in January 1918, called for 'a federation of the Soviet Republics of Russia', the RSFSR constitution adopted in mid-1918 contained no effective federal elements. The consolidation of Bolshevik rule over Ukraine and the conquest of Armenia, Azerbaijan and Georgia in 1920–1 necessarily intensified the debate over the structure of the state. Stalin proposed the 'autonomisation' plan to reduce the newly conquered states to the status of Russia's existing autonomous republics (Tataria, Bashkiria, Kazakhstan and Turkestan). Lenin, however, concerned by the alleged chauvinist and arrogant behaviour of Bolshevik officials in Transcaucasia, on 26 September 1922 rejected the autonomisation plan in favour of the creation of a new federation, and as a first step the three Transcaucasian republics were federated into one.

The Union Treaty of 30 December 1922 creating the USSR brought together four union republics: the RSFSR, Ukraine, Belarus and the Transcaucasian Soviet Federative Socialist Republic; together with 26 autonomous areas, 22 of which were in Russia.[4] The first Soviet constitution of January 1924 was marked by a centralising ethos, with Russia's governing institutions mostly converted into the corresponding USSR body. The policy of *korenizatsiya* (indigenisation), however, adopted by the Twelfth Party Congress in 1923, sought to root Soviet power in native elites and encouraged the use of indigenous languages, but by the early 1930s state policy had changed to renewed Russianisation. Over the years the territorial organisation of the Soviet Union changed kaleidoscopically, with endless arbitrary transfers, mergers and new entities created. By 1991 the number of union republics had risen to 15: 3 emerged as a result of the disintegration of the Transcaucasian Federation (Armenia, Azerbaijan and Georgia); 5 Central Asian republics as a result of carving up the territory of the RSFSR (Kyrgyzstan, Tajikistan, Turkmenistan and Uzbekistan, while Kazakhstan technically is only partly in Central Asia); and 4 had been incorporated into the USSR during the Second World War (Estonia, Latvia, Lithuania and Moldova). While some formerly autonomous areas became union republics, others did not, even though they were larger. When the question of raising the status of some autonomous republics was discussed in the run-up to the adoption of the new constitution in 1936, Stalin listed three necessary factors to become a union republic:

1   Sufficient population, considered to be over one million.
2   Compactness of population, which excluded the Jews who were scattered throughout the USSR.
3   Location on the borders of the USSR, in case of secession. This provision excluded the Tatars and Bashkirs, who in terms of size and compactness of population deserved to become republics. This remains a source of bitterness for Tatarstan to this day.

Russia, too, had changed, and the country that in 1991 became the 'continuer' state to the USSR was far smaller than in 1922, having donated territory to Ukraine and the Central Asian republics. The geographical area of the RSFSR under Soviet power had decreased both in absolute and in comparative terms: if in 1922 the RSFSR comprised 94.7 per cent of the territory of the USSR, by 1991 this had fallen to 76.2 per cent. In terms of size, the USSR had become rather more a union of equals, divided up into 53 different types of national-territorial units: 15 union republics and 38 autonomous republics, *oblasts* and *okrugs*. Russia replicated the federal-unitary structure of the USSR (see Figure 11.1); in 1990 it consisted of 88 administrative units, 73 of which were primary and 15 were secondary (i.e. subordinated to one of the former), reflecting the hierarchical *matryeshka* doll-like construction of Soviet federalism.[5] There was, moreover, a considerable disparity between the historical and the actual ethnic borders between the peoples.

This distinctive form of national-territorial federation was intended neither to promote the emergence of ethnically pure nation-states nor, on the contrary, to allow the emergence of multinational 'nations' within the framework of the ethno-federal areas. They were seen as no more than a transitional stage in the long-term goal of complete state unity, passing through an initial stage of 'coming closer' (*sblizhenie*) to result ultimately in complete fusion (*sliyanie*), on a world scale if possible. In the meantime, however, rather than being a union of equal and sovereign peoples, Soviet federal policy was based on a strict hierarchy of nations, with some privileged to have a state in their name, while other ethnic groups failed to qualify for the honorific of 'nation' and instead were called 'nationalities' (*narodnosti*). While the 1989 census listed 128 nationalities, only 68 formally made up the 53 ethno-federal units. Ethnic Russians made up just over half (50.78 per cent) of the Soviet Union's population of 290,938,469 in July 1990. They were followed by Ukrainians at 15.45 per cent, Uzbeks at 5.84, Belarusians at 3.51 and Kazakhs at 2.85 per cent (see Table 2.1). The official language was Russian, but the country was host to over 200 languages and dialects, at least 18 of which had more than one million speakers.[6]

As the USSR disintegrated the ethno-federal republics were drawn into the struggle between the union centre and the republics. In the Law on the Delimitation of Powers between the USSR and the Subjects of the Federation of April 1990 Gorbachev gave Russia's autonomous republics the right to join any new Union Treaty on terms equal with the union republics. The elevation of the political status of the republics was later rejected by Yeltsin as a threat to Russia's territorial integrity.[7] Hoping to use second-tier federal units to counter-balance the growing autonomy of first-tier republics, Gorbachev

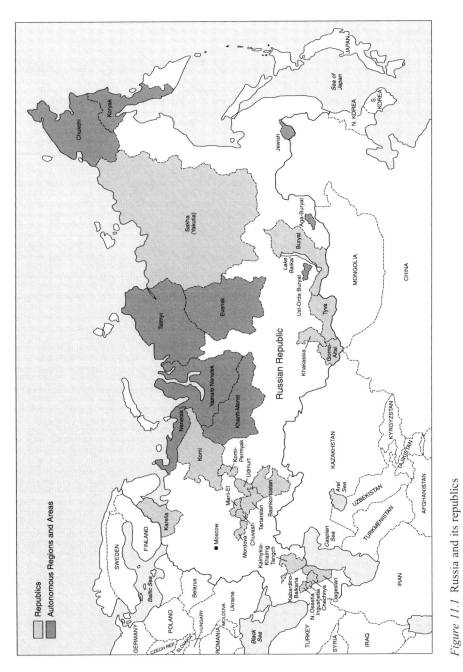

*Figure 11.1* Russia and its republics

instead provoked the union republics to assert even greater sovereignty claims. Russia was in the vanguard of this, but at the same time Yeltsin sought to prioritise a civic identity and loyalty to a democratic Russian state over sub-national ascriptive ethnic or regional loyalties. He was willing to renegotiate the relationship between Russia and its republics and championed the achievement of sovereignty from below on condition that they remained loyal to the Russian state.

For most of the period the Soviet national-state system maintained a precarious balance and survived because the CPSU exercised real power. Declarations of republican sovereignty and the Russian Decree on Power of June 1990 unwittingly accelerated the destruction of the Soviet state. The main target of these declarations was the communist regime, which had sat uncomfortably above the union republics as some sort of virtual sixteenth republic, but the victim was Soviet state unity. While a viable post-communist federation or confederation might have been feasible,[8] in the event, the destruction of communism was accompanied by the disintegration of the USSR (see Part I). The August coup destroyed the final shreds of legitimacy of attempts to 'renew' the communist system and at the same time delivered a devastating blow against Gorbachev's attempts to save the union.

### Ethno-federal structure and composition

Sovereignty declarations in 1990–1 were accompanied by the 'republicanisation' of Russia; the constitution was amended on 15 December 1990 to delete the word 'autonomous' in the title of Russia's 16 republics, and they simply became 'republics forming part of the Russian Federation'. On 3 July 1991 the Supreme Soviet elevated 4 of the 5 autonomous *oblasts* (Adygeya, Gorno-Altai, Karachai-Cherkessia and Khakassia) to the status of republics and they were removed from the jurisdiction of the krais to which they were formerly subordinate.[9] This brought the number of republics to 20, leaving only the Jewish autonomous *oblast*. The number of republics rose to 21 when on 4 June 1992 the Supreme Soviet split the Chechen-Ingush republic into two. The 21 national republics comprise 15.2 per cent of the population and 28.6 per cent of Russia's territory. Most of the autonomous *okrugs* also declared themselves sovereign, trying to free themselves from the control of the corresponding *oblast* or krai to become subjects of federation in their own right (Table 11.1). As we shall see, under Putin the move was in the direction, to merge the autonomous *okrugs* with the *oblast* of which they are part (Chapter 12).

Russia's federal components and their status are listed in the constitution (Article 65.1), and changes to their status do not require a constitutional amendment. Russia's federalism is organised on two principles: territorial and ethno-territorial. The territorial principle alone applies to the two federal cities (Moscow and St Petersburg), the 49 *oblasts* (before Putin's mergers) and the 6 krais (the latter differ little from *oblasts* except that they were once border regions). The remaining 32 units of the federation are defined by unstable ethno-territorial characteristics: 21 republics (see Table 10.2), one autonomous *oblast* (Birobijan) and ten autonomous okrugs (see Table 11.1). The 32 ethno-federal territories occupy 53.3 per cent of Russia's territory but (in 1989) only 16.7 per cent of the population.[10]

Ethnic Russians make up the overwhelming majority of the country's population but find themselves in the anomalous position of not having an ethno-federal area

*Table 11.1* Autonomous *oblasts* and *okrugs*

| Names of component | Titular nationality % | Russians % |
|---|---|---|
| Jewish autonomous *oblast* (Birobidjan) | 4.2 | 83.2 |
| Agin-Buryat autonomous *okrug* | 54.9 | 40.8 |
| Chukchi autonomous *okrug* | 7.3 | 66.1 |
| Evenk autonomous *okrug* | 14.0 | 67.5 |
| Khanty-Mansi autonomous *okrug* | 1.4 | 66.3 |
| Komi-Permyak autonomous *okrug* | 60.2 | 36.1 |
| Koryak autonomous *okrug* | 16.5 | 62.0 |
| Nenets autonomous *okrug* | 11.9 | 65.8 |
| Taimyr (Dolgan-Nenets) autonomous *okrug* | 13.7 | 67.1 |
| Ust-Orda Buryat autononous *okrug* | 36.3 | 56.5 |
| Yamalo-Nenets autonomous *okrug* | 4.2 | 59.2 |

*Source*: *Argumenty i fakty*, No. 13, March 1991, p. 1, where the administrative divisions are those of 1989, but the figures are updated 1989 census returns reflecting the situation of early 1991.

of their own – hence the calls by some nationalists either for the establishment of a 'Russian republic', or for the abolition of the territories of ethnic minorities. Out of a total RSFSR population of 147.02 million in 1989, 119.87 million (81.53 per cent) were ethnic Russians: of these 108.06 million (90.2 per cent, or 73.5 per cent of the total RF population) lived outside ethno-federal units; while 11.8 million (9.8 per cent, 8.02 per cent of total RF population) lived within the national-state territory of some other nationality. The nearly twelve million ethnic Russians living in the ethno-federal territories of others comprise 45.7 per cent of the population of these areas (see Table 10.1) and constitute a source of potential Russian nationalist mobilisation.

Some peoples have a 'republic' and others not: 33 national groups have some sort of territorial home (though some live in great communal dwellings like Dagestan) and 63 do not. The have-nots include Russians and some of the less numerous peoples. Equity would suggest that all should be on an equal footing, irrespective of whether they have a republic in the 'near abroad' – 7.8 million compatriots of the titular nationalities in the 14 former union republics live in Russia, including 4.4 million Ukrainians (see Table 10.1); or in the 'far abroad': Germans (821,000), Koreans (107,000), Poles (95,000), Greeks (92,000), Finns (47,000) and a few other peoples; or Jews who have a nominal homeland abroad (Israel) and one in Russia, Birobijan (the Jewish autononous *oblast*).

At the time of the 1989 census the titular nationality comprised an absolute majority of the population in 8 of the 31 ethno-federal units of that time,[11] a comparative majority in 3,[12] and in the other 20 ethnic Russians were in the majority (Tables 10.1–10.3). In the 16 autonomous republics the titular nationalities comprised only 42 per cent of the total population; in the autonomous *oblasts* 22 per cent; and in the autonomous *okrugs* only 10.5 per cent, largely as a result of the heavy in-migration of Russians and other peoples. The total population of the 41 nationalities with their own or sharing ethno-federal areas is 17.71 million (12.05 per cent of the total population of the RSFSR), but of these only 10.32 million (58.3 per cent, or 7.02 per cent of total RF population) live in their own titular federal unit (Table 10.1).[13] As for the 21 republics in Russia today:

- The titular population comprises over 50 per cent of the population in only seven: Chechnya, Chuvashia, Dagestan (where Avars, Dargins, Kumyks, Lezgins and Laks

make up 73 per cent of the population), Ingushetia, Kabardino-Balkaria, North Ossetia and Tyva.
- In eight of the republics Russians comprise the majority: Adygeya, Buryatia, Gorno-Altai, Karelia, Khakassia, Komi, Mordovia and Udmurtia.
- In the other six republics (Bashkortostan, Kalmykia, Karachaevo-Cherkessia, Marii El, Sakha (Yakutia) and Tatarstan) no group has an absolute majority.
- The dispersion quotient is also marked by great variations: over 90 per cent of Yakuts, Tyvans, Kabards and Balkars live in their republics, while at the other extreme two-thirds of Tatars and Mordvins and nearly half of Chuvashis and Maris live outside their titular republic. A total of 9.7 million people live outside their nominal republic (see Table 10.2).[14]

The status of the autonomous okrugs remains ambiguous. Article 5 of the constitution asserts that they are equal to the other units of the federation, while Article 66 subordinates them to the *oblast* or krai in which they are located. In addition, some of the okrugs are extremely rich in natural resources (oil and gas), like Khanty-Mansi and Yamal-Nenets in West Siberia, while others are very poor. Not surprisingly, the rich *okrugs* have sought absolute independence from the *oblasts* of which they form part, but so far only Chukotka has achieved this goal, separating from Magadan *oblast* in June 1992. Like the republics, the autonomous *okrugs* were established in the name of titular ethnic groups, but the eponymous nationality makes up over 50 per cent only in Komi-Permyak and Agin-Buryatia, while Russians make up the majority elsewhere (Table 10.2). Under Putin there was considerable debate over the fate of the autonomous *okrugs*, with views divided over whether they should be fully subordinated to the host *oblast*, or whether they should become separate units. As we shall see in Chapter 11, a number of regions merged. The status of the last remaining autonomous *oblast* is equally perplexed. Birobijan was established in the inhospitable Far East by Stalin as a homeland for the Jews, but today they comprise only 4.2 per cent of the population and represent only 1.7 per cent of Russia's Jews. The *oblast* separated from Khabarovsk krai on 25 March 1991, and under Putin discussion centred on it reintegrating with its former host.

### The potential for conflict

The complexity of minority issues in Russia is daunting. The rich diversity of Russian ethnic composition means that much of the population has multiple identities with overlapping ethnicity, religion, culture and language. As noted, the 1989 census identified 128 ethnic groups, although 16 had a population of fewer than 5,000. There are 26 groups among the peoples of the North alone, ranging from the Nentsy numbering 34,200 to the Entsy at 200. Table 10.1 demonstrates the overwhelming predominance of the ethnic Russians at 81.5 per cent of the population, followed a long way behind by the second largest group, the Tatars at 3.75 per cent. The 2002 census now listed 182 peoples.

While there remains a devastating potential for Russia to split up, the figures above suggest a picture that differs in several respect from the nationality problems of the USSR. The majority of Russia's republics lack a clear demographic basis to aspirations for independence, and to date a trigger mechanism for disintegration has been lacking. However, territories where the titular nationalities are the strongest are found on the periphery: in the North Caucasus the Islamic bloc of Dagestan, Chechnya, Ingushetia, Kabardino-Balkaria, together with Buddhist Kalmykia and Christian North Ossetia; and in the Far East Tyva on the borders of Mongolia, and Agin *okrug*. The Volga and Kama republics form a single contiguous territory in the centre of Russia (see Figure 11.1), but in Chuvashia and Marii-El Russians make up a clear majority. In Tatarstan Tatars comprise 48.5 per cent of the population and Russians 43.3 per cent, but only a third of all Volga Tatars live in Tatarstan. The independence of some of the republics at the margins of the Federation, like Chechnya or Tyva, might not destabilise the fragile unity of the country; whereas the secession of a republic in the heartlands, like Tatarstan, could stimulate a snowball effect tearing the unity of the Federation apart.

Woodrow Wilson was asked during the Paris peace conference in 1919, 'Does every little language have to have a state all its own?' The answer for the USSR in 1991, as in Eastern Europe in 1919, appeared to be 'yes'; whereas in Russia today a somewhat different dynamic operates – or so the leadership believes. In America Theodore Roosevelt had tried to transcend ethnic identities – Italian-Americans, Hispanic-Americans, Anglo-Americans – to forge a nation of *Americans*, whereas the current trend towards multiculturalism has reversed assimilationist policies. For historical reasons the question in Russia cannot be posed in quite the same way, and we have advanced the notion of pluriculturalism to capture this difference. The Bashkirs, Tatars and others were long established, and in many cases predated the arrival of the Russians themselves; but at the same time the existence of Tatar-Russians, Bashkir-Russians and many more is an established fact. This is reflected in the two terms used to denote 'Russian' in the language: *Rossiiskoe* means 'of Russia', used adjectivally, giving rise to the noun *Rossiyanin*, a citizen of Russia of whatever ethnicity; whereas *Russkii*, the noun, denotes those who are ethnically Russian.

The *korenizatsiya* policy of the 1920s had contributed much to the development of the national consciousness of the peoples of Russia, and in particular had consolidated national cultures and scripts. From the 1930s onwards, as we have seen, schooling in native languages was reduced and the policy of national development reversed. With the collapse of the Soviet Union policy returned to that of the 1920s, with the difference that the earlier nation-building was now accompanied by state-building; for many peoples in the republics the restoration of cultural symbols and culture was not enough and they now sought full-blooded statehood. The former communist regime had always been able to invoke the concept of class to trump 'nationalism' (often denigrated as 'bourgeois'), but Russia could not so easily delegitimate national aspirations. In Russia the defence of the integrity of the state has been asserted on the basis of free and equal citizenship, a civic concept that transcends national differences, although it is not able to transcend cultural specificities.

The Russian leadership from 1990 sought to prevent the 'Balkanisation' of Russia. The central question was to define a new relationship between the many peoples of Russia and the state. The ethno-federal legacy left a heavy burden, with political inequalities not only between regions and national areas, but between the autonomies themselves. The 16 autonomous republics in the RSFSR had had their own constitutions but (in contrast to the 15 union republics) no right of secession, whereas the 5 autonomous *oblasts* and the 10 autonomous okrugs, quite apart from the mass of ordinary *oblasts*, had no constitutions and even fewer rights to self-government. This legacy of inequality in national relations represented the single most urgent problem facing the new government. Some peoples (like the Chechens and Tatarstan) sought to become nations in their own right, and tried to do this within the framework of traditional ideas of statehood. Not all of the peoples in the Russian Federation, however, could or even wanted to achieve statehood. The emphasis for the majority moved from 'national self-determination', taking the form of state-building, towards forms of national-cultural self-development. The rediscovery of national identity is at the same time the remaking of this identity in post-Soviet conditions where *all* societies face a crisis of values and viability.

The division of Russia into national areas did not 'solve' the national question but exacerbated it. The question of national development, instruction in native languages and so on, cannot be reduced to the question of statehood, since so many people live outside 'their' state (an argument made about the USSR as a whole). Not only do a large proportion of people with their own titular republic live outside their nominal area, but the national areas themselves are home to many other peoples (primarily Russians). By the mere fact of their presence Russians are perceived as a threat to native languages and traditions, representing an ever-present danger of cultural assimilation. In most areas, however, Russians never considered themselves the bearers of an imperial creed but sought to escape hardship at home, to find work and better wages, or were deported involuntarily. The absence of counter-mobilisation to the nationalism of some of the titular nationalities is striking. The strong vote for Zhirinovsky in some of the national areas, however, revealed ethnic Russian fears.[15] Just as in the elections to the First and Second Dumas in 1906 and 1907, where the greatest support for Russian nationalist parties came in the 15 *gubernii* of the Pale of Settlement and border areas with mixed populations, so too in the elections for the revived First Duma in December 1993 support for Russian nationalists came from areas of mixed settlement. However, in later elections opposition to the ethnocratic territorial organisation of the country was not a significant factor.

Russia is now an entire borderland, the distinguishing feature of post-imperial identities. The very existence of Russia as a state has been questioned. Ryszard Kapuscinski in his book *Imperium* formulates the problem succinctly:

> In short, following the disintegration of the USSR, we are now facing the prospect of the disintegration of the Russian Federation, or, to put it differently; after the first phase of decolonization (that of the former Soviet Union) the second phase begins – the decolonization of the Russian Federation.[16]

The strongest exponent of this view is Rafael Khakimov, one of Tatarstan president Mintimir Shaimiev's chief advisers in the 1990s and still an influential figure. He espoused the 'decolonisation' model, contrasting a Moscow-based officialdom and 'a provincial, colonial nation living in another world'.[17] In his view, as the regions struggled for greater cultural and economic autonomy and achieved ever more legal sovereignty, Russia itself would gradually disappear:

> Russia will increasingly become an ephemeral notion limited to rather vague emotional slogans. There is no hope of preserving Russia in its earlier condition. Russia's borders have lost their legitimacy. There are no legal norms whereby its approximate borders could be defined ... Regional interests and the idea of regionalisation offer a way out of the impasse for Russia.[18]

For Khakimov Russia as a geopolitical reality was destined to disappear. This is certainly not the way that things look from the perspective of Moscow. The attitude identified by Kapuscinski remains strong:

> For in such a state as the former USSR (today, CIS, tomorrow ...?) there exists a certain class of people whose calling is to think exclusively on an imperial scale, and even more – on a global one. One cannot ask them questions like 'What's happening in Vorkuta?' for they are utterly unable to answer them. They will even be surprised: And what is the significance of it? The Imperium will not fall because of anything that is happening there!... Between the Russian and his Imperium a strong and vital symbiosis exists: the fortunes of the superpower truly and deeply move him. Even today.[19]

As we shall see when we discuss foreign and security policy (Part V) a great power mentality is pervasive in Russia. Yet, on the basis of our discussion above, we argue that the decolonisation model is not an appropriate one for Russia. Russia may have displayed aspects of an imperial state, but its mix of nationalities suggests that some sort of multinational nation had emerged.

The constitution now recognises all territories as multinational, guaranteeing equal rights for all of Russia's citizens irrespective of where they find themselves. The problem, however, arises when it comes to the question of collective rights. While all the peoples of Russia have the right to national and cultural development, the political form in which this can be expressed remains ambiguous. Russia is considered a state of all of its citizens, irrespective of their nationality, but the ethno-federal legacy of the Soviet period is difficult to reconcile with this civic conception of equal citizenship (an issue we shall return to in Chapter 12). The fragmentation of citizenship was particularly resented. A survey in Komi republic revealed that 60 per cent of the ethnic Russians considered themselves primarily citizens of Russia rather than of the republic.[20] The ethno-federal system itself remains a potent element stoking the fires of inter-ethnic conflict (although it is neither a sufficient nor a necessary condition for such conflicts). Attempts, however, to separate the national question from the problem of territorial autonomy would in the short run only precipitate conflict. Of all the chalices bequeathed by the Soviet regime, ethno-federalism was perhaps the most poisoned.

## Russian federalism

Russia's federal character in the Soviet period was derived not from the regions where the majority of the population lived, which effectively lacked federal representation, but from the national republics. The system was a mixed ethno-federal and unitary one and thus very different, say, from the United States, where representation is uniformly federal-territorial. How was Russia to move from an ethno-federal system to a genuine federal-territorial system in which *all* of Russia's territories would become subjects of federation? Opinion divided between those who sought to make all the components of Russia equal subjects of federation, and those who tried to maintain a hierarchy in the relationship between the republics and the rest. The debate over the new federal treaties reflected the struggle between two different visions, one focusing on individual rights in a democratic state, while the other prioritised national rights loosely identified with the existing ethno-federal regions. The debate is one familiar to France where exponents of the Jacobin tradition, for example, oppose the granting of autonomy to Corsica on the grounds that this would subvert the principle of republican equality.

### Towards the Federal Treaty

Learning from the fate of the USSR, which had responded too late to the problem of nationalism, the First Russian CPD in May 1990 decided that the Russian federal system should be renewed; the Declaration of State Sovereignty of 12 June 1990 recognised 'the need for a significant extension of the rights of the autonomous republics ... and regions of the RSFSR'; and the Supreme Soviet Presidium on 17 July proposed a timetable for a Federal Treaty. A draft was ready for the Third CPD to adopt in March 1991, but the vigorous anti-federalist lobbying of a group of deputies forced it to be redrafted. The fourth draft of the USSR Union Treaty, published three days before the coup, made provision for a Russian treaty to regulate its own inter-national relations. The disintegration of the USSR and the problems encountered in adopting the new Russian constitution placed even more of a premium on achieving an agreement to prevent the disintegration of the Russian Federation.

The debate focused on what was to be the subject of the Russian federal system? If only national-territorial areas, then what role would the regions play, and even more, what about peoples without territory? Sakharov had suggested making all 53 Soviet national-territorial units subjects of federalism in his draft constitution for the Union of Soviet Republics of Europe and Asia. It was not clear why 53 republics should represent the 128 census nationalities, especially when ethnic boundaries did not coincide with the national ones and where the titular nationalities were often in a minority in the republic that bore their name. To counter the threat of secession by Lithuania and other republics Gorbachev responded by getting the USSR Supreme Soviet in April 1990 to adopt a law on the 'Delimitation of Powers' between the USSR and the subjects of the federation equalising the rights of autonomous republics with those of union republics. This meant that autonomous republics could now negotiate on equal terms with the republics of which they formed part. The idea was to hang a sword of Damocles over republics that threatened to secede; if they tried to leave the union, they would be faced by the threat of secession within the secession.

It was in part to counter Gorbachev's threat that Russia declared its state sovereignty on 12 June 1990 while at the same time promising extensive sovereignty for its own autonomous republics. Russia's declaration of state sovereignty *vis-à-vis* the USSR was thus accompanied by declarations of sovereignty by its own national areas. On 20 July, North Ossetia declared itself a union republic, albeit as part of Russia. Karelia on 9 August declared its sovereignty but did not change its status, while Khakassia on 15 August unilaterally raised its status to an autonomous republic. On 29 August Komi and on 30 August Tatarstan declared themselves sovereign, followed by Udmurtia on 20 September and Yakutia on 27 September.[21] What these declarations meant in practice remained to be discovered, but it soon became clear that a declaration of sovereignty by no means signalled its achievement. Russia's autonomous republics sought to join Gorbachev's Union Treaty process in their own right, an idea at first supported by Gorbachev to undermine Yeltsin's power base – even if it meant the destruction of the Russian Federation. Resentment over this lingered throughout the 1990s.

It is for this reason that the autonomous republics most active in seeking sovereignty were also those that most actively supported the coup in August 1991, with the leaderships in Tatarstan, Kabardino-Balkaria and Chechen-Ingushetia actively supporting the putschists. In Chechnya a lingering Sovietism persisted until well into the 1990s; president Johar Dudaev always argued that he would be happy for Chechnya to become a union republic in the USSR, but not a republic of Russia (*mutatis mutandis*, this is the position of Abkhazia *vis-à-vis* Georgia, and for the same reason). What is often forgotten is that later, in his enthusiasm to achieve a renewal of the Soviet Union through the Novo-Ogarevo process in the spring and summer of 1991, Gorbachev simply confirmed the rights of the 15 existing Soviet union republics as the subjects of the proposed Union Treaty, and in effect washed his hands off their own internal secessionist problems.

It was as part of the attempt to out-bid Gorbachev, however, that on a visit to Tatarstan in August 1990, following his election as chairman of the Russian parliament, that Yeltsin declared 'Take as much independence as you can', and he went on to suggest that if this meant secession from Russia, then 'your decision will be final'.[22] In Bashkortostan soon after he once again urged the local authorities to 'take as much power as you can swallow'.[23] In his speech to the Fifth CPD on 28 October 1991 Yeltsin argued that

> The process of self-determination of peoples began even before the revolution of 1917, but was interrupted by crude force for many decades. It is now entering its decisive phase. A new national consciousness is forming in the Russian people, which is democratic in its very essence.[24]

It was all very well to urge local sovereignty in a bid to counter Gorbachev's overtures to Russia's republics, but how was this 'freedom' and 'self-determination' to be institutionalised, and would it be democratic and compatible with the unity of the state? Yeltsin was to find that the nations of Russia, which under the Soviet system had enjoyed various degrees of formal autonomy, now tried to convert their rights into genuine powers. While the Karelians, Dagestanis, Buryats and Yakuts sought to extend their autonomy to control resources on their territory, the Chechens and certain groups in Tatarstan sought outright independence.

One of the concrete manifestations of sovereignty was the 'presidentification' of Russia's republics, once again following the example set by Yeltsin himself. Tatarstan led the way, electing a president on the same day as Russia (12 June 1991). By the end of 1991 presidents had been chosen in Kabardino-Balkaria, Marii El, Mordovia, Chechnya and Tyva, and with other republics moving in the same direction. Tatarstan moved the furthest in translating its declaration of sovereignty into practice, having chosen not only a president but also a new name (formerly Tataria) and a coat of arms, and sought economic sovereignty by establishing its own bank and bringing former union enterprises under its own jurisdiction. The only other republic to have set on the same path was Chechnya. The key issue everywhere was control over local property, natural resources and budgets, especially taxation.

In the struggle to shape a new post-Soviet federalism 'democrats' like Yelena Bonner (Sakharov's widow) argued that 'The choice is either the creation of a democratic state with guarantees to all the peoples of the federation of the right to self-determination, and protection of this right, or disintegration in accordance with the same former USSR scenario.'[25] Radical liberals insisted that Russia could avoid the fate that had befallen the USSR only by granting full autonomy to the republics, whereas national democrats and patriots responded that it was this logic that had led to the break-up of the USSR. Instead, they insisted that since the ethnic borders of Russia only roughly corresponded to the existing borders, and because every single region of Russia was multi-ethnic to one degree or another, rights should be individual rather than national. Russian nationalists revived the Whites' Civil War slogan of Russia 'united and indivisible' (*edinaya i nedelimaya*), but the sentiment was shared by most of Russia's new leaders.

Official policy in the early period was criticised for constantly reacting to crises rather than developing consistent principles. Galina Starovoitova, Yeltsin's adviser on nationality issues until October 1992, placed her hopes on the development of an effective federal system, but in the meantime argued in favour of giving the republics a free rein so as not to provoke conflict. The State Committee for Federalism and Nationalities under Shakhrai took a harder line, insisting that national self-determination was to be dependent on two other principles of international law: human rights and the inviolability of borders. The Committee's policy was based on a number of principles: the equality of all peoples living in the federation; the genuine development of federalism in Russia; the depoliticisation of nationality policy; reliance on the legally formed authorities in the components of the federation, whether the centre liked them or not; the indisputable priority of political methods in resolving national conflicts; accepting the link between economic and nationality policy; and consistency in nationality policy.[26] According to the liberal MP Vladimir Lysenko, the state was to ensure the neutrality of the federal centre in inter-ethnic conflicts, a moratorium on border changes, ban the creation of new federal components through the division of existing units, assist the stabilisation of political elites in the republics by advancing moderate nationalists, managers and entrepreneurs to leadership positions, and prevent the fusion of state and mafia-criminal structures in the national areas.[27] By contrast, Ramazan Abdulatipov, the chair of the Supreme Soviet's Council of Nationalities, insisted that the revival of the national life of the peoples of Russia was an essential part of the formation of civil society and the establishment of a legal state: 'We consider national rebirth as the combination of the national idea with general human interests and democratic principles'. He insisted that in a multinational society the state should not stand above the various ethnic groups, and he condemned those who sought to replace the national principle by the territorial one. He agreed that the priority was individual human rights, but this should not infringe national rights.[28] The points made above indicate the range of issues discussed at this time.

Federalism came to be seen as the only way Russia's unity could be preserved while guaranteeing autonomy for its peoples. Federalism has a long history in Russia, although not always described as such. The Northern Society of what became the Decembrist movement advocated a federal system for Russia along American lines, including the separation of ethnicity from the system of territorial representation, whereas the Southern Society, by contrast, opposed all hints of federalism and explicitly favoured the assimilation of national minorities,[29] a view that finds its advocates today. The treaties signed between the Tsar and the governments of peoples entering the empire, like the Caucasian khans and Central Asian emirs, contained provision for a division of powers between the centre and the locality, the hallmark of federalism. Various national areas of the old empire had certain rights and privileges, allowing local self-government and limiting the prerogatives of Tsarist *chinovniki*. These early elements of federalism were undermined during the centralising and unitarist period of the second half of the nineteenth century, as the supranational principles of Tsarist imperial statehood began to give way to a nation-building statism, yet did not disappear entirely. The Bolsheviks had at first condemned the concept of federalism, but were soon forced to incorporate it in their state-building but, as we have seen, federal forms were undermined by a unitary practice. In drafting Russia's new constitution Yeltsin insisted on three key principles: that human rights were to be guaranteed throughout Russia, including the republics; the unity of Russia must be maintained; and the constitutions of the republics should not contradict the Russian constitution.[30] He failed to uphold these principles, and it was left to Putin to reassert them.

The major obstacle to adopting the constitution was disagreement over what was to be the subject of federation. The draft of October 1991 weakened the old ethno-territorial division of Russia by proposing two forms of representation: ethno-federal from the *republics*, which would not necessarily be the same as the existing autonomous republics; and federal-territorial, as in the USA or Germany, from *zemli* (lands, or in German *Länder*). A highly regionalised Russia was to emerge with some forty units, the republics and the *zemli* (whose relative status remained to be determined). All of Russia for the first time would become a subject of the federation and not just specified ethnic parts.[31] Trying to steer a course between those who argued for the re-establishment of a unitary state (in the form of the restoration of the Tsarist *gubernii*), and extreme ethno-federalists, encompassing not only secessionists in Tatarstan or Chechnya but also Russian nationalists who called for the creation of an ethnic Russian republic, the draft appeared to satisfy neither. On the one hand, it was attacked for undermining the unity of the country by conferring extensive rights on the titular republics, and indeed for infringing the rights of Russians living in them. On the other hand, the attempt to equalise the rights of republics and lands was interpreted as an attack on the privileges of the former. The draft represented a move away from the traditional Soviet prioritisation of the ethnic dimension in state-building, which had granted statehood to all sorts of ethnic groups to whom the principle was often alien and pointless; but having tasted statehood, the ethno-federal territories would not give it up without a struggle – the hallmark of path dependency.

The October 1991 draft constitution reflected the view that Russia was a *constitutional* rather than a *treaty* federation: the state sovereignty of Russia only needed to find a constitutional and federal form; it was not formed by contracts between its members. Russia was a multinational state that had come into being over the centuries, and thus membership was not a matter of choice or based on a voluntary contract. This did not exclude the signing of a Federal Treaty between the republics of Russia and the state as a whole, but did not give the republics the right of secession since they were already part of a pre-existing Russian state. Thus the draft condemned the treaty path to a new constitution, which would have given all the subjects of the new federation the choice whether to join or not. According to Rumyantsev, this would not only have caused endless conflicts but it would also have denied that Russia was *a priori* already a 'sovereign state created by the peoples historically living in it'.[32] Russia had never been a treaty federation (unlike the USSR) and therefore none had the right to secede; and neither would they be given a choice of whether to join. Tatarstan, Tyva and Chechen-Ingushetia had never formally signed to join the RSFSR or the USSR, and were now bitter that they would not be given the option of choosing to enter the Russian Federation as signatories of a new treaty.[33]

Post-communist Russian state-building was thus torn between three principles.

- The first suggested that all national-territorial formations should be abolished in their entirety, and that Russia should become a unitary state and be divided into simple administrative regions like the Tsarist *gubernii*, the approach suggested by Stalin in his autonomisation plan and advanced by patriots and even more vigorously by nationalists like Zhirinovsky. Advocates of 'gubernisation' insist that a unitary state is not necessarily a centralised one, and point to the example of France where regional devolution has eroded Napoleonic centralism. In Spain since the death of Franco in 1975 a hybrid type of federalism has emerged with the devolution of authority to 17 self-governing provinces; but the lack of historical identity of some of the regions suggests elements of 'false federalism'.
- The second view absolutised the federal principle and sought to divide Russia into fully fledged republics and *zemli* with equal rights. Distinctions between ethnically based units and a purely territorial form of federalism would be eliminated.
- The third view, advanced by the leaders of Russia's republics, sought to maintain the existing hierarchy of federalism, with the ethno-federal units at the top.

The 1991 draft constitution took the second path and weakened the ethno-federal principle in favour of a de-ethnicised federalism. This led to protests in the republics by advocates of the third path, and later versions of the constitution veered to the third option, making concessions to the national elites in the titular republics, although not repudiating the principle of equalising the rights of the subjects of the federalism. The special status of national republics was retained but the rights of Russia's regions were enhanced.

Yeltsin had earlier favoured the division of Russia into some 8–10 large regions to avoid nationality clashes and separatism, and Rumyantsev had favoured the division of Russia into *zemli* and republics with equal rights. This had been opposed by the national republics who wanted more rights in *comparison* with the Russian *oblasts*, even though they were gaining extensive rights in comparison with the past. The national republics were united on this, irrespective of their ethnic composition. Karelia, a republic in which the titular nationality made up only 10 per cent of the population, sought exactly the same rights as Tatarstan or Tyva with much larger proportions of the titular nationality. Behaviour was defined by status rather than ethnic composition. The rise of regional separatism later added to this leapfrogging battle of relative sovereignties.

This balance between privileges and rights was enshrined in the three federal treaties (known collectively as the Federal Treaty), signed on 31 March 1992 and ratified by an overwhelming majority by the Sixth CPD on 10 April.[34] The treaty allowed a significant degree of decentralisation, providing for joint jurisdiction over education, environmental protection and conservation, healthcare and natural resources, while recognising certain areas as the sole prerogative of the subjects. The treaty recognised three types of federal subjects (see Figure 11.2):

- Twenty (now 21) national-state formations (formerly autonomous republics) as sovereign republics within the Russian Federation.
- Fifty-seven administrative territorial areas (*krais*, *oblasts*, as well as the cities of Moscow and St Petersburg).
- And 11 national-territorial areas (autonomous *oblasts* and autonomous *okrugs*).

*Figure 11.2* The regions and republics of European Russia

All had equal rights and obligations, but the republics were allowed the attributes of statehood: constitutions and laws, elected Supreme Soviets (parliaments), supreme courts, and, if they so wished (which most did), presidents.[35] With the elevation in 1991 of 4 autonomous *oblasts* to the status of republics the total rose to 20, and of these 18 signed the treaty. Tatarstan, which had earlier voted for self-rule, and the Chechen Republic, which had declared independence from Russia in November 1991, refused to sign. Tatarstan insisted on a separate bilateral treaty between itself and Russia as equal sovereign states. Bashkortostan had threatened not to participate but at the last moment agreed to sign when granted additional budgetary rights.[36]

The Federal Treaty did not signify the creation of a new state, since such a state was taken to have existed for centuries; and neither did it denote the transformation of the state into a federation, since Russian statehood had long contained elements of federalism; but was an attempt to define the powers of the federation and its subjects.[37] The treaty rendered the subjects of federation equal in a juridical sense, yet the republics were granted more of the attributes of statehood and greater economic powers than the regions.[38] In contrast to the old Soviet constitution, the treaty did not grant the republics the right to secede but bound them together while granting greater powers and freedoms. The treaty was not intended to act as a substitute for the constitution, and instead was incorporated, with some amendments, into the constitution of the time as a special section. Moscow retained the right to control defence and security and to set federal taxes, while the signatories now gained some control over natural resources and formalised their borders. They could now also conduct foreign trade on their own. The extent of their control over natural resources and the right to levy taxes remained unclear and caused endless conflicts later – including a joint declaration by the presidents of Bashkortostan, Tatarstan and Sakha (Yakutia) that the federal authorities ignored the legitimate rights and interests of the republics.[39]

Once again a form of ethno-federalism was confirmed in Russia despite hopes to avoid this route. The new Russian federalism now developed on a constitutional-treaty basis, a hybrid that internalised all sorts of contradictions. It appeared absurd to retain three different types of subjects of federation, yet 'asymmetrical federalism' appeared to be the only basis on which the Russian Federation could survive. Under asymmetrical federalism components of the federation have different competencies and status, whereas in a symmetrical federation they are equal.[40] There are well-grounded fears, however, that asymmetrical state structures give rise to conflicts, since not all components are willing to accept the disparities in status and prerogatives. It may even provoke the emergence of dual federalism, with one or more states becoming entirely distinct from the others. This was the process that engendered the division of Czechoslovakia, provoked regional conflicts in Spain between the so-called nationalities and provinces, and which placed the Belgian state (divided into three separate language communities) under enormous pressure as Flanders gained many of the attributes of statehood.

The Federal Treaty did not put an end to debates in Russia about the form of its federalism. Questions of property and taxation remained vexed, the fundamental question over whether Russia should be a territorial rather than an ethno-national federation had not been resolved, and an unstable hierarchy of federalism had been established. The 21 republics were endowed with the appurtenances of a state, but the others were not. Tatarstan's constitution affirmed that it was a state 'associated with Russia',[41] and the constitutions of some of the other republics (namely Tyva, Karelia and Yakutia-Sakha) declared the primacy of local laws over Russian ones.[42] The struggle between executive and legislative power in Moscow allowed the regions to ignore presidential decrees and legislative acts and weakened economic links. In 1993, for example, Moscow collected only 40 per cent of the tax revenues due to it from the regions and republics,[43] and over two dozen refused to pay the centre their federal tax obligations. The confusion allowed considerations of short-term advantage to predominate over juridical principles of unified and equal state-building for all of Russia.

### The constitutional basis of the new federalism

Drafts of the constitution both encouraged the aspirations of Russia's republics for sovereignty while at the same time limiting these aspirations, a tension still not satisfactorily resolved. Strengthened by his victory in October 1993, Yeltsin took a more assertive line towards the regions and republics of Russia and in effect reneged on what he had been forced to concede during the struggle with Gorbachev and parliament. In particular, the word 'sovereign', incorporated into the Federal Treaty and which a number of republics had adopted to describe themselves, was struck from the constitution on the grounds that one state could not have two sources of sovereignty. The constitution adopted on 12 December 1993 finally gave legal form to Russia's federal system. In terms of Riker's notion of a 'federal bargain', which he defines as 'a bargain between prospective national leaders and officials of constituent governments for the purpose of aggregating territory, the better to lay taxes and raise armies', Russian federalism is deficient. It does meet Riker's criterion that there must be at least two levels of government ruling the same land and people; and to a degree his stipulation that each level has at least one area of action in which it is autonomous (although this autonomy has tended to take asymmetrical and contingent forms, rather than being formalised in the federal bargain); but the guarantee, although enunciated in the constitution, of the autonomy of each government in its sphere has been only weakly observed.[44]

The Federal Treaty was excluded from the 1993 constitution, although the basic principles of decentralisation, joint and sole jurisdictions, remained. The new constitution, which took precedence over the Federal Treaty, took a more restrictive view of these rights. Although the definition of the republics as 'sovereign states' was dropped from the text, the federation structure continued to apply different criteria to various units despite the formal claim that all federal components are equal (Article 5.1). The rights of Russia's federal units were significantly equalised and made subject to the laws and decisions of federal authorities. The principle of 'asymmetrical federalism', the keystone of the Federal Treaty, was in principle abandoned (although as we shall see in Chapter 12, it is very much alive in practice). No longer were some subjects of the federation 'more equal' than others – at least in theory. While the provisions of the Treaty were reflected in the new constitution, the text itself was no longer bodily incorporated to underline the principle that Russia is a federation based on a constitution and not on a treaty. The constitution regularised the hybrid federalism that had been emerging in Russia, based partly on national areas (like Belgium and India) and partly on areas lacking any national significance (as in Brazil, Germany and the USA). This mix of national and territorial federalism was accompanied by declarations (Article 5) on the equality of all the subjects of the federation; when in fact they had greatly differing rights. The republics, for example, have their own constitutions, governments, parliaments, presidents and other attributes of statehood denied the territorial formations; the latter, however, have the right to issue their own charters. The constitution tried to move away from the old Soviet primacy given to the ethno-federal organisation of the state, a principle that was largely meaningless under communist rule. The new document sought to prioritise civil over collective ethnic rights, and at the same time tried to prevent ethnic differences becoming the foundation of local or central statehood, a development that could only exacerbate centrifugal tendencies.

Regions and republics were now guaranteed significant areas of autonomy as long as their legislative acts did not contradict the Russian constitution or federal laws. Articles 71–3 of the constitution lay out the respective powers of the federal authorities and the regions. Article 71 subordinates civil law, the court system and the procuracy to the federal authorities; Article 72 outlines the elements of joint jurisdiction, including the control and use of natural resources; and Article 73 ascribes all that is not specified in the previous two articles to regional jurisdiction, although this is vague and does not specify what these were. Putin's struggle against non-compliance has been waged within the terms of reinstating the primacy of Article 71, but the danger arose that the provisions of Articles 72 and 73 would be undermined.

The long-standing dispute between republics, on the one hand, and between regions and territories, on the other, was not resolved, and debates over Russia's state structure continue. In contrast to the republics, the powers of the remaining 68 subjects of the federation appeared residual, sharing certain listed powers and enjoying other unspecified prerogatives not conflicting with the national state (Article 76.6), but there was no mention of any detailed regulatory or financial powers that they could exercise independently. Republics can elect presidents and adopt constitutions, while regions often have governors and adopt 'charters'. Regions sought to narrow the difference, while republics fought jealously to preserve the differential.

# 12 Segmented regionalism and the new federalism

> In every age justice has been called the keystone of the social edifice. By acting towards each other justly, the citizens maintain the condition of trustfulness and friendship which is the basis of an unforced and fruitful cooperation; by acting with justice towards each and all, the public authority wins the confidence and respect which render it effective.
>
> (Bertrand De Jouvenal)[1]

Segmented regionalism was characterised by the erosion of constitutional principles of a single legal and economic space. Regional authorities took advantage of the weakness of the Russian state under Yeltsin to develop a highly variegated set of policies and political regimes. The concept of asymmetrical federalism disguised the way that national norms guaranteeing individual rights, legal standards and the development of a national market were undermined by strong regional executives, often little constrained by their own representative assemblies. Federalism was increasingly undermined by the development of decentralised segmented regionalism, a process that Putin sought to reverse. His attempt to reconstitute the state, however, was torn between compacted and more pluralistic forms of federal development. The struggle against segmented regionalism once again undermined the development of federalism, but now from the other extreme, and in taking the form of traditional centralism threatened the development of Russian democracy as a whole. Federalism, defined as the constitutionally entrenched separation of powers between national government and sub-national units, became trapped between segmented regionalism and the compacted reconstitution of the state. Under Putin the central authorities claimed the entirety of sovereignty, although federalism is all about finding ways in which sovereignty can be shared between the federal government and sub-national units. Theories of federalism insist that this should not undermine the ability of the federal government to provide leadership, while allowing the subjects of the federation to develop political solutions appropriate for their needs. Centralism as such is not inherently anti-federal, but a balance must be retained between the prerogatives of the various levels of governance.

## Segmented regionalism

Regional politics in the 1990s became extremely diverse, both in type of governmental system and in regime characteristics, and some of this continues to this day. Most republics have a president, whereas most *oblasts* have a governor. The legislative bodies in each region (the collective term we shall use to describe Russia's federal units) were also composed in diverse ways and have different powers, stipulated by regional constitutions and charters. As for the political characteristics, some regions were relatively democratic, whereas in others authoritarian regimes emerged. All took advantage of the weakness of the centre under Yeltsin to seize powers and a degree of sovereignty that in certain cases posed a threat to the continued existence of the Russian state. Instead of an effectively integrated federal system, a type of segmented regionalism emerged. Yeltsin managed regional affairs by a mix of concessions and personal links, whereas under Putin regional laws and statutes were made to conform more to the Russian constitution and legislation. The powers of regional actors in national politics were curbed. The debate continues over whether Putin's reforms represented the development of federalism or its repudiation in favour of traditional Russian centralism. Local government, meanwhile, remained a relatively neglected area, over-shadowed by the powerful regional bosses and limited by inadequate funding.

### The organisation of power

Weakening central power under Brezhnev had been accompanied by the commensurate growth of the power of regional elites. Even before the coup the CPSU was losing power, and the more farsighted communist officials were already shifting over to posts in the local state system and later reinvented themselves as democratic leaders. The end of the communist regime allowed these regional elites, in particular in the republics, to consolidate their authority, albeit now in a democratic guise. Traditional elites, in alliance with some of the new social forces, underwent a dual adaptation comparable to that experienced by political parties: they adapted to the new market and political conditions; and at the same time ensured a convergence between elite interests and the uncertainty engendered by the new electoral politics. Neither project met with uniform success, yet regional elites showed remarkable ingenuity in subverting democratic forms and reducing electoral uncertainty.

Yeltsin-style authoritarianism never quite developed into full-blown dictatorship but equally never quite submitted itself to popular accountability and constitutional and legal restraints. The phenomenon was replicated at the regional level. An extremely heterogeneous pattern of regime types emerged, ranging from the relatively democratic in Novgorod, Arkhangel'sk, Samara and St Petersburg, to the outright authoritarian in Primorsk (Maritime) *krai* under Yevgeny Nazdratenko and Kalmykia under president Kirsan Ilyumzhinov. There was also diversity in types of state-political structure. Udmurtia was a parliamentary republic (until a referendum in early 2000), Tatarstan was a fully fledged presidential republic, Dagestan was governed by a form of consociational democracy in which a State Council sought to balance and represent the ethnic diversity of the republic, while Moscow city replicated the 'super-presidentialism' of the central government itself. This diversity in part reflected local traditions, the dynamic of elite relations, and the ethnic and social composition of a particular republic, and in turn affected policy outcomes.[2]

Regional government remains part of the state system, whereas local-self government is separate from the state. In the period of constitutional stalemate of 1991–3 the regions duplicated the national power system, with the heads of administration appointed by Yeltsin and the regional soviets subordinated to parliament. Only after the events of

3–4 October was the old system of soviets abolished, and new regional legislative bodies created. Below we will briefly discuss the main instruments of power in the regions.

### Yeltsin's 'presidential vertical'

From 1991 presidential envoys (*predstaviteli prezidenta*) were appointed to the regions to monitor the work of the newly-appointed governors.[3] In a few cases, as in Nizhny Novgorod, Moscow and St Petersburg, the presidential envoy was also the governor. The envoys were likened to the Bolshevik system of commissars, who monitored the political reliability of former Tsarist officers in the Red Army during the Civil War. The decree of 22 August 1991 stated that envoys were to ensure that local legislation was compatible with national laws, and could recommend the dismissal of local officials who undermined national policy, and they were to report back to the president.[4] Their basic task was to ensure local compliance with central policies. Envoys could impose presidential decrees directly, avoiding the local bureaucracies. Rather contradictorily, they were enjoined not to interfere in local administration or to issue orders covering the given territory.[5] Separate instructions limited the powers of the presidential envoys in the national republics of Russia.[6] The state inspector was to oversee the work of the representatives as well as coordinate the work of local executive bodies. They were ordered to 'facilitate' the observance of federal laws, decrees and presidential instructions.[7] The aim was to establish a supervisory authority that could act as an autonomous presidential vertical chain of authority. They were present in some 80 of the 89 regions by the time that they were subsumed into Putin's reform of the 'presidential vertical' in 2000 (see below).

### Regional executives and their election

The vacuum created by the fall of the CPSU and its once mighty network of *obkom* first secretaries was filled by the appointment of regional heads of administration, who soon became known as governors (*gubernatory*). Governors up to 1995 were directly appointed rather than locally elected, and most were former *oblast* Party leaders, provoking Yeltsin's democratic allies to talk of 'the revolution betrayed'.[8] The appointment of governors was intended to be an interim measure until the regional elections due in December 1991, but these elections were repeatedly postponed.[9] Only Moscow and St Petersburg had been able to elect their mayors, on the same day as Yeltsin was first elected president of Russia (12 June 1991). On 17 September 1995 Yeltsin once again suspended the regional electoral process, decreeing that governors be elected in December 1996 (that is, after the presidential elections due in June 1996) and legislatures only in December 1997. Later twelve exceptions were made to allow regional elections in December 1995, and second mayoral election in Moscow and St Petersburg on 16 June 1996. The mayor of St Petersburg, Putin's mentor Anatoly Sobchak, however, moved the elections forward to 19 May to wrong-foot his opponents, but the strategy backfired and one of his deputy mayors, Vladimir Yakovlev, took over in the city. Putin resigned as vice-mayor, and soon stepped on the political escalator in Moscow that would take him to the presidency. As the wave of gubernatorial elections gathered forced, the number of appointed administrative heads gradually decreased. In the autumn of 1996 alone, 52 executives faced election, joining the handful which had already been elected. Elected governors (unlike presidential appointees) could no longer be dismissed by the federal authorities; once elected, they enjoyed a power base separate from the president. Governors usually had a say in appointing the heads of federal agencies to be found in every federal subject. Under Putin long-formulated plans to deprive them of this right were activated (see below).

Elections affected not only the regions but also national politics. Governors automatically became members of the Federation Council, as did the chairs chosen by the newly elected legislatures. It is for this reason that the centre took great pains to influence regional elections, and pro-Yeltsin sitting governors used all the powers of incumbency to retain their jobs. Nevertheless, a number of pro-Yeltsin incumbents were defeated, but once in office oppositionists were forced to come to terms with Moscow, since most were in a position of financial dependency. The classic case was Sverdlovsk governor Eduard Rossel, who was elected in August 1995 as a defender of the idea of a semi-autonomous 'Urals Republic', yet went on to become a staunch supporter of Yeltsin's re-election as president. The significant turnover of regional executives indicates that the electoral process did have a certain bite. Out of the total of 148 elections of regional executives between 1995 and 2000, 65 (44 per cent) incumbents lost. The trend, however, was for incumbent governors to marshal their resources to greater effect in electoral races, and the chances of incumbents winning improved.[10] The law limiting governors to a maximum of two terms was passed on 19 October 1999, to come into effect on 19 October 2001, giving the governors a two-year grace period.[11] In the event, on 25 January 2001 the Duma adopted a generous amendment to the law. The first term of the governor was to be counted as the one starting after 19 October 1999, allowing 69 regional executives to run for a third term, and in 17 cases a fourth. Mayor Luzhkov in Moscow, who had been re-elected in 1996 and once again in December 1999, could stand for yet one more term, while Shaimiev in Tatarstan could seek two more terms. This represented a major capitulation to the regional lobby, although a further amendment banned governors from forcing pre-term elections by resigning and then standing again.

The vicissitudes of electoralism encouraged some governors to contemplate giving up whatever legitimacy they may have gained through the electoral process and return to the old system of appointment from the centre. In return, governors sought greater powers of appointment over mayors of regional centres and heads of districts, thus re-establishing what was called the 'presidential (or executive) vertical' all the way from the Kremlin to the local level. A notable expression of this trend was the letter of three governors to Putin in February 2000 calling for such a reform, with the necessary constitutional amendments to be enacted through a Constitutional Assembly, spiced with the call for the presidential term of office to be extended to seven years.[12] Elections fostered regional separatism, something they considered could only be overcome by recentralisation.[13] For others, like Konstantin Titov of Samara, such a change represented 'a detailed plan for the liquidation of democratic achievements in Russia', undermining the emergent democratic political links in the federal system and once again reasserting administrative ties.[14] Under Putin this 'detailed plan' was implemented.

*Regional legislatures*

Following the October 1993 events Yeltsin dissolved local soviets and ordered that new elections be held to reconstituted regional assemblies. The decree of 9 October 1993 proposed radical changes to local assemblies.[15] In the *oblasts* they were to be reduced in size from 2–400 to some 15–50 deputies, who were to be full-time legislators, while in the republics legislatures tend to be larger, with some 100–130 deputies. On 22 October 1993 Yeltsin called for local and regional elections to be held between December 1993 and the following spring, but his decree established only the broadest of 'basic guidelines', allowing the regional authorities (in most cases the governor) to establish detailed electoral arrangements. The balance of power between the regional legislative bodies and governors remained unclear. The decree of 22 October 1993 gave the new regional assemblies (usually called assemblies or dumas, with a few at first sticking with the traditional name of 'soviet') the right to pass laws, something denied the old regional soviets. At the same time, however, the decree gave local governors, many of whom were appointed by Yeltsin, a great deal of authority over the new regional parliaments. Local laws were not to contradict federal laws, presidential decrees or governmental instructions, a stipulation that was widely flouted until Putin began his campaign to establish a 'single legal space' throughout Russia.

Decentralisation clearly did not enhance democracy, and indeed allowed regional authoritarian regimes to thrive, and thus Putin's reassertion of central authority was welcomed by many. Legislatures throughout the 1990s were over-shadowed by regional executives and enjoyed little legislative autonomy. Some, however, did move into opposition to the local executive, a trend that increased in the 2000s. Already the regional parliaments in St Petersburg, Krasnoyarsk, Irkutsk, Tver and Sakha asserted themselves against the local governor, a trend that the Kremlin sought to encourage. Under Putin there were vigorous attempts to ensure that those working for the executive branch were not allowed to sit in regional legislatures, on the grounds that the practice violated the division of powers. Mixed systems, where some deputies were elected through PR systems and the rest in single-mandate seats, were already in operation in Kaliningrad, Krasnoyarsk and Sverdlovsk, but were now generalised. Regional legislatures are now required to elect half their members on the basis of party lists, depriving governors of the control that they typically enjoyed over the selection of members in single-mandate constituencies. The new law on parties adopted in 2001 (see Chapter 7) prevented regional parties (usually under the control of the governor) from participating in regional legislative elections while encouraging national parties to play a more active part in regional politics.

### Segmented regionalism in practice

Mikhail Alexseev notes that 'The specter of regional separatism has haunted Russian politics since the collapse of the Soviet Union in 1991'.[16] Segmented regionalism was underpinned by competing sovereignty claims. The crisis of the state and the economy allowed some of the republics to expand their *de facto* sovereignty by adopting laws that created a legal space that became increasingly distinct from that established by Moscow. In the vanguard of this process, dubbed 'disassociation by default', were Tatarstan, Bashkortostan, Khakassia and Yakutia. The unifying role of the military was lost, and indeed, the army became increasingly dependent on the regional authorities. The federal authorities were unable to guarantee basic civil rights in the regions, and even lost control over regional branches of state agencies. The local offices of the procuracy, the MVD and other ministries fell into the hands of governors and local presidents. Only the FSB appeared able to withstand 'capture' by regional authorities. Segmented regionalism was generated by historical, material and social factors and not simply by the strategic choices of post-communist central and regional elites. However, while federal asymmetry reflected the diversity of the country, it did not explain the legal and juridical disparities between the country's regions. In the 1990s federal relations developed largely as a function of the immediate political needs of the presidency. The lack of genuine reciprocal and transparent relations between the centre and the localities was one of the most significant failures of Yeltsin's presidency. As his regime gave way to Putin's, a whole series of issues remained problematical. We examine some of them below.

### Subject-level constitutions and charters

By the late 1990s at least 50 of the 89 local constitutions and charters contradicted the federal one, while a third of local legislation violated in one way or another federal legislation. The constitutions of Bashkortostan, Tatarstan and the regional charter of Tula *oblast* were exemplary cases of subjects claiming rights not allowed for in the national constitution, derogating from the principle of equality between subjects of the federation. Article 1 of Bashkortostan's constitution, adopted in December 1993, stated

> The Republic of Bashkortostan has supreme authority on its territory, independently defining and conducting domestic and foreign policies, adopting the Bashkortostan constitution and its laws, which have supremacy on its entire territory.

Komi's constitution granted special rights to citizens of the republic who were ethnic Komi, stipulating that the head of the republic and deputies to the legislative assembly had to be citizens of Komi, while its citizenship laws themselves contravened the national constitution. One of Putin's immediate concerns was to bring the republican constitutions and regional charters into line with the Russian constitution. Bashkortostan proved the most resistant to bringing its constitution into line with that of Russia, fearing that doing so would reduce Russia once again to a unitary state.

### The fragmentation of legal space

According to the Justice Ministry, an examination in 1997 of 44,000 regional legal acts, including laws, gubernatorial orders and similar documents, found that nearly half did not conform with the constitution or federal legislation.[17] Sergei Stepashin, at the time Minister of Justice, in December 1997 noted that his ministry had analysed 9,000 laws adopted in the regions, and claimed that a third contradicted either the Russian constitution or federal legislation. On the same theme, the Prosecutor General, Yuri Skuratov, noted that nearly 2,000 regional laws had been revoked for contradicting the constitution, but warned that Russia lacked sufficient 'levers' to ensure compliance at the regional level with the rulings of the Constitutional Court.[18] In addition, subjects of the federation signed agreements amongst themselves, bypassing the centre, which further fragmented Russian economic and political space.

### Power-sharing bilateral treaties

In a departure from the principle enunciated in the constitution, the signing of the treaty between Tatarstan and Russia on 15 February 1994 suggested that Russia was indeed a treaty rather than a constitutional federation. The treaty affirmed Tatarstan's right to have a constitution, tax system, foreign policy and foreign trade policy. During Yeltsin's presidency 46 power-sharing treaties were signed between the leaders (not, it should be noted, by the subjects as a whole) of 42 individual regions and the federal authorities, accompanied by 260 specific agreements. The treaties formalised the emergence of asymmetrical federalism where the rights of separate regions were negotiated on an *ad hoc* basis. As far as the central authorities were concerned, the negotiation of bilateral treaties inhibited collective action by regions and macro-regional groupings. The terms of many of these treaties, included in various annexes and annual supplements, were not made public, and their net result was to accentuate the asymmetries in federal relations. The bilateral treaties allowed customised deals between the centre and the subjects, and to that degree Yeltsin had a case in arguing that they 'strengthened Russian statehood',[19] yet they could not but undermine basic principles of constitutional equality and political transparency.

### Supra-regionalism and regional development

The division of Russia into 89 regions was considered by many to be excessive, prompting repeated plans to merge them into larger (supra-regional) units while at the same time prompting the creation of inter-regional associations. In his presidential campaign of June 1991 Yeltsin had argued for the division of the country into some 8–10 large economic regions, and the idea had been incorporated, as we have seen, into the October 1991 draft constitution in the form of *zemli*. It was at this time that Moscow, and Yeltsin personally,[20] supported the creation of regional associations, in part to counterbalance the sovereignty movement of republics and regions.[21] Dating from the Soviet period, Russia had 11 economic regions, each closely tied to the national administrative system,[22] but from 1990 they were effectively superseded by the creation from below of 8 Inter-regional Economic Cooperation Associations.

The most effective associations were those most distant from the centre - the Far East, Siberia and the Urals - where regionalism was infused with the separatist spirit that had already been evident at the time of Russia's earlier disintegration during the Civil War. The Siberian Accord (*Sibirskoe soglashenie*) was established on 2 October 1990 and brought together all 19 administrative regions of East and West Siberia (see Figure 12.1). It was the most effective in integrating regional and nationality politics. The borders of some of the associations changed in order to correspond more closely with the local definition of the region rather than the economic definition taken from the Soviet state planners. In Siberia there was even talk of the need to 'decolonise',[23] accompanied by demands for greater control over Siberia's rich natural resources, the right to conduct foreign trade directly, and an end to what was called colonial exploitation by Moscow.[24]

Rossel, in 1995 the exponent of the creation of a 'Urals Republic', in the run-up to the 2000 presidential election advocated the consolidation of Russia's 89 regions into larger macro-regions; the existing eight regional associations could become the organisational base for the future federation.[25] Putin ultimately adopted a variant of such an approach in the creation of the seven federal super-regions. The associations had been established to coordinate the actions of their members, and thus to increase their leverage, but they failed to act as cohesive bargaining agencies. During Primakov's premiership

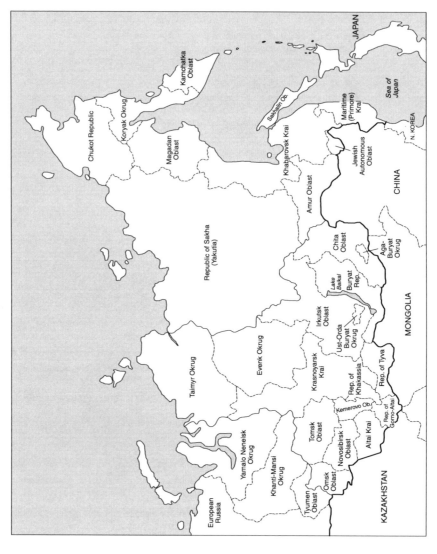

*Figure 12.1* Siberia and the Russian Far East

(September 1998 – May 1999) the heads of the associations joined the presidium of the government, and Stepashin continued the practice, which was of enormous symbolic significance but little practical consequence. With Putin's reorganisation of the country into seven federal districts the existing inter-regional associations, including the most active like Siberian Accord, Great Volga and Great Urals (*Bolshoi Ural*), were marginalised and lost much of their *raison d'etre*. This was exacerbated by the lack of coincidence between the borders of the federal districts and the inter-regional associations. Several regions, for example, that had traditionally been considered part of the Urals (Bashkortostan, Udmurtiya, Perm and Orenburg) ended up in the Volga federal district, while Volgograd became part of the Southern FD.

## Fiscal federalism

The asymmetry in federal relations was reflected most sharply in budgetary matters. Although fiscal matters can never be fully symmetrical, there is a long way for Russia to go before the procedure for distributing transfers among regions becomes both transparent and accurate, with the clear enunciation of the formulae whereby budget revenues are collected and distributed. The struggle over the allocation of tax revenues at the point of collection and from the federal budget became the defining indicator of Russia's failure to establish itself as a genuine federation.

The principles underlying inter-regional transfers have been the subject of considerable debate.[26] The whole notion of 'donor' or 'subsidised' region depends to a large degree on definitions, on what is included and what is left out in making these calculations. By May 1999 only 13 regions were calculated to be donors,[27] but this did not mean that all the others were recipients: about a third received nothing from the centre. In addition, the various bilateral agreements discussed above allowed differences to emerge in the amounts of tax revenue transferred to the centre. Tatarstan, for example, passed on only 50 per cent of its VAT revenues to the federal budget, while other regions transferred 75 per cent of what is the most effectively collected tax in Russia.

The fundamental fact of fiscal dependency for most remained, although the degree to which the centre used the system of transfer payments for overtly political purposes has been questioned.[28] The leading exponent of the 'politicisation' thesis regarding fiscal flows is Daniel Treisman, who has argued that during Yeltsin's rule transfers were used as 'bribes' to encourage subordination among the more fractious regions rather than as 'rewards' for those who demonstrated loyalty.[29] Treisman argues that the central authorities operated a policy of 'fiscal appeasement' to gain the loyalty of regional leaders. Potential separatist ambitions were bought off in a policy that, paradoxically, rewarded not loyalty but rebelliousness. Although not efficient in economic terms, political stability was thereby achieved.[30] Treisman's approach, while raising important issues, suggests a competence in Moscow in managing regional affairs that is probably exaggerated. Budgetary transfers were only one part of the story of fiscal flows between the centre and the regions.

Others have argued that transfers were more depoliticised and reflected relatively objective criteria of need, rather than acting as a mechanism of punishment and rewards.[31] Lavrov and his 'Fiscal Transparency' team in 1999 examined the allocation of federal and public financial resources, analysing not only budgetary distribution (the focus of Triesman's work) but also off-budget outlays (e.g. for social insurance and pensions).

The team quantified federal expenditure in the regions and the aggregate tax burden, and above all the proportion of public spending in the unit that was derived from the interregional allocation of funds. Contrary to the traditional view that only between 10 and 12 regions were 'donors', Lavrov's team suggested that there were more self-sufficient regions than conventionally believed; about 25 of the 89 regions contributed more to the federal budget than they received in state spending. Examination of the scale and nature of extra-budgetary flows began to fill in one of the largest 'blank spots' in Russian politics, with enormous implications for the development of regional policy. The debate shifted from how to squeeze money out of the handful of allegedly super-rich regions to placate the vast majority of the supposedly indigent, but on how to formulate a balanced policy of regional economic development and political sustainability.[32]

It was Moscow's enduring control over the allocation and disbursement of funds to the regions that was often considered the main cement holding the federation together. Regions dependent on the centre for subsidies, whatever their political complexion, were forced to establish good relations with the Kremlin to ensure the continued flow of funds. The adoption of the budget provided an annual spectacle of bargaining and deals. The lack of transparency of financial flows under Yeltsin encouraged corruption and barter. The development of the Federal Treasury system contributed to the gradual improvement of the management of federal finances; by 1998 over 60 per cent of all expenditures were channelled through the Treasury. Monetary flows were centralised and instead of the federal government transferring money to regional administrations, which often took a cut and exercised discretion in allocating funds, the Treasury now makes payments direct to agencies disbursing, for example, payments to veterans. Putin's reforms signalled a shift of economic power, above all between the regions and the centre, and we shall return to this below.

### Economic differentiation and the fragmentation of the national market

Since 1991 the economic independence of Russia's regions has increased considerably: regional and republican governments now account for 50 per cent of tax raising and 70 per cent of government spending. Despite the Soviet regime's commitment to regional equalisation, there were marked disparities in the level of economic development and standards of living, with the national areas tending to be at the bottom of both scales. The 1990s saw increased differentiation between regions in the speed and scale of reform, exacerbating existing differences.[33] Regions able to exploit raw materials (like oil and gas rich Tyumen) or which act as gateways for Russia's booming trade with the world economy (like Moscow) are doing well, while those dominated by agriculture were locked in deep depression throughout the 1990s. The development of a genuine capitalist national market would encourage a type of unity from below, whereas the regions which pursued a slow model of economic reform tended towards economic autarchy and often political separatism.

The growing economic divergence between regions provided an economic basis to federal asymmetries. Some regions have access to world markets through the sale of energy, raw materials or basic finished industrial goods, giving them an independent resource in the federal bargaining game. Central to the development of segmented regionalism is the political economy of the post-Soviet period. Economic 'reform' in the 1990s was not so much a transition from the Soviet forms of economic planning to the market but rather endless exploitation of the opportunities opened up by the transition process itself. Martin Nicholson notes:

> From heady beginnings, when they acquired control over the wealth-creating assets of the former Soviet Union, regional leaders have become locked into an economic system that is neither 'socialist' nor 'capitalist', but a battle of vested interests in which normal economic indicators, including money, play little part.[34]

At the heart of regional politics was the coalition of political and business interests that proved resistant to federal interference. This was particularly strong in the Volga republics, with Tatarstan's government, for example, taking control of the regional economy: 'In early 2000, about 65 per cent of the region's wealth was under the control of the governing political elite, which thus also constituted the region's economic elite.'[35] There was also an ethnic dimension, with ethnic Tatars making up 80 per cent of the governing elite in 2003.[36]

Throughout the 1990s regions tried to impose restrictions on the movement of goods and foodstuffs. The August 1998 financial crisis stimulated further the 'economisation' of regional politics. Regions and republics, forced back on to their own resources, saw themselves increasingly as autonomous economic subjects and less as part of a single national market.[37] Regional responses fell into two categories: measures designed to take control of financial flows, including the refusal to pay taxes to the central budget; and laws that tried to control the market by regulating prices and the movement of goods. Many regions stopped remitting tax revenues to Moscow, and a number introduced price and other controls over their economies. The national market appeared to be breaking down. Many other non-market responses were implemented as regions took advantage of the crisis in the payments system to increase their autonomy. Some of these measures were temporary and primarily defensive in character as the interdependence of central and regional economies became clear. Nevertheless, an underlying trend towards the imposition of regional administrative controls remained. On 24 June 1999, for example, Kirov *oblast* became the third region in Russia, after Khabarovsk krai and Tyumen *oblast*, to impose price controls on selected food products, industrial goods and services like rented housing, heating and public transport.[38]

The creation of a national market became one of the central planks of Putin's regional policy. The general weakening of the power of individual regions during his presidency had important economic consequences, in particular in the struggle against Russia's 'virtual economy' (the network of barter and non-payments) that was very much regionally based. At the same time, the federal government began to revoke many of the tax concessions that it had granted under Yeltsin.

## The regionalisation of foreign policy

Regions began to emerge as international actors. In 1991–5 alone, Russian regions signed over three hundred agreements on trade, economic and humanitarian cooperation with foreign countries, undermining Moscow's monopoly on foreign relations and shifting attention away from high diplomacy to the pressing needs of Russia's regions. Some republics, like Tatarstan, pursued their own foreign policies, while the views of regions on international questions cannot be ignored. In the Far East, for example, the Primorsk *krai* Duma, supported by the assertive Nazdratenko, in March 1996 requested that the Constitutional Court review the May 1991 Soviet–Chinese border agreement that resulted in the transfer to China of about 1,500 hectares of disputed territory. Other Far Eastern regions categorically refused to contemplate the possible return to Japan of the four contested Kurile Islands (called by Japan the Northern Territories, see Chapter 16). While some regions inhibited problem-solving, particularly those in the Far East, others like Karelia and Pskov acted to stabilise their regional foreign relations by establishing warm relations with their neighbours (in the case of Karelia in the framework of the EU's 'Northern Dimension'). Over half of Russia's regions are borderlands, and need the support of the federal authorities in dealing with their neighbours. The exclave of Kaliningrad, indeed, could not be more of a borderland, separated from the rest of Russia by Lithuania and Belarus.

Regions on occasions effectively exercised a veto on foreign policy. This was particularly in evidence during the Kosovo war of 1999, when Shaimiev of Tatarstan threatened to send Tatar volunteers to support the Muslim Kosovars if Russian nationalists sent volunteers to assist the Serbs. The prospect of Russian fighting Russian in the Balkans, in the context where some 20 million Russian citizens had some Islamic heritage, brought the government and public opinion back from the brink of ethnicising Russian foreign policy.[39] The preferences of Russia's regional leaders became part of the complex tapestry of Russia's foreign relations.

To coordinate regional and federal foreign policy, in October 1997 the Duma adopted a law ensuring that regional authorities liaised with the Foreign Ministry over any negotiations with a foreign government.[40] A special department was established by the ministry dealing with inter-regional affairs, with branch offices in regions and republics that were particularly active in foreign affairs. A Council of Regions for International and Foreign Economic Ties was established; a forum used by the foreign minister, Igor Ivanov, on 30 January 2001 to warn governors that the government planned to improve its oversight of their foreign political and economic policies.[41] The principle that only the federal government had the right to sign international treaties (*dogovory*) was jealously guarded, and upheld by numerous judgments of the Constitutional Court.[42]

Segmented regionalism undermined state-building and the emergence of a unified national market, legal space and Russia's coherence as an international actor. The ambiguities in the federal system were exploited by actors in the regions to enhance their privileges and powers, while the central leadership was more concerned with political advantage than the coherence of the state. It was this segmentation of political, economic and juridical development against which Putin set his face.

## Putin's 'new federalism'

The Yeltsinite regional bargain provided the regions and republics a free hand as long as they did not threaten secession.[43] As in the Ottoman and Habsburg empires, local privileges were granted in return for loyalty. The development of civil society was inhibited since these were privileges granted not to individuals but to corporate groups. The free hand extended to the manipulation of elections (until the abrogation of the results of the elections for the head of Karachaevo-Cherkessia in May 1999, no election result had been rescinded), allowed the political elites of titular ethnic groups to consolidate their dominance, and permitted various types of authoritarian regimes elsewhere. Even in Novgorod under Mikhail Prusak, typically contrasted favourably with neighbouring Pskov, Dinello argued that consensus there was 'vested in an authoritarian political model in which rigidities are moderated by a charismatic and enlightened governor'.[44] She argued that it was this model that was being applied to the rest of Russia by Putin. In the context of the segmentation of regional politics, individual rights were easily usurped.[45] Segmented regionalism threatened the rights of minorities and of individuals. It was in response to this that the countervailing republican (in the Jacobin state-building sense) agenda represented by the national state was asserted. Yeltsin's traditional style of managing the regions, where relative independence and selective privileges had been granted in return for support for the Kremlin at the federal level, now gave way to a period of federal activism. In his book *First Person*, Putin had stressed the importance of an independent judiciary together with greater federal control over the regions,[46] and now he implemented this programme.[47]

### Federal districts and presidential envoys (polpredy)

The centrepiece of the new 'state-gathering' policy was Putin's decree of 13 May 2000 dividing Russia into seven large administrative districts.[48] They were to part of what came to be called the 'power vertical'. Putin's hero, Peter the Great, had divided the Russian empire into eight regions and established the institution of governor general in 1708. Putin's innovation did not formally change the existing territorial-administrative divisions, but the establishment of an administrative layer between the federal centre and the regions reduced the significance of the latter. The new federal districts (FDs) are headed by presidential envoys (*polpredy*) appointed by the president, thus undermining the principle of regional democracy, and are directly subordinate to the president. The aim was to restore the 'executive vertical', but in effect a 'triangle' was established with the new FDs added to relations between the regions and Moscow. The *polpredy* organise the work of federal agencies in the regions, with particular attention to the law enforcement bodies, monitor the implementation of federal policy, provide the federal authorities with information on what is going on in the regions, and advise and make recommendations on federal appointments. They also work with the eight old inter-regional associations to devise social and economic policies, although the fact that the borders of the two entities do not coincide makes such a 'coordinating' role extremely difficult. The envoys have far greater powers than the old representatives,[49] 'monitoring the implementation' rather than facilitating the observance of federal laws, decrees and presidential instructions.[50]

The new federal districts largely coincided with those of military districts, suggesting a certain 'militarisation' of federal relations (Figure 12.2). With only two exceptions (Nizhny Novgorod instead of Samara, and Novosibirsk instead of Chita), the new federal centres coincided with the headquarters of the military districts.[51] No less significantly, the borders of the seven federal regions corresponded exactly with the districts of the Internal Troops of the MVD. It was, moreover, noteworthy that no ethnic republic was made the centre of a federal district, although the post in the Volga FD had been offered to president Shaimiev of Tatarstan. The seven presidential representatives appointed on 18 May, moreover, reinforced the military/security tone to the measure. Only two were fully civilian figures: Sergei Kirienko and Leonid Drachevsky.[52] Many of their staff as well came from military or security background. Putin's decree of 30 January 2001 placed

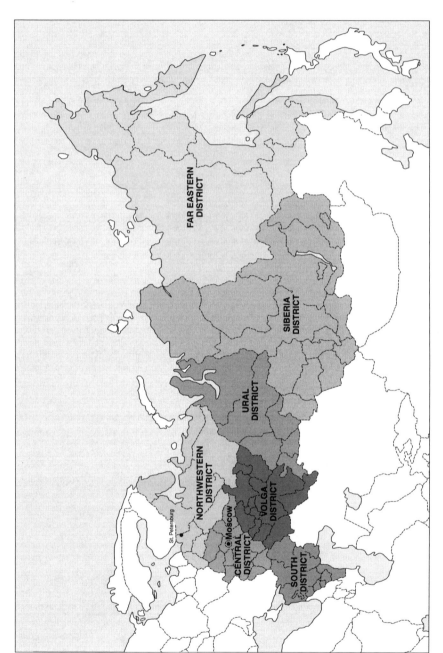

*Figure 12.2* The seven federal districts

the seven presidential representatives directly under chief of staff (at the time Voloshin, later Sergei Sobyanin), ensuring that the GKU retained a role, albeit much reduced. The representatives sought expanded powers to control budgetary flows and even to establish their own governments, but their efforts in this direction were curtailed. The envoys officially were guided in their work by the constitution, federal laws, presidential orders and the instructions of the chief of staff. They became members of the Security Council and met regularly with the president, and to a degree became political actors and economic managers in their own right rather than simply overseers.

The FDs were created by presidential decree rather than through a law or constitutional amendment, and thus the juridical basis for the new system remained precarious. Their creation was para-constitutional in the sense that they represented a change to the constitutional order without changing the letter of the constitution. Any attempt formally to 'constitutionalise' the change would be fraught with difficulties, given the complexity of changing the constitution. Since the change affected only the president's own administration and did not alter the powers of the governors or restructure the Russian Federation itself, the constitutional question was avoided. The *polpredy* report directly to the president, and they in turn, as noted, appoint inspectors to each of the regions within their jurisdiction. While the reform signalled that Yeltsin's tolerance of diversity and asymmetry in federal relations was over, it did not yet indicate that an effective way had been found of ensuring effective national governance and the subordination of the whole country to the constitution.

The seven FDs gradually came to be filled with content and took on a range of political and administrative functions. They are part of a long Russian tradition of appointing governor generals, as outlined in a book edited by one of the new-style governors, Victor Cherkesov.[53] The *polpreds* were deeply involved in regional, above all gubernatorial, elections, and later in the appointment of governors, although their efforts met with variable success. One of their most important administrative tasks was to coordinate the federal agencies and to rebuff regional state capture. Important federal-level agencies like the treasury and the tax ministry all adapted to the new structure of government. Similarly, the Procurator General set up office in each of the new federal districts, as did the justice ministry and the judicial system as a whole. The Soviet practice of rotating the postings of public servants was restored to ensure the homogeneity of public administration, and thus to reinforce the powers of the central state. Innumerable 'colleges', commissions and councils were established to coordinate federal administration and personnel policy at the regional level. In addition a 'security council' was set up in most of the FDs, to coordinate the work of security and police agencies. Smaller versions of the national State Council brought together the governors of the regions comprising the FDs.

The federal districts changed the terms of regional bargaining with the centre – by interposing a new layer in between the centre and the regions separatist sentiments were blunted and regional leaders constrained by the agents of the 'power vertical'. Conflicts between the federal centre and the regions were now to a degree displaced to the level of relations between the federal districts and individual regions. Putin's reforms to the federal system were based on a complex system of supports and alliances and it would be a great simplification to suggest that they have 'failed'. Officially, the *polpredy* were part of the federal level of government and were not intended to govern but to supervise (*kontrol'*) the work of federal bodies in the regions. In practice the FDs changed the dynamics of regional politics, effectively curbing the political pretensions of the governors to be national players and depriving them of control over federal administrative agencies in the regions. In many ways the envoys were remarkably effective, forcing legal changes, providing a forum for macro-regional coordination, resolving a number of cardinal administrative and personnel issues and emerging as active political players. They also provided the president with a chain of support, especially in the management of the security and legal systems at the regional level.

### The Federation Council

Soon after the announcement of the creation of the federal districts, in a televised address on 17 May Putin announced that he would submit a package of laws to the State Duma designed 'to strengthen and cement Russian statehood'.[54] 'The common task of all these acts', according to Putin, was 'to make both the executive branch and the legislative branch truly working, and to fill the constitutional principles of the separation of powers and the unity of the executive vertical with absolutely real content'.[55] The origins of Putin's federal reforms lay in the various debates since the mid-1990s, but he now gave these ideas flesh through a number of initiatives at this time, notably changes in the way that the upper house of Russia's bicameral parliament, the Federation Council (FC), is formed (see Chapter 9).

The first convocation of the Federation Council in 1993 had been formed by direct election in the regions, but a law adopted in 1994 made the heads of the regional executive and legislative branches directly members of the upper house. Now Putin returned to a variant of the 1993–5 system, to allow the senior figures to 'concentrate on the specific problems facing their territories'.[56] The Federation Council is now composed of two permanent representatives from each region, one nominated by each region's executive branch and one by the legislature. The new 'senators' are delegates of the regional authorities rather than popular representatives. The reform of the Federation Council demonstrated Putin's peculiar mix of strength and weakness. He achieved the reform that he desired, above all achieving a full-time upper legislative chamber and the more realistic separation of powers (by removing the heads of the regional executive branch from the national legislature), but in doing so he considerably weakened the authority of the upper house, a problem compounded by the establishment of the State Council. As we have seen, the present system of forming the FC is undoubtedly unsatisfactory, and even more so with the introduction of appointed governors. Mironov and others have frequently raised the possibility of restoring direct elections. Another issue that needs to be resolved is the role of parties in the assembly. Despite grasping the problem of the FC at the beginning of his presidency, fundamental issues had not been resolved by the time Putin left office.

### Dismissal and dissolution

A bill in 2000 provided a mechanism whereby the heads of regions could be removed and regional legislatures dissolved if they adopted laws that contradicted federal legislation. Although in principle the courts already enjoyed the power to dismiss governors, two court decisions were required stating that the governor had violated federal law. The attempt to strengthen this right proved extremely difficult, especially since it had to be approved by the Federation Council, the very body whose membership was under threat.

The bill sought to give the president the right to dismiss governors who violated federal laws on more than one occasion. In introducing the bill, the presidential representative in the Duma, Alexander Kotenkov, averred that 'at least 16 governors' faced the prospect of criminal prosecution.[57] In the event, the Duma on 19 July 2000 adopted the legislation allowing the president to dismiss regional leaders and to disband local parliaments. On 4 April 2002 the Constitutional Court confirmed the president's right to fire governors and the State Duma's power to disband regional legislatures. The sacking power became moot once the system of appointing governors was introduced in 2004 (see below).

### The end of the sovereignty of sub-national republics

In a decision adopted on 7 June 2000 the Constitutional Court declared unconstitutional the sovereignty declarations adopted by most of Russia's republics.[58] The ruling dealt specifically with the case of Gorno-Altai, but clearly had wider implications. In its judgment, the Court took a rather narrow state-centred view of sovereignty, arguing that 'the constitution of the Russian federation does not allow any kind of state sovereignty beyond the sovereignty of the Russian Federation', and went on to assert that 'the subjects of the Russian federation do not have sovereignty, which from the start belongs to the Russian Federation in general'.[59] The ruling against any devolution of sovereignty to the republics was justified on the grounds of equity: it would, they insisted, be unfair for such an imbalance to persist *vis-à-vis* the other subjects of the federation (reflecting a classic postulate of the French republican tradition). In a further ruling the Constitutional Court supported the Putinite principle that only the federal government had the right to establish courts and determine criminal procedures, thus denying the regions the right to set up their own courts or to establish rules for their operation. The stick, bent so strongly towards the republics in the period of the 'parade of sovereignties' in 1990–1, was now pushed back the other way.

### Legal conformity

Under the premiership of Stepashin (May-August 1999) the long-awaited law, devised earlier in part by Putin, 'On the Principles of Dividing Power Between the Russian Federation Government and the Regions' (henceforth regional law) was finally adopted.[60] It stipulated that all new federal and regional laws had to be adopted in conformity with this law, and that all previously adopted legislation and treaties had to be brought into line within set periods. The law reinforced attempts to establish a unified national system of the administration of justice. The Constitutional Court played a key role in interpreting the writ of the constitution in disputes between regional and federal prerogatives. The national judicial system acted as a barrier, however weak in some places, to the emergence of regional despotisms. It was this obstacle to the fragmentation of law that Putin sought to strengthen. By mid-2001, according to justice minister Yuri Chaika, 94 per cent of regional laws had been brought into conformity with federal legislation.[61] A meeting of the Security Council in June 2001 chaired by its new secretary, Vladimir Rushailo, however, noted that legislation in Tatarstan, North Ossetia, Kabardino-Balkaria, Komi and Pskov still diverged significantly from federal norms, while 57 articles of the constitution of Sakha (Yakutia), which specifies Russian, Yakut and English as state languages, contradicted the national constitution.[62]

Decrees issued on 11 May 2000 demanded that Bashkortostan, Ingushetia and Amur bring their laws in line with the Russian constitution and national legislation.[63] On 16 May another decree was issued with respect to Smolensk *oblast*.[64] Bashkortostan was the most egregious case of divergence from federal norms, and the decree now ordered the republic to amend its constitution and regional laws, above all provisions concerning citizenship and the powers of the republican president, including the stipulation that the republican president must speak Bashkir (effectively excluding the candidacy of a representative of the large Tatar and Russian communities in the republic). The republican constitution had authorised regional participation in international alliances and organisations, as well as permitting agreements with foreign partners and the exchange of diplomatic representatives. The republic's constitution contained articles that overstepped 'the limits of joint jurisdiction' and ran 'counter to the foundations of federal arrangements, including principles of the spread of the Russian Federation's state sovereignty to its entire territory'.[65] Bashkortostan now turned out to be the most resistant to bringing its constitution into line with that of Russia, fearing that doing so would reduce Russia once again to a unitary state. In neighbouring Tatarstan 357 amendments were made to the republic's constitution, following intense bilateral negotiations between Putin and Shaimiev, and the revised version was adopted as a new constitution in April 2002. Shaimiev was guaranteed considerable autonomy as long as he supported United Russia and delivered the appropriate election results.[66]

A federal law in 2003 obliged all of Russia's regions to ensure that all local laws that contradicted federal legislation had to be removed by mid-2005. The reassertion of federal law sought to ensure that Russia became a single legal space, with the principles of legality and individual rights enshrined in the constitution enforced throughout the country. This legal offensive against segmented regionalism sought to bring regional charters, republican constitutions and all other normative acts into conformity with the constitution and federal law. However, there was widespread resistance to the harmonisation campaign, including the usual foot-dragging as well as more overt opposition.[67] Speaking at a meeting of the Council of Legislators (representing regional assemblies) on 16 March 2006, Putin argued that regional legislation could help improve the quality of national laws, but he emphasised that 'strengthening the unity of legal space is our most important national priority'. He noted that only ten regions had brought their laws fully into conformity with federal norms, and that in many of the regions that had failed to do so 'these infringements lead to restrictions on the rights and freedoms of citizens. This is absolutely inadmissible'.[68]

### *Independence of the judiciary*

In early 2000 the Chair of the Supreme Court, Vyacheslav Lebedev, announced that henceforth all courts - from the top down to the regional and lower courts - were to be financed solely from the federal budget. The aim was to eliminate the courts' financial dependence on regional governments, something that obviously compromised their independence. At the same time, the salaries of judges were to be raised to improve their level of 'professionalism' and 'honesty'.[69] The federal authorities at this time won a court victory that allowed courts of general jurisdiction (with the Supreme Court at the apex of this system) to rule on the constitutionality or illegality of regional constitutions and laws.

### The end of bilateral treaties

The new federalism was characterised by the end of the bilateral treaty process. The federal authorities insisted that they were not international treaties, but their precise juridical status was not specified. Did these various treaties take priority over federal laws, supplement them, or trump them? The regional law of June 1999 formalised the procedures for the adoption of power-sharing treaties, stressing above all that every-thing was to be done openly, thus forbidding secret clauses and sub-treaties. This law, together with one adopted in October 1999, substantially changed the legal environment and rendered power-sharing treaties redundant as a way of managing federal relations. Although treaties with Tatarstan and other regions later were renewed, bilateral treaties became an outmoded way of managing federal relations and no more were signed after 1998. On 26 June 2001 Putin established a commission to examine federal relations as a whole, and the role of the treaties in particular, under the leadership of his close colleague, Dmitry Kozak. The latter made no secret of his view that most of the treaties contradicted federal law and would have to be changed to establish a 'single legal space' in Russia. In anticipation of negative findings, a number of regions repudiated their treaties (for example, Perm, Ulyanovsk, Nizhny Novgorod and Marii El in July 2001), to ensure, in their words, 'the superiority of the constitution and federal law'.[70] Between 21 December 2001 and 20 May 2003, 33 treaties were renounced. Tatarstan, Bashkortostan, Sakha were extremely reluctant to follow suit, since their treaties gave them considerable priv-ileges in keeping taxes and over the natural resources in their regions, while Sverdlovsk governor Rossel noisily defended his treaty.

The revocation of the bilateral treaties was part of the process of ensuring more rational and uniform regional administration. In his state-of-the-nation speech on 18 April 2002 Putin noted that of the 42 regions that had such agreements, 28 had already been revoked.[71] A treaty with Yakutia was signed on 26 September 2002 modifying the 1995 treaty. That left only 9 treaties with 12 of the staunchest regions, including some key republics. A law of 7 July 2003 ordered that unless all existing treaties were renewed in conformity with existing legislation within two years, they would be rendered invalid. Since none were able to do so, despite attempts by Yakutia, they all lapsed on 8 July 2005.

Although the time of a 'treaty federation' had gone, there were two exceptions. The first was the renewed treaty with Tatarstan, ratified against considerable opposition by the Duma on 9 February 2007 but vetoed by the Federation Council on 25 February 2007. Dominated by Mironov's Just Russia, the upper house argued that numerous clauses in the new treaty contradicted the constitution and even threatened the existence of the federation. In the event, on 11 July 2007 the Federation Council overwhelmingly endorsed a new power-sharing agreement and on 26 July Putin signed the document. It gave the Tatarstani authorities extended rights in economic, cultural and environ-mental issues, as well as joint management of its energy resources by federal and republican authorities. The republic was allowed to insert a Tatar-language page into passports, but ultimately the treaty did not restore most of the economic privileges of the earlier era. Long-drawn out discussions with Chechnya tried to formalise its excep-tional status in the Russian Federation with a bilateral treaty. Putin had promised the republic extensive autonomy before the referendum adopting the constitution in 2003, and discussions over a new treaty began in 2004. Delays were provoked by Moscow's fears of granting excessive powers and privileges to the Chechenised leadership in the republic, above all in the economic and taxation spheres. As prime minister in 2005–6 Ramzan Kadyrov had been particularly keen to assert the republic's control over the oil industry. The *siloviki* in the Kremlin and their allies did not trust Kadyrov, and opposition to a power-sharing treaty with the republic was led by Igor Sechin in the PA, Mironov in the FC, and Viktor Ilyukhin, head of the Duma's security committee. One of Kadyrov's first acts once the Chechen parliament had formally approved his nomination as president on 2 March 2007 was to renounce the idea of a special treaty.

### *Fiscal federalism*

The attempt to recreate a national market became one of the central planks of Putin's new federalism. The general weakening of the power of individual regions during his presidency had important economic consequences, in particular aiding the struggle against the 'virtual economy' (the network of barter and non-payments) that was very much regionally based. At the same time, the federal government began to revoke many of the tax concessions that it had granted under Yeltsin. On 26 July 2000 the second part of the new Tax Code was overwhelmingly approved by the Federation Council (128 to 13), even though it caused an immediate fall in regional tax revenue. The main features of the tax package were a flat rate 13 per cent income tax, a minimum 5 per cent unified social tax, the raising of some excise taxes, and the amending of the law on value added tax. Instead of the regions keeping 15 per cent of VAT, it was now to be transferred in its entirety to the federal centre. The 4 per cent turnover tax, raised mostly in the regions, was abolished. All regions apart from Moscow benefited from another change operating from 2002: firms now pay part of their taxes in the region where they actually work rather than where they are registered. The establishment of a social programme co-financing fund means that every rouble spent by regions on social issues is matched by one from the federal authorities, irrespective of the level of income in the region. The practice of 'unfunded mandates', costs that are imposed on regional administrations without sufficient resources to cover them, were to be phased out.

The new Tax Code provided for much greater redistribution of revenues between the regions than had hitherto existed. Not surprisingly, the poorer regions (the great majority) supported the bill, while the richer minority, led by Moscow mayor Luzhkov, argued against it. The federal government would receive 70 per cent of tax revenue, leaving 30 per cent to the regions instead of the 50 per cent they received earlier. The government now pursued an active regional policy: concentrating more resources and redistributing them as part of a conscious strategy of levelling some of the disparities between regions. The lion's share of tax and duties revenue went to the centre, including VAT receipts, income taxes, excise and customs duties, and natural resource taxes. All that was left for the regions was transport tariffs, a portion of profit taxes, property and gaming taxes. In 1999 federal transfers to regions represented 9 per cent of total federal spending, in 2001 18 per cent, but by 2007 it represented about a third of all spending.[72] The formula for this redistribution was far from clear, with half going out according to known criteria to support various programmes, whereas the other half was discretionary, and thus to a degree arbitrary. Tatarstan, Bashkortostan and the North Caucasus did well out of this system, together with St Petersburg and some Siberian regions. The whole system of inter-budgetary transfers, designed to avoid misappropriation, encouraged game playing, with regions downplaying their own performance to gain extra funds.

The economic gap between regions was increasing despite growing transfers. Very few of Russia's regions have achieved economic self-sufficiency, with a dozen of the most successful regions accounting for over 50 per cent of Russia's GDP. By 2006, 70 out of Russia's 88 regions were receiving subsidies from the centre, with most regional budgets weighed down by deficits. In a report to the State Council Krasnoyarsk governor Alexander Khloponin reported that 'the gap between regions in terms of per capita GDP, by which the figure for the richest regions was 64 times that for the poorest in 2000, approached a factor of 300 in 2005'. The intractable problems in the North Caucasus (Figure 12.3), with a spreading insurgency in the region combined with grave social tensions and ethnic conflicts, provoked Kozak, the presidential envoy to the Southern federal district, to suggest that the degree of federal devolution should be in inverse proportion to the level of subsidy that they received from the centre: 'The more money the centre provides, the less regional power.'[73] From January 2007 an external administrator in Moscow assumed some responsibility for the management of subsidised regions. This is 'federalism as you pay', and represents central intervention on a drastic scale, effectively undermining the federal division of powers. In 2007 a more coherent regional policy was implemented, designed to encourage successful regions while preventing the poor ones from sinking entirely, while those in the middle would get targeted developmental support. Regional performance is tracked by Rosstat, the national statistics agency.

### Institutional uniformity

We have noted above the diversity in institutional forms that had developed in the 1990s. Russia had a rich variety of regional legislatures: some were bicameral while others were unicameral, some deputies were professional and paid, while others were volunteers, and electoral systems also vary. This was now reversed and a single model for all regions imposed. This meant, for example, that the bicameral assemblies in Adygeya, Dagestan and Kabardino-Balkaria were abolished, while in Dagestan consociational elements were dropped in favour of the standard model of an appointed governor nominated by Moscow. However, the single design was not imposed everywhere, with Chechnya being granted the exceptional right to create a bicameral assembly.

### Regional governors: from election to appointment

In his 13 September 2004 speech Putin argued that the most important factor in strengthening the state was 'a unified system of executive power in the country', a unity that in his view came from Article 77 of the 1993 constitution. The war on terrorism, he insisted, was a national task, and hence the 'unity of actions of the entire executive power vertical' had to be unconditionally assured. He proposed that the regional executives were to be elected by the legislative assemblies of the territories 'at the representation of the head of state'. This replicates the manner in which the Russian government is formed, but represented a reversal of Putin's earlier view. In his question and answer session with the Russian people on 19 December 2002 Putin stated that 'I have no desire to place appointed officials in charge of regions', arguing that appointments were a phase in Russian history

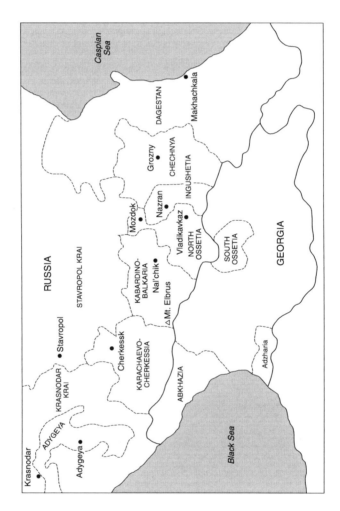

*Figure 12.3* North Caucasus

that the country had passed, and added that 'The leaders of regions are elected by the people in direct secret elections. That is what the constitution prescribes, and that is how it should stay.'[74] It was on this basis that opposition leaders like Vladimir Ryzhkov insisted that the proposal was unconstitutional, citing the 18 January 1996 Constitutional Court ruling on the Altai case stating that representatives of one branch of government (in this case the legislature) cannot be in charge of forming another (appointing the governor), arguing that this would infringe the principle of the separation of powers. In strictly constitutional terms, the direct appointment without the involvement of regional legislatures would be more in accord with the Altai ruling; but that would remove entirely local consultation and *ex ante* accountability.

The federal law of 11 December 2004 established the system whereby the president nominates a candidate for the post of governor no later than 90 days before the end of the incumbent governor's term, and there are opportunities for consultation between the president and the legislature before a candidate is nominated. Regional legislatures have two opportunities either to reject or approve a candidate, who must be over 30 years of age and is appointed for a 5-year term. Over half of the relevant assembly must support the nominee for the candidate to become governor. If a regional legislature twice fails to approve the presidential nominee, at the third attempt the president is entitled to appoint an acting regional head for up to 6 months and to dissolve the legislature by decree, with new elections to be held within 120 days of the decree entering into force. Dissolution, however, may only take place after a month-long cooling-off period for discussions between the president and legislators. Appointed governors are permitted to serve more than two consecutive terms, thus the interminable debates on two-term limits at a stroke were rendered anachronistic.[75] A presidential decree of 27 December 2004 provided more detail about appointment procedure, specifying that the *polpred* in federal districts would prepare a short list to be examined by the Presidential Administration, which would select two candidates for the president to consider. Consultations would then take place (it was not clear with whom) and materials would be examined (it was not clear which), and the candidates had to issue statements agreeing to be considered for the post.[76] Governors appealing directly to the president were initially relieved of the latter stipulation, although by a decree of 29 June 2005 this was changed.[77] In the system's first year no regional assembly rejected a nomination, and very few were rejected thereafter.

The appointment of governors undoubtedly reduced the autonomy of the regions, and raised the question whether the new system is compatible with federalism. On 21 December 2005 the Constitutional Court ruled that the new procedures were not a violation of 'the principle of the division of powers and federalism … *in the current historical circumstances*' (italics added).[78] This decision has been seen to indicate the spinelessness of the Constitutional Court *vis-à-vis* the authorities, and thus its inability to act as a bulwark against authoritarianism.[79] Popular opinion, moreover, favoured the continued elections of governors.[80] In his state of the nation address of 25 April 2005 the president suggested that governors could be nominated from among regional leaders or representatives of parties winning provincial elections, an idea he touched on several times later. Based on this idea, a law adopted by the Duma on 31 December 2005 allowed the majority party in regional legislatures to nominate a candidate, something that will undoubtedly enhance the status of these assemblies.[81] In his televised press conference on 31 January 2006 Putin singled out the adoption of the law allowing victorious parties at the regional level to participate directly in the formation of the executive authorities as one of the major achievements of 2005, insisting that the new system was 'far from the appointment of executive heads from Moscow.' The new system, in his view, would allow the appointment of governors who were 'sensitive to regional problems, but who were also vitally aligned with national interests.'[82]

Appointed governors became little more than ordinary bureaucrats dependent not on the wishes of the electorate but on the federal executive.[83] In some cases individuals were appointed who would never have won an election, but who were individuals of ability and integrity. This was the case with the appointment of Mukhu Aliev in Dagestan in February 2006. However, the weakening of the democratic basis for regional executives threatened the federal separation of powers and the status of the post. Ever-fewer governors figured on the list of most influential Russian politicians. The abolition of term limits allowed some long-standing governors further to extend their incumbency, as with Shaimiev's reappointment in March 2005. An egregious case was that of Murtaza Rakhimov of Bashkortostan, whose 16 years in power was extended by another 5-year term in October 2006. With parliamentary and presidential elections coming up, Putin clearly wanted a trusted figure in charge of this important republic. Despite Putin's attempt to institutionalise and formalise federal relations, they remained as personality-driven as before.

### Regional party and election systems

The weakness of party representation at the regional level under Yeltsin was striking. In 1998 only 635 (18 per cent) of the 3,481 elected deputies had been nominated by political parties, overwhelmingly from the CPRF.[84] Despite Putin's attempt to extend the reach of the national party system to shape regional politics, the trend in the early part of his leadership was if anything in the opposite direction. Fewer governors were elected who explicitly declared their party affiliation, and ever more declared independents were elected to regional legislatures.[85] The influx of the representatives of big business into regional legislatures sharpened the struggle for the redistribution of resources.[86] The emergence of a dynamic presidency put all parties in the shade, and at the regional level party groups, however active, found it hard to have any effect on governor-business networks.[87] Regional assemblies had traditionally been dominated by executives and powerful business or other local elites, and Putin now sought to break up these local blocs that had together too often in his view conspired to undermine the writ of the constitution.

The 2001 law on parties abolished the right of regional parties to be registered as political parties, and thus to contest regional or national elections. We noted above the end of the legal sovereignty of federal regions, however defined, and this measure now undermined the political sovereignty of regions. Regional elites could conduct politics only through participation in national parties, and until the creation of Just Russia this was primarily through the 'party of power,' United Russia. This of course limited their freedom of manoeuvre, which was undoubtedly part of the intention. Putin sought to achieve the homogenisation of political space, which in positive terms can be seen as the creation of a single political community. Russian federalism, however, was stripped off yet another element of the diversity that is characteristic of federalism as a principle.

Amendments to the law on elections of July 2002 stipulated that regional executives had to be elected in at least two rounds, while from July 2003 elections to regional legislatures follow the national pattern: half of their members are elected from party lists proposed by national parties; and the other half are elected from single-mandate districts. The introduction of party-list elections allowed central politicians to exert more influence over regional elections, an area where governors had hitherto predominated. At the time the legislation was passed few of the fifty-odd parties registered at the national level had vibrant regional networks, and even the active ones were usually dominated by the local governor. This now began to change as parties merged and consolidated their resources, but this could not prevent the predominance of United Russia in regional elections until challenged by Just Russia. The 7 per cent national representation threshold was introduced into a large number of regional electoral systems, further consolidating the predominance of a handful of national parties. The changes were accompanied by the abolition in some places of minimum turnout requirements. Independent regional politicians had earlier been able to fight single-mandate seats in Duma elections, but they now had to fight their way on to national party lists, where they had to negotiate various gatekeepers. The ability of independents, well-known in their regions, to enter the national legislature, is reduced. At the same time, regional elections are now held across the country twice a year (March and October), which diluted specifically regional issues.

### Merging of regions

In December 2001 a federal constitutional law was adopted that permitted regions to merge, laying out detailed procedures that were amended in November 2005 to allow governors, in consultation with the president, to initiate referendums. Under Putin regional unification was of two sorts. The first involved the merger of two ordinary regions, with the idea, for example, of unifying Pskov and Novgorod, and St Petersburg with its surrounding Leningrad region. None of these discussions came to anything. The second form was the attempt to end the *matreshka* doll element of Russian regionalism by merging national autonomies in a compound region with the nominal outer layer of the doll. A number of compound regions were transformed:

- The process was led by the merger of Perm region and the Komi-Permyak autonomous okrug to create Perm krai on 1 December 2005.
- Referendums approving merger also took place in 2005 in the Evenk and Taimyr autonomous okrugs in Krasnoyarsk region to create a unified Krasnoyarsk krai on 1 January 2007.
- The Koryak autonomous okrug and Kamchatka *oblast* merged to create Kamchatka krai on 1 January 2007.
- The referendum on 16 April 2006 in the Ust-Orda Buryat AO and Irkutsk region approved merger, although it had been quite a struggle for Putin to push this merger through. The Buryats in their small AO feared the loss of an independent identity, but in the event they became part of the Greater Irkutsk Region that came into being on 1 January 2008.
- Plans continue to merge Chita region with the Aginsk Buryat autonomous okrug to create the Trans-Baikal krai.
- In Arkhangel region merger attempts were opposed by the oil-rich Nenets AO, fearing the loss of economic privileges if it merged with the poorer region.

- Plans to reconstitute the old Chechen-Ingush republic were opposed by the Ingush.
- The Republic of Adygeya was equivocal about merging with Krasnodar krai, with the local elites fearing the loss of their status. With just 24 per cent of the population, the ethnic Adygs held the majority of public offices, a situation that began to provoke a long-delayed reaction from Russians. Merger would shift powers of patronage out of Adygeya to the larger unit.[88]
- The referendum in October 2006 on the merger of the Altai krai with the Altai Republic was accompanied by major protest action by Altais, who feared losing their identity, and merger plans were shelved. This demonstrates the limits to Putin's alleged 'authoritarianism', and indeed highlights his gradualist approach to such issues.[89]

By January 2007, 6 regions had merged, reducing the total number of subjects of federation to 86. The formal explanation for the mergers was to simplify administrative and economic management. However, there were fears that the underlying motive was to dissolve the ethnic republics, above all on the Volga and in the North Caucasus. The mergers were reminiscent of the ideas advanced by Vladimir Zhirinovsky for a return to a unitary state of the type that existed in imperial Russia. As he notes, Russia was divided into 8 provinces under Peter the Great, into 40 under Catherine the Great; and had 56 *guberniya* just prior to the 1917 revolution.[90] Although Putin's style is incremental and para-constitutional, at a certain point such dramatic changes to Russia's territorial organisation will require a wholesale constitutional revision.

### Local self-government and the delineation of powers and functions

In a follow-up measure to earlier reforms of federal relations, on 26 June 2001 Putin established a commission to examine federal relations as a whole, and the role of the treaties in particular, under the leadership of his close colleague and deputy head of the presidential administration, Kozak. The unsatisfactory condition of local government was a strong reason for its creation. The commission sought to develop the legislative basis for the division of power between the federal, regional and local levels of government. The constitution's assignment of a number of responsibilities to joint jurisdiction had proved to be a recipe for confusion, and now the idea was to draw up a list of functions and designate them to specific levels. The aim was to establish a common set of rules for all regions and to provide them with equal rights. The 22-member commission included a number of governors, and sought to proceed, in a manner typical of Putin, by consensus with regional leaders. The commission sought to delineate what bodies were responsible for what at each of the three levels (national, regional, municipal) of governance. The issue of resources and division of taxes was central to this. The issue of the accountability of public bodies was also at the centre of the commission's work, with an attempt to clarify lines of financial and public accountability.

The fourth sphere focused on the work of local self-government. Russia in 2002 had 153,000 local self-government units (including sub-units within regions and municipalities), with 90,000 comprising fewer than 100 people and 24,000 with fewer than 1,000. The commission recommended that smaller units should be merged to create some 30,000 bodies, with none with fewer than one thousand people. By contrast, many large towns lacked municipal self-government bodies. A new standardised system able to fulfil its responsibilities and with adequate resources was to be introduced. Each unit of local government would be divided into an executive (*uprava*) and legislative (*munitsipalitet*) branch, with most funding going to the former (typically 90:10). Unfunded mandates would no longer be allowed, raising fears that the reform would lead to sharp cuts in social programmes.[91] The two-year legislative process came to an end with the adoption of a new law (law 133) on local self-government on 6 October 2003, with implementation to begin on 1 January 2006, with some provisions delayed until 2008.[92] There was now to be a uniform system, with 'settlements' (*poselniya*) at the lowest level, for the first time granting villages certain powers of self rule. They in turn are grouped into some 24,000 'municipal formations', doubling the number of old municipalities, while large cities retained their existing powers to govern themselves. A key point of contention was the allocation of enterprises, the main source of revenues, between the regions and municipalities. By mid-2006 about half of Russia's regions had implemented the provisions of the new system. In the event, the complexity of the new system, including the demarcation of the borders of the new local government districts, led to the postponement of the wholesale implementation of the new law until 2008–9.

## Segmented regionalism and asymmetrical federalism

While no federation can be completely symmetrical (for example, in terms of population and area), very few give political form to asymmetries. In Russia there is a formal power asymmetry enshrined in the differing prerogatives granted republics and regions and further codified in power-sharing agreements.[93] In the 1990s the old hyper-centralised Soviet state gave way to the fragmentation of political authority and contesting definitions of sovereignty. A complex and unstable balance was drawn between the claimed prerogatives of the centre and the normative and *de facto* powers of the regions. The tension between central and regional claims concerned not only practical issues of governance and finances, but also focused on fundamental competing sovereignty claims. The evolving practice of 'asymmetrical federalism' affected the very definition of the state. A distinctive type of 'segmented regionalism' emerged, whereby Russia in effect had 90 governments. The federal authorities at the centre entered into asymmetrical bargaining relations with the other 89 'subjects of the federation', one of which (Chechnya) claimed outright independence. Some went so far to argue that under Yeltsin Russia had turned into a federation of mini-dictatorships in which freedom and human rights were abused by regional leaders, who in some cases were little more than representatives of organised crime.

The federal separation of authority was undermined by spontaneous processes of segmented regionalism.[94] The development of asymmetrical federalism may well have provided a framework for the flexible negotiation of individual tailor-made solutions to Russia's diverse ethnic and political composition,[95] but it failed to do this within the framework of universal norms of citizenship or republican notions of equality. Instead, segmented regionalism fragmented the country legally, economically and, implicitly, in terms of sovereignty. By the end of Yeltsin's term in office Russia was beginning to become not only a multinational state, but also a multi-state state, with numerous proto-state formations making sovereignty claims *vis-à-vis* Moscow.[96] The country was increasingly divided into segments, not only spatially but also in terms of the fragmentation of political authority. Overlapping jurisdictions and fragmented administrative and legal practices led some to suggest that Russian politics had become 'medievalised'. The emergence of a national party system was stunted by the proto-state claims made by regional executives, their ability to control patronage resources and to influence electoral outcomes. The Federation Council, moreover, gave regional elites a powerful hold on the national decision-making process and, while providing a focus for a common political discourse, ensured a regional veto on national issues.

Attempts in the 1990s to build federalism from the top down were countered by the regions which managed, *de facto* if not yet *de jure*, to ensure a significant bottom up devolution of power.[97] All federations are designed to constrain central political power, but not all do so with equal effect. In Russia, whatever the nature of the local regimes themselves, regions acted as a check on the central authorities; a type of spatial separation of powers emerged that to a degree compensated for the inadequacy of the vertical separation of power in the new constitutional order. In this context, however democratic the reconstitution of the Russian state may be, the weakening, if not the removal, of this 'fourth pivot' in Russian government (in addition to the classical trinity of the executive, legislative and judiciary), weakened the democratic pluralism of the Russian constitutional order. Segmented regionalism and asymmetrical federalism provided a more effective check on executive authority than the relatively weak legislature and judiciary, but this had little in common with the federal separation of powers.

This was the situation facing the incoming president, Putin, on coming to office in 2000. His response was to appeal to the principle of 'the dictatorship of law', and in particular the unimpeded flow of constitutional and juridical authority throughout the territory of the Russian Federation. Sub-national sovereignty claims were thereby rendered illegitimate, even though federalism as a principle is all about shared sovereignty. Fundamental issues were occluded by Putin's attempts to reconstitute the state, above all the question of the form of state sovereignty. Was Russia to become a genuine federation, in which law would be defined in accordance with the normative spatial division of sovereignty; or would it take the form of *de facto* regionalism, where an effectively unitary state grants rights to devolved units, in which case a very different definition of sovereignty would operate?

Under Yeltsin regional regimes came to exert considerable autonomous authority over their 'fiefdoms'. Putin's reassertion of central authority in defence of the writ of the constitution represented the defence of a particular vision of democracy. His aim was to place the constitution at the centre of the political process in regional relations. For some this was no more than a new form of Russia's traditional centralism; others argued that it offered an opportunity to move away from asymmetrical federalism towards a more balanced form. Asymmetrical federalism not only granted differential rights to regional leaderships, but effectively established different gradations of democratic citizenship to those living in different parts of the country. The attempt to achieve a universal and homogeneous type of citizenship lay at the heart of Putin's attempt to reconstitute the state.

Putin's new federalism thus entailed a range on institutional innovations, but above all a new philosophy of central-regional relations. The old segmented regionalism was undermined, although far from overcome, but the new federalism was very much a top-down process of political reform. Putin was well aware of the unbalanced nature of the new division of powers, and in July 2005 he suggested that appointed governors could regain up to 114 powers taken from the elected governors,[98] and at the same time he granted governors the right to confirm (although not to reject) federal appointments to regional branches of national ministries, including the MVD, and the justice and emergency situations ministries.[99]

Putin's reforms of the federal system had mixed results. The old segmentation has decreased, with regional laws and republican constitutions beginning to converge with federal constitutional and legal norms, the state's own agencies in the regions were brought back under central control, and some of the more egregious centrifugal tendencies checked. However, regional reforms have not entirely been able to overcome institutional confusion, and in some cases instead of being resolved these contradictions have intensified. For example, the reform of the Federation Council raised in sharper form the idea that it should be formed through direct elections. There was clearly a breakdown of the principle of the separation of powers when the president appointed a governor (even with regional input and consent), then this governor delegates a representative to the upper chamber, a body designed to act as a check on the executive. A new type of 'circular flow of power' had been established in which presidential power became self-perpetuating. New tensions have emerged, as between the presidential envoys and the government: the envoys have been urged to ensure federal control over ministerial branches in the regions but the representatives themselves do not sit in the cabinet. Relations with the presidential administration are not always smooth, while relations with the governors are structurally unstable.

Putin's reforms are centralising insofar as they seek to fulfil the liberal republican ideal of equality of law across the whole territory, but in practice they have managed to reproduce new forms of segmentation, but at a higher level. Institutional fragmentation continues, and instead of a power 'vertical' being established, we have instead a power 'triangle', intensifying bureaucratic conflicts and complicating public administration. The problem, however, is more than institutional. As Elena Chebankova notes, '[T]he problem of Russian federalism is not of a structural character. It stems rather from a serious deficiency in processes and, therefore, it is cultural and ideological.'[100] In other words, while Russia is formally a federation, the spirit of federalism is missing. All federations are designed to constrain central political power, but not all do so with equal effect. In Russia, whatever the nature of the local regimes themselves, regions acted as a check on the central authorities; a type of horizontal separation of powers that to a degree compensated for the inadequacy of the vertical separation of powers. Although Putin may well have sought the democratic reconstitution of the state, the weakening of the regional 'fourth pivot' acting as a check on the central authorities undermined the democratic separation of powers. The compacted reconstitution of the state endangered democratic and federal pluralism. The interests of regime perpetuation undermined pluralistic state reconstitution.

# Part IV

# Economy and society

Russia's economic transformation in the 1990s was accompanied by largely negative economic indicators: falling living standards; high inflation, budget deficits, capital flight; a greater fall in industrial production even than during the great depression in the United States in the early 1930s, a fall in overall GDP of 42 per cent, high unemployment and a massive growth in income inequality, with the richest 10 per cent earning 13 times more than the poorest 10 per cent, a gap that by 2006 had increased to 15.3 times. Large sections of economic life became criminalised and entered various shades of the black economy, accompanied by great difficulties in collecting taxes. Privatisation allowed an already privileged class to consolidate its position by the transformation of public goods into private wealth, and allowed a small group of oligarchs to plunder the national economy. A type of rent-seeking capitalism emerged where power and government influence was used to leverage advantageous deals. The low point of all of this was the partial government default on its debts in August 1998, a crisis that saw numerous banks go under and people for the second time in a decade losing their deposits. This proved to be the turning point, and by the time Putin came to power in 2000 the economic tide had turned. Buoyed by high energy prices, his leadership saw an annual average rise in GPP of about 7 per cent. Demographic indicators remained starkly negative, with a high death rate accompanied by a birth rate that remained well below the replacement rate, but a new mood of social optimism emerged that reflected the sense that the worst of the transitional period was over. A market economy had been established, although still distorted by monopolies and increasing state intervention, and Russian companies invested ever more abroad. The establishment of capitalism in Russia entailed a cultural revolution in manners and mores, yet a new self-confidence began to emerge as the experience of the communist epoch began to fade into historical memory and people once again began to believe in a future that would not be more painful than the past.

# 13  Russian capitalism

> Gaidar's reform secured macroeconomic change, namely the destruction of the old economy. It was a wildly painful break, surgically crude, with the rusty grinding sound of pieces of old parts and mechanisms being ripped out together with the flesh, but the break occurred. Most likely, it simply could not have happened any other way. We had virtually nothing to work with apart from Stalin's industry, Stalin's economy, adapted to the present day. And its make-up dictated precisely that sort of a break: over the knee. The system was destroyed in the same way that it was created.
>
> (Boris Yeltsin)[1]

By 2001 the World Bank had taken Russia off the 'crisis list'. Russia had become a market economy. By 1998 Russia was ranked tenth in the world in terms of purchasing-power parity (PPP), below Brazil but above Mexico.[2] Russia's integration into the world economy was 'shallow', mostly accounted for by a rise in trade with the developed economies and focused primarily on primary materials and energy exports. Nationalists argued that Russia's economy had become 'Kuwait-ised'. Deeper integration would be accompanied by more FDI and structural changes in the economy. Under Putin production became more profitable, and certainly more politically expedient, than asset-stripping, especially in the context of high commodity prices. The 'initial accumulation of capital' phase appeared over as enterprise managers sought to add value rather than seize cash flows and export commodities. The great challenge facing Russia was to restore the micro-economic tissues of an entrepreneurial and active society combined with market-enhancing macro-economic policies. The weakness of the banking system and contract law and the presence everywhere of street hawkers and market hustlers, robber taxi drivers and organised crime, gave birth to the image of the 'Wild East', a riotous free-for-all on the fringes of the emerging market. This in turn gave way by the time Putin left office of a state once again trying to implement an anachronistic model of state-directed development.

## The road to the market

The fall of the Berlin Wall ended the political division of Europe, but it exposed the economic one. Two Europes still faced each other, one relatively prosperous, the other confronted with the legacy of a failed economic experiment. By some reckonings the Soviet Union in 1991 was comparatively as far, if not further, behind the leading Western countries as Russia had been in 1913. The Soviet system stormed into the industrial age but failed to respond to the challenges of post-industrialism. Only under Gorbachev was the assault against the market tempered but the search for a distinctive socialist economics was not abandoned. After the August 1991 coup economic reform gave way to the marketisation of the entire system. There is no single optimal path of transition and the question of sequencing – the relative priority between liberalisation, stabilisation, privatisation and restructuring – had to be determined in the course of the reforms.[3]

### The pre-history of economic reform

The Soviet economic crisis had been exacerbated by *perestroika* but had long been evident. There had been a sharp decline in growth rates since the mid-1970s, accompanied by the growth of debt and budget deficits. The anti-alcohol campaign of 1986–7 and its attendant revenue losses was only one element in a larger crisis in which enterprises and ministries took advantage of the weakening centre to obtain cheap investment funds from the central budget. The problems, in the words of Anatoly Chubais, were 'only the summit of a prolonged socioeconomic structural crisis connected with the decay of the centrally planned economy'.[4] The decay, however, had not been terminal and many studies suggest that the Soviet economy could have limped on for a good few years until destabilised by reform.[5]

Russia contributed 61 per cent of the USSR's GNP, and thus on its own over-shadowed the other 14 republics. Even before the 1991 coup Yeltsin had begun the painful process of disengagement from the Soviet economy. On 3 September 1990 premier Ivan Silaev outlined the Russian government's programme, envisaging a speedy transition to the market although acknowledging that this would be impossible without coordination among all the republics. The programme, which ran to over a thousand pages, advocated a new structure to replace the ministries for separate industries, and an inter-republican economic council. Despite its length, the programme lacked clear criteria for implementation and was greeted by a divided government and personal conflicts. It was at this time that Gorbachev rejected the '500 days programme' for a Soviet-wide staged transition to the market, and thus Russia's resolve to go it alone was stiffened. By November 1990 the Russian parliament began implementing its own economic reforms, beginning with an important law regulating agriculture. The Russian government unilaterally cut by 80 per cent its 1991 budget contribution to the Soviet treasury. However, the period up to August 1991 was marked by frustration as Russian programmes came into conflict with Soviet ones, and the economic crisis only worsened. With the fall of the Soviet Union the Russian economics team inherited a yawning budget deficit, a mountain of roubles accumulated as a result of years of monetary and fiscal laxity, and a debilitating system of price controls. The result was empty shops, low labour productivity and rampant inflation.

The lack of clarity over what exactly was the subject of economic reform, Russia or the Soviet Union, continued to impede progress. The Inter-Republican Economic Committee headed by Silaev, with Yavlinsky one of its key advisers, sought to maintain an integrated economy. Their efforts led to the signing by eight republics of an economic treaty on 8 October 1991 in Almaty.[6] The treaty stressed private ownership, free enterprise and competition, and committed the republics to marketisation and restricted government interference. They were forbidden unilaterally to take control of shared property or to erect trade barriers between themselves. The rouble was to remain the common currency, but members were allowed to have their own currencies if it did not harm the rouble.[7] The treaty in essence repeated the provisions of the rejected Shatalin-Yavlinsky 500-day plan of August 1990, but in the new circumstances of independent states it did not really offer viable measures to deal with the economic crisis. The main problem was that it dealt with the external aspects and not with the root causes of crisis in each of the republics. Hopes for a federal reserve banking system, an economic arbitration court and all the other trappings of a federal union were probably unrealistic given the obstacles to maintaining political union. The independent republics, led by the Baltic republics, instead began putting up customs barriers. Ukraine declared that it would establish its own currency and other republics considered taking similar measures.

The break-up of the union dislocated regional patterns of economic specialisation and destroyed the national market.[8] The vertically integrated Stalinist economy encouraged the manufacture of goods in gigantic plants in an attempt to benefit from economies of scale, and the production of key items for the whole USSR were concentrated in a limited number of plants. When some pharmaceutical plants were closed in 1989–90 because of their high pollution levels, they soon had to be reopened because they were sole suppliers of items necessary for medicines. However, a debate continues over the extent of economic dependency between the republics, with suggestions that this was exaggerated by Gorbachev and his associates in their attempt to prove the desirability of the Union.[9] A study of the Baltic republics, for example, argued that their dependence on the rest of the Union was not as critical as had been thought, and certainly nothing that normal economic contracts could not cover.[10] It has been estimated that the disruption of trade with CIS countries contributed 10 per cent to Russia's overall economic decline in the early 1990s.[11]

The CIS documents signed in Minsk and Almaty in December 1991 were vague on economic integration. The paradox emerged that the republic with the greatest potential for independent economic development, Russia, remained the most committed to a larger economic unit. Russia provided nearly 67 billion roubles in subsidy to the other republics in 1989, and in 1988 was the least dependent on trade with the other republics. Russia sold its energy and raw materials relatively cheaply, and paid for consumer goods at inflated prices. Russia stood to gain most from a shift to the use of the dollar in inter-republican trade. The desire of the other republics for economic separation was politically motivated, though in the long term they were probably right to believe that they could manage their own resources and enterprises better than distant Moscow could under the old regime. They feared Moscow's domination in whatever shape it came, benign or malign, subsidy or exploitation. Only the Central Asian republics sought to maintain the old links since they were clear net beneficiaries of subsidies from Moscow, but even they soon developed their own economic strategies.

The Soviet legacy to Russia was a heavy one indeed. The structural reorganisation of the Russian economy took place against the background of a sharp decline in real incomes and production, the latter falling in the USSR as a whole by 17 per cent in 1991, and in light industry, hit hardest by the cuts in imports, output fell by 40 per cent.[12] In comparison, in 1932, the hardest year of the Great Depression in the USA, GNP fell by only 14 per cent. In Russia national income fell by about 5 per cent in 1990 and 9 per cent in 1991.[13] Pavlov's government had been marked by fiscal and budgetary anarchy and rising budget deficits. This was exacerbated by local authorities refusing to contribute to republican funds, and republics reneging on commitments to the Union budget, in particular the central stabilisation, pension and social security funds. Credits were received from the State Bank, which in turn only encouraged the printing presses to work faster. The problem of the USSR foreign debt burdened the transition, having risen under Gorbachev to $77 billion ($60 billion to Western creditors and $17 billion to Asian and East European countries) by late 1991.[14]

In the early 1990s long-term structural crisis turned from a latent to an actual one. Financial problems became catastrophic, and this more than anything else hastened the demise of the USSR. The Soviet inflation rate quadrupled in 1991, reaching some 700 per cent by the end of the year. The chairman of the State Bank, Viktor Geraschenko, warned in early December that only enough funds remained for a few days' of expenditure, a crisis precipitated by the Russian parliament's objections to the Bank's policy of printing money to meet commitments. Yeltsin agreed to bail out the union government, but at the price of a tough budget strategy and the transfer of the Soviet Ministry of Finance to Russian jurisdiction. On 20 November the process was accelerated when Yeltsin in effect took over all the remaining union economic ministries, disbanding several of them, and imposing Russian control over all strategic natural resources. Thus Russia, despite itself, was forced to take over Soviet economic institutions, but was in danger of finding itself in the position of responsibility without power since little positive could be done until there were new budget laws, effective taxation, credit and monetary policies.

### *Facets of economic reform*

As the USSR moved towards oblivion Russia drew up a fully fledged independent economic policy. Yeltsin outlined his programme to the Russian parliament on 28 October 1991.

- Economic stabilisation based on tight monetary and credit policy, strengthening of the rouble (although one of the major problems was the influx of roubles from the former union republics) up to the creation of a separate Russian currency to protect the economy.
- Price liberalisation.
- Privatisation and the introduction of a mixed economy with a growing private sector, accelerated land reform.
- Reorganisation of the financial system, tight control of budget expenditure, reform of the tax and banking systems.[15]

Yeltsin promised 'to stabilise the situation' and then to 'begin the process of rejuvenation', although he admitted that the measures would be unpopular but expected there to be an improvement by autumn 1992. This was a programme for radical changes in both ownership and management of the Russian economy that drew much on the Polish experience of shock therapy.

On 1 November the CPD granted Yeltsin wide powers (valid until 1 December 1992) to be used to promote reform. Presidential decrees on such matters as banks, property and land reform, taxation, currency and so on were to be submitted to parliament, and if not rejected within seven days they became effective; otherwise they were to be discussed by parliament within ten days.[16] On 6 November Yeltsin reorganised the government, stating that for the duration of radical economic reforms the president would also act as head of the 'government of reforms' himself. A new Russian Council of Ministers with 23 ministers was appointed, and the country prepared itself for yet another grand attempt at social engineering.

### Liberalisation (shock therapy)

There are two basic philosophies of the transition to the market. One urged the need for 'shock therapy' and a 'big bang' on the Polish model, implemented by finance minister Leszek Balcerowicz from 1990. In addition, only this option would gain the backing of the West, and with it vital political and financial assistance. Shock therapists drew the conclusion from Gorbachev's reforms that half-measures are often worse than none. The other line, which we can dub 'evolutionists', advocated a 'soft landing' comprising controlled price rises, demonopolisation, gradual privatisation and assistance to enterprises to tide them over the transition. Yavlinsky at the head of the social democratic Yabloko party in particular favoured a sequence beginning with the break-up of monopolies, and only then followed by price liberalisation; while the leftist and nationalist groups continued to believe in massive state subsidies. In the event, Russia's road to the market began with a vigorous 'big bang', but then began to draw on elements from the evolutionist school.

The idea behind 'shock therapy' is that countries plagued by years of planning, state ownership and bureaucracy have to be jerked into the mainstream of market reforms. This is to be achieved by the rapid liberalisation of prices, removal of subsidies, expenditure cuts and severe reductions in money supply. To use Janos Kornai's term, the aim is to overcome 'soft budget constraints', to ensure that considerations of bottom line profitability was restored to economic life.[17] The aim was for goods that had previously been hoarded to find their way back to the shops and thus for queues to decrease, deterred by the high prices if not eliminated by the sufficiency of goods. Higher prices would encourage production, and a revived private sector would gradually bring supply and demand into line. Price rises would then stabilise, and the economy would then begin to move out of recession. In practice, the immediate result of shock therapy in Bolivia, Poland, Russia and elsewhere has been an explosion in prices, a rapid rise in unemployment and a steep fall in production, although quite soon the positive effects did become apparent as queues for deficit goods disappeared and the new incentives for production kicked in.

The theory was condemned by the veteran economist John Kenneth Galbraith as 'simplistic ideology'. He argued that the neo-liberal reliance on the market to the exclusion of any major role of the state was primitive economics.[18] Shock therapy places intolerable strains on the economy and society, and companies that in other conditions might have fought their way to viability are forced to close for lack of liquidity. The fall in production is matched by spiralling prices and the population sees its savings disappear and endures yet more suffering. Living standards, already low, plummet, and tight budgetary constraints means that there is a lack of funds to provide adequate social security for the growing army of the unemployed and needy. The sheer speed of the transition intensifies the suffering and the whole fragile tissue of democratic institutions is placed under almost intolerable strain. It took Germany ten years to move to a market economy after the war, and Britain retained price and other controls into the 1950s. In Russia the economic shocks of the 1990s brought the very legitimacy of market economics into question.

In defence of his strategy, Gaidar stressed that Russia had little choice, given the disastrous circumstances in which the country found itself as it became independent in late 1991: grain reserves down to four months supply, foreign currency and gold reserves were exhausted, and the whole country lacked credit-worthiness. The old system was completely paralysed and the new one did not work. In these conditions, he insisted, all talk about a soft, evolutionary approach to reform was meaningless. His strategy was based on a three-year programme, but in the event he was out of government within thirteen months. Those countries which had three years of consistent reform, such as Poland, Estonia, the Czech Republic, Latvia and Lithuania, enjoyed an economic upturn by the end of the period, whereas in Russia the premature relaxation of policy undermined any immediate benefits. According to Gaidar, the problem was not that Russian reforms were pursued too dogmatically, but that they were pursued without consistency and firmness.[19]

Gaidar's political position was always exceptionally weak. Appointed deputy prime minister in charge of economic policy on 7 November 1991, he became first deputy prime minister on 2 March 1992, acting prime minister on 15 June 1992, and was dismissed on 14 December 1992 (returning briefly to the economics portfolio in late 1993). Nevertheless, he was the architect of the first stage of Russia's economic reforms. His policy was marked by a commitment to traditional International Monetary Fund (IMF) precepts including a balanced budget, the reduction of inflation, cutting back subsidies, exposing the domestic economy to the world market and raising energy prices. He and his neo-liberal allies tended to idealise neo-classical economic theory and denigrated the role of the state and other regulatory institutions of contemporary capitalism.[20] Given the weak and faction-ridden nature of the Russian state at this time, he had a point.

In late 1991 wage limits were lifted, restrictions on foreign economic activities eased, minimum wages set, all customs barriers introduced by individual regions banned, VAT set at 28 per cent, guidelines for privatisation in 1992 adopted, and much else besides. Then on 2 January 1992 came comprehensive price liberalisation, with prices freed from administrative control on about 90 per cent of retail prices and 80 per cent of wholesale prices. On 29 January the restrictions on trading, imposed in the 1920s, were lifted and soon kiosks sprouted on streets everywhere. Ambitious targets were set to reduce the budget deficit, which by some estimates reached a fifth of GDP in 1991, and to achieve a balanced budget by the end of the year. Monetary policy was tightened, and attempts made to bring the flood of roubles under control. Bread, milk, vodka, medicines, rents, public transport and the price of some utilities remained controlled, and from March 1992 local councils had the right to impose local controls as long as they paid for any subsidies. From May 1992 energy prices were increased, but because of political fears not up to anything demanded by the IMF and as late as 2001 energy prices in Russia were still only a third of world prices.

The January measures were a mixture of price liberalisation and price reform, raising prices rather than letting the market find a natural level balancing supply and demand. Demand was damped down by what for most Russians were exorbitant prices, but too little was done to free the supply side of the economy, with only desultory moves towards privatising the retail sector and breaking the stranglehold of monopolies. Reforms to price structures appear to have operated mainly in one direction – price increases. Consumer price inflation rose sharply, by 245 per cent in the month of January alone before falling back to 10 per cent in August;[21] at which point the government's attempt to resolve the problem of inter-enterprise arrears stimulated a new wave of inflation, rising to a monthly 25 per cent by the end of the year. By November 1992 prices had risen 22-fold, whereas wages had only increased 10-fold.[22] Total inflation in 1992 was 2,500 per cent, in 1993 840 per cent and in 1995 130 per cent before falling back to 11 per cent in 1997. An incomes policy had been an essential element of shock therapy in Poland, but in Russia the government considered wage controls politically unfeasible and unnecessary since the wage-price spiral was not the central element fuelling inflation. The impact of the price rises was cushioned by savings and accumulated goods, but these were soon exhausted; the loss of savings, indeed, became one of the most bitter charges against Gaidar's economics.

Shock therapy in the short term provokes a sharp drop in manufacturing production. In Poland industrial output fell by 37 per cent from 1990 before beginning to pick up in late 1992, but the decline was worse in Russia because shock therapy was applied to an economy already in very deep recession. Industrial output in Russia plummeted by 20 per cent in 1992, compared with a fall of 11 per cent in 1991. Production was hit by the tight squeeze on investment: the aim was to destroy the old inefficient system rather than to construct anything new.[23] In conditions of extreme monopolisation, instead of firms cutting prices to compensate for falling demand, they cut output and raised prices. Between 1990 and 1995 GDP fell by some 50 per cent, compared to a cumulative fall of some 31 per cent in American GNP during the Depression.[24] Despite the temptation to blame shock therapy for this fall, countries (like Ukraine) that tried a 'soft landing' into economic reform fared even worse.

## Stabilisation and crash

Already from mid-1992 political pressures forced a shift from liberalisation towards stabilisation. Fears of a social backlash meant that energy prices were raised only 5-fold in April 1992, despite the demand of the IMF to raise them to world levels. Tight monetary and fiscal policies were pursued to restrain inflation and to stabilise the value of the rouble against international currencies. The Russian budget deficit, nevertheless, tended to rise as the government eased its public sector spending restrictions and raised state sector wages. The management of the economy was reorganised, with the new Ministry of the Economy absorbing the old general ministries like Gosplan and Gossnab, the state supply system abolished in January 1992. The Ministry of Industry took over some two dozen branch industrial ministries, while others were turned into concerns, trusts, associations and the like, but still modelled as ministerial departments. Large debts were run up between companies, primarily between the old state industries and the military-industrial complex, because they could not sell goods to consumers, who had no spare cash, because they had been unwilling to sack workers or to cut down on overheads, but above all because they in effect gained credit by not paying for goods received. The economy for most of the 1990s appeared paralysed, with factories waiting for orders from ministries in Moscow that no longer existed. Lax fiscal and political controls encouraged 'rent-seeking', defined as 'any activity designed to exploit a monopoly position or to gain access to government subsidies, as opposed to profit-seeking in a market with competitive firms'.[25] The whole system, moreover, was permeated by corruption as managers looked to their own interests rather than those of their enterprises, and sought ways of profiting from the crisis by transferring ownership to themselves and associates on the cheap, by purloining foreign currency income, intercepting cash flows and in general by exploiting the opportunities of a system stuck between the plan and the market, neither 'socialist' nor 'capitalist'. Joel Hellman characterises this as a 'partial reform equilibrium' where the winners of the first phase of reform seek to protect their gains by obstructing further change.[26]

One source of opposition to Gaidar's liberal policies came from the industrialists, represented above all by the Russian Union of Industrialists and Entrepreneurs (RUIE), largely made up of the directors of the large state enterprises who favoured a slower pace of reform and more government subsidies. Another came from opposition democrats like Yavlinsky, who insisted that it was a mistake for the government to liberalise prices before privatisation and competition had been introduced. His warnings were correct in that monopolies took advantage of the liberalisation to raise prices and cut production, the opposite of what the reform policies were meant to achieve. A third source of opposition came from parliament, who demanded the replacement of the young academics in government with 'professionals'. The appointment on 30 May 1992 of Chernomyrdin, chairman of Gazprom, as energy minister was a response to these demands, reflecting the reformers lack of a solid parliamentary base. The government reshuffle of June 1992 led to concessions to the industrial lobby in the form of writing off debts and increased monetary emissions, stoking inflation yet more.

The challenge to neo-liberal policies finally succeeded when on 14 December 1992 Chernomyrdin replaced Gaidar as prime minister. While most of the radical 'government of reforms' remained, a change of tack was promised with more credits for state industry, and on 5 January 1993 limits on profits on some consumer goods and services were announced in an attempt to keep prices down. In the event, Chernomyrdin's economic policy did not differ all that much from Gaidar's. The policy of tight credit and monetary policy was restored, and financial stabilisation and the strengthening of the rouble became his priorities. The First Duma from 1994 proved receptive to the logic of centrist economic reform, and in December 1995, as noted, for the first time since 1991 a budget was adopted before it was due to come into operation.

The 1993 constitution grants the Central Bank of Russia (CBR), previously subordinated to the Supreme Soviet, a degree of independence from the legislature. It determines the money supply within the framework of a commitment to the stability of the rouble. Its director is hired or fired by the State Duma, but only on the president's recommendation. Thus the CBR gained some room for manoeuvre, above all from parliament, but enjoys nothing like the degree of independence enjoyed by the Bundesbank or the Federal Reserve Bank in America, or even the Bank of England since 1997. Few restrictions were placed on capital flows in and out of the country. The final demise of the rouble zone followed the CBR's currency reform of July 1993, giving Russia effective monetary and credit control, and by 1995 almost all the other republics had introduced their own currency.

Stabilisation was marked by a roller-coaster of booms and busts. A notable low point was 'black Tuesday', 11 October 1994, when the rouble lost over 20 per cent of its value, largely as a consequence of an earlier loosening of monetary policy and, it was suspected, because of machinations by bankers. The rouble swiftly recovered its value but its vulnerability was exposed and between September 1994 and January 1995 it lost half its value. By 1998 the rouble was effectively stabilised within a dollar corridor, with inflation reduced to tolerable limits. The major problem, however, was to achieve full rouble convertibility, without which Russia would attract little foreign investment because of difficulties in repatriating earnings, given the natural limits to barter or counter-trade.

The whole policy depended on the West in the form of debt restructuring and stabilisation funds. Debt relief released valuable foreign currency to finance imports and stabilise the currency, while standby loans are a crucial element in providing a source of non-inflationary financing. Russia gained full membership of the IMF and the World Bank on 27 April 1992, after some debate over the size of Russia's quota in the IMF that sets its capacity to borrow, and thus became eligible for loans. In the 1990s IMF assistance totalled some $24 (£13.5) billion, tied to a set of conditions including tight monetary and fiscal policies, reductions in the budget deficit, cutting credits to loss-making enterprises, establishing the legal framework for private ownership, reforming the farm and energy sectors, servicing debts to the West and establishing a unified exchange rate for the rouble. Although direct credits to state firms were phased out from 1994, subsidies continued to flow to agriculture while high tariffs (for example, on imported automobiles) protected domestic manufacturers.

Between mid-1995 and mid-1998 money supply and exchange rates remained stable, but ultimately severe fiscal imbalances undermined monetary stability and led to the end of the rouble-dollar anchor. In the 1990s direct state subsidies to enterprises were largely replaced by debts. Tax shortfalls led to budget deficits (including the deficits of the federal budget, the regional budgets and social security) that the government tried to finance in a bacchanalia of state bond issues (GKOs) whose ever higher-interest rates could not be sustained indefinitely, provoking the crash of August 1998. The ensuing devaluation improved the competitiveness of the Russian economy and allowed significant growth to take place from 2000 (see Table 13.1) as import substitution gave a boost to domestic manufacturers and suppliers.

### Privatisation

The main purpose of privatisation is to break the dependence of enterprises on the state budget. Subsidies and easy access to bank credits fuel inflation and undermine the credibility of reform. However, privatisation is as much a political act as an economically expedient one. The destruction of the old monopolies and their corporate dependence on the state not only begins to create a capitalist market but also entails the destruction of the associated bureaucracy. For Chubais, the deputy prime minister at the head of the State Committee for the Administration of State Property (*Goskomimushchestvo*, GKI) responsible for privatisation, the programme was designed to create a new class with a stake in property and thus make society less susceptible to political demagogy. In his address to the nation on 19 August 1992 Yeltsin described privatisation as the 'ticket to a free economy'. Private property was considered the basis of a civilised society and the foundation on which democracy could be built.

The Soviet economy was the most monopolised in the world. Up to a third of all industrial enterprises were absolute monopolies, producing goods that no other company in the USSR produced. The system was characterised by 'the "super-monopolism" of state power' in production, in the sphere of management, in trade and supply and in research and development.[27] This was why Yavlinsky and others argued that denationalisation had to be accompanied by demonopolisation, to stop privatisation simply transforming state monopolies into private ones. As in Britain, however, privatisation tended to precede the break up of monopolies, and in most cases simply achieved the transfer of a state monopoly into the private sector where they could impose punitive charges on captive customers. The state committee for anti-monopoly policy, a body independent of the government, vetted all company registrations valued at more than 50 million roubles. The anti-monopoly legislation, however, was relatively ineffective and pursued with a singular lack of vigour, and demonopolisation tended to take spontaneous rather than planned forms.[28] Monopolies, however, affected only certain industries, and overall the concentration of industry was not that much greater in Russia that in the United States. The problem in Russia was 'the missing fringe of small firms', the source of technical innovation, competition and job creation.[29]

The aim of privatisation is to overcome the amorphous nature of state property: allegedly belonging to all, it belongs to no one. The intention is to personify it in the form of concrete owners or known corporate agencies while creating a new class of property owners (in our case, 'new Russians' and oligarchs). The presidential decree on the Privatisation of State and Municipal Enterprises in the RSFSR of 29 December 1991 set ambitious targets for privatisation, but little was said about demonopolisation.[30] The Government Programme of Privatisation of June 1992 was the main document outlining Russia's privatisation programme.[31] Strategic and defence enterprises, utilities and those with over 10,000 employees could only be privatised, if at all, with the government's approval. All small enterprises (the 200,000 enterprises with up to 200 employees, most of which were owned by local or municipal authorities) were to be sold through competitive auctions, commercial tender competitions or lease buy-outs. Large enterprises (with 1,000 to 10,000 employees) were to be transformed into joint-stock companies (corporatised), after which their shares were to be sold or distributed according to the provisions of the mass privatisation programme. Medium-sized enterprises could adopt either the direct sale or corporatisation method. Three main approaches were available for disbursing the assets of joint-stock companies, while a fourth sought to involve the mass of the population.

- The first was for collectives to receive up to 25 per cent of non-voting shares free, and another 10 per cent of voting shares at a discount, while managers could buy up to a fifth of voting shares for a nominal sum.
- The second was for workers and managers to purchase 51 per cent of normal shares in closed sales. This was the preferred option for most companies, but since the workers' shares could not be held collectively they were easily over-shadowed by management, allowing the enterprises effectively to be taken over by their own administrations.
- The third option applied only to medium-sized enterprises and allowed a managing group to privatise an enterprise while ensuring solvency and employment for at least one year; the managing group could buy 30 per cent of voting shares, while 20 per cent was sold to workers and managers at preferential terms.[32]
- In addition, in August 1992 the government began to issue privatisation vouchers with a nominal value of 10,000 roubles. Citizens were given investment coupons,

that is, registered securities enabling them to buy shares or management shares at preferential rates of the 6,000 medium and large companies earmarked for corporatisation in 1992 and privatisation in 1993. The coupon method does not create additional capital or strengthen the management of companies, but instead was meant to symbolise the advent of 'popular capitalism'. In the event, instead of creating a new class of shareholders, voucher privatisation turned into a disaster as the management companies set up to manage the popular shareholdings simply stole the shares; very few ever paid out any dividends; and the whole process boosted the development of oligarchical capitalism as a few holding companies scooped up the millions of vouchers.

Much of the debate over privatisation focuses on the issue of equity. If state enterprises had earlier belonged to the people, then how was their formal ownership now to be translated into real ownership? The argument that enterprises should be given to their workers was flawed since those in viable enterprises would benefit far more than those in the service sector or bankrupt plants. The debate was often couched in terms of equity versus efficiency, though some argued that giving away shares combined both efficacy and equity and would at the same time build up popular support for the reforms.[33] Others favoured the most rapid disbursement of state assets to establish a critical mass early on in the reform process.[34] Milton Friedman, however, insisted that ownership meant not only assets but also liabilities, and that old illusions would be perpetuated if the first step on the road to the market was giving people something for nothing instead of having to provide something in return.[35] The giving away of state property to workers might well undermine both efficiency and equity since those who did not work in a state enterprise or had retired would be at a disadvantage, and the value of enterprises in any case varied sharply.[36]

Privatisation turned out to be a highly complex affair in which genuine problems were compounded by an almost obsessive fear of foreign penetration of the economy allied with the attempt to avoid the Soviet mafia buying up land and enterprises with their ill-gotten gains. The latter consideration failed in the most spectacular way, and privatisation was accompanied by massive insider dealing and the 'grabbing' (*prikhvatizatsiya*, a pun on the Russian word for privatisation) of public wealth by what were to become 'oligarchs'. In one respect, however, privatisation was easier in Russia than elsewhere since the process was little affected by reprivatisation, the restitution of property. Russia's former owners were for the most part dead, and their heirs scattered to the four corners of the earth. Changes in property relations took a number of forms, of which outright privatisation was only one. The other options were leasing arrangements, worker-management schemes, the so-called '*nomenklatura* privatisation' whereby managers and former political officials took the best of the state enterprises, and the creation of new businesses. Leasing, holding companies and the like appeared to be at best a half-way stage, a type of pseudo-privatisation.

Privatisation always has a directly political purpose. The aim here was to make the transition to the market economy irreversible by creating a class of property owners while at the same time making firms more efficient and market-oriented. In addition, rapid state-sponsored privatisation sought (unsuccessfully) to pre-empt factory directors from appropriating choice parts of the state economy. The majority of privatised enterprises were not sold to the public but in workforce elections, encouraged by their managers, voted for the option that allowed staff to buy 51 per cent of the stock at a fixed price. Rather than outside owners coming in and shaking out factories and sacking staff and managers, control remained within the factory gates. Voucher privatisation was followed from mid-1994 by a second stage focusing on key aspects of enterprise restructuring and with more emphasis on private sector development, including the transition to cash privatisation, the attempt to achieve more efficient corporate management, and the accelerated development of securities markets and legal reforms. Enterprises were now encouraged to raise investment resources on the open capital market, and at the same time cash auctions and investment tenders for stakes in the newly privatised companies and for blocks of shares held by the state in privatised enterprises accelerated. Attempts were made to attract foreign investment, but continuing capital flight depressed investment.

Local authorities played a key role in the privatisation process, especially in the housing and retail areas. Moscow insisted on control over privatisation in the city, and even safeguarded for itself the right to renationalise enterprises in the capital. Enterprises had traditionally provided a range of social facilities such as subsidised canteens, crèches, housing and hospitals, which they considered a form of hidden taxation on their enterprises and thus refused to pay taxes to the state. These non-productive social services were gradually transferred to the local authorities, but the latter often lacked the resources to maintain them.

By early 2001, 130,180 enterprises formerly owned by the state had been privatised, representing exactly two-thirds of the total. The attempt to conduct privatisation without strict controls by the executive and judicial authorities allowed a small group of economic managers and new capitalists to seize the lion's share of state property. The 'shares for loans' scandal of 1995–6 allowed the oligarchs to consolidate as a class. It was clear that not enough was charged for privatised assets. If in Russia privatisation revenues per capita in the 1990s were \$56.40, in Hungary they reached \$1,252.80.[37] Russian capitalism took on carpet bagging forms, interested in short-term gains, rent seeking and asset-stripping. A distinctive type of 'comprador capitalism' emerged. Putin, however, set his face against renationalisation and insisted that there would be no redistribution of property. He did, however, ensure that privatisation took place more fairly and that the state received its due share by holding competitive auctions. He also tried to ensure cross-subsidy. For example, in 1999–2000 Oleg Deripaska and his associates at the head of Russian Aluminium were allowed to take control of 70 per cent of Russia's highly lucrative aluminium industry in exchange, it appears, for a commitment to support the Russian automobile industry. Russian Aluminium went on to buy enterprises such as the massively loss-making GAZ car plant in Nizhny Novgorod, with its 100,000 workers, corrupt management, outdated product lines and huge burden of social expenses, and began its modernisation.[38]

Putin's administration began to change the way in which the government functioned, above all strengthening the power of the federal government at the expense of the regions. The measures, as we have seen above, included the creation of the seven new federal districts, the strengthening of the federal treasury and the federal prosecutors, and changes in the management of the natural monopolies (including Gazprom and RAO UES, the electricity monopoly). The government's control over the management of these companies was strengthened. The new push for reform suggested that the 'partial reform equilibrium' identified by Hellman could be overcome by an outside force, in this case a rejuvenated presidency.

## The Russian economy today

The liberalisation, stabilisation and privatisation of the 1990s created the basic legal framework of a market economy. The achievement is impressive, yet major problems remained as Putin took office. The rights of creditors, for example, were poorly defended, above all because of the cumbersome procedure whereby the courts take the assets of debtors and only after an auction provide some of the returns to the creditor. This made debt financing (which is part of investment) highly problematic. In addition, the rights of minority shareholders over management have been too weak to prevent asset stripping or to exercise accountability over corporate managers; majority shareholders rode roughshod over minority shareholders, encouraging 100 per cent investment. There remain major gaps in the law, for example over intellectual property rights and the land code. The main problems facing Putin in the economic sphere were enterprise restructuring, public finance, the banking system and corporate governance. The development of an operational market economy in Russia required the strengthening of the rule of law, the development of legislative standards and frameworks, and attention to the social aspects of a modern Western economy. Several years of strong growth (Table 13.1) brought Russia's GDP by late 2007 to 102 per cent of that of 1991, but still slightly lower than the 1989 peak.

On 28 June 2000 the plan devised by the Minister for Economic Development and Trade, German Gref, and his research centre was adopted by the government and represented an integrated plan for the modernisation of the Russian economy and society. It sought to make social benefits more targeted, with pensions linked to contributions. A more benign business environment was to be created by reducing licensing, streamlining investment decisions and introducing international accounting standards for the

*Table 13.1* Russian economic performance since 1990

| Year | GDP change (%) against preceding year | Industrial production (% year on year) | Inflation |
|------|---------------------------------------|----------------------------------------|-----------|
| 1990 | −3.0 | −0.1 | 78 |
| 1991 | −5.0 | −8.0 | 138 |
| 1992 | −14.5 | −18.0 | 2,323 |
| 1993 | −8.7 | −14.1 | 844 |
| 1994 | −12.7 | −20.9 | 202 |
| 1995 | −4.1 | −3.3 | 131 |
| 1996 | −3.6 | −4.0 | 21.8 |
| 1997 | 1.4 | 1.9 | 11 |
| 1998 | −5.3 | −5.5 | 84.4 |
| 1999 | 6.4 | 8.1 | 36.5 |
| 2000 | 10.0 | 9.3 | 20.2 |
| 2001 | 5.1 | 4.9 | 18.6 |
| 2002 | 4.7 | 3.7 | 14.0 |
| 2003 | 7.3 | 7.0 | 12.0 |
| 2004 | 7.1 | 7.3 | 11.7 |
| 2005 | 6.4 | 4.0 | 10.9 |
| 2006 | 6.9 | 3.9 | 9.0 |
| 2007 | 7.6 | 6.5 | 11.9 |

*Sources*: Grinberg, 'Desyat' let sistemnoi transformatsii', *Nezavismaya gazeta*, 22 December 1999, p. 4; RFE/RL *Newsline*, 3 January 2001; RIA Novosti, various dates.

corporate sector. The plan committed the country to global integration, although its aspirations for accelerated World Trade Organisation (WTO) membership proved rather premature.[39] Although strongly diluted by the government, echoes of the plan resound in the following policy areas.

### Finances

#### Tax policy and collection

The state's punitive exercise of *its* property rights through taxation, that in some cases exceeded 100 per cent of what was being taxed and thus encouraging barter, was compounded by selective enforcement. This was remedied by the introduction of international standards reflected in Part I of the new Tax Code, establishing the basic relationship between tax-payers and the authorities. On 26 July 2000, the second part of the new tax code was overwhelmingly approved by the Federation Council, despite the fact that it would cause an immediate fall in regional tax revenue. The main features of the tax package were a flat rate 13 per cent income tax (the lowest in Europe), a minimum 5 per cent unified social tax, a 2 per cent social charge on wages, the raising of some excise taxes, and the amending of the law on VAT.

The failure to collect taxes in the 1990s undermined the basic sinews of the state and forced the government to resort to high-interest short-term borrowing, precipitating the crash of August 1998. Tax evasion (or avoidance) is always a problem in federal states, where the very structure of politics engenders suspicion of the centre. The tax service itself was chronically under-funded, with only 200,000 ill-equipped tax inspectors. Above all, the high level of distrust between the state and its citizenry encouraged tax avoidance since there was no confidence that the monies collected would go to public benefit. The new Tax Code improved matters, liberalising and simplifying the tax system. Tax collection in 2000 increased by 60 per cent to reach 20.7 per cent of GDP.[40] With some 60 per cent of business at that time out of the taxation zone, the level of taxes was largely irrelevant. Tax issues have now become far more prominent among business concerns, for the simple reason that taxes now have to be paid.

#### Budget deficits/surpluses

For most of the 1990s Russia ran severe budget deficits, and sought ever more creative ways of covering the gap between spending commitments and income. Only in 2000 did Russia finally achieve a budget surplus (some $6 billion), compared with the enormous deficits of earlier years. The government refused the demands of the left in the Duma to divert funds in the 2001 budget to provide state support for the manufacturing sector or for increased social spending, provoking the ire of the communist opposition. By 2006 Russia was running a 7.5 per cent budget surplus, with 45 per cent of budget revenue coming from energy export duties.[41] Part of the reason for this was the low level of state spending, which as a share of GDP had barely risen from the extremely low level of 1999, despite the huge rise in revenues.[42] The National Projects did begin to invest in infrastructure and human capital, but investment in the provision of public goods like health and education was wholly inadequate to make up for past shortfalls.

*The banking system and mortgages*

Up to August 1998 Russia had some 1,800 banks, but the 20 largest banks alone controlled 58 per cent of the total assets in the banking system.[43] Russian commercial banks did not engage in the normal financing of economic enterprises but instead focused on the speculative pursuit of short-term interest. In 2000 the Central Bank withdrew the licences of 36 banks, reducing the number to 1,316.[44] Before his assassination on 13 September 2006, Andrei Kozlov, first deputy chair of the Central Bank, had been working to close down questionable banks, shutting 90 out of 1,200, including 33 in the summer of 2006 alone. A more customer-oriented banking service began to emerge, and gradually confidence in the banking sector was restored, demonstrated by the growth in retail deposits in real terms. Yet banks play little part in financing investment, and many banks still operate largely as the financial arms of enterprises. The Gref plan called for the restructuring of the banking system, consolidation into a smaller number, the establishment of a more robust regulatory system and easing restrictions on the participation of foreign banks and a system of deposit insurance.

All of this began to transform the banking sector. By 2006 about 600 Russian banks were offering mortgages, double the number in 2005. An enormous demand for housing fuelled a construction boom, accompanied by sharp rises in apartment prices, doubling in the big cities between 2004 and 2006. Putin made affordable housing one of his four national priorities. Much of the nation's housing stock is in need of renewal, with about 60 per cent over 30 years old. Russia has an average of 21 square metres housing per person, compared to between 40 and 60 metres in Europe and the US. At the same time, Putin recognised that earlier policies had led to the loss of personal bank savings, and although he argued that the country could not afford to compensate savers in full, the government did apply a rolling policy of repayments, with the ultimate aim of providing recompense in full.

*Bankruptcy*

Denationalisation is usually accompanied by bankruptcy laws allowing previously subsidised but unprofitable companies to go to the wall. In September 1991 for the first time a mine in Donetsk was declared bankrupt, unable to pay its debts and the banks unwilling to extend further credits.[45] Thus began the process of hardening the budget, but the various bankruptcy laws, above all that of 1998, remain open to abuse, above all because creditors have little incentive to recover their claims. Bankruptcy proceedings often turned into another form of asset stripping.

*Inflation*

Inflation was the bugbear of the reforms of the 1990s, approaching hyper-inflation at certain times, but as a result of stabilisation policies was brought under some sort of control. By 2000 inflation had fallen to 20.2 per cent for the year. Part of the reason for the fall was the increasingly tight control over the banking system. The application of neo-classical macroeconomic policies in the Putin years, despite windfall energy rents, reduced inflation to 9 per cent in 2006.

*Domestic and foreign direct investment (FDI)*

The decline in the rate of investment far exceeded the decline in output during the early years of radical reform. The absolute level of investment between 1990 and 2000 fell by 75 per cent. The great deficit of investment resulted in an exhausted capital stock and massive cumulative productivity shortfalls that will cast a long shadow into the future. The inadequacy of the banks meant that most investment came from the enterprises themselves. The investment climate, however, improved under Putin. In 2000 investment in fixed capital reached 17.7 per cent, up from 5.3 per cent in 1999.[46] One of the reasons for this is that it was clear that there would be no grand redistribution of property and therefore owners could now turn to running their businesses for long-run profitability, rather than short-term asset-stripping. Investment in fixed capital today exceeds GDP growth, but at 19 per cent is still quite low relative to GDP and thus inadequately compensates for the shortfall of the 1990s. By late 2006 total accrued foreign investment exceeded $130 billion, with $35 billion in foreign ($10 billion of which was FDI) and $10 billion in domestic investment having been attracted in that year alone. There had been a small net capital inflow in 2005, which in 2006 rose to an inflow of over $30 billion, and in 2007 to $45 billion.[47]

At first wary of foreign direct investment (FDI), especially in larger firms, the Russian government later sought to attract foreign investors. For this a strong legal and financial system was required, as well as a reasonably stable political environment. In 2000 FDI rose to $12 billion, a growth of 20–5 per cent over the previous year. However, like the foreign investment boom of 1997–8, this includes investments in Russian stocks, including Russian-owned companies quoted on non-Russian stock markets. The share of FDI comprised by direct investment in new plant and equipment is still remarkably low for a country the size of Russia. In 2006, for example, Russia attracted $10 billion in FDI, compared to over $70 billion in China, and Russia's FDI totals less than 5 per cent of the total FDI that has flowed into China. Most foreign investment goes into trade and public catering as well as into the food industry, while the fuel industry received a relatively small proportion because of problems protecting minority share-holder rights and repatriating profits. By late 2006 total accrued foreign investment was about $130 billion.

*Capital flight*

Corporate capital flight took place through export and import contracts involving transfer pricing, the non-repatriation of export revenues and the distortion of information. Capital flight was stimulated by weak property rights, the lack of domestic investment opportunities and tax evasion. No accurate figures are available, but it is estimated that at least $20–30 billion of corporate capital left before August 1998. There were other types of capital flight as well, above all in cash, amounting in total to several hundred billion dollars. Annual losses to Russia in illegal capital flight in the 1990s averaged $25–30 billion. The weakness of the rouble and the fragility of the banking system encouraged people to hoard dollars, often kept in accounts abroad. Small businesses would try to avoid paying taxes by buying cash dollars as a means of payment. As a result Russia's stock of cash dollars are estimated to be $60 billion, equalling the $50–70 billion that the US Treasury estimates is held in cash dollars in America itself.

Among the other positive economic indicators of Putin's early rule, capital flight in relative terms (as a proportion of export earnings) declined, and there was a reversal of capital flight. An early indication of this was the growth in domestic investment. At the same time, cash flows at the federal level are now much more tightly controlled, above all through the establishment of the Federal Treasury and a more effective tax system. A new law against money laundering in mid-2001 tightened supervision over financial transactions. The permissive environment towards corruption typical of the Yeltsin years now gave way to the struggle for a new probity in public affairs encouraging some 'return flight', above all from Russian accounts in places like Cyprus. The liberalisation in currency transactions from 1 July 2006 reduced much of what in the past had been labelled capital flight.

### Foreign debt

In 1991 Russia's foreign debt totalled $120 billion, one-third of which was held by the 19-strong Paris Club of state-to-state creditors and the rest with the London Club of commercial creditors. By 2001 Russian sovereign debt (excluding private foreign debt by Russian enterprises and banks and the foreign debt of regional and local governments) had risen to some $150 billion. In 1990 Russia's sovereign debt represented 10.4 per cent of the country's GDP; by July 1998 this figure had risen to 31 per cent; only to rise to 113 per cent in December 1998, then falling back sharply. The debt carried over from Soviet times was $103 billion, and it was this component that particularly angered those in Russia who argued that the debt burden prevented productive investment and the maintenance of services.

Debt repayment peaked in 2003, when the country was due to pay $17 billion, but early repayments reduced the total and the anticipated debt repayment shock did not happen. In 1998 debts came to 130 per cent of GDP, some 60 per cent when Putin came to power in 2000, and fell to 35 per cent in 2003 and to the extraordinarily low level of 18 per cent in 2006 – on average in the EU debt represents 60 per cent of GDP. Windfall energy revenues were used to pay back creditors, which had the additional advantage of being non-inflationary. In 2006 the Paris Club debt to creditor states was paid off, and the total foreign debt had fallen to $47.8 billion by mid-2007, saving billions in annual interest payments. Under Putin there was no default of the sort that had hit Russia in 1998, and the country's credit rating rose steadily.

### Gold and foreign exchange reserves

Gold and foreign exchange reserves rose from $12 billion in 2000 to $410 billion by mid-2007, the third largest in the world after China ($875 billion) and Japan ($852 billion), with Taiwan ($257 billion) relegated to fourth place.[48]

### Stabilisation fund

A 'stabilisation fund' was created on 1 January 2004 to collect export duties and extraction tax from the price of oil exceeding $27 a barrel (initially $20), and reached

$150 billion by the end of 2007, or 10 per cent of GDP. It was initially kept in a rouble-denominated account in the Central Bank but in 2006 was fully converted into foreign currencies and invested in AAA-rated government securities. The attempt to 'sterilise' this money and to set up a counter-cyclical fund was a prescription in all good macro-economic textbooks, but the temptation to draw on the fund for current expenditure was enormous. A World Bank report in April 2006 recommended that Russia should invest the energy windfall in stocks and bonds outside Russia, which would provide a source of income for decades ahead even when the oil price had fallen, and this is what Russia did. As the report noted, 'Future textbooks on Russian history will likely evaluate the economic policies of the current government to a large extent on how effectively it manages the country's growing oil wealth.'[49] In February 2008 the funds were divided into a Reserve Fund to cushion the budget with liquid assets, and a National Welfare Fund (based on the Norwegian Future Generations Fund) to be invested in blue-chip companies.

### External economic assistance

The European Bank for Reconstruction and Development (EBRD) was established in May 1990 to provide risk capital for the transition economies, and over the years supported specific sectors and enterprises in Russia. The main source of economic assistance, however, came from the IMF, while the World Bank invested significantly to restructure strategic industries such as coal mining. External official assistance to Russia has been small in relation to Russia's GNP (0.3 per cent in 1996, and declining thereafter). However, in 1997 one-sixth of the federal budget deficit was financed from external official sources. By 2000, however, this source of deficit coverage had almost dried up.

### Foreign bond issues and initial public offerings (IPOs)

Russia's unexpectedly successful bond issue in November 1996 raised a billion dollars on the global market. Moscow's first international issue since the 1917 Bolshevik revolution was heavily oversubscribed, with bids totalling two billion on an offering that had originally been expected to be pitched at a cautious 300 million dollars. The issue boosted the financial credibility of the country, struggling in its negotiations with the IMF over Moscow's failure to meet its structural adjustment terms on a three year 10.2 billion dollar loan package. It appeared to give Russia a new source of budget finance, and opened the way for Russia's city authorities and major industries to issue their own bonds, raising the infrastructure investment they could not get from the state or on the domestic money market. In the event, the August 1998 crash disappointed hopes that this was the way to unblock the investment logjam in the country, which was holding up industrial and infrastructure development at all levels. In the 2000s Russian companies became ever more active in raising capital on foreign markets, to the point that by 2006 Russia came third in the world through IPOs, raising $18 billion, a long way behind the leader China ($56.6 billion) and America ($34.1 billion) but a growing presence. The market of choice for Russian companies was the London Stock Exchange.

### Trade and enterprise

*Foreign trade*

A presidential decree of 15 November 1991 and later measures decisively broke with the old state monopoly on foreign trade by liberalising foreign economic relations, and regulating flows by tariffs rather than quantitative restrictions. Trade patterns changed dramatically, with a shift away from the former Soviet markets towards Western Europe. By 1994 Russian trade with the EU was worth almost double that with the CIS and by 2006 represented over 50 per cent of its exports. The formation of the Eurasian Economic Community (see Chapter 18) and other integrative initiatives boosted Russia's trade with the former Soviet republics, especially Belarus. Russia's trade surplus in 2000 reached $69 billion, the best performance since Gorbachev's first year in power in 1985. The trade structure, however, was unbalanced, consisting mainly of energy and raw material exports and the import of consumer goods. Every $1 rise in the price of a barrel of oil represents a $1 billion increase in government receipts. High energy and commodity prices, however, are only part of the story. Imports in early 2001 were still 40 per cent lower than pre-August 1998 levels, reflecting the enormous amount of import substitution that had taken place after the devaluation.

The Jackson-Vanik amendment to the 1974 US Trade Act linked US-Soviet trade and economic agreements with civil rights and freedoms in the Soviet Union, in particular the right to emigrate. In practice, the amendment restricted deliveries of some high technology goods to the USSR and later to Russia. The American government favoured lifting the amendment since the mid-1990s but has been blocked by Congress, although suspended annually by presidential action. While Russia enjoys most-favoured nation status, it does not have permanent trading relations, and thus acts as a permanent threat to economic ties, although the symbolic issue is probably far more important. In March 2006 Congress repealed the amendment for Ukraine while leaving it in place for Russia. With Russia's imminent membership of the WTO, the issue of regularising trade relations with Russia became even more pressing.

*World Trade Organisation (WTO) membership*

Russia was the last of the major industrial countries to join what had become by 2007 a 149-member organisation. Russia applied in 1993, but it was only under Putin that serious negotiations started. The debate divided the Russian business community, but Putin was unambiguously of the view that only through membership could Russian industry be modernised. Membership would allow Russian goods non-discriminatory access to foreign markets, allow Russia to use the WTO dispute settlement procedures, provide greater security for investors, and give Russia a voice in international trade negotiations, as well as symbolically marking Russia's entry into yet another international organisation. Certain sectors stood to lose, above all agriculture, light industry and manufacturing, as tariff barriers would have to be brought down. WTO membership would force manufacturing quality to rise if these goods were to find international markets, and even the domestic market would become more competitive as foreign goods gained greater access. Russia's average tariffs were remarkably low by international standards, some 11.7 per cent, and these were to be reduced even further by 2010, including for foreign-made aircraft. Membership would affect certain sectors particularly hard, like the aluminium producers enjoying cheap electricity from the massive hydroelectric schemes in Irkutsk *oblast* (Bratsk). Entry would also open up the financial sector, which in any case had seen ever greater penetration by foreign companies, accounting for about a fifth of Russian banking by 2007.[50] Energy companies favoured WTO entry since it would open up Western markets for them, as it would for the timber industry, occupying fifth place in the country's GDP. Overall it was anticipated that membership would raise GDP by 3 per cent.

Putin pushed ahead with WTO membership, but his ambitious entry date of 2003 proved unfeasible as Russian entry turned into a political football,[51] bringing to the surface a deep current of anti-Russian sentiment in the West. The EU imposed tough conditions on Russian entry, including ratification of the Kyoto Protocol. By early 2006 Russia still had to complete negotiations with Australia, Colombia (the sticking point for these two was sugar) and the US, with the latter demanding that Russia abolish customs duties on aircraft imports, grant access for foreign banks and insurers to operate in Russia directly, and the strengthening of intellectual property rights, notably to prevent of copyright violations (although DVD piracy was greater in both China and Mexico, who were already members of the WTO). The WTO itself was wracked by disputes over farm trade and pharmaceuticals, and the Doha Round, focusing on liberalisation in the service sector, ran into the sands. What appeared to be America's excessively politicised approach in the final stages of the negotiations, linking WTO membership with an ever more bizarre list of concerns ranging from Russian policy to Iran to the price of yogurt in Moscow, alienated Russian officials. Even Putin became irritated, noting at a meeting with entrepreneurs that the US demands were artificial. As he put it in his typically vivid style, Western markets 'are completely limited. They chatter about free trade but in fact everything is closed, and you can't worm your way in there'.[52] Putin's hopes of announcing membership at the G8 summit in July 2006 were disappointed. The shifting criteria prompted a growing backlash and the idea that membership could be postponed indefinitely. The final hurdles in negotiations with America were surmounted and an 800-page agreement was signed on 19 November 2006 that differed little from the agreement that had been ready to sign at the time of the G8 summit.[53] In Washington, as in Moscow and in Brussels earlier, politics appeared to trump economics,[54] and as membership was even further delayed sentiment in Russia moved ever more against joining.

*The fuel and energy complex (FEC, in Russian TEK) and the Dutch disease*

Putin's early years were accompanied by extraordinarily favourable economic circumstances, and Russia was a major beneficiary of the commodity-price boom of the early twenty-first century. Above all, the price of oil remained high, bringing in enormous revenues and endowing Russia with a large trade surplus. The price of oil rose from its 1998 trough of $12 (in part the reason for Russia's crisis that year) to average $61 in 2006. By 2006 Russia's oil and gas industries accounted for 35 per cent of Russia's exports but 55 per cent of export revenues, 40 per cent of gross fixed investment, and through taxes 52 per cent of all revenues to the state treasury, up from 25 per cent in 2003. In June 2006 for the first time Russia extracted more oil than Saudi Arabia.[55] By 2006 energy production represented 16–20 per cent of Russian GDP. Although energy exports played a critical role in Putin's mini 'economic miracle', this should not be exaggerated. As one commentator put it, 'It would be wrong ... to state that the growth in the Russian economy in the last seven years reflects nothing else than the boom in oil prices'.[56] A study by the Rand Corporation suggested that increased energy rents accounted for between one-third and two-fifths of economic growth between 1993 and 2005.[57] The substantial rise in real incomes fuelled a consumption boom that in turn generated economic growth.

The large role played by the export of energy and other natural resources threatened the country with the 'Dutch disease'. The term describes the situation when large trade and current account surpluses cause a country's exchange rate to rise in real terms, either because the price of foreign exchange is forced down by the surplus or because inflows of foreign currency produce inflation. The strong currency and inflationary pressures make the export of other goods uncompetitive, and render imports cheaper than domestically produced goods. Thus what apparently look like healthy trade surpluses strangle domestic manufacturing and foster industrial stagnation. There were elements of this Dutch disease in Russia before the devaluation of 1998, and is an ever-present threat. Putin's attempts to achieve structural reform of the economy, however, combined with fiscal discipline, notably the establishment of the Stabilisation Fund, helped reduce the inflationary pressures. The decision to ease foreign exchange surrender requirements in mid-2001 eased real appreciation pressures, but the rouble exchange rate continued to rise, increasing the competitive pressure on the rouble.

## Information and communications technology

Russia has an obsolescent communications infrastructure, but the Russian internet is one of the fastest growing in the world. Russian software services are among the most technically innovative, based on a traditionally high level of programming culture and habituation to levels of virtual reality.

## Entrepreneurialism and small business

Although Putin encouraged the development of small and medium enterprises (SMEs), and simplified the registration procedures to encourage more start-ups, the weight of the bureaucracy and lack of developed financial services meant that the sector only grew slowly. By 2005 the 979,000 SMEs made up 94 per cent of all businesses in Russia.[58] Over the same period their share of total employment rose from 45 to 47, and market share rose from 40 to 47 per cent.[59] SMEs in Russia account for less of total GDP than is typical for more developed economies. In America 60 per cent of GDP comes from SMEs, in Japan the figure is 74 per cent, but in Russia only 17 per cent comes from the sector.[60] Russia has fewer than a million SMEs, whereas Poland has four times as many with only a quarter of the population. However, Vladimir Kontorovich has argued that low population density across large parts of the country inhibits small business development, and that the density of small businesses around large conurbations like Moscow and St Petersburg follows Western patterns. Nevertheless, the weight of start-up registration formalities, payments for numerous licences and permits, the burden of arbitrary fire and health inspections, and the ever-present fear of the mafia stifled the development of this sphere. However, in many regions the SME is the predominant source of tax revenues, since large business were registered in the capitals or offshore. There is also a very large individual entrepreneur sector operating in grey markets that contribute much to regional economies, notably in the North Caucasus.

*Debureaucratisation*

Under the leadership of Gref, the Ministry of Economic Development and Trade sought to reduce the number of activities requiring licences. The multitude of permissions required to undertake even the most minor of economic activities was one of the main factors inhibiting the development of small businesses and fostering rampant corruption. According to one estimate, up to a tenth of the prices paid by consumers went towards paying for these 'administrative barriers'.[61] Gref had initially hoped to reduce the number of licensed activities from 341 at the federal level (if regional licences are included the number would reach at least 500) to 50. After extensive lobbying, however, this figure rose to 102 activities requiring licensing, and a number of powerful agencies were exempted from the new regulations.

*Free economic zones*

Thirteen free economic zones had been established in Russia by the end of 1991, encompassing some 18 million people, 12 per cent of the total population of Russia.[62] Later the concept of these zones was questioned, in particular because of the money laundering opportunities they provided, and their status was weakened. A new type of economic zone was introduced by Putin, but without some of the extreme tax privileges granted earlier.

## Agriculture

The legacy of the Soviet regime was particularly heavy in agriculture. Since Stalin's decision to launch forced collectivisation in 1929, Soviet agriculture had suffered a 'permanent crisis',[63] and was characterised by George Kennan as the 'Achilles heel' of the Soviet economy.[64] This crisis was marked by low productivity of land and workers, gross wastage, and food shortages that on occasion reached famine levels, as in Ukraine and the Donbass in the early 1930s and again in 1946. Average crop yields 1975–90 were a third of those typical in America, and much of what was grown was squandered since it could neither be harvested nor stored correctly. Some 80 per cent of potatoes spoilt during harvesting, and then over a half of what was left rotted in storage. The USSR lost as much grain as it was later forced to purchase from abroad, 30–40 million tonnes. The lack of good farm machinery meant that 66 per cent of work was carried out by hand. The shortage of housing and socio-cultural facilities in the villages gave rise to an extraordinary internal migration in which 27 million people left the villages for towns in the 20 years from 1965. Thousands of villages lie deserted, and others are populated only by the old, drunk and infirm. The agrarian sector of the economy had been 'treated as a type of internal colony out of which resources were pumped for the development of towns and industry'.[65] Agrarian relations had been refeudalised and a distinctive type of new serfdom emerged.

Agrarian reform was therefore high on the agenda in the transition from communism and is an essential element in the restoration of private property and market forms of economic coordination.[66] However, the concept of agrarian reform is ambiguous, and can mean a simple division of land between different proprietors and users with the emphasis on the development of private ownership (land reform in the narrow sense);

or it can mean the reorganisation of agrarian relations in their entirety affecting not only land ownership but the whole structure of the agro-industrial complex. Both would be long and hard. The international trend is towards larger farms, so a radical shift to small farms in Russia could well reduce its comparative advantages. One of the options for the collective and state farms, commonly practised in Hungary and the Baltic, was to transform themselves into joint stock companies, and for some to be reorganised into something like the Danish and Dutch producers cooperatives. Marketing for smaller concerns could be assisted by processing and distribution cooperatives, popular in both France and Italy. Above all, a land bank like the Credit Agricole in France is essential. Some of this has been achieved, in particular around the big cities where the opportunities are greater to provide dairy and vegetable products for the urban market.

The attempt to transform peasants into farmers, as under Stolypin, faced numerous obstacles, not least of which was the reluctance of the mass of the peasantry to lose the traditional support of the collective farm. Land is but one component of agriculture, and the private farmers, lacking seeds, equipment and credit, faced an uphill struggle for survival. The absence in the 1990s of a land market giving farmers the right to buy and sell inhibited the development of private farms. The Law on the Land passed by the Soviet CPD in March 1990 refused explicitly to endorse the concept of private property in land, but it marked a considerable advance in accepting 'lifelong ownership, with the right of bequeathal' (Article 3) as long as the land was used 'for family smallholdings, personal cultivation' and so on (Article 20).[67] Yeltsin's government went further and committed itself to the break up of the collective and state farms and the creation of a system of small private farms.

Land remained outside the purview of the privatisation programme outlined above. The ban on the resale of land and limitations on land entitlement remained in place until the early 2000s, despite attempts to force the issue by holding a referendum. Only in 2001 was a new and relatively liberal land code adopted by the Duma: despite the desperate warnings of its communist opponents, the new code allowed the buying and selling of no more than 10 per cent of the country's land. By that time, state support for agriculture had fallen some 20-fold since 1991, representing only 1.7 per cent of budgetary expenditure.[68] The Federal Land Registry announced on 3 January 2001 that some 130 million hectares of land in Russia had become privately owned in the previous decade. At that time there were 43 million landowners who owned some 8 per cent of the country's total land surface.[69] Most of these were not private farms but small peasant holdings and cottage (*dacha*) plots. In contrast to the Baltic republics and the Western marches of the Soviet Union, the great mass of Russia had never known a system of consolidated family farming. Before 1929 peasants in effect owned land, but in the form of strips governed by the commune and subject to periodic redistribution. After 1991 the aim was not to reprivatise or reconstitute the family farm system, but to build it from scratch and thus to complete what Stolypin had tried to achieve when he was prime minister between 1906 and his assassination in 1911. By 2005 there were still only 257,400 private farms in Russia, 20 per cent of which were under three hectares, producing 18 per cent of Russia's grain, and only 2.4 per cent of meat and poultry and a meagre 3 per cent of milk.[70] A total of 60.5 million of Russia's 77.5 million hectares devoted to agricultural crops were owned by various types of agricultural organisations, while 5 million belonged to household farms and 12 million to private peasant farms.[71]

The obstacles facing the independent farmer are formidable. Not only do they lack tools, seeds, fodder, breeding stock and so on, but they also face hostility from the collective farms and in many cases from the villagers themselves and there are probably no more than a quarter of a million, mostly in European Russia and particularly in the Volga and North Caucasus regions. Agrarian reform entails a revolution in the countryside, and is resisted not only by the agricultural bureaucracy but also by a rural population accustomed to the security provided by the traditional neo-feudal agrarian system. The most active people had long ago been killed or moved to the cities. Agricultural bureaucrats seized the new opportunities to sell off land for housing and country cottage (dacha) development. The collective and state farms were the centre of local life and the population; pensioners, agrarian specialists, local schools, and much else, all depended on the network of social and economic relations that centred on them. Without the farm village society and economy are in danger of collapse.

## Evaluation of market reform

The notion of shock therapy strictly speaking applies only to the first months of 1992, and thereafter lax money supply undermined economic stabilisation until the tight money supply policy of 1994–5 forced down inflation – and living standards. Slow progress was made in reform of the energy, transport, banking and utility sectors. After a decade of nearly unbroken economic decline (see Table 13.1) Russian GDP per capita fell from 39 per cent of the EU average in 1990 to only one-fifth (22 per cent) in 1997.[72] By 1998 industrial production had fallen to 46 per cent of the 1989 level. By comparison, at that time the Czech Republic was 80.4 of the 1998 level.[73] Russia had fallen out of the top 40 in the table of countries listed by GDP at PPP per capita.[74] Economic reform staggered forward in response to short-term crises and needs.

Despite the tendency to view developments through apocalyptic spectacles, and given the appalling starting conditions and the lack of a coherent reform programme this is understandable, Russia had, nevertheless, made significant advances on the road to a market-based economy. In June 2002 the United States officially declared that Russia was a market economy, in November the EU followed suit, while in October the country was removed from the blacklist of the Financial Action Task Force (FATF), a 29-nation agency established by the OECD in 1989 to fight against money laundering. As one survey put it:

> The role of the state in controlling the economy has been vastly reduced, domestic prices and foreign trade have been extensively liberalised, and monetary and fiscal policy is increasingly moving towards operational standards typical of market economies.[75]

Yeltsin insisted that the great achievement had been the change in popular attitudes, the weakening of the dependency syndrome and an awareness that the transition to the market was now, after so many false starts, for real and that new opportunities existed.[76] Attitudes had indeed changed, and even the CPRF no longer supported a return to the command economy and accepted a role for foreign investment. There has been little public protest, and the level of strikes has never risen above that of 1991. Russia began to be reintegrated into the world economy, becoming a fully fledged member of the G8 group of advanced industrial nations in 2002 and hosting the G8 summit in July 2006. A structural transformation of the economy has taken place, with cuts in defence spending, the rise of a vigorous financial services industry and the growth of the service sector, rising from 33 per cent of GDP in 1990 to over 60 per cent in 2006. The reforms gained a self-sustaining character, having learnt some of the rudiments of the operation of a market economy. Powerful interests are now bound up with the continued marketisation of the economy. The process, however, requires political stability, a clear legal framework and the development of self-regulatory mechanisms to avoid the endless repetition of the scandals and excesses of the early reform years.

The success of economic reform is measured by the stimulation of economic activity, the modernisation of the structure of industry, competitiveness on world markets, rising living standards, a stable and convertible currency, and budgetary stability. The bill for inefficiency should no longer to be paid by the consumer but shifted back to the monopolist industrial structures, forcing them to reduce excessive costs and increase production. Marshall Goldman explains 'why economic reforms in Russia have not worked'. Shock therapy in his view failed to stimulate the supply side of the Russian economy and instead sucked in imports.[77] Economic growth requires an institutional setting that allows 'low-cost transacting' and the enforcement of property and contractual rights and obligations.[78] An effective state in economic terms would collaborate with business elites but would remain relatively insulated from particularistic societal pressures.[79]

Much was made of the unsalubrious 'primary accumulation of capital' phase of early Western capitalism: Russia, it is argued, is only experiencing a delayed version. If this is the case, the best policy would be sound money, minimal and simple laws, straightforward regulation and basic taxes to unfetter Russian entrepreneurialism and allow it to race 'ahead of our Western form of corporate capitalism, which has grown flabby and slow. It is possible to imagine a future of Russian capitalism that asserts itself in the early 21st century as the envy of the world'.[80] However, the law of uneven development would suggest that stages are not repeated but jumped, and while capitalism was new to Russia, it was not the early stages of capitalism that Russia needed. The structure of modern capitalism as a world system has changed radically.

At the turn of the millennium Russia faced the danger of the development of a type of comprador capitalism in which small elites with external links exploit resources to the benefit of foreign capital rather than developing a solid indigenous industrial and commercial structure. Russia had great difficulties in establishing an adequate market environment because of structural and cultural factors. In conditions of high transaction costs in a market plagued by corruption, banditry, political opportunism and fiscal instability, entrepreneurs sought to maximise immediate returns to the detriment of long-term investment. Rather than trading acting as the nucleus and source of capital for a productive market economy, it might end up as the substitute for a genuine market system. Rather than acting as a motor of development, the system was in danger of becoming endemically corrupt in the manner of some Third World countries. Russia finds it very difficult to break out of the cycle of misdevelopment.

Instead of the state falling prey to economic magnates with political ambitions (the so-called oligarchs), under Putin the tables were turned and state took on a more predatory character towards the new economy. The year 2003 saw Yukos and Sibneft try to create an oil company with a combined market capitalisation of $35 billion – from companies that had been privatised by Mikhail Khodorkovsky and Boris Berezovsky eight years earlier for merely $259 million. The new company would have had the world's largest reserves of oil and been fourth in production terms.[81] Although the government initially approved the merger,[82] plans to sell a large stake abroad and fears that the new company would be able to influence government policy led to the dismantlement of Yukos, a process driven by the state-owned Rosneft. The head of Yukos, Khodorkovsky, was put on trial for tax evasion and fraud, and in 2004 was sentenced to eight years in gaol. The state once again firmly entered economic life. In 2006 Gazprom was used to revise the 1994 production-sharing agreement in the Shell-led Sakhalin-2 oil and gas project. In December 2006 a deal was reached whereby Shell's stake fell from 55.5 per cent to 27.5, while the stakes of Shell's Japanese partners Mitsui and Mitsubishi fell to 12.5 and 10 per cent, respectively, while Gazprom's rose to 51 per cent plus one share. In the energy sector the state became ever more prominent, although this was not renationalisation but 'deprivatisation'. In general, however, by 2006 privately owned companies represented 80 per cent of all enterprises, while in the state's share fell to 4 per cent. Over the previous decade employment in private enterprises rose by 41 per cent, while falling by 15 per cent in state enterprises.[83]

The modernisation of Russian industry involves not only the creation of a national market and regional specialisation to overcome the vertical centralisation of Soviet planning, but also overcoming the problem endemic to mature industrial powers, that of old 'rustbelt' industries. Even if Russian economic reforms were successful, the problem of the old coal and steel industries would remain, affecting in particular Kuzbas in Siberia (Kemerovo region) and the Urals. In the short term, regional fragmentation accelerated, exacerbated by the uneven embrace of market relations. Existing regional imbalances in standards of living and incomes have been exacerbated, and prices vary greatly even between neighbouring towns. Land reform was most effective in the South, whereas in the North and the non-Black Earth regions they marked time. The great majority of new businesses and joint enterprises are found in Moscow, St Petersburg, Yekaterinburg and Nizhny Novgorod, whereas traditional industrial areas, quite apart from the political complexion of the regional leadership, find it difficult to adjust to competitive market conditions. An area like Udmurtia, with three-quarters of its workforce employed in military enterprises, cannot survive without state orders and subsidies, and a rapid transition to the market is out of the question.

For most of the 1990s IFIs encouraged Russia to reduce the role of the state in the economy through deregulation and liberalisation, but by the end of the period the opinion had shifted towards a greater appreciation of the role of the state in economic development, including more state intervention in areas like foreign exchange controls and, possibly, protective tariffs. Above all, Western advice had focused on macroeconomic stabilisation, while micro-economic management issues had been neglected. No one was suggesting that the state should return to the role of direct economic manager, and indeed despite the headline figure that 60 per cent of Russia's economy had been transferred into private hands in the 1990s, the state's role in the economy remained large (nearly 100 per cent in agriculture, mining and defence, 60 per cent in banking and 50 per cent in health). While liberalisation was achieved relatively swiftly, the economy still remained heavily monopolised. Half of Russia's companies do not compete with imported wares, with a third competing only with other Russian companies, serving a primarily regional market.[84]

Under Putin attempts were made to incorporate the population into the new system. During his presidency GDP increased by 60 per cent, and incomes almost doubled, with wages growing by an average annual 13 per cent in real terms from 2002. However, this could not disguise the growing gap between rich and poor, with 53 of the wealthiest magnates concentrating over $400 billion of capital assets in their hands, about a third of GDP.[85] The privatisations of the 1990s had not been fully legitimated, and Russian capitalism retained a brittle quality that may not withstand external or domestic shocks. The highly concentrated nature of the Russian economy had worsened: if in 2000 1,200 companies produced 80 per cent of GDP, by 2006 fewer than 500 were producing the same amount.[86]

In his last work Mancur Olson stressed the role played by the state in the development of markets, identifying what he called 'market-augmenting governments'.[87] In Russia in the 1990s there was, to put it mildly, tension between market-augmentation and economic destruction. By the end of Yeltsin's presidency Russia had a functioning market economy, but a heavily distorted and criminalised one. Putin's administration sought to reconcile market development with state reassertion to achieve economic growth, but there was the danger that the threat of state capture would give way to business capture by a predatory state. Putin believed in an activist state in economic affairs, but the model of state-directed development accompanied by the advancement of 'national champions' was reminiscent of an earlier model of economic life before the era of globalisation and intense international economic integration and competition. As so often in Russia, the country moved from one extreme to another. It would be up to Putin's successor to find the optimum balance between market forces and the state.

# 14 Society and social movements

> No society can surely be flourishing and happy, of which the far greater part of the members are poor and miserable.
>
> (Adam Smith)[1]

Democracy is as much a social and cultural project as a political one: it cannot be built in the air, in the minds of intellectuals and politicians, but needs to be rooted in society itself. As Solzhenitsyn put it: 'Stolypin believed that it is impossible to create a state governed by laws without first having an independent citizen: social structure precedes any political programme and is a more fundamental entity.'[2] After 74 years of the Soviet regime the social basis for democracy in Russia was at best ambiguous. As Sergei Shakhrai, the state legal adviser at the time, put it:

> We have no middle class of property owners upon which to build a stable government. If I have something to lose: my work, my apartment, my family, my dacha, my car, my savings, then I will be a support for the state and of a stable social stratum. Unfortunately, our society has not progressed to that stage yet.[3]

The basic principle of the reformers was, to quote Solzhenitsyn again, that 'there can be no independent citizen without private property'.[4] As we saw in the previous chapter, private property has been established in Russia, however tenuous its legal guarantees, but the citizen of democratic Russia (whose views we shall examine in the next chapter) has had a decidedly tough time since 1991.

## Social structure and dynamics

In Russia democracy came before the development of a bourgeoisie, and as Barrington Moore long ago observed, 'No bourgeois, no democracy.'[5] The existence of a substantial middle class is no guarantee of democracy, as Germany discovered in the inter-war years, but to date there has been no liberal democracy without a capitalist social structure. A traumatised and unequal society jeopardised the building of democracy in Russia, while the weakness of social organisations, like trade unions and professional bodies, undermined political pluralism. While the concept of transition refers properly to political change, Russia entered a period of accelerated social transformation affecting all aspects of class and elite relations, the family and social groups. The marketisation of social relations undermined not only the achievements, however rudimentary, of the Soviet welfare state, but also challenged the whole network of existing social relations and cultural values.

## *Demography*

Russia suffers from a severe demographic crisis, with the population declining by about 700,000 a year. Between 1991 and 2007 Russia's population fell by 5.7 million from 148 to 142.3 million on 1 May 2007 (see Table 14.1), accompanied by a 6 million fall in the number of children. If present tends continue, projections suggest that Russia's population will fall to 133 million by 2015 and to only 85 million in 2050. While Russia may be the world's largest country in terms of area, it holds only seventh place in terms of population and if the estimate for 2015 is correct, Russia will fall to the world's fifteenth most populous state.[6] The decline has not only economic but also security implications, threatening the country's ability to maintain a large conscript army and its comparative geopolitical pre-eminence. The demographic situation in Ukraine and Belarus is comparable to Russia's whereas in Central Asia and the South Caucasus, in particular in Kazakhstan and Turkmenistan, the birth rate is booming.

Natural population increase has been falling for at least a quarter of a century, reflecting the pattern common to most developed industrial societies where planned parenting

*Table 14.1* Resident population of USSR and Russia (urban/rural)

| Year | Total population (million) | Of whom | | | |
|---|---|---|---|---|---|
| | | Urban | | Rural | |
| | | Million | % | Million | % |
| *USSR* | | | | | |
| 1979 | 262.4 | 162.9 | 62 | 99.5 | 38 |
| 1989 | 286.7 | 189.2 | 66 | 97.5 | 34 |
| *Russia* | | | | | |
| 1979 | 137.4 | 94.9 | 69 | 42.5 | 31 |
| 1989 | 147.0 | 108.0 | 73 | 39.0 | 27 |
| 1990 | 148.0 | 109.2 | 74 | 38.8 | 26 |
| 1993 | 148.6 | 108.7 | 73 | 39.9 | 27 |
| 1996 | 148.3 | 108.3 | 73 | 40.0 | 27 |
| 2001 | 146.3 | 107.1 | 73 | 39.2 | 27 |
| 2002 | 145.6 | 106.7 | 73 | 38.9 | 27 |
| 2003 | 145.0 | 106.3 | 73 | 38.7 | 27 |
| 2004 | 144.2 | 105.8 | 73 | 38.4 | 27 |
| 2005 | 143.5 | 104.7 | 73 | 38.8 | 27 |
| 2006 | 142.8 | 104.1 | 73 | 38.7 | 27 |
| 2007 (1 May) | 142.3 | | | | |

*Source*: *Russia in Figures: 2006* (Moscow, Rosstat, 2006), p. 72. Data unless specified is for 1 January.

*Note*: Data for 1993, 1996, 2001 and 2002 have been adjusted in the light of the 2002 census.

*Table 14.2* Births, deaths and natural movement of Russian population

| Year | Births | Deaths | Natural change | Infant deaths under 1 year old | |
|------|--------|--------|----------------|--------|--------|
| | | | | '000 | Per 1,000 live births |
| 1960 | 2,782,000 | 886,000 | 1,896,000 | — | — |
| 1970 | 1,904,000 | 1,131,000 | 773,000 | — | — |
| 1980 | 2,203,000 | 1,526,000 | 677,000 | — | — |
| 1985 | 2,375,000 | 1,625,000 | 750,000 | — | — |
| 1990 | 1,989,000 | 1,656,000 | 333,000 | — | — |
| 1992 | 1,587,600 | 1,807,400 | −219,800 | 29.2 | 18.0 |
| 1993 | 1,379,000 | 2,129,300 | −750,300 | — | — |
| 1994 | 1,408,200 | 2,301,400 | −893,200 | — | — |
| 1995 | 1,363,800 | 2,203,800 | −840,000 | 24.8 | 18.1 |
| 1996 | 1,304,600 | 2,082,200 | −777,600 | — | — |
| 1997 | 1,259,900 | 2,015,800 | −755,900 | — | — |
| 1998 | 1,283,300 | 1,988,700 | −705,400 | — | — |
| 1999 | 1,215,800 | 2,140,300 | −924,500 | — | — |
| 2000 | 1,266,800 | 2,225,300 | −958,500 | 19.3 | 15.3 |
| 2001 | 1,311,600 | 2,254,900 | −943,300 | 19.1 | 14.6 |
| 2002 | 1,397,000 | 2,332,300 | −935,300 | 18.4 | 13.3 |
| 2003 | 1,477,300 | 2,365,800 | −888,500 | 18.1 | 12.4 |
| 2004 | 1,502,500 | 2,295,400 | −792,900 | 17.3 | 11.6 |
| 2005 | 1,457,400 | 2,303,900 | −846,500 | 16.1 | 11.0 |

*Sources*: *Naselenie SSSR, 1988* (Moscow, 1989), p. 40; *Demograficheskii ezhegodnik 1991* (Moscow, Goskomstat, 1992), p. 55; *Rossiya v tsifrakh* (Moscow, Goskomstat, 2000), p. 70; *Russia in Figures: 2006* (Moscow, Rosstat, 2006), pp. 28, 75.

and affluence has seen a dramatic decrease in the size of families. In 1960 the RSFSR had seen natural population growth of 2 million,[7] in 1985 749,500, whereas in 1992, for the first time since the war, there was a natural population decline as deaths outnumbered births by 190,000 (Table 14.2).[8] In 1994 the population declined by 920,000,[9] a fall that was offset by in-migration from the former Soviet republics (see below), but the total population still fell by 124,000. In Russia the fall in the number of women in the primary childbearing age group, the lack of confidence in the future, increased levels of stress in a changing society and declining living standards provoked a sharp decrease in the fertility rate (the average number of children born to a woman between the ages of 15 and 50), falling from around two between the 1960s and the late 1980s to 1.17 in 2001, well below the replacement level of 2.14.[10] The average family has not two but one child, thus falling below the level of natural population replacement. Russia still has a very high abortion rate (up to half of all pregnancies end in termination), rendering up to one-third of Russia women infertile. Russia's birth rate is about 9.95 per 1,000 people, while in the United States it is 14 per 1,000 but only 8.3 per 1,000 in Germany.

The decreasing birth rate, falling by 13 per cent in 1992 alone, was accompanied by a dramatic rise in the mortality rate; the death rate from unnatural causes alone rose in that year by 8 per cent.[11] In 2000, deaths exceeded births by 930,000, accompanied by declining in-migration. By 2007 the death rate reached 14.65 per 1,000 people, compared to 8.2 in the US and 10.6 in Germany. The infant mortality rate (for children up to the age of one) peaked at 19.9 per 1000 in 1993, much higher than the average for

*Table 14.3* Life expectancy at birth

|      | Total population | Males | Females |
|------|------------------|-------|---------|
| 1992 | 67.8 | 61.9 | 73.7 |
| 1995 | 64.5 | 58.1 | 71.6 |
| 2000 | 65.3 | 59.0 | 72.3 |
| 2001 | 65.2 | 58.9 | 72.2 |
| 2002 | 65.0 | 58.7 | 71.9 |
| 2003 | 64.9 | 58.6 | 71.8 |
| 2004 | 65.3 | 58.9 | 72.3 |

*Source*: *Russia in Figures: 2006* (Moscow, Rosstat, 2006), p. 76.

developed countries.[12] By 2006 the infant mortality rate had fallen to 15 per 1,000 live births, but this compares to just 6.5 in the US, and just 4.1 in Germany.[13] Infant mortality is highest in Ingushetia, with 34.7 children dying before the age of one, and lowest in Samara *oblast* with 10.1 dying in that period.[14] These figures provoked national-patriots to argue that Russia was victim of planned genocide, and that democracy was no more than a Western plot to undermine the genetic basis for Russian life.[15] By 2000 the birth rate had begun to rise for the first time in many years, to 8.7 per 1,000, compared to 8.4 in 1999.[16] This was further encouraged by a range of measures announced by Putin in his annual address to the Federal Assembly in May 2006 designed to encourage women to have larger families. Monetary payments increased exponentially with every child born.

The starkest symptom of the social crisis was the declining life expectancy of Soviet men, ranked 54th out of 56 countries that supplied data in 1989. Average male life expectancy fell from the peak of 65 in 1986[17] to the trough of 57.6 in 1994,[18] to stabilise at 58.7 by 2007, compared to 76.6 in the euro area (see Table 14.3). The State Statistics Committee in 2001 forecasted that if current trends continue only 58 per cent of men aged 16 at that time will reach 60. The committee's experts noted that this was little better than life expectancy in 1897 when 56 per cent were expected to reach 60. Russian life expectancy had peaked in 1985–6 at 64.91 for men and 74.55 for women.[19] Female life expectancy compared to men was higher but had also declined from 75 in 1986 to 71.2 in 1994 rising to 71.8 by 2007, compared to 82.8 in the euro area. Average life expectancy in Russia in 1992 was 68, falling to 64 in 1994 before rising slightly to 65 by 2007 compared to 75.5 in America (72 for men and 69 for women). There is a marked variation within Russia, with life expectancy in rural areas in general lower, and with regional disparities, with the situation worst in the Far East and Eastern Siberia, and best in the North Caucasus and the Volga region. Life expectancy in Moscow (71) and the autonomous districts in Tyumen *oblast* (68) were higher than the national average of 65, whereas in the least developed regions of Tyva it was 56, and in Chita, Amur and Pskov *oblasts* it was (59–60). There are also differences between the former Soviet republics, with the highest life expectancy in Armenia at 68 years for urban dwellers, and the lowest in Turkmenistan at 61.

There are many reasons for high Russian male mortality rates, ranging from workplace and traffic accidents, the prevalence of heart disease, a high suicide rate (rising from 39,150 in 1990 to 61,886 in 1994),[20] and violent deaths (rising from 16,000 to 26,000 over the same period). In 1999 alone 580,000 Russians died of non-natural causes (accidents, poisonings, murder and suicide), 27 per cent of all deaths. High rates of tobacco addiction and the instability of family structures play their part. One of the main factors, however, is alcohol abuse, with *per capita* consumption in Russia for the first time exceeding that of France in 1993. Between 1986 and 2007 alcohol consumption of the population tripled, rising from 5 to an astonishing 15.2 litres (26 pints) of pure alcohol per capita for the over 15s.[21] By 2005 Russia had 2.3 million registered alcoholics, and every third death is attributable in one way or another to alcohol abuse.[22] Gorbachev's anti-alcohol campaign had dramatically misfired, encouraging the production of low-grade moonshine liquor (*samogon*), and the abolition of the centuries-old state monopoly on vodka production in 1992 (as part of Russia's commitment to economic liberalisation) saw prices fall dramatically.[23] Since 1995 there have been numerous attempts to restore the vodka monopoly, both for fiscal and health reasons. The deeper causes of Russia's alcohol dependence, however, still have to be treated, with some arguing that it was a response to the authoritarianism of society and its profound inequalities, while others, like the sociologist Igor Bestuzhev-Lada, insisting that the system itself was responsible for alcoholism, and that the only cure was the democratisation of society and the development of a citizenry responsible for its own actions.[24]

The higher death rate for men led to a sharp gender imbalance, with 10.3 million more women than men in Russia's population of 143.5 million by 1 January 2005.[25] The age structure was also unbalanced, with the proportion of the population above working age rising from 29.1 per cent in 1993 to 38 per cent by 2001. There are 38.2 million pensioners in Russia today (26.6 per cent of the population), but many are forced to continue to work. Plans to raise the retirement age, currently 60 years for men and 55 for women, have been delayed since such a small proportion of men survive to pension age. For every 1,000 people of working age, there are 770 non-working (pensioners and children under 16). The nearly two-fifths of Russia's population who are pensioners are an important factor in electoral politics, tending to be more keen on casting their votes on election day and allegedly taking a more conservative approach than the rest of the population, which in Russian conditions means voting communist. As the protests against the monetisation of welfare benefits in early 2005 showed, if Russia were to have a revolution it would be a 'grey' rather than an 'orange' one.

### Occupational and class structure

While the events of August 1991 were dramatic and came to symbolise the fall of the old regime, the Soviet system had already undergone a long decay since at least the death of Stalin in 1953. The old authority system underwent significant evolution, and at the same time an embryonic new pattern of social relations began to emerge. The protracted degeneration of the old system became a factor in shaping the new order as features like patronage networks, corruption and clientelism became endemic. The long transition allowed morbid systems of social irresponsibility to become firmly lodged in the body social as a pseudo-civil society regulated not by law but by the anti-law of customary practices took shape. The emergence of powerful criminal networks in the lee of decaying Party authority, the evolution of the political *nomenklatura* appointments mechanism into a corrupt social phenomenon, the development of a shadow economy

*Table 14.4* Employment structure in 1989

| Occupation | Millions | % |
|---|---|---|
| Total employed | 70.0 | 100 |
| *Of whom*: | | |
| Workers | 45.0 | 64.3 |
| Employees | 21.0 | 30.0 |
| Collective farmers | 4.0 | 5.71 |

Source: *RSFSR v tsifrakh v 1989g.* (Moscow, Finansy i statistika, 1990), p. 21.

preyed on by protection rackets and living off the inefficiencies of the state economy, all this and more shaped the social subject of the transition.

The 74 years of the Soviet regime had churned society as if it had gone through a concrete mixer. Tatyana Zaslavskaya argued that instead of the social structure having become simpler, it had in fact become more complex than comparable capitalist societies. Groups, classes, elites, workers, peasants, and indeed whole peoples, were displaced, mixed up and thrown down. Instead of the organic growth of social complexity and differentiation over a more or less steady pattern of development, the USSR had telescoped decades of modernisation (and an ideologically driven pattern of mismodernisation at that) into just a few years. The alleged *lumpenisation* of the Soviet population was accompanied by a type of negative egalitarianism in which society was levelled down to the lowest common denominator, distinguished not by equality of opportunity but by an equality in poverty impatient of complex solutions.[26] Social ties today show great signs of instability; the very fabric of society has been torn and the process of healing will take decades.

The old regime recognised three great groups in society depending on their relationship to property and the means of production: the two classes of workers and peasants and the stratum of the intelligentsia. The working class had grown from some 1.7 million in Soviet Russia in 1920 to 45 million in 1989 (see Table 14.4). Stalinist industrialisation created a massive working class and the emergence of a Soviet technical intelligentsia, while collectivisation destroyed the peasantry as a class and encouraged a mass exodus to urban areas. From the 1950s to the 1970s, an average each year of some 1.7 million people fled the devastated countryside to seek new opportunities in towns.[27] In the early 1990s, 26 per cent of the population lived in rural areas, a proportion that rose as life in the cities became tougher for certain sections of the population, above all pensioners. By 1989 out of a total Soviet population of 284.5 million there were 117.24 million (41.21 per cent) workers and employees, 19 per cent of whom were employed in agriculture and forestry.[28]

Russia began its post-communist journey with a higher proportion of its workforce in state employment than in most other republics. Post-communist Russia underwent a rapid change in occupational structure (Table 14.5). The USSR had been an 'over-industrialised' economy, and from 1991 the proportion of GDP coming from the production of goods fell from 60 to 36 per cent in 2006, while the contribution of the service sector, including trade and transport, rose to 59 per cent, with 5 per cent of GDP still coming from agriculture. Total employment in the same period fell from 72 million to 64.5 million, with the fall sharpest in the industrial sector, falling a third

*Table 14.5* Economically active population, unemployment and employment type

|  | 1992 | 1995 | 2000 | 2002 | 2004 | 2005 |
|---|---|---|---|---|---|---|
| Economically active population million (%) | 75.06 (100) | 70.74 (100) | 72.33 (100) | 72.42 (100) | 72.91 (100) | 73.81 (100) |
| *Of which:* employed in economy | 71.17 (94.8) | 64.05 (90.5) | 65.28 (90.2) | 66.27 (91.5) | 67.13 (92.2) | 68.60 (92.1) |
| *Of which:* unemployed | 3.89 (5.2) | 6.68 (9.5) | 7.06 (9.8) | 6.15 (8.5) | 5.77 (7.9) | 5.21 (7.1) |
| Total employed, million (%) | 72.07 (100) | 66.41 (100) | 64.33 (100) | 65.36 (100) | 66.41 (100) | 66.94 (100) |
| State and municipal | 49.66 (68.9) | 27.94 (42.1) | 24.36 (37.9) | 24.19 (37.0) | 23.58 (35.5) | 23.19 (34.6) |
| Private | 14.05 (19.5) | 22.84 (34.4) | 29.66 (46.1) | 32.50 (49.7) | 3.44 (51.8) | 35.74 (53.4) |
| Social organisations | 0.58 (0.8) | 0.47 (0.7) | 0.53 (0.8) | 0.50 (0.8) | 0.44 (0.7) | 0.44 (0.7) |
| Mixed Russian (without foreign participation) | 7.58 (10.5) | 14.73 (22.2) | 8.05 (12.5) | 6.15 (9.4) | 5.63 (8.5) | 5.22 (7.8) |
| Mixed with joint Russian and foreign participation, and foreign | 0.19 (0.3) | 0.43 (0.6) | 1.73 (2.7) | 2.02 (3.1) | 2.34 (3.5) | 2.34 (3.5) |

Source: *Russia in Figures: 2006* (Moscow, Rosstat, 2006), pp. 83, 82.

from 21 to 14 million. At the same time, a middle class appeared to have emerged. Some 20–5 per cent of Russians have three of the five characteristics of being middle class: a certain income level, ownership of some property, some savings, a certain educational level, and a perception that they were 'successful and worthy members of society'.[29] Nearly half of the middle class works in the public sector. In Russia the middle class remains primarily an income category and not yet a hegemonic cultural force that could demand the rule of law and democratic governance.[30]

## Migration and refugees

The late twentieth century has been dubbed 'the age of migration', and the Soviet and post-Soviet experience confirms the view that processes of global change have stimulated a new wave of population displacement.[31] Population movement in the post-Soviet area is marked by the following processes.[32]

### Returnees

People returning to their homelands from which they had been expelled by Stalin. The category of returnees includes Germans expelled from the Volga at the beginning of the

Second World War, Crimean Tatars expelled to Central Asia, and a number of North Caucasian peoples, including the 23,000 Meskhetian Turks now trying to re-establish themselves in Krasnodar *krai*. In their once and future home regions there were few jobs or houses for them, registration laws applied in a heavy-handed manner, and the new populations typically were hostile. Since 2004 about 11,000 have left the region to settle abroad.

## Ingathering

A broad phenomenon of 'ingathering', the consolidation of ethnic and national groups, has been under way since the fall of communism. Many Ukrainians and Belarusians left Russia to help rebuild their own countries, while Kazakhs left the war in Tajikistan to return to their homeland. However much the idea is now denigrated, in a feeble and distorted form the Soviet Union had created a new community of peoples, where a Georgian could freely study in Moscow and then go to work in Kiev, and the failure of the CIS to establish common citizenship forced every ethnic group back into the laager of national myth-making and imagined identities.[33] The process was accelerated in the case of Georgians by the punitive measures imposed on them in Russia as a result of deteriorating relations with the Russophobic regime led by Mikheil Saakashvili in Tbilisi. In 2006 over 6,000 Georgians who had long been resident in Russia were forced to leave. At the same time, as a result of conflicts and under-development, ethnic Russians left the North Caucasus. The majority of ethnic Russians left Chechnya in the early 1990s, and overall the number of ethnic Russians in the region fell from 1.36 million in 1989 to 950,000 in 2002, and the number has fallen since then.[34]

## Russian out-migration

Since the 1970s there had been a drift of Russians away from the other Soviet republics, and in the 1990s this accelerated, peaking in 1994.[35] In that decade over 8 million people moved to the RF from the former Soviet republics, significantly reducing the total of 25 million Russians who found themselves outside Russia in 1991. Before the disintegration of the USSR Russians occupied half of the top positions in agencies and ministries in Kazakhstan, but the proportion soon fell dramatically as Russians left and the new class of officialdom took on a Kazakh face. According to incomplete official figures, 600,000 Russians moved to Russia in 1992, 560,000 in 1993 and over 700,000 in 1995. Anti-Sovietism had often tended to take the form of anti-Russianism, and now this inglorious tradition took on a new intensity. Russians in Uzbekistan, for example, were now categorised as *pieds noirs* even though many had lived there for generations. The structure of the old relationship between the metropolis and the periphery meant that few had learnt Uzbek; Russian had been the language of higher schools, factories and top level politics. Russians made up a growing number of internal migrants between the former union republics. By late 1992 half the Russians of Tajikistan had left, together with a third from Azerbaijan. Some three million ethnic Russians had left the former Soviet republics since 1991, one of the largest migratory movements since the Second World War. While there was undoubtedly some discrimination against them, a survey by the Russian

Minorities Research Centre found that only 9 per cent of ethnic Russians abroad expressed concern about their ethnic rights. Economic worries appeared to be a far more potent source of concern.[36] The CIS agreement on pensions provoked an estimated migration of two million people to Russia to take advantage of the more generous benefits.[37]

In the mid-1990s it was estimated that some 10 out of the 25 million Russians abroad wished to migrate to Russia, but were prevented by lack of funds.[38] A new wave of out-migration affected Turkmenistan in the early 2000s, as the country's maverick leader, Niyazov, refused to accept Russian educational qualifications. Nowhere are Russians and Russian speakers recognised as ethnic minorities. The flow, however, declined and in 2000 it compensated by only 17 per cent the decline in Russia's population from excess deaths over births, a proportion that had fallen to 6.3 per cent in the first four months of 2001, reflecting the lowest in-migration for the period 1992 to 2000. Russian in-migration into Russia, which in 2000 numbered 200,000, is the main reason why Russia's overall population had only declined by 2 per cent since the fall of communism. For the donor countries, however, the natural demographic losses were compounded by this out-migration. Kazakhstan suffered the most, losing about a million Russians since independence (about 8 per cent of its population). The migrants tended to be more urban and better educated, and now the rural part in Kazakhstan's 14 million population is a greater proportion of the total than it was in 1991. Belarus was the least affected by migration, where Slavs are a larger majority than in Russia itself, and the population remained stable at about 10 million. Ukraine's population had fallen about 5 per cent since independence: in 2000 deaths outnumbered births by two to one accompanied, as in Russia, by a declining birth rate.

In a speech in Novosibirsk on 17 November 2000 Putin had argued that Russia's demographic shortfall could be compensated by labour immigration from the former USSR. He had in mind some of the 20 million-odd ethnic Russians in the CIS and the Baltic states and not non-Slavic ethnic groups, above all 'persons of Caucasian nationality'. By inviting Russians in neighbouring states to migrate to Russia the economic and military security of those states was challenged and their own state-building endeavours undermined. Russia's ability to manage in-migration in any case was questionable, lacking housing and jobs for those already resident. The speech did, however, signal a shift in emphasis as Russia's 'compatriots' in the former Soviet states were now perceived less as a political lever against those states than as an economic resource for Russia, a theme to which Putin returned on numerous occasions later.

### Economic migration

Economic migration, including a drift from the harsh Siberian North to more temperate climes, has characterised the post-communist era. Economic migration took place both within countries and between them in the former Soviet space. In Russia alone by mid-1994 there were some two million economic migrants forced to move by lack of work and the decline of areas of marginal economic activity. In the six months to May 1994 alone some 500–600,000 people moved out of the Russian Far North and the Far East,[39] and between 1992 and 1999 the population of the Far East declined by 10.9 per cent, with Chukotka *okrug* alone registering a fall of 48 per cent. A growing number of foreigners arrived to work in Russia; 213,000 alone in 2000.

*Illegal immigrants*

By 2001 there were an estimated 1.5 million illegal immigrants in Russia.[40] The bulk of these were Chinese in the Far East, with a large number of Vietnamese in various urban centres across the country.

*Urban/rural drift*

We have noted above that the long-term migration from rural areas to the towns has now moved in reverse as city dwellers now head for the countryside.

*Refugees and internally displaced persons (IDPs)*

Refugees became a mass phenomenon in the former USSR, with numbers rising from an estimated 422,000 in 1988 to some two million by 1994 from the former Soviet republics, mainly from areas of inter-ethnic conflict,[41] most of whom settled in South European Russia (see Table 14.6). The category of those fleeing actual or implied threats of war and other catastrophes includes so-called ecological refugees, in particular those fleeing the contaminated areas around Chernobyl. Armenians and Azerbaijanis fled the other's territory, and people sought to escape the wars in South Ossetia, Abkhazia, Transdniester and Central Asia. By February 1992 there were officially 220,000 refugees (overwhelmingly Russians) in Russia, with some 15 per cent of the 294,000 ethnic Russians and 60,000 Russian speakers registered by the 1989 census as living in Chechnya leaving in the year after the coup,[42] and most of the rest soon after, to leave only 70,000 by the time of the 2003 census. Russians also left neighbouring Dagestan, with their proportion in the total population falling from 9.21 per cent in 1989 to 5.6 per cent in January 2001.[43] The number of Russian refugees from the other republics reached 460,000 by September 1992, with 50,000 arriving in August alone as Russians fled the fighting in Abkhazia, while some 30,000 of the total came from Kazakhstan and 13,000 from Kyrgyzstan.[44] By May 1994 there were 860,000 registered refugees in Russia.[45] Attempts by Russia to sign treaties with other republics regulating the status of Russians were resisted. There were few arrangements for the payment of compensation and so, for example, the Russians who left in a mass exodus from Baku in 1991 received

*Table 14.6* Refugees and forced resettlers

|  | *Total* |
|---|---|
| 1995 | 271,977 |
| 2000 | 59,196 |
| 2002 | 20,504 |
| 2003 | 4,726 |
| 2004 | 4,291 |
| 2005 | 8,914 |
| Total registered up to 1 Jan. 2006 | 168,711 |
|  | Of which |
|  | 168,253 resettlers since 1 July 1992 |
|  | 458 refugees since 20 March 1993 |

*Source: Russia in Figures: 2006* (Moscow, Rosstat, 2006), p. 79.

nothing from the Azerbaijani authorities. As the conflict in Chechnya gathered pace from the early 1990s almost the entire Russian, Armenian and Jewish communities, which had been long established there, were forced to leave. In late 2006 there were still 20,070 IDPs from Chechnya in temporary settlements in Ingushetia, and another 30,000 elsewhere, with an estimated 200,000 Chechens living as IDPs within Chechnya itself.

Yeltsin had promised refuge for all Russians who wanted to live in Russia, but in fact Russia was in no position to offer jobs, homes or even passports to the Russians who suddenly found themselves 'abroad'. Some 9.5 million of Russia's own long-term residents were waiting for housing. The status of 'refugee' in Russia remained ambiguous. Only the disabled, pensioners, women and children received food coupons and housing while most refugees were treated as strangers in their own land. They increasingly encountered the hostility of local populations, in particular Cossacks, in the struggle for scarce housing, food and jobs.

*Emigration out of the former USSR altogether*

The constitution guarantees Russians the right to emigrate, and large numbers have taken advantage of this, but not as many as was once feared. A total of 2.5 million emigrated from the Soviet Union in the four decades after the war, but in 1987–90 alone over a million left.[46] Soviet emigration rose from 39,000 in 1987 to almost 500,000 in 1990, and in 1991 the figure reached 700,000. A study in March 1991, however, found that 75 per cent of the population had no intention of emigrating, and of the rest 15 per cent thought in terms of a short visit abroad and only 2 per cent firmly considered emigration, which, although a relatively large proportion of the population, in the circumstances is not that high.[47] Apart from Jews and Germans, Russians did not leave in great numbers, and in fact Russia was a net population gainer (Table 14.7). The liberal foreign travel law (initially passed for the USSR on 20 May 1991 and then adopted by Russia) came into effect on 1 January 1993 and entitled all Russian citizens to a foreign passport, provided they were not on trial, engaged in military service or privy to state secrets. The new passports were valid for a fixed term, rather than the old documents which necessitated a fresh exit visa for each trip. Despite fears about a flood of Russian economic migrants, the expected mass tide of emigration did not take place.

*Table 14.7* International migration

| | Arrivals to Russia | | | Departures from Russia | | |
|---|---|---|---|---|---|---|
| | *Total* | *Of which from CIS* | *From other countries* | *Total* | *Of which to CIS* | *To other countries* |
| 1997 | 597,651 | 571,903 | 25,748 | 232,987 | 146,961 | 86,026 |
| 2000 | 359,330 | 346,774 | 12,556 | 145,720 | 82,312 | 64,408 |
| 2001 | 193,450 | 183,650 | 9,800 | 121,166 | 61,570 | 59,596 |
| 2002 | 184,612 | 175,068 | 9,544 | 106,685 | 52,099 | 54,586 |
| 2003 | 129,144 | 119,661 | 9,483 | 94,018 | 46,081 | 47,937 |
| 2004 | 119,157 | 110,374 | 8,783 | 79,795 | 37,017 | 42,778 |
| 2005 | 177,230 | 168,598 | 8,632 | 69,798 | 36,109 | 33,689 |

*Source: Russia in Figures: 2006* (Moscow, Rosstat, 2006), pp. 77–8.

Most former Soviet bloc countries in Eastern Europe had no visa requirements (until membership of the EU forced them to put up barriers) but tightened restrictions against the hundreds of thousands of Russians who came officially on tourist visits but failed to leave on time.

*Asylum*

In 2005, 21,633 appeals were lodged to gain asylum in foreign countries, a large proportion of them people escaping Chechnya to seek refugee status elsewhere. In 2006, the flow decreased to just over half this number, reflecting relative stabilisation in Chechnya. Russia itself was not a generous granter of asylum status, and often made it difficult for those seeking refuge to gain access to the Federal Migration Service. In 2005, just under 4,000 people were granted asylum, and, in 2006, this fell to little over 3,000. The Russian government, however, tended to avoid *refoulement*, the return of people to countries where they feared persecution. Although the government worked with the International Organisation for Migration (IOM) and the UNHCR to ensure compliance with international norms, the status of asylum seekers and refugees in Russia was a deeply uncomfortable one.

## Welfare and incomes

In the post-communist-era budgetary constraints forced a retreat of the welfare state, but the basic infrastructure remained remarkably unchanged and during Putin's second term welfare spending increased sharply. In the 1990s there had been a sharp debate over the degree to which the inevitable hardship resulting from economic reform should be compensated: how generous should the system of social provision be to protect the weaker sectors of society? At one extreme were the neo-liberals, who accepted that economic reforms would inevitably entail a high social cost. They advocated complete deregulation and minimal controls on the free market and condemned rationing systems as distorting the operation of the market. On the other side, the left insisted that full-scale free market economic policies could not be applied to Russia in its fragile state. In the event, a middle course was adopted, seeking to maintain a minimum threshold of welfare benefits but imposed cuts in the general level of social provision. Repeated promises to inject a 'greater social content' into the reforms were defeated by the equally harsh imperative of financial stabilisation.

Only under Putin were there attempts to ensure the payment of wages and pensions on time. The introduction in 2005 of the four national projects injected major funds into health, education, agriculture and housing. The outcome of over a decade of post-communist development was a mixed one, and while certain groups saw their working conditions and living conditions deteriorate, for some professional groups standards improved.[48] In terms of the United Nations' Index of Human Potential, Russia by 2001 had put an end to its long decline and moved up from 62nd to 55th place,[49] a trend confirmed by the strong improvement registered by the Human Development report on Russia issued by the United Nations Development Programme in 2007.[50] The report noted that only about a quarter of the country's population lived in regions with an HDI above the national average, although it noted that poverty had halved since economic growth had been restored.

## Health

Soviet healthcare had always been lamentably under-funded, despite attempts during *perestroika* to improve the situation. The USSR spent only about 3.6 per cent of its GNP on healthcare, half that of most West European countries and a third of the sum spent in the United States. The reforms undermined already low wages, and the provision of medicines and equipment became even more sporadic. Following the fall of communism, funds devoted to health fell to 1.8 per cent of the Russian budget in 1994, and traditional shortfalls and inequalities in the standard of provision were exacerbated.[51] Standard facilities had never been very high but now deteriorated further, while staff were demoralised by low pay and lack of resources and medicines. For all but the richest, standards of healthcare fell sharply. The health infrastructure began to revive in the 2000s. In 2007, Russia had 4.3 doctors per 1,000 people, compared to 3.9 in the euro area.

Cases of infectious diseases increased sharply in the early reform years, with tuberculosis once again prevalent in the majority of Russia's regions. The breakdown of mass immunisation allowed diptheria to return, while the spread of cholera was facilitated by antiquated water and sewage systems. According to official statistics, the number of drug addicts rose 12-fold following the collapse of the USSR, with 300,000 registered addicts in 2006. International experience suggests that the real number is ten times the number registered, which in Russia would make the figure three million or 5 per cent of the population. The incidence of HIV infection peaked in 1991 with 80,000 new cases, and then fell to 35,000 new cases reported in 2004, but thereafter once again increased with 40,000 new cases in 2006. HIV is more prevalent in wealthy regions. By May 2007, 402,000 Russians had been registered HIV positive since 1989 although well over a million could be living with HIV, with the proportion of women infected rising from 20 per cent in 2001 to 44 in 2006.[52] It is clear that Russia faces a major crisis, exacerbated by the shared use of needles by drug addicts and by widespread popular ignorance about the nature of the disease.

## Housing

The onset of market relations exacerbated the housing crisis inherited from the Soviet Union. According to official statistics, in Moscow alone in 1994 there were 30,000 homeless people, but the actual figure may well have exceeded 100,000, while in Russia as a whole some 4 million were estimated to be homeless.[53] Out of a population of some 8 million in Moscow, some 8 per cent still live in communal flats – *kommunalki* – in which numerous tenants share the kitchen and bathroom. Their number is declining, however, as tenants are moved out and the apartments converted into large and highly desirable flats.

## Social security

The USSR's highly developed social security system was gradually eroded. Budgetary constraints forced a radical overhaul of social security to target it towards low income groups and to improve the social safety net. While 'Benefit programs must provide security but at the same time discourage dependence on the state', the optimum balance is something that eludes most developed societies let alone the former communist states.[54] The main thrust of reform was to lessen direct dependence on the state budget by developing employer insurance schemes with employee contributions for health, pensions and unemployment benefits.[55]

### *Wages, incomes and poverty*

The transition to the market economy meant changing the whole social landscape. Enterprises under the old system were more than production units offering only pay but also provided food, housing, holidays, medical and childcare. Local authorities, short of money themselves, could take over only a fraction of these responsibilities. The economic reforms challenged what the Chinese called the 'three irons' of the Maoist era: the lifelong job, lifelong wage and lifelong position. This was balanced by the 'iron rice bowl', a minimal but secure standard of living. Marketisation now challenged the traditional pattern of work, wages and job security.

Money wages in the Soviet Union by 1991 had fallen far below even the miserly rate of neighbouring countries. Khasbulatov stressed that the Soviet state had been a super-exploiter, giving only 7 to 15 per cent of the labour value back to the worker in the form of wages, whereas under capitalism workers received 60–70 per cent.[56] The economist Matlin argued that the Soviet government had long been waging an economic war against its own people, a war which had intensified during *perestroika*. By 1991, surplus value reached 210 per cent of wages, rising from 126 per cent in 1985 and 102 per cent in 1908 under the allegedly exploitative Tsarist regime. The methodology on which these figures are based can be disputed, but the trend is clear: late communism was twice as exploitative as late Tsarism. Matlin argued that 'The political revolution of August [1991] should be followed by an economic revolution, dismantling the state monopoly of the means of production.'[57]

Economic reform imposed new hardships and provoked the further pauperisation of society. The prices of goods, including basic foodstuffs, began to approximate world levels, yet the average monthly pay remained at absurdly low levels. As the economic reforms began to bite, money wages tended to fall even lower in relative terms and wage differentials increased sharply as the transition to the market sharply exacerbated social inequalities. In 1992, at the beginning of the reforms, the incomes of the lowest 10 per cent of the population represented 6 per cent of overall monetary income of the population, while the top 10 per cent received 40 per cent (6.6 times more); in 2000, the share of the poorest 10 per cent had fallen to 2.4 per cent, while that of the richest accounted for 32 per cent of income (a difference of 13.3).[58] By 2007 the gap had increased to 15.6, compared to the US figure of 15.9 and the British average of 13.6.[59] Those with access to foreign currency and goods, or employed by a successful enterprise, could become relatively rich very quickly, while those tied to a state wage and pensions saw their position further eroded. In 2000, 30 per cent of the population was living below the poverty level, a proportion that had fallen to 15 per cent in 2007.

The old system of subsidised housing, transport, childcare and much else rendered the money wage part of income relatively less important,[60] but now the end of generalised subsidies meant that money wages had to cover far more of individual needs. Access to quality healthcare, pre-school facilities and even education now increasingly had to be paid for. The government found itself trapped since wage rises could only be met by increasing budget expenses in the form of subsidies, and this would only return the whole process to square one. The government negotiated a tortuous path between the pressures of the IMF for financial stabilisation, on the one hand, and the ability of the Russian people to endure yet more hardship on the other. The dash for the market was tempered by attempts to cushion some of the painful effects of the transition for vulnerable groups by ensuring at least a survival income.[61] Miners in the Kuzbas region of Siberia and elsewhere engaged in industrial action at various times (for example, in the 'rail war' of 1998), and fear of working-class protest clearly influenced budgetary priorities. This was to a degree self-defeating since increased wages without commensurate rises in productivity only fuelled inflation.

Only a relatively small proportion were the 'winners' in the transition, while the vast majority in the short term saw their incomes shrink and their job security eroded. Millions lived below the poverty line throughout the 1990s, but the whole notion and the appropriate level of such a 'line' has been much debated. In Russia it is based on level of household income required to maintain a minimum level of consumption, but the actual income in many families is often hidden from the authorities and as the tax system began to bite was usually under-stated, quite apart from wide regional variations. Real income did not fall dramatically in the first years of liberalisation because of inflationary budgetary emissions, but the imposition of a tight money policy saw real incomes fall in 1995 before gradually rising until 1998, and thereafter they plunged as a result of the financial crisis, and in 2000 still remained 20 per cent lower than in 1998 despite rises in wages and welfare payments under Putin.

Poverty and inequality increased markedly. Some 15 per cent of the Russian population still live in poverty (according to the UNDP criterion for the transition countries of $4 per person per day). The poor are concentrated in particular groups (families with more than two children, female single-earner families) and in particular regions (lowest in Moscow and St Petersburg and highest in the North Caucasus, Siberia and the Far East). While Muscovites enjoyed incomes 3.3 times higher than the average in other regions, and only eight other regions exceeded the average, residents in Ingushetia and Ust-Orda Buryat Autonomous *okrug* had average incomes that were only a quarter of the national average.[62] Employment is not necessarily the antidote to poverty, especially when there are long delays in wage payments and their level can be minimal. Two-thirds of the adult poor were working in 1996. As a result of the improvement in Russia's overall economic performance in 2000 the number of 'utterly destitute' declined from 60 million to 46 million, but still one-third of Russia's population were left below the poverty level.[63] By 2007, some 20 per cent of the population still fell below the poverty line.

### Unemployment

Despite claims that the USSR had beaten the problem of unemployment in the 1930s, and concerns over labour shortages in the 1980s, unemployment had in fact been disguised by endemic overstaffing in Soviet enterprises leading to the low labour productivity typical of the extensive model of economic development. The structure of the Soviet labour force, while broadly corresponding to trends elsewhere, nevertheless, revealed a high proportion engaged in manual labour, some 50 million out of a 133 million-strong labour force (with another 7 million involved with the armed forces). Until the RSFSR Law on Employment of 19 April 1991 it was a crime not to work.[64] For most of the Soviet years there had been a relatively free movement of workers, but there had not been a labour market as such.

Unemployment increased but its scale was less than some of the more apocalyptic predictions had suggested, although for a society unaccustomed to any official unemployment the phenomenon itself was shocking. On 1 January 1996, 2.3 million people (3.1 per cent of the working population) were registered as unemployed, an increase of 690,000 over the previous year, while some 5.9 million people (8.1 per cent) were jobless.[65] After a surge of unemployment following the financial crisis of 1998, official unemployment fell from 7.4 million in June 2000 to 6.6 million a year later.[66] In 2002, Russia had a 10.2 per cent unemployment rate, but by 2006 this had fallen to 6.6 per cent, a total of 1.63 million people. The scale of 'hidden unemployment', however, is difficult to estimate but probably affected another 10 million. The official unemployment figures, as in other countries, have been criticised by bodies like the International Labour Organisation who condemned the bureaucracy involved in registering with the Federal Employment Service.[67] Unemployment was worst in Ivanovo *oblast*, dominated by the crisis-ridden textile industry predominantly employing women, where joblessness is five to six times higher than the national average. Unemployment was also particularly high in Ingushetia, Norilsk in the Far North, timber and logging towns, and previously secret defence industry towns.[68] By 2005, a quarter of those of working age in the southern federal district were unemployed, with an astonishing 65 per cent unemployed in Ingushetia including a youth unemployment rate of 94 per cent.

While the conventional view attributes the absence of mass unemployment to the lack of restructuring, changes in the structure of employment, the shift to new and more dynamic sectors of the economy may well have absorbed labour surpluses. The anticipated catastrophic rise in unemployment, moreover, was averted by weak or non-existent bankruptcy laws and the reluctance with which enterprises shed staff, especially in small towns with only one enterprise. Wages ultimately were paid by state subsidies, acting as a huge form of hidden unemployment benefit. With the end of the Soviet regime it might have been thought that the army of bureaucrats, some 80 per cent of whom were women, would become redundant, but the Russian administrative apparatus continued to burgeon. By October 2006, Russia had 74.6 million economically active people, 52 per cent of the country's population.

New placement and retraining schemes were launched, the benefits system simplified, and Russia's 2,300 employment exchanges run by the Federal Employment Service (itself only established in April 1991) began to be modernised and the 10,000 staff retrained to cope with the influx of 'customers'. The emphasis was on developing an effective placement service, retraining for displaced workers, and financial incentives to employers to take on hard-to-place workers.[69] Thirty-seven million people had passed through its doors by 2001, half of whom had been found jobs.[70] Many of those who lost their jobs felt no need to go to a labour exchange since they could find jobs on their own, but as the traditionally taut labour market became much slacker demand increased for the range of specialist services provided by such centres.[71] In the long term, in the light of the demographic changes discussed above, it was anticipated that by 2015 Russia would experience a labour shortage of some ten million.

## Social movements

One of the key questions of the democratic transition in Russia was how society was to be integrated into the post-communist political order. The old gulf between workers and intellectuals had been partially bridged as the new Soviet technical intelligentsia had emerged, but independent labour politics had been delegitimised and incorporated, like the women's and youth movements, as part of Soviet 'transmission belt' politics in a monstrously bureaucratised trade union movement. In the post-communist era the whole notion of class politics was in bad odour because of its association with the discredited Soviet regime, and the new pluralism was highly segmented. The experience of democratisation in Russia demonstrated that the autonomous representation of social interests was subsumed into a broader process of regime consolidation, and independent civil society associations were eclipsed.

### *Labour and trade unions*

Lenin in 1920 had talked of trade unions and other mass organisations acting as 'transmission belts', relaying Party policy to the people, and under Stalin this was achieved with a vengeance for all social organisations, including the youth movement (Komsomol) and women's organisations. The trade union movement, organised in the form of the All-Union Central Council of Trade Unions (VTsSPS) in the Soviet period was a vast bureaucratic organisation whose leadership was appointed by the Party and whose role was reduced to little more than provider of rest homes, special rations, holiday vouchers, pensions and welfare entitlements. In 1933 Stalin transferred the social insurance fund to the unions, and from that time they remained a core element of the Soviet Party economic system. The VTsSPS administered a large part of the social security budget, but this only served to underline the administrative nature of the organisation: functions that in most countries are undertaken by special ministries were fulfilled in the USSR by a body nominally representing workers' interests.[72] Although under the post-Stalin leadership mass organisations became a little more responsive to the needs of their members, they remained heavily bureaucratised with a relatively low status in the Soviet pecking border.

On 11 July 1989 the first major strike of the Kuzbas and other miners demonstrated that *perestroika* was no longer simply a revolution from above but had now to accommodate itself to worker activism from below.[73] The miners' strike, moreover, swept away any residual belief that the CPSU was in any serious way a party of the working class. A year later these same miners staged an avowedly political strike calling for the resignation of Ryzhkov's government and for radical reforms. These strikes demonstrated that the nascent workers' movement, at least in this area, were fighting not for any renewed form of 'the dictatorship of the proletariat' but for a broad democratic programme.

In the 'phoney democracy' phase in 1991–3 the official trade union movement was reformed and de-étatised, while the new trade unions were subject to the factionalism and splits typical of the pseudo-parties. An independent trade union movement emerged and numerous unions were established.[74] The first was the Independent Miners' Union (NPG) established in Donetsk in October 1990, but later it was plagued by divisions and financial scandals. One of the largest trade union organisations was the Moscow Federation of Trade Unions (MFPS), claiming the affiliation of 39 unions with 5.7 million workers.

Another active union was Sotsprof, which originally called itself socialist but later simply called itself a 'social' trade union and supported Yeltsin's dash for the market. The General Confederation of Trade Unions (VKP) sought to act as an umbrella organisation throughout the CIS but remained embryonic. The main process, however, was for old unions to rename themselves and to try to adapt to new conditions, now without state subsidies, compulsory membership and stripped of some of their social functions. The leadership of the new unions were often the same as the old Soviet ones. Unions in Russia are regulated by a separate law to that governing NGOs, and in conformity with international norms, unions operated under a relatively light registration regime and there are no minimum membership requirements, although to be legally licensed a minimum membership of three is required. By 1 January 2005 Russia had no fewer than 57,515 trade unions. However, in June 2006 the Federal Registration Service asserted that normal NGO provisions apply also to unions, which at a stroke increased the 'accountability' burden.

Although a plethora of independent new unions were formed, the vast majority remained under the umbrella of what was now called the Federation of Independent Trade Unions of Russia (FNPR), the successor of VTsSPS, created in March 1990, with some 60 million affiliated members out of a total Russian labour force of some 70 million organised in 40 All-Russian unions. The FNPR perpetuated the traditions of the old union movement, including collective membership of whole industries, covering managers as well as workers. The FNPR, at first chaired by Igor Klochkov, protested against Gaidar's neo-liberal policies and attempts to impose a wage freeze, insisting on 'market wages for market prices'.[75] Klochkov was replaced by Mikhail Shmakov, the head of the MFPS, at the time of the October 1993 events, and he remained at the head of FNPR into the Putin era. While broadly supportive of the Russian government's attempts to transform the economy, he insisted that this should not primarily be at the expense of working people. While workers retain the right to form and join trade unions, the dominant position of the FNPR to this day limits this right. The FNPR boasts that 46 per cent of the country's workforce of 74 million are unionised, and of this about 95 per cent belong to the FNPR (about 29 million members). In the last decade the FNPR's membership has fallen by about 10 million. The FNPR is closely affiliated to various political structures, and while nominally independent acts as a powerful instrument of neo-corporatist practices.

In 1993 the government took back the social insurance budget, but this only threw the union movement into dependence on employers.[76] Old Soviet habits, when trade unions were part of the *troika* of management and party bosses to ensure the fulfilment of the five-year plan, lingered on.[77] In keeping with his corporatist instincts, Yeltsin effectively integrated the FNPR into the regime. The idea of social partnership was formalised by the establishment in January 1992 of the Tripartite Commission on the Regulation of Social and Labour Relations, bringing together organised labour, management and the state, with the brief to review and set wage levels and to mediate in labour disputes, and helped establish the system of quarterly indexing of minimum wages and pensions.[78] Russian welfare payments and salaries in the state sector are calculated as multiples of the minimum wage, set by the Tripartite Commission and influenced by the Duma. The defence of workers' interests played little part, but in return workers could not be sacked, however poorly they worked. This neo-Stalinist bargain, where 'the workers pretend to work and the state pretends to pay them', is today reflected in relatively low official unemployment rates. Under-employment rather than unemployment became chronic as workers and management present a common front against outsiders, and workers become ever more dependent on management, acting as a barrier to collective action.[79] Reflecting the under-development of Russian parties, in the 1995 and 1999 parliamentary elections trade unions sought directly (albeit in loose electoral alliances) to achieve representation in the Duma, but by 2003 they lost an independent voice and threw in their lot with United Russia. A far more profound problem facing unions, however, was their shifting social and political role, lacking credibility in the workplace and in society at large.[80]

The new Labour Code which came into force on 30 December 2001 sought to modernise labour policy by relaxing some of the restrictions inherited from the Soviet period to create a more flexible labour market. Collective bargaining was limited to the unions representing a majority of the workers in an enterprise. Employers had more scope to agree fixed-price labour contracts, and the hiring and firing of workers was made easier. The minimum wage was set at the subsistence level. The greatest criticism of the new Code was directed against its regulations concerning the role of trade unions in labour relations. As in other countries, the drive for labour market flexibility eroded workers' rights. Employers were granted greater rights to sack workers without the approval of the unions, as well as hiring workers on fixed contracts without granting them social benefits. Not surprisingly, this neo-liberal approach to labour issues raised considerable controversy, although there were compensatory features: the minimum wage must be no lower than the subsistence level; workers should receive two-thirds of their wages if the enterprise stops as a result of the actions of employers; and employers pay penalties if there are delays in wage payments. Some of the inconsistencies of the 2001 Code were ironed about by amendments adopted in 2006. There was more emphasis on ensuring that employers implemented the appropriate labour legislation, and labour rights became more secure.

In conditions of dramatic economic decline, huge wage inequality and mass impoverishment the persistence of social peace in the 1990s is surprising.[81] Economic liberalisation severely weakened the bargaining position of workers, and under Putin the consistent rise in real wages turned organised labour into one of his strongest supports. Remarkably, in May 2000 no strikes at all were recorded, and this pattern continued for most of Putin's presidency. While the law enshrines the right to strike, extremely complicated procedures govern disputes and thus render most strikes technically illegal. Strikes require the approval of a majority vote at a meeting comprising at least two-thirds of all staff, including management. Strikes are banned in certain sectors, including the railways, air traffic control and government agencies. A public interest clause in case of strikes stipulates that essential services must be maintained in case of a dispute. Of the strikes that do take place, most are provoked by the non-payment of wages and have been organised by strike committees rather than by the official unions.

Trade unions were transformed from instruments of the state to instruments of collective bargaining, facing the employers in the form of the RUIE. The major challenge facing the union movement was to transform itself from a bureaucratic state agency to the organisational core of the labour movement.[82] The FNPR represented no more than part of the political *nomenklatura*, allied to the enterprise directorate and more interested in elite-level intrigues than the membership. The FNPR moderated its criticisms of the government out of fear that it would lose its extensive network of sanatoria, rest homes and hotels, worth a fortune at market prices. It is for this reason that a number of unions, often calling themselves 'free' to distinguish themselves from the old-style unions, were established, and in contrast to the old unions did not allow members of management to join.[83] Trade unions do not figure significantly in workplace life and according to polls is one of the least trusted social organisations.[84] The intelligentsia on the whole kept itself well apart from the struggle for free trade unions, while political parties have almost no role to play in labour struggles. Privatised enterprises often try to eliminate organised labour altogether from the workplace. The labour struggles that accompanied the rise of Western capitalist democracy will no doubt once again be re-enacted in Russia.

### *Gender politics*

Functionalist approaches tend to examine women in three roles, as workers, mothers and homemakers, and is standard when studying Soviet society. The early Bolsheviks considered that gender inequality would be overcome if women were absorbed into social production, and if children's upbringing and daily life were socialised, accompanied by a socialist camaraderie in relations between the sexes. Experiments with new forms of daily life were soon suppressed. In the early 1930s the separate women's departments (*zhenotdely*) in the Party were closed and the 'women's question' was declared resolved. The 'thaw' of the 1950s and 1960s revealed that the question was far from over, and later analysis revealed that on all the main indices of social achievement and psychological freedom women were at a disadvantage compared to men.[85]

The participation rate of women in paid employment in the Soviet Union was one of the highest in the world, at around 90 per cent. In the period of extensive economic growth the proportion of women in the Russian workforce peaked in the 1970s at 53 per cent, but as the economy began to shift to a more intensive form of development the proportion fell to 52 per cent in 1987[86] and by 1990 was down to 48 per cent and continued to fall as reform increased female unemployment. Women made up 60 per cent of Soviet specialists with higher and secondary special education, constituting 58 per cent of all engineers, 67 per cent of doctors, and up to 91 per cent of librarians. Even though half a million women in the USSR were directors of enterprises, institutions and organisations,[87] there was both vertical and horizontal professional segregation. Within the workplace the usual 'glass ceiling' on promotion was in place; the higher one went in an administrative or professional hierarchy, the lower the proportion of women. Women predominated in less qualified work and nurturing professions and received on average a third lower wages than men. Women are barred from some five hundred jobs, from coal mining and senior positions in the Navy, and quotas on female police officers remain.

There is a large literature that suggests that women are the losers of Russia's new transformation, although more nuanced studies reveal a more complex picture.[88] As workers, women were made redundant before men and often with lower benefit rights. In the early years of reform the average unemployed person in Russia was a woman with higher or specialised education in the 35–40 age group with one child.[89] Women, who had traditionally made up half of the Russian workforce, accounted for 75 per cent of the officially unemployed; three out of every four people who lost their job were women.[90] Wages in the highly 'feminised' professions, moreover, fell below the living minimum, leading to strikes by teachers, healthcare workers and textile workers. Post-war Soviet economic development drew on women instrumentally, as the last great reserve army of labour (together with the peasantry), but as soon as labour shortages gave way to labour surpluses, the alleged emancipatory benefits of paid employment were soon forgotten and the other two roles of women, as mothers and homemakers, were once again stressed. The low birth rate had already prompted Gorbachev to argue that the Soviet regime's attempt 'to make women equal with men in everything' by putting them to work on construction sites, offices and factories had been at the cost of 'their everyday duties at home - housework, the upbringing of children and the creation of a good family atmosphere'. The strategy therefore was 'to make it possible for women to return to their purely womanly mission'.[91]

But as homemakers, too, women are under enormous pressure.[92] The lack of housing, alcoholism, the frighteningly high incidence of male violence against women (unofficial reports suggest that 36,000 women are beaten by a husband or partner every day), and the stultifying social atmosphere places the family at risk, with a divorce rate three times higher than the European average. Whether the appeal to the traditional values of the patriarchal family is an adequate response may be doubted. The level of domestic violence is shocking. According to official statistics, some 12,000–16,000 women die each year from domestic violence, comparable to the total deaths in the Afghan war.[93] The average Russian family is also changing: it increasingly lacks the clear predominance of either the male or female side; it is increasingly nuclear as the tradition of living with parents and grandparents wanes; it is often childless or one child; and it is increasingly single parent as, typically, the woman struggles to bring up a child as the man (especially in the villages) lies drunk. Children tend to be economically dependent on their parents for longer than in the West because of housing shortages, low wages and other labour market inflexibilities. Changing perceptions of morality have given rise to an exceptionally large proportion of marriages being provoked by the pregnancy of the bride, and it is these marriages that prove to be the most unstable, with the child almost always staying with the mother. If in 1960, 12 out of every 100 marriages ended in divorce, by 1990 an extraordinary 42 out of every 100 marriages failed.[94] In 2005, for every 10 marriages there were 6 divorces.[95] Fewer than a quarter of divorced women enter into a second marriage within 10 years of divorcing, thus millions of children live in one-parent families without the benefit of the father's influence, and usually without any male role models at all.[96]

The division of labour in homes remains traditional, with women doing most of the domestic chores and taking primary care of children.[97] Thus the well-known phenomenon of the 'double burden': a full shift at paid work and then several more hours of unpaid work looking after the home and (in the old days) queuing for goods. The reform period saw the rapid deterioration of social facilities, including the destruction of social services like childcare and pre-school nurseries or their commercialisation, placing them far beyond the reach of average families. The birth of a child usually means giving up paid work altogether. The electoral bloc Women of Russia noted that 3 million single women in Russia had to rely on their earnings alone. Their wages had declined relative to men's: if earlier women's wages were nearly 70 per cent men's, by December 1993 they had declined to about 40 per cent.[98]

As citizens, too, women have largely disappeared from national leadership. Under the old regime quotas were reserved for women, and they comprised from a third of the total deputies (in national) to half (in local) soviets. A third of the deputies elected to the eleventh convocation of the USSR Supreme Soviet (1984–9) were women, and the partial removal of quotas led the proportion elected to the USSR CPD in March 1989 to fall to 15.7 per cent.[99] With the full abolition of quotas in the March 1990 elections to the Russian Congress the proportion of women fell to just 5.5 per cent.[100] The trend was briefly reversed in the December 1993 elections, largely due to the efforts of the Women of Russia electoral association which won 8.13 per cent of the party-list vote.[101] The proportion of women in the Federal Assembly rose to 10.8 per cent, but this figure masks the disparity between the First Duma, where women comprised 13.1 per cent of the total (58), and the Federation Council, elected on a first-past-the-post system where only 5.1 per cent were women.[102]

The Women of Russia bloc was a unique attempt in Russia for a women's party to appeal directly to women as a specific constituency.[103] The bloc, however, failed to breach the 5 per cent threshold in 1995, leading to a fall in women's representation in the Second Duma to 46 (10.2 per cent).[104] In the 1999 Duma election only nine of the 26 electoral associations had women in the top three of their party lists and there were no women in 74 of the 225 single-mandate districts. As a result, only 21 women were elected in SMDs and only 15 became deputies through the list system, giving a total of 36 (8 per cent).[105] Table 9.2 shows a slight increase of women in the Fourth Duma to 44 (9.8 per cent), but still very low. A similar pattern is found in the Federation Council, in which there were only ten women out of some 176 senators in 2006. In a quarter of regional legislatures women comprise less than 5 per cent of membership, and in fewer than a tenth make up over 20 per cent. In the Perm and Orenburg regional legislatures between 1999 and 2004 there was not a single woman. The larger and wealthier regions tended to have fewer women elected, while female representation was highest in the Far East federal district. The problem is not that there are any legal obstacles to women entering political decision-making arenas; it lies in the realm of attitudes and multiple obligations. It appears that democracy is indeed particularly gendered in the transitional stage.

It would be misleading to suggest that women were simply passive victims of the transformation. Opportunities for women to participate in the rich socio-political life of post-communist Russia, in the new political parties, trade unions, business life, protest movements and human rights groups, increased as much as for anyone else.[106] Even here, though, women were under-represented, especially in leading bodies. A strictly numerical approach does not always reflect reality, and there is no doubt that qualitatively women played an important part in the democratic movement. However, as in the West, women tended to be absent at the point where decisions are taken: 'Where there is power there are no women; where there are women, there is no power.'[107] Some women, like Ekaterina Lakhova, the head of the Women of Russia Duma faction, took an active part in issues like renewing Russia's Family Code (regulating marriage and family matters) and the former Yabloko deputy Elena Mizulina played an outstanding part in the life of the Duma as deputy chair of its legislative committee, drafting for example amendments to the Criminal Code. In government Valentina Matvienko was a long-serving minister for social welfare. In December 2000 the only female governor of a Russian region, Valentina Bronevich of the tiny Koryak autonomous *okrug*, lost her seat. In 2002 Putin advanced Valentina Matvienko to become governor of St Petersburg, and in the Fourth Duma Lyubov Sliska served as first deputy speaker while Svetlana Orlova was a deputy chair of the Federation Council. Irina Khakamada courageously stood against Putin in the 2004 presidential election.

Women's interests are weakly articulated in the political system because, among other things, women's organisations are weak. The fall of the Soviet regime led to the dissolution of some of the old bureaucratic women's organisations, and no new dynamic organisation was able to take its place. The Soviet Women's Committee survived with the new name of the Russian Union of Women and kept its lavish headquarters, but without subsidies it was forced to take up commercial activities. It was one of the main sponsors of the Women of Russia bloc. A women's movement began to take shape at the grassroots, but there were numerous social and political factors inhibiting its development. If the social democrats of the past had argued that 'the women's question' was just one aspect of the emancipation of labour as a whole, so in the post-communist transition the emphasis has been on the achievement of democratic and citizenship rights for all. Women's activity was channelled into the struggle for democracy, just as once before it had been subordinated to the struggle for socialism. Rather than building strong collective organisations, women in post-communist Russia have tended to adopt individual strategies. This may well reflect what has been called the 'escape from forced emancipation' typical of Soviet-type systems, marked by an allergy to public engagement.[108]

The problem of gender differentiation did, however, generate three main forms of women's political activity. The first was the development of numerous local associations and pressure groups that campaigned for various measures or focused on particular issues. Brutal conditions for conscripts and the horrors of the Chechen war stimulated the creation of the Union of Committees of Soldiers' Mothers and similar organisations. The Soldiers' Mothers organisation, indeed, was one of the most impressive independent social organisations in post-communist Russia. Myriad women-centred NGOs were funded by Western donors, fragmenting not only coherent work in the area but also undermining the development of a cohesive civil society.[109] The second form was involvement in some of the existing women's organisations, to try to turn them from bureaucratic structures into genuinely responsive organisations not only *for* women but also *of* women. The third was the attempt to create genuinely independent new structures. One of these was the Centre of Gender Studies of the Academy of Science, established in early 1990 and directed by Anastasiya Posadskaya, which analysed demographic and social problems of women in Russia and acted as a link between Russian and Western feminists. However, despite the direct threat posed by marketisation to women (in economic, social and identity terms), there was no upsurge in a politicised women's movement. Posadskaya noted that state policies were still designed *for women* and not programmes of *women themselves*.

As in other spheres, the question remained whether the 'modernisation' of Soviet women would necessarily repeat Western patterns, or whether Russian modernity might differ in significant ways from that prevalent in the West. Why should sexual identity become gender identity?[110] The question is often raised of Russian women's own consciousness of their own interests in the three spheres mentioned above (work, motherhood, family) and as individuals or part of a feminine community. In refusing to adopt Western criteria of feminism, had they in some way internalised their own subjection, or was their refusal to adopt Western ways of thinking a reflection of a deeper cultural difference between Russia and the West?

### Environmentalism

Marxists traditionally looked upon nature as a resource to be plundered in the service of humanity. Holloway notes that 'Land, air, and water were as much victims of Stalin's ruthless policies as the people of the Soviet Union were. "We cannot expect charity from nature," Stalin said. "We must tear it from her."[111] The environmental movement played a central role in popular mobilisation during *perestroika*, and indeed throughout the communist era environmentalists had acted as a residual source of social consciousness and responsibility. The outstanding plant biologist Academician Nikolai Vavilov, for example, had tried to defend the autonomy of science against the depredations of Trofim Lysenko, but had failed and was arrested in June 1940 and died of starvation soon after.[112] He was not alone, and the courage of the earth scientists prompted Douglas Weiner to describe the discipline as 'the Gulag of freedom'.[113] In a certain sense the biologists and allied disciplines of the Soviet period can be described as the kernel of civil society waiting for more propitious circumstances to germinate.

These better times proved to be Gorbachev's *perestroika*. A multitude of environmental groups emerged arguing that communism had been as much an environmental disaster as it had been a political and economic one.[114] A study by the state statistics agency, Goskomstat, revealed that 100 million tons of pollutants were discharged into the environment annually in the 5 years to 1991.[115] Commercial felling of forests at some 2 million hectares a year far exceeded the replacement rate, which in *taiga* growing conditions in any case is very slow. The indiscriminate use of chemical fertilisers and pesticides laid waste great tracts and contaminated rivers and ground waters; the deserts of Dagestan and Kalmykia had increased from 15,000 to a million hectares in a generation; in the Arctic tundra overgrazing had led to the loss of 40 million hectares of pasture (an area larger than Germany); the wildlife of Eastern Siberia has been devastated by factory pollution; the level of the Aral Sea is falling by one metre a year; the closed Caspian Sea is filling with poisons; Lake Ladoga (Europe's largest lake, near St Petersburg) is dying from nitrate and phosphate poisoning; on the high seas the USSR had systematically lied about slaughter of a large part of the world's protected whale population, dumped nuclear waste into the Sea of Japan, and discarded seven nuclear submarines and an ice-breaker, six of them in the shallow sea around Novaya Zemlya between the Barents and Kara Seas, north east of Murmansk; and the sad list could go on.[116] The cumulative effect of these disasters has a devastating effect on public health.

Nikolai Vorontsov had been the first non-communist Soviet minister, given responsibility for the environment in 1989, and he increased spending on environmental protection to 1.3 per cent of GNP. But this had little impact on the gross pollution of most industrial cities, with the worst affected like Kemerovo, Bratsk and Norilsk exceeding by ten times permitted levels of air pollution.[117] Alexei Yablokov became the Minister for the Environment in the new Russian government, a man who had long fought for environmental causes and had been the first chair of the Soviet branch of Greenpeace. Russia faced a daunting task in overcoming the disastrous environmental legacy of the old regime. The loss of biodiversity was matched by the human health hazard posed by the crisis, and Yablokov calculated that 20 per cent of the country's population lived in ecological disaster zones and another 35–40 per cent in ecologically damaged conditions.[118] Oldfield identifies two schools of thinking about environmental issues in post-communist Russia: the 'catastrophists', who highlight the awful problems; and the 'transitional' approach, which suggests that the transition to the market and democracy, accompanied by the growth of civil society and environmental movements, would gradually lead to improvements. Oldfield is of the first school, noting that although overall pollution levels have fallen, largely because of the deindustrialisation that accompanied the market reforms of the 1990s, the overall quality of the environment has improved little.[119]

Russia faced the dilemma shared by other post-communist countries, namely the balance to be drawn between environmental policies and the costs in economic and job terms. It was all very well to advocate the closure of environmentally hazardous plants and industries, but how would the economic losses be covered, and where would the new jobs for those made redundant come from? Who would pay for the closure of the giant pulp and paper mills threatening Lake Baikal in Southern Siberia, the deepest freshwater lake on earth containing one-fifth of the world's freshwater and home to 1,500 plant and animal species, 1,200 of them found nowhere else in the world? The main form of industrialisation in Siberia was resource extraction, and with the acute pressure for foreign currency logging of the fragile *taiga* forests, half of the world's coniferous forest and over one-fifth of all forest (being twice as large as the Amazon rainforests), was set to increase. Korean, Japanese and American firms increased their presence despite the resistance of local authorities and the native peoples, and who would police environmental laws, prevent the erosion of soils and silting of rivers, prevent the loss of animal habitat and make up the losses in hard currency earnings for raw timber exports?[120]

The disintegration of the USSR jeopardised Soviet environmental and conservation legislation as each republic sought maximum advantage for itself, leading, for example, to the return of sea fishing of sturgeon in the Caspian, banned in 1962 by the Soviet Ministry of Fisheries.[121] The collapse of the Soviet economy, however, also had a beneficial environmental impact, as plants closed and industrial activity declined, but deindustrialisation is hardly a long-term solution to the crisis. The tension between environmental security and economic well-being is an acute one in countries in economic crisis.

In his drive for administrative rationalisation, one of Putin's first acts on coming to power was the abolition of the State Committee for Environmental Protection, dissolved on 17 May 2000. The task of environmental protection was transferred to the Ministry of Natural Resources, a move that many considered akin to placing the fox in charge of the hen coop. The old Committee, it must be stressed, had been criticised for its sometimes intrusive (some argued exploitative) interference in business, for example the development of the energy resources on Sakhalin, motivated (it was claimed by its opponents) by the opportunities afforded by the need to receive its approval for bribery. At the same time, the State Committee on Forestry was also eliminated. The appointment of Alexander Gavrin, who had close links with Lukoil, the country's biggest oil producer, as energy minister added further to the impression that business had captured government. The Ministry of Natural Resources is charged with the development of the country's natural resources, and its responsibility now for environmental issues exposed it to redoubled pressure from business, local authorities, foreign concerns and environmental lobbyists.

Environmental concerns in Putin's Russia became entwined with the political struggle to reassert presumed state interests against foreign companies The Rosprirodnadzor agency, although subordinated to the natural resources ministry, under its deputy director, Oleg Mitvol, showed its teeth in a number of cases, notably in 2006 on the alleged environmental damage caused by the Sakhalin-2 energy project, developed by a consortium headed by Shell and in conflict with the Russian government over the terms of its 1994 production-sharing agreement (PSA), signed at a time of Russian weakness. Critics argued that environmental abuses were used to wrest control of the project from foreign companies, and to give Gazprom a controlling share.[122] Mitvol, a businessman who had made his fortune in the 1990s before entering government service, was even willing to take on Gazprom, accusing it of serious environmental violations. The instrumental use of environmental issues by the state undermined the autonomy of the environmental movement. This was seen most clearly when Russia acceded to the Kyoto Protocol. As part of the deal to get EU approval for Russia to join the WTO, the Duma ratified the Kyoto protocol in October 2004, allowing it to come into force in February 2005. Putin did show an awareness of environmental issues, notably when in 2006 he insisted that the route of the East Siberia – Pacific Ocean (ESPO) oil pipeline should be routed far to the North of Lake Baikal to avoid a potentially disastrous oil spill polluting the lake. Ultimately, however, environmental concerns were not high up Putin's list of priorities, as demonstrated by the lack of urgency in developing a viable 'state strategy for sustainable development', in draft form since 2002. In Russian '*ustoichivoe razvitie*' refers more to viable or stable rather than to sustainable development.[123]

The issue was particularly acute concerning nuclear power. The explosion at the Chernobyl plant on 26 April 1986 was dreadful proof of the dangers of nuclear technology in the hands of an irresponsible state.[124] The USSR had 53 nuclear power stations operating in 1991, most of a primitive design lacking concrete container systems. The presence of such a dome at the RBMK-type Chernobyl power plant might have contained much of the radiation released following the explosion. In republics like Russia, Ukraine, Lithuania and Armenia nuclear power played a crucial part in the energy balance. Russia's 28 nuclear power stations supply 11.8 per cent of the country's energy needs (18.9 GWe Gigawatts electric), while Ukraine's 15 supplied 25 per cent (13 GWe). Ukraine suffered from chronic energy shortages, amassing enormous debts to Russia for oil and gas deliveries, and insisted it could not close the remaining two working reactors at Chernobyl (which supplied 7 per cent of Ukraine's electricity) until the West helped pay for alternatives, like a gas-fired power station. In Armenia the Metzamor station was taken off line in March 1989 in the wake of the December 1988 earthquake, but returned to active service in 1995. Thus while many reactors should close on environmental grounds, to do so would leave cities cold in the harsh winters. The energy shortage, exacerbated by falling output of oil, gas and coal, led Russia's powerful 'Minatom' agency in December 1992 to propose an increase in nuclear power output to 37 GWe by 2010 by completing unfinished plants and constructing new ones.[125] Yablokov called the plan 'unacceptable from the legal, ecological, economic and political points of view',[126] but the severity of the energy shortfall was such that there was no guarantee that his warning would be heard, especially since nuclear power was a smaller component of Russia's energy balance than in many developed Western states.[127] In his annual address to parliament on 26 April 2007 Putin stated that 'Thirty nuclear power plants were built in the country during the Soviet period. And we need to build another 26, based on the latest technology.' He proposed 'setting up a corporation to integrate nuclear power enterprises operating on domestic and foreign markets'.[128] A new nuclear age was dawning, in Russia as in the West.

The legacy of past nuclear irresponsibility could not be avoided. The problem of radioactivity was the greatest single catastrophe afflicting the country. Some 8,000 people had died as a result of the Chernobyl explosion, and contamination affected large parts of Ukraine and 40 per cent of Belarus – provoking movements for national independence – as well as 16 regions of Russia. The sarcophagus containing the damaged Reactor 4 at Chernobyl, moreover, is in danger of disintegrating.[129] In Moscow itself leakage from nuclear plants and research institutes make certain parts of the city extremely dangerous. Some six hundred miles of the Yenisei downriver from Krasnoyarsk-26 are heavily contaminated since in the past water from the cooling towers in a military plant producing plutonium went straight into the river. The legacy of atmospheric nuclear tests still affect parts of Siberia downwind of the Semipalatinsk test site in Kazakhstan. An explosion in tanks containing nuclear waste in 1957 at the Chelyabinsk-40 installation cast radioactive materials over a wide area, and another explosion at Kyshtym near Chelyabinsk in 1976, kept secret for twenty years, contaminated a large part of the Urals. And everywhere there were Chernobyls waiting to happen, in old nuclear power stations and secret nuclear factory towns like Chelyabinsk-65.

The fall of communist power did not resolve the environmental crisis but made possible analysis of its scale. A whole series of new problems arose in conditions of marketisation, weak state power and energy shortages.[130] The Russian government was conscious of the relationship between economic transformation and environmental factors, adopting a Law on Protecting the Environment on 19 December 1991,[131] and sought to develop cooperation with the other CIS states on environmental policy.[132] The Law on Specially Protected Natural Areas, finally ratified by Yeltsin on 14 March 1995, was the cornerstone of measures to regulate the protection and use of specially protected areas. Russia already had strictly protected Nature Reserves (*Zapovedniki*), established some seventy years ago, National Parks (set up in 1983), Special Purpose Reserves (*Zakazniki*), Nature Monuments, and some others, and the act now introduced a new type of protected area, Regional Natural Parks (analogous to State Parks in the United States). The act drew a clear distinction between the federal and regional level of protected areas, a particularly important delineation at a time of privatisation, with the *Zapovedniki* and National Parks to remain federal property, while the *Zakazniki* were under regional control.[133] The *Zapovedniki* were the heart of Russia's conservation policy and biological diversity, whereas some of the other areas were virtually 'paper parks', encroached upon by the increasing number of small landowners, farmers and herders, quite apart from the pressure of mining, logging and other business interests.

The constitutional provision (Article 42) that 'Each person has the right to a decent environment' is far from being fulfilled. Democratisation acts as a two-edged sword in the field of environmental politics. On the one hand, it makes possible the relatively honest appraisal of environmental problems, allows the mobilisation of lobbies and groups, and promotes public participation in legislative acts. On the other hand, powerful new corporations and business lobbies emerge to exploit natural resources, private entrepreneurs encroach on protected areas, the capacity of the state to regulate and implement environmental programmes weakens, and the resources available for conservation and rehabilitation decline. The Russian case demonstrates clearly, however, that environmentalism is not the preserve of affluent Westerners but is a global concern.[134]

## Para-constitutionalism and non-governmental organisations (NGOs)

The reconstitution of state authority in the 2000s was accompanied by ever tighter regulation of public life in general, and civic activity in particular. The Putin presidency was characterised by the growth in the bureaucracy and the intensification of the depoliticising trend that had been a feature of Yeltsin's rule. The regime assumed that it knew best, and that public engagement was a luxury that the country could ill afford. This technocratic ethos did not repudiate democracy, but it did encourage a para-constitutional bypassing of the constitution. Putin's system was legalistic, but it often acted in a spirit contrary to that of constitutionalism.

### Para-constitutionalism

Russia's 1993 constitution does finally do what a constitution is supposed to do: establish the basic principles of the polity and define the roles of the institutions of government. At the heart of the idea of modern constitutionalism is the separation of powers, and this the 1993 document does, although this separation in various aspects is unbalanced. The logic of Russian politics, however, in practice tends to be based on principles other than divided governmental powers inherent in constitutionalist approaches. Genuine constitutionalism, characterised by vertical and horizontal accountability, is still struggling to be born.[135]

An administrative regime has emerged between the structures of the constitutional state and the accountability structures of civil society, above all parties and parliament. Para-constitutional behavioural norms predominate that, while not formally violating the letter of the constitution, undermine the spirit of constitutionalism. This is a feature that was already identified in American presidentialism in the 1980s,[136] and it has if anything intensified since then. As in America, para-constitutional behaviour gets things done, but is ultimately counter-productive because its reliance on bureaucratic managerialism undermines popular trust and promotes self-interested behaviour on the part of elites. This is more than the politics of duplication that was prevalent under Yeltsin, notably in the case of the development of the Presidential Administration as a type of surrogate government. During Putin's presidency the practices of para-constitutionalism have been sharply accentuated. His regime has been careful not overtly to overstep the bounds of the letter of the constitution, but the ability of the system of 'managed democracy' to conduct itself with relative impunity and lack of effective accountability means that it is firmly located in the grey area of para-constitutionalism.

A number of the key institutions involved in the practice of para-constitutionalism under Putin. The first is the establishment of the seven federal districts in 2000 (discussed in Chapter 12). The second is the establishment of the State Council in September 2000, a body comprised of the heads of Russia's regions, but running in parallel with the upper chamber of Russia's parliament, the Federation Council (Chapter 9). The third para-constitutional body is the Presidential Council for the Implementation of the National Projects established in autumn 2005 to advance the four national projects announced that September. The projects were to see major investment in housing, education, health and agriculture, and were to be overseen by one of the putative presidential candidates, the head of the presidential administration and soon afterwards first deputy prime minister

Dmitry Medvedev, who also headed the Council's presidium. The Council is chaired by the president and consists of 41 members, and was responsible for an initial budget of $4.6 billion. A number of ministers are on the Council, above all those in the areas affected, together with the seven federal envoys and the chairs of the two houses of parliament. Later demographic issues were taken up by the Council. The Council is obliged to meet in full session at least once a year. It does not have a budget as such, but its advice is usually followed by the Duma and the various ministries and it is thus much more than an 'advisory' body. The Council worked in parallel to the government and clearly undermined the authority of the prime minister. By bringing together the various executive and legislative agencies in this way, the Council also undermined the separation of powers.[137]

The fourth main para-constitutional body is the Public Chamber. In his speech of 13 September 2004 Putin argued that a Public Chamber would act as a platform for broad dialogue, to allow civic initiatives to be discussed, state decisions to be analysed and draft laws to be scrutinised. It would act as a bridge between civil society and the state. On 16 March 2005 the State Duma overwhelmingly adopted the law on the creation of the Public Chamber by 345 votes to 50; it was signed into law by Putin on 4 April; and it came into effect on 1 July.[138] The Chamber was established as a type of 'collective ombudsman',[139] although its powers are purely consultative. Its duties included the review of draft legislation and the work of parliament, and the monitoring of federal and regional administrations. It offers non-binding recommendations to parliament and the government on domestic issues, investigates possible breaches of the law and requests information from state agencies. The Chamber has 126 members: one-third is selected by the president, intended to be authoritative individuals who would be neither politicians nor businesspeople; the second group is nominated by the first from national civic associations; and once in office these two groups in turn choose the remaining third, representing regional non-governmental organizations. The body's funding and offices are allocated by the Presidential Administration. Putin appointed the first tranche of 42 members in September 2005, including representatives of the major religious confessions, sports figures, academics, policy analysts, scientists and NGO representatives. In November the first group selected the second, consisting of various voluntary assistants and civic activists; popular personalities, journalists and sportspeople; prominent lawyers; and business leaders.[140] The third tranche came from regional activists. The creation of the central Chamber was followed by the creation of similar bodies in the regions.

The new Chamber worked in cooperation with the state, a characteristic of Russian civil society, but on numerous occasions, as in the conflict over the adoption of the NGO law (see below), the Andrei Sychev bullying case in the military, and the development of the Butovo district in Moscow, it demonstrated that it was not afraid to stand up to the authorities. The Chamber also had an uneasy relationship with the Duma. The public Chamber introduced a new channel of public accountability against overbearing officialdom, and thus usurped what should have been one of parliament's key roles. Work that should properly have been the preserve of the State Duma was transferred to this new body, a type of non-political parliament. The existence of the Public Chamber could not but diminish the role of parliament, which should act as the primary tribune for the expression of popular concerns.

The system of surrogates is not provided for in the constitution, although it does not violate the letter of the constitution. Para-constitutional accretions to the constitution were designed to enhance efficacy but in practice undermined the development of a self-sustaining constitutional order and the emergence of a vibrant civic culture and civil society.

### NGOs and their regulation

In his Federal Assembly address of May 2004 Putin spoke of NGOs 'fed by an alien hand'. Concerns had increased in the wake of the Ukrainian Orange revolution of autumn 2004 that NGOs were being supported from abroad to continue the wave of 'colour revolutions', seen already in Serbia with the overthrow of Slobodan Milošević in October 2000, then in the 'rose' revolution in Georgia in November 2003, which brought Mikheil Saakashvili to power, and again in Kyrgyzstan in the 'tulip' revolution of February 2005, which saw the overthrow of president Askar Akaev. The fear that Western-sponsored civic activism would be used as a battering ram to achieve 'regime change' provoked Alexander Lukashenko to clamp down on the flickering remnants of independent NGO activity in Belarus. The American strategy of supporting civil society organisations to achieve regime change through people power was also applied in Iran. Boris Berezovsky, the oligarch exiled in London, was calling for Putin's overthrow, by illegal means if necessary. It was in this context that Putin issued warnings that the unmonitored financing of political activity from abroad was impermissible.

The new law focused above all on ensuring the depoliticisation of NGOs, to be achieved through intense vetting during a complex registration procedure, and much tighter financial monitoring. Branches of foreign NGOs were to register under the same rules as applied to Russian bodies. The law provoked a storm of criticism from Russian human rights organisations, foreign politicians and organisation, including the European Parliament, which urged Russia to ensure that the law conformed to Council of Europe standards. The Public Chamber, at that point still only two-thirds formed, appealed to the Duma to postpone discussion of the law until the full Chamber had a chance to examine its provisions, and in general clearly disapproved of the speed with which the law was being rushed through. Ella Pamfilova, the head of the Presidential Council for Civil Society Institutions, and Vladimir Lukin, Russia's human rights ombudsman, criticised the law. The general principle of regulating NGO activity was not in question, but the point is that the law should be transparent and immune to arbitrary interpretation, and in turn should serve to make the activities of Russian NGOs more transparent and accountable.

These protests had an effect, and the law adopted by the Duma on 23 December 2005 no longer required branches of foreign NGOs to re-register as local bodies, but officials would still be allowed to ban them if they threatened 'Russia's sovereignty, independence, territorial integrity, national unity and originality, cultural heritage and national interests'. The law was published on 17 January 2006 and came into effect on 10 April.[141] Russia's NGOs had to register with the Federal Registration Service within six months of the bill becoming law, but if they wished to continue to operate informally they did not need to register as legal entities. A court decision is required before an individual can be prevented from establishing an NGO, whereas earlier the authorities could deny registration if they simply suspected the founder of extremism or money laundering. Organisations have to provide detailed reports on the spending of foreign funds, even if the money is used for philanthropic purposes. The new accountability measures had a positive side-effect in encouraging professionalism in NGO activity and the improvement in NGO governance. The new measures encouraged the payment of trained accountants to manage NGO funds, and fostered managerial and financial discipline. It was clear, however, that the wording of the law remained far too vague, leaving the authorities with almost unlimited discretion in deciding whether to register an NGO or to close it down. In March 2006 the Prosecutor General's Office froze Open Russia's account, on the grounds that the new NGO law prohibits someone who has been prosecuted (in this case Mikhail Khodorkovsky) from being the founder and sponsor of a public organisation. Open Russia had been one of the most generous sources of funding for NGOs in Russia. At the same time, the complexity of bureaucratic requirements inhibited the formation of organisations, in a field well known for the rapid turnover of groups. Access to foreign sources of support became more complicated.

# 15 Cultural transformation

> I think that Russia can only be Russia. It is neither Asian nor European. It is just Russia.
>
> (Alexei Podberezkin)[1]

Accompanying the political, social and economic revolutions was a no less profound transformation of the cultural sphere. Instead of the closed, introspective and heavily administered Soviet system, a more open, pluralistic and free society began to emerge. The financial and institutional basis for this freedom, however, remained tenuous. The censorship of the communist years was abolished, but new constraints emerged, above all, financial. The press may have cast off one form of oppression, but reliance on wealthy benefactors or subsidies imposed new limitations. The role of the intelligentsia as the 'conscience of the nation' also gave way to attempts to find new ways to survive in a free but relatively impoverished society. Religious freedom was restored, but here, too, fears that Russia was becoming exposed to excessive foreign evangelism led to the imposition of new restrictions. While the old political order may have changed in 1991, the people remained the same although their attitudes and views evolved. How can democratic institutions function democratically if societal values remain in some way antithetical to Western democratic values? The old forced ideology had gone, but the country appeared to experience a crisis of values.

## The media

*Glasnost* (openness) had been the defining characteristic of Gorbachev's *perestroika*: society came to know itself and its own past, and in so doing appeared to lose itself.[2] Revelations about Soviet crimes and follies undermined faith in the regime; *glasnost* acted as a profoundly disintegrative force. The revelatory aspect of *glasnost* continued into the post-Soviet era, but its impact was reduced since the new facts were now part of history rather than politics. Nevertheless, some of the details revealed following the fall of the old regime retained their power to shock, especially when the executioners spoke out. A former NKVD chief Vladimir Tokarev described in chilling detail how it took a month for NKVD troops in Kalinin (Tver) to shoot 6,295 Polish officers one by one. He revealed that 3,897 had died in a similar fashion in Katyn and 4,403 near Kharkov, a total of 14,595.[3] It was only in 1990, and then without a hint of repentance, that the Soviet regime had admitted that they, and not the Nazis, were guilty of the murders in April 1940.[4]

*Glasnost* gave way to freedom of speech and the press, confirmed by the liberal Law on Press Freedom of 12 June 1990. *Glasnost* had been subversive of the old regime and had undermined social consensus, or at least made vivid the absence of consensus. Now, the new freedom contributed to the creation of a distinctively Russian public sphere and focus for social discourse. Freed from censorship, the new quality papers acted as a forum for debate of public issues. Freedom of the press acts as a major form of control over executive power, and papers now took great pride in calling themselves the 'fourth estate'. Papers like *Nezavisimaya gazeta* (*The Independent*), for example, gloried in its freedom to act as a forum for debate. Its own position was a liberal patriotic one, acting as the mouthpiece for the democratic intelligentsia. The new Russian Law on the Press debated in autumn 1991 was in certain respects less liberal than the Soviet one, allowing the ministry to close a newspaper down if it had been 'warned' twice, but after protests the law that came into effect on 6 February 1992 extended press freedoms and now included provisions against monopoly ownership.[5] The freedoms that had begun during *glasnost* now blossomed into genuine freedom of speech and the press, and the variety of publications and the openness of their content was unparalleled in Russia's history.

The press struggled to adjust to post-communist conditions. If earlier they had been subject to political restrictions, they had at least been subsidised and shielded from market forces. The media moved from peddling lies to pursuing profits, with an intervening stage of the enthusiastic half-truths of *glasnost*. In the first period after the coup the press still faced the monopoly distributor of newspapers and journals, *Soyuzpechat*, and later distribution remained a problem, with the major central papers rarely available for purchase in the regions. The supplier of newsprint enjoyed a monopoly, and did not hesitate to take advantage of it by raising prices. Higher prices sharply reduced subscriptions, a trend that was only reversed in the late 1990s. In March 1992 *Pravda*, the flagship of the Bolshevik movement since Lenin founded it in 1912, ceased publication until it reappeared with the help of a loan from a Greek millionaire. The other of the two great Soviet newspapers, *Izvestiya*, the paper of the USSR parliament, developed an authoritative liberal voice.

The price of freedom was economic hardship, and papers were forced to enter the marketplace and take on advertising, while some in addition sought to attract readers by dropping the high-minded asceticism (however hypocritical) typical of the communist press and moved resolutely downmarket with a diet of sex and scandals. The government found ways of subsidising sympathetic papers, while in the regions governors created their own subservient media groups. This was particularly threatening to freedom of expression, since 70 per cent of subscriptions are now to local newspapers. The ideal would be press freedom and government subsidies that would shield the papers from commercial pressures and the ensuing compromises, but, as in the West, this was not to be. The dissemination of propaganda gave way to the pursuit of profits, and the prestige of the press fell accordingly. The fall of communism allowed the media to escape from state ownership, but few remained genuinely independent. One by one the oligarchs snapped up media outlets. Following a financial crisis in August 1996, for example, *Nezavisimaya gazeta*, whose very name proclaims its independence, was taken over by one of the most predatory of Russia's post-communist tycoons, Berezovsky. The under-developed condition of the advertising industry and its later concentration in just a few hands means that it is difficult to retain commercial independence. Even *Moskovskie novosti*

(*Moscow News*), which for most of the 1990s maintained its independence by a mix of income from sponsorship and advertising, in the 2000s fell prey to the oligarchs.

In the 2000s the persecution of the Radio Liberty reporter Andrei Babitskii, the retired Navy captain and environmental reporter Alexander Nikitin, of the popular muckraking reporter Alexander Khinstein and others, all appeared to signal the end of the luxuriant but dirty profusion of press liberties that had emerged in the late 1980s and somehow survived under Yeltsin, although much of it had become bent to the will of the oligarchs. Babitsky had been arrested in Chechnya and then held incommunicado for a month before being exchanged for some Russian prisoners to the Chechen insurgents. On his release in Dagestan, he was accused of having false documents and was banned from leaving the country. The information regime imposed on reportage of the second Chechen war took contemporary Western informational practices in times of warfare to new extremes. It appeared that any non-official reporting of the war could be construed as 'anti-state activity'. The raid by masked tax police on the offices of NTV, the only national inde-pendent TV station, on 11 May 2000, followed by Vladimir Gusinsky's imprisonment for four days, suggested a sustained assault against press freedom. Gusinsky was no more corrupt than other oligarch, but he was the head of an independent media company that was critical of Putin and 'the family'.

As some moguls bought up existing media outlets, others established new ones, while bodies like Gazprom set up its own voice in the form of Gazprom-Media. It was this media conglomerate that bought a large stake in Gusinsky's NTV, and later under Putin took a controlling interest in the television company. Berezovsky never made any secret of the fact that he 'never in the course of the decade viewed the mass media as a business', instead considered it 'a powerful lever of political influence'.[6] This was something that Putin, too, understood, and acted accordingly. The Gazprom-Media empire was used by the Putin regime to discipline the media while not resorting to outright censorship or authoritarian control. In June 2005 Gazprom-Media bought *Izvestiya* from the 'oligarch' Vladimir Potanin, followed by a decline in the quality of its news coverage. Nothing was done to prevent discussion (although usually in relatively small circulation newspapers) of controversial issues. The case of Alexander Ivanov, the son of the then defence minister Sergei Ivanov, who hit and killed a pedestrian on a crossing, or the abuse of judicial procedures in the Khodorkovsky case, gained considerable coverage. The two newspapers formerly owned by Berezovsky also changed hands. In August 2005 *Nezavisimaya gazeta* was bought by Konstantin Remchukov, an assistant to German Gref.[7] *Kommersant*, owned by Berezovsky from 1999 to February 2006, also began to lose its once-famed objectivity. Berezovsky sold the paper to Badir Patarkatsishvili, an oligarch resident in Georgia who was *persona non grata* in Russia, and in August 2006 it was bought by the magnate Alisher Usmanov, the owner of a number of steelworks and also head of Gazprominvestholding, a fully owned subsidiary of Gazprom. The editor also changed at this time.

The electronic media followed the same trajectory as the press: first a renaissance during *glasnost* and the early post-communist years, the latter marked by the develop-ment of independent television and radio, followed by financial crises, commercialisation and oligarchical control, although here the paths diverged: unlike the press, television re-entered a phase of state 'influence', if not control. Under a deal agreed between the Soviet and Russian presidents, Channel 2 became a purely Russian channel (RTR), and later the first channel (Ostankino) became the basis for an interstate television network for the CIS (ORT), today known simply as Channel 1. Television lost some of its Reithian earnestness and desire to educate that it had gained in the years of *perestroika*; in market conditions, it now sought to entertain as much as to enlighten. The creation of Gusinsky's NTV marked a radical departure from Soviet traditions. The station was marked by its fearless reporting of the first Chechen war, although in Yeltsin's 1996 re-election campaign it threw in its lot with the regime. NTV was particularly critical of Putin and all his doing in 1999–2000, until finally subordinated to Gazprom in April 2001. It was never clear whether the struggle over control of NTV was primarily about finances or politics. The removal of Leonid Parfyenov from NTV's thoughtful 'Namedni' programme in 2004, however, signalled yet another nail in the coffin of lively independent broadcasting.[8]

By 2007 Russia had 1,100 television channels (5 major networks and 3 nationwide channels), 670 radio stations and 53,000 periodicals, half of which were financed by foreign capital. The internet became a major source of information, with 7 per cent of Russians logging on every day according to one survey.[9] Central television remained the main source of information for 85 per cent of the population,[10] and hence the care with which the Kremlin ensured that the right messages were broadcast. The main television channels – Channel One (formerly ORT), Russian Television, TV-Center and NTV - were firmly under Kremlin control, while Ren-TV was only slightly less obsequious in endlessly reporting on the activities of the authorities. From 2004 all panel discussions were pre-recorded, allowing provocative comments to be edited out. In its Press Freedom Index for 2006, Reporters Without Borders ranked Russia 147th out of the 168 countries it examined, lodged between Singapore and Tunisia.[11] The murder of the investigative journalist Anna Politkovskaya in Moscow on 7 October 2006 (Putin's birthday) brought the issue of media freedom to the fore. This murder was only one of a series that included the killing of the Forbes journalist Paul Klebnikov on 9 July 2004. Since 2000, thirteen Russian journalists had been murdered by paid assassins. There is no evidence that the Russian federal authorities were involved in these killings, but they did stand accused of not having investigated these murders with adequate vigour and of having tolerated the conditions that allowed these murders to happen.

The news agencies also underwent a radical reorganisation after the coup. The Novosti Information Agency was brought under the wing of the Russian Information Agency to form RIA-Novosti, which sought to become a non-political news gathering organisation like other world press agencies such as Reuters or Agence France Presse. The major problem was that Novosti had been an unprofitable organisation, having been subsidised by the Soviet state and other organisations including the KGB, and in order to become profitable many foreign publications were closed, including *Soviet Weekly* in Britain, whose last issue came out on 5 December 1991. Independent agencies such as Interfax and Postfactum also served much the same market, and the vigorous work of these agencies remains testimony to the continued pluralism in the Russian news market.

'Thick journals', periodicals that enjoyed a long history in Russia as the forum for the intelligentsia but which had died out in Britain in the early twentieth century, enjoyed a renaissance in the heady days of *glasnost* in 1988 and 1989 but now once again fell upon hard times. They were forced to put up cover rates and the number of subscribers fell. Subscriptions to *Novyi mir* (*New World*) fell from 2.5 million at the height of *perestroika* to 250,000 in 1992, *Znamya* (*The Banner*) from 1 million to 250,000, and *Druzhba narodov* (*Friendship of Peoples*) from 1.2 million to 90,000. At the thin end of the thick publications, numerous political and social journals were transformed by the fall of the regime. After the coup some of the former communist periodicals engaged in some astonishing breast beating. *Partiinaya zhizn'* (*Party Life*), for example, distanced itself from the Central Committee, whose mouthpiece it had long been, or at least, of its '*nomenklatura* core'. The editorial insisted that this small group of 'imposters' had claimed to speak on behalf of the whole Party, hence the journal had often published the 'hypocrisy, banalities and malicious conceits of the partocratic jargon'. The journal, now under the control of its workers, exclaimed, 'thank God, that this excrescence (*narost*) on the body of society has been removed'.[12] The journal went on to rename itself *Delovaya zhizn'* (*Business Life*), and thus completed one of the more astonishing transformations of the transition to post-communism in Russia. Even more breathtaking for its sheer audacity, however, was the transformation of *Kommunist* into *Svobodnaya mysl'* (*Free Thought*), though under the auspices of the Gorbachev Foundation it lived up to its name and today under its editor Vladislav Inozemtsev provides some of the most thoughtful analysis of contemporary Russian public life.

The integrity of the media in the West has also been questioned. As Stjepan Mestrovic notes, 'postmodernist journalism has abandoned the notion of seeking truth in reporting'.[13] A study of the state of media freedom in Russia concluded that 'each region violates media freedom differently but each of them does so'. According to the survey, Moscow and St Petersburg were rated to be most free, with the ethno-federal republics at the bottom.[14] Media freedoms remained fragile in the centre as well, with threats that the government would be given the powers to license publications, a power that could easily be used to limit freedom of speech. The Information Security Doctrine of 9 September 2000, developed by the Security Council, revealed a defensive and security-dominated approach to media freedoms, listing a whole range of 'threats to the informational security' of the country,[15] and was followed by a renewed spy scare and increasing attempts by security agencies to control the informational sphere.

## Culture and the intelligentsia

The lifting of censorship and the other controls during *perestroika* raised expectations that society would enjoy an explosion of long-repressed creativity. While the flood of hitherto suppressed facts about the Soviet past and discussion of previously taboo subjects raised the circulation of the 'thick journals' and the press, by 1989 interest was waning. *Perestroika* was not accompanied by a cultural renaissance, and indeed by 1991 some critics began to talk in terms of the 'death' of Soviet and Russian literature.[16] The Soviet regime in its heyday had produced works of more universal value than a literature that veered between obsessively grimy and introspective works, on the one hand, and escapist writings, on the other.

The political revolution and the market posed dramatic challenges to the whole intellectual and cultural life of society. The USSR Academy of Sciences had long been criticised not only for being an elite establishment, absorbing almost all research funds and thus starving universities and colleges, but also that it was a grossly inefficient body. Whole institutes had produced little in the way of worthwhile research for years, and yet took their wages, bonuses, housing and rations. Attempts by the USSR Academy of Sciences to become independent of Russia were scotched soon after August. As Yeltsin noted, 'Then, the USSR Academy of Sciences, 96 per cent of whose institutions and scholars are in Russia, tried to become an organisation independent of Russia. Now the situation has changed dramatically.'[17] In a decree of 21 November 1991 Yeltsin created a Russian Academy of Sciences (RAS), and all members of the old academy joined automatically. The new academy faced a severe financial crisis and its institutes were forced to find alternative income to supplement state subsidies. As with the press, freedom was gained at the price of financial security. Attempts in the late Putin years to bring the Academy under some form of state control, in return for greater financial security, were rebuffed.

In the early post-communist years the educational system also suffered from a crisis of financing and re-orientation, but under Putin became the focus of one of the 'national projects'. The fabric of schools had decayed in the last Soviet years, and only within the framework of the national projects was modernisation and extensive staff training undertaken. Once again, as in the early 1980s, the educational system in the early 2000s faced a major reorganisation.[18] Universities are now allowed to take a certain proportion of paying students to help subsidise the rest. Russia witnessed a veritable boom in higher education in the post-communist years, with an early decline in the number of students more than compensated by a massive expansion in the proportion of young people entering the system. By 2007, Russia was spending 3.8 per cent of GDP on education, compared to the euro area average of 4.81. A particularly acute problem is the gulf between higher education and the economy, with universities turning out over a million graduates every year whose skills often fail to meet the requirements of a modern economy. University libraries lacked resources to update their collections, and it was only with the help of the Soros Foundation that 56 per cent of higher education establishments had been endowed with internet centres.

In the last years of *perestroika* the two streams of Russian culture, in exile and at home, came together, and in the post-communist era they fused as the divisions of the revolution and the Civil War healed. Yeltsin began his visit to the United States in June 1992 by telephoning Solzhenitsyn and asking him to return home after 17 years of exile. Solzhenitsyn had resolutely refused to have anything to do with *perestroika*, but now that the communist regime had fallen he returned home in 1994. Vladimir Voinovich, Andrei Sinyavsky, and many other émigrés visited the motherland, and Russian cultural figures could now travel freely abroad. The magazine *Kontinent*, edited in Paris since 1974 by Vladimir Maximov, moved to Moscow and sought to reflect religious concerns and the problems of the intelligentsia. Its new editor, Igor Vinogradov, noted that the magazine would discuss problems of Russian national consciousness in the new conditions and whether indeed there could be a 'special path' for Russia, avoiding 'the real dangers of Western civilisation'.[19] One of Putin's first acts on coming to power was to visit Solzhenitsyn, and this symbolised the 'patriotic' tone of his presidency. Solzhenitsyn reciprocated, and on numerous occasions endorsed Putin's way of reconstituting the state.

The disintegration of the USSR was reflected in the Byzantine manoeuvrings within the organised writer's movements. The liberal Union of Russian (*Rossiiskie*) Writers was bitterly opposed to the RSFSR Writers' Union, dominated by extreme nationalists, while the old USSR Writers' Union gave way to a new Commonwealth of Unions of Writers, which itself later split. The struggles reflected the extreme politicisation of writers and literature as a whole, but the farcical plots and counter-plots within the cultural establishment discredited them all. The intrigues surrounding the Russian Booker

Prize perpetuated in new form old conflicts. While the views of writers were sought after and valued during *perestroika*, the fall of the old regime was accompanied by their marginalisation and indeed the devaluation of culture as a whole. Crude commercialisation, the shortage of paper for journals and books, the high prices, all played their part in the alleged decline of literature. However, the displacement of ideological constraints by the demands of the market was only one aspect of the problem. By 1991 much of the suppressed or exiled literature had been published, but the new wave of writers at first proved decidedly thin. This gradually gave way to a vibrant new literature in whose vanguard were writers like Victor Pelevin, whose *Babylon* (in Russian *Generation P*) is a satire on Western influences on contemporary Russia, and the Yukio Mishima-like figure of Eduard Limonov, whose nationalism ultimately led him to the Lefortovo gaol in 2001. His National Bolshevik Party adopted a virulent rejectionist stance, and became one of the most active parts of the 'Other Russia' opposition bloc from 2005. The popularity of the writings of Boris Akunin, whose series of Erast Fandorin detective novels set in the late nineteenth century, has been interpreted as serving the needs of a nascent Russian middle class.[20]

The Russian intelligentsia changed as *perestroika* progressed, and became increasingly engaged with the political life of the country to the extent that a large number of the former intelligentsia became leading members of the new elite. But as a class the intelligentsia suffered during the transition to more market-oriented forms of social life. The enormous number of institutes and network of privileges of the old USSR Academy of Sciences were cut back as budget cuts took their toll. The intelligentsia had enjoyed a brilliant swansong during *perestroika*, when for the last time the Soviet regime courted them and Gorbachev sought to enlist them as allies in the struggle against the bureaucracy, but this was only the glare of a star in its death throes.

In Eastern Europe the intelligentsia had by and large survived, though the old bourgeoisie had been destroyed, and thus an invaluable link with the past and with the West remained.[21] In Russia the old middle classes had been destroyed, but a multi-layered intelligentsia had emerged from the debris of the old system. The core of the cultural intelligentsia maintained traditional values of scholarship throughout the Soviet period, and indeed took on some of the hegemonic functions of the bourgeoisie. But in a way traditional for Russia, its values were isolated from society and because of the peculiarities of the Russian state formation were unable to combine a programme of democratic reforms, state modernisation and national aspirations. The intelligentsia had played a leading role during *perestroika*, but at the same time as a group had become irrevocably split. The divisions of the Russian intelligentsia reflected the contradictions of the Russian state system in its entirety.

In democratic societies the intelligentsia as such is fractured between academic, media, and other groups in the diverse patterns of modern life. The old Soviet middle class had been unique in that it was not so much based on property but on occupation and strategic location in the reproduction of cultural values, above all the creative and scientific intelligentsia. Against the background of hyperinflation and falling incomes Boris Saltykov, the Deputy Prime Minister in charge of science and education, talked of the 'disintegration of the middle class', a process Khasbulatov called 'the lumpenisation of society'.[22] The old Russian *ésprit de corps* of the intelligentsia waned. Its economic security eroded and its cultural superiority undermined, the liberal intelligentsia began to adopt nationalist positions.[23] The transition to the market was accompanied by the decline of the traditional Russian intelligentsia and the erosion of middle-class lifestyles: the crisis affected both the producers and consumers of culture.

## Religion and the state

In his appeal to Russians living abroad Yeltsin stressed the religious basis to Russia's national tradition. He spoke of 'reviving all the good things that were lost after [the Bolshevik revolution of October 1917], all that which made Russia Russia'. These included 'the Russian spiritual heritage, ravaged by the senseless and pitiless ideological struggle'.[24] Already in June 1988 church and state had achieved what was in effect a new concordat when Gorbachev allowed the celebrations of the millennium of the Russian Orthodox Church (ROC) and the authorities thereafter sought the assistance of the church in establishing the moral basis for a new order. In the elections of March 1990, 300 priests of various denominations were elected to soviets at all levels. *Perestroika* allowed a revival of the organisational life of the ROC and by late 1990 11,940 parishes came under the jurisdiction of the Moscow Patriarchate, 1,830 of which had been registered in the first 9 months of that year alone.[25] The reconsecration of churches was often accompanied by moving acts of social reintegration, and in Kazan 10,000 joined in the first service at the returned cathedral. The USSR Council for Religious Affairs, which had exercised harsh supervision over the church for decades, was finally disbanded in December 1991.

One of the gravest problems facing ROC was coming to terms with its compromised relationship with the Soviet state and its penetration by the KGB. For decades ROC had been ruled by an ecclesiastical *nomenklatura*, and the election of Patriarch Aleksy II, a man considered reliable by the old regime, to replace Patriarch Pimen in June 1990 appeared a continuation of old ways. The collapse of the USSR finally made possible the revelation of the names of the KGB 'agents in cassocks' in the Orthodox hierarchy (which included Metropolitan Filaret of Kiev), and the way that the KGB had tried to influence the World Council of Churches.[26] The ROC, however, had survived one of the cruellest onslaughts against religion in history, and later became one of the most trusted public bodies in Russia.[27]

As the Soviet Union disintegrated, so did the territorial unity of Orthodoxy as Moscow's pastoral authority was challenged by numerous national movements. The Uniate or Ukrainian Greek Catholic Church in Western Ukraine practised Orthodox rites but acknowledged the authority of the Roman Pope. By mid-1990 the Uniates, headed by Cardinal Libichevskii since 1984, claimed jurisdiction over some 1,400 parishes and had taken over all of the Moscow Patriarchate's churches in Ivanovo-Frankovsk and all but one in Lvov. The Pope's visit to Ukraine in June 2001 for the Uniate church represented the culmination of the hopes of many generations, whereas for Moscow it appeared to aggravate old sores. The Ukrainian Autocephalus Orthodox Church (UAOC) also grew rapidly and by mid-1990 claimed 300 parishes, some 200 of which were in the Ivanovo-Frankovsk region. With the independence of Ukraine Metropolitan Filaret of Kiev, representing the Moscow Patriarchate's Ukrainian Orthodox Church (UOC), was placed in an increasingly difficult situation until finally his alleged earlier collaboration with the KGB made his position untenable. Under a cloud of nationalistic rhetoric, supported by president Leonid Kravchuk, he made the UOC autocephalus and thus beyond Moscow's jurisdiction. The Ukrainian government supported a division that even the French revolutionaries had not contemplated by trying to establish a separate Catholic Church in France. In Russia itself Suzdal and other communities transferred their allegiance to the Free Russian Orthodox Church (under the jurisdiction of the New York-based Russian Orthodox Church Abroad, ROCA), while the True Orthodox Church (the part of the Catacomb Church that did not join the Free Orthodox Church) enjoyed a significant revival. While Patriarch Aleksy II called for reconciliation with ROCA, the leaders of ROCA insisted that the Moscow Patriarchate had for too long been the tool of a Godless regime and should publicly repent. One step in this direction was Aleksy's recantation in 2003 of the patriarchate's 1927 declaration of loyalty to the Soviet atheist regime. On 17 May 2007, the two churches formally reunited, putting an end to the long schism and marking, as Putin put it, an important step towards 'rediscovering the lost unity of the Russian people'.[28]

The opening of the borders made Russia fertile ground for missionaries and representatives of organised religion. Roman Catholic and Protestant churches developed their organisations, while the big cities were host to numerous fringe groups ranging from Hare Krishna, old Russian paganism (banned since 1552) and Freemasonry. The Hasidic community successfully campaigned for the return of the collection of manuscripts known as the Shneerson books, kept in the Lenin Library since being illegally confiscated in the 1920s. The wealth of the Unification Church of Sun Myung Moon, established in Korea in 1954, against the background of Russian poverty allowed it to exert a strong influence, as did various American Baptist and evangelical organisations. Post-communist religious life was marked by

> the amazingly ready credulity of the general public in the face of any self-styled preacher of 'spirituality' which is quite understandable in a country where the extermination of several generations of religious philosophers and theologians led to the oblivion of the fact that Reason has its own rules not only in the secular world, but also in the domain of religion.[29]

It was the fear of foreign penetration that provoked the 'Law on Freedom of Conscience and Religious Associations', adopted in September 1997, which sought to place barriers in the way of foreign proselytism. A distinction was drawn between 'traditional' and 'non-traditional' religions, with Orthodoxy, Islam, Buddhism and Judaism in the former category, while various 'cults' and 'sects' were in the latter. Religious *organisations* were granted certain privileges (such as the right to own property, employ people, conduct charity work and maintain formal international relations) that were denied religious *groups*. All religious bodies were to be registered, with particular stipulations concerning groups that that had been in Russia for less than fifteen years. Some groups, above all Jehovah's Witnesses and some Baptist churches, claimed that regional authorities placed obstacles in the way of registration, while attempts to block the registration of the Salvation Army on the grounds of its 'obvious militarism' were later reversed by the courts. Despite extensions to the deadline for registration, by 31 December 2000 13,922 congregations had been approved, while 3,000 had failed to register (mostly because they had ceased to exist or failed to present the necessary documentation) and were disbanded.[30] It is clear that the need to re-register was not as discriminatory as some had feared. Indeed, a study found that by mid-2001 there were over 20,000 congregations, compared to fewer than 5,000 in 1990, suggesting a religious flowering in Russia both in number and diversity.[31] Official figures reveal that on 1 January 2006 there were 22,513 religious organisations registered in Russia, of which 12,214 were official Orthodox, 706 other Orthodox, 251 Roman Catholic, 3,668 Islamic, 284 Jewish and 197 Buddhist.[32]

In January 2005 the 1997 law was amended to conform to new rules on the registration of other legal entities. The amended law requires all registered religious organisations to inform the federal registration service within three days of changes in its leadership or legal address. Failure to comply with this burdensome requirement can lead to deregistration. Despite the intrusive legislation, by December 2005 the Ministry of Justice had registered the 22,513 religious organisations, with local courts largely permitting non-traditional groups to register. Some did encounter problems, however, notably the Salvation Army (its military-style moniker alarmed the Russian authorities), the Moscow branch of the Church of Scientology, and the Jehovah Witnesses, remained under significant pressure. The Hizb ut-Tahrir was banned by the Supreme Court in 2003 as a terrorist organisation.

The influence of the church on society was significantly extended. Thousands of Sunday schools have been established, and numerous religious, philanthropic and charitable organisations visited hospitals, cared for the old, the indigent and the unemployed, looked after orphans and distributed food aid. Over 100 Russian Orthodox brotherhoods were established, reviving a tradition dating back to the Middle Ages, concerned with religious and philanthropic work. Many of these brotherhoods, however, adopted extreme nationalist and even racist positions. The Orthodox priesthood also played its part in the development of a new business class. In the prevalent conditions of lawlessness and rudimentary business ethics, enterprises managed or monitored by priests were among the few that could be trusted. This was a rather literal application of Weber's and Tawney's views on the role of the 'Protestant work ethic' in the rise of capitalism,[33] though the part played by the Orthodox priesthood in the restoration of the cultural values and motivations of capitalist accumulation might be considered anomalous. In general, the ROC only slowly adapted to new conditions, and its social philosophy remained a profoundly conservative one.[34]

According to the constitution (Article 14.1), 'The Russian Federation is a secular state. No religion may be established as the state religion or a compulsory religion.' In the 1990s, however, it was clear that the four 'traditional' religions were favoured, with their representatives given prominence on state occasions, such as presidential inaugurations. Of the four, Orthodoxy was clearly given primacy. This was reflected in the Preamble to the September 1997 law, which acknowledged that Russia was a secular state but recognised the special role of Orthodoxy in Russian history and culture. Similar formulations were adopted in Georgia (for Georgian Orthodoxy) and Mongolia (for Buddhism), and implicitly followed in Poland (for Roman Catholicism). These churches were not 'established' in the British sense, yet their pre-eminence was recognised. Putin made no secret of his affiliation with ROC, and although he tried to ensure equal treatment for other established religions, it was clear that Orthodoxy was more equal than the others.

## Political culture and public opinion

The attitudes and values engendered by the political socialisation of the earlier era, both official and unofficial, cast a long shadow over the new politics. While a type of democratic politics is formalised at the level of the state, the question focuses on whether it is adequately integrated into the patterns of daily life. Eckstein spent his academic life examining the problem of 'congruence' between social attitudes and state institutions, and post-communist Russia proved a particularly complex case study.[35] The question whether Russia enjoys the prerequisites (and indeed, the nature of the prerequisites themselves) for democracy remains open.

One of the more popular approaches of the earlier age was the notion of political culture, and in particular the question of the civic culture, the ideas and attitudes that sustain a political system.[36] Political culture refers to the values, perceptions of tradition and history, and beliefs about politics held by individuals. Seven decades of communist dominance, a period that itself followed only the briefest of political openings in the first years of the twentieth century, inevitably raises the question whether the Russian people themselves have the appropriate mental approach and attitudes to sustain the democratic experiment. There is a significant school of thought arguing that, given Russia's background, the Russian people could hardly be ready for democracy, having experienced collectivist socialisation and a manipulated political system all their lives. For Biryukov and Sergeev, the key to Russia's political culture is the concept of *sobornost'*, a pre-political attachment to collectivism, anti-individualism and hostility to pluralistic representative institutions.[37] Lukin takes this argument further, suggesting that the political culture of Russia's 'democrats' was little more than an inverted form of that held by the communists, hoping to replace one form of monolithic power with another (their own), failing to understand the deeper meaning of democratic pluralism. Although the anti-communist insurgency used the language of democracy, it did not really understand the deeper meaning of the terms that it so glibly threw around.[38] An opposed view argues that even within the old order, whose legitimation was democratic if in practice it fell far short of classical liberal democratic practices, a democratic consciousness had been maturing, fostered by the modernisation advanced by the regime itself. The shift from a predominantly peasant and rural society to an urban, literate and highly educated one could not but transform public values.

Political culture can be used in several different senses, including popular attitudes towards government and questions of political behaviour, but one of the most common ways of applying the term is to compare the degree to which historical factors determine present behaviour both at the elite and the popular levels.[39] In all communist countries, however, there was a choice of pasts, and it was easy to find elements that confirmed the historical continuity of the regimes then current rather than stressing the ways that they had repudiated the past. The past, like facts, is created in the eyes of the beholder. There are many Russian pasts reflecting its Asiatic and European identities. In the nineteenth century Russia was torn between Slavophiles like Alexei Khomyakov and Ivan Kireevsky who stressed Russia's communal, Orthodox and traditional ways against Westernisers like Konstantin Kavelin, Boris Chicherin and, on the socialistically inclined wing, Alexander Herzen and Vissarion Belinsky, who rejected appeals to Russia's uniqueness and insisted that the only road to the future lay through Europe. In the twentieth century the country once again was divided between liberals espousing the development of individualism, the rule of law and the market and socialists of various stripes espousing collectivism, egalitarianism and constraints on the market, if not its abolition in its entirety.[40] Arguments that rely on political culture as the independent variable tend to become circular and tautological: explaining what exists in terms of past legacies, but failing to explain mechanisms of change and adaptation.

Putnam demonstrated that beneath apparently similar political institutions, deeper social structures and behavioural patterns can differ sharply, even in a country as small as Italy.[41] His approach has been criticised as being back to front: it was not political culture that shaped the evolution of political institutions, but divergent institutional development shaped political culture.[42] While Russia is many times larger, the Soviet regime imposed a relatively similar experience of industrialisation and modernisation across the country, although in regions like the North Caucasus traditional patterns remain a living presence. Russia's past is multi-layered, and faced with the current challenge of modernisation and democratisation its history is once again being trawled to find elements that can sustain the new democratic experiment. The view of Russia as eternally autocratic has now given way to one which suggests that there were popular and philosophical constraints on autocratic rule.[43] Nicolai N. Petro stresses that:

> [B]efore Peter the Great the Russian ideal of 'good government' was not absolutism, as the political culture approach suggests, but a strong (autocratic) government constrained by religious and national tradition to serve the will of the people. Peter weakened these traditional constraints, but the populace never forgot them. The rift between the popular ideal of good government and the political reality of Imperial Russia was just beginning to heal when the October 1917 revolution seemed to dash popular aspirations for democratic government.[44]

From this perspective, advocates of the view that there is profound continuity from the pre-Soviet period to the present have to identify precisely which strand of the past they have in mind. There is also a fatalistic element to the continuity thesis, in that Russia's twentieth century was certainly not a period of the glorious triumph of democracy but a succession of social cataclysms and political breakdowns.

The contrasting views of Russia's past were reflected in the many dimensions of Russian popular thought as reflected in public opinion polls. It was clear long before the end that the Soviet regime had lost the confidence of the 'brightest and the best'.[45] A large-scale poll in March 1991 found engineering-technical workers the most dissatisfied social group with conditions of daily life, but reasonably satisfied with their work.[46] This may well explain why the majority (58.4 per cent) at the time favoured the market though only a small minority (12 per cent) thought that it would have a positive effect on their enterprise.[47]

Public opinion and values have been much analysed since the fall of communism (see Bibliography). The upsurge in public confidence following the coup soon evaporated. In a broad survey of public opinion in April 1992 only 13 per cent responded that their life was shaping up well in the new conditions, 63 per cent said tolerably, while the rest ranged from bad to very bad. At the same time 33 per cent insisted that the situation in the country was alarming or close to a crisis, 60 per cent called it a crisis or disastrous, while only 3 per cent considered the situation normal. Thus there was a gulf between people's perceptions of their own tolerable circumstances and the disastrous state of the country.[48] By the time of the first anniversary of the coup 55 per cent of Muscovite supporters of the White House accepted that their hopes had been disappointed, 19 per cent were unable to answer, while only 26 per cent considered that their hopes had been fulfilled.

There had been a shift in sympathies, and now only 42 per cent (compared to 62 per cent a year earlier) supported the democratic forces, though still only 7 per cent (compared to 4 per cent earlier) supported the putschists, while just over 50 per cent were indifferent or could not answer.[49] The early period of post-communism in Russia was therefore marked by a sharp rise in disillusionment with the new political system and the market.[50]

Society was left disoriented and alienated by the changes, yet it appeared that they did not threaten the market or democracy. The informal networks that had sustained people during the turmoil of *perestroika* helped people adjust to the collapse of the USSR and the emergence of a new order. Above all, public attitudes were permeated by a thorough democratism, for the institutions of democracy if not for the democrats themselves. A study in Yaroslavl' examined whether Russian political culture was compatible with the establishment of democratic institutions and discovered substantial support for democratic values and institutions.[51] A follow up study a decade later confirmed the earlier argument: there were deeper popular roots to democracy than the pessimistic school would suggest.[52] There appeared to be a high degree of social consensus on basic values like non-violence, the democratic resolution of conflict, and economic reform. This might suggest that there was little chance for a nationalist or neo-communist government coming to power, and the desire for strong government did not entail support for authoritarianism.[53]

Popular attitudes to private enterprise, private employment (long considered to be tantamount to 'exploitation'), and the transition to the market as a whole were far more favourable than stereotypes would allow.[54] The standard image was one of hostility, though it soon became clear that this had been much exaggerated. Yakovlev in October 1991 argued that 'Equality in poverty is the major obstacle to any social progress; it was the great invention of the ruling class, cementing its unlimited powers.'[55] A widespread popular passivity was identified, but this was not so much apathy as demobilisation, a calculated response to circumstances. The problem appeared to be that 'Many wanted to live in a market-democratic society, but rejected the steps, means and methods required to create such a society.'[56] A persistent theme was support for some sort of reconstituted USSR. Any number of polls demonstrated a sense that some sort of natural community had been destroyed in 1991, but at the same time there was no agreement over the nature of a possible reconstituted state. Just as in 1990–1 the majority had been in favour of retaining some sort of union of republics, few had favoured the existing structure,[57] and it was Gorbachev's inability to reconcile these two positions that led to disintegration, so later integrationists like Zyuganov could not find an adequate formula in which to frame aspirations for unity. A nationwide survey in February 1992 found that over 40 per cent preferred a reformed or even a restored USSR. Freedom of speech was considered by 71 per cent as the greatest achievement of the new system, but a significant proportion thought that within five years these freedoms would be curtailed. The concept of 'social justice' changed its meaning and was now used not as it had been by the democrats, to condemn the privileges of the elite, but by the conservatives to justify slowing down the reforms to avoid the development of excessive inequality. So from a revolutionary slogan, the term was converted into a conservative one.[58]

Political demobilisation served the reformers well, and the political emancipation of society was not accompanied by popular activism that might have jeopardised the policies that were considered to be in the people's long-term interests. The new political system, despite its many problems, was more stable than many had anticipated, especially in the absence of any serious alternative. Clearly, age, gender geographical location and occupation all affected views. Repeated polls suggest a relatively positive attitude to the West, but perhaps more significant is the strong correlation between age and attitudes, with the young far more open than the older generation.[59] One finding from opinion surveys was the rejection of force as a method to solve political disputes. Between 45–50 per cent of the population strongly rejected the use of extraordinary measures, and 80 per cent opposed the use of military force even in the most critical situations.[60] The strength of democratic commitment, however, was another matter.[61] Under Putin support for building up the power and might of Russia tempered the desire to integrate with the West.[62] On this issue, and on most others, there was no evidence of a gulf between elite and popular values; in fact, there was a remarkable coincidence.[63]

The detailed empirical study by Miller *et al.* suggested that political values and support for democratic political systems differ little between East and West Europe. Although there are numerous minor differences, there was no sustained East/West division correlating to different historical experiences and contemporary political values. In terms of attitudes to liberal values, the rule of law, tolerance for minorities, multi-party elections, the state's role in the economy, socialist values, nationalism and cultural conformity, there was little to choose between Britain and states emerging out of Tsarist, Ottoman or Habsburg rule. A large majority in all the states surveyed, including Russia, supported liberal and democratic values as well as the institutions embodying these values, and this was reflected in structured voting patterns. All this suggested that

> there was no evidence that the people of the former Soviet Union and East Central Europe were not ready for democracy... the lines of division that have excited so many theorists and historians seem remarkably faint in terms of contemporary political values.[64]

The traumas following the fall of communism provoked a return of former communists, but this in itself did not suggest opposition to democracy as such. Of course, those social groups and regions which lost the most in the transition, above all the aged and workers (especially agricultural workers, working in a sector locked in almost permanent recession) were the most deeply alienated from market reforms, and proved the most consistent supporters of revived communist parties. By contrast, those who benefited the most, the young, the urban and those employed in the private sector, repudiated socialism most strongly and were the bedrock of support for the new democratic order. Thus it was not historical legacies that determined political values, but the experience of the transition itself.

Similar findings are reported by Colton and Mcfaul. They take issue with the popular view that Russians prefer order above democracy, although there is plenty of polling evidence (which they cite) that could support such a view. However, while they demonstrate that Russians are dissatisfied with the actual operation of Russia's democratic institutions, this does not betoken a repudiation of democracy itself. Asked in broad terms whether they support democracy or not, 64 per cent came out in support.[65] More detailed examination of attitudes towards core elements of democracy like freedom to elect the country's leaders and freedom of speech revealed high levels of support (87 per cent).[66] When it came to a choice between order and liberty, Russians were not enthusiastic once again to discard their freedoms.[67] In confirmation of the findings of other research, there was a strong correlation between age and attitudes, with the older generation, not surprisingly, more attached to the Soviet system (and its values) than younger people. Putin's supporters, moreover, were not in any way more authoritarian than voters for any of the other candidates in the 2000 presidential election. In sum, there was a 'chasm between democratic attitudes and inadequately democratised institutions',[68] but not a repudiation of democracy itself.

## The reshaping of values

Values became disoriented as all the old certainties and articles of faith were undermined. The crisis affects far more than the collapse of the aspirations of the communist project and the social life support systems of the socialist regime. By the time the old system expired in 1991 the number of true believers had been sharply reduced, and communism had became more a way of life than an attractive goal, and indeed the more that communism receded as a goal, the more attractive it became as a way of life. The relatively cheap housing, energy and transport, the almost free telephones for local calls, the subsidised crèches and nurseries and holidays, the stable irrationality of the economic system and the strongly ordered social and cultural life, all provided a relatively congenial environment for the citizens of late communism - as long as they kept their mouths shut in public. Alexander Zinoviev argued that

> Ibanskian [i.e. Soviet] society is one which, in practice, has no effective institution of political rights. The reason is that it does not produce or reproduce on a large scale individuals capable of becoming the subjects of political law...The few political individuals who appear from time to time are subjected to persecution not because of a bad political law, but because of the absence of any political law.[69]

Both Yeltsin and Putin struggled to provide some core to changing conceptions of national identity. Already in 1996 Yeltsin had urged his aides to find a 'national idea' around which the country could unite: 'There were various periods in the Russian history of the twentieth century – monarchy, totalitarianism, *perestroika* and, finally, the democratic path of development. Each stage had its own ideology. We do not have it.' He allowed one year for the new idea to emerge.[70] Although in his 'Russia at the Turn of the Millennium' article Putin insisted that 'I am against the restoration of an official state ideology in Russia in any form',[71] on several occasions he returned to question of what should constitute the core principles of a revived Russia. He insisted that the basis of social accord would be patriotism: 'Large-scale changes have taken place in an ideological vacuum. One ideology was lost and nothing new was suggested to replace it.' He insisted that 'Patriotism in the most positive sense of this word' would be at the core of the new ideology.[72] Soon after the 1999 Duma elections Putin went further in specifying the elements of this ideology: 'It is very difficult to strive for conceptual breakthroughs in the main areas of life if there are no basic values around which the nation could rally. Patriotism, our history and religion can and, of course, should become such basic values.'[73] In his *Millennium* article Putin identified Russia's 'traditional values' as 'patriotism', *'gosudarstvennichestvo'*, (statehood) and 'social solidarity'. He defined patriotism as 'a feeling of pride in one's country, its history and accomplishments [and] the striving to make one's country better, richer, stronger and happier'.[74]

Putin's nation-building thus focused on four key elements. At its heart was an integrative patriotism that rejected the exclusivity associated with the concept of nationalism but instead encompassed pride in Russia's diversity, its history and its place in the world. This was to be buttressed by a strong political authority (statehood, *gosudarstvennost'*) that could maintain internal order, the integrity of the country and assert the country's interests abroad. Third, the pragmatic patriotism was to be supra-ethnic and statist, and it was on this basis that segmented regionalism was attacked to create a homogeneous constitutional space in which the ethnocratic rights of titular elites were to be subsumed into a broader political community. As Fish puts it, recentralisation was part of Putin's agenda of 'separating ethnicity from identity'.[75] And finally, the new nation-state was to be socially just. There was not much here about a rights-based liberalism, yet the lack of emphasis on pluralism and individual human and civic rights was balanced by Putin's emphasis on the rule of the law. His ideology was liberal conservatism.

A nation only exists when it shares a set of symbols and orientations towards its own history. In the 1990s Russia had remained bitterly divided in this respect. Putin sought to reconcile Russia's various pasts to overcome the divisions between Reds and Whites, Greens and Blacks. As we have seen (Chapter 10), this was most vividly in evidence in the adoption of the country's symbols and anthem.[76] As for the individuals who lived through the transformation of Russian society, the problem of integrating various layers of experience and socialisation was no less acute. Under communism it had been easy to shed personal responsibility, since the Party-state claimed total responsibility. People were thus in a distinctive way free of personal responsibility, a form of infantilism. While Zinoviev was right in asserting that the laws of the Soviet regime had become ever distant from real practices in daily life, he was mistaken to suggest that the system reflected the social characteristics of the psychological types inhabiting its universe. In other words, the system was not derived from the existence of a particular character type, but *homo sovieticus* was a morbid symptom of the system itself. Change the system, and *homo sovieticus* would soon die out.

The Soviet citizen lived according to a self-evident counter-rationality which generated a stable pattern of counter-values which did not so much oppose the Soviet system as ignore it. The counter-values came to predominate after August 1991, but these forms of resistance reflected the subject of resistance and reproduced some of its values in an inverted form. It was this network of counter-values rather than the Soviet values in which few believed that was shaken during the hard transitional period following the fall of the old system.[77] The belief in democracy as a universal panacea, faith in the West, trust in international institutions and guarantees of human rights, belief in the value of the word and rational argument to avoid conflict, were undermined by the economic collapse, the inadequacy of the West's response and by the various conflicts that erupted across the former Soviet Union. Underlying much of the unease about the accelerated integration into world society and to the market economy was the fear that Russia's 'uniqueness' might be lost. This is a fear shared by the Japanese, Chinese and other major civilisations faced with the apparently relentless tide of Americanisation. Some of these fears were articulated by Solzhenitsyn and the patriots. New forms of resistance to Western capitalist modernity will no doubt emerge in Russia as they have in the West with the development of the 'anti-globalisation' movement. In Russia, however, capitalist democracy has first to be built before a coherent opposition can be sustained.

The dissolution of the old order necessarily meant the partial dissolution of the subject of society, 'man', since the self is to a degree shaped by the relationship to society. The reordering of society meant a reshaping of its subjects. As far as the national-patriots were concerned, the liberal experiment in Russia in fact meant the dissolution of the subject as they scrabbled to join the grazing herd of Nietzsche's 'Last Men', a fate which they did not even develop themselves but borrowed from abroad. If there is anything worse than slavery, they argued, it is to borrow the slavery of others - Marxian socialism earlier, and now market liberalism. While the creation of a market economy posed unprecedented challenges, the transformation of society was no less dramatic. The elite structure was reformed and traditional cultural and social values were undermined as commercial relations affected the media, education and the very identity of individuals. While the *homo economicus* gradually squeezed out the *homo sovieticus*, it was not clear what would be the scope for the broader political and social community. The citizen and the bourgeois both now emerged, but what would be the relationship between the two?[78] Mediating between the two a powerful regime emerged, once again managing and directing society.

# Part V

# Foreign, security and neighbourhood policy

Russia is different not only from the other former Soviet states, but also from countries comparable in size and population. It is different not only because of historical dominance of its region and its geopolitical role in Europe and Eurasia, or because of its strategic significance as the world's second largest nuclear power, or because of its political weight associated with its status as a permanent member of the UN Security Council, or because of its crucial role as energy supplier to Europe. These are important factors, but above all Russia is different because it perceives itself to be different. For some policy-makers in the West, above all in the corridors of power in the United States, the gulf between Russia's ambitions and its rather more modest realities became increasingly irksome. Russia's pretensions to be a 'great power' were derided and the country was urged to render its attitudes and policies rather more commensurate with its decreased territorial space, economic resources and comparative military potential. Russia, however, was more than just another European state, a view reflected in any number of comments and official documents. For example, Anatoly Utkin at the USA and Canada Institute argued that Western advice that Russia should 'forget about our past greatness and become another Brazil' ignores the fact that '150 million don't perceive themselves as Brazilians'.[1] The Russian government's Medium-Term Strategy on relations with the EU argued:

> As a world power situated on two continents, Russia should retain its freedom to determine and implement its domestic and foreign policies, its status and advantages as a Euro-Asian state and the largest country of the CIS, and independence of its positions and activities at international organisations.[2]

This striving for autonomy and recognition as a global player was repeated in innumerable documents and was increasingly translated into policy. Russia gradually recovered from the traumas of the 1990s, and buoyed by a growing economy and a greater sense of self confidence, the country sought to assert itself in world and regional politics. However, this resurgence was greeted with suspicion and fear. It was not clear how the post-Cold War international system, dominated by a single superpower, could incorporate a revived great power.

# 16 Foreign policy

Russia's misfortune lies in this: Russia and Europe live in different historical times.

(G. P. Fedotov)[1]

The fall of communism overshadowed perhaps an even more epoch-making event, the disintegration of a geopolitical unit that had lasted some five hundred years, in comparison with which the reign of communism had been a mere interregnum. The geopolitical and strategic balance not only of the post-Second World War era but of the whole epoch since the Congress of Vienna in 1815 came to an end. Russia's long climb from local, regional, continental and then to global power was suddenly dramatically reversed. The dissolution of communism ended one set of problems associated with global confrontation in the Cold War, but the disintegration of the Soviet Union raised no less epochal issues. Would the inherent instability of Russo-European relations for the last four hundred years give way to a new partnership?[2] Would the new Russia be able to define a post-imperial and post-communist national identity and integrate into global economic and political processes? What sort of 'normality' in international and regional affairs was normal for Russia? These questions were hard enough for the weak Russia of the 1990s, but were no less complex for the revived power of the 2000s.

## The evolution of foreign policy

One does not have to be a full-blooded constructivist to argue that the shaping of foreign policy is to a large degree determined by the way that a country defines itself and its place in the world. Before any coherent foreign policy based on 'national interest' could be defined, Russia had to achieve a minimum consensus on its evolving national identity and priorities. The interdependence of foreign and domestic policy in the post-communist era was explicitly closer than ever before as Russia sought a favourable international climate to assist economic reform and to facilitate its reintegration into the international system. In the first period Russian foreign policy was thoroughly 'domesticated', with domestic reform taking priority over any remaining global ambitions, but gradually the outlines of a more 'balanced', or as others would put it, a more assertive if not aggressive, policy took shape.

Russian foreign policy since independence has passed through six main stages. Each was marked by contradictory goals that imbued policy with what we shall call an 'essential ambiguity', often reflected in what appeared to be irresolution and muddle. We use the term 'essential' because the conflicting aims were structured into the very situation and could hardly be avoided if a complex policy was to be pursued; and 'ambiguous' because they reflected the profound and unresolved (and probably insoluble) civilisational and geopolitical choices facing Russia. The foundations on which choices would be made were themselves contested: would economic development be the priority, or the struggle to restore Russian dominance in Eurasia, or would the attempt to maintain good relations with the West while asserting the country's autonomy predominate? Russia's size, location, and history generated multifaceted if not contradictory foreign policies.

### The emergence phase: before the coup

Even before the 1991 coup the outlines of an independent policy had emerged, yet the problem of defining Russia's separate interests distinct from those of the USSR had not been resolved. Yeltsin's election to chair the Russian CPD on 29 May 1990 and the declaration of Russian state sovereignty on 12 June set the scene for a debate over Russia's national interests and over the shape of its foreign policy. Already by October two central principles had emerged: that Russia would seek friendly relations with the other Soviet republics in a renewed union; and that Russia wished to return as an autonomous force in world politics, defending its status as a great power but at the same time seeking 'to occupy a worthy (*dostoinoe*) place in the community of civilised peoples of Eurasia and America'.[3]

A separate Russian diplomatic service was re-established in October 1990, and in November Andrei Kozyrev was appointed foreign minister. From 1974 to 1990 Kozyrev had worked in the Directorate of International Organisations in the Soviet Ministry of Foreign Affairs (MFA), and thus it is not surprising that he later placed so much emphasis on international institutions. He also came to be known as an 'Atlanticist', someone in favour of close links with America. Kozyrev argued that Russian policy would no longer be based on ideology or messianic ambitions but common sense and the realistic evaluation of concrete needs. He developed new approaches to international issues, even though policy, in this area as in most others, remained in Yeltsin's hands. Russia's first independent acts reflected the blurred distinction between foreign and domestic policy, namely the signing of treaties with Ukraine on 19 November, Kazakhstan on 21 November and with Belarus on 18 December 1990. The treaties recognised the signatories as sovereign states, and declared that their relations would be based on principles of equality, non-interference and the renunciation of the use of force, and that they would establish diplomatic relations with each other. Soviet and Russian foreign policy began to diverge as Russian diplomacy sought to facilitate the radical transformation of society and to defend what came to be seen as Russian national interests separate and distinct from those of the Soviet Union. During Gorbachev's visit to Japan in April 1991, for example, Yeltsin made it clear that the USSR could not negotiate a return of the four disputed Kurile Islands without consulting Russia.

Yeltsin's defence of the concept of a sovereign and independent Russia, presented so eloquently during his presidential campaign in June 1991, however, was conceived within the framework of a renewed union. Russia sought not the disintegration of the union but its transformation on the basis of a renegotiated treaty, retaining a system of collective security, a coordinated foreign policy, and the maintenance of a common economic, transport and employment space. To this end Russia took an active part in the nine-plus-one negotiations for a new union treaty and was committed to signing the documents on 20 August when the coup intervened. Russia's assertion of an independent foreign policy, therefore, was considered compatible with a renewed union with its own federal government. This is a clear example of the 'essential ambiguity' of Russian policy since it was difficult to see how mutually exclusive claims to sovereignty could be reconciled within a single state.

### The establishment phase: August to December 1991

The nine-plus-one union renewal process was derailed by the events of August 1991 and never gained momentum thereafter, despite Gorbachev's last ditch attempts to transform the USSR into a Union of Sovereign States (see Chapter 2). The tension between a decaying Soviet and an embryonic Russian foreign policy provoked only confusion and frustration.

Following Eduard Shevardnadze's resignation as Soviet foreign minister on 20 December 1990 Alexander Bessmertnykh had been appointed in his place, but during the coup he had wavered. He in turn was replaced by Boris Pankin, the former ambassador to Prague and one of a handful of Soviet envoys who denounced the putschists without hesitation. Pankin notes the atmosphere:

> In those days the common obsession that gripped our entire leadership was with the idea of becoming a 'civilised state'. The issue of being patronised or humbled did not arise. In fact giving advice to the Soviet Union was a pastime that had been positively encouraged by the highly sociable Shevardnadze, who in all his contacts with the West seemed more ready to be polite and accommodating than to stand firm.[4]

Pankin, however, proved to be only a temporary appointment, and although he fought to defend the Soviet foreign affairs establishment and modified some of the cuts imposed on the MFA, he was accepted neither by the Soviet foreign affairs community nor by the emerging Russian one. The Soviet MFA began to wither away, despite attempts to 'democratise' its ruling collegium and its reorganisation into a Ministry of External Relations after merger with the Ministry of Foreign Trade. The reappointment of Shevardnadze on 19 November 1991 as minister of external relations represented Gorbachev's last desperate attempt to restore his crumbling authority.

Conflicts between the USSR and Russia were provoked not only by institutional rivalries but also over policy issues. Russia influenced the decision in September 1991 to remove the Soviet training brigade from Cuba, the decision to halt arms sales to Afghanistan on 13 September, and the restoration of diplomatic relations with Israel on 24 October 1991, 24 years after they had been broken off after the Six Day War of June 1967. Germany, hitherto Gorbachev's keenest supporter, in November 1991 welcomed Yeltsin on a state visit as he sought to secure economic assistance for Russia's promised reforms. The visit signalled that Russia had returned to the international community as a nation in its own right.

By the end of the year Russia had swallowed up the Soviet state. On 18 December 1991 Yeltsin brought the Soviet diplomatic service under Russian control, and on 22 December the Soviet foreign and defence ministries were abolished. The Soviet Ministry of External Relations was merged with Russia's, and Shevardnadze once again left political office until he entered the political fray in his native Georgia, where he served as president from 1992 until he was overthrown in the 'rose' revolution of November 2003. Yeltsin placed himself at the head of the Russian MFA, and Gennady Burbulis took over routine operations. Russia inherited the mantle of responsibility and sought international recognition for its new role. Russia was recognised as the 'continuer' state to the USSR, taking over responsibility for Soviet treaties and obligations and above all for the Soviet strategic arsenal (see Chapter 17). Russia was more than just a 'successor' state, but became the residual legatee of all the authority that was not devolved to the other republics. A vivid manifestation of Russia's dissolution in the Union was that whereas Ukraine and Belorussia as well as the USSR took seats in the UN as founding members (according to a deal agreed with Stalin in 1945), Russia had been left firmly in the cold. Now Russia took over the USSR's seat as one of the five permanent members of the 15-member UN Security Council (UNSC), giving it a right of veto. The permanent seat on the UNSC became one of the most important symbols of Russia's claim to great power status.

### The 'romantic' phase, January 1992–February 1993

Freed from the burden of the union, Russia re-entered the world stage and by January 1992 had already been recognised by 131 states. Addressing the Russian MFA on 27 October 1991, Yeltsin set two main aims for Russian policy: to secure favourable external conditions for domestic political and economic reforms; and to overcome the legacy of the Cold War and to dismantle confrontational structures.[5] Both policies were laced with ambiguities: to what degree would economics (reform at home and global integration) be placed above national interests, however defined; how would this attempt to reap the 'peace dividend' be compatible with Russia's claimed great power status; and why was nothing said about forging a new relationship with the former Soviet states? Questions such as these have led to this period of Russian foreign policy being dubbed 'romantic', allegedly excessively pro-Western at the expense of Russia's own interests and at the price of the neglect of its own 'backyard' in the CIS. The so-called 'Atlanticist' orientation of Russia foreign policy at this time allegedly undermined Russia's national interests in its neighbourhood and in the world at large.

National-patriots, centrists and democratic statists alike were to varying degrees sceptical about the viability of the Soviet successor states, and insisted that Russia should direct its policy far more actively towards them. Post-communist Russian nation-building was profoundly influenced by the question of the 25 million Russians (however defined) who had suddenly found themselves 'abroad', and the claimed defence of their rights and status permeated domestic politics. The Russian leadership was hesitant to adopt ethnicity as a factor in inter-state relations and thus allegedly abandoned their compatriots abroad; by the same token the sanctity of the new international borders and the sovereignty of the new states was acknowledged. This did not, however, prevent the blurring of the distinction between domestic and foreign policy when discussing relations with the former Soviet states, especially when Russian strategic interests were concerned. The widespread use of the term *blizhnee zarubezh'e* (near abroad) for the former Soviet republics suggested that these countries were somehow in a different category from genuinely foreign countries.

Kozyrev noted that 'the second Russian Revolution unfolded in a favorable foreign policy setting',[6] and proceeded on the assumption that military force was no longer relevant as an instrument of policy. This view was immediately contradicted by the dominant role that the Russian military played in shaping policy in the near abroad as the foreign ministry all but abdicated responsibility in the area. Kozyrev on several occasions condemned the military and the 'party of war'.[7] With the onset of a deep Western economic recession in the early 1990s and Germany's preoccupation with absorbing its new Eastern territories, the international environment deteriorated. Western funds became more limited, and in any case the bulk went to the 'old' Eastern Europe (above all Hungary, Poland and the Czech Republic, what later became the 'new' Europe). Whether justified or not, there was a palpable sense of disappointment in Russia as early hopes of a rapid transformation with Western help evaporated. A new Marshall Plan was certainly not forthcoming. This period has been dubbed 'romantic' but it might better be characterised as idealistic, in the sense that it sought indeed to base policy on a set of universal ideals based on human rights, national self-determination, and the belief that the end of the Cold War was a common victory. Soviet ideology had given way to a democratic idealism, and policy remained removed from the harsh geopolitical realities of the world in which the newly independent Russian state found itself.

### The reassertion phase, March 1993–December 1995

Post-communist Russian foreign policy is marked by great continuity in strategic goals, focused above all on achieving international economic integration and recognition of the attributes of a great power, but there have been several tactical turning points. One of these took place towards the end of 1992 and into early 1993. The opposition condemned Kozyrev's alleged servility and 'romantic' obsession with the West and his failure to formulate an effective policy towards the former Soviet republics. As far as the national-patriots and centrists were concerned, allegiance to the principles of a cosmopolitan liberal universalism threatened Russia's very existence as a state. Russia now began explicitly to assert a hegemonic concept of its 'vital national interests' in the near abroad, coupled with a reassertion of Russia's great power status in the world at large. It was at this time, Pavel Baev notes, that 'geopolitics successfully replaced communist ideology as the conceptual basis for Russia's foreign policy'.[8] This brought the concept of *Realpolitik* firmly back into the lexicon of foreign policy discourse, displacing the idealistic universalism of the *perestroika* years. Gorbachev's 'new political thinking' and 'common European home' became increasingly associated with capitulation and retreat, and there was now a new concern with defending what were taken to be Russia's vital interests.

In March 1992 Stankevich and other proponents of an active post-imperial Russian foreign policy sponsored a Russian Monroe doctrine, defining the whole area of the former Soviet Union as one vital to Russian national interests.[9] This approach was further developed in August 1992 in the first 'Strategy for Russia' report of the Council for Foreign and Defence Policy (SVOP), established by Sergei Karaganov, the deputy director of the Institute of Europe. The document argued that Russia's interests were not necessarily the same as the West's, and indeed, that the gap between the two would probably increase; and as a corollary, the focus of Russian policy should shift from the West to the near abroad from whence the main challenges to Russian security would come. Thus the document advocated an 'enlightened post-imperial course' that could balance the relationship with the West and Russia's concerns in the near abroad.[10] In a speech to the Civic Union conference on 28 February 1993 Yeltsin for the first time made explicit Russia's claim to have a 'vital interest in the cessation of all armed conflicts on the territory of the former USSR', and appealed to the UN 'to grant Russia special powers as the guarantor of peace and stability in this region'.[11] In 1993 the new line was formalised in the 'Foreign Policy Concept' drafted by the Security Council, which once again declared Russia to be the guarantor of stability in the former Soviet Union. While the international community was reluctant to endorse Russia's special role, it was unwilling to intervene itself and thus *de facto* Russia was granted a free hand to impose its own order in the post-Soviet space – with the important exception of the Baltic states.

Kozyrev's own position evolved, with his enemies accusing him of a chameleon-like opportunism to maintain his post, usually involving uncritical support for Yeltsin. Kozyrev sought to combine two apparently contradictory principles. On the one hand, he sought to 'guarantee the rights of citizens and the dynamic socio-economic development of society'; on the other, he insisted that Russia was 'a normal great power, achieving its interests not through confrontation but through cooperation'.[12] By late 1993 Kozyrev had adopted a more sharply defined empire-saving strategy, insisting that Russia had the right to intervene to prevent the country 'losing geopolitical positions that took centuries to achieve'.[13] Alarmed by the appeal of Zhirinovsky's nationalistic rhetoric in the December 1993 elections, much of the Russian political elite incorporated some of his ideas into their own programmes. The attempt to make Russia a democracy *and* a great power became the central principle of Russian policy from early 1993, but these aims (typical of the essential ambiguity characteristic of Russian policy) were not entirely compatible. Kozyrev now argued that Russia could be a democratic post-Cold War great power pursuing a non-ideological definition of national interests while accepting that this could sometimes entail elements of competition with the West. This tough approach was vividly manifested in Kozyrev's refusal in November 1994 in Brussels to sign documents already agreed with NATO concerning the Partnership for Peace (PfP) programme. Attempts by the West to discredit the pursuit of Russia's 'normal' great power interests by forever raising the spectre of a revival of the Cold War, according to Yeltsin a month later at the Budapest summit of the OSCE in December 1994, threatened precisely to lead to the emergence of a 'cold peace'.[14] Kozyrev left the Russia's Choice faction in the Duma when they condemned the onset of war in Chechnya. Kozyrev became a proponent of the reconstituted ideology of power, but this did not mean the abandonment of all of his earlier views and he remained committed to a viable relationship with the West. Despite his partial conversion to a great power ideology, his critics continued to characterise his foreign policy as confused and amateur.[15]

Kozyrev's new-found statism not only undermined his credibility as a liberal but also damaged his ability to function as foreign minister. At home his stand was widely interpreted as yet another manoeuvre to stay in power, while abroad his credibility, already undermined by the indeterminacy of Russian policy in the Bosnian war (1992–5), imbued Russia's foreign policy with a damaging unpredictability.[16] National-patriot and neo-communist denunciations were roused to fever pitch by his weak response to the threat of NATO expansion and the bombing of Serb positions in Bosnia in August 1995. Despite his alignment with 'pragmatic nationalists' Kozyrev remained committed to a constructive relationship with the West, refusing to accept that the latter remained the threat it had been during the Cold War. In the December 1995 elections Kozyrev retained his single-member seat in Murmansk; faced with the choice of leaving the foreign ministry or giving up his seat, he chose the former and on 5 January 1996 resigned. Thus a distinctive era in Russian foreign policy came to an end.

### Competitive pragmatism, January 1996–9

The new foreign minister was the former head of the Foreign Intelligence Service, Yevgeny Primakov. A specialist on Middle Eastern affairs, Primakov had risen high in the former regime, holding senior positions in the academic world and becoming a candidate member of the Politburo. He had been Gorbachev's envoy to the Gulf charged with averting war following Iraq's occupation of Kuwait in August 1990. Although foreign policy is a presidential prerogative, the change of ministers inevitably altered the tone and modified the substance of policy. Primakov had been highly critical of the West, and thus his appointment was welcomed by the communists and nationalists in the Duma. While seeking to maintain good relations with the West, Primakov sought to reassert Russia's position in China, the Far East and with its traditional allies in the Middle East. Primakov took a substantive view of Russia's national interests and insisted that the country was not only a great power but also the cornerstone of a multipolar international community.[17] His four priority tasks for Russian foreign policy were to create the external conditions to strengthen Russia's territorial integrity; to support integrative tendencies within the CIS; to stabilise regional conflicts (above all in the former USSR and Yugoslavia); and to prevent the spread of weapons of mass destruction.[18] The key concept of Primakov's stewardship of foreign policy was 'pragmatism', yet this was of a distinctive type that we characterise as 'competitive'.

As prime minister between September 1998 and May 1999 Primakov remained a guiding influence on foreign policy, although the new foreign minister, Igor Ivanov, had views of his own. During the Kosovo crisis of 1999 Ivanov was willing to employ some harsh anti-Western rhetoric, yet was careful not to back Russia into a corner. While expressing support for the Serbs in general and Slobodan Milošelvić in particular, the Russian leadership retained its freedom of manoeuvre and did little to help the Serb leader. In June 1999 Russia helped broker the peace deal between the NATO allies and Milošević, after 74 days of bombing from 24 March. Russian foreign policy pragmatism remained even after Primakov's forced retirement from government.

### From new realism to new Cold War, 2000–8?

On coming to power Putin retained Ivanov as foreign minister, yet an appreciable change took place in foreign policy. Although elements of Primakov's 'competitive pragmatism' remained, policy now lacked the groundless assurance that Russia was a great power, and that it was the West's misfortune not to recognise this. Following a meeting of the Security Council on 24 March 2000 devoted to Russia's new Foreign Policy Concept, Ivanov commented that the document was 'more realistic' than its 1993 predecessor.[19] The Concept was adopted on 28 June 2000 and combined a commitment to international integration with assertions about Russia's great power status.[20] Although almost all the elements were there before, Putin's foreign policy was marked by a more sober appreciation of reality and of Russia's real as opposed to idealised interpretations of its interests. In a keynote speech to the MFA on 26 January 2001 Putin urged that Russian diplomacy had to focus more on promoting the country's economic interests abroad, while at the same time improving its image.[21] The new realism was no less ambitious in its own evaluation of Russia's role, but was marked by a realisation that the means were lacking to maintain what was considered Russia's rightful place in the world. Putin stressed the need to rebuild the domestic economy, while at the same time sought to achieve by diplomacy what was lacking materially. He engaged in a round of high-profile visits (some thirty in his first year as president) as he took the management of foreign affairs into his own hands. However, the tangible benefits of his globe-trotting appeared slender, and ultimately only accentuated not Russia's global role but its difficulty in sustaining that role. By the end of Putin's two-term presidency a newly self-confident and gauchely assertive Russia encountered growing hostility in the world, giving rise to fears of a new Cold War.

The phases discussed above were marked by an unstable extremism: the assertion of Russian autonomy undermined the viability of the USSR; the establishment phase precipitated the collapse of the USSR by reducing Gorbachev to little more than a figurehead; the 'romantic' phase exaggerated dependence on the West; the reassertion of Russian interests failed to build a stable and predictable relationship with the international community; competitive pragmatism endangered the very real achievements of Kozyrev's foreign policy in normalising relations with the world at large; while the new realism was based on the dangerous illusion that international affairs are governed by reciprocity and recognition of the genuine interests of great powers. All of these excesses reflected the fundamental problem of inserting a democratising Russia into an existing international order as an equal. This problem has not yet been resolved.

## The structure of policy-making

Soviet diplomacy had traditionally had two faces: one focused on the professional diplomats in the Soviet MFA, characterised by expertise in negotiation techniques, conflict management and the like; the other, inspired by the residual internationalism of the socialist system, was organised by the Communist Party's International and other departments. Shevardnadze had limited the prerogatives of the latter and by the end of *perestroika* foreign policy had firmly shifted from the Party to the state and was concentrated in the hands of the specialists in the Soviet MFA. Already by August 1991 the Party organisation had been abolished in the Russian MFA, and the merging of the Russian and Soviet MFAs in late 1991 was accompanied by the 'deideologisation' of the new ministry. This was designed above all to improve its professionalism and to ensure that the ministry worked to defend Russia's national-state interests. The cause of international revolution was officially pronounced dead.

The Russian MFA inherited the buildings and diplomatic staff from the old regime. Kozyrev moved into the luxurious offices in the foreign ministry building on Smolensk Boulevard and set about rebuilding the Russian diplomatic service. Up to 1991 about two-thirds of Soviet embassy staff abroad were also on the payroll of the KGB.[22] The Russian MFA was restructured to reflect the new priorities of foreign policy. The traditional confused system of administrations (*upravleniya*) and sections (*otdely*) was replaced by a more ordered system. Thirteen departments (*departamenty*), overseen by deputy ministers, nine functional administrations (*upravleniya*) and three services (*otdely*) were initially established. The old regional administrations were transformed into seven departments: Europe, North America, Central and South America, Africa, the Near East, the Asia-Pacific region, and South West Asia. There were also departments for International Organisations and Global Problems of International Humanitarian Assistance, and Cultural Cooperation. The departments dealing with information and the press were significantly upgraded. Of particular significance was the creation in April-May 1992 of a department for relations with CIS countries, a belated recognition of the importance of this area of what had now become foreign policy. Over the years the management of relations with post-Soviet states changed frequently, until by the end of Putin's presidency a deputy prime minister was placed in charge of coordinating work in this crucial area.

In February 1992 Yeltsin subordinated the 'power' and 'political' ministries to the presidency, bringing the MFA and the ministries of defence, internal affairs, security, justice and some others firmly under his control.[23] Numerous presidential agencies and advisory groups were spawned to formulate the main lines of foreign and security policy and to supervise the current work of the ministries, reducing the foreign ministry to not much more than a specialist executive agency. Even though Yeltsin in November 1992 made the MFA responsible for coordinating Russia's foreign policy, confusion remained as individuals and institutions, above all the Supreme Soviet under Khasbulatov, sought to pursue their own foreign policy agendas. Under Putin elements of this confusion remained as the Security Council under Sergei Ivanov took on an enhanced role before relapsing back into its typically passive role, while the MFA (in the eyes of critics) appeared to become little more than a glorified travel agency organising Putin's many trips abroad.

The adoption of the 1993 constitution confirmed the president's pre-eminent role. Article 80.3 baldly states that the president 'determines the basic guidelines of the state's domestic and foreign policy', Article 80.4 stipulates that he or she 'represents the Russian Federation within the country and in international relations', and Article 86 specifies that the president 'exercises leadership of the foreign policy of the Russian Federation' (Article 86a), conducts negotiations, signs international treaties (Article 86b) and instruments of ratification (Article 86c), and accepts letters of diplomatic accreditation (Article 86d). The president decides membership of the Security Council, chairs its sessions and is the final arbiter of Russia's military doctrine. The president, in consultation with parliament, nominates ambassadors, and has the right to appoint and dismiss members of the government, including those responsible for foreign policy. The government's powers over foreign policy are limited, authorised only to implement measures for 'the realisation of the foreign policy of the Russian Federation' (Article 114.1e). In other words, it is intended to do little more than to implement policies coming from the presidency. The work of the MFA in the new conditions was formulated by a presidential statute of 14 March 1995, subordinating it to the president but delegating to it 'the development of the general strategy for Russian foreign policy'.[24]

This was reflected in the reduced foreign policy role assigned to parliament. Formally, the State Duma's functions are restricted to approving or rejecting international treaties (Article 106d), while the Federation Council authorises the use of Russian troops abroad

(Article 102.1d). Both issues could prove controversial. Parliament's foreign policy role, however, is broader than the above would suggest. Above all, the committee system ensures that foreign policy issues remain firmly within the purview of deputies. The FC's committees for foreign affairs, CIS affairs, and security and defence policy are complemented by the Duma committees for foreign affairs, defence, security, CIS affairs and links with compatriots. The anti-Western majority in the First Duma, and even more in the Second, forced foreign policy to adopt the language of 'struggle' between Russian and Western interests. The espousal of Russia as a 'great power' often meant that 'ideological dogma had priority over common sense'.[25] With a supportive majority in the Third and Fourth Dumas, the president's foreign policy initiatives were now reinforced by a solid parliamentary base.

Many other organisations play their part in the foreign policy process. In addition to the domestic security agencies and the Foreign Intelligence Service, the Security Council at various times has taken an active foreign policy role. The SC under Sergei Ivanov became one of Putin's main institutional supports, until Ivanov moved on to become defence minister, at which point the SC, first under Vladimir Rushailo and then the former foreign minister Igor Ivanov, once again went into decline. With the creation of the Russian Ministry of Defence in May 1992 older Soviet patterns of rivalry between the foreign and defence ministries re-emerged. Kozyrev insisted on the primacy of the foreign ministry, and warned (unsuccessfully) against the military becoming an autonomous force in areas such Transnistria.[26] On several occasions, as in Abkhazia and elsewhere, it appeared that Russia had two foreign policies, an official presidential one and another pursued by the military. Yeltsin's debt to the military following the October 1993 events only increased their scope for independent initiatives. Under Putin the military had little influence in foreign policy formation, although its peace-keeping role in post-Soviet Eurasian conflicts meant that hints of the old duality remained.

The country was marked by the proliferation of non-governmental 'think tanks', lobbying pressure groups, pseudo-academic research institutes established by retired or dismissed politicians, and money-making ventures launched by institutes of the Academy of Sciences to augment the meagre funds available from the state. By far the most important, however, was SVOP, founded in June 1992 'as a public organisation of politicians, entrepreneurs, civil servants, media figures and academics whose purpose is to support the development and implementation of strategic conceptions for the development of Russia, its foreign and defence policies'.[27] In the words of its director, Karaganov, its task was to coordinate the contending proposals to create 'a stable political centre in the country'.[28] Membership ranged across the political spectrum, encompassing academics, Duma deputies and politicians. Its first report (noted above) called 'A Strategy for Russia',[29] strongly influenced the evolving debate over Russia's foreign policy and place in the world, while its second report in May 1994 had even greater resonance (see below).[30] In anticipation of a change of leadership, from late 1998 the council commissioned its third major study of the problems facing Russia, designed explicitly as a programme for the new president. The report was published in 2000, just in time to be used by the new leader, and dealt (in its own words) not only with Russia's eternal question of 'what is to be done?', but focused above all on 'how it is to be done'.[31]

In contrast to the Soviet era, and indeed even under Gorbachev, policy-making was now a much more open and pluralistic process. Some regional and republican leaders (in particular Tatarstan) also sought to sustain foreign policy initiatives, but the scope for this was limited by the Federal Treaty of 31 March 1992, which unequivocally reserved to the federal government responsibility for foreign policy, and by the 1993 constitution (although as we saw in Chapter 12, this did not stop some regions trying to develop autonomous foreign policies of their own). The MFA in December 1994 established a Consultative Council of Russian Federation Subjects on International and Foreign Economic Relations to coordinate local initiatives. To curb international freelancing by regional elites, the Duma in January 1999 adopted a law stipulating that regional authorities must liaise with the MFA in negotiations with a foreign government.[32] A special department was established by the ministry dealing with regional matters, with branch offices in regions and republics that were particularly active in foreign affairs. Only the federal government has the right to sign international treaties (*dogovory*), a principle upheld by numerous judgments of the Constitutional Court.[33]

Institutions and social forces sought to influence policy through lobbying, press campaigns and other normal features of pluralistic politics. However, the politicisation of foreign policy had some negative consequences as crude representations of complex foreign policy decisions became part of domestic political struggles (a typical feature of the Western foreign policy process), adding yet another layer of unpredictability. Foreign and security policy became part of an intensive public debate reflected in the print and electronic media. The emergence of active domestic constituencies concerned with foreign policy limited the range of options available to the leadership. Despite the new pluralism, post-communist Russia reproduced aspects of Soviet, if not Tsarist, patterns of foreign policy-making. Once again the cabinet of ministers was reduced to executing policies taken by the Tsar, Politburo or president, with its functions largely focused on economic issues. Decision-making in the Soviet system might have been cumbersome, with foreign-policy decisions coordinated between the relevant ministries, Central Committee departments and the KGB, but at least policy was marked by consistency. Russian policy, however, was characterised by lack of coordination and often contradictory purposes. In its second policy statement 'A Strategy for Russia', SVOP was bitterly critical of the fragmentation of foreign policy-making:

> None, even the most elementary strategy for the defence and realisation of the national interests of the country, can be implemented under the present condition of the institutions intended to formulate and implement it... Each official enjoys the freedom to have his own policy. This situation not only weakens the position of the country but also disgraces it. This is one of the most difficult challenges for Russian foreign policy.[34]

Although foreign policy prerogatives were concentrated in the hands of the presidency, the presidential apparatus itself under Yeltsin was divided into competing factions seeking to influence the president.[35] The presidential system included a number of analytical centres and presidential assistants for foreign policy. These special advisers could not substitute for a solid bureaucratic structure combining expertise with the ability to control decision-making and implementation, although under Putin the system mostly worked in a more coordinated manner than before. Even then, the 'presidential' foreign policy structure could not effectively replace the role of the MFA and other ministries in the formulation and implementation of policy. The foreign, defence and intelligence ministries represented concentrations of information, expertise and experience, and with their own policy agendas, while powerful business interests and occasionally regional leaders tried to impose their agendas. The erratic jerks in Russian foreign policy reflected not only conceptual shifts but changes in the relative weight of various governmental agencies. The new pluralism encouraged the fragmentation of policy-making.

## The debate over foreign policy

By late 1991 Russia had lost much of the territory for which it had fought for centuries. Peter the Great's defeat of the Swedes at Poltava in 1709 gave Russia access to the Baltic ports, and in particular Riga. Catherine the Great's defeat of the Ottoman Turks gave Russia access to the ports of the Black Sea, above all Sevastopol in the Crimea. Victory in the Second World War gave the USSR an extended security zone reaching as far as Berlin. In 1991 Russia's military-strategic expansion not only ended but collapsed, and the 'gathering of the lands' went into reverse as the rump Russian state in the West was reduced to not much more than Muscovy under Ivan the Terrible in the sixteenth century. From an imperial point of view, the collapse of communism and the disintegration of the USSR was a defeat for Russia. It lost its warm water ports in the Baltic republics, and now had to rely on Kaliningrad, separated from Russia by Belarus and Lithuania, St Petersburg, not really a natural harbour, and the ice-bound ports of Murmansk and Arkhangel. The retreat from the Baltic and the Black Sea pushed Russia Eastwards away from Europe and the Middle East and back into the Eurasian heartlands. It is against this background that the debate over Russian foreign policy unfolded.

### *Ideology, interests and values*

Empires have fallen before, but never one armed with nuclear weapons. While a strong Soviet Union had been a threat to the rest of the world, a weak Russia was equally dangerous because of the damage it could do itself and its neighbours. It has indeed been argued that Russian foreign policy in the 1990s took on the characteristics of the 'tyranny of the weak', threatening economic and military anarchy if it did not receive substantial assistance from the West and was not accepted into global economic structures.[36] From the Russian perspective, however, things looked very different. Sergei Rogov, the Deputy Director of the Institute of the USA and Canada, noted that 'Today the country has no enemies, but neither does it have reliable allies capable of and prepared to render support in trying times'.[37] As far as he was concerned, Russia had failed to achieve a 'civilised' divorce with the former Soviet states, giving rise to a zone of instability around Russia, and neither had it been able to defend its status as a great power. Russia's relative friendlessness continued into the decade, and Rogov's comment could be equally applied to the state of affairs at the end of Putin's presidency.

From 1990 a separate Russian foreign policy emerged, but as time passed it appeared that more and more elements were borrowed not only from the Soviet Union but also from the pre-revolutionary era. Foreign policy evolved away from the so-called 'liberal universalism' of the early period towards a more vigorous assertion of Russian great power national interests. There was no consensus, however, on what precisely constituted Russia's national security and other interests. The liberals saw them as lying in close ties with the West and peace with its neighbours; the centrist groupings sought greater reliance on indigenous economic and military resources to buttress a rather broader vision of Russia as a great power; the national-patriots envisioned Russia as a type of superpower in regard to its neighbours and in the world at large, to be achieved by restoring aspects of the old administrative command system; the neo-communists more explicitly sought to re-establish the Soviet system and the Soviet geopolitical space; for nationalists the key lay in asserting the dominance of ethnic Russians; while neo-imperialists promised easy solutions to a disappointed people but threatened Russia's neighbours and provoked once again the image of Russia, whether communist or not, as the permanent enemy. Each vision of Russia's national security interests reflected profound differences in thinking about what it means to be a Russian and what Russia itself means. As Igor Ivanov noted, 'The rethinking and definition of the country's national interests continued throughout the 1990s'.[38] Foreign policy would be unstable and contested as long as no new orthodoxy could emerge or be imposed.

What are Russia's national interests, and what form should their espousal take in the international system? Would Russian foreign policy indeed become something new or would traditional great power and Russian imperial traditions reassert themselves? Gorbachev's foreign policy, managed by Shevardnadze, was conducted within the framework of what was called the 'New Political Thinking' (NPT). Russian foreign policy continued some of its concerns, such as ending political and military divisions, reintegration into the world community and the demilitarisation of foreign policy, but at the same time qualitatively new issues emerged. It no longer made sense to talk of the deideologisation of foreign policy, of a world divided into 'two camps', however interdependent, or of the conflict between the social systems of capitalism and socialism; but at the same time the idea of 'multi-polarity' sought to impose new lines of division. The concept of a multi-polar world is a code word in effect for the perpetuation of the Cold War and global bloc conflict by other means.

Now, more than ever before, there was a blurred distinction between domestic and 'foreign' policy. Foreign policy was a field over which domestic politics was fought, but while various interests sought to exert their influence, policy remained firmly in the hands of the president and his ministers. The challenge now was to redefine Russian national interest in the new geopolitical circumstances of the post-Cold War world and the disintegration of the USSR. But before national interest could be established, the nature of Russia itself had to be defined. The interests of a national democratic state are very different from a neo-imperial Russia, and it would be hardly appropriate to talk of the national interests of a Russia dissolving once again into the principalities of the fourteenth and fifteenth centuries. Does Russia have constant geostrategic, political or ideological interests, and what social groups should mould a new Russian national interest?[39] Pre-revolutionary imperial messianism asserted that Russia had not only a military but also a spiritual mission to bring enlightenment to neighbouring peoples and the world, while the Soviet Union defined itself as the harbinger of international socialism. Russia's national identity began to be reformulated as a state rather than as an empire. But even some of those who accepted the birth of a nation insisted on the retention of Russian universal values, threatened allegedly by the rush to embrace the West, and that Russia retained a 'mission' if not a messianic purpose.[40] The debate in essence was over a new ideology of foreign policy for Russia, one that could inform day-to-day policy formulation and provide a convincing rationale for strategic planning.

A distinction should be drawn between national and state interests, since national interests may well be opposed to those of the state.[41] In contemporary foreign policy, it is state interests that predominate over those of the nation, yet in post-communist countries the distinction remained blurred. Estonian nationalists and extreme Russian patriots sought to identify the interests of the state with those of a particular national group. Talk of the 'national interest' in a multinational state can be misleading, and for this reason it has been argued that the term 'fundamental interests' may be more appropriate.[42] Mythical ideas of the homogeneity of national interests overlook the conflicting interests of contemporary civil society, and indeed the ability of nationalists and communists to subsume conflicting social interests into a single plane of national struggle testifies to the relative under-development of civil society in Russia. Pozdnyakov goes so far as to argue that national interests and state interests are identical.[43]

At the centre of the debate over Russian foreign policy was the attempt to define Russia's relationship with Western civilisation and strategic concerns. Failure to deal with this question in 1917 led to the fall of the Provisional Government. Russia's subservience to the West, above all in honouring its commitments in the Great War, allowed it to be pressured by the French into launching the disastrous Galician offensive in June 1917. National-patriots in the 1990s accused Yeltsin's government, too, of selling Russia's interests short by kowtowing to the West, begging for assistance and alienating Russian lands and islands. A new Russian isolationism emerged, warning against 'over-Westernisation' and the 'Americanisation' of foreign policy. They stressed the need for native (*samobytnyi*) traditions and questioned the need for Russia's 'return' to Europe and reintegration into the world economy. The dominant centrist view, however, can be formulated as 'the road to our future passes through the West but does not stop there': joining the world but on Russia's terms, not as a supplicant but as an equal, retaining Russia's own identity and defending its interests. This was a view that Putin sought to implement.

### Eurasianism and the world

Opinion divided over whether Russia constitutes a separate civilisation or whether it is no more than a variant of 'world civilisation', usually considered synonymous with the West. The emergence of a 'new Eastern Europe' of Ukraine and Belarus separating Russia from the rest of Europe stimulated the 'Eurasian' tradition in Russian philosophy, and indeed the tension in Russian national identity can be interpreted in the light of a struggle between Atlanticists and Eurasianists.[44] The latter shared Dostoevsky's view that Russia should concern itself with dominance in Asia rather than dreams of European integration: 'In Europe we are hangers-on and slaves, but in Asia we walk as masters.' The old debate resurfaced between the Westernisers, oriented towards Western values and Russia's integration into European processes, and the Slavophiles, stressing Russia's native traditions and distinct culture. Tibor Szamuely argues that before the revolution and again today Russian thinkers

> would not have accepted the idea of the Russian past having been just a part of a single, uniform, homogenized European experience... Whether they gloried in this difference and strove to perpetuate it, like the Slavophiles, or yearned for a decisive

break with tradition, like the 'Westernisers', all alike recognised that Russia had merely been in Europe, but not of it.[45]

Likhachev takes issue with Szamuely's view that Russia is the only European country that 'owed virtually nothing to the common cultural and spiritual heritage of the West'.[46] He insists that Russia was part of European development, owing its religion and much of its culture to Orthodox Christianity and borrowing early concepts of statehood from the Scandinavians.[47]

Eurasianists argue that Russia is not part of European civilisation but represents a separate and distinct civilisation of its own acting as the 'balance holder' between Europe and Asia.[48] They deny the need for Russia to integrate into Europe, civilisationally part of which, they argue, it had never been.[49] The Eurasianists revived the geopolitical school of thinking, developed by Halford Mackinder in the early part of the century, according to which Russia encompasses most of the 'geographical pivot of history', acting as the balance holder in the World Island.[50] As far as they were concerned, Russia was a bridge between Western and Eastern civilisations. The modern Eurasianists, drawing on the thinking of their predecessors in emigration of the early 1920s, question uncritical pro-Westernism and advocate a reorientation of policy towards the countries of the former Soviet Union. Stalinist xenophobia, in their view, had given way to a condition that Krizhanich had already diagnosed in Russia three centuries earlier: 'Xenomania (*chuzhbesie* in our language) is an obsessive love of foreign people.'[51] Sergei Goncharov, a researcher at the Far East Institute, noted that

> today, we are moving away from total confrontation with the West toward an equally total fraternisation. In the process, we sometimes overstep the bounds of reason in our desire for alliance... The idea of the primacy of human rights is being turned into an absolute as zealously as the earlier concept of 'class interests' was.

He advocated a policy of 'rational egoism' that placed the success of domestic reforms over any other considerations, even though this might lead to measures that displeased the West.[52] Eurasianism thus represented the moderate face of the Russian rejection of the West.

Of all the Slavophiles Peter Chaadayev was the most pro-European, a sympathy accompanied by a denigration of Russia. In his first *Philosophical Letter* he wrote 'We do not belong to any of the great families of humanity, to either the West or the East, and have no traditions of either. We exist outside time.'[53] It was this attempt to emulate the West by vilifying Russia that so incensed sections of society following the fall of communism. Pozdnyakov, one of the leading exponents of Eurasianism, pointed out that no sooner had the socialist utopia died out than a host of new ones sprang up to replace it, including '*mondialiste* Westernisers whom Russian national traditions tell nothing whatever – are pushing Russia into Europe', and he insisted that 'it would be very wrong and, in fact, dangerous to forget that Russia's history, the history of the formation of our society and state, differs *entirely* from that of Western Europe'.[54]

There are many strands of Eurasianism, including a pragmatic Eurasianism that simply reflects the fact that Russia is both a European and an Asian power; neo-Eurasianism, with a more imperialist and at times semi-fascist inflection that minimises the East as a substantive force while playing up geopolitical factors and the denigration of the West;[55]

an inter-civilisational Eurasianism, focusing on Russia's multi-ethnic identity,[56] and a mystical Eurasianism that sharply distinguishes the mega-region as the spiritual counter-point to Western degradation.[57] Putin if anything is a pragmatic Eurasianist, but even this is tempered by his unequivocal Europeanism and he has little truck with Eurasian-ism's characteristic anti-Westernism, however wary he may be of Western hegemonism. Elements of all four positions informed Russia's foreign policy under Putin, but a mod-ified form of neo-Slavophilism predominated, no longer so much concerned with the development of a Slavic identity but focused on Russia's autonomous development in partnership with the West but reasserting its great power status. Dmitry Trenin argues that China's growing strength in the East and the instability of the Islamic South, means that Russia's only geopolitical future lies with the West, including accelerated integration with the EU and solid relations with the United States.[58] Trenin stresses that Russia's integration with the West has to take into account national peculiarities, and thus the liberal project of Westernisation had to adopt a patriotic form.[59]

The debate over Eurasianism is essentially a debate over paths of development and the principles of political and economic reform. Zagorsky stresses, however, that the concept of the West is no longer confined to Europe or America but includes Japan, South Korea and other newly industrialised countries, none of whom had renounced their own civilisations but had become part of the synthesis of global civilisation. The concept of Russia as a bridge is therefore meaningless, since links between Germany and Japan could quite happily by-pass Russia. Eurasianism is a bridge leading nowhere.[60] The debate, however, clearly signalled, as Mark Frankland has observed, 'that the natural relationship between Russia and Europe is more likely one of rivalry than of unbroken cooperation'.[61]

### Drawing the line

Russia's attempt to formulate a new international doctrine took place in a relatively benign international environment, with no direct threats to its integrity and no global threat of the sort that had derailed the democracies in the 1930s.[62] This did not, however, prevent the emergence of a movement in both domestic and foreign policy challenging the liberal-democratic view dominant in the first post-communist period, which was firmly oriented towards the West and the global institutions of the post-war world. This provided fuel for those who argue against the 'democratic peace' hypothesis,[63] and in particular those, like Jack Snyder, who suggest that democratising states pose a threat to peace.[64] A recent study, indeed, has argued that not only is the presence of democ-racy no guarantee of peace, under certain conditions it may even enhance the potential for war.[65]

Russian foreign policy developed against the background of a debate over the structure of international relations in the late twentieth century and in the era of the so-called 'long war' against terror. The democrats espoused a normative approach, insisting that ethical and moral considerations had an important part to play in international affairs. They were attracted by the concept of world society, and sought to integrate Russia into the existing system of international institutions. The national-patriots held to a more traditional view, stressing the primacy of the national interest in a 'realist' world in which foreign policy was determined by the power of states. The neo-communists incorporated patriotic themes into a programme that sought not only to reconstitute the Soviet Union but to reassert its superpower status. The realities of power rather than the pursuit of justice dominated the thinking of the centrists and the regime. But whose power? The realist pursuit of alleged national interests in an international system dominated by nation-states was tempered by a world covered by a multitude of international non-governmental and governmental international organisations. The unravelling of Stalin's 'hyper-realist' foreign policy ultimately led to the collapse of the USSR as the Baltic and other forcibly incorporated republics took their revenge. The lesson appears clear: there is nothing more unrealistic than brute realism.

Russia was torn between remaining a *status quo* power or becoming a revisionist power. Russia had been the greatest loser of the territorial settlements of the Soviet years and was thus potentially a revisionist power. In addition, a type of 'Versailles syndrome' emerged whereby the democrats were alleged to have betrayed Russia's national interests in the exit from communism, above all in signing the Belovezh Accords in 1991 that consigned the USSR to the dustbin of history. As with Britain earlier, the loss of empire is accompanied by the search for a new role. McFaul and Goldgeier argue that post-communist Russian foreign policy does not follow the pattern anticipated by realist thinking. According to them Russia has become a 'joiner', and does not conform to the 'balancing' stance anticipated by classical realist theory.[66] For Ambrosio, a state can either try to balance the major power in the international system, or bandwagon with it: the choice depends on the structure of the environment and the country's political culture. In Russia's case he identifies three strands: the Atlanticists, favouring alignment with the United States and the West (the bandwagoners); the imperialists, who favour the reassertion of Russia's power in opposition to the West (the balancers); and the neo-Slavophiles, sharing the sentiments of the imperialists but who stress the development of the country's Slavic identity.[67]

The lesson about the limits of realism had been well learnt by Putin. While his foreign policy can certainly be located within the framework of classical neo-realism, this differed from Primakov's 'competitive pragmatist' realism. Putin's 'new realism' sought far more to engage with the Western-oriented international system, although on its own terms. Putin's new realism is concerned not so much with balancing as joining, while at the same time tempered by neo-Slavophile concerns about autonomy and uniqueness, and pragmatic Eurasianist notions of balance between East and West. As Tsygankov puts it, 'Russia's attitude is essentially accommodationist', and in contrast to earlier policy the country did not try to exploit the threat posed by unipolarity by forging a counter-alliance.[68] The focus of Russian policy was post-imperial state-building. Like all post-imperial states, however, relations with former partners and subordinates are uneasy. The new realist pattern was already established during Yeltsin's presidency, but his realism became coloured by a specific definition of pragmatism that retained much of the classical competitive approach to realism in foreign policy. Under Primakov the concept of a multipolar world was used to accentuate need to move away from the allegedly excessive unidirectional (American-centred) foreign policy of earlier years, and it encouraged a diplomacy based on competitive pragmatism.

Putin's new realism placed rather less emphasis on multipolarity, although it did not disappear and was expressed in the June 2000 Foreign Policy Concept. While stressing the need to extend cooperation with NATO, the document insisted that the alliance limited the security role of any other pan-European institution.[69] The emphasis now was rather more on multilateralism, trying to manage the international system in an inclusive and consensual manner, rather than the competitive dynamic inherent in the concept of multipolarity. It was only under Putin that engagement with the West moved onto a more cooperative basis, although relations continued to be soured by the regime question – the nature of the political system emerging in Russia.[70] The new realist consensus, however, by the end of Putin's presidency began to unravel from both ends: the West's refusal to accept Russia on its own terms; and Russia's own increased assertiveness. One of the great historic opportunities for reconciliation had been missed.

## Russia and the world

Russia sought to find its place in the world at a time when, unfrozen from the Cold War, international relations remain in flux. Long-term processes have come to fruition whereby economic strength is a more accurate measurement of power than narrowly defined military power. Economic weakness undermined Russia's aspirations to become a great power until the economic resurgence of the Putin years endowed Russian policy with a new confidence. While Moscow was invited as a guest to G7 meetings and in 2002 was invited to become part of what became G8, in matters concerning the management of the global economy the group tended to operate as 'seven-plus-one'. The gulf between Russian aspirations and capabilities remained, while the gap between what Russia considered was its appropriate place in the world, and what the dominant powers were willing to accept, also yawned ever larger. The tension between Russia's ambition to become a major regional and world power and its relative economic weakness generated numerous tensions. The ambition itself became the driving force for policy, but as long as the gulf remained between Russia's aspirations and capacities Russia's role in the world would remain characterised by 'essential ambiguity'. The tension if anything worsened as the gap between ambition and capacity narrowed. By 2007 Russia had become the world's tenth largest economy, but the failure earlier to integrate Russia into the dominant international system now generated endless tensions that provoked much discussion about the onset of a new Cold War.

### United States of America

The fall of Soviet communism made possible the global hegemony of the single remaining superpower, but at the same time it removed any over-riding purpose to this predominance. The Soviet MFA had long been torn between 'Americanist' and 'Europeanist' tendencies, and while during *perestroika* European policy had been revived, the concentration on America in the old game of superpower politics remained. Reflecting growing economic links, it was only natural that Russia focused more on the European aspects of its foreign policy, although care was taken not to neglect other spheres and the relationship with America remained crucial. The meeting in Vancouver in April 1992 between Yeltsin and Clinton was the first ever 'superpower' summit devoted not to overcoming confrontation but to economic issues. Yeltsin's visit to Washington in June 1992 dispelled the lingering reservations that characterised Soviet-American relations even at their best and marked the confirmation of Russia's status as a partner in world affairs. In his address to Congress on 17 June Yeltsin drew a thick line under the past, insisting that communism, 'which spread everywhere social strife and brutality, which instilled fear in humanity', had collapsed never to rise again. Yeltsin insisted that Russia had made 'its final choice in favour of a civilised way of life, common sense and the universal human heritage'. For good measure, he stressed that 'The freedom of America is now being upheld in Russia.'[71]

Points of tension, however, remained. The lack of coordination between Russia's aggressive arms sales and foreign policy led on several occasions to conflict, as over the proposed sale of submarines and nuclear power technology to Iran and cryogenic engines to India. The economic depression in the final period of Bush senior's term in office and his weak leadership meant that the euphoria of the end of the Cold War was not translated into effective policies to assist the rehabilitation of Russia and other post-communist states. The Clinton presidency pursued a 'Russia first' policy, but this was not translated into much more than support for Yeltsin personally. The role of American assistance and support for Yeltsin's version of reform has been much criticised.[72] Plans to expand NATO to Eastern Europe (see Chapter 17), the war over Kosovo and American plans for (National) Missile Defence (NMD), which led to the American repudiation of the 1972 Anti-Ballistic Missile (ABM) treaty in December 2001, brought Russia's apparent national interests into confrontation with those of America.

Russia's dramatic choice to join the 'coalition against terror' after the events of 11 September 2001 built on earlier developments. Putin was the first to telephone president George W. Bush after the al-Qaeda attack, and he offered not only sympathy but stressed that Russia would stand full-square with the United States in the struggle against international terrorism. In the Iraq crisis Russia sought to act as mediator between Europe and America, a role Britain had traditionally tried to play. Russia, like France, insisted that any war against Iraq should be conducted under the aegis of the UN, and that the legitimate interests of Russia (and France) in the country should be respected in a post-Saddam Iraq. Russia found itself torn between the two faces of the West: the interventionist Anglo-American bloc and the Franco-German 'axis of peace'.[73] In populist terms, these could be dubbed the 'wild West' and the 'normative West'. Putin's second term was marked by increasing tensions in Russo-American relations. Attention remained focused on traditional areas of cooperation, notably security and non-proliferation of weapons of mass destruction, although energy supplies became an increasingly important mutual concern. Russia's supply of technology and materials for Iran's nuclear energy programme, as well as its arms sale programme, including the supply of anti-aircraft missiles to Syria, caused considerable acrimony. In 2006 Russia's arms exports rose to $6.4 billion, with China and India alone accounting for 80 per cent of this, although Russia sought to diversify its markets and supplied weapons to over 60 countries, including to some of America's traditional markets in the Middle East. Putin centralised sales of hardware, technologies and services into a single agency, Rosoboroneksport, with only the Sukhoi and MiG aerospace companies remaining independent.[74] American support for the various 'colour' revolutions in Georgia, Ukraine and Kyrgyzstan seemed to pose a threat to Russia itself, especially when American officials openly declared the strategy of using civil society to overthrow legitimately elected governments. It appeared that the US was trying to build an arc of containment around Russia, stretching from the Baltic in the North to Central Asia.

A report at the time noted: '[T]he gap between glowing rhetoric and thin substance has grown. This shallowness leaves US-Russian ties bereft of constituencies wider than leaders and a few highly placed government officials and increasingly vulnerable to growing choruses of skeptics'.[75] The authors argue that the fashionable distinction drawn between 'interests' and 'values' in foreign policy was a false one, insisting that the way that a state defines its interests reflects its values: hence 'disagreements between Russia and the US reflect differences in how we frame and define our interests'.[76] In Russia there was a renewed stress on self-sufficiency and sovereignty, while America asserted its global hegemony in ever more strident tones. This was reflected in the Council on Foreign Relations Independent task force report of early 2006, which subjected Russian policy, and ultimately Russia itself, to sustained criticism, insisting that Russia was taking the 'wrong direction'.[77] As far as many Russians were concerned, 'What really upsets the United States is Russia's unique role in the global energy market.'[78] Talk of a 'strategic alliance' between the two countries was redundant, especially since it appeared that there was no common vision or shared set of values.

The speech of vice president Dick Cheney at a conference of East European leaders in Vilnius on 4 May 2006 argued that 'opponents of reform are seeking to reverse the gains of the last decade, and warned Russia against its alleged abuse of the energy instrument: 'No legitimate interests is served when oil and gas become tools of intimidation or blackmail, either by supply manipulation or attempts to monopolize transportation'. He conceded that 'None of us believes that Russia is fated to become an enemy', but he insisted that 'Russia has a choice to make', the 'return to democratic reform'.[79] The content of the speech and its hectoring tone provoked a storm of protest in Russia. The upheavals in Georgia and Ukraine placed US-Russian relations under strain and challenged Putin's definition of 'new realism', especially when it came to competition for influence over CIS states. Dmitri Trenin sums this up well:

> Western relations with Russia can no longer be described in terms of integration, as it is traditionally understood, that is, gradually drawing Russia into the Western institutional orbit. For that, there is neither particular demand on the part of Russia nor sufficient supply on the part of the United States or the EU. NATO and the EU, which were so successfully used with regard to the countries of Central and Eastern Europe, will have to remain idle in the case of Russia. The famous 'double integration elevator' cannot take Russia aboard because Western institutions simply do not have the capacity to do so.[80]

Putin's second term was over-shadowed by fears of the emergence of a type of post-ideological Cold War, in which Russia's alleged democratic back-sliding (the regime question) was used to isolate Russia. In 2007 the planned deployment of elements of the Missile Defence shield in Poland and the Czech Republic revived the worst memories of the Cold War and the struggles of the 1980s over intermediate nuclear weapons. According to Georgi Arbatov,

> Towards the end of the Soviet Union there was virtually no anti-American sentiment in Russia. But then these rosy expectations changed into doubts, disappointment, and suspicion. What was actually inevitable has now become clear: that the political interests of Russia and America are different and rarely coincide in reality.[81]

Events in Iraq and Iran, combined with the eastward enlargement of NATO and Russia's assertion of its own vision of its place in the world, appeared to place Russia and the West in opposed camps once again.

### Russia and the European Union (EU)

The European direction of Russian foreign policy was repeatedly stressed by Russian presidents, but was only fitfully implemented. At a press conference in Paris on 17 April 1991 Yeltsin stressed that Russia could 'play a unique role as a bridge between Europe and Asia and that it can contribute towards extending the area of European cooperation, particularly in the economic field, from the Atlantic to the Pacific'.[82] Russia's economic weakness inhibited the development of this programme, but its openness to the international economy gradually bore tangible fruit. Russia's links with the EU were strengthened, but this was to be a long and hard road. Russia signed a Partnership and Cooperation Agreement (PCA) with the EU on 24 June 1994, but because of the Chechen war it only came into effect in 1997 and would take many years for its potential to be fulfilled. The EU delayed the signature of a trade and cooperation agreement, while the Parliamentary Assembly of the Council of Europe suspended membership procedures.[83] The head of the Council of Europe, Daniel Tarschys, insisted that as long as Russia ignored 'basic rules and standards' of human rights it would be inappropriate for Russia to join.[84] However, following the elections of December 1995 Russian membership was approved on the grounds that 'integration is preferable to isolation'. Russia on 28 February 1996 became the 39th member of the Council of Europe.

The *Common Strategy of the EU on Russia,* adopted at the Cologne summit on 4 June 1999, was intended to guide EU policy-makers for an initial period of four years, although its implications would last far longer than that and the document was to be periodically reviewed by the European Council.[85] The *Common Strategy* identified four 'principal objectives' facing Russia:

* The 'consolidation of democracy, the rule of law, and public institutions', together with 'the emergence of civil society'.
* The 'integration of Russia into a common European economic and social space', which required the development in Russia of an 'operational market economy'.
* The third element was the establishment of 'cooperation to develop stability and security in Europe and beyond', based on the recognition that Russia and the EU had a common interest in achieving this.
* And finally, a number of issues were considered 'common challenges on the European continent', including a common energy policy, the management of resources, nuclear safety, environmental problems, organised crime, money-laundering, and trafficking in human beings and drugs.[86]

The Russian government formulated its own views on Russian-EU relations, in part as a response to the EU's *Common Strategy*, in the document *Medium Term Strategy for the Development of Relations Between the RF and the EU (2000–10)*. As the EU's most important neighbour, there were a range of issues that required common management: minority problems, migration, border and customs issues, and perhaps above all the consequences of EU enlargement itself.[87]

Russia took a deliberately benign view of Europe, in part as a challenge to the near-permanent edge of rivalry and competing aspirations that characterised Russo-American relations. Russia was mostly positive about EU enlargement, while at the same time condemning NATO expansion (see Chapter 17). Policy towards what had formerly been known as 'Eastern' Europe was now subsumed into larger European policy, as indicated by the single department for Europe in the MFA. In 1989–90 these countries shrugged off their Sovietisation; and relations between them and Russia began on a new footing. Even as the USSR declined, Russia had been pursuing a distinct East European policy of its own marked by common democratic aspirations. Yeltsin's first official visit to the region was to Czechoslovakia in May 1991 in which he moved far beyond Gorbachev's 'regret' over the invasion of the country in 1968 and instead called it a 'gross mistake and interference in Czechoslovakia's internal affairs'. On 29 August 1991 Kozyrev condemned the armed intervention in Hungary in 1956 in equally harsh terms. The enlargement of 1 May 2004 brought eight former communist countries into the EU fold (Estonia, Latvia, Lithuania, Poland, Czech Republic, Slovakia, Hungary and Slovenia), while on 1 January 2007 Romania and Bulgaria joined. Despite earlier attempts to appeal to common values and to lay to rest some of the ghosts of the past, relations with the region were strained, in particular in reaction to Russia's perceived use of energy as an instrument of foreign policy. According to Sergei Yastrzhembsky, the deterioration in Russo-EU relations had been provoked by the accession of the former communist countries, who had allegedly 'brought the spirit of primitive Russophobia' to the EU.[88] The conflict with Estonia in May 2007 over moving the Bronze Soldier Soviet war memorial brought into play primitive emotions on all sides, but most disturbing was the EU's inability to 'Europeanise' its neophytes and instead it was in danger of amplifying 'ancient hatreds' and reinforcing one-dimensional historical narratives.

The EU failed effectively to allay Russia's sense of grievance over the Russian minorities in Estonia and Latvia, and indeed, sense of betrayal by the West. Quite why the EU should endorse assimilationist policies in the Baltic when the whole normative basis of the EU favours multicultural integration elsewhere remains to be explained. Putin's successor could well pursue policies more in the spirit of *ressentiment*. As Hanna Smith notes, 'The concept of ressentiment is often used to describe a situation where the ruling elite accuses foreign powers of trying to weaken it. It is often also based on suspicion that stems from insecurity about one's own identity, and a feeling of being looked down upon by others'.[89] It was understood that Russia's entry into the EU would not be considered in the immediate future, although it was not inconceivable. Kasyanov insisted that at some point Russia could become a member as part of its general effort to promote a common European space.[90] European fears about 'empire overstretch' were much in evidence over discussion about Turkey's membership of the EU, while the idea of Russia's membership was relegated to some point on the horizon. Instead, Russia fell into the category of a larger Switzerland or Norway, associated with the EU but not enjoying the membership privilege of being able to shape its rules. The PCA expired on 30 November 2007, but could be automatically extended unless either side gave notice of its termination. During the Finnish presidency in late 2006 it was agreed that the new Stability and Cooperation Pact would take the form of a Strategic Partnership Treaty between the EU and Russia, encompassing energy issues and a range of new instruments, to provide for a genuine strategic partnership.

On 11 March 2003 the European Commission adopted the 'Wider Europe' Communication, outlining a new framework for relations over the next decade with Russia, the Western NIS (Belarus, Ukraine, Moldova) and the Southern Mediterranean including Israel and the Palestinian Authority.[91] Russia wished to have nothing to do with the programme when it later became the European Neighbourhood Policy (ENP).

These countries do not have the immediate prospect of EU membership, but they now share a border with the EU. The aim of the ENP is to surround the EU with a ring of friendly states while encouraging them to adapt to European norms and standards. This would be achieved by opening up its markets to neighbours and facilitating the free movement of goods, services, people and capital within the region. At the same time, the ENP policy ruled out these countries becoming EU members in the near future. The Western Eurasian states, above all Ukraine, were disappointed about being lumped in with North Africa and the Middle East, whose membership of the EU has been ruled out by Brussels. The possibility of accession for West Eurasian states has not been excluded, but the ENP does not mention it. The countries feared that the EU's policy of 'deepened cooperation' instead of 'integration' would be applied to them for the long term as well.

Even without membership, the shadow of the EU fell ever more strongly over the countries to the East. A dramatic reorientation in Russia's trade patterns took place, shifting from Eastern to Western Europe, with the EU by 1993 becoming Russia's biggest export market, and by 2007 53 per cent of Russian trade was with the enlarged EU. Russia has 27 per cent of the world's gas reserves, mostly found in Siberia, and supplied a third of Western European gas needs, and was the primary supplier to Turkey. With a developed network of supply pipelines to Europe, Russia supplies 50 per cent of all gas imports and also supplies the EU-27 with one-third of its oil needs. This stimulated the search for alternative sources of energy to avoid excessive dependence on Russia, and prompted fears that the existing dependence has blunted EU criticisms of perceived democratic failure in Russia. The brief interruption in gas supplies in the first days of 2006 as part of a pricing dispute with Ukraine was taken as a 'wake-up call' to diversify supplies. At the same time, over 60 per cent of Russia's export revenues come from energy, and the bulk of that is exports to the EU, and Russia derives 40 per cent of its budget from the sale of natural resources to the EU. It is clear that Russia is as dependent on the EU as the EU is on Russia for its energy supplies. The establishment of an Energy Dialogue in October 2000 attempted to regulate this system of mutual dependency, dealing with issues like security of supply, energy efficiency, infrastructure (above all pipelines), investment and trade. However, the energy dialogue did not become an energy partnership, especially since Russia refused to ratify the transport protocol to the 1994 Energy Charter Treaty, which sought to regulate the energy market in Europe.

The 2004 enlargement brought the EU to the borders of Russia and raised new problems in its wake. There were major questions over access, the visa regime and other issues concerning the Kaliningrad exclave, separated from Russia by Lithuania and Belarus. On 11 November 2002 an agreement allowed the use of a Facilitated Transport Document (FTD) system from 1 July 2003 for Russian citizens travelling between Kaliningrad and other parts of Russia. The 31 May 2003 St Petersburg Russia-EU summit adopted the four common spaces concept: economic, external security, justice and home affairs, and research and culture. While practical work on the four spaces continued, above all in the form of 'roadmaps' adopted at the May 2005 Moscow summit, EU-Russian relations in this as in other spheres appeared unable to move beyond the stage of 'dialogue' towards 'partnership'. By the time of the Samara EU-Russia summit in May 2007 relations had deteriorated to the point where all sides agreed that it would be pointless to begin negotiations on the Strategic Partnership Treaty to replace the PCA, even if a Polish veto on the negotiations started was lifted. The enlargement to encompass ten former communist countries had changed the character of the EU, away from a normative peace-creating body towards one with a stronger and more regressive foreign policy agenda. As a consensus organisation the EU had to take into account the fears and resentments of the new members, while the ability of the 'old Europe' large states to shape the policy agenda was reduced. Germany's ability to act as intermediary between East and West was reduced.

In a widely circulated article on the EU's fiftieth anniversary in 2007, Putin noted the strategic importance of the EU while noting the limits to that relationship. He quoted Dostoevsky's definition of Russia's European mission: 'Being a true Russian will ultimately mean bringing reconciliation to Europe's contradictions', and in his own words Putin argued that 'I strongly believe the full unity of our continent can never be achieved until Russia, as the largest European state, becomes an integral part of the European process.' He insisted that 'The development of multifaceted ties with the EU is Russia's principled choice', but added that there were limits to this: 'It is true that in the foreseeable future, for obvious reasons, we have no intention of either joining the EU or establishing any institutional association with it.'[92] Early hopes that greater Russian integration would be ultimately crowned by accession now gave way to managing a long-term process of integration without accession.

### Asia

Following the fall of communism the 'Asianist' orientation of Russian policy gained in importance, with Russia attaining the status of a full ASEAN dialogue partner in July 1997 and joining the Asia-Pacific Economic Cooperation (APEC) forum in 1998. The problem, however, was that Russia tended to use Asia and the East as little more than a 'crowbar for relations with the West'.[93] Although two-thirds of Russia lies beyond the Urals its economic and demographic centre of gravity lies firmly in the West. Policy appeared to reflect Brzezinski's view that Russia's only serious geostrategic opportunity to play an important international role and to modernise itself lay in Europe.[94] Russia's self-image, moreover, was European and global, and only marginally Asian. The economic and demographic gap between the Russian Far East and Asia was large and growing, particularly since Russia's potential as a supplier of energy resources, above all oil and natural gas, was difficult to realise. Russia is clearly a potential major player in Asia Pacific, but its role there lacked definition. Russia remained a subaltern player in the emerging Asia-Eurasia community, although the energy resources of Central Asia and the Caucasus and the establishment of an East-West transport corridor connecting Asia and Europe could make Russia an essential part of this Asian-led community. As the late Akino Yutaka put it:

> The old corridor of the Trans-Siberian Railway runs between fifty and sixty degrees latitude, while the new corridor, tracing the ancient Silk Road, will run between forty and fifty degrees latitude.[95]

While Lenin may have argued that 'geographically, economically and historically, Russia is not only a European country but an Asian one as well',[96] it was unclear what form this dual identity would take.[97] Russian power was asymmetrical, with its strategic position secure as long as it had nuclear weapons but a marginal economic force other than in energy and raw materials supplies.

Fear over the fate of the under-populated and isolated Eastern regions of the country, sharing a 4,300 kilometre-long border with China, remained a top concern. The population of the Russian Far East is 8 million and that of Siberia 25 million, and both are decreasing, whereas Northeast China's population is approaching 300 million. The population of the three provinces closest to Russia (Heilongjiang, Jilin and Liaoning) have a combined population of 80 million, provoking Russian concern about massive inflows of people from China. The major obstacle to Russia's integration in the affairs of the Asia-Pacific region, now that the fear of communism was lifted, was its own weakness and economic disintegration, ethnic unrest and separatist tendencies. In contrast to the rapid development of the Pacific region as a whole, the Soviet Far East remained backward and under-developed. Under Gorbachev economic and political ties with China and other Pacific countries had begun to improve and mutual trade grew rapidly. The Chinese road of authoritarian modernisation combining political conservatism and economic radicalism attracted many in Russia. Russian and Chinese views on international relations converged in condemning residual Cold War thinking, the threat posed to world peace by 'hegemonism' and power politics, in opposition to the strengthening of the military blocs and alliances of the Cold War era, and the inequitable international economic order that harmed the interests of developing countries. Both claimed to defend a universal concept of security that abandoned Cold War mentalities and group politics in favour of multipolarism. Numerous military and technology agreements were signed on arms sales, military cooperation and the modernisation of some of the 256 factories built by the Soviet Union in the 1950s. Sino-Russian relations did not quite bloom into the 'strategic partnership' mooted by Primakov and others in Russia, for the simple reason that China's economic predominance (by 2000 its GDP was five times that of Russia), demographic weight and potential military power were perceived as posing a potential threat to Russia. Bilateral relations, however, became the closest ever in their history. The establishment of the Shanghai Cooperation Organisation (SCO) at a summit in Shanghai on 14–15 June 2001 as a regional mechanism for security and cooperation, comprising Russia, China, Kazakhstan, Kyrgyzstan and Uzbekistan, brought China into Central Asian politics and under-scored the 'strategic partnership' between Russia and China (Chapter 18).

The conflict over the Kurile Islands, called by Japan the Northern Territories (Habomai Islands, Iturup (Etorofu), Kunashiri and Shikotan Islands), occupied by the USSR since 1945, weakened Japan's participation in international funding for Russia's reforms, though Japan remained Russia's third largest trading partner. The Russo-Japanese Treaty of 1855 placed Sakhalin Island under joint control, but in 1875 Russia gained control over the whole island in exchange for the Kurile Islands. The Treaty of Portsmouth in 1905 ceded Southern Sakhalin to Japan in exchange for Russia gaining the Southern Kurile Islands. Southern Sakhalin was known as Karafuto until it was annexed by the USSR at the end of the Second World War, and at the same time in September 1945 the USSR reoccupied the Southern Kurile Islands after Japan had surrendered and in violation of the Neutrality Pact, leaving Japan with nothing except an abiding sense of injustice. The Joint Declaration of 1956 stipulated that the USSR would return Shikotan and Habomai Islands to Japan and diplomatic relations were re-established, but in response to the revision of Japan's security treaty with the United States in 1960 the USSR reneged and denied the very existence of a territorial problem. For Japan the question was motivated neither by economic or security concerns but by the very principle of territorial integrity; similar feelings informed Russia's refusal to give up territory.

Public opinion in the islands themselves suggested that at least a third would be willing to come under Japanese sovereignty if the terms were right, but public opinion in Russia opposed any territorial concessions. In 1991 Yeltsin proposed a five-stage approach to the question; a recognition that the problem existed; then Russia would declare the islands a free economic zone, where the Japanese would be given preferential treatment; the demilitarisation of the islands, entailing the closure of the many Russian bases; and fourth, agreements would be reached between Japan and Russia on economic, trade, social and cultural issues. These four stages would take some twenty years, and by the fifth stages new leaders would appear who would be able to cut the Gordian knot.[98] At the 'no-neckties' summit between Yeltsin and the Japanese prime minister Ryutaro Hashimoto in Krasnoyarsk in November 1997 both sides committed themselves to signing a peace treaty by 2000. However, this was not achieved and the problem remained active into the Putin era.

### The 'Third World' and the rest

In contrast to difficult relations with Japan, Russia inherited and maintained India as the main partner and ally in Asia. A treaty on friendship and cooperation signed in January 1993 sought to build on Soviet-Indian ties but at the same time to make them mutually beneficial by discarding the old logic of exclusive geopolitical alliances. Russia remained India's main supplier of arms, including advanced tanks and warplanes. Relations with the developing world starkly posed the question of how to define the 'national interest'. The 'burden of achievement' in Central Europe, the costs of supporting 'client states' from Cuba to Vietnam, and the disastrous war in Afghanistan, all undermined the Soviet consensus on foreign policy that had underlain its drive to become a global superpower. During *perestroika* the NPT allowed universal humanistic concerns to challenge the old view that international relations was the class struggle on a global scale. The theoretical basis for Soviet support for Third World revolutionary states was undermined by the view that development was now seen as having to precede socialism, rather than socialism being the key to unlocking development. The vigorous debate over Soviet Third World policy resulted in Soviet disengagement under Gorbachev.[99] Soviet troops were withdrawn from Afghanistan in February 1989, and the traditional relationship with Cuba became much more strained. Solzhenitsyn called these countries 'insatiable squanderers of our wealth',[100] and Soviet aid to Afghanistan, Angola, Cuba, Ethiopia, Kampuchea and Mozambique was cut. Disengagement became a rout, but as its own policy became more assertive Russia once again sought to reforge old alliances. Russia's reduced weight in world affairs was vividly in evidence in the Middle East conflict. Although one of the sponsors of the Madrid peace process, it was squeezed out of attempts to regulate the Palestinian war in the 2000s.

As the post-Soviet 'continuer' state, Russia assumed not only the treaty, financial and other obligations of the USSR, but also many of attitudes and ambiguities of the former superpower. Russia inherited the institutions of the Soviet Union together with uncertainty about its proper place and role in the world. Kozyrev stressed the distinction between 'the normalisation of relations with other countries and normal relations with them', noting that Gorbachev had begun the first task but it was up to Russia to complete the second. At the heart of the new foreign policy was the idea of Russia as a 'normal great power', one 'that does not rely on threats (like the USSR) but at the same time knows how to live in a world that is not conflict-free'.[101] The notion of 'great power' is itself contentious, and Russia's claims to be one inevitably alarmed its neighbours. While the idea of 'normality' in this context acted as a normative acknowledgement of acceptable forms of behaviour, it could not be anything but ambiguous. The Russian case seems to demonstrate that democratisation does not necessarily provoke aggressive foreign policies, but neither does it resolve problems of integration, status and geopolitical interest. The redefinition of national interest proved to be an open-ended process in which the struggle between liberal and national-patriotic approaches reflected the larger struggle over Russia's identity and place in the world.

# 17 Defence and security policy

> The wolfhound century leaps at my shoulders,
> But I am no wolf by blood.
> (Osip Mandelstam)[1]

The USSR was one of the world's most militarised states, with five million men under arms in 1988 and another four million employed in defence industries and with some 15–20 per cent of Soviet GDP devoted to the upkeep of this vast 'state within a state'.[2] The well-known saying that 'The USSR did not *have* a military-industrial complex, it *was* one', reflected a frightening truth. Not only were economic resources diverted towards supporting the country's enormous military establishment, but the system of conscription and patriotic education made the military the cornerstone of national identity.[3] *Perestroika* represented the repudiation of the logic of Cold War, and by rejecting a security-dominated foreign policy suggested that domestic politics and the economy would also be demilitarised. The disintegration of the USSR was soon followed by the division of the Soviet armed forces as the newly independent republics created their own military systems. Russia was burdened with the legacy of Soviet imperial power, a bloated defence sector and, perhaps most significantly, a military establishment accustomed to getting its own way. Russia tried to forge a new military establishment, able to deal with contemporary security challenges and responsive to the changed demands of society. Could a new model of civil-military relations be forged in post-communist Russia, and with it a demilitarised sense of national purpose?

## The end of the Soviet armed forces

With the fall of communism the Soviet Armed Forces were no longer a military threat but a source of social and political instability to the countries that had sacrificed so much to give them birth. Attempts to maintain a single CIS command after 1991 were soon undermined by the aspirations of republics like Ukraine to create their own armed forces, fuelled by fears that a Russian-dominated military could be used to threaten the newly won independence. In his study of the end of the Soviet armed forces, Odom calls his chapter dealing with these events 'The Illusion of the CIS Armed Forces'.[4] Russia itself had been reluctant to create its own armed forces, yet by early 1992 was forced to embark on this path. Russia now began to disengage its forces from neighbouring countries while asserting control over the huge nuclear arsenal, and at the same time began to reconstruct its own armed forces for new tasks.

## The end of the Soviet Army

What was to be done with the Soviet Army, most of it deployed in Russia and which in ethos and tradition appeared antithetical to the principles of the new democracy? After the coup the General Staff in Moscow was left virtually without a master; there was an army, but no state.[5] Yeltsin sought to gain the allegiance of the high command by promising to keep the army intact, but following the disintegration of the USSR this proved both meaningless and counter-productive as morale and discipline plummeted. Russia ultimately simply renamed the Soviet Army the Russian Army, and thus incorporated the best as well as the worst of the old traditions. The great majority of its officers (80 per cent) were Russian and some 90 per cent, including almost all senior officers, were members of the Communist Party. Russia was left to deal with the problems bequeathed by the old regime, with forces stationed not only in the former Soviet republics but also in Germany and Poland.

Already in December 1991 Ukraine, Azerbaijan and Moldova had announced plans to create their own armed forces. Kravchuk in December 1991 declared himself commander-in-chief of all forces on Ukrainian territory, some half a million men. Instead of seeking the removal of Soviet forces (the policy pursued by the Baltic states), Ukraine assimilated the Soviet Army (including some of the best equipped front line forces and aviation) to its own purposes. In January 1992 all forces on its territory were required to take an oath of allegiance to the republic, something done with surprising alacrity by soldiers in the Kiev, Odessa and Carpathian Military Districts (MDs). Some 40 per cent were Russian, and they were faced with the choice of pledging allegiance to Ukraine or returning to an uncertain but in most cases hard future in Russia. Ukraine's decision in June 1992 to deport military officers who refused to take the oath of loyalty demonstrated the irrevocable breakdown of the concept of CIS forces.[6] Ukraine now had Europe's second largest army, with ground forces of 308,000 in 1994.[7]

The successor republics gradually took over their own security and foreign policy. In Russia the problem of ethnicity and divided allegiances played little role since the officer corps was overwhelmingly Russian. The emergence of a Russian national army, however, was retarded by the role played by the Joint Command and by a residual belief that Russia would be the centre of some larger unit. Instead, the republics created their own armed forces and the CIS failed to establish a security structure similar to NATO. The Collective Security Treaty signed in Tashkent on 15 May 1992 was limited both in scope and the countries involved (see below). The CIS was reduced to dividing Soviet military assets between the former republics.

The former Soviet defence minister, Dmitry Yazov, was implicated in the coup, and his replacement, Yevgeny Shaposhnikov, immediately launched a purge in the ministry.[8] He later became the commander-in-chief of what became known as the Joint Command, formally accountable to the CIS Council of Heads of State, but in practice the absence of any effective CIS command mechanism meant that he worked closely with Yeltsin.[9] The Joint Command was responsible for control over strategic nuclear arms, the coordination of military doctrines and reforms of CIS states, and the resolution of armed conflicts both within the CIS and along its borders.[10] The Bishkek summit in October 1992 agreed to

*Figure 17.1* Central and Eastern Europe

develop a joint military security concept as well as a new command structure for CIS forces.[11] Ukraine, however, sought to escape from the old security system centred on Moscow, and attempts to maintain the CIS Joint Command as the core of a common security system soon foundered, and on 15 June 1993 it was abolished. Thus the Soviet armed forces, victorious over Nazi Germany but also destroyer of aspirations for a more humane and democratic socialism in Budapest in 1956 and Prague in 1968, finally died (Figure 17.1).

### Creation of the Russian Army

Russia was one of the last CIS states to have its own army. Yeltsin's decree on the formation of a Russian Ministry of Defence on 16 March 1992 named himself acting defence minister, and on 7 May he finally ordered the creation of a Russian Army with himself as commander-in-chief.[12] On 18 May General Pavel Grachev was appointed minister of defence. As commander of the Soviet Airborne Forces he had obstructed the plotters in August 1991, and was appointed a deputy USSR defence minister and head of Russia's Defence Committee, having operational command of Russian forces when

Yeltsin was acting defence minister. In the event, Grachev lacked any strategic sense of how to conduct military reform, as well as demonstrating himself to be an incompetent tactician as demonstrated by the repeated blunders he committed in the first Chechen war from December 2004.

Hopes that a civilian defence minister would be appointed and that the defence ministry would become a civilian department were disappointed.[13] The Law on Defence adopted by parliament after long debate in September 1992 defined the scope of military activity and imposed a strict system of state control over the military, but attempts to enshrine the principle that only a civilian could occupy the post of minister of defence were defeated at the last minute. The first deputy minister, however, was Andrei Kokoshin (responsible for relations with the defence industries and scientific-military policy), who was a first-rate academic defence specialist, and indeed the first civilian to be appointed to a leadership position in the armed forces since the 1920s. The majority of appointments to senior posts, however, reflected the predominance of traditionalists. The appointment of Boris Gromov, formerly commander of the Soviet Army in Afghanistan, as deputy defence minister was widely interpreted as a concession to hardliners. We shall discuss the various other defence ministers below.

It was only under Putin on 28 March 2001 that a civilian defence minister, Sergei Ivanov, was appointed, albeit a man with a security background. On 15 February 2007 Ivanov was promoted to first deputy prime minister, responsible for overseeing Russia's military-industrial complex, through the Military Industrial Commission formed in 2006, and aspects of the civilian economy, in particular the engineering sector. Under Ivanov the defence budget quadrupled, but he had never been popular with military officialdom. The new defence minister was Anatoly Serdyukov, who had headed the Federal Tax Service since 27 July 2004, and before that in 2000–1 had run the tax service in St Petersburg in a notoriously harsh manner before becoming deputy tax minister. His 'market-based' brief was to sort out the financial affairs of the defence ministry, a task hardly likely to inspire devotion from the officer class. Serdyukov's appointment meant that for the first time in independent Russia an entirely civilian person was appointed as defence minister, but he lacked any military or diplomatic experience, although on his appointment he did take an intensive course in military leadership at the General Staff Academy. His priority was the improvement of financial management and more rigorous oversight over the spending of state funds.[14] Serdyukov's appointment was a clear sign that Putin would assert even tighter personal control over military and security issues.

The new Law on Defence of 24 April 1996 defined the role of Russia's armed forces and made it clear that a number of other agencies could also be called on for defence purposes (Article 1.4, section 1). In addition to the 1.1 million regular forces, these include 150,000 in the border guard service, about 190,000 Interior Ministry troops, about 4,000 in special FSB units, some 10,000 presidential guards, 54,000 in government communications and information bodies, and 50,000 railway troops.[15] The transformation of the Soviet Army into a Russian one was not accompanied by the sort of reforms in organisation and mentality that affected the rest of society. Instead, the Russian Army remained a monument to traditional Russian and Soviet values, including a strongly developed sense of self-preservation, a culture of secrecy (as demonstrated over its handling of the sinking of the *Kursk* nuclear submarine in August 2000), its self-ascription as the enshrinement of the highest values of society, its commitment to maintaining

Russia as a 'great power', and above all a sense of its own superiority *vis-à-vis* the civil authorities.

### The Conventional Forces in Europe (CFE) Treaty

The CFE treaty was signed in Paris on 19 November 1990 by the 22 NATO and former Warsaw Treaty Organisation (WTO) nations (the number of signatories later rose to 29). The treaty, ratified by the Russian parliament on 8 July 1992, stipulated that the Russian Army and Navy had to be reduced from 2.8 million men to 2.1 million by 1995 and placed restrictions on the number, type and deployment of weapons and forces: indeed, of all the signatories only Russia (and Ukraine) faced restrictions on where weapons could be stationed on their own territory (the flank limits). Germany was allowed a maximum of 375,000 soldiers, and Ukraine's ratification of the CFE Treaty in July 1992 limited its forces to 250,000.[16] In Tashkent in 1992 the Soviet CFE quota was divided between the successor states. The CFE treaty set strict limits to the number of conventional forces West of the Urals, and placed a ceiling on the number of forces Russia could have on its Northern (St Petersburg MD) and Southern (North Caucasus MD) flanks. Much Treaty Limited Equipment (TLE) was eliminated by the time the treaty came into force in November 1992, and even more was destroyed in advance of the full implementation of the treaty in July 1996. Russia also redeployed significant forces beyond the Urals, outside the scope of the CFE treaty. Russia was limited to 1700 tanks in European Russia, a sixth of the Soviet total.[17]

Moscow sought to revise the treaty, in particular the Northern and Southern flank limits, on the grounds that what had been negotiated for the USSR was inappropriate for an independent Russia, whose security and geostrategic problems had changed so dramatically. Russia hoped to replace the treaty with a more general European arms-control agreement that would limit military research and development expenditure. Above all, Russia requested greater flexibility in the deployment of its forces to meet its new security needs, in particular in the North Caucasus (including Chechnya), transformed from a rear MD in the Soviet era to a frontline zone of conflict covering Russia's only access to the Black Sea and the Caspian. The West conceded that the CFE treaty placed particularly severe restrictions on Russia and the limits were slightly revised in late 1995, and a full review in May 1996 granted Russia three extra years to comply. The treaty was modified in 1999 to take into the post-Cold War realities. However, only four countries – Russia, Belarus, Ukraine and Kazakhstan – ratified the modified treaty, and 'NATO newcomers such as Slovakia [in fact Slovenia] and the Baltic republics', Putin noted in his address to the Federal Assembly on 26 April 2007, 'had not joined the CFE treaty altogether'. He rejected the link made by the Western powers between ratifying the treaty and Russia's Istanbul commitments stipulating the withdrawal of Russian forces from Georgia and Transnistria. Putin announced a moratorium on Russia's implementation of the treaty, arguing that it made no sense for Russia to observe its conditions when they were ignored by NATO. He warned that Russia would repudiate the treaty in its entirety if no progress was made in ensuring its full implementation.[18] The emergency conference of the OSCE states, convened at Moscow's request, in Vienna on 11–15 June 2007 rejected Russia's demand that NATO countries should ratify the treaty by 1 July 2008, and in December 2007 Russia withdrew from the treaty.

## The great retreat

The dissolution of the WTO in June 1991 and the disintegration of the USSR accelerated the retreat of what had now become Russian forces not only from Central Europe but also from large parts of what had formerly been home territory. In the former East Germany, covering 22 per cent of contemporary Germany, 375,000 troops of the Western Group of Forces (WGF) remained. By June 1991 all Soviet forces had left Hungary and Czechoslovakia and the last Russian combat troops left Poland in October 1992; in 1993, however, 250,000 remained to be repatriated from Germany, Poland, the Baltic and Transcaucasia.[19] Finally, 49 years after the Soviet flag had been hoisted over the Reichstag, the last Russian troops left Berlin on 31 August 1994. The date symbolises the end of an epoch: the Cold War, the division of Europe and superpower 'overlay' over the destiny of European states.

Russia became the successor not only to the Soviet Union, but also to the geopolitical realities that had created the Russian empire earlier. Russia *de facto* became a neo-imperial power not by choice but by history. How could Russia shed this burden while maintaining its long-term strategic interests? The definition of these interests, as we have seen, was contested, but Russia's role as a regional power was to some degree thrust upon it by the escalation of regional conflicts. The removal of forces from Moldova, for example, was complicated by the insurgency in Transnistria. An agreement was reached on 10 August 1994 for the removal of all Russian forces from Moldova within three years, but Moscow on this occasion, as in the future, dragged its feet over fulfilling its commitments. The vast stockpile of munitions, equipment and weapons was only slowly removed, and Russia's last 500 troops in 2007 were ostensibly kept to guard the matériel.

The Baltic republics asserted that the enforced stationing of troops on foreign soil was a violation of international law: as long as 'foreign' troops remained the three republics could not feel fully independent. In late 1991 there were some 25,000 former Soviet troops in Estonia, 60,000 in Latvia and 40,000 in Lithuania. Negotiations on their removal embittered relations between the new democracies. Grachev in June 1992 argued that the troops could not be withdrawn until housing had been provided for them in Russia, a process that would take several years. Neither was it clear who would pay the pensions of the former military personnel living in these republics. The negotiators were caught between extremists on both flanks: in Russia the national-patriots and neo-communists urged Yeltsin to take a firmer line against the Baltic states; whereas nationalists there insisted that Russia remove the forces immediately. Up to mid-1992 Russia treated the Baltic forces as a single unit, but at that point indicated that it would be willing to contemplate the speedier withdrawal from Lithuania because of its more amenable approach to citizenship issues.[20] Despite attempts to link military withdrawal to civic rights, the number of Russian troops continued to decline because falling conscription meant that soldiers who had completed their tour of duty were not replaced: by the end of 1992 all but 50,000 of the troops had gone. The removal of troops was completed in Lithuania by the end of August 1993, and the last Russian troops withdrew from Estonia and Latvia by 31 August 1994. Thus the North-West Group of Forces ceased to exist, and Russian troops in Kaliningrad (the Eleventh Army) now came directly under the command of GHQ Land Forces. By August 1994 some 1.5 million troops had been redeployed to Russian territory from Eastern Europe and the former USSR: no significant Russian forces were stationed outside the former Soviet Union.

The 'great retreat' affected parts of the Russian Federation proper. Following the abortive intervention in Chechnya in November 1991, when some 500 troops were sent and then summarily withdrawn, Russia removed its forces from the republic but left behind enormous quantities of matériel and arms, to be used by the insurgents in the war from December 1994. Russia removed its forces from Nagorno-Karabakh, and in May 1992 an agreement was signed with Azerbaijan on the withdrawal of all Russian forces within two years. The relocated troops faced a hard fate in Russia, competing for housing, jobs and pensions with those released by earlier cuts. Many of the 30,000 officers and their dependants withdrawn from Hungary and Czechoslovakia lived in converted barracks while the troops lived under canvas, with many junior officers living below the poverty line. The pitiful plight of forces from CIS countries was graphically illustrated by the case of the 104th Airborne Division, relocated from Ganja in Azerbaijan to Ulyanovsk in 1993. In their 'home' country, the troops were treated almost as invaders and faced difficulties in finding housing and integrating into the local community.[21]

The retreat encompassed not only the physical return of troops but also a decline in the prestige and morale of the armed forces in their entirety. The military profession was no longer an attractive one, and many officers left for better-paid jobs in the growing private sector. The retreat was accompanied by the erosion of discipline, with many officers taking up entrepreneurial activities to create 'military-commercial clans' specialising in the sale of weapons and equipment. By 2001 there were some 10 million unlicensed weapons in private hands. Corruption in the Russian Army was accompanied by the illegal sale of military property through underhand deals between the military supply service and commercial interests.[22] It was while investigating corruption in the WGF that the journalist Dmitry Kholodov was murdered in Moscow in 1994 by a suitcase bomb, planted, it is alleged, by officers trying to cover up massive illicit arms sales. Mass demobilisation and desertion, moreover, threatened stability throughout former Soviet territory.

The increased assertiveness of Russian foreign policy from 1994 was accompanied by attempts to put an end to the retreat. Russia's redefined security policy now sought to keep some military bases in the 'near' and 'far' abroad. Overseas, USSR/Russia since 1979 had enjoyed the rent-free lease of Cam Ranh Bay naval base in Vietnam, but following the failure to reach an advantageous deal once the lease expired in 2004 Russia pulled out, signalling the end of its aspirations to maintain a blue-water navy in the Indian and Pacific Oceans. Russia still paid $200 million a year to maintain the Lourdes listening post in Cuba, monitoring US communications. Putin's decision to close the post (it ended its work in January 2002) reflected a deeper choice that the Cold War had really ended. Nearer to home, the Skrunda radar station in Latvia was closed in 1998 and replaced by the new strategic radar site 'Volga' in Barnaovichy in Belarus. Twenty-eight Russian bases proper remained in the CIS. In Belarus an air force regiment remained at Zyabrouka;[23] the Russian military presence was indeed strengthened as the joint Belarus-Russia state began to take shape. There are two bases in Armenia (Erevan and Gyumri), but none in Azerbaijan although Russia leases the giant Lyaki (Gabala) early-warning radar installation. A long-running dispute with Ukraine over the status of the Black Sea fleet stationed in the Crimea was settled for a time in 1997, with Russia leasing the facilities until 2016. The loss of Crimea was perhaps the most painful blow to Russia's pride. The deepwater port of Sevastopol was founded in 1783 by General Alexander Suvorov following eleven wars with the Ottoman Empire, and endured two legendary sieges – the first during the Crimean War of 1854–6, and the second during the Second World War. Russia was also forced to leave the Balaklava nuclear submarine base.

The four bases in Georgia were the most contentious. At the Istanbul summit on 19 November 1999 as part of the adapted CFE treaty Russia agreed to close two of the four by 1 July 2001. Russia fulfilled its obligations concerning the Vaziani base and airport near Tbilisi (the former headquarters of the Transcaucasus Group of Forces, GRVZ), and the departure of the final Russian presence from Tbilisi on Christmas day 2005 brought to an end two hundred years of a Russian garrison presence in the capital, established in November 1799. By June 2007, Russian forces had been completely evacuated the base at Akhalkalaki, established by the Imperial Russian Army in 1910 near the Ottoman border, with some matériel transferred to the Russian base in Gyumri in neighbouring Armenia. This left two bases as the bone of contention, preventing the Western powers ratifying the adapted CFE treaty. At Gudauta in the breakaway Abkhaz region the local population allegedly insisted on Russia retaining the base as the headquarters for peace-keeping operations, although it was due to have closed by 1 July 2001 according to the adapted treaty. The presence of a residual Russian force in Transnistria remained the biggest obstacle to the ratification of the 1999-adapted CFE treaty. By the mid-2000s no more than 30,000 men remained in the near abroad, engaged in various peace-keeping operations (notably in Abkhazia) and in the bases. By 2007 some 11,000 soldiers were in Tajikistan alone (primarily the 201st Motor Rifle Division, which were Russia's contribution to the Rapid Deployment Force of the Collective Security Treaty Organisation (CSTO, see next chapter), policing the border with Afghanistan and maintaining the fragile regime. As the president, Imomali Rakhmon (formerly Rakhmonov), put it, for Tajikistan 'Russia is our chief strategic ally'.[24] The establishment of a Russian airbase at Kant, near Kyrgyzstan's capital Bishkek, in October 2003 within the framework of the CSTO signalled the beginning of the end of the great retreat.

## Military and security doctrines

Like most other countries, Russia periodically assesses the threats to the country, the various risks facing its policy-makers, and evaluates the most appropriate responses. These views are reflected in major documents, drafted by the Security Council. Their significance should not be exaggerated, since policy is usually reactive and spontaneous rather than the emanation of deeply thought strategies, yet they do provide some indication of the evolution of official thinking.

### *Military doctrine*

The former chief of the general staff and a noted reformer, General Vladimir Lobov, argued that a 'military doctrine does not exist by itself [but] is part of the overall state doctrine' affecting the economy, science, politics and foreign policy.[25] As Scott McMichael puts it, 'Soviet military doctrine functioned as a virtual surrogate for what the West would call national security policy.'[26] Like America's regularly revised National Security Strategy, Russia's Military Doctrine deals not only with narrowly military issues but provides an overview of the strategic challenges facing the country. It provides a useful gauge to measure the concerns of the Russian leadership.

Russia's military doctrine has been in a constant process of evolution. The first draft of May 1992 built on the changes introduced into the USSR's doctrine (last revised in 1987), above all in its overwhelmingly defensive orientation, the absence of residual notions of class struggle, and its rehabilitation of the concept of 'national security' and 'national interests'. Some of the old concerns, however, remained, albeit in a new guise, particularly in the notion of 'some states and coalitions' (i.e., the USA and NATO) who still seek to dominate the world. The deployment of foreign troops into countries bordering Russia was considered a direct military threat, while attacks on Russian-speaking populations in other CIS countries would give Russia the right to intervene on their behalf.[27] The struggle between parliament and president prevented this draft being adopted.

A revised version, called 'The Main Provisions of the Military Doctrine of the RF', was adopted on 2 November 1993, a modified version of which was adopted in 1997. The 1993 document stressed that Russia's vital interests 'in no way involved the security of other states'. The doctrine stressed the need for conflict prevention, the territorial integrity of states, respect for their sovereignty and non-interference in their internal affairs. Learning from the October events, 'separate' military units could now be deployed to support interior troops in internal conflicts or to support border troops in particular cases, provisions utilised to allow Russian forces to intervene in Chechnya. In contrast to Russia's draft Military Doctrine of May 1992, which placed a heavy emphasis on military cooperation within the CIS, the Doctrine approved in November 1993 made only one brief mention of the CIS. Another key change from the earlier draft was the shift in threat perception, now identified as coming from local wars. The Russian Army was to defend Russia's 'territorial integrity', but it was not clear where the borders lay. The doctrine formalised the view of the former Soviet republics as part of Russia's extended security zone and tried to endow the CIS with a military dimension, with Russia acting as a type of garrison state on behalf of the other members. The army, however, could only move in with the consent of the government involved, but Russia's 'peace-keeping' operations (see below) sometimes blurred the principle of impartiality or neutrality in disputes. The doctrine made no mention of civil or parliamentary control over the military, and had little to say about the role of the army in Russian society. The doctrine, even though it had moderated some of the postulates of the earlier draft, reflected the 'great power' thinking of the Defence Ministry. While declaring Russia's peaceful intentions, the doctrine nevertheless revealed an underlying bloc mentality and a deep sense of insecurity.[28]

The focus in the 1997 version was on internal and local conflicts as the main threat to the state. The involvement of NATO in the Balkans crisis in 1999 raised the profile of the Russian military and there were signs that it was able to increase its leverage over politicians. During the bombing campaign against Serbia Russia announced that it would be reviewing its military doctrine to take into account the possibility of large-scale ground warfare, something that had been discounted earlier. A stronger role for nuclear deterrence was also suggested, the need for forces abroad (above all in Belarus) was argued, and there was greater support for the demands of the generals for an increased military budget. Anti-Western sentiments among the population were mobilised to achieve promises for greater military spending. Russia's militaristic response to the Kosovo crisis, however, alarmed its allies in the CIS and only six renewed the Tashkent Collective

Security Treaty when it came up for renewal in 1999. Despite Russia's attempts to lead a boycott of NATO's fiftieth anniversary celebrations in Washington, DC, in April 1999, only Russia and Belarus stayed away while all the other countries appeared even more eager to attend. The Kosovo crisis was for Russia a domestic crisis of the first order, revealing the limits of its authority on the world and regional stage while at the same time exposing the way that nearly a decade reform had provoked anti-Western sentiments, something that the Soviet regime with its huge propaganda apparatus had been unable to do. Russian policy and public sentiment was motivated less by sympathy for the Serbs than by fear that the power imbalance in the post-Cold War order threatened the autonomy of less powerful states, amongst which Russia (together with China) now found itself.

A revised Military Doctrine was prepared by the General Staff and was signed into effect by Putin on 21 April 2000.[29] Although adopted in the Putin era, its concerns were those of the Primakov years. The 'no first use' of nuclear weapons postulate, already weakened in the 1993 doctrine, was given added detail, and reflected the deeper sense that Russia's conventional forces would not be able to repulse any attack. As part of the reassessment of the risks facing the country the document called for the forward deployment of troops outside Russian territory. The focus was on the war on terrorism, reflecting the beginning of renewed warfare in Chechnya.

The Security Council began work on a new Military Doctrine in early 2007.[30] Drafts reflected the deterioration in the climate of international politics. Discussion focused on the perceived strengthening of military blocs, notably NATO, and how Russia could best respond. In the past Russia's frequent statements against NATO enlargement had been signally ineffective. The revised doctrine also reassessed the nature of threats to Russian national security, and warned of the danger from America to Russia's interests in post-Soviet Eurasia. There were suggestions that the new doctrine would remove the article asserting Russia's right for a pre-emptive nuclear strike, which had been adopted at a time of Russia conventional military weakness. There was also talk of shifting the emphasis away from conventional war towards guerrilla warfare. The priority of ensuring adequate defence capacity, irrespective of domestic economic conditions, was reasserted. In March 2007 the Security Council announced that it no longer considered global terrorism the main threat, which now came from international structures, primarily NATO.[31] The intense discussions over the content of a new security doctrine at this time reflected the struggle for the soul of Russian politics and its perception of the world.

### Security doctrine

Although a Law on Security had been adopted on 25 March 1992,[32] this dealt with the internal arrangements of the power agencies and it was only in 1997 that the Security Council produced a more strategic document. The document was relatively optimistic about the possibility of a multilateral world system, about Russia's ability to be absorbed as an equal into the new system of global security, and the relative low level of threats to Russia. The shock of the Kosovo war, NATO enlargement and a growing sense of Russian self-confidence prompted the development of a revised version. Russia's new Security Concept had been prepared by the Security Council under Putin's leadership, and was approved by presidential decree on 10 January 2000.[33] While there is much overlap between with the Military Doctrine there are also plenty of incompatibilities, but both failed to develop a coherent programme of military reform.[34] It was this gap that allowed the very public clash between the defence minister Igor Sergeev and chief of General Staff Kvashnin in July 2000 over the relative priority of strategic forces (defended by Sergeev) or whether they should be cut to provide extra resources for conventional forces (Kvashnin's view).

The 2000 document reflected deep concerns about the external environment. The August 1998 economic meltdown revealed Russia's vulnerability to speculative international financial markets, the use of NATO forces with an unclear UN mandate to bomb Serbia between March and June 1999, NATO's enlargement in March 1999 to encompass Poland, Hungary and the Czech Republic, strategic arms control tensions and renewed war in Chechnya, all provoked a rethinking of the international environment. The Concept expanded the list of external threats to Russia's security, noting in particular the weakening of the Organisation for Security and Cooperation in Europe (OSCE), the UN and the CIS. The document described the tension between a multipolar world, in which relations are based on international law and an acceptance of a significant role for Russia, and attempts by the US and its allies to carve out a unipolar world outside of international law. Talk of 'partnership' with the West disappeared, and instead more emphasis was placed on more limited 'cooperation'.

## Nuclear politics and non-proliferation

With the fall of communism the instruments of the Cold War became a greater threat to world peace than the systems that had given them birth. Nuclear weapons lost much of their strategic significance but the race to possess them and the difficulty of disposing of them provoked regional rivalries and international concern. India and Pakistan in 2000 became confirmed nuclear states, while Israel and some others are 'threshold' states, ready to join the five permanent members of the UN Security Council as nuclear states. A number of 'rogue' states, above all North Korea, demonstrated missile capacity, while Iran's development of a nuclear power industry had the potential to be used as a cover for the development of an atomic military nuclear capacity. It was against these two that the United States sought to develop Missile Defence. In January 2007, the US announced plans to deploy a missile base in Poland and a radar facility in the Czech Republic, allegedly to counter possible attacks from Iran or North Korea.

The modest cuts of about one-third envisaged by the Start-1 Treaty of 31 July 1991 were surpassed by a number of proposals later that year. While nuclear weaponry lost some of its political value in East-West relations, among the successor states nuclear issues involved delicate power plays and the management of symbolic relationships. The four nuclear successor republics (Russia, Ukraine, Belarus and Kazakhstan) and the West were agreed that nuclear proliferation should be avoided and that Russia should emerge as the only successor nuclear state, but, as usual, the devil is in the detail. The Almaty inaugural meeting of the CIS on 21 December 1991 vowed to maintain unified control over nuclear weapons: the president of Russia was granted the exclusive right to use them but only with the approval of the other three nuclear states. Shaposhnikov, as supreme commander of CIS forces, took over control, sharing the firing codes with Yeltsin. This arrangement did not last long, and the day after the decision by the CIS defence ministers on 15 June 1993 to disband the Joint Command, Shaposhnikov was relieved of the 'nuclear suitcase'.

The proliferation of nuclear technologies threatened global security, and in the former USSR they became a source of political instability.[35] The USSR left an arsenal of 27,000 nuclear weapons, about two-thirds of which were strategic and the rest tactical.[36] There were fears that weapons could find their way to what were then nuclear 'threshold' states like Pakistan, Iran, Iraq and Libya. In addition, some 900,000 people were involved in the maintenance of the USSR's thermonuclear arsenal, with perhaps 2,000 people with knowledge of nuclear weapons design and some 3–5,000 with experience in plutonium production or uranium enrichment.[37] Defeat in 1945 had allowed America to attract German experts in missile technology, so now there were fears that the collapse of the USSR would lead to the proliferation of nuclear technology. The only consolation was that the medium-range weapons had already been destroyed under the terms of the 1987 Intermediate Nuclear Forces (INF) Treaty.

At the December 1991 Almaty meeting Ukraine and Belarus agreed to join the 1968 Non Proliferation Treaty (NPT) as non-nuclear states, and only Kazakhstan hesitated in agreeing to the withdrawal of nuclear weapons from its territory. However, under pressure from a vociferous pro-nuclear lobby Ukraine later modified its approach. Ukraine regarded military policy as part of the overall struggle for independence, and thus had second thoughts about unilaterally undermining its bargaining position by renouncing nuclear weapons.[38] The prime minister and from June 1994 president, Leonid Kuchma, had for ten years been the manager of the world's largest missile plant (Yuzhmash) and insisted that Ukraine had the technical means to maintain its missiles. Ukraine sought political control over the 176 missiles with some 1,200 warheads 'temporarily' on its territory.[39] Kazakhstan and Ukraine suspected, probably correctly, that while they had nuclear weapons Russia and the world would negotiate more respectfully with them. By mid-1992 all tactical nuclear weapons had been moved to Russia, but Ukraine and Kazakhstan equivocated over the removal of strategic nuclear weapons. The pro-nuclear lobby insisted that in exchange for surrendering its arsenal Ukraine should receive certain security guarantees. What form these guarantees could take was unclear, and the issue damaged Ukraine's international standing. The Lisbon Protocol of 23 May 1992 made Belarus, Kazakhstan and Ukraine partners to the Start-1 Treaty, together with Russia and the USA, and all three pledged to join the NPT as non-nuclear states.[40] Despite misgivings Kazakhstan finally joined the NPT and Ukraine, too, joined as a non-nuclear weapon state on 5 December 1994.

Despite much opposition, the Russian parliament ratified the Start-1 Treaty on 4 November 1992 (which expires in December 2009), but already a more radical version was being prepared. Yeltsin described the Start-2 Treaty signed in Moscow on 3 January 1993 as 'surpassing all other disarmament treaties in its scale and importance', while president George Bush Snr, taking his final bow on the world stage, saw the treaty as marking the definitive end to the Cold War and the start of a 'new world of hope' in which 'parents and children would have a future far more free from fear'. A total of some 17,000 nuclear warheads were to be destroyed, and the American and Russian strategic arsenals were to be cut to between 3–3,500 warheads each by 1 January 2003, less than half the total agreed by the Start-1 Treaty. These cuts of a combined total of some 21,000 strategic weapons would take place in two stages and included the elimination of all land-based intercontinental ballistic missiles with multiple and independently targeted warheads (MIRVs), notably Russia's 10-warhead RS-20s (known in the West as the SS-18, Satan), either through straightforward scrapping or through conversion to a single warhead (to a maximum of 90) by adapting the launching pads. Within ten years the number of submarine-based missiles (SLBMs), the main American deterrent, was to be capped at 1,750. This committed America to destroying about half of its 432 Trident I and II missiles with their eight warheads apiece. Several Russian demands, largely motivated by considerations of economy, were taken into account in formulating the treaty, such as its plan to adapt 90 SS-18 launch pads to take SS-25s, and to convert 105 of its six-warhead SS-19s into single-warhead weapons.

The agreement signalled that the Cold War was truly over, and that arms control had entered a qualitatively new phase with deep cuts reducing the number of superpower ballistic warheads from the peak of 26,331 agreed by the Salt Agreement of 1988 to a little over 6,000 in 2003. Russia broke with the fundamental principle of Soviet military doctrine, namely the need to maintain nuclear parity with the United States. Deterrence as such had ended in 1991 when most missiles had stopped being targeted on each other. It would be a long path, however, from signing to implementing Start-2; not only was there significant opposition in the Duma, which sought to link the issue to NATO enlargement, but the sheer cost of decommissioning placed yet more strain on an over-stretched budget. In a strange reversal of roles some of the funds were provided by the US, in particular through the Nunn-Lugar programme. In the event, one of the first acts of Putin's presidency was to convince the newly compliant Duma to ratify the Start-2 treaty, which it did in early 2000. By then there was talk of a further Start-3 process, but negotiations were compromised by American plans for the 'son of Star Wars' (National) Missile Defence (NMD) shield, enthusiastically supported by president George W. Bush. Russia feared that Missile Defence would provide the Americans with unilateral strategic invulnerability, concerns that were exacerbated by America's unilateral abrogation of the 1972 Anti-Ballistic Missile (ABM) treaty in December 2001. Even America's European allies were concerned that the scrapping of the 1972 ABM treaty would provoke a new arms race.

These tensions did not prevent the signing of the Strategic Offensive Reduction Treaty during Bush's visit to Moscow on 24 May 2002, with each side pledging to reduce their stockpile to no more than 2,200 warheads by 31 December 2012. Although the treaty allowed warheads to be dismantled rather than destroyed and there was no verification procedure, the Duma ratified what became known as the Moscow Treaty on 14 May 2003. Russia and America have a common interest in preventing nuclear proliferation because, apart from the dangers involved, the more countries with nuclear weapons, the less influence for them. The optimum level of their nuclear arsenals, however, remains a matter of debate. Despite the awesome dismantlement costs involved, it was Russia that in 1995 had suggested negotiations for a Start-3 treaty to reduce nuclear arsenals to some 1,000 warheads each; sufficient for retaliation, but not enough for a disabling first strike. On 1 January 2007 Russia had 927 nuclear delivery vehicles and 4,162 nuclear warheads for strategic missiles, while the United States owned 1,255 and 5,866, respectively, just below the cap of 6,000 warheads imposed by Start-2 and well below the 1,600 ballistic missiles and strategic bombers allowed by the treaty.[41]

Faced by the deterioration of its conventional forces, however, Russia became more rather than less dependent on nuclear weapons. In the late 1990s Russia successfully tested the Topol-M nuclear missile, with a single warhead, and began its deployment in the 2000s. This complemented the ageing SS-18s, with 10 warheads each, as the main instrument of deterrence. Russia found it increasingly difficult to maintain the triad of nuclear systems, air, sea and land, with the submarine-based systems in particular becoming obsolescent. By the mid-2000s, according to an American study, Russia had 58 per cent fewer ICBMs than the Soviet Union fielded at the end of the Cold War, giving America strategic superiority.[42] In response, Russia accelerated the modernisation of its nuclear arsenal, including updating its Iskander Cruise missile and in May 2007 successfully test-launched the new RS-24 ICBM, capable of carrying up to 10 warheads and designed to replace the RS-18 (SS-19, Stiletto) and SS-18 missiles. American plans to deploy interceptor missiles in Poland and a radar shield in the Czech Republic threatened to turn Europe, once again, into a 'powder keg', as Putin put it.[43]

The Soviet commitment to no first use of nuclear weapons was dropped in the Security Doctrine adopted in 2000, and the debate over whether conventional or nuclear weapons should take priority paralysed military reform. While the possession of nuclear weapons on its own does not guarantee a state 'great power' status, Russia's position as the world's second nuclear power does add a certain authority to its foreign policy. The larger picture is the onset of a new nuclear age, disappointing the hopes of those who had hoped that the end of the Cold War would lead to a gradual denuclearisation of strategic planning.

## Military reform

Military reform focuses on two key issues: *professionalisation*, above all devising a new relationship with personnel; and *modernisation*, covering command structures, technical organisation and equipment. The fundamental shift was from a huge conscript army of the Soviet type towards a smaller and more professional force able to deal with the multitude of threats facing the country. No longer was there an over-riding strategic threat from the massed armies of the West but a variety of concerns encompassing terrorism, migration, weapons and narcotics smuggling.

### Professionalisation

In 1991 Russia had 196 divisions, but of the 30-odd remaining today no more than 10 are combat-ready. Grachev sought to reduce the armed forces from the 3.4 million in 1991 to some 1.5 million, no longer a conscript but a mobile, professional army. By 2007 the number in the regular army (Ground Forces) had fallen to 1.13 million, accompanied by another 300,000 Interior Troops (VV) organised in 29 interior divisions and 15 brigades, while numbers in the police had grown 1.5 times to some 333,000. The functions of the VV had also changed, with fewer engaged in protecting objects and people's security, and more devoted to preventing mass unrest – a change that gave rise to the view that Russia had once again become a police state. Military reform for much of the 1990s was reduced to troop cuts. This was reflected in the view of the outgoing defence minister, Sergeev, in February 2001 that the basic guidelines for military reform would involve cutting the armed forces by 365,000 and defence ministry employees by 120,000 over five years,[44] a commitment reaffirmed by Sergei Ivanov.[45] The problems ran far deeper than simply numbers, however. The catastrophic condition of the Russian military was revealed in the first Chechen war from December 1994, when hastily scrambled units only met on the way to the republic, and with over half of those sent to fight having never fired live shells with their tanks and guns. A spate of resignations accompanied the onset of war, by officers well aware that troops and equipment were not ready. In the first months of the war the army lost 1,146 soldiers killed and another 374 reported missing.[46]

The shortage of personnel was a constant refrain. As an army made up largely of conscripts, the military authorities opposed attempts to limit the length of military service or to extend exempted categories. Yeltsin in May 1995 extended the period of compulsory military service from 18 months to two years, and ended certain student exemptions. Putin once again limited student exemptions and re-introduced military education into the educational system. In 2008 compulsory military service was reduced to one year, with a further nine types of deferment categories abolished. Nevertheless, an army of 1.1 million requires some 350,000 conscripts a year, and double that number when the length of service is one year, a physical impossibility with Russia's demographic decline and health problems. Reformers seek the abolition of conscription and the creation of a wholly professional army, an aim conceded by Yeltsin during his re-election campaign in May 1996 but then deferred. The Soviet armed forces had always been designed as a mass army, with millions of reservists to be called up when required, and this tradition remains strong today.

This is one reason why the law on alternatives to military service, a right guaranteed by the constitution, was so long delayed. There could be no serious military reform until a law on alternative civilian service (ACS) was adopted. Debates in the Duma over the law in 2001 focused on the length of alternative service for those without higher education: international practice is for it to last twice as long as service in the army. The law adopted in July 2002 came into effect on 1 January 2004 and was the harshest of all those proposed to the Duma and faithfully reflected the concerns of the military. Applicants for ACS have to prove to the conscription commission that military service is against their convictions. ACS will normally be served outside the applicant's region of residence. ACS in civilian bodies lasts 42 months (for those with higher education, 21 months), while in military bodies it lasts 36 and 18 months, respectively. The punitive nature of the ACS law provoked liberal deputies in the Duma to try to amend the law to allow men to undertake ACS in their home regions.

Personnel shortages are caused not only by the high percentage of those due for conscription who are automatically granted deferment (such as those in higher education) or exempted on health or social grounds, but above all by the low number of those actually answering conscription orders - not much more than a quarter annually. The quality of those drafted was often low, with little education, poor health and, not infrequently, criminal records. In 2005, 40 per cent of draftees were found to be unfit for military service because of physical or metal disabilities. Quite apart from low pay and conditions, the Soviet Army suffered a dreadful record of bullying (hazing) known as *dedovshchina*. In the second half of the 1980s some 15–20,000 conscripts died 'noncombat' deaths,[47] and in 1991 alone, according to official figures, 5,500 CIS servicemen (mostly conscripts) died through suicide, beatings or accidents, while 98,700 were wounded.[48] About 1,000 conscripts committed suicide annually throughout the 2000s as a result of various barbaric initiation ceremonies and *dedovshchina*. According to official data (which now has to be published annually), in 2005 1,067 servicemen died non-combat deaths, more than in four years of conflict in Chechnya where 1,049 died between 2002 and 2005.[49]

It was in response to this that in June 1989 the first committees of soldiers' mothers were established to exert pressure on the authorities to enforce a decree allowing students to defer military service.[50] In the 1990s the Union of Committees of Soldiers' Mothers became one of the most active pressure groups in society, exposing the savage way that the authorities dealt with conscripts and casualties in the Chechen wars. In addition, the demographic trends that we noted in Chapter 14, in particular the extremely low Russian birth rate, makes it increasingly difficult to maintain a large conscript army, with ever fewer males reaching recruiting age annually. As a result most units are at best half-manned and the number of officers sometimes exceeds the number of conscripts. In 2001 there were more senior officers than junior officers, and one officer for every two soldiers. The development of a 109,000-strong NCO cadre of sergeants was essential to reduce the violence within the army and to provide the core of an all-volunteer service, and all NCOs were to be contract soldiers (*kontrakniki*, who sign up for fixed-term service contracts). In the 2000s training was improved and more units were combat ready. The aim was to create a more mobile, professional and technologically sophisticated army.

Some saw the solution in the creation of ethnic and regional units, which were traditional for the Russian Army, while others sought to combine this with a purely professional force. A professional army, however, requires higher spending on improved salaries and the like. The introduction of contract service represented a move towards the transition, with the 78,000 contract soldiers by 2007 making up an estimated one-third of Land Forces, concentrated primarily in technical and logistic units, while combat units, including those designated for peace-keeping operations, remain severely understaffed. *Kontrakniki* sign up for three years, and although they may come directly from civilian life the intention was to allow conscripts who had served their term to become professional soldiers. The cost of a contract serviceman is much higher than a conscript, and their quality tend to be low, attracting those who were unemployable in other professions. Fewer than a fifth of *kontrakniki* re-enlist, alienated by poor pay and primitive living conditions.

### Modernisation

For much of the 1990s there was a stalemate in devising a coherent reform strategy. Sergeev, the former head of the Strategic Rocket Forces, favoured reliance on nuclear weapons, but was opposed by chief of the General Staff, Anatoly Kvashnin. At the heart of discussion was a fundamental disagreement over the requisite structure of Russia's armed forces. By 2000 Russia had four services: the three common to most countries, the Air Force, the Navy and Ground Forces, plus the Strategic Rocket Forces (SRF) that had earlier incorporated the Air Defence Forces (ADF). The SRF remained an independent unit because of the extreme danger posed by unsanctioned actions, requiring exceptionally high skills and discipline in its personnel. The military insisted that the experience of other countries could not be blindly copied since Russia faced distinctive geostrategic challenges in the context of its own history and traditions.[51] Putin re-established the Chief Command of Ground Forces, disbanded in 1998, and reduced the number of services to three by merging the SRF into the traditional air, land and sea structure.

Military reform at first was conducted against the background of a severe economic crisis and tight budgets, with sharply reduced defence spending, halving in real terms by 1995 and with only $7 billion spent on defence in 2001. Such low expenditure meant reduced procurement of new weapons and equipment, shortages of fuel and spare parts and inability to conduct training and exercises. In 1992, for the first time since the reign of Peter the Great, Russia failed to begin the construction of a single warship.[52] Speaking to the State Duma in November 1994, Grachev claimed that only 40 per cent of the Russian Army's armaments could be classified as modern,[53] a proportion that fell to some 10 per cent by the year 2000. In 2001 arms procurement represented only 6 per cent of total defence expenditure, contrasted to the minimum of 20 per cent in NATO countries. The loss of technological edge and financial muscle threatened to bar Russia from genuine great power status, something that Putin sought to prevent. Russian law establishes a minimum of 3.5 per cent of GDP to be devoted to the military, but under Putin spending stabilised at around 2.6 per cent. In absolute terms there were significant increases in budgets, by about a third each year, reflecting the growing economy, and in the first seven years of his leadership spending on the military increased five-fold. Defence expenditure in 2006 was 15 per cent of budgetary expenditure, down from the 24 per cent in 1994, but in absolute terms much higher. According to Putin, between 2000 and 2006 army financing increased by three and a half times, which in absolute terms by 2006 was $30 billion.[54] This was 25 times less than that spent by the US and half that spent by China.

In one of his last acts as defence minister, Sergei Ivanov announced a significant enhancement of the procurement programme, with the phased introduction of new ships, aircraft and armour, as well as the strategic weapons mentioned above. He outlined an ambitious programme for defence rearmament over the next decade that would see 45 per cent of military hardware being renewed.[55] Defence procurement was to rise sharply, including the purchase by 2017 of a new system of ICBMs and tactical rockets, 50 strategic bombers, 31 ships, advanced tanks and new air defence systems. The aim was to restore strategic parity with the West. Presenting his plans to the Duma on 7 February 2007, Ivanov insisted that the issue was 'modernisation, not reform of the army', since the word reform, he asserted, 'gives us an allergic reaction'.[56] Later that month Ivanov was promoted to become a first deputy prime minister, in which role he announced the revival of the Glonass satellite navigation programme, based on a system of 24 satellites, to be completed by 2009. In February 2007 Putin signed the decree creating the United Aviation Corporation, combining all national civilian and military aircraft companies, including MiG, Sukhoi, Tupolev and Ilyushin. The new company was to be chaired by the former defence minister Ivanov. A similar plan was announced to consolidate Russia's shipbuilding industry, encompassing 160 shipyards and shipbuilding plants, into three giant holding companies, with the biggest, the United Industrial Company, also to be chaired by Ivanov. Three-quarters of Russia's shipbuilding capacity was military. The outlines of a rearmament programme were in place, which while modest in comparison with combined Western defence expenditure nevertheless signalled the onset of a new era of militarisation.

## Civil–military relations

Civilian control of the military has been crucial in all previous transitions, notably in Latin America and Southern Europe. Even in Spain, the much-admired democratic transition, everything was put in jeopardy in 1981 when some army officers seized parliament. In the post-communist world a decade after the fall of communism Chris Donnelly noted that 'there is not a single Central and Eastern European country today which has a civil-military relationship and a reorganized armed forces which it can consider satisfactory'.[57] In Russia civilian control over the military sphere was at best partial. The Soviet regime had created a military machine whose scope was unprecedented in peacetime but had always been careful to ensure Party and state control over the ambitions of the generals. Marxism-Leninism asserted the primacy of the Party over the military but at the same time its view of permanent conflict with capitalism served to justify the maintenance of the huge military establishment and imbued it with prestige and purpose. With the dissolution of the communist regime traditional forms of control disappeared, and at the same time the prestige and morale of the armed forces plummeted. In the apparently 'post-military' post-Cold War world, the very basis of the military-society relationship has changed: in the past, involvement in the military through conscription and civil defence was a token of citizenship; now, economic citizenship has taken on a much higher profile. Military intervention in politics can take different forms. For some it means resolute action against the civilian leadership, something which has not yet taken place in Russia. However, there are softer forms of intervention, primarily taking the form of undue influence over the budget and policy process, visible above all in foreign relations.

During *perestroika* the military had become increasingly politicised as the old unity gave way to dissonance of *glasnost* and the rise of republican separatism. The demise of the old Soviet political organs (above all the Main Political Administration) left officers prey to influences from beyond the military. Organisations like the All-Russian Officers Union, registered in February 1992, headed by Vladislav Achalov and Stanislav Terekhov were anti-government, accusing it of indifference towards corruption, dismissing officers for political reasons (above all for criticism of Grachev himself), and for presiding over Russia's military decline.[58] While claiming a membership of 30,000 officers, in fact Terekhov's organisation was minuscule but this should not disguise the fact that the armed forces were rife with anti-government sentiments. According to military sociologists in November 1992 only 19 per cent of servicemen supported the government, while its policies were opposed by 56 per cent.[59] The reconstituted Russian military authorities fought to reverse the politicisation of the army, including a ban on party activity in the ranks, the forced resignation of those actively involved in political life (a dispensation that appears to have been dropped in the December 1995 elections) and the prohibition on army trade unions.[60]

Defeat in the Second World War had destroyed the military establishments and militarist traditions in Germany and Japan, leaving the civilian state to concentrate on domestic economic development. In Russia the Soviet military establishment remained largely intact at independence in 1991, and it fell to the new state to begin the arduous task of civilianising politics. The state itself, however, was in certain respects weaker than the military; as Donnelly points out, 'large bureaucratic institutions continue to function irrespective of the lack of government... the armed forces hierarchy was increasingly determining its own agenda'.[61] The military definition of state security and the militaristic ethos of the ruling class remained to be challenged. The functional equivalent of defeat in war is humiliation in peace (the Versailles syndrome). As if the great retreat was not enough, the military discovered that involvement in domestic conflicts was extremely damaging. Every intervention acted as a self-inflicted blow on prestige and morale: the Tbilisi massacre of 9 April 1989; the brutal occupation of Baku in January 1990; and the seizure of the television tower in Vilnius and other events in the Baltic in January 1991.

The civilian leadership usually retreated behind a cloud of obfuscation and equivocation, while the army was left to explain the corpses. The army's half-hearted involvement in the coup of August 1991 salvaged its pride, but all these events demonstrated once again the dangers of trying to solve the political agendas of others by military means. The military adopted a policy of 'neutrality' in domestic political struggle. General Lobov argued that 'people in uniforms should not engage in party activities, nor in political battles in parliament at any level'.[62]

This explains why in October 1993 the army was so reluctant to become involved, and it took several hours of pleading by Yeltsin at the Ministry of Defence to get the military to suspend the formula 'the army is outside politics' and to agree to an assault on the White House.[63] The October events revealed the desperately divided condition of the Russian Army. The force of just 1,700 was drawn from five separate divisions in the Moscow MD. To ensure loyalty tank crews were made up almost entirely of officers, and at least half the infantry were officers or senior NCOs.[64] The military's involvement in resolving the October 1993 crisis led to much speculation that they would thereafter enjoy a disproportionate influence in policy, whereas in fact the effect was short lived. The military gained few of the anticipated rewards like increased budgets, an end to personnel cuts and a harder line in the near abroad. Already low morale was further undermined by the Chechen campaign, which did little to enhance Grachev's personal standing. A poll of 615 generals and colonels in August 1994 revealed fewer than 30 per cent trusted Yeltsin, and under 20 per cent had any faith in Grachev, while half said they trusted Generals Lebed and Gromov. As far as their political attitudes were concerned, 80 per cent of these top ranking officers favoured an authoritarian form of government and 64 per cent dismissed Western-type democracy as unsuitable for Russia.[65] Andrei Nikolaev, the former head of the border guards and later a Duma deputy, is typical of the forthright way that military personnel in Russia, both active and retired, voice their views; in his case, in a book that condemned America's and NATO's 'pretensions for world dominance'.[66]

According to the Russian constitution, defence, like foreign policy, is a prerogative of the president. The president is commander-in-chief of the Armed Forces of Russia, operating through the General Staff. The so-called 'power ministries' are directly responsible to the president and not the prime minister. The power ministries include the Ministry of Defence as well as numerous other services including the MVD, the SVR and the FSB. Yeltsin retained the power of appointment to these services, without requiring parliament's approval. The Security Council is the main military and political body controlling Russia's defence establishment, while the Ministry of Defence is responsible for developing and implementing military, technical and personnel policy. The president tries to ensure that the Security Council, bringing together the heads of the leading power ministries, is headed by a loyalist – hence Lebed's rather short tenure as head between August and October 1996. The appointment of the loyal Vladimir Putin as head on 29 March 1999, at a time when the government was headed by Primakov who had a tense relationship with Yeltsin, was a case in point. Russia's Defence Ministry liaises through the CIS Defence Council of Ministers where appropriate. The prime minister and parliament can exert considerable practical influence over defence policy through control of budgets and the Duma's defence committee. The status of the armed forces is regulated by the Law on Defence of 24 September 1992 and with a revised version signed into law on 1 June 1996. The Law restricts the army to external defence only, thus its involvement in the Chechen wars was technically illegal.

Harmonious civil-military relations reflect stable social relations, while social crisis gives rise to tension, and this was certainly apparent in Russia. Civil-military relations in the Yeltsin years were managed by Yeltsin himself, although he never took a great deal of interest in military affairs, unlike his successor who was a career security officer. Yeltsin effectively retained control over the armed forces and denied access to any other politicians, but their subordination to his authority was not unquestioned, as demonstrated in October 1993. A major problem remains oversight over unit commanders; the weakening of the Soviet system of Party and instructor oversight has left lower level officers as virtual tyrants over their fiefdoms. Another problem is the great autonomy enjoyed by the system of military justice, headed by the Chief Military Prosecutor, a post that is formally part of the national judiciary yet in practice virtually independent.

The appointment of the civilian Sergei Ivanov as defence minister in 2001 broke with tradition (although under Brezhnev the civilian CC secretary Dmitry Ustinov had been defence minister), but the fact that he was a Putin loyalist perpetuated another tradition. The appointment of Lyubov Kudelina as deputy defence minister in charge of the defence ministry's budget and finance department reinforced the attempt to civilianise military affairs, an appointment that is particularly important since defence consumes one-fifth of the state budget. As we have seen, Serdyukov's appointment as defence minister in February 2007 was unequivocally a civilian appointment, and signalled the clear subordination of the military to the civilian leadership. Among other things, it was designed to guarantee that the military kept out of any potential succession crisis as Putin gave up the reins of power.

The political views of servicemen are an important factor in electoral politics.[67] In the mid-1990s there were 1.8 million military personnel; about 7 million members and relatives of service families with the right to vote; some 7–9 million employed in military-industrial enterprises, military research institutes and agencies, with families; some 20 to 21 million service pensioners and the families of veterans of the Great Patriotic and other wars; and some 2 million Russian Cossacks.[68] Today the armed forces and related groups make up to 40 million people out of a total electorate of about 107 million, and this is leaving out of account those employed in security agencies, which could well add another 10–15 million people. In broad terms, the voting pattern of the military was oppositional in the 1993 and 1995 electoral cycles, but swung round in conformity with broader patterns to support Putin and his allies from 1999 through to 2008. Voting patterns were distorted in 1993 because ballot boxes were placed directly in barracks, whereas in later elections soldiers joined with the mass of citizens in general polling stations.

For understandable reasons, the military favoured the preservation of the defence industries and Russia's great power status. The military establishment continued to act as an important player in foreign policy, and in particular in relations with the 'near abroad' (as in Transnistria and Abkhazia) and also over relations with Japan. The weakness of central authority meant that the reconstituted Russian military enjoyed considerable autonomy, and allied with the still powerful military-industrial officials, tried to shape policies. The military at times appeared to be making its own policy. The Far Eastern MD, for example, had its own agenda in relations with China, while some regional commanders appeared intent on pursuing their own interests, often associated with the development of various enterprises. This was not so much warlordism as a distinctive form of military capitalism. However, by a mixture of inducements and turning a blind eye, the post-communist authorities were able to keep the military out of politics, except when called upon in moments of crisis. Despite its involvement in heavy-handed 'peace-keeping' operations abroad and a radical intervention in domestic politics in Moscow and Chechnya, Lambeth argues that 'The military nonetheless remains a responsible and stabilizing force in Russian society.'[69]

The establishment of parliamentary committees overseeing security policy and the budget (and with it military expenditure) facilitates civilian control over the military. However, the establishment of political controls primarily requires effective political institutions, and Russia has not yet reached that stage. The other side of the equation, the professionalisation of the military, also requires competent state structures. The absence of the latter encouraged the military itself to enter politics, as witnessed by the large number of soldiers participating in the December 1995 elections. General-Lieutenant Lev Rokhlin, commander of forces in Volgograd and veteran of the Afghan and Chechen wars was placed third on the Our Home is Russia list. Rokhlin became an ardent oppositionist in parliament until murdered (allegedly by his wife) in 1998. He headed the Duma's defence committee, which became the virtual headquarters of the virulently anti-Yeltsin 'Movement in Support of the Army'. Divided between parties and tendencies, however, 'the military' as such lacked a single voice, and thus diminished the incentive to enter the political arena by forceful means. The military 'opposition' to Yeltsin, if it can be called that, took two main forms: 'the professionals' (Gromov, Lebed, Rokhlin); and the 'irreconcilables', mainly consisting of retired officers (including generals Makashov and Achalov, and the ex-KGB officer Sterligov). The appointment of General Igor Rodionov, formerly head of the General Staff Academy, as defence minister in July 1996 brought the professionals into the centre of military and security affairs, as did Sergeev's appointment later. Both, however, could not forgive Yeltsin for the defeat in Chechnya in 1996 and the declining role of the military in society. The second Chechen war, according to Baev, in this context should be seen

> not just as an attempt by the top brass to take revenge for the defeat of three years earlier, but as part of their larger effort to restore the 'proper' place of the army in society and check further degradation of the military structures.[70]

Putin was able to halt the decline of the armed forces, but creating a modern army would take at least a generation.

## New security paradigms

In a speech in Berlin on 12 December 1989 James Baker had spoken of 'a new architecture for a new era', a new structure for European and international security. This rather inflexible imagery foreshadowed one of the abiding features of post-communist Europe, namely the crisis of the institutions created during the Cold War to conduct and regulate that conflict. While communist Cold War organisations dissolved, those in the West not only survived but sought to expand their roles. The largely non-negotiated nature of the post-Cold War peace (noted in Chapter 16) was reflected in an institutional conservativism that sought to keep existing organisations while imbuing them with a new content.

Russia, however, became the champion of institutional revisionism, seeking at first to renegotiate the European security system by enhancing the role of the OSCE - as long as it was constrained by rules of consensus. In the event, Russia became deeply disillusioned not only with the OSCE, but with the whole trend of post-Cold War security arrangements. From being a status quo power, as the 2000s progressed signs of a new revisionism became apparent.

### Organisation for Security and Cooperation in Europe (OSCE)

In line with its reinvigorated European policy, Russia was an active participant in the web of institutions once labelled by Soviet writers the 'all-European process'. This included the CSCE, established in Helsinki in 1975, which with the end of the Cold War entered a period both of deepening and widening. Following the Paris Conference in November 1990 it acquired a headquarters and secretariat in Vienna, a Secretary General (supporting the work of the Chairman-in-Office), a Senior Council, a Permanent Council, a centre for the prevention of conflicts, a human rights commissioner, and an office for free elections (which later became the Office for Democratic Institutions and Human Rights based in Warsaw, specialising in constitution-making and election monitoring), and in May 1992 the CSCE Parliamentary Assembly was established. The body itself was renamed the *Organisation* for Security and Cooperation in Europe (OSCE) at the Budapest Review Conference in December 1994 to reflect its greater institutionalisation. Russia took over the Soviet seat, and total membership rose dramatically to 53 with the accession of the Baltic states in September 1991, all of the former Soviet states in January 1992 (except Georgia, which joined a few months later), and the post-Yugoslav states. The accession of the Central Asian states imbued the OSCE with the Eurasian character of Russia itself. It was far from clear, however, whether the OSCE was capable of dealing with the complexity of Eurasian politics.

Expectations that the OSCE would play a growing role in the post-communist world, expressed in the lofty language of the 'Charter of Paris for a New Europe' of 21 November 1990, were disappointed. Despite greater institutionalisation, including a modification of decision-making to allow 'consensus minus one', the OSCE remained but one among many competing institutions. The Americans favoured NATO, whereas the Maastricht Treaty of 1992 envisaged a strengthened role for the defence arm of the EU, the Western European Union (WEU), as the European Security and Defence Identity (ESDI) began to take form, formulated as one of the Maastricht pillars of the EU: the Common Foreign and Security Policy (CFSP). The OSCE played little part in conflict resolution in Nagorno-Karabakh (although its Minsk group sought to act as a mediator). Many argued that the hasty widening of the OSCE allowed membership to some former Soviet (and Yugoslav) states that did not meet accepted human rights standards and thus diluted the OSCE's human rights role. Contrary to the high hopes of 1990, the OSCE failed to become a community for the civilisational integration of Europe based on a common set of values. The notion of 'values' was used instrumentally as the outlines of a new confrontation between East and West took shape. As Zagorsky points out, insofar as the division of Europe was not yet over but had only taken on new forms,[71] the CSCE remained an important forum for the regulation of relations between the Eastern and Western parts of the Eurasian landmass. In gaining a stronger institutional framework the OSCE seems to have lost some of its original spirit of flexibility and consensus.

Russia's calls for a comprehensive system of collective security based on the OSCE, proposed formally in July 1994, were clearly designed in part to oppose plans for NATO expansion. If the OSCE were indeed to become the main vehicle for post-communist European security, then NATO enlargement would become meaningless. While perhaps never seriously believing that it could become an effective pan-European security organisation, Russia sought to expand the OSCE's political responsibilities and thus diminish NATO's influence and consolidate Russia's influence in European affairs. This early enthusiasm for the OSCE by the mid-2000s had turned into bitter criticism. The main Russian charge was that instead of acting as a regional security organisation focused on themes, such as minority rights and migration issues, it had become little more than an instrument of the Western powers to critique developments in post-Soviet Eurasia. At the international security conference in Munich on 10 February 2007 Putin denounced what he called 'attempts to turn the OSCE into an unsophisticated instrument to promote the foreign-policy interests of individual countries, or groups of countries, towards other countries'.[72] The Russian government was particularly exercised by the work of the ODIHR, which had criticised the conduct of most elections held in post-Soviet Eurasia, with foreign minister Lavrov calling it a 'politicised organisation'.[73] In his last annual address to the Federal Assembly on 26 April 2007 Putin called on the OSCE to return to its real mission, and take up the issue of the planned US deployment of a missile defence system in Poland and the Czech Republic 'as part of this organisation's political and military dimension'. As Putin noted in his characteristically pithy way: 'It is time for us to give the OSCE real substance and have it address the issues of genuine concern to the peoples of Europe rather than just hunting for fleas in the post-Soviet area.'[74] In the event, the OSCE did take up discussion of the planned missile shield deployment in Eastern Europe. At that point America's already rather weak commitment to the OSCE flagged even further.[75]

### NATO, Russia and enlargement

Despite Russia's equivocations and early attempts to play the OSCE 'card', the fundamental question remains unanswered: if there is no longer a security threat from any European power, then why should NATO expand?[76] The subtext to the whole question of NATO enlargement is whether the West was now to be a genuine partner or whether it still represented a threat to Russia - and *vice versa*. The relationship between Russia and NATO and the question of the latter's expansion to the East (and in particular to the 'middle abroad', the states of Central and Eastern Europe) became one of the most thorny issues in Russia's post-Cold War relationship with the West.[77] With the demise of its old adversary, what was now the point of NATO, and was it possible for Russia to join? While NATO remained the only effective coordinating body for the defence policies of its members, and inhibited the revival of the old balance-of-power politics that had so often brought war to Europe, its role remained a matter of discussion. NATO had always been a defensive alliance, but the problem lay in the definition of the security risks facing Europe. Was Russia part of the problem or part of the solution to European security? And as for Russian membership, a long-term commitment to this end would echo the visionary statesmanship that had brought the EEC into being after the Second World War, as a way forever of preventing war between European powers, but it would effectively reduce NATO to little more than the OSCE. The very existence of an expanded NATO would create a permanent source of tension in the centre of Europe; as Kozyrev put it, 'NATO's advance toward Russia's borders cannot but be seen as a continuation, though by inertia, of a policy aimed at containment of Russia'.[78] The need to contain Russia was made explicit in 2007 by the former prime minister of Ukraine, Yuliya Timoshenko, when she argued 'The West must seek to create counterweights to Russia's expansionism and not place all its chips on Russian domestic reform.'[79]

The renegotiation of European security, with perhaps the launching of a European Treaty Organisation (involving the USA, Canada and perhaps Japan), would prevent NATO itself becoming a threat to European security; but without NATO the paralysis in European security that had allowed the First and Second World Wars would be repeated. For good or ill and however ineptly, it was NATO that finally halted Serbia's killing machine in Yugoslavia. The creation of the EU's 60,000-strong Rapid Reaction Force by 2003, designed to act separately but in alliance with NATO, began to remedy Europe's lack of security coherence, much to Washington's alarm. At the same time, NATO took over responsibility for military affairs in Afghanistan in 2006. It was clear that NATO enlargement and its new role have to be seen in the context of the EU's emerging defence identity, as well as broader issues like missile defence, and arms control and non-proliferation agreements.

Twice before the USSR had sought, admittedly half-heartedly, to join NATO (Georgy Malenkov in the 1950s and Gorbachev in the 1980s), but with the fall of communism the question could be realistically posed. On a visit to NATO headquarters in Brussels in late October 1991 General Alexander Tsalko, deputy chair of Russia's Defence Committee, went so far as to suggest that Russia might join the organisation, initially at consultative level.[80] In late 1994 Boris Fedorov insisted that 'Russia must join NATO', arguing that membership would mean the end of US dominance in the organisation and would counteract Germany's growing power. Russian membership, moreover, would signal the genuine end of the Cold War and further guarantee democratic development in Russia.[81] In an interview with the BBC on 5 March 2000 Putin once again entertained the possibility that one day Russia could join NATO, albeit on 'equal terms'. The sentiment was reiterated by Vladimir Lukin, the former head of the Duma's foreign affairs committee, who argued that the optimal solution would be 'the widening of NATO to Vladivostok'.[82] Even if the principle of Russian membership were to be conceded, numerous economic, military and technical problems would have to be resolved before membership could be taken seriously. NATO itself veered between the outright rejection of the notion of Russian membership and a cautious welcome of the idea.

Even if the necessity for NATO is demonstrated, did it need to expand? For many in Russia enlargement represented a breach of faith by the West since it appears that assurances were given to Gorbachev during talks over German unification that there would be no expansion. Enlargement, moreover, could be represented as Germany's traditional *Drang nach Osten* in a new form.[83] Faced with the resolute wish to join by the Eastern European states themselves, Yeltsin equivocated. During his visit to Warsaw in August 1993 Yeltsin had said 'go ahead' when asked about Poland's prospects for membership of NATO. This stance was rapidly modified on his return to Moscow. Despite some initial uncertainty about its attitude, Russia finally insisted that any expansion would have to meet tough conditions, including a ban on the forward deployment of NATO forces and bases. Russia's objections were not so much a way of keeping Eastern Europe within Russia's security orbit but arose out of the obvious geopolitical consequences of expansion without commensurate commitments. In the event, the Czech Republic, Hungary and Poland did join in April 1999, although celebrations at the same time of NATO's fiftieth anniversary were rather muted as a result of the war in Kosovo. Russia's objections to the integration of the new members into the alliance's military structure were not accepted; of NATO's 19 members, only France is not part of the unified military command and Spain is only partly integrated. In the event, the three new members did not change their relationship with Russia, just as Norway's or Turkey's membership (two other of Russia's neighbours) had not done earlier.

The question then shifted to the problem of second-wave enlargement. The ten potential members between the Baltic and the Balkans in May 2000 met in Vilnius and urged NATO to enlarge further in a single fell swoop. The 'Vilnius Ten' sought to pool information and resources, to avoid mutually destructive competition, and to lobby together for swift accession. President Bush in a speech in Warsaw on 15 June 2001 held out the vision of a rapidly expanding NATO 'from the Baltic to the Black Sea'. At a second meeting of the Vilnius Ten in Estonia on 10 July 2001 they insisted that aspirant countries should be judged on their qualifications and not on their 'geography or history'. The NATO summit in Prague on 21–2 November 2002 went for the 'big bang' approach and invited almost all the former communist states to join, with the exception of those in the Balkans. In April 2004 the three Baltic republics (Estonia, Latvia and Lithuania) joined along with Slovakia, Slovenia, Romania and Bulgaria. The door was left open for a further enlargement that would include at the minimum Croatia, and possibly Albania and Macedonia, while Serbia, Montenegro and Bosnia in the long term were potential members. More worrying for Russia were the aggressive attempts to join by Ukraine and Georgia. Ukraine on 23 May 2002 announced that it would seek membership of NATO, although its leadership admitted that it would take at least eight to ten years for this to be achieved.[84] Following the orange revolution of autumn 2004, the new president Viktor Yushchenko sought to achieve an accelerated timetable for Ukrainian membership. In Georgia president Mikheil Saakashvili quite explicitly couched Georgia's NATO aspirations in term of containing a putative Russian threat. This formulation could not but be destabilising for broader European security.

The further advance of a powerful military alliance to its borders became increasingly unsettling for Russia, especially since many of the former Soviet bloc members sought to use the alliance as an instrument to take revenge against what they saw as their former overlord. In addition, the placing of elements of a missile defence system in Central Europe posed a direct threat to Russian security, despite America's hollow protestations that they were directed against Iran and North Korea. From Russia's perspective, NATO expansion would jeopardise its attempts to have good relations with both East and West Europe and would in effect signal its exclusion from equal participation in the European security regime. Russia's concerns can be summarised as follows:

- The extension of NATO to the East undermined the role of universal organisations like the UN and the OSCE.
- Enlargement was accompanied by a redefined role for the alliance that increased emphasis on missions outside the geographical zone of responsibility of the Alliance.
- NATO enlargement weakened the security of the alliance itself by re-establishing lines of division within Europe that could not but be directed against Russia.

- It would undercut the existing arms control regimes, above all the European disarmament architecture and its fundamental unit, the adapted CFE treaty.
- Regional security tensions were exacerbated, above all with the entrance of the Baltic states, thirty per cent of whose population are ethnic Russians. Would the Kaliningrad region become a 'bridge' between East and West or a 'military bridgehead'?
- Enlargement increased Russia's isolation and risk excluding it from decision-making in Europe, possibly precipitating a post-ideological Cold War, the 'cold peace' that Yeltsin had warned of at the OSCE Budapest Summit in December 1994.
- Instead of deepening the demilitarisation of foreign policy promised by the end of the Cold War on the basis of common civilisational values, NATO enlargement insists on its members making an 'adequate contribution' to collective defence in accordance with Article V of the 1949 Washington Treaty establishing NATO, and thus risks squandering the peace dividend.

In response to these concerns, NATO sought to manage enlargement in a way that achieved the goal but did not alienate Russia entirely. The Rome summit of NATO in November 1991 established a North Atlantic Cooperation Council (NACC), and on 20 December 1991 it held its inaugural meeting. NACC's membership included 36 countries stretching from Vancouver to Vladivostok, including all the members of NATO and the former Soviet republics. The idea was to extend a 'shadow of security' over the region without offering concrete defence guarantees. The body remained more shadow than substance, however, and NACC in 1997 was transformed into the Euro-Atlantic Partnership Council (EAPC) as a consultative forum for crisis management, proliferation issues and much more.[85] Attempts by the EAPC to encroach on the OSCE's (and indeed, the UN's and the CIS's) prerogatives in peacekeeping and post-conflict rehabilitation were firmly rebuffed by Russia, although it welcomed attempts to enhance the EAPC's role in the field of civil emergency planning (CEP). Committed to expansion, the dilemma for NATO was how to do so without driving Russia back into hostility. A temporary solution was the Partnership for Peace (PfP) initiative, launched by NATO on 10 January 1994, considered a prerequisite for membership although participation did not guarantee membership. Whereas EAPC is a multilateral body, operating like the OSCE largely by consensus, PfP represented a series of bilateral agreements. By April 1995, 26 countries had signed up to the programme, ranging from Albania to Uzbekistan,[86] but although all members were formally equal some were clearly on the fast track for membership. Thus PfP was simultaneously a way of managing NATO enlargement and delaying it. It was not clear whether PfP could indeed become a bridge rather than a barrier across Europe. Russia signed the Partnership Framework Document on 22 June 1994, when Kozyrev conceded that Russia 'had no fundamental objections' to NATO enlargement, but delayed signing the associated Individual Partnership Programme.

As the price for expansion Moscow sought a formal expression to the much-touted post-Cold War idea of a 'strategic partnership' between the West and Russia, a permanent forum for consultation with NATO and a voice in security developments in Central Europe, something that in any case had been emerging within the framework of the OSCE and in the form of bilateral meetings. Russia, moreover, sought guarantees that prevented the forward positioning of nuclear weapons or the stationing of alliance forces in these countries, arrangements that already existed for Norway. The Western powers, however, firmly rejected Russia's attempt to achieve a special relationship with NATO that might allow it to veto eastward expansion, but accepted that it should spring no surprises on Russia. This sparring finally resulted in the signature of the Russia-NATO Founding Act on 27 May 1997,[87] followed on 9 July by the signing of the Charter on Distinctive Partnership between NATO and Ukraine. The Founding Act established a Permanent Joint Council (PJC) as a forum for Russian-NATO discussions, typically meeting at the level of foreign ministers or at ambassadorial level, discussing issues like those associated with the continuing crisis in former Yugoslavia. The PJC in the short term was seen as a damage-limitation exercise – to make NATO expansion more palatable to Russia by allaying its fears about the forward deployment of nuclear weapons and NATO troops in the new member states – but its scope was more ambitious: to

> provide a mechanism for consultation, coordination and, to the maximum extent possible, where appropriate, for joint decisions and joint action with respect to security issues of common concern.[88]

Tensions over NATO intervention over Kosovo in 1999, indeed, had derailed the work of the PJC for a period. As a sign of improving relations, in February 2001 NATO opened an information office in Moscow, the counterpart to the Russia's rather large mission to NATO headquarters at Mons.

The establishment in June 2002 of a reconstituted NATO-Russia Council built on the 1997 Russia-NATO Founding Act, but instead of the model being 19 NATO members relating to Russia singly, the new 'NATO at 20' elevated Russia symbolically to equal rank with all the others and thus represented yet another step attempt to transcend the Cold War. The issues to be dealt with by the new body included the struggle against terrorism, proliferation of weapons of mass destruction, management of regional crises and peacekeeping, anti-ballistic missile defence and search-and-rescue operations. Even though the Cold War had once again ended, Russia was still treated as a special case and the unwieldy character of the new body reduced its ability to deal effectively with complex issues. The aim was to bring Russia into an enlarged security community while stopping short of actually inviting it to join the organisation.

The issue of third wave enlargement once again embittered relations between Russia and NATO. The evident desire for countries such as Georgia and Ukraine to join the organisation would bring NATO to Russia's borders on three sides. The strength of concern was reflected in the non-binding parliamentary resolution adopted on 7 June 2006 warning that 'Ukraine's accession to the military bloc will lead to very negative consequences for relations between our two fraternal peoples'.[89] The message was reinforced that day in the Duma by foreign minister Sergei Lavrov's warning that while former Soviet states could decide their own fate, 'the accession to NATO of such countries as Ukraine and Georgia would mean a colossal geopolitical shift'. He argued that Russian policy towards the former Soviet states had become more coherent: 'Yes, we regard these states as independent and sovereign. And that is how we are going to shape our relations with them. One vivid proof of this is the transition to market principles of pricing in trade, including trade in energy'.[90]

NATO enlargement became the defining issue in Russian foreign policy and did much to shift Russian public opinion away from the democratic and internationalist values that had informed the early period of independence.[91] NATO involvement in former Yugoslavia vividly illustrated Russia's marginalisation and raised fears that Russia itself might anticipate the same treatment if it stepped too far out of line. The NATO alliance was formed to counter a danger that had disappeared but its continued existence appeared to run counter to Russia's long-term strategic interests. The issue of NATO expansion served to forge an almost unique consensus among all wings of Russian politics. According to Karaganov, 'NATO's plans for expansion mean a potential new Yalta … By accepting the rules of the game that are being forced on her … Russia will lose.'[92] Some in Moscow responded by insisting that if NATO expanded, then Russia should create its own new military bloc made up of the former Soviet republics and other countries that objected to an aggressive NATO on their borders – but there were few takers (except Belarus, and even that country by 2006 was looking for new strategic partners) to the invitation. Russia's attempts to renegotiate the post-Cold War order met with little success. Quite apart from the institutional conservatism of the West, Russia's initiatives were often poorly prepared and ill-thought out. The prospect of a post-communist Cold War threatened to erode the fragile peace achieved with the fall of the communist regimes in 1989–91.

# 18 Commonwealth, community and fragmentation

> The disappearance of the Soviet superpower, oppressive to its subjects as it was, has created a dangerous imbalance of power among its former components and between them and their neighbours. Possibility of serious conflicts arise. Russia, which by any definition is a Great Power in the classical sense, is bordered by the much weaker states which have broken away from the Soviet structure. As with water, power will find its level.
>
> (Elie Kedourie)[1]

The disintegration of the Soviet Union brought 15 independent republics onto the world stage. This ranks as an event of unparalleled historical importance, shifting the balance of power on the Eurasian landmass and altering the global system of international relations. The very concept of the 'near abroad', as noted, suggested some sort of intermediate status between sovereign statehood and traditional dependence for Russia's new neighbours. Russia was linked by centuries of political and human contacts with these new states but now had to find new forms of interaction. While the USSR might have collapsed with relatively little violence, the disintegration of the great empires of the past suggests that the biggest danger comes from conflicts between successor states and the threat of outside countries seeking to take advantage of the power vacuum. The arbitrariness of the borders, the intermingling of peoples and nations, and a host of unresolved problems, including energy imbalances and transport networks, provided fertile ground for conflict.

## The Commonwealth of Independent States (CIS)

The ambiguities in Russian policy towards the successor states, 12 of which including Russia came to be members of the CIS, was one of the main charges against the liberal foreign policy of the early post-communist years. The nature and purpose of the CIS was contested. The CIS was not itself a state in the conventional sense and neither was it a subject of international law. Its member states actively pursued their own independent foreign policies, intended often to distance themselves from their former partners, above all Russia. Russian policy sought to incorporate the former Soviet states (excluding the three Baltic republics) into an expanded security zone and sphere of vital interests, while the other states sought to defend their sovereignty and independence. The CIS did not become the successor state to the USSR, and there is no CIS foreign policy and no CIS 'national interest'. Instead, there are divergent foreign policies in constant uncomfortable interaction with each other. Each member regards economic and foreign policy, and increasingly security policy as well, as its own preserve. The CIS has been a success to the limited extent that the states have not come into violent conflict with each other, but the area has been characterised by the diversification of economic dependencies, the development of regional alliances and associations in line with traditional cultural affiliations, and the search for protectors and sponsors abroad.[2] There is no agreement among its members about the proper role for the CIS, and thus it is very unlikely to evolve into something akin to an Eastern EU.

### Organisation and development

Attempts to create a Union of Sovereign States in the post-coup period soon came to nothing. The draft treaty of November 1991 still provided for some form of power-sharing between a reconstituted centre and the republics,[3] but the other republics feared that the new centre would recreate patterns of domination; Russia appeared to be assuming the mantle of leadership cast off by the old union. As we saw in Chapter 2, the Ukrainian vote for independence on 1 December 1991 sealed the death warrant for the union treaty process, and on 8 December the leaders of the three Slavic republics announced the creation of the CIS (see Figure 18.1).

The CIS played a critical role in managing the transition to independent statehood, yet few of the objectives proclaimed in the CIS treaty of December 1991 were achieved. Commitments to coordinate their foreign policy, to maintain a common economic space, to coordinate transport and communications system, and to retain open frontiers and guarantee freedom of movement for all CIS citizens were only partially fulfilled.[4] Two opposing views took shape: the first, supported by Gorbachev, argued that the CIS should create supranational executive bodies and accelerate integration;[5] while the second defined the CIS as a temporary intergovernmental coordinating and consultative body designed only to provide a civilised mechanism for the 'divorce' of the former Soviet republics. While the CIS registered a 'negative' success in preventing a total collapse of former ties, positive achievements were meagre but nevertheless real. A significant body of CIS law has been developed, establishing basic normative standards across the region.

Russia became the 'continuer' state of the USSR in diplomatic terms and in international law, but for the other 'successor' states the term suggested that Russia expected to become the dominant partner. The disintegration of the USSR posed endless questions about the division of assets, capital, institutions and the armed forces. Above all, there was the problem of determining the citizenship of the heterogeneous populations of the new republics. The division of resources proved less of a problem than had been anticipated, and operated on the principle that what was in the republics belonged to them, and what was in Russia belonged to Russia even though both sides might have contributed to its development. As for the division of foreign assets, all the CIS states agreed to exchange their share in return for Russia assuming their part of the USSR's foreign debt.

The provisional accords of 8 December 1991 stipulated that the CIS headquarters was to be in Minsk, the capital of Belarus. The CIS coordinates policy through a Council of Heads of State (CHS), which meets at least twice a year and works by consensus, and a Council of Heads of Government (CHG), which meets four times a year and focuses on economic coordination. The presidency of both councils rotates. Individual

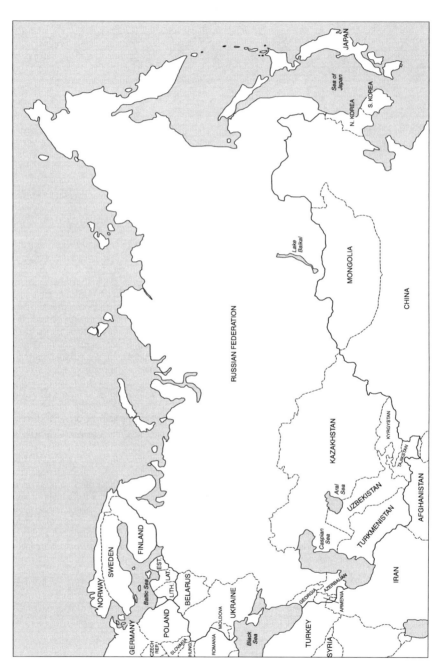

*Figure 18.1* Member states of the CIS

member states have the right to veto decisions of the councils. In 1992 the councils each met eight times and signed some 275 agreements, though most were of a declaratory nature and lacked implementation mechanisms, and about half dealt with military matters. These agreements and later ones formalised not the deepening of relations between states but regulated their separation. Although in December 1991 it was agreed that decisions would be taken by consensus, in practice delegations could easily opt out. The Tashkent summit of 15 May 1992 adopted the formula 'consensus-minus-one', and simple majority voting for procedural issues. Even that proved too restrictive, and any state could simply declare that it was not interested in a particular decision and was thus exempted. Selective participation in signing agreements became standard practice, with only 7 out of 11 member states signing the relevant document on the establishment of the CIS Interparliamentary Assembly at the March 1992 Kiev summit, only 6 signing the Collective Security Treaty in Tashkent in May 1992, 8 delegations approving the 6 July 1992 Moscow Agreement on the status of the Economic Court, and the same with most other accords.[6] No agreement was achieved on the imposition of sanctions for the non-observance of treaty commitments.

Documents adopted by the CIS were primarily of two types.[7] The great majority fell into the category of *modus vivendi* agreements designed to prevent a total collapse of the infrastructure of the old union. They dealt with such issues as energy, transport, payment of pensions, border forces, customs regulations and so on, and were signed by most members. While possibly contributing in the long-term to integration, in the short term these agreements did little to promote the development of a common space but merely regulated the assertion of national sovereignty and tried to avoid a complete collapse of the old economic area. The second category consisted of agreements establishing coordinating bodies such as the Collective Security Council, a Council of Defence Ministers, a Customs Council and some two dozen others. Most tried to regulate inter-state economic relations, dealing with such issues as rail transport, statistics, energy, science and technology, and the like. Azerbaijan refused to sign agreements in the defence sphere, and from March 1992 opted out of agreements on coordinating bodies in socio-economic affairs as well. Ukraine was little more enthusiastic about the common institutions of the CIS and, together with Moldova and Turkmenistan, these four states were the most opposed to the institutionalisation of the CIS. They insisted that the CIS was an inter-governmental rather than a supranational organisation.

Negotiations in late 1992 over a revised CIS Charter defining the rights and obligations of member states were riven by disputes over human rights, economic and other issues. At the Minsk summit on 22 January 1993 seven out of ten members approved the CIS Charter providing for a 'multispeed' CIS, allowing those countries which wished to achieve deeper integration to do so without excluding those who favoured a slower pace. While the CIS remained under-institutionalised, a rudimentary permanent executive body was established in the form of a Coordinating and Consultative Committee assisted by over 30 inter-state, inter-governmental and inter-departmental coordinating agencies covering such issues as foreign policy and the environment. It was clear, however, that a two-tier CIS was emerging. Ukraine, Moldova and Turkmenistan never ratified the Charter but continue to participate in CIS work. The establishment of the CIS Interparliamentary Assembly on 27 March 1992 was designed to address this problem. Given final shape by a Convention signed on 26 May 1995, the Assembly makes no attempt to reflect the political views of its members, and is not a statutory body of the

CIS but an autonomous international organisation. Although the CIS has a range of institutions, most lack formal and substantive authority. Typical is the post of Executive Secretary, who has minimal powers and cannot be compared to an executive General Secretary of an international organisation.

### Diversification and utility

The CIS was marked by a differentiation process in which three groups of states emerged. The first was a core comprising Russia, Kazakhstan, Kyrgyzstan, Tajikistan and Uzbekistan (Figure 18.2). These countries were the most willing to sign the union treaty in 1991 and now signed most agreements, and appeared most devoted to the concept of the CIS evolving into a closer community of nations. Nazarbaev, indeed, urged the creation of a new union, and after the August coup lamented the failure to unify the economy while giving all the states complete independence in matters of foreign and domestic policy.[8] Nazarbaev's idea of a confederal union, later called the 'Eurasian Union', was supported by Gorbachev.[9] The emergence of this core group led some to suggest that the CIS would become no more than a Russian Central Asian bloc. Indeed, the Eurasianists argued that since Ukraine had driven a wedge between Russia and Europe, Russia should pursue a less Western-oriented policy and concentrate on links with the Central Asian states to ensure Russian predominance in Eurasia. In contrast to the Atlanticists, who considered that Russia should aim to join the core states of the industrialised North as quickly as possible, the Eurasians considered that Russia's natural allies were to be found in the South. The suggestion in 2007 made by the

*Figure 18.2* Central Asia

Kyrgyzstan prime minister, Felix Kulov, that the country should form a confederation with Russia seemed to confirm the Eurasian argument.[10] Although the idea was greeted with scepticism, no one disputed that Kyrgyzstan had become Russia's key ally in the region.

The second group was made up of Armenia (Figure 18.3) and Belarus; they began by being sceptical members of the CIS but became its most ardent supporters. Both at first were selective in signing agreements and were wary of the creation of supranational CIS bodies; they supported cooperation within the CIS, but sought to avoid being caught up in a political and military alliance. Belarus at first tried to reduce its Eurasian ties but under president Alexander Lukashenko from 1994 became committed to closer ties with Russia, signing a bilateral treaty on 2 April 1996 (the first of a series) committing both states to closer integration. A decade later, however, little had been achieved (see below), and conflicts over energy supplies soured the whole project. Armenia was isolated from the heartlands of the CIS by Georgia and Azerbaijan, and was aggrieved that the CIS was powerless to resolve the Nagorno-Karabakh conflict or to ameliorate its own grievous economic hardship. Its very isolation later rendered Armenia one of Russia's strongest allies, and in return received arms (some of it clandestine) and other forms of support. However, even though, by 2007, 160 documents had been signed between Russia and Armenia formalising close ties, economic links remained weak (only $240 million annual trade turnover) and there were many sources of tension, including resentment in Armenia that its debts to Russia had been paid by the transfer of ownership of its energy sector.

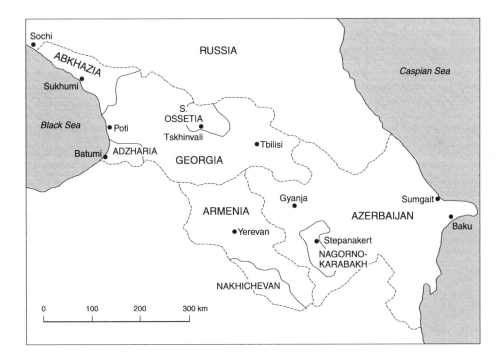

*Figure 18.3* South Caucasus

Armenia increasingly saw its future lying in closer ties with the EU, and believed that the EU would provide a mechanism to restore relations with Turkey. An increasing proportion of the Armenian population, moreover, approved of closer ties with NATO.[11]

The third group was made up of Ukraine, Turkmenistan, Azerbaijan and Moldova (Figure 18.4). Ukraine made no secret of its desire to become a 'normal' European state, and behaved as though it was embarrassed by Russia's Asian tail dragging it back in geography and time. Ukraine unequivocally opposed attempts to strengthen CIS institutions and fought hard against Russian dominance in the organisation but offered little in the way of a positive programme. Just as Austria and Bavaria had opposed Prussian domination of the German Confederation in the nineteenth century, so today Ukraine is determined to resist the hegemony of the stronger power and opposes Russian domination in Eurasia. Ukraine thus sought to make the CIS as weak as possible, with no permanent status and a minimal staff, rejected outright the idea of a unified armed force, and objected to the CIS Charter which envisaged supranational Commonwealth structures.

Turkmenistan adopted an independent stance secure in the enjoyment of its income from its gas fields. Dominated by an increasingly bizarre leader-dominated system until the death of Saparmurat Niyazov in December 2006, Turkmenistan became something of an international pariah. Only under its new leader Gurbanguly Berdimukhamedov did

*Figure 18.4* Ukraine

some sort of normalisation take place, although the country remained oriented towards Russia. Azerbaijan and Moldova at first appeared to be temporary members of the CIS, waiting only for an appropriate moment to leave. The 6 July 1992 Moscow summit warned that if they did not ratify the CIS Treaty they would not be admitted to the next summit. On the eve of the Bishkek summit of 9 October 1992 the Azerbaijan parliament voted unanimously against ratification and thus left the organisation.[12] Moldova, too, failed to ratify the Almaty accords, but left some room for manoeuvre and continued to participate selectively in the work of the CIS. Moldova's relations with the CIS and Russia are filtered through the prism of the Transnistria conflict. At the time of the August 1991 coup a group seized power in this sliver of land on the East bank of the Dniester, one-third of whose population were Russians, and then for the next two decades challenged Moldovan sovereignty over the breakaway territory.

The development of the CIS was marked by the bilateralisation of relations between member states, undermining multilateral attempts to solve problems on a Commonwealth-wide basis.[13] Turkmenistan from the first was sceptical about the value of the CIS, refusing to sign agreements on economic, collective security, financial and other issues, and instead Niyazov relied on bilateral rather than collective agreements. Kravchuk and Kuchma on several occasions insisted that Russo-Ukrainian relations would develop on a purely bilateral basis, while the numerous agreements between Belarus and Russia allowed the former to steer clear of any political or military bloc. Bilateralisation was not altogether incompatible with the existence of the CIS, but this would be a CIS limited to the orderly management of transition to nation-states rather than one committed to finding multilateral solutions to common problems, let alone the attempt to establish a new community on confederal principles. Those (like Turkmenistan, Kazakhstan and Azerbaijan) with oil and/or gas sought to buttress their political independence by links with Western partners to exploit reserves, but the sheer enormity of the stakes in the geopolitics of energy policy served in some cases to undermine the room for manoeuvre, faced by Russia's refusal to be cut out of either the exploitation or transportation of Caspian oil.

Countries like Ukraine encouraged the development of bilateral relations to undermine the development of the CIS as a coherent multilateral organisation. In practice the process was double-edged and raised the danger of the creation of a new union dominated by Russia. Reflecting the highly centralised nature of the old USSR, bilateral relations between the peripheral countries developed slowly and the great bulk of agreements focused on Russia. Links were closest between the core members of the CIS, and agreements on friendship, cooperation and mutual assistance were signed with Kazakhstan, Uzbekistan and Kyrgyzstan. Russia became the centre of a dense web of relationships which rather than enhancing the authority of the CIS began to act as a substitute for it. Russia became the military, economic and political core of a new union that might at one stage dispense with the CIS altogether. Although Putin began his leadership by repeating standard nostrums about the importance of the CIS, it was clear that as part of his 'new realist' review of foreign policy, in the words of Sergei Ivanov, the 'accelerated development of the Commonwealth into a fully fledged international association is not possible in the near future', and as a consequence Russia would pursue its interests 'first of all through the development of bilateral relations with CIS countries'.[14]

Despite fears that the whole CIS project might collapse, it soon became clear that it performed certain important functions. Russia, certainly, found it a useful foreign policy instrument, and sought to ensure the survival of the organisation. Following the overthrow of Abulfez Elchibei's nationalist government in 1993, Azerbaijan agreed to rejoin the organisation. Hard on the heels of the military debacle in Abkhazia in 1992-3, Georgia finally agreed to join the CIS in 1993. This brought membership to twelve, with only the three Baltic states outside. Lacking an effective institutional framework, the CIS was an intergovernmental rather than a supranational body. There was no consensus among the member states over the way that the CIS should evolve. The debate over the CIS Charter revealed basic conceptual differences in attitudes, with one view expressed most forcefully by Kazakhstan stressing the need to establish a more coherent community, while others equally firmly argued that it should be little more than a forum for inter-governmental consultation on specific issues. Policy represented less a coherent vision of development than the lowest common denominator of agreement between groups of countries with radically different views on its evolution and future.

### Russia and the CIS

The Commonwealth is fundamentally lopsided by Russia's sheer size and cultural pre-dominance, with Russian becoming the *lingua franca*, and the fears that this raised in its neighbours (see Table 18.1). The experience of the Russian Empire followed by 70 years of Soviet power, with Russification used as the cement of empire, was hardly a strong basis on which to build a community based on trust. The absence of strong coordinating institutions engendered an atmosphere of constant crisis. Russia tended to view Soviet

*Table 18.1* Territory and population of former Soviet republics, 1 January 1990

|  | *Territory in km2* | *% of USSR* | *Population (1000)* | *% of USSR* | *% urbanised* |
|---|---|---|---|---|---|
| Former USSR | 22,403 | 100.0 | 288,624 | 100.0 | 66 |
| Russia | 17,075 | 76.2 | 148,041 | 51.3 | 74 |
| *Baltic:* | 175 | 0.7 | 7,993 | 2.8 | 70 |
| Estonia | 45 | 0.2 | 1,583 | 0.5 | 72 |
| Latvia | 65 | 0.3 | 2,687 | 0.9 | 71 |
| Lithuania | 65 | 0.3 | 3,723 | 1.3 | 68 |
| *Western Eurasia:* |  |  |  |  |  |
| Moldova | 34 | 0.2 | 4,362 | 1.5 | 47 |
| Belarus | 208 | 0.9 | 10,259 | 3.6 | 66 |
| Ukraine | 604 | 2.7 | 51,839 | 18.0 | 67 |
| *South Caucasus:* | 186 | 0.8 | 15,880 | 5.5 | 56 |
| Armenia | 30 | 0.1 | 3,293 | 1.1 | 68 |
| Azerbaijan | 87 | 0.4 | 7,131 | 2.5 | 54 |
| Georgia | 70 | 0.3 | 5,456 | 1.9 | 56 |
| *Central Asia:* | 3,994 | 17.8 | 50,250 | 17.4 | 49 |
| Kazakhstan | 2,717 | 12.1 | 16,691 | 5.8 | 57 |
| Kyrgyzstan | 199 | 0.9 | 4,367 | 1.5 | 38 |
| Tajikistan | 143 | 0.6 | 5,248 | 1.8 | 32 |
| Turkmenistan | 488 | 2.2 | 3,622 | 1.3 | 45 |
| Uzbekistan | 447 | 2.0 | 20,322 | 7.0 | 41 |

*Source*: Economist Intelligence Unit, *CIS: Country Report*, No. 2, 1992, p. 11, modified.

property and institutions as its own; the other republics had to build theirs from scratch. In the army, the diplomatic corps and the foreign trade offices of the USSR Russians had predominated, and with the end of the USSR they transferred their loyalties to Russia. For the other nationalities there could be no such easy transition, and loyalty to an amorphous CIS was no substitute for their own nationhood. Naturally, this gave rise to resentment, leading to fears that the CIS would be abandoned altogether(see Table 18.2).

Russia in 1992 had been hesitant to take the lead in pursuing the integration of CIS states, fearing accusations of neo-imperialism, and concentrated on political and economic links with the West, but for the rest of the decade and into Putin's presidency became the main champion of integration within the CIS framework. Industrialists sought closer union between the CIS countries, and the Civic Union indeed called for the establishment of a collective organ to unify economic, cultural and scientific policy.[15] Under pressure at home and goaded by enthusiastic integrationists like Nazarbaev in Central Asia, Yeltsin became increasingly aware that there was no escaping close links with the former Soviet republics. In February 1993 Yeltsin called on the international community to grant Russia special powers as the guarantor of peace and stability in the former USSR, and the Security Council's adoption of the document 'Basic Directions of Foreign Policy' in April 1993 reaffirmed Russia's commitment to the unity of the area. Russian foreign policy towards the successor states advanced on three fronts at the same time: the attempt to preserve and strengthen the CIS; the consolidation of relations with the core states in a type of 'Eurasian union'; and the bilateralisation of relations. For a period in the late 1990s Russia's prioritisation of the CIS was given physical shape in the form of a separate ministry for CIS affairs. It proved unable to install coherence in Russia's relations with its neighbours, and one of Putin's first acts was to abolish it and return responsibility to the foreign ministry, although later he reinstated the post of deputy prime minister responsible for CIS affairs.

Russian domestic opinion was fundamentally divided over the CIS. National-patriots and some neo-communists regarded the CIS as a fundamentally illegitimate creation born out of the forced collapse of the USSR. Discussion of the CIS often served as a cover to condemn the disintegration of the USSR: 'Masquerading as a foreign policy issue, it is actually a vehicle for deploring Russia's loss of empire.'[16] By endorsing the CIS, Russia accepted restraints on its freedom of manoeuvre in its relations with the other republics, limitations which enraged the opposition who felt that the interests of Russia as a whole and the rights of Russians abroad were being neglected. They viewed the creation of the CIS as the denial of Russia's status as a great power, evidence of Russia's 'withdrawal into Asia' and alienation of primordial Russian lands. While denouncing the 1991 Minsk Accords, the CPRF favoured the recreation of the Soviet Union and barely mentioned the CIS in its electoral programmes. NATO expansion prompted efforts to transform the CIS into a counter-alliance to NATO. In his decree on CIS strategy of September 1995 Yeltsin stressed that the CIS was a 'priority area' for Russia, although he noted that this should be based on mutually beneficial economic cooperation.[17] The decree called for the transformation of the CIS into a fully fledged collective security alliance, much to the alarm of other members, especially the provision that no CIS state would be allowed to join any military alliances aimed at another CIS state.

Kuchma's election as Ukraine's second post-communist president in 1994 was in part a reaction to Kravchuk's anti-Russian rhetoric, although Kuchma in practice found his pro-Russian options limited. His election did, however, lead to improved relations and in

Table 18.2 The CIS in 2007

| | Territory, km2 | % of CIS | Capital | Population | % of CIS | GDP, US$ bn | Leader, start date |
|---|---|---|---|---|---|---|---|
| Russia | 17,075,000 | 77.25 | Moscow | 142,893,540 | 51.02 | 733.0 | Vladimir Putin, 31 Dec.1999 |
| Moldova | 34,000 | 0.15 | Chisinau | 4,466,706 | 1.59 | 2.6 | Vladimir Voronin, 4 April 2001 |
| Belarus | 208,000 | 0.94 | Minsk | 10,293,011 | 3.67 | 28.5 | Alexander Lukashenka, 20 July 1994 |
| Ukraine | 604,000 | 2.73 | Kiev | 46,710,816 | 16.68 | 81.5 | Viktor Yushchenko, 25 Jan. 2005 |
| Armenia | 30,000 | 0.14 | Yerevan | 2,976,372 | 1.06 | 6.6 | Robert Kocharyan, 30 March 1998 |
| Azerbaijan | 87,000 | 0.39 | Baku | 7,961,619 | 2.84 | 14.0 | Ilham Aliev, 31 Oct. 2003 |
| Georgia | 70,000 | 0.32 | Tbilisi | 4,661,473 | 1.66 | 5.2 | Mikheil Saakashvili, 25 Jan. 2004 |
| Kazakhstan | 2,717,000 | 12.29 | Astana | 15,233,244 | 5.44 | 52.6 | Nursultan Nazarbaev, 1 Dec. 1991 |
| Kyrgyzstan | 199,000 | 0.90 | Bishkek | 5,213,898 | 1.86 | 2.2 | Kurmanbek Bakiev, 14 Aug. 2005 |
| Tajikistan | 143,000 | 0.65 | Dushanbe | 7,320,815 | 2.61 | 2.1 | Emomali Rakhmon(ov), 6 Nov. 1994 |
| Turkmenistan | 488,000 | 2.21 | Ashgabat | 5,042,920 | 1.80 | 16.2 | Gurbanguly Berdimuhammedov, 14 Feb. 2007 |
| Uzbekistan | 447,000 | 2.02 | Tashkent | 27,307,134 | 9.75 | 10.8 | Islam Karimov, 24 March 1990 |
| Total | 22,102,000 | 100 | | 280,081,548 | 100 | 955.3 | |

Source: Russia Profile, Vol. 4, No. 4, May 2007, pp. 20–1, modified.

May 1997 Russia signed a ten-year Treaty on Cooperation and Friendship with Ukraine, accompanied the following February by a Treaty on Economic Cooperation. Many of the stipulations, particularly of the latter, were not fulfilled, but the treaties placed the bilateral relations, symbolically at least, on a firm footing. Ukraine's agreement to allow Russia basing rights for the Black Sea Fleet in Sevastopol until 2017 also helped put to one side one of the thorniest issues in their relations. The August 1998 crisis accelerated trends in relations within the CIS that were already evident. Trade within the CIS, for example, had fallen sharply after 1991 and now declined further. Trade was hampered by payments arrears and the prevalence of barter arrangements, used above all to pay for Russian natural gas deliveries to Belarus and Ukraine. By the end of the decade none of the former Soviet states had regained their 1990 output levels, whereas countries like Poland and Hungary in Central Europe surged forwards. Only in the 2000s was strong economic growth recorded across the region.

Although the CIS was unlikely to act as the motor of reintegration, an increasing proportion of the Russian population regretted the break-up of the Soviet Union. If, in 1992, 69 per cent were in this category, by the time of the tenth anniversary of Gorbachev's referendum on renewing the union, which had been overwhelmingly supported, 79 per cent in 2001 spoke in favour of the union. Over the same period, the percentage not regretting the end of the union fell from 32 to 15 per cent. If a new referendum were to have been held on the tenth anniversary of the first, then 72 per cent would have voted for the unification of the former Soviet republics, although it must be stressed that 58 per cent did not believe in the possibility of such a re-unification, although 30 per cent did.[18] When in his state of the nation speech on 25 April 2005 Putin spoke of the break-up of the Soviet Union as 'the greatest geopolitical catastrophe' of the twentieth century and a 'tragedy for the Russian people', he was expressing the sentiments of a large majority of the Russian people.[19] It should be stressed that he discounted any attempts to try to restore the Soviet Union in any shape or form. On a visit to Armenia in early 2005, indeed, Putin referred to the CIS in the past tense, and from the summer of 2005 Russia stressed that relations with post-Soviet Eurasia had to be placed on a strictly economic basis.

Russia remains one of the strongest supporters of the CIS because, among other things, it fulfils a number of essential tasks. It limits the damage caused by the disintegration, and through *modus vivendi* agreements helps avoid the total collapse of economic, infrastructural and human ties. The CIS also legitimates Russia's presence, including the deployment of military forces, in Commonwealth countries. Through the CIS Russia regulates the conflicts in Abkhazia and Transnistria, though it must be admitted that bilateral approaches predominate. The CIS retains the potential for the creation of future structures of cooperation between areas that were once part of a single state. Russia, however, remains torn over whether it is simply an equal member of the Commonwealth, or whether because of its size and traditions it should act as *primus inter pares*. Ukraine in particular is determined that there would be no new centre, whether one created by the CIS itself, and even less if Russia were to claim the honour. Once again the question focused on Russia's foreign policy priorities. If Russia's key foreign policy objective is to move from the periphery to the core of the world economy, this can only be achieved through natural economic processes and not by diverting scarce resources to unrealistic plans to make Russia the centre of a reconstituted Eurasian union. The definition of Russia's foreign policy depends on the understanding of global processes in their entirety. If one were to accept that the post-Cold War world is defined by the marketisation of world power, in which military and nuclear power have declined in importance relative to economic achievements, then Russia should abandon its military-industrial complex and concentrate on advanced economic modernisation and globalisation and turn its back on the CIS. This was the view of the Atlanticists, but was contested by the Eurasianists. Under Putin there was an attempt to place relations between CIS on a more solid economic base, but the mixture of politics and economics became even more complicated, notably in the various 'gas wars' with Ukraine, Belarus, Georgia and others. Politics and economics can never be entirely separated, but it was clear that no adequate model had been found in post-Soviet Eurasia during Putin's presidency.

One of the key principles of Putin's relations with CIS states was his emphasis on conservative legitimism. In domestic affairs from the very first he stressed that he would not change the constitution and would abide by its stipulations, and in technical terms he has done just this, and this principle has also been applied to post-Soviet Eurasia. This led him to support authoritarian leaders, such as Islam Karimov in Uzbekistan and Alexander Lukashenka in Belarus, establishing a type of latter-day 'holy alliance' against colour revolutions. Following the killings in Andijan on 13 May 2005, when Tashkent suppressed an alleged armed insurrection in the city when several hundred died, Uzbekistan restored close links with Russia, in particular in the sphere of energy policy, and requested the removal of American bases from the country. Putin's legitimist approach is reinforced by his aversion to revolutionary changes of power and by issues of geostrategic advantage. Putin's over-emphatic support for the succession of power from Leonid Kuchma to Viktor Yanukovych in Ukraine in late 2004 ignored the fact that the final winner, Viktor Yushchenko, had forged strong economic and political ties with Russia when he had been prime minister earlier. In relations with the former Soviet states, however, this has not made him a neo-Brezhnevian, and Russia's lack of intervention in support of Askar Akaev at the time of the 'tulip' revolution in March 2005 made clear that no updated version of the Brezhnev doctrine was in the offing, despite the threat of pre-emptive strikes beyond Russia's borders made in the aftermath of Beslan. Russia in the CIS was a profoundly *status quo* power, but the struggle to maintain the *status quo*, including Russian predominance, necessitated the adoption of ever more radical measures as new powers sought to enter the region.

The debate over the future of the CIS is at the same time a debate over the past, and in particular whether the disintegration of the USSR had been inevitable. If the USSR had always been an illegitimate construct, then its dissolution was final and irrevocable; but if the USSR did represent, in however attenuated a form, some primordial unity of the Eurasian land mass, then attempts to recreate some sort of successor body are legitimate and not simply an expression of Russian neo-imperialism. While the CIS consists of countries with very different cultures and levels of economic development, the main splits do not occur on these lines but because of conflicting elite strategies. Integration entails giving up sovereignty, but before being given up it has to be achieved, and this is the phase through which the former Soviet republics are now passing.

### Evaluation and prospects

Without a government or its own armed forces, and with no mechanism to ensure that its decisions are implemented, the CIS is an unloved child of the break-up of the Soviet Union. Created hurriedly in December 1991 without prior negotiations over the division of assets, questions of citizenship or the fate of the army, the CIS has survived but not prospered. Ukraine continues to see the CIS as little more than a way of achieving a 'civilised divorce'. The CIS remains a hybrid stranger on the international scene. Created in large measure to satisfy Ukraine's desire for sovereignty, Ukraine paradoxically was the most reluctant of CIS partners. The CIS had been formed to keep Russia and Ukraine in a single political space when the attempt to create a new union had failed, but this founding condition thereafter acted as a brake on further development.

There are some profound structural reasons for the failure of the CIS to develop as a full-scale integrative organisation. The first is the presence of powerful zones of integration in the neighbourhood of the region, which act as alternative poles of attraction. Second, the general level of development of the area is more like that of Latin America, where the movement of finished and semi-finished products comprises about half of trade, whereas in the EU it is 80 per cent, creating an economic transnationalism that in due course became the basis for further political integration. In the CIS agricultural and raw materials represent the bulk of trade, and these primary products tend to repel each other since they are competing for the same markets. The third factor has become increasingly salient, namely the division of the CIS countries into exporters and importers of energy resources. The energy exporters like Russia, Kazakhstan, Turkmenistan and Azerbaijan seek markets outside the CIS where prices and profits are higher, although access to these markets creates new patterns of dependency between themselves. The transit CIS countries are increasingly perceived as obstacles to be overcome rather than partners, hence the onset of a period of 'gas wars' and the like, when Russia in particular tried to shift relations on to more market-oriented terms. Putin on numerous occasions from 2005 complained about Russia's annual $3.5 billion subsidy to Ukraine in the form of cheap energy.[20] Countries without natural resources try to sell finished products. Thus 78 per cent of Ukraine's exports are finished goods, 74 per cent for Belarus and 44 per cent for Georgia. However, the quality of much of this production is too low to be competitive internationally hence they rely on the CIS market; while the importing countries increasingly seek better-quality Western goods, even if more expensive.[21] Since 1990 the proportion of intra-CIS trade has fallen from 60 to 18 per cent. The list could be extended but the point is clear: there are some profound structural impediments to CIS integration, and these reinforce the rather weak political desire for unity in the CIS region.

Despite the lack of clarity over the role of the CIS and these various obstacles, certain achievements can be credited to it. As Yeltsin pointed out, the CIS was a form of relations between states fated to live together. Many frontiers have only gradually become full state borders, and a visa-free regime is still in operation (with the exception of Georgia). The CIS as an institution has moved neither in the direction of closer economic integration, in contrast to the EU to which it is sometimes mistakenly compared, nor to tighter security cooperation on the model of NATO. Rather than facing external threats the main danger comes from internal conflicts. The regular CIS summits provide a framework for leaders at least to talk. As Putin noted in his 1 February 2007 press conference, the Minsk summit a few months earlier had allowed him to discuss some of the most difficult question with Georgian president Mikheil Saakashvili, including whether the CIS was needed at all, and allowed some of the tension to be defused.[22] The coordination of foreign policy and the maintenance of a common economic space were soon forgotten, a common currency zone did not survive, and attempts to maintain a single juridical space throughout the CIS were undermined. Comparisons with the short-lived French Commonwealth, created on the basis of a referendum in 1958 and dissolved two years later, is instructive. However, the independent Francophone countries retain a deep affinity with France, and Russia could hope that it, too, could play a hegemonic cultural role in Eurasia, though it was precisely such aspirations that so alienated countries like Ukraine. At the minimum, the CIS provides a framework for conflict deflation, if not resolution.

## Regional organisations

Russia has devoted nearly two decades searching for effective instruments to institutionalise links with willing CIS partners. Russia is the only state involved in every CIS regional grouping, except those with an anti-Russian edge. The former Soviet states can be arranged along a spectrum, with the Baltic option at one end signifying a complete break with the past, refusal to have anything to do with the CIS, accompanied by what were ultimately successful attempts to join Western European institutions like NATO and the EU, and the Belarus variant at the other end, denoting the attempt to recreate some sort of post-Soviet political community with Russia at its core. Even Belarus after an energy dispute with Russia in late 2006 became a rather less enthusiastic proponent of Eastern integration. As the Baltic option became increasingly attractive (and possible) for a number of countries, so their interest in the continuation of the CIS as anything more than a very loose umbrella organisation declined. Attempts to supplant the CIS by organisations with less ambitious goals but with more achievable remits, however, were not that successful either.

### *Collective Security Treaty Organisation (CSTO)*

At the CIS summit in Tashkent on 15 May 1992 the Collective Security Treaty (CST) was signed by Armenia, Kazakhstan, Kyrgyzstan, Russia, Tajikistan and Uzbekistan, with Azerbaijan, Belarus and Georgia joining in 1993. The refusal of Ukraine and other countries to sign once again revealed the deep divisions. The Tashkent Treaty stipulated that aggression against one of the signatory parties would be considered aggression against them all, but it was less a multilateral military and political alliance than a way of legitimating Russian military assistance to the signatory states.[23] The Tashkent meeting also agreed on the distribution of CFE Treaty limits among the newly independent states. The CST represented one of the very few successful attempts to build a broad multilateral body within the framework of the CIS, having by 2001 established a 2,500-strong rapid deployment force. It also reflected the weakness of such bodies, and Azerbaijan, Georgia and Uzbekistan never took part in any of its activities and abandoned it altogether in 1999. The remaining countries divided into three operational groups: Russia and Belarus in the West, Russia and Armenia in the Caucasus, and Russia, Kazakhstan, Kyrgyzstan and Tajikistan in Central Asia.

To overcome earlier inadequacies, on 14 May 1999 the CST was transformed into a Collective Security Treaty Organisation (CSTO), similar in form to NATO, and on 7 October 2002 its Charter was adopted a the Chisinau summit. The CSTO at that time united Armenia, Belarus, Russia, Kyrgyzstan, Kazakhstan and Tajikistan, and Uzbekistan 'rejoined' at the CSTO summit in Minsk on 23 June 2006. The new organisation is managed by a number of executive bodies, including a Council on Collective Security, comprising the heads of state, as well as councils of foreign and defence ministers as well as a Joint Military Staff. The tripartite regional structure was preserved, but now the aim was to pour some operational content into what had been a largely political organisation. The Central Asian rather than Western focus remained, with Russia deploying aircraft to the Kant airbase near Bishkek in Kyrgyzstan. In May 2003 the CSTO was given ambitious security tasks, including a joint military command in Moscow, a rapid reaction force, a common air defence system and 'coordinated action' in foreign, security and defence policy.[24] Putin sought to legitimise the CSTO by establishing direct contacts with NATO.[25] While the anti-Western Lukashenka greeted the creation of the CSTO as a counter-weight to NATO, few really believed that a new geopolitical force was emerging in the East as the successor to the Warsaw Pact.

### *EurAsian Economic Community (EAEC or EvrAzES)*

The Customs Union of 1994 built on the agreement of 14 March 1992 and promised free trade between Russia, Kazakhstan, Belarus and Kyrgyzstan, with Tajikistan joining in January 1999. On 26 February 1999 Belarus, Kazakhstan, Kyrgyzstan, Russia and Tajikistan signed a treaty to establish a Customs Union and Common Economic Space, providing the framework for the free movement of goods, capital, services and people. By contrast with the EU's moves towards the creation of a single market in 1986, this treaty specified neither a timeframe nor created an instrument to push through its objectives.

To overcome these problems on 10 October 2000 these same countries signed a treaty strengthening their existing customs union, and at the Minsk summit in 2001 the Customs Union was transformed into the EurAsian Economic Community (EAEC). The aim was to establish a free trade and unified customs system, and to coordinate relations with the WTO. A number of institutions were to promote these goals, including an Interstate Council, its highest body, an Integration Committee, a Parliamentary Assembly, an EAEC Arbitration Court, together with a permanent secretariat to service the organisation. A system of weighted votes was introduced, giving Russia a clear predominance. Ukraine and Moldova gained observer status in 2002. At the EAEC summit on 25 January 2006 Uzbekistan joined the organisation, underscoring the country's geopolitical shift towards Russia and the strengthening energy partnership between the two. In 2006 the EAEC merged with the Central Asian Cooperation Organisation.

### *Joint Economic Space (Edinoe Ekonomicheskoe Prostranstvo, EEP)*

A Joint Economic Space (EEP) was announced on 23 February 2003, and Russia took the lead in ensuring that the relevant documents were signed on 19 September 2003, uniting the more advanced economies of Russia, Ukraine, Belarus and Kazakhstan. The idea was to create a free trade zone to facilitate the free movement of goods, services, capital and labour (on the model of the EU's Single European Act of 1986). Ukraine, a key member of any Eurasian economic community, agreed to participate but in the ratification process added so many conditions that its membership remains highly qualified.

Bilateral trade between Russia and Ukraine reached $16 billion in 2004, an increase of 40 per cent over that attained in 2003, and made Ukraine Russia's third-largest trade partner after Belarus and Germany. Despite close economic ties, Ukraine was ambivalent about the EEP, fearing that it could jeopardise links with the EU, concerns that were intensified after the orange revolution in late 2004. Plans to establish a supranational body mooted at the Astana summit in September 2004, together with the adoption of 29 policy documents, alarmed Ukraine's new leadership. Russia, Belarus and Kazakhstan by mid-2006 were ready to sign the documents creating the EEP, and hoped that in due course Ukraine would join. As it became clear that EU membership would at best be a long-term prospect, Ukraine was even willing to consider the idea of membership in Kazakhstan's idea of creating a Eurasian Economic Union, united by a single currency.

### Organisation for Democracy and Economic Development (GUAM)

The most vivid evidence of the decline of the CIS was the creation in October 1997 of the GUAM group of states (Georgia, Ukraine, Azerbaijan and Moldova), prefigured a year earlier by an Azerbaijani initiative at the Vienna OSCE summit. With the accession of Uzbekistan in April 1999 the group for a time became GUUAM. Their initial concern was to ensure Russian compliance with force limitations within the framework of the CFE treaty, and more broadly to resist Russian security policy and contain its influence in the post-Soviet region. The anti-hegemonic group was concerned in particular with the various secessionist conflicts and Russian troops on their territories. The long-term aim was to stay outside Russia's orbit and Russian-dominated bodies like the Collective Security Treaty and the Eurasian Economic Community. The development of GU(U)AM acted as a counter-weight to what its members suspected were Russia's hegemonic ambitions within the CIS. At the Yalta summit in June 2001 GUUAM became an organisation with its own secretariat and headquarters, and the Charter adopted at that meeting outlined GUUAM's goals as the development of reciprocal trade, the creation of a GUUAM free trade zone, and support for transit routes between Europe and Central Asia. The top decision-making body was the conference of heads of state, to meet annually in Yalta, the permanent site of GUUAM summits. Ukraine, the main mover behind the organisation, would provide organisational support for the body. Soon afterwards GUUAM was recognised as an international regional organisation.

Uzbekistan by early 2000 had clearly cooled towards the body, wanting Russian assistance in its struggle against 'Islamic extremism', while Moldova feared antagonising Russia and, now led by a neo-communist government, suffered from multiple vulnerabilities. By the time of the organisation's second summit on 19–20 July 2002, again in Yalta, the Uzbekistan leader, Islam Karimov, stayed away. The meeting went ahead and agreed to rename the organisation the Black Sea-Caspian Initiative, and took further plans to establish a free trade area, now comprising only the four countries. Discussions also centred on the development of oil pipelines bypassing Russia, one of the main *raisons d'etre* of GUAM. Following the Andijan massacre in May 2005, Uzbekistan formally withdrew.

At the Kiev summit on 23 May 2006 GUAM was formally relaunched as an international organisation, and was once again renamed, this time as the 'Organisation for Democracy and Economic Development – GUAM'. The Kiev Declaration talked of a common commitment to 'the creation of a regional space of democracy, security, and stable economic and social development', reaffirmed the intention to strengthen relations with NATO and the EU, and signed the new organisation's Charter and created a number of new policy-making and executive bodies, including the Council of Heads of State. Membership was to be open to other countries, possibly including Bulgaria and Romania.[26] The president of Ukraine, Yushchenko, was elected as the inaugural Secretary-General, a Secretariat was established in Kiev, and its new Charter focused on the development of democracy, the rule of law and human rights, and significantly, 'to cooperate actively in settlement of unresolved conflicts in a number of GUAM states that undermine sovereignty, territorial integrity and independence of those States…'.[27] The summit called for increased cooperation with NATO and the EU, with greater economic cooperation to complement its original focus on security. In particular, reducing dependence on Russian oil and gas became a core aim, together with the development of a free-trade zone and customs union. A year later, however, neither Ukraine nor Moldova had ratified the Charter.

America strongly supports the GUAM initiative as part of its strategy of isolating Russia and to push it out of its traditional sphere of influence in the Caucasus and Central Asia.[28] A type of neo-containment policy was pursued in the former Soviet South while the integration of Moscow into Western institutions was proceeding in the North. Ukraine was a willing accomplice, and indeed instrument, of this strategy. Just as Russia had anti-Western hardliners, the West had those (many of whom were to be found among the neo-conservatives in George W. Bush's entourage) who insisted that Russia remained a real threat and all should be done to ensure that it never rose to great power status again. Democracy became quite explicitly an instrument in foreign policy strategy.

### Community of Democratic Choice

This took concrete form in the establishment of the Community of Democratic Choice in Kiev in December 2005, although its aims and terms of reference remained vague. By 2006 this had evolved into the Union of Democratic States, comprising the Baltic republics, Poland, Czech Republic, Slovakia, Hungary, Ukraine, Moldova, Romania, Bulgaria and Georgia. The contours of a new division of Europe were in place, with only Azerbaijan and Turkmenistan undecided. A huge new *cordon sanitaire*, was in the making, to be reinforced by the extension of NATO to all of these countries. A conference of these countries in Vilnius on 4 May 2006, as noted, heard US vice-president, Dick Cheney, lambaste Russia for allegedly using energy as 'tools of intimidation or blackmail, either by supply manipulation or attempts to monopolise transportation', and he warned Russia to stop its democratic backsliding.[29] The harsh tone of the comments was reminiscent of the Cold War, although their lack of balance or judgment was something new. The commentator Vyacheslav Nikonov warned that 'Once an escalation like this starts there's no telling where it will end.'[30] In his address to the Federal Assembly a few days later on 10 May Putin enigmatically remarked that 'The wolf knows whom to eat … and is not about to listen to anyone', a reference to America's overbearing manner.[31]

### Unification with Belarus

Regional alliances were not able to substitute for bilateral links, the most intense of which was with Belarus beginning with the signing of the April 1996 agreement on unification. There was strong and consistent public support for unification with Belarus, with 62 per cent in favour in 1997 and 72 per cent in November 2000, while on average only 15 per cent were opposed.[32] Russia's link with 'Europe's last dictator',[33] Lukashenka, was understandable in purely *Realpolitik* terms, but did little to enhance Russia's reputation as a democracy. Putin rejected Lukashenka's plan of 10 June 2002, insisting that unification should not be at the 'expense of Russia's economic interests'. As a recent study of the Russian-Belarusian relationship pointedly puts it, 'I love you, you pay my rent.'[34] Putin refused to countenance Lukashenka's demands that Belarus, whose economy was only 3 per cent of Russia's, would have 'rights of veto, sovereignty and territorial integrity' unless Russia had them too, and spoke against creating 'a supranational organ with undefined functions'.[35] Although integration issues dominated Belarusian politics throughout Lukashenka's presidency, support for unification among Belarusian citizens dropped significantly. If in 1994 45 per cent were in favour, by 2002 this had fallen to 16 per cent.[36]

The population had clearly become accustomed to independence, while the elite feared being reduced to little more than provincial officials in a joint state. Putin himself had no guilt complex about destroying the old USSR, a sentiment that certainly influenced Yeltsin earlier, and neither did he need integration with Belarus to increase his political capital in Russia. Putin, however, insisted that 'the Belarusian and Russian peoples are brotherly people in the full sense of this word', and stressed the close economic links between the two countries and that Russia could be strengthened by unification with Belarus as part of the 'movement of the Russian Federation – both territorial and demographic – in the direction of Europe'. The main thing, however, he insisted was that 'the form and methods of the unification should be beneficial for both the Belarusian and Russian peoples'.[37] In the event, no such formula could be found. Lukashenka was concerned that Russia would simply absorb Belarus, noting in 2004 that 'we cannot return to the humiliating suggestion of Belarus being incorporated into Russia'.[38] Russia feared granting Belarus control over economic and monetary policy in the joint state, and was not too keen on paying for the privilege of integrating with Belarus. While the Belarusian economy was certainly dependent on Russia, above all in the sphere of energy, Lukashenka tried to ensure that it did not fall into the hands of Russian big business, and this was yet another reason for his resistance to privatisation and insistence on pursuing the 'Belarusian economic model'. The agreement signed on 27 January 2005 for the supply and transit of gas was remarkably generous to Belarus, especially in the context of the sharp increase in prices to Ukraine and other states as they moved to 'market levels', and heightened speculation that the ultimate plan was for Russia to take over the Belarusian gas supply network, Beltransgaz. Energy was a potent weapon, and indeed Putin promoted Russia as an 'energy superpower', but as the conflict with Ukraine in the first days of 2006 demonstrated (when the spigots were turned to encourage Ukraine to accept a new gas pricing structure), it could backfire if used too forcefully and undermine Russia's image as a reliable supplier and reasonable partner.

Numerous Union State bodies have been created, and over two hundred interstate agreements signed. At its twenty-ninth meeting in January 2006 the parliamentary assembly of the Russia-Belarus Union drafted the Constitutional Act of the new state, to act as a type of 'pre-constitution' before a proper constitution was adopted. The Act did not envisage a single leader to head the union but a Supreme State Council, chosen in part through elections and delegation from both national parliaments. Facing elections in March 2006, the move was designed to bolster Lukashenka's position. However, the budget of the Union State increased by only 17 per cent to 3.9 billion roubles, the resources of an average small district in Russia. Revenue, moreover, was drawn from industrial enterprises on Union-wide significance and the repayment of loans earlier issued by the Union State, hardly the way to fund a new state entity.[39] While processes of legal harmonisation and economic integration languished, there was greater success in the security and foreign policy fields, although a union state was not required for these. Any expectations that genuine union would take place while Putin and Lukashenko were leaders were dashed by the energy pricing dispute between the two countries in January 2007. Lukashenka began to look for new alliances and tried to move out of Russia's orbit.

### The Shanghai Cooperation Organisation (SCO)

The 'Shanghai Five' was established in 1996 by Russia, China, Kazakhstan, Kyrgyzstan and Tajikistan, and at a summit in Shanghai on 14–15 June 2001 it was reformed as the Shanghai Cooperation Organisation (SCO) as a regional multilateral mechanism for security and cooperation, comprising the original five joined in 2001 by Uzbekistan. The meeting adopted a Charter and Constitution, and established a permanent secretariat. The SCO Charter pledges 'non-interference and non-alignment', while seeking to establish 'a new political and economic order'. The June 2004 Tashkent summit expanded the SCO's activities, establishing a Regional Anti-Terrorism Structure (RATS) to deal with drug trafficking and trans-national insurgencies, whose office relocated from Shanghai to Tashkent in 2005. In August of that year Russia and China held their first ever joint military exercise.

The SCO's establishment brought China into Central Asian politics and under-scored the shift away from a 'strategic partnership' between Russia and China, as expressed in the treaty signed by Yeltsin and Jiang Zemin in 1996, towards a more pragmatic relationship based on shared interests and concerns. The SCO was the antithesis of the liberal universal principles proclaimed by the leading Western powers, and instead took a hard-headed realist approach to international politics based on interests rather than 'values'. Although not yet a mutual defence pact, it could well develop into a political and security bloc to rival those in the West. At the SCO summit in Astana in July 2005 the call for the United States to remove its forces from Central Asia was adopted, followed swiftly by Uzbekistan's request for American troops to leave the Kharsi-Khanabad (K-2) base on the border with Afghanistan. At that meeting India, Iran, Mongolia and Pakistan were granted observer status, while America's application was refused. Belarus later applied for observer status, and there were plans to give the observers full membership, and to rename and reform the organisation. The SCO has emerged as a regional political, security and economic bloc with the potential to counter American influence in the region, and complements the work of the CSTO to block the extension of Western influence in Russian, Chinese and Central Asian security matters. By 2006 even India had established a base in the region: the Ayni (Farkhor) airfield near Dushanbe, operated together with Russia and Tajikistan.

In terms of population, area and resources, the SCO overshadows NATO and the EU, and it dwarfs traditional security organisations in the region. Enjoying a large proportion of the world's oil and gas reserves and armed with nuclear weapons, the group has been dubbed 'OPEC with bombs'.[40] China's developing economic ties in Central Asia, focusing on energy and pipelines but broadening out into manufacturing, trade and banking, were accompanied by its strategic goal to minimise Western influence in the region.[41] This was a concern shared by Russia, although China's own growing weight in the area could not but worry Moscow. The SCO served to keep the US out of Central Asia, and to provide a security cover for growing Chinese penetration into the Central Asian economies. China was concerned to ensure control over energy supplies from the region, and did so by paying over the odds for energy resources and infrastructure, and by offering soft loans to Central Asian partners. China was also exercised by the 'Three Evils' – religious fundamentalism, terrorists and 'splittists' (that is, secessionists).[42] The organisation's main stated goal was to foster cooperation to settle border disputes, promote economic links and to deal with regional problems such as drug-trafficking. Nevertheless, the military dimension remained prominent, and suggested that the grouping would ultimately be rather more ambitious than posing as a pole of *autonomy* but could well become an *alternative* to the American-dominated system. This trend would undoubtedly intensify if Russia's relations with the West continued to deteriorate.

Russia under Putin had initially been most concerned with enhancing bilateral ties with China while improving relations with the West. Meeting with limited success in the latter strategy, Russia look more positively on the enhanced leverage offered by the SCO. The development of the SCO rendered the notion of a new 'great game' in Central Asia even more anachronistic. Instead of the struggle between rival great powers, the outlines of a new global polarisation began to emerge. The common approach to world affairs and common concerns brought Russia, China their regional allies together. They shared common approaches to issues such as joint security, energy, cooperation in the struggle against terrorism and separatism, and Islamist militancy. Condemned by its critics as a 'club of dictators', the SCO, despite the original intention of its founders, could well become the core of an alternative bloc to NATO and the US-dominated alliance system.

# Part VI

# Dilemmas of democratisation

The adoption of the constitution in December 1993 furnished Russia with the normative framework for the development of a liberal and democratic society. The genesis of the constitution, however, in a bloody struggle between the legislative and executive branches of government, stamped the new order with a political mark of Cain. The new constitutional system, nevertheless, provided Russia with the main institutions of a modern representative democracy and established the parameters within which democratic politics could be conducted. The constitution allowed the development of genuine parliamentarianism while defending liberal principles of human rights and the separation of powers. The principle of popular sovereignty, at the heart of the democratic insurgency against the communist regime, was reaffirmed, although its representation was partial and the ability of society to hold the authorities accountable was tenuous. In this part we will stand back from the detailed analysis of institutions and policy and examine some of the larger issues and processes affecting Russia's struggle for democracy.

# 19 Problems of transition

A weak state is a threat to democracy in no less a degree than a despotic power.

(Vladimir Putin)[1]

Gogol ends his satire on Tsarist Russia, *The Government Inspector*, with the image of a careering troika (three-horse carriage) dragging Russia no one knew whither: 'And where do you fly to, Russia?' This troika has still not yet been tamed, and its final destination remains a mystery. The country in 1991 may well have set its compass for capitalist democracy, yet the storms and turmoil of the succeeding years have taken Russia into unfamiliar territory. It is not quite a fully fledged consolidated democracy, since the rule of law remains too weak and the ability of executive and bureaucratic agencies to insulate themselves from popular accountability and control too high. Nor would it be accurate to talk about Russia having endured a failed democratic transition, since it is far too early to consider the present system as the end point of Russia's post-communist evolution. Russia is not an authoritarian state, although there are undoubtedly elements of authoritarianism. It is a hybrid system with considerable scope for further democratic evolution, or indeed the establishment of a harder authoritarian order. In this chapter we examine the historical and theoretical problems associated with the concept of democratic transition, and in the final chapter analyse the tribulations of democracy in Russia. As we shall see, approaches focusing on modernisation and development are misleading in suggesting an inevitable outcome that can by no means be assumed. The view that Soviet-style politics could be cast off to expose a nascent capitalist democracy was misleading, but not entirely erroneous. There *are* profound continuities between the Tsarist, Soviet and post-Soviet eras in Russia, but at the same time there are enormous discontinuities and innovations. It is precisely the analysis of the dynamics of change and continuity that can reveal the sources of Russian political evolution. A democratic Russia could not emerge fully formed like Minerva from the brow of Zeus; but neither is the country forever in thrall to its tragic yet glorious past.

## The challenge of history

It is often argued that Russia's failure to come to terms with its past is the greatest obstacle to the development of a consolidated democracy. According to the historian Yury Afanas'ev, 'The public consciousness has not yet reached the required level. That there existed a certain regime and that a return to it is out of the question is acknowledged only by individuals, not as yet by the society.'[2] Nostalgia for the past was entertained not only by the communists but also by the great mass of the people. The memory of the past, however, was selective: both in terms of choosing the particular period that suited present tastes; and in reinterpreting the significance of each particular epoch. In adopting the Tsarist double-headed eagle as the state emblem, the Soviet national anthem (with new words) as Russia's official hymn, and the 'democratic' tricolour as the national flag, Putin sought to achieve the reconciliation of the various national myths. History remains central to post-communist Russian culture, with the flood of memoirs showing no signs of abating. Most newspapers and journals have a section devoted to Russia's past, there are numerous historical series on television and many volumes of archival documents are being published. The past, its selection, interpretation and dynamics, however, remains a problem for contemporary Russian politics.[3]

The speed of the collapse of the communist system, as with the destruction of Tsarism in February-March 1917, took most observers by surprise. When in 1913 the Romanov dynasty celebrated its 300th anniversary, the throne and empire appeared solidly in place; yet a mere four years later both lay shattered. When Gorbachev came to power in 1985 the Communist Party and the Soviet system appeared firmly ensconced; and once again just seven years later communist rule had dissolved and the Soviet Union had disintegrated.[4] Tsarism had been unable to survive the strains inflicted by the Great War, but in the Soviet case the absence of war made the collapse all the more astonishing. In a time of peace one of the world's great geopolitical powers dissolved politically and disintegrated territorially. The Cold War played its part: the attempt to challenge the capitalist democracies for world leadership and to match their combined military potential provoked a severe case of 'imperial overstretch', to use Paul Kennedy's phrase.[5] But the dissolution of the Soviet regime owed as much to its fundamental internal incoherence as to external factors. From a neo-institutional perspective, a strong case can be made that the structures of accountability and policy-making became so narrow that ultimately they lost contact with the society that they sought to manage. Political power became responsible to a narrow 'selectorate' and was unable to respond to the enormous social changes that it had itself provoked through industrialisation and the broad programme of post-Stalin modernisation.[6]

Isaac Deutscher had long argued that Stalinism would be its own gravedigger, having set in motion social changes that would undermine the authoritarian political system. Khrushchev responded by trying to re-energise the revolutionary spirit of Bolshevism, while Brezhnev tried to buy off any potential demands for political inclusion by promising improved standards of living in return for political passivity. The stability that was at the heart of Brezhnev's rule undermined the system's potential to adapt to the changes that it had set in motion. According to Roeder, the Bolshevik 'constitution' (the rules that governed the Soviet system from the early revolutionary years into the post-Stalin era; not to be confused with the official constitutions adopted in 1924, 1936 and 1977), imposed severe institutional constraints on the USSR's adaptability.[7] The debate continues whether we can still call the late Soviet regime totalitarian.[8] In social terms, *perestroika* exposed the contradictions between the attempt to transcend the market and the realities of the command economy in which informal economic activity and corruption were rife; between the abolition of private property that condemned the mass of the population to a universal 'equality in poverty' and the luxuriating privileges of the political elite; between the progressive claims to political leadership by the Communist Party and its own crude manipulations of political decision-making; and above all between the regime's claims to a monopoly of truth and the mountain of lies on which it rested.

The Soviet regime went the way of the Romanov dynasty earlier and entered the dustbin of history; but what was to take its place? Max Weber in the early years of this century had been sceptical about the possibility of democracy in Russia,[9] and many today are equally doubtful given Russia's past. The history of reform in Russia provides 'many examples of opportunities missed and reform initiatives wrecked on the rocks of popular indifference or hostility or the resistance of powerful groups in society to the loss of their privileges'.[10] Equally pertinent, given the apparent adaptation of contemporary reforms to traditional patterns, is Crummey's observation about 'the ease with which initiatives for change can be sucked into the morass of traditional administrative habits and ways of thinking'.[11] The hopes of the era of 'great reforms' of the 1860s under Alexander II, under pressure from the terrorism that culminated in the Tsar's assassination in 1881, gave way to the reaction of the 1880s under Alexander III. The aspirations vested in the February 1917 'bourgeois democratic' revolution soon gave way to the disappointment of the Provisional Government and the calculated brutality of the Bolsheviks from October of that year. The three main reform periods of the Soviet regime, the New Economic Policy of the 1920s, Khrushchev's thaw of the 1950s, and Gorbachev's *perestroika*, all dissolved into disappointment. Against that background, it is hardly surprising that the prospects for democracy today are not considered bright.

Russia is not the only European country where the passage to political modernity has been traumatic; Weber had been as sceptical about the prospects for democracy in Germany as he was for Russia. Studies of the origins and dynamics of the Nazi regime offer a useful comparative perspective on Soviet developments.[12] Recent studies have rejected orthodox Marxist interpretations of Nazism as an instrument of monopoly capital, but at the same time the standard liberal view of Nazism as a temporary archaic regression in the onward march of modernisation is equally untenable. Like the Lenin-Stalin regime in Russia, the Nazi state was propelled towards ever more radical measures by its inherent instability.[13] Structural and institutional factors complement approaches based on political culture or social psychology. In post-war Germany the alleged 'totalitarian personality' appears to have adapted remarkably swiftly to democratic mores after 1945, although as late as 1968 Ralf Dahrendorf argued that high rates of political participation masked a qualitatively flawed political socialisation: 'Democratic institutions are accepted; but they remain external, distant, ultimately irrelevant ... Democratic behaviour becomes ritualised, a mere observance of external demands, a "duty" of citizenship.'[14] The 'unpolitical German', as Dahrendorf put it, at least made a show of political participation whereas in post-communist Russia reform was thrown onto 'the rocks of popular indifference'. It is usually assumed that the unpolitical character of the German people facilitated authoritarian rule; what then will Russian 'anti-political' tendencies yield?[15]

While most post-communist countries could aspire to return to some indigenous model of development, however mythologised, Russia's pre-communist past was both more distant in time and more ambivalent.[16] P. Pestel', one of the leaders of the Decembrist uprising of 1825 (often considered the first blow in the revolutionary struggle for democracy in Russia), advocated a type of 'autocratic modernisation' in which 'Modernisation seemed a far more urgent goal than democracy or human rights.'[17] Russian history demonstrates that every attempt to achieve a 'leap' into modernity in fact only delayed the achievement of the desired modernisation, and indeed, the whole history of Russia from 1825 can be seen as a struggle between the opposed principles of revolution and gradualism – and only gradualism has provided tangible and enduring achievements, such as the legal and *zemstvo* (local government) reforms of the 1860s. In Russia's last great opening to the West, between 1885 and 1913, industrial production grew at an overall annual rate of 5.7 per cent, and in the four years before the Great War, growth reached 8 per cent per annum. In those years Russian wheat exports represented a quarter of the world market, and rye over two-thirds.[18] In politics, too, the standard image of the Tsarist regime as brutal and stifling has been tempered by the idea of the role of 'constrained autocracy' in Russian history.[19]

This was a period of enormous achievements in art and literature, the Silver Age of Russian poetry, a period of brilliant social analysis by religious philosophers such as Nikolai Berdyaev, Sergei Bulgakov and Semyon Frank, thinkers who ultimately provided the most sustained rejection of the revolutionism typical of the Russian intelligentsia of that time in the *Landmarks* (*Vekhi*) collection of 1909.[20] Schools of jurisprudence developed and a law-based although not democratic state emerged. A modest form of parliamentarianism was created, legal reforms established elements of a law-based state, and economic growth brought Russia to the forefront of the European states.[21] It was these achievements that were lauded by Stanislav Govorukhin in his film *The Russia that We Have Lost*, which played to packed houses in the early 1990s and helped launch his political career. While it was natural to portray the Tsarist era as some sort of golden age in contrast to the age of mass murder that followed, and undoubtedly represented a necessary corrective to the tendentious picture of Tsarism presented by the Soviet regime, the new representation, however, once again failed to explore the tensions in the old society. Eighty per cent of the population, for example, were peasants governed by customary law and relatively insulated from the modernising processes that were transforming the rest of society.

These tensions led to the fall of Tsarism in February 1917 and allowed the Bolsheviks to seize power in October of that year. Instead of moving from autocracy to democracy the 'transition' in 1917 was from Tsarism to communism. Peter the Great's revolution had stimulated the development of what Richard Pipes calls the 'patrimonial' state, where the whole country is considered the property of the ruler.[22] This pattern was reinforced by the communist revolution, and even more than under Tsarism the autonomy of civil associations like trade unions, political parties and public organisations was undermined. The Russian Orthodox Church was humbled and market relations and private property as economic institutions were abolished. Thus in the late twentieth century, when democratisation and economic modernisation were once again on the agenda, their social and institutional bases were even more tenuous than in 1917. In these circumstances, the conflict between ends and means would once again inevitably come to the fore. Yeltsin from the late 1980s many time stressed that it would be impossible to reform the socialist system. In the wake of the October 1993 events, not without some irony, Yeltsin argued that 'we have said farewell to the illusion of giving socialism a human face'.[23] This may well have been true, but the corollary of abandoning an evolutionary exit from communism, of the sort proclaimed by Gorbachev, was a return to the revolutionism that had played such a devastating role in Russian history before. It is no accident that the sub-title of Reddaway and Glinski's magisterial study of the Yeltsin era is 'Market Bolshevism against Democracy':[24] the market, like communism earlier, was to be imposed by authoritarian means. Like the socialist revolution of the earlier age, the democratic project was built from the roof down.

Russia's past is multi-layered, and faced with the renewed challenge of finding an appropriate model of modernisation following the fall of communism the country's history was once again trawled to find elements that could sustain the democratic experiment.[25] Obolensky argues that Russia's conservatism has deep roots in certain psychological constants of mass consciousness, including anti-personal social attitudes, a social inferiority complex, the lack of moral regulators of social behaviour, and the weak development of a normal work ethic, although even he concedes that there is a countervailing 'syndrome of modernisation'.[26] The view of Russia as eternally reactionary has been challenged by the argument that there were popular and philosophical constraints on autocratic rule. The political culture approach might suggest that democracy and civil society are somehow alien to Russia. This would be unduly deterministic, and Petro indeed writes of two competing political cultures in the Russian tradition whereby 'democracy, or *narodovlastie* in Russian, had deep roots in Russian history'.[27] Nevertheless, the historical failure of liberalism and democracy to strike institutional and social roots has many later parallels. The two themes that dominate today, the absence of a social basis for democracy and the need for authoritarian government in the transition, were common already in 1917.[28] On several occasions Yeltsin drew the analogy:

> If you are looking for historical parallels, I would compare the present time with the period in which the Provisional Government was in power, especially after June 1917. Despite its many mistakes and faults it sought to establish a democratic republic in Russia. Then the Bolsheviks prevented this and led the country into a bloody civil war. Now, 76 years later, the Russian people have the first real possibility of a free choice of the way forward.[29]

Alexander Yakovlev, one of the architects of *perestroika*, warned of the parallels between the renewed attempt at democracy in Russia and the catastrophe of 1917, arguing that the new leaders were repeating the mistakes of the February revolution. Gorbachev had failed to use presidential power to secure a deideologised politics during *perestroika*, and once again the 'democratic forces', in Yakovlev's view, 'do not have any extensive programme of civil transformations to withstand the possibilities of authoritarianism'. The new democrats failed to build on and advance the achievements of *perestroika*, which, in Yakovlev's view, 'managed to overthrow Bolshevism's autocracy, abandon the permanent war against our own people and the war with the people of Afghanistan, and step back from constant nuclear confrontation with the whole world'. Land reform had been delayed and economic mismanagement had plagued both the democracy of 1917 and post-1991. A mere eight months after the overthrow of the autocracy a new and more dreadful enslavement was imposed, a failure according to Yakovlev that sprang from the inability to develop the foundations of democracy. A civic culture based on compromise and dialogue had not emerged, and instead the mass-meeting democracy only reinforced intolerance and 'the bacillus of moral decay'. In the 1990s as in 1917 'the only path left is to overthrow ourselves, our infinite intolerance towards others, and our pitiful slobbering. Oh, how we hate others for our own laziness, foolishness and ignorance'.[30]

Is post-communist democracy in Russia in danger of going the way of the Provisional Government in 1917? Quite apart from the absence of war and a wholly different external environment, internally the country has changed. The legacy of the Russian imperial state was a semi-industrialised peasant economy, weak civic institutions, a society prey to a disintegrating army, an alienated working class and an intelligentsia tempted by utopian promises of a thorough reordering of society on a non-capitalist basis.[31] By contrast, the collapse of the Soviet state in 1991 revealed a rich network of civic and public associations and a counter-culture, although lacking the legal and social bases of civil society, oriented towards liberal democratic forms of political representation and the restoration of the market. When Soviet authority crumbled there was not the anarchic vacuum that characterised events in 1917 but a shadow society (admittedly, heavily deformed) and a republican government ready to take the place of the old system.

No country can entirely escape the tyranny of the past, but history usually contains numerous seeds for the future, some of which may lie dormant for centuries. The Russian historical record is not wholly negative, and precedents can be found for the separation of powers and the principles of responsive governance. Russian history is not simply a story of a 'strong state' and 'weak society', but of unique attempts to find a synthesis of the two on the snow-bound and indefensible Eurasian landmass. There were elements of a 'usable past' in Russian traditions that could generate and sustain liberal and democratic forms of interaction between state and society. What use would be made of them by the country's new leaders is another question.

## Transitional justice

The 'Nuremberg question' has haunted all post-communist states. To what degree were the perpetrators of the mass murders and other crimes of the communist regime to be brought to account, as some of the Nazis were in the Nuremberg trials in 1945–6? To what extent was the plea 'only obeying orders' admissible? How deep should the purging of the past go? The fundamental question is whether the choices are to be framed in absolute moral terms, with justice to be sought on behalf of the victims, or whether the problems of one regime (the victor) sitting in judgment on another (the defeated one) would distort both equity and legitimacy. Russia's hybrid transition makes the question of transitional justice particularly acute; although the old regime was overthrown, in personnel terms and within the framework of international law for its state obligations, it was at the same time perpetuated.[32] For Solzhenitsyn 'A public admission by the Party of its guilt, its crimes, and its helplessness would at least be the first step towards alleviating the oppressiveness of our moral atmosphere.'[33] Shortly after the coup Yakovlev argued that 'Democracy is not thirsty for revenge',[34] and Gorbachev also insisted that there should be no witch hunt.[35] Some democrats, however, insisted that there should be a public trial of the leading bodies of the CPSU, which 'had for decades imposed a terroristic regime on the country', and called for lustration laws (from the Latin *lustratio*, purification by sacrifice) against top Party and KGB officials to prevent them occupying responsible posts.[36] In early 1993 Democratic Russia proposed its version of a lustration law, based on Japanese experience, to ban former *apparatchiks* from jobs in certain sensitive occupations, a policy, they argued, that would provide space for a genuinely new administrative class to emerge.[37] As we have seen, this did not take place, and instead the Soviet-style bureaucracy flourished in post-communist Russia.

There have been 14 Truth Commissions of various sorts, notably in South Africa and El Salvador, as part of the development of 'restorative justice'.[38] There have been none, however, in the post-communist world. Neither truth nor reconciliation could be achieved through the mechanism of a special agency. Any serious decommunisation process, accompanied by dismissals and in certain cases trials, would involve unimaginable numbers and was liable to tear society, and indeed family and friends, apart, and sow misery and discord. Prosecutions for war crimes are always of the defeated by the victors, thus rendering judicial equity questionable.[39] In Poland the first post-communist government from August 1989 led by Tadeusz Mazowiecki drew a 'thick line' under the past, but the line did not hold and in May 1992 legislation allowed the exposure of the names of politicians and state officials who had collaborated with the communist regime.[40] A new wave of decommunisation was launched in 2006 under the presidency of Lech Kaczynski, with some notable victims including the putative bishop of Warsaw, and even the name of the great writer Ryszard Kapuscinski was traduced through allegations of collaboration with the secret police. The lustration law of October 1991 in Czechoslovakia affected more than 250,000 top officials and allowed the past of journalists and others to be exposed in a merciless process that judged people guilty until proven innocent and which led many, including president Vaclav Havel, to regret that the law had been adopted at all.[41] In the court of public opinion innocence is almost impossible to prove. Instead of 'drawing a line under the past', in the former East Germany the new authorities vigorously pursued secret police collaboraters.[42] The law from 1 January 1992 gave all citizens access to their Stasi dossiers, some six million of which were in the archives covering half the adult population. Many former dissidents and respected individuals (including the writer Christa Wolf) were accused of collaboration and many lost their jobs despite protestations of innocence. Legal and administrative mechanisms to enable people to defend themselves were inadequate.[43]

The long shadow of the secret police poisoned post-communist politics. As the Poles discovered, Party officials and state functionaries who did not need to be pressed into its service would not have secret police records, and neither would the millions who kept silent and thus acquiesced in what Solzhenitsyn called 'the lie'. Only those who tried to resist were the subject of police pressure; and now their sufferings were to be prolonged by the moral crusade of the new leaders, most of whom had not fought against the regime when it had been dangerous to do so. During the '*épuration*' (purification) following the liberation of France in 1944 some 11,000 people accused of collaboration were executed, usually without trial, and the same happened in Italy after the fall of the Salo Republic. If popular vengeance were to be unleashed against the perpetrators of the Bolshevik crimes a new bloodbath would sweep Russia. Demands by the democrats for lustration laws were resisted by the Russian authorities, perhaps fearful of their own pasts. Yeltsin took the view that former communists had to be employed (unless they had committed a specific crime) since they represented the largest pool of professionalism. Putin's coming to power acted as a type of vindication of the old ruling class and in particular its security wing.

The political use of decommunisation campaigns was vividly illustrated by the timing of the report issued by the 'Commission for the Rehabilitation of the Victims of Political Repression', established by Yeltsin and headed by Yakovlev. Issued 'coincidentally' two weeks before the December 1995 Duma elections, the report called for the rehabilitation of those who suffered in the communist anti-religious persecutions. The report estimated that some 200,000 religious figures had been murdered by the Soviet regime for their beliefs, 40,000 churches had been destroyed, half the country's mosques and over half of the Jewish synagogues.[44] The timing suggested that the aim was to discredit the communists, and Yakovlev made no secret of his hopes that the report would undermine their prospects.[45] This instance of a decommunisation struggle being used for instrumental anti-communist purposes was the last attempt to date of the successor regime to distance itself from the Soviet past.

Putin allowed formal destalinisation to continue, above all through Yakovlev's Presidential Commission on Rehabilitation of the victims of Stalin's crimes, but he did little to encourage the destalinisation of national consciousness. Russia's official position that the Soviet occupation of the Baltic republics in 1940 had been legitimate and legal enraged the local populations and was one factor in provoking the intense conflict with Estonia in 2007 over moving the Soviet war memorial called the Bronze Soldier.[46] Human rights organisations such as Memorial, created on 30 October 1988, continued to explore Stalin's crimes by seeking out mass graves, and by honouring the memory of the dead in various ways, yet its work was under constant threat and increasingly relied on the support of foreign donors. The FSB did not encourage investigation of the sins of its predecessors. Putin's selective destalinisation was in evidence in the limited scholarly access allowed to the Kremlin's Presidential Archive (formerly the Politburo's archive). However, Nanci Adler is only partially correct in suggesting that 'It is much riskier and more destabilising for a regime to disinter skeletal memories that are embedded so closely to the foundations on which it still rests',[47] since the contemporary Russian state (unlike Gorbachev's Soviet Union) certainly does not fundamentally rest on Soviet foundations. The resistance to full-scale destalinisation is not so much systemic as cultural and generational.

The problem of identifying who was guilty for the years of suffering inflicted on the population was even more acute than in Germany. With the disintegration of the USSR the moral question arose, as it did in Germany: if the state and system on whose behalf the crimes were committed no longer exists, to what extent is the guilt transferred to the successor (even more so the continuer) state that has repudiated the principles in whose name the crimes were committed? The guilt, shame and responsibility of a society that on the whole had condoned the crimes, if only by silence, etched themselves onto the post-communist national consciousness. Perhaps less ethically correct, but probably the only practical option, was to behave as the Germans did once the Cold War came into full swing in the late 1940s; ending the prosecution of Nazis, stopping the *épuration* and re-employing fascist officials in Italy. In Russia this approach was based not only on pragmatic considerations, but also on the moral revulsion against Bolshevik absolutism. Sergei Kovalev, the former head of the parliamentary and then the presidential human rights committees, opposed all attempts to divide society into the 'clean' and 'unclean', arguing 'There are no judges among us, not a single one. Everyone is to blame'.[48] The moral rejection of the Bolshevik cause was no longer accompanied by the denial of the humanity of Bolshevism's servants. In his film *The Inner Circle* Andrei Konchalovsky raised the issue of the degree to which the sources of Stalinism were to be found in the people themselves. Did not the ordinary people play a part in creating the conditions that made their victimisation possible?

## Models of transition

The Czechoslovak reform communist Zdenìk Mlynáø argued that change in what was the Soviet Union should be incremental: any sudden destruction of the existing system would be extremely dangerous.[49] However, the system did collapse and reform gave way to transition. The changes that had begun during *perestroika* in relations between the individual, social groups, the state and society were intensified. Market relations and democratic institutions were to be built in parallel. While postmodernism, according to Jean-Francois Lyotard, is about the end of 'meta-narratives', then the post-communist era is still firmly located in the modern epoch since developments after the fall of communism are interpreted through at least three such narratives: transitology, modernisation theory and globalisation.

### *Transition and democratisation*

The notion of 'transition' suggests the almost inevitable achievement of the desired end, something that in Russian conditions can by no means be guaranteed. The idea of 'transition to democracy' reinterpreted in a liberal form the old communist view that history has a meaning and purpose, and that the end point is intelligible to observers. It was this historicism that Francis Fukuyama reinterpreted in a liberal guise.[50] Russia is in a transitional period, but there can be no certainty about the shape of the new polity that will emerge. While the collapse of Soviet socialism demonstrated the futility of trying to abolish the market and the inadequacies of central planning, and indeed discredited the whole notion of the socialist transcendence of the capitalist social system, the larger question of the new social and political order that would replace it remains open.

In this context it is useful to distinguish between two approaches. The first can be labelled *teleological transitology* and tends to the view that there is only one permissible, and indeed possible, outcome to the post-authoritarian transformation process, namely some variety of liberal capitalist democracy. The great variety of outcomes in the post-communist world and elsewhere suggests that we are certainly far from 'the end of history', and liberalism is far from being accepted as a universal value. The second approach is rather more modest in its claims and can be called simply *technical transitionism*. The focus here is on the appropriate institutions and processes that can make a modern capitalist democracy work. The political science literature devotes considerable attention on how to 'craft democracy'.[51] The following are particularly important:

1  The choice of electoral system, with the central focus on the choice between majoritarian or proportional representation, or the balance between the two.[52] Sartori has described the electoral system as 'the most specific manipulative instrument of politics'. As Robert Moser notes, 'if this is true, then decisions involving electoral arrangements of new democracies are the most important decisions leaders of these new states will make'.
2  The structure of assemblies; above all whether they will be unicameral or bicameral. The formation of the upper house remains problematic even in some mature democracies (Germany, UK), and still a matter of sharp contention in Russia's nascent democracy.

3    The development of political parties and party systems. The development of strong parties and a stable party system is considered one of the essential features of a viable democracy.[53]

4    The choice of political system: presidential, semi-presidential, parliamentary or some hybrid.[54] There has been a wide-ranging debate in recent years about the relative merits of parliamentary and presidential systems.[55] There would appear to be a general consensus that parliamentary systems are more stable than presidential ones, and more conducive for democratic outcomes.

5    One of the most important institutional variables is the nature of the state form: federal or unitary.

Russia has faced all these questions, and by the end of Putin's presidency it was clear that very few of these issues had been satisfactorily resolved.

Samuel Huntington has described the current period as the third great democratisation wave in the modern era, each followed by a reverse wave: with the first lasting from 1828 until about 1922, when Mussolini's march on Rome set the trend for a decrease in the number of countries that could be considered democratic; the second phase began with the Allied victory in 1945 and encompassed decolonisation but ran out of steam in the early 1960s, with military takeovers in Latin America and authoritarian regimes coming to power in Africa and Asia; and the current wave began in 1974 with the Southern European transitions, continued with redemocratisation in Latin America, and was accelerated by the fall of the communist regimes in 1989–91 and the appearance of the concept of 'good government' throughout the world.[56] Experience would suggest that most seeds of democracy fall on stony ground.[57] Democracy cannot be established without some degree of societal acceptance.[58] Regime change in Latin America has followed a cyclical pattern, and the fall of a regime like the Shah's in Iran did not open the door to democracy.

A large literature has emerged concerning transitions in Latin America, Southern Europe and elsewhere, and we can do no more than indicate some of the salient issues.[59] O'Donnell and Schmitter demonstrated that no transition to democracy has taken place without major cleavages within the authoritarian regime itself, in particular between 'hardliners' and moderates.[60] Gorbachev's *perestroika* had indeed been torn by numerous cleavages, with reactionaries, conservatives, reform communists led by Gorbachev himself, and a growing band of radicals, all proposing divergent visions of the future. By 1990 reform communism had exhausted itself and Gorbachev found himself hopelessly exposed and hostage to the conservatives as he sought to shield himself from the reactionaries. The room for 'pacts' and other negotiated strategies of regime transition disappeared. The political cleavages of the final Soviet period were not replicated in the sovereign Russian state, and thus the foundations for a more pluralistic politics were missing. Instead, a dangerous unanimity appeared to reign, reflected in the overwhelming votes for Russian sovereignty on 12 June 1990 and for the dissolution of the Soviet Union on 12 December 1991. Yeltsin was able to place himself at the head of a relatively formless broad popular movement rather than a political party, and out of this emerged the problem of the lack of accountability that still plagues Russia's democracy. Yeltsin was able to use the radicals and the popular aspirations for a democratic society, but once he had achieved power neither his former colleagues in the democratic movement nor the representatives of mobilised civil society were able to exert control over him.

The red and brown oppositions tended to be anti-systemic, and thus could not provide the necessary impetus for pluralistic politics.

The Soviet transition did, however, share certain characteristics with the one analysed by Alfred Stepan where the success of the 'liberal' line depended on the presence of a moderate and intelligent opposition, giving critical support to the within-system reformers. This is to the advantage of both, since the moderate opposition can gain at the expense of more radical oppositionists, and the 'liberals' can ward off the assaults of the hardliners.[61] There were major differences, however, since such a model can only work where the regime has a modicum of viability and is able to evolve, whereas the Soviet regime was in an advanced condition of decomposition and the state itself divided between the centre and the republics. While the leverage exerted by the liberals with the support of the conservatives was sufficient to neutralise the reactionaries for a time, the whole struggle within the Soviet system was outflanked by the new political pivot based on the republics. The August coup meant the defeat not only of the conservatives but also of the moderate within-system reformers, above all Gorbachev. The initiative passed to those outside the system who had launched an insurgency against it. The dialectic between 'republicanisation', the emergence of sovereign and later independent republics in the last years of the USSR, and 'democratisation', the struggle for popular inclusive sovereignty and accountable government to replace the Communist Party, led to the overshadowing of the latter. Independence for many (and this was even stronger in republics like Georgia and Ukraine) became a higher immediate political priority than democracy.

A political transition is about building democratic institutions; but it is about much more than this, notably the need to find a solution to the geopolitical challenges facing the democratising state. The Weimar constitution in inter-war Germany had been a model of democratic institution-building, yet by the early 1930s had palpably failed either to root itself in the affections of the German public and political elite or to provide an effective framework for the solution of social and political problems or to deal with the country's place in the world. Hitler's rise to power in 1933 reflected the devastating role of the irrational in politics and the vulnerability of new democracies to demagogic ideologies. It also demonstrates that the challenge of democracy in a former great power must take into account intangible factors of national esteem and find a way of integrating the country in an appropriate manner in the international system. This was not achieved in the interwar years for Germany, and it has not been done for Russia today.

As decolonisation gathered pace Western social scientists examined the problem of change in authoritarian regimes, the establishment of political order and how democracies achieve stability, questions which have a renewed relevance today with the fall of communist regimes.[62] Several models have been employed which trace the sequence of events that allowed democracies to emerge, notably the study of Northern Europe by Dankwart Rustow. State boundaries were established early on in the process but not without numerous wars. The struggle then shifted for dominance within the states, marked by civil wars, coups and internecine warfare until at last, exhausted, the political elites agreed on rules for choosing leaders. It required a few more decades for these rules to be internalised. In what Rustow calls the 'preparatory phase' competing parties are organised on the basis of unresolved class conflict and who struggle inconclusively over issues of meaning to them, but generally abide by the rules of the game. In the 'decision phase' compromises on political participation and procedures are reached, and in the 'habituation phase' politicians and citizens come to accept these procedures.[63]

In post-communist countries the preparatory and decision phases have been reversed, with no prolonged period of struggle and compromise to prepare for democratic means of conflict-resolution. Seven decades of communism in Russia denied the people any experience of competitive, multi-party politics. In certain respects, however, Russia is going through both phases simultaneously, and the country remains in the 'preparatory phase' where the struggles between the centre and localities and between the executive and legislative branches, involving profound issues of constitutional structure, have to date been waged by groups who have broadly-speaking abided by basic democratic norms (with the exception of the events of October 1993 and the Chechen wars). Whereas in the 1930s both the left and right condemned what they considered were the discredited and degenerate rules of parliamentarianism and readily took to the streets, in Russia today the only legitimate source of authority is the law and the constitution, and, however much honoured in the breach, the great majority of political actors claim allegiance to these principles.

According to Claus Offe, post-communist countries faced a 'triple transition': the first concerned the definition of citizenship, deciding on who would be 'in' or 'out' of the nation-state and the extent of the borders of that state; the second focuses on the constitution (in the broadest sense) of the polity, the system of governance and administrative practices; while the third is concerned with distributional issues, the parameters of the welfare state and the struggle for resources by organised interests. The decisional logic and the timescales of the three levels differ: the first is long drawnout and involves passions and emotions; the second should be governed by reason and takes decades; while the third is immediate and is determined by power and ego.[64] Although Offe was talking of East Central Europe, these issues are no less central for Russia. However, in addition to establishing a bounded nation, a constitutional polity and deciding on the parameters of the welfare state and the distribution of public goods, Russia faced some additional and more intense challenges: the struggle for a civil society; the transition to a market economy; and the reconstitution of national consciousness to overcome both the legacy of imperial thinking at one extreme, and the problem of minority separatism at the other. The rebuilding of political, economic and administrative structures in Russia would inevitably be long drawnout and attended by national, social and political upheavals. The modernisation of the economy involves the separation of the economy and the polity and the establishment of a new relationship between the two.[65] In the event, the simultaneous transformation of the economy and polity was partial and allowed enclaves of late modernity to coexist with more traditional areas.

There has been a lively debate over the relevance of classical third wave 'transitology' to the post-communist states. Valerie Bunce has argued that in the latter the scale of the tasks is so much greater and the depth of the transition so much more intense, that to compare the earlier transitions in Southern Europe and Latin America with those in Eastern Europe is fundamentally misleading.[66] Rather than the post-communist transitions representing a continuation of the 'third wave', they constitute a fourth wave of their own.[67] The exit from authoritarianism and the struggle for democracy in the post-communist states, it is suggested, is very different from that found elsewhere.[68] Logically, the argument could be taken even further and the post-Soviet transitions (with the possible exception of the Baltic republics, which were only fully incorporated into the Soviet Union in 1944) should perhaps be distinguished from the Central European countries as distinctive 'fifth wave' transitions. The length and depth of the communist experience in the USSR meant that civil society and entrepreneurialism were rooted out far more thoroughly than in the countries that had only relatively recently become communist. In addition, as suggested above, the dialectic between state-building and democratisation in the exit from authoritarianism was distinctive. Indeed, it could be argued that the Soviet Union in its last days under Gorbachev was *more* democratic than the majority of the successor regimes. From 1991 the logic of the national revolutions appeared to run contrary to the dynamism of democratisation. The degree to which this is true of Russia is a matter of considerable controversy.

Rustow's question remains valid: 'What conditions make democracy possible and what conditions make it thrive?'[69] One condition is a stable national and territorial identity, something still lacking in Russia. The delineation of borders precedes the establishment of democracy, but with continuing plans for a union with Belarus, rhetorical commitment to the deepening of integration within the CIS, and dreams of the reconstitution of the USSR, Russia's borders remain negotiable. With the disintegration of the USSR it became clear that the vessel for democracy would be the 15 national states, but in Georgia, Russia and some other republics the debate over borders (both internal and external) is by no means over. Chechnya at first refused to accept its status as a republic within Russia, and some other republics (notably Tatarstan) seek expanded sovereignty. The very nature and scope of Russian federalism remains contested.

Studies of transitions suggest that the struggle between well-entrenched forces can either lead to stalemate or force the creation of institutional arrangements to regulate the struggle.[70] This assumes agreement about the basic 'rules of the game', and it also assumes the presence of autonomous actors with defined social constituencies. The relative amorphousness of the Russian social formation, however, undermines this autonomy and promotes neo-corporatist statism. For example, press freedom is not just a matter of good press laws but also requires an independent financial base for media syndicates. In the West this is derived from advertising revenue, but in Russia the 'oligarchs' stepped in where the market failed, until Putin in turn began to discipline the oligarchs and state-oriented media conglomerates, such as Gazprom-Media, came to the fore. It would take years for democratic rules and conventions to find their expression in organised social interests and in society at large.[71]

### Modernisation and mismodernisation

The relationship between economic and social structures and political authority and rulers, a subject that preoccupied Max Weber, is still not clear. Modernisation theorists would suggest that the Soviet system had been its own gravedigger, modernising society to the extent that it could no longer be constrained by the authoritarian carapace of the Soviet regime. The maturation of Soviet society now led on to the democratic revolution, but the nature of Soviet modernisation was highly ambivalent and so too was its relationship to democracy. Whereas in nineteenth-century Britain democracy was grafted onto a liberal system of property and law, in Russia political democracy was in search of a social base. Soviet-style modernisation was of a distinctive sort that I have dubbed 'mismodernisation'; not to suggest that there is necessarily only one correct form of modernisation, but to reflect the widespread view of Russia's post-communist leaders that the Soviet economy was an inappropriate one in the contemporary world.[72] In his speech of 28 October 1991 Yeltsin observed that the economic basis for statehood had to be sought through land reform, privatisation and the market: 'We have defended political freedom; now we have to give economic freedom.'[73] The democratic revolution came before the bourgeois revolution; political changes preceded the economic and social basis on which they could be rooted. The state itself not only had to maintain order but to take upon itself 'the organisation of enrichment'.[74] This it did in a grand way under Yeltsin – for some. Putin also was unequivocal about the distorted economic structure that Russia inherited from the Soviet system:

> *The current difficult economic and social situation in the country is the price that we have to pay for the economy we inherited from the Soviet Union* [italics in original]. But then, what else could we have inherited? We had to introduce market mechanisms into a system based on completely different standards, with a gigantic and distorted structure. This was bound to affect the progress of the reforms.
>
> We had to pay for the excessive focus of the Soviet economy on the development of the raw materials sector and defence industries, which negatively affected the development of consumer production and services. We are paying for the Soviet neglect of such key sectors as information science, electronics and communications. We are paying for the absence of competition between producers and industries, which inhibited scientific and technological progress and rendered the Russian economy non-competitive in world markets. This is the price to pay for the impediments and bans on initiative and entrepreneurship of companies and workers. Today we are reaping the bitter fruit, both material and intellectual, of past decades.[75]

Modernisation theory was at its most popular in the 1950s and 1960s and suggested two things: echoing Marx, that the more developed societies only showed the less developed ones their own future (the unilinear thesis); and that the social effects of modernisation have certain ineluctable political consequences (the spillover thesis). Over the years Lipset has advanced a cautious version of the spillover thesis.[76] In later years modernisation theory appeared discredited: societies showed a variety of developmental trajectories, and some failed to develop at all; and the effect of socio-economic development on politics was far from clear. After years on the margins, however, modernisation theory was defended by one of its leading exponents, Lucian Pye, who insisted that it was one of the most effective ways of studying the transition from authoritarian regimes. He did warn, however, that democratic outcomes were by no means assured but depended on the outcome of the struggle between national political cultures and the 'world culture' of modernisation.[77] Pye's warning is a necessary corrective to the assumption, so common in 1989, that the fall of the communist regimes would lead to the triumph of liberal values based on economic and political freedom.

Post-communist modernisation theory sought to take into account national peculiarities and distinctive types of modernisation.[78] This is not the place for an extended discussion of the concept of modernisation, but it should be stressed that the whole notion of modernity is ambivalent, and the features that distinguish being 'modern' to being 'non-modern' or traditional have been much contested.[79] Modernity takes many different shapes and forms, and although there may well be a growing underlying convergence (the 'evolutionary universal' noted in the literature) towards the creation of a 'world society', there are plenty of pockets of exceptionalism. Fukuyama argued that there were no sustained universal alternatives to liberal democracy, and Rustow argued that 'A tide of democratic change is sweeping the world',[80] but in many countries the tension between universalism and particularism remains unresolved.

Since Peter the Great Russia has sought to achieve comparability with the West, but in its own way. Under Sergei Witte and Stalin Russia pursued an early industrial pattern of modernisation based on factories and the extensive exploitation of resources and labour. This continued until the fall of the communist regime despite much talk of the 'scientific-technological revolution'. Some sectors like aerospace and parts of the military-industrial complex did make the transition to late industrial patterns, but on the whole the Soviet economy remained locked into an outmoded pattern of industrial activity based on iron and coal technologies. The post-industrial modernisation current in the West is based on the application of information and bio-technologies, the development of service and knowledge-based industries, the shift to the conservation of resources and nature, and the predominance of the consumer over the producer. The overall lack of modernisation of the Soviet economy and polity gave rise to the systemic crisis at the end of the 1980s: enough modernisation had taken place to provoke the systemic crisis identified by Roeder; but this modernisation was of a stunted and distorted type that left the Soviet economy lagging ever further behind the complex modernisation taking place in the West.

Rather than being 'under-developed' in the classic 'Third World' pattern, the Soviet industrialisation drive resulted in a distinctive 'Second World' form of 'misdevelopment'. Extraordinary economic achievements coexisted not only with grotesque waste and catastrophic environmental damage but with distinctly inappropriate technologies for the general level of development of the society. Space missions were launched from the Baikonur cosmodrome, for example, among a people brutalised beyond all measure in Kazakhstan: a third of whom had died during collectivisation in the 1930s and then whole nations, like the Chechens, were dumped in their midst in the 1940s. Factories were built in the wrong place producing goods that people did not want, while the queues lengthened for goods that people needed. Post-communist Russia was faced with the problem not of development as such but of redirecting an already recognisably modern economy from a Second into a First World path. Authors like Ickes and Gaddy suggest that in certain respects it would be easier to allow the old industrial economy to decay and to start from scratch instead of squandering yet more resources on trying to save 'value-subtracting' enterprises.[81]

Attempts at modernisation under Tsarism and the Soviet regime endowed Russia with a relatively developed economic and social infrastructure. The real task from 1991, it appeared, was the *remodernisation* of the economy to make it compatible with world standards. Remodernisation, moreover, was more than just an economic project but also entailed the radical reconstitution of society and the values on which it was based. As Karl Polanyi had long ago argued, the shift to the disciplines of a modern industrial economy from the late eighteenth century in Britain had required a fundamental cultural revolution to market-oriented values, what he called 'the great transformation' – and this is what now faced Russia. Polanyi argued that the 'free market' was an artifact created and sustained by laws that defended private property rights, the law of contract and the rules of market competition, restraining monopolies while advancing the culture of capitalism.[82] For Russia, this meant that the focus of the state's activity was to shift from war and security to market regulation and social arbitration. For patriots, this was seen as part of Russia's Westernisation, but the transformation was deeper than that and could take specifically Russian forms, just as capitalism in the Far East took on Asian characteristics.

Russia's mismodernisation affected not only the economy but also politics and society. As far as society was concerned, Russia lived simultaneously in the modern world and in a world of preindustrial mentalities that survived perhaps more there than elsewhere, shielded from the restless change and reinventions of modern capitalism by statist and autarkic forms of development. Russia appeared to live in several time-worlds simultaneously: traditional family patterns, clan relationships and ethnic affiliations coexisted with the modern world of contractual relationships and individualism. In Russia the peasantry, the great repository of national traditions and culture, was destroyed during collectivisation, but just as ethnic communities were sustained by the Soviet form of ethno-federalism and the passport regime, so traditional relations were reinvented in apparently modern forms of social interaction. The Communist Party itself was a modern invention, yet its structures of rule harked back to early modern patterns of political dominance;[83] and the collective farm appeared post-capitalist yet operated according to the all-embracing rules of a distinctive type of primitive feudalism. Social structures had a dual signification; modernising, yet at the same time adapting to a new type of traditionalism.

Modernisation theorists suggested a strong relationship between socio-economic development and political pluralism. O'Donnell and Schmitter, however, deny the view that a higher level of socio-economic development is a necessary or sufficient condition for the establishment of a pluralistic political system. For them questions of leadership and the political conditions necessary for the stabilisation of democratic processes are in the final analysis decisive. The more developed Latin American countries like Argentina had until recently failed to establish stable democratic systems, whereas a less developed country like Peru had, once again until recently, been more successful. The reverse thesis is no more accurate, that political pluralism is a necessary or a sufficient condition for socio-economic development.[84] Thus one of the more cherished illusions of the *perestroika* years, that Gorbachev's reforms represented the maturation of the USSR's socio-economic development, were placed in doubt.[85] Structural factors certainly help shape the context of post-communist developments but they are not determining. Few generalisations can be made about the relationship between socio-economic structures and political institutions and behaviour; specific historical and cultural factors have to be taken into account.

The transformation in Russia was predicated on the view that not all capitalist countries were democratic, as the experience of Franco's Spain or Hitler's Germany demonstrated, but all democratic countries were capitalist or at least based on some form of market system.[86] Moore agreed with 'the Marxist thesis that a vigorous and independent class of town dwellers has been an indispensable element in the growth of parliamentary democracy', although as we noted in Chapter 14 it may be a necessary but is not a sufficient condition.[87] Numerous American political scientists have stressed the connection between democracy and economic growth.[88] In a perverse way, they reiterated Marx's argument that liberalism and private property were two sides of the same coin. The debate on political development of the post-communist countries stressed the need to restore private property to anchor liberal democratic development in a network of social relationships, and above all in the self-interest of a property-owning class. An economic view of liberalism took precedence over political liberalism.[89] Classical American social science suggests that a substantial middle class is the bastion of stability, progress and democracy; and post-communist policy was designed to build up such a middle class. Privatisation was intended to overcome amorphous social ownership and to create a class of shareholder capitalists, but this was far from making a nation of stakeholder citizens. Privatisers assumed that in Russia the new class of property owners would behave as in post-war Western Europe and North America. Privatised property did begin to generate a new bourgeoisie, but when one of its leading exponents, Mikhail Khodorkovsky, began to make political claims on behalf of the class power of the new order, Putin quickly reasserted the prerogatives of the state. As for the broader development of the middle class, the liberal-Lockean assumption that it will act with moderation, pragmatism and responsibility may prove unfounded.

On the political level misdevelopment meant that Russia's political stage was populated with bodies that carried the same name as those in the West, like political parties, trade unions and so on, but had a very different content. Parliament, too, had to cast off the primitive unanimity imposed by the communist regime, but conflict for the sake of conflict was an equally corrupt expression of political life.[90] The rebirth of politics, therefore, necessitated new bases of political consensus, and this was something that Putin tried to provide. The alternative modernity represented by communism had been demonstrated to be internally incoherent and only sustainable by coercion, and Russia's economic and social misdevelopment was now accompanied by a painful process of remodernisation. The speed of the collapse of communist power, however, left the society unprepared and thus borrowing from the West became the norm; but civilisations cannot be borrowed from abroad or transplanted wholesale into existing societies. Putinism in this context represented the adaptation of reform to Russian conditions.

### Globalisation versus nativisation

The transition in Russia is often considered part of a global democratic revolution in which dictatorships have found it increasingly difficult to isolate themselves from 'the global trend of intensifying communication and economic integration'.[91] The theory (if that is what it can be called) of globalisation represents little more than a variant of modernisation theory, suggesting the irresistible spread of a global capitalist culture forged by ever greater and faster financial and information flows, with nation states reduced to little more than providing a propitious environment for investment, a trained and docile workforce, and political stability.[92] The fate for a large part of the world is not globalisation but marginalisation. The share of world trade of the 49 least-developed countries (LDCs) fell in the 1990s from a measly 0.48 per cent to an even more pathetic 0.4 per cent.[93]

The tension between global and national cultures is increasingly becoming the main line of political confrontation in the post-Cold War world, and takes distinctive forms in post-communist countries. Jadwiga Staniszkis has identified two main tendencies in the transition: the 'globalists' who favour Westernisation and marketisation; and 'populists' who seek to keep the changes within the bounds of what they perceive to be domestic traditions and national interests, retaining a large degree of state control.[94] The question of when a democrat, responsive to popular demands, becomes a populist is a moot one.

Russian presidential policy under Yeltsin at first fell firmly within the globalist framework but was gradually forced from 1994 to make concessions to the 'populists' at home. One of the dynamic contradictions of Putin's leadership is that he appealed simultaneously to patriotic sentiments while committed to liberal marketisation and openness to the West.

Underlying much of the unease about the accelerated integration into world society and to the market economy is the fear that Russia's 'uniqueness' (*samobytnost'*) might be lost. This is a concern shared by the Japanese, Chinese and other major civilisations faced with the apparently relentless tide of globalisation, a phenomenon which for many is no more than another name for Americanisation. These fears in Russia were articulated by patriots, the Communist Party and many others who considered 'democracy' little more than a cover for the loss of national identity and subordination to an amorphous cosmopolitanism. Zyuganov explicitly drew on Samuel Huntington's notion of the 'clash of civilisations' superseding the Cold War ideological struggle to justify his defence of 'the Russian idea'.[95] If Bolshevism in Russia was one form of resistance to Western modernity, then his national communism is another.

Post-communist Russian politics was marked by the struggle between contrasting policies of globalisation and nativisation, although in many instances these views were complementary. For some nativists Russian identity was bound up with notions of a strong state, giving rise to the *derzhavnik* (great power) tendency, but for other nativists (like Solzhenitsyn and Likhachev) Russian identity was more closely bound up with cultural and social values. Support for native traditions, therefore, did not necessarily exclude integration into global economic and social processes. Staniszkis takes a more irreconcilable line, however, taking it as axiomatic that Russian problems of identity and state formation throughout history were resolved through external expansion. In her view, the end of the Soviet Union meant that 'real' expansion (military and political conquest) was replaced by symbolic forms (posturing and manoeuvring to defend Russia's status) until the Chechen war meant that this mimicry was abandoned and traditional forms of state-building were restored. Power allegedly shifted from the Atlanticist to the Eurasianist faction.[96] The argument fails to take into account the powerful countervailing currents in Russian political life. Russian policy often looked confused and contradictory because it *was* confused and torn by contradictory pressures. It is true that Russia's political elites at the centre adopted expansive concepts of military and economic security that encompassed much of the former Soviet territory, but at the same time this policy was pursued on the whole within the formal diplomatic channels available to any power. Russia was notably hesitant about taking Belarus back into the fold, and Ukraine's suspension of Crimea's constitution in 1995 met with a remarkably muted response consistent with the view that the question was Ukraine's internal affair. Under Putin the reassertion of Russian great power ideology was at first accompanied by a 'new realist' attempt to integrate into the international system, and the apparent failure of this strategy and the onset of elements of a new Cold War owes as much to Western intransigence as to Russian obstreporousness.

The very balance between security and democratisation appears to have changed. Russia's history since the Mongol conquest has indeed been marked by a dialectic between external security and internal repression, the fear that domestic divisions could lead to external subjugation. While the end of the Cold War for a time reduced the external threat, the sense of a society under siege did not disappear. Those in favour of authoritarian solutions at home have a vested interest in exaggerating the dangers from

abroad. Unlike the earlier Time of Troubles between 1605 and 1613, when foreign powers took advantage of the dissolution of the regime to seize Moscow, the West has been
broadly supportive of the Russian regime since 1991, although under Putin the reassertion of Russia's perceived geopolitical interests resulted in vigorous attempts to discredit
the democratic credentials of the regime. A satisfactory balance in Russia's relations
with the West has not yet been found. While claims that Russia in the 1990s unconditionally capitulated to the West and ceded its diplomatic and trading (above all arms)
positions are exaggerated, there remains a perceived lack of balance in the relationship
that provoked the post-ideological Cold War discussed earlier.

International factors indeed play a crucial role in democratising transitions. Laurence
Whitehead observes that the most successful transitions are those that do not challenge
the existing alliance system, and which reinforce existing political and economic links.[97]
Events in Eastern Europe, and even more so in the USSR, not only forced the establishment of new security structures and a new balance of power in the region and in
the world as a whole, but even questioned existing borders and gave rise to the birth
of new states. The transition in Eastern Europe and Russia entailed a total transformation of their socio-economic systems and network of international relations. As we have
seen, the extension of NATO to include some of the USSR's former allies provoked an
extended and profound debate in Russia. New forms of geopolitical competition began
to undermine Russian democratisation.

In the contemporary world the debate over the legitimate limits to the scope for markets and the values which inspire them takes the form of a struggle between nativism
and globalisers. Christian socialists have long argued that 'The market system has to be
guarded by moral values if it is not to play havoc with society';[98] and the sentiment was
echoed by various nativising political trends that together comprise various alternative
models of development, including the much-vaunted 'Asian' one. At the centre of the
debate is the proper role of the state. In some Far Eastern countries not only have the first
stages of industrial development been directed by the state, but authoritarian political
systems placed limits on the democratic process on the grounds that fragile communities
required a paternalistic political shield to restrain the destabilising effects of popular
participation. This was certainly the view of the advocates of 'managed democracy' in
Russia, accompanied later by the 'sovereign democracy' view that international competition required the assertion of state power. Markets require states, but for Russia the
major problem was to decide how big the state should be in conditions of economic
and political inter-dependence. Most agreed that the overweening socialist state should
be diminished, but to what extent should its powers be redirected to strategic planning,
discretionary industrial support, infrastructural development, and so on? Attempts to
apply a neo-liberal programme anywhere is fraught with dangers, but in Russia, with its
long tradition of patriarchal community reinforced by the egalitarian rhetoric of Soviet
communism, it was doubly so. But the problem was deeper, and just as the institutions
and practices of democracy take time to develop, so too the culture of market relations,
as Polanyi argued, needs time to mature.

It is useful to compare the democratisation project in Russia with experiences elsewhere. In Africa there has been a long-term failure to institutionalise the democratic
process compensated by the over-bureaucratisation of government.[99] At the same time,
the states are relatively weak because of their inability to find ways of integrating social
structures and interests into the larger state system.[100] Single-party regimes and military

intervention were long considered the only antidotes to ethnic conflict and secessionism. African experience clearly demonstrates that ethnocentric or unilinear models of modernisation have to take into account the spontaneous generation of traditional patterns. In Russia the institutionalisation of civic activity appeared to take root very quickly, overcoming political misdevelopment, yet its fragility encouraged the creation of an authoritarian carapace to manage the transition.

The growing class divisions, the emergence of a concentrated monopolistic pseudo-capitalist elite, semi-privatised and state-owned industries allowing as if by sufferance a capitalist sector, and the absence of a strong middle class reminded many of Latin American patterns.[101] There small elites maintained their rule with the occasional intervention of the military when societal and political contradictions became too great. Russia's destiny appeared not Western Europe but an unstable political order built on a corrupt and unequal social system. This model does have some points in its favour, yet the differences between earlier Latin American patterns and the Russian situation are significant. In Russia, for example, the military did not serve as the midwife of the new polity and therefore lacked the legitimacy to intervene directly in politics. Russia did not have a stable society based on an oligarchic property system developed over the centuries and linked to foreign concerns. The civilian political elite in Russia was able to achieve a relative autonomy from social and military elites, and indeed its isolation was part of the problem and necessitated the generation of alliances and patronage systems with the emerging elite structure. Russia generated its own synthesis of tradition and modernity, of old and new elites, of legal-rationality and charismatic rule.

The enormous destructive creativity and creative destructiveness of Western civilisation embroiled all other cultures and civilisations in its expansive dynamism. Other societies either had to find a way of incorporating Western values within a transformed tradition; or find that tradition ruthlessly subverted and granted only a pastiche of civilisational independence. Russia had been one of the first to confront the problem, and spent much of its modern history inventing strategies to cope with it. After the fall of communism the problem returned with redoubled force. Old debates between Slavophiles and Westernisers, patriots and liberals, were not simply exhumed but re-energised to confront the problems of post-communist Russia, and indeed to respond to universal problems of modernity and modernisation. The liberals were portrayed as a fifth column hastening the disintegration of Russian civilisation; whereas the patriots portrayed themselves as the zealots defending the last citadel of the nation's spiritual identity. The paradox of Russia's post-communist Communists is particularly vivid here: a movement that had begun life as internationalist in the 1990s became patriotic and anti-globalist.

Barrington Moore described three main routes to the 'modern world'; the path of 'bourgeois revolution' that combined capitalism and parliamentary democracy; the reactionary capitalist path that culminated in fascism; and the peasant and/or communist road. The failure of the last two in the twentieth century leaves only the first, although in this respect many are called but few are chosen. The 'modern world' for the great majority and a growing proportion of humanity appears elusive, and the most common path in large parts of the world appears to be underdevelopment (both political and economic) and an inability to reach 'modern society' but to live forever in its shadow. This may be the fate of some of the post-soviet republics, and possibly Russia itself.

# 20  Democracy in Russia

It is absolutely ridiculous to attribute to the high capitalism which is today being imported into Russia and already exists in America – this 'inevitable' economic development – any elective affinity with 'democracy' let alone with 'liberty' (in *any* sense of the word). The question should be: how can these things exist at all for any length of time under the domination of capitalism? In fact they are only possible where they are backed up by the determined *will* of a nation not to be ruled like a flock of sheep.

Max Weber[1]

The problems facing the Russian transition have now become clear, but their solution rather less so. It is still too early to know whether the reconstruction of Russia will take longer than the post-war rebuilding of Germany or Japan, but we do know that it will not be any easier. We cannot even be sure what the end point of this new Russian 'time of troubles' will be: liberalism, neo-socialism, or some new type of authoritarianism. In the years covered by this book Russia underwent a revolution, but a revolution of a distinctive type: mostly not accompanied by bodies of armed men on the streets but a profound revolution of adaptation to a set of norms and governing principles devised elsewhere but at the same time also generated by profound domestic aspirations and pressures. The ambiguity in the reception and incorporation of these norms – of liberal democracy, a market economy and private property, an autonomous arena of public association and a public sphere, individualism and human rights, and international integration – was reflected in the contradictions apparent in Putin's presidency. Rhetorically committed to all of the above, in practice political and social pressures intervened to weaken their fulfilment. A revolution represents a change in power, property and of the ruling class. Russia has undergone an incomplete revolution: the structure of power has changed; property relations are being transformed; but the ruling class and some of its traditional principles of governance remain in place. In this chapter we will provide a brief concluding assessment of the achievements to date.

## Problems of democracy

In the 1990s Russia became caught up in multiple processes of accelerated transition focusing on changes in politics, economics, national identity and culture. The Russian Federation, while in certain respects the successor to the Russian Empire and the Soviet Union, differed from its predecessors politically (in trying to become a democracy), economically (in trying to place market relations at the centre of economic life), geographically (Russia had never existed in its present borders) and civilisationally (joining the international community as an equal). The attempt to change every-thing simultaneously provoked numerous contradictions. Democratisation, for example, entailed the creation of forms of representative government based on popular sovereignty and the rule of law, while the challenge of economic modernisation posed a some-what different set of challenges – privatisation, stable property rights, the weakening of Soviet welfarism, market prices for public goods – whose resolution at times appeared incompatible with democratisation; while the demands of state-building came into con-tradiction with the principles of national self-determination. The Bismarckian Second Reich in Germany at the end of the nineteenth century had been a *Rechtsstaat* (law-based state) rather than a democracy, and post-communist Russia assumed aspects of such an 'illiberal' democracy.

Moore defines democracy as: 'a long and certainly incomplete struggle to do three closely related things: 1) to check arbitrary rulers, 2) to replace arbitrary rules with just and rational ones, and 3) to obtain a share for the underlying population in the making of rules'.[2] In the 1990s Russia only imperfectly achieved these objectives for a variety of reasons. Political demobilisation and problems in structuring political associations was one factor, the hesitant development of democratic state institutions another, while leadership factors were perhaps determining. At the same time, Russia appeared to be a pre-state society in which a pre-political society lived according to its own logic and internal structures. Society appeared to impose its rules on the state, rather than the other way round; while the state once again, as so often in Russia's past, increasingly divorced itself from civil society.

One of the most acute observers of the development of democratic states, Alexis de Tocqueville, argued that the political institutions of America reflected the spirit and ethos of the people.[3] Democracy is both a system of government and a way of life; and it is not clear how democratic institutions could be grafted on to a society whose traditions were apparently antithetical to democratic norms (but see Chapter 15). The mere presence of numerous political parties and a democratic constitution are no guaran-tee of democratic practices. Democracy can only with difficulty be 'built from the roof down' but requires elements of a civic culture like toleration and restraint in society to allow the growth of democracy from below. Tocqueville had warned against 'democratic despotism', although he insisted on the need to create a social state in which popular beliefs (*moeurs*) would sustain a 'free social state'. He noted in *Democracy in America* that 'In America, free mores have made the political institutions freely; in France it is up to the free political institutions to create the mores.' In Russia, too, the political institutions of post-communism were faced with the challenge of developing the social basis on which they could rest. Democracy, in other words, had to create the conditions for its own existence.

The very concept of democracy became an element in intra-elite power struggles and lost much of its allure to society and to the elites themselves. A survey of deputies in legislative assemblies in a sample of Russia's regions (Khabarovsk, St Petersburg and Volgograd), for example, found that out of 89 asked, 43 insisted that Russia could not be characterised as a democratic state, 32 tended to that view, while only 12 answered in the affirmative.[4] How can we explain the emergence of this high level of disenchantment? Part of the problem is the distinction, drawn by Larry Diamond and others, between electoral and consolidated democracy: consolidated democracy is when the practices of government are in conformity with the substantive stipulations of the legal-normative provisions of the constitution (see Table 20.1).[5] The attempt to remake Russian democracy was bound by bureaucratic institutions and traditions. The 'new' political order was a peculiar hybrid: on the one hand, adapting old state structures to new conditions; and, on the other, introducing genuinely new ideas and approaches. It is the unstable balance between these two elements that caused so many problems in the first post-communist years and gave rise to 'a contradiction between the content and form of state power'.[6] The democratic state-building slogans of the early years were trampled in the rush for power and privileges of a narrow political and social elite. While the achievements of democratic institutional building in Russia are substantial and real, they are mediated by asymmetries in access to power and weaknesses in the accountability of that power to society's representatives.

The political system was marked by the following features. First, although formally the presidency under Yeltsin gained enormous powers, its authority and powers were fragmented; the presidential system was prey to factionalism and competing policy lobbies. Under Putin the presidency sought to re-assert its autonomy while at the same time differentiating the state from the economy and unmediated social pressure. Second, the fragmented nature of political authority allowed the 'power' and political ministries, the only bodies with the bureaucratic muscle, to devise and pursue their own agendas and policies, often in contradiction to officially proclaimed policy. Third, the government was relatively marginalised, concerned mainly with the economy. Fourth, while parliament emerged as an effective legislative agency, its political influence was relatively weak because authority had been transferred to the presidency and the government. In terms of principal-agent theory, the accountability of the agent (the executive authorities) to the principal (the sovereign people's representatives in parliament) was extraordinarily weak. Fifth, the numerous political parties did not yet add up to a viable multi-party system. In short, a modified bureaucratic politics model clearly applies to post-communist Russian politics.

Democratisation is usually defined as the extension of mass democracy through active citizenship. The stunted development of popular representation in Russia and the limited reach of parties means that, although formally a democracy, the quality of democratic

*Table 20.1* Five arenas of consolidated democracy

| Arena | Conditions |
| --- | --- |
| Civil society | Self-organising groups, movements and individuals. Articulates values and advances interests. |
| Political society | Legitimate contestation for public power, above all through political parties in multi-candidate elections. |
| Rule of law | Constitutional governance regulated by courts and an impartial judiciary. |
| State efficacy | A usable bureaucracy and governing elite that defends an impartial view of state interests; effective tax and budget processes. |
| Economic society | Set of norms and laws that regulate relations between the state and the market. |

*Source*: Adapted from Juan J. Linz and Alfred Stepan, *Problems of Democratic Transition and Consolidation: Southern Europe, South America, and Post-Communist Europe* (Baltimore, Johns Hopkins University Press, 1996).

life in Russia remains impoverished. Political parties serve more as a means of communicating within the elite and of mobilising ideological and political resources in intra-elite struggle than a way of representing social interests. The communicative functions between state and society are fulfilled more by the mass media, various lobbying groups and by presidential agents than by parties. Parties are an expression of the attempt to institutionalise the diverse interests of civil society, but Russia's fragmented pluralism allows parties only fitfully to achieve this function. No efficient mechanism exist to channel popular feelings into legislative affairs, or then to support parliamentary politics in society. The formation of a structured party system is inhibited by the intrinsic weakness of Russian civil society, by the institutional framework of government, and by the general failure of the legal order to defend the autonomy of social interests. While Putin's reforms of the party system sought to overcome the atomisation of the Russian party system, it failed adequately to ensure the autonomy of the representative system. Some of the cruder forms of the antagonism between state and society ended with the fall of the Soviet system, but the gulf between power and the individual remained. A structured party system is an essential element in pluralist democracy, but only the rudiments of such a system have emerged in Russia.

## Regime politics

The tension between the weakness of the Russian constitutional state (characterised by the inadequate independence of the judicial authorities and poor accountability procedures) and the hypertrophy of the state apparatus promoted the development of what we call 'regime politics'. The elimination of the political monopoly of the CPSU in Russia was not replaced by multi-party governance as such but by a regime system in which power was concentrated in the instruments of executive authority in an unstable relationship with legislative power, popular movements and powerful social interests. The pluralism of the system (however distorted) is not in doubt; what is questionable is the degree to which open democratic forms of adjudicating interests have been institutionalised. The factors which inhibit the development of a multi-party system are not necessarily the same as those which hinder the development of a functioning democratic system, but one way or another the fate of democracy depends on the integration of the new political forces into the system of government (see Table 20.2).

While the main structural features of the old system have disappeared (the one-party state, the command economy, the ubiquitous security system), elements of what Rigby called 'bureaucratic crypto-politics' has continued in a new form.[7] A number of public policy spheres – parliament, the media, business, think tanks and the like – interact but above them all stands a system focused on the presidency. A variety of terms have been advanced to describe the mix of authoritarianism, corporatism, liberalism, managerialism and democracy that has emerged, characterised as authoritarian democracy in the first edition of this book. In the general literature, however, one of the best-known terms is 'delegative democracy'. In weakly established democracies a leader can become so strong that he or she can ignore those who they are meant to represent. O'Donnell characterises these countries as having 'delegative' rather than representative democracy with the electorate allegedly having delegated to the executive the right to do what it sees fit for the country.[8] Thus a government emerges that is 'inherently hostile to the patterns of representation normal in established democracies' by 'depoliticising the population

*Table 20.2* Schematic overview of regime politics

| | |
|---|---|
| 1 | *The state*: The sphere of constitutionality, impartiality and affective loyalty. |
| 2A | *Government*: The arena for decision-making on the basis of political choices and policy debate; government in typical democracies is characterised by the presence of an institutionalised opposition and thus a political process. The government is constrained by a variety of *ex post* and *post facto* accountability mechanisms, above all through a representative assembly. Intra-governmental relations are the subject of much political science debate, and in particular the most effective system to ensure accountability. The distinction between state and government is maintained, even if by a variety of legal fictions, although in practice they have an enormous practical significance. |
| 2B | *Regime*: A government becomes a regime when some fundamental aspects of effective accountability are missing. Democratic transition is all about the shift from regime to government. The regime tends to colonise the institutions of the state, and thus undermines the autonomy of its practices. |
| 3 | *Governance*: This tends to be technocratic and bureaucratic, and thus depoliticised. In the era of globalisation governance has gradually supplanted government, with hived-off agencies carrying out much of the work once conducted by governmental ministries. The state tends to take on a greater regulatory role, often managed by unelected and weakly accountable quangos. |
| 4 | *Civil society and public sphere*: This is where the formal institutions of democracy are rooted in diverse forms of civic engagement and a political culture of responsibility. If demos-development takes place at the level of the nation state, this is the arena for citizen-building. |

except for brief moments in which it demands its plebiscitary support'.[9] A large literature deals with questions of the efficacy and justification of delegative democracy in the context of the developing world, focusing on questions like the function of authoritarian institutions in economic policy-making and the related issue of the role of democratic representation and representative institutions. The evidence suggests no clear conclusion that authoritarian forms of modernisation (as in Taiwan or Singapore) are more effective than in democratic societies, and indeed contemporary thinking highlights the increasing costs associated with authoritarian policy-making.[10]

In Russia the concept of delegative democracy has been fruitfully applied to the study of regional and central politics.[11] It does not, however, adequately convey some of the nuances of the post-communist syndrome, where the elite structure is unstable, social interests fluid, and the relative autonomy of the ruling elite much stronger than, for example, in Latin America, the region for which the term was first devised. Another term that has been used to describe the emerging Russian reality is Fareed Zakaria's notion of 'illiberal democracy'.[12] According to Zakaria, states like Germany in the nineteenth century were ruled by law but were not democracies, and until its reincorporation into China, Hong Kong was also an illiberal democracy. Russia, too, is in principle governed by the norms established by the constitution and the law, but the quality of its democracy remains decidedly thin. However, the tension between economic and political liberalism is blurred by the use of the term, and although it does provide some insights, does not capture the distinctive features of post-communist Russian politics.

We argue that the concept of regime politics best captures the complexity of Russia's semi-consolidated democracy (see Table 20.2). Regime politics limits the scope of democratic consolidation but cannot be defined as full-blown authoritarianism. The 1993 constitution now lies at the basis of the polity, committing Russia to liberal rights and freedoms, the separation of powers, federalism and the rule of law. Although often honoured more in the breach than in practice, these commitments remain at the centre of Russian political life. However, there is a tension, on the one hand, between the formal arrangements outlined in the constitution and succeeding normative acts, what we may call the political system, and, on the other hand, the regime that until Yeltsin's resignation on 31 December 1999 centred on the president himself, his family and associates, and a group (conventionally called 'the oligarchs') that were able to take personal advantage of the grand redistribution of state property to enrich themselves and to become key players in the new system.[13] Yeltsin himself was re-elected in 1996 with the collective support of the oligarchs, who put aside their own divisions to rally around the defence of Yeltsin's regime, fearing that a victory of the CPRF led by Zyuganov would put an end to their dominance. In the event, Yeltsin's second term was characterised by policy drift, Yeltsin's own physical incapacity, and a growing demand for changes to the polity through constitutional reform.

Under Yeltsin there was no clear distinction between the regime and the state, and both succumbed to clientelistic pressures exerted by powerful interests in society, some of whom (above all the so-called oligarchs) the regime itself had spawned. The oligarchy and its allies represented a fusion of financial and industrial capital with direct access to government. The traditional distinction between the market and the state was eroded, and lobbying interests enjoyed an extraordinarily close relationship with government. Russian politics became characterised by the salience not so much of the formal institutional structures of government and management but by informal relationships. Above all, given the weakness of the state, the emergence of what might be termed quasi-state actors became particularly important. For example, the banks (including the Central Bank), and the large energy companies (above all Gazprom), acted as substitute sinews of the state, providing financial resources not available through taxation, and served as indirect enforcers of federal policy, while at the same time ensuring that federal policy was not hostile to their interests. Under Putin the perceived excessive access by big business to the state was ended and the regime was reconfigured. However, it still remained weakly constrained by the norms of the constitutional state or limited by the accountability mechanisms of the representative system.

The tension between system and regime was also one between formal and informal political relationships, between law and politics, and between the institutionalisation and personalisation of political authority. In regime politics personalised leadership inhibits the development of institutions. Behind the formal facade of democratic politics at the level of the state, the regime conducts itself largely free from genuine democratic accountability and popular oversight. If under the Soviet system a 'party-state' had emerged, where the CPSU exercised leadership and prevented the state from gaining political autonomy, then we can describe the system that emerged in the post-communist era as a 'regime-state', where the regime focused on the presidency exerts extra-constitutional authority over the political system as represented in the institutions of the state. Political practices that were once associated with 'the Party' are now exercised by 'the regime'. The result is the continued debilitation of the state, unable to assert the principles of the constitutional autonomy of the state *vis-à-vis* the regime.

We apply the concept of 'regime' to describe not the character of the system as a whole but in the word's other meaning, of a relatively small group of political leaders gaining a certain independence of systemic constraints. Political integration in post-communist Russia takes place at the level of the regime rather than at the level of the political system (the state). The political system is regulated by constitutional norms, laws and judicial decisions; the regime, however, operates according to patterns of personalised ties, patron-client relations and the perpetual struggle to ensure that pluralism remains constrained. The consequences of this pattern of politics are threefold:

1   Although political institutions are established, political processes remain under-institutionalised. They are focused on personalised ties rather than administrative procedures.
2   The greater the institutionalisation of the political system, the more ordered is the state. In Russia, however, not only does the regime undermine the routinisation of systemic power, it is also more broadly parasitic on the state itself. Indeed, an ordered state would threaten the very existence of the relatively autonomous regime. The crisis of the post-communist Russian state, among many other factors, is in part at least due to the emergence of the regime. The state, to use Michael Mann's terms,[14] was unable to develop its infrastructural resources in any consistent way, and instead, at moments of crisis, resorted to the use of despotic force (October 1993, Chechnya) in defence of the regime if not of the state itself. The infrastructural power of the regime is corruption, bribes, electoral manipulation, and indeed the systematic subversion of the constitutional principles of the political system itself. In short, power remains power, and is not converted into authority. Any legitimacy that the regime may have is derived from the delivery of certain public goods, for example rising standards of living, the reduction of wage arrears, and certain intangibles such as the restoration of great power consciousness. These are contingent factors, and given an economic downturn or serious foreign policy failures, could lead to the withdrawal of popular support.
3   In an effective liberal democratic society there is a strange alchemy whereby power is converted into legitimate authority. This alchemy works in other respects as well, above all in the sphere of political economy. Marx devoted his life to understanding the mysterious way that money is converted into capital. In Russia's capitalism this transformation of money into capital has barely begun.[15] Money is only gradually becoming capital, and economic relationships remain heavily administrative rather than determined by the rationality of the juridico-market framework. In a semi-marketised and heavily bureaucratised economy like Russia's personalised links act as the substitute for genuine market relations.

Political and economic interests remain thoroughly entwined. This, however, is not corporatism of the traditional type since each of the three elements traditionally associated with it (the state, employers and labour) were too weak taken individually or together to strike and maintain corporatist deals. Instead, a 'regime system' emerged based on informal but regularised relationships between the major societal interests and the unclear separation between political office and economic concerns. This is accompanied by a hybrid type of 'regime democracy' in which democratic proceduralism is tempered by the manipulation of democratic processes. Russian democracy is not a sham, but neither is it consolidated.

Post-war Japan has also been characterised by a form of regime politics, institutionalised until 1992 by the dominance of the Liberal Democratic Party (LDP) in the Diet and by innumerable informal links with business and other constituencies. A comparison with pre-1989 Italy is also useful. Even the much-vaunted French presidential system is riven by problems and gave rise, according to one observer, to 'the death of politics' under president François Mitterrand, marked by the centralisation of government, the fusion of administrative and political elites, the dominance of the head of state and the corresponding marginalisation of the prime minister, the cabinet and parliament.[16] In Mexico the Party of the Institutional Revolution (PRI) dominated politics for seven decades, and acted not only as the source of patronage but also as the crucible for the aggregation of factional interests.

These international comparisons put into perspective 'culturalist' interpretations of post-communist Russian political development. While Russian traditions, and in particular the legacy of institutional confusion and arbitrariness, played an important part in forming the mental world of those who shaped the post-Soviet system, these traditions on their own are an inadequate explanation for these developments. Reissinger *et al.* have proposed, in a different but equally fruitful context, what they call a 'political economy' perspective which stresses 'the evolving concrete material interests of different members of society during a time of rapid change'.[17] Factors like intra-elite conflict and the political economy of economic reform as much as inherited cultural norms shape post-communist political development. Inherited elites seek to maximise their economic advantages in a time of dramatic opportunities, but equally they seek to underwrite their gains in the political sphere; legal guarantees on their own at a time of 'revolution' (if that, indeed, is what Russia is engaged in) are barely worth the paper on which they are written. Thus the regime system has emerged as a function of the inadequate differentiation between politics and economics and as a response to the political needs of the dominant groups in post-communist Russia.

Regime politics in the post-communist context, however, is not like traditional authoritarianism, and the regime cannot insulate itself from aspects of modern liberal democratic politics like media criticism, parliamentary oversight (if not accountability) and, above all, from the electoral cycle. The legitimacy of new regime-state rests firmly on its commitment to the classical postulates of liberal democracy and to the capitalist economy. Thus regime-type politics looks both ways: backwards to old-style command politics and the bureaucratic regulation of the economy (hence the enormous opportunity for rent-seeking by elites with access to the regime); and forwards, towards the genuine separation of powers, the differentiation of politics from economics, the subordination of politics to law, and the genuine application of democratic choice in elections. Regime politics thus represents a hybrid system, not foreclosing further development towards democracy but at the same time replicating many of the practices associated with the past, although in radically new forms and based on an entirely different legitimating idiom. This is the very mixed legacy of nearly two decades of political change and explains why very different evaluations of this period are possible.

## Leadership and regime change

Yeltsin was above all a master politician, pursuing several policies, often mutually exclusive, simultaneously, and playing off groups and institutions against each other. For most of his rule Yeltsin's appointments were tactical combinations to maintain a balance pivoted on himself. Yeltsinism, like the regime that it led, looked in two directions at once: forwards towards democracy, international integration and a less bureaucratised and genuinely market economy; while at the same time it inherited, and indeed not only perpetuated but also reinforced, many features of the past – the pervasiveness of bureaucratic arbitrariness in politics and the economy, knee-jerk anti-Westernism, pervasive patron-client relations rather than meritocracy, and widespread corruption. This was the legacy facing Putin, and although he continued many features of the regime politics typical of the Yeltsin era, he subjected that regime to significant change.

### Yeltsin's farewell

While it is not unusual for there to be a qualitative difference between the first and second terms of a presidency, no one could have predicted quite how the different the two would be in Yeltsin's case. If in the first term Yeltsin still retained the capacity for policy innovation, in the second he became reactive and lost strategic direction. We now know that Yeltsin's health first started to deteriorate badly in 1995, and soon after his re-election in June-July 1996 he was forced to carry out a multiple heart bypass operation. From at least March 1997 and the establishment of the government of 'young reformers' (represented above all by Boris Nemtsov) it was clear that Yeltsin's main priority was the succession. It is this factor that helps explain the rapid succession of prime ministers from March 1998, when Chernomyrdin was sacked and Sergei Kirienko was appointed in his place.

The MP and political commentator Vyacheslav Nikonov argued that 'we will only be able to talk of Russia as a democratic or civilised state when the country for the first time in its thousand-year history has a constitutional change of power'.[18] In the event, the dénouement to Yeltsin's presidency was as dramatic as the way in which it had been conducted. In his resignation speech of 31 December 1999 Yeltsin asked for forgiveness:

> Not all our dreams came to fulfilment … we thought we could jump from the grey, stagnatory totalitarian past to a light, rich and civilised future in one leap. I believed that myself … But it took more than one jump.

Yeltsin stressed that he was not resigning for health reasons, although it had long been clear that he had been losing his physical powers. Yeltsin's resignation reflected his view that an opportunity had arisen for him to leave the scene without endangering his political achievements. One of Putin's first moves as acting president was to sign a decree granting Yeltsin and future presidents immunity from criminal prosecution, arrest, search or interrogation. The former president was entitled to 75 per cent of his monthly salary, state protection for himself and his family, and access to VIP lounges in Russia's airports, railway stations and ports.[19] While the interests of the country may have been served by Yeltsin's premature exit, democracy was not best served by the timing. As Yeltsin himself admitted in his resignation speech, his premature exit meant that Russia would not see one democratically elected leader transfer power to another in direct accordance with the expectations laid down in the constitution. Instead, there was an attempt to pre-empt the choice of the voters by transferring power to a designated successor for whom the most benign political environment had been established. However, the succession did take place according to the constitutional norms established earlier in the decade, and this was no mean achievement.

For all of its many faults, the Yeltsin era, on the political level at least, was one that did not foreclose the option of democratic development. The basic democratic openings of the late 1980s and early 1990s were not entirely lost, although by the end of the decade undermined. Parliament had not developed effective monitoring mechanisms over the executive, media freedoms were being eroded, in the regions various political fiefdoms were being established, the legal system lacked funding and autonomy, the security services once again began to emerge as an independent political force, and in general the quality of political relations had been degraded by the tawdry pursuit of narrow institutional and personal self-interest. Yet a basically cooperative relationship had been established with the West, no one had been prosecuted for views expressed in the media, and basic political freedoms and rights could be exercised. As the Yeltsin era entered its closing stages, the basic question remained: did the system established by Yeltsin have an evolutionary potential, or did Russia once again have to enter a period of revolutionary upheaval?

### Putin's 'third way'

The accession of Putin to the presidency suggested that the answer was 'no'. He came to power committed to the maintenance of the existing constitutional system, although as we have seen in his early years he engaged in significant para-constitutional change (as in the establishment of the seven federal districts, the State Council and later, the Public Chamber). Putin's politics were centrist, but of a distinctive kind. For Victor Sheinis victory in the December 1999 Duma elections went to a 'quasi-centre',[20] whose basic policy orientations were right-wing (i.e. liberal) economics and left-wing politics: economic liberalism accompanied by statist great power politics. Privatisation and other economic reforms would continue, but allied to the continued iron grip of the bureaucracy over the 'market'. According to him, the elections revealed 'the minimal movement towards a self-sustaining civil society' and 'the isolation of the political class from the deep layers of society'. This gulf between the power system and society was something noted by many other commentators. This is why Sheinis' notion of a quasi-centre is so suggestive. It does not come from a historical convergence on the centre ground of policy, but from the opportunistic cooptation of policies to ensure regime survival.

A genuine 'third way', according to Giddens, is derived not simply from the repudiation of idealised notions of left and right, reflected in traditional class politics, but from attempts to create a genuinely radical politics of the centre.[21] While the 'third way' in the West was an attempt to come to terms with the apparent exhaustion of traditional social democracy and represents an attempt to renew it, Russia's third way, or genuine politics of the centre, is drawn from an older tradition, liberal conservatism. Writers like Peter Struve and Semyon Frank were drawn on to sustain the emerging consensus over a Russian 'third way' based on support for the reconstitution of state authority while continuing market reforms and international economic integration. Under Putin the outlines of a distinctive Russian 'third way' emerged, although shot through with contradictions. The politics of Russia's third way emerge out of traditional 'centrist' positions but the degree to which they represent a development of them is unclear.

Putinism reflects the political amorphousnous of the quasi-centre but at the same time potentially transcends it. His intensification of the reforms after 2000 represented a second wave of liberal transformation of Russia. The framework, however, was more statist than under Yeltsin, leading to suggestions that his policies represented a programme of authoritarian modernisation; attacking economic institutions and social practices inherited from the Soviet period while reasserting elements of Soviet-style centralisation. Putin systematically dismantled the system of checks and balances that had been established during Yeltsin's rule, basing his power on both bureaucratic and charismatic elements. Putin himself remains an enigma. It was clear that support for Putin in the 2000 presidential elections was not based on any real appreciation of his policies, since other than the vigorous pursuit of the war in Chechnya, it was unclear what these policies were. Instead support went to mythologised conceptions of what he was taken to represent: youth and vigour in contrast to Yeltsin's senescent debility; the impersonal pursuit of Russian national goals as opposed to selfish and irresponsible pursuit of enrichment and aggrandisement of personal power by Yeltsin and his acolytes; the continuation of economic reform accompanied by a crackdown on corruption, lawlessness and banditry; good relations with the West based on genuine partnership rather than Russian kowtowing to Washington. Some of these mythologised representations turned out to be accurate but, perhaps more importantly, the extraordinary speed and scale of his rise reflected Yeltsin's own political trajectory in the late 1980s, suggesting the need for hero figures in Russian politics, unconnected with parties, programmes or specific interests.

Putin's room for manoeuvre was limited, with the scope for radical political intervention and change constrained by earlier institutional development and by Russia's socio-economic structure. In his 'Russia at the Turn of the Millennium', which we have already cited, in the last days of 1999 Putin was evidently trying to move beyond traditional amorphous definitions of centrism towards a more radical future-oriented model.[22] Putin committed himself to the maintenance of the existing constitution, a policy of political stabilisation accompanied by capitalist modernisation, and the attempt to return Russia to a native model of development. His basic approach was a statist and socially oriented model of liberal capitalism. He did not directly challenge the economic and political privileges and semi-feudal power of the neo-*nomenklatura* elite, although he did distance it from direct access to the state and thus undermined one of the central elements of Yeltsin-style regime politics. Putin sought to transform his broad but shallow political support into a genuine political coalition, but his tendency to rely on administrative methods to do so undermined the autonomous development of representative parties and interests in society. Putin's leadership represented the triumph of a nativist strand of liberal patriotism; but as the development of the national liberals in late nineteenth century Germany showed, there are many dangers associated with this combination.

## A struggling democracy?

Yelena Bonner criticised Yeltsin for not taking stronger action following the coup in 1991: Yeltsin should have discarded democratic principles for the sake of expediency, dissolved the Russian parliament, and held new elections. This would have made possible economic reform and constitutional government. 'We lost our August victory … The hope that it could be built on and developed by parliamentary means was Yeltsin's main historic error.[23] Sergei Stankevich, a political adviser to Yeltsin in the immediate post-coup period, talked of 'Russia's lost decade of reform'. While Poland had turned the economic corner in 1994 and thereafter registered strong growth and low inflation, Russia remained on an economic and political precipice even after steady economic growth resumed in 2000. Political stabilisation in Poland was based on the rise of a middle class that provided some 60 per cent of the country's GDP, while in Russia whatever advances had been made by the middle class were knocked back by the August 1998 crisis and were only slowly restored thereafter. In Russia the presidency, in Stankevich's words, waged 'a permanent Cold War against parliament' and 'regional barons' pursued separatist agendas, facilitated by the lack of a national party system. After a lost decade of reforms Russia, in Stankevich's view, the country had returned to almost the same situation it had been in at the beginning of the 1990s, with the difference that the idea of reform itself had been discredited.[24]

### Weimar Russia

The tension between democracy, order and economic liberalisation remain unresolved. The apparent democratic consensus among the political elite in the early post-Soviet period soon dissolved and gave way to a complex interaction between democratisation and authoritarianism. Agreement on the basic rules of the political game at the fall of communism was undermined by the struggle between the president and parliament that led to October 1993, and doubts over the legitimacy of the new constitution and disagreement over its provisions means that the 'polity' question, the shape of the constitutional order, remains open. The factionalisation of politics, the concentration of power in court attendants and bodyguards, the arbitrary rule of bureaucrats, the growth of corruption and the unpredictability of government suggested that Russia's democratic experiment has run into the sands. The fundamental question is whether the constitutional order inaugurated in the early 1990s is robust enough to allow political and constitutional evolution within its framework, or whether some new system should be devised. As so often in the past, the choice lay between evolution and revolution.

Rather than 'the transition' inexorably leading to a liberal democracy of the Western sort, by the end of Putin's presidency there was fear that the democratic aspirations of the *perestroika* years and the achievements of the early post-communist period were being undermined. The moral outrage that had been the hallmark of popular politics during *perestroika* gave way to political demobilisation. The concept of democracy remains tarnished, while the word is still often used as a term of opprobrium. The credibility gap between the statements of the leadership and the realities of daily life gave rise to what has been called a 'mistrust culture' and a pervading sense of social nihilism. While socialism in the early Soviet years had been built with enthusiasm, capitalism was now being built with resignation and a sullen sense of betrayal.

The long shadow of 1917 warned of the danger from the left, while the destruction of inter-war German democracy provided an equally strong warning of the threat from the right. A constituency for non-democratic authoritarianism and populism clearly existed in the form of disgruntled communists and chauvinistic nationalists, fuelled by the loss of a clear national purpose and by squabbling elites. The rejectionists considered the Belovezh Accords an act of treason akin to the alleged betrayal of the military by civilian politicians in Germany in 1918–19, and this was gradually woven into a national-patriotic counter-myth which considered Yeltsin, and increasingly Putin too, as 'traitors' to Russia. Extremist forces lurked to left and right waiting to take advantage of social unrest and economic dislocation, much as Hitler took advantage of the weakness of the Weimar republic. Before his death in 1920 Max Weber had voiced doubts about the viability of democracy in Germany following the collapse of the Second Reich in 1918, and insisted that Germany needed a strong leader of a plebiscitary or Caesarist type like Bismarck.[25] The fate of Weimar Germany and the rise of Hitler seemed to bear out Weber's pessimism.

The applicability of the 'Weimar Russia' scenario, however, should be tempered by the fact that the world of the 1990s and 2000s is a very different one from that of the 1920s or 1930s, or indeed from the world torn by war in 1917. The growth of economic interdependence, a dense network of human rights legislation and international organisations, all raise the threshold of toleration that extremist reaction would have to negotiate. In addition, for all its faults the Soviet regime had appealed to a form of democratic legitimacy and values that were supportive of democracy, whereas the Wilhelmine Reich had espoused militaristic and elitist values. Nor is it clear what the social basis for fascism or a recrudescent communism in Russia would be. The middle class in Weimar Germany never really accepted 'bourgeois democracy' in the interwar years, whereas in Russia the nascent middle class and the intelligentsia aspire to live like their counterparts in the West. The analogy with inter-war Germany is instructive but not wholly appropriate. A society that has just freed itself from 70-odd years of dictatorship is hardly likely to embrace another so soon; the idea of dictatorship remains deeply unpopular among Russians. While the values of order and democracy are often contrasted in public opinion polls, it seems clear that a combination of both is the desired social ideal for the mass of Russians.

### *Towards democracy?*

Russia today has a hybrid political system, combining elements of both democracy and authoritarianism. The freedoms that had begun during *glasnost* blossomed into genuine freedom of speech and the press, and the variety of publications and the openness of their content is unparalleled in Russia's history. Censorship is explicitly forbidden and only the courts can permanently ban newspapers, and then only on specific grounds and after due warning. However, the assault against the privileges of certain oligarchs under Putin appeared to threaten the independence of radio and television. Corruption marred the development of Russia as a democracy. While the old regime lacked freedom, it did at least ensure a degree of security. The new freedoms after the fall of communism have been accompanied by such a degree of job and physical insecurity that many yearn for the old days. The interpenetration of organised crime and politics led some to argue that Russia's second revolution had been 'stolen' by an unholy alliance of communists-turned-speculators and the criminal underworld.

The hybrid nature of authoritarianism democracy in Russia arose out of the conflict between ends and means and had a dual function: to undermine the old structures of social and political power, while at the same time to provide the framework for the growth of democratic forms that could ultimately stand on their own. The second or maturity phase of the democratic revolution is marked by free and *fair* elections, the establishment of the 'civic culture' of toleration and institutionalised conflict over resources and decisions, and a peaceful and fully constitutional change of government. Regime-based politics probably only represents a phase in Russian politics, and sources of weakness became increasingly apparent. The development of a more robust and autonomous party system, for example, would offer an alternative means of national integration and popular representation. Under Putin, moreover, federal politics became more insulated from the pressures of economic interests, and the presidency operated less as a free-loading operator in the interstices of the state and society, as it had done under Yeltsin, but as part of a state order seeking support in society.

The fall of communism was one of the greatest events in European and Asian history. The disintegration of the USSR was accompanied by the reversal of the centuries-long Russian process of the 'gathering' of the lands. While the transitions in some of the East European countries entailed elements of redemocratisation, the reprivatisation of property and the reliberalisation of social relations as a whole, there was little 're' about Russia's transition, except the rediscovery and recovery of native memory and indigenous traditions and remodernisation. The social, economic and political infrastructure of democratic and liberal systems had to be built for the first time with building blocks that had been thoroughly subverted by the Bolshevik attempt to create an alternative modernity. Ken Jowitt notes the multiple fragmentation in what he calls the post-Leninist world, and stresses the ambiguities in the political culture:

> To put it bluntly: the Leninist legacy, understood as the impact of Party organisation, practice, and ethos, *and* the initial charismatic ethical opposition to it favour an authoritarian, not a liberal democratic capitalist, way of life; the obstacles to which are not simply how to privatise and marketise the economy, or organise an electoral campaign, but rather how to institutionalise public virtues.[26]

The dramatic changes in the economy and polity would be inadequate if the public side of human identity was not also cherished, and a way found to establish a balance between 'ethics' and 'interests'.

While to all intents and purposes 'the transition' in Russia is largely over, it is still too early to talk of the establishment of a functioning democracy. The multi-party system is embryonic, the legal system mired in the problems of the past, and elections have been less than fair. Solzhenitsyn condemned Russia's new 'false democracy' and described Russia's retreat from communism as 'the clumsiest and most painful possible' imposing yet another 'heartless experiment on unhappy Russia'.[27] The very project of democracy did not command universal legitimacy. For many, like Metropolitan Innokenti of Khabarovsk, democracy in Russia was a transitional phenomenon and would in time disappear altogether to be replaced (perhaps in a generation or two) by something more in the Russian tradition of *sobornost'*. For national patriots, liberal democracy is antithetical to Russian traditions and cannot provide a solution to problems that are distinctively Russian.

So does Russia have no more than a simulacrum of democracy, a parody of the rule of law, trapped in a cycle of 'democratisation' but unable to achieve democracy itself? There are no guarantees that the moment of liberation following the fall of communist power will be anchored in effective democratic institutions and processes. The greatest achievement of the post-Soviet system in Russia is not the establishment of democracy, a task that will take many years and which in any case is ambiguous, but the restoration of the autonomy of politics, the beginning of open contention over policy and the role of the state. The restoration of politics means the end of the totalitarian impulse and is the first but essential step on the road to liberal democracy. The Russian transition is an attempt to provide an institutional framework for pluralism in society, to guarantee property rights and to overcome Russia's isolation from global processes. While democratic institutions have appeared, it will take longer for the democratic culture and economic structures that can sustain them to emerge, for the unwritten rules of convention to reinforce the written word of the constitution. The first post-communist Russian leaderships laid the foundations of a new political order in the belief that Russia could only enter world civilisation if it remade its own. At the beginning of the twenty-first century it is clear that both Russia *and* the world face challenges that cannot be resolved in isolation from each other.

# Appendix    The Russian constitution

We, the multinational people of the Russian Federation,

   united by a common destiny on our land,

   asserting human rights and freedoms and civil peace and concord,

   preserving historically established state unity,

   proceeding from the generally recognized principles of the equality and self-determination of peoples,

   revering the memory of our forebears who passed down to us love and respect for the Fatherland and faith in goodness and justice,

   reviving the sovereign statehood of Russia and asserting the immutability of its democratic foundations,

   seeking to ensure the well-being and prosperity of Russia,

   proceeding from responsibility for our homeland to present and future generations,

   recognizing ourselves as part of the world community,

   adopt the CONSTITUTION OF THE RUSSIAN FEDERATION.

## Section one

### Chapter 1 Foundations of the constitutional system

*Article 1*

(1)   The Russian Federation-Russia is a democratic federative rule-of-law state with a republican form of government.

(2)   The names Russian Federation and Russia are of equal validity.

*Article 2*

The individual and his rights and freedoms are the supreme value. Recognition, observance and protection of human and civil rights and freedoms is the obligation of the state.

*Article 3*

(1)   The holder of sovereignty and the sole source of authority in the Russian Federation is its multinational people.

(2)   The people exercise their authority directly and also through bodies of state power and bodies of local self-government.

(3) The supreme direct expression of the authority of the people is the referendum and free elections.

(4) Nobody can arrogate power in the Russian Federation. The seizure of power or the arrogation of powers are prosecuted in accordance with federal law.

## Article 4

(1) The sovereignty of the Russian Federation extends to the whole of its territory.

(2) The constitution of the Russian Federation and federal laws are paramount throughout the territory of the Russian Federation.

(3) The Russian Federation ensures the integrity and inviolability of its territory.

## Article 5

(1) The Russian Federation consists of republics, krais, oblasts, cities of federal significance, an autonomous oblast and autonomous okrugs which are equal components of the Russian Federation.

(2) A republic (state) has its own constitution and legislation. A krai, oblast, city of federal significance, autonomous oblast or autonomous okrug has its own charter and legislation.

(3) The federal structure of the Russian Federation is based on its state integrity, the unity of the system of state power, the delimitation of areas of responsibility and powers between bodies of state power of the Russian Federation and bodies of state power of the components of the Russian Federation, and the equality and self-determination of the peoples in the Russian Federation.

(4) All components of the Russian Federation are equal with each other in inter-relationships with federal bodies of state power.

## Article 6

(1) Citizenship of the Russian Federation is acquired and terminated in accordance with federal law and is uniform and equal irrespective of the basis on which it is acquired.

(2) Each citizen of the Russian Federation possesses all rights and freedoms on its territory and bears equal obligations stipulated by the constitution of the Russian Federation.

(3) A citizen of the Russian Federation cannot be deprived of his citizenship or of the right to change it.

## Article 7

(1) The Russian Federation is a social state whose policy is aimed at creating conditions ensuring a worthy life and free development of the individual.

(2) In the Russian Federation people's labour and health are protected, a guaranteed minimum wage is established, state support is insured for the family, mothers, fathers, children, invalids and elderly citizens, the system of the social services is developed, and state pensions, allowances and other guarantees of social protection are established.

*Article 8*

(1)  In the Russian Federation the unity of the economic area, the free movement of goods, services and financial resources, support for competition and freedom of economic activity are guaranteed.

(2)  In the Russian Federation private, state, municipal, and other forms of property enjoy equal recognition and protection.

*Article 9*

(1)  The land and other natural resources are utilized and protected in the Russian Federation as the basis of the life and activity of the peoples inhabiting the corresponding territory.

(2)  The land and other natural resources can be in private, state, municipal or other forms of ownership.

*Article 10*

State power in the Russian Federation is exercised on the basis of the separation of legislative, executive and judicial powers. Bodies of legislative, executive and judicial power are independent.

*Article 11*

(1)  State power in the Russian Federation is exercised by the president of the Russian Federation, the Federal Assembly (the Federation Council and the State Duma), the government of the Russian Federation and the courts of the Russian Federation.

(2)  State power in the components of the Russian Federation is exercised by the bodies of state power formed by them.

(3)  The delimitation of areas of responsibility and powers – between bodies of state power of the Russian Federation and bodies of state power of components of the Russian Federation is effected by the present constitution and the Federation Treaty and other treaties concerning the delimitation of areas of responsibility and powers.

*Article 12*

In the Russian Federation local self-government is recognized and guaranteed. Within the limits of its powers local self-government is independent. Bodies of local self-government do not form part of the system of bodies of state power.

*Article 13*

(1)  In the Russian Federation ideological diversity is recognized.

(2)  No ideology may be established as the state ideology or as a compulsory ideology.

(3)  In the Russian Federation political diversity and a multiparty system are recognized.

(4)  Social associations are equal before the law.

(5)  The creation and activity of social associations whose objectives and actions are directed towards the forcible alteration of the basic principles of the constitutional

system and the violation of the integrity of the Russian Federation, the undermining of the security of the state, the creation of armed formations, or the fuelling of social, racial, national or religious strife are prohibited.

## Article 14

(1) The Russian Federation is a secular state. No religion may be established as the state religion or a compulsory religion.
(2) Religious associations are separated from the state and are equal before the law.

## Article 15

(1) The constitution of the Russian Federation has supreme legal force and is direct-acting and applies throughout the territory of the Russian Federation. Laws and other legal enactments adopted in the Russian Federation must not contradict the constitution of the Russian Federation.
(2) Bodies of state power, bodies of local self-government, officials, citizens and associations thereof are obliged to observe the constitution of the Russian Federation and the laws.
(3) Laws are subject to official publication. Unpublished laws are not applied. Any normative legal enactments affecting human and civil rights, freedoms and duties cannot be applied unless they have been officially published for universal information.
(4) The generally recognized principles and norms of international law and the international treaties of the Russian Federation are a component part of its legal system. If an international treaty of the Russian Federation establishes other rules other than those stipulated by the law, the rules of the international treaty apply.

## Article 16

(1) The provisions of the present chapter of the constitution form the basic principles of the constitutional system of the Russian Federation and cannot be altered except by the procedure laid down by the present constitution.
(2) No other provisions of the present constitution can contradict the basic principles of the constitutional system of the Russian Federation.

## Chapter 2 Human and civil rights and freedoms

### Article 17

(1) Human and civil rights and freedoms are guaranteed in the Russian Federation in accordance with generally recognized principles and norms of international law and in conformity with the present constitution.
(2) Basic human rights and freedoms are inalienable and belong to each person from birth onwards.
(3) The exercise of human and civil rights and freedoms must not violate the rights and freedoms of others.

*Article 18*

Human and civil rights and freedoms are direct-acting. They determine the meaning, content and application of laws and the activity of the legislative and executive branches and of local self-government and are safeguarded by justice.

*Article 19*

(1)   All are equal before the law and the courts.
(2)   The state guarantees equality of human and civil rights and freedoms regardless of sex, race, nationality, language, origin, property and position, place of residence, attitude towards religion, convictions, membership of public associations and also other circumstances. Any forms of restriction of citizens' rights on grounds of social, racial, national, linguistic or religious affiliation are prohibited.
(3)   Men and women have equal rights and freedoms and equal opportunities to exercise them.

*Article 20*

(1)   Each person has the right to life.
(2)   Until its abolition the death penalty can be prescribed by federal law as the supreme penalty for particularly grave crimes against life, the accused being granted the right to trial by jury.

*Article 21*

(1)   The dignity of the individual is protected by the state. Nothing may be grounds for disparaging it.
(2)   No one must be subjected to torture, violence or other brutal or humiliating treatment or punishment. No one may be subjected to medical, scientific or other experiments without their voluntary consent.

*Article 22*

(1)   Each person has the right to freedom and inviolability of the person.
(2)   Arrest, taking into custody and keeping in custody are permitted only by judicial decision. An individual cannot be detained for a period of more than 48 hours without a judicial decision.

*Article 23*

(1)   Each person has the right to inviolability of his private life, individual and family privacy, and defence of his honour and good name.
(2)   Each person has the right to privacy of correspondence, telephone conversations and postal, telegraph and other communications. Limitation of this right is permitted only on the basis of a judicial decision.

*Article 24*

(1)   The collection, storage, utilization and dissemination of information about a person's private life without his consent are not permitted.
(2)   Bodies of state power and bodies of local self-government and their officials are obliged to ensure that each person has the opportunity to see documents and materials directly affecting his rights and freedoms unless otherwise provided by law.

*Article 25*

Dwellings are inviolable. No one is entitled to enter a dwelling against the wishes of the persons residing there except in cases prescribed by federal law or on the basis of a judicial decision.

*Article 26*

(1)   Each person is entitled to determine and indicate his own nationality. No one may be compelled to determine and indicate his own nationality.
(2)   Each person has the right to use his native language and to the free choice of language of communication, education, instruction and creativity.

*Article 27*

(1)   Each person who is legally present on the territory of the Russian Federation has the right to travel freely and choose his place of stay and residence.
(2)   Each person may freely travel outside the Russian Federation. The citizen of the Russian Federation has the right to return without impediment to the Russian Federation.

*Article 28*

Each person is guaranteed freedom of conscience and freedom of religion, including the right to profess any religion individually or together with others or not to profess any, and freely to choose, hold and disseminate religious and other convictions and to act in accordance with them.

*Article 29*

(1)   Each person is guaranteed freedom of thought and speech.
(2)   Propaganda or agitation exciting social, racial, national or religious hatred and enmity is not permitted. Propaganda of social, racial, national, religious or linguistic supremacy is prohibited.
(3)   No one may be compelled to express his opinions and convictions or to renounce them.
(4)   Each person has the right freely to seek, receive, pass on, produce and disseminate information by any legal method. The list of information constituting a state secret is determined by federal law.
(5)   The freedom of mass information is guaranteed. Censorship is prohibited.

*Article 30*

(1)   Each person has the right of association, including the right to create trade unions to protect his interests. The freedom of the activity of public associations is guaranteed.
(2)   No one may be compelled to join or to remain any association.

*Article 31*

Citizens of the Russian Federation have the right to assemble peacefully without weapons and to hold meetings, rallies and demonstrations, processions and pickets.

*Article 32*

(1)   Citizens of the Russian Federation have the right to take part in the administration of the state's affairs both directly and via their representatives.
(2)   Citizens of the Russian Federation have the right to elect and to be elected to bodies of state power and bodies of local self-government, and also to take part in referendums.
(3)   Citizens deemed incompetent by a court and also those detained in places of imprisonment by sentence of a court do not have the right to elect and to be elected.
(4)   Citizens of the Russian Federation have equal access to state service.
(5)   Citizens of the Russian Federation have the right to take part in the administration of justice.

*Article 33*

Citizens of the Russian Federation have the right to appeal personally and also to send individual and collective appeals to state bodies and bodies of local self-government.

*Article 34*

(1)   Each person has the right to make free use of his abilities and property for purposes of entrepreneurial activity and other economic activity not prohibited by law.
(2)   Economic activity directed towards monopolization and unscrupulous competition is not permitted.

*Article 35*

(1)   The right of private ownership is protected by law.
(2)   Each person is entitled to own property and to possess, utilize and dispose of it both individually and together with others.
(3)   No one may be deprived of his property except by court decision. The compulsory expropriation of property for state requirements may be carried out only if full compensation is paid in advance.
(4)   The right of inheritance is guaranteed.

*Article 36*

(1)  Citizens and their associations are entitled to hold land in private ownership.
(2)  Owners freely possess, utilize and dispose of land and other natural resources provided that this does not damage the environment and does not violate the rights and legitimate interests of others.
(3)  The conditions and procedure for the use of land are defined on the basis of federal law.

*Article 37*

(1)  Labour is free. Each person has the right freely to dispose of his abilities for labour and to choose a type of activity and occupation.
(2)  Forced labour is prohibited.
(3)  Each person has the right to work in conditions meeting the requirements of safety and hygiene and to receive remuneration for labour without any discrimination and of not less than the minimum pay prescribed by federal law, and also the right to protection from unemployment.
(4)  The right to individual and collective labour disputes utilizing the methods of solving them prescribed by federal law, including the right to strike, is recognized.
(5)  Each person has the right to leisure. Persons working on the basis of a labour contract are guaranteed the working hours, days off and holidays prescribed by federal law and paid annual leave.

*Article 38*

(1)  Maternity and childhood and the family are under the state's protection.
(2)  Concern for children and their upbringing are the equal right and duty of the parents.
(3)  Able-bodied children who have reached the age of 18 years must look after disabled parents.

*Article 39*

(1)  Each person is guaranteed social security in old age, in the event of sickness, disability or loss of breadwinner, for the raising of children, and in other cases prescribed by law.
(2)  State pensions and social benefits are prescribed by law.
(3)  Voluntary social insurance, the creation of additional forms of social security and charity are encouraged.

*Article 40*

(1)  Each person has the right to housing. No one may be arbitrarily deprived of housing.
(2)  Bodies of state power and bodies of local self-government encourage housing construction and create the conditions for exercise of the right to housing.

(3)   Housing is provided free or at affordable cost to low-income and other citizens indicated in the law who require housing from state, municipal and other housing stocks in accordance with the norms prescribed by law.

## Article 41

(1)   Each person has the right to health care and medical assistance. Medical assistance in state and municipal health care establishments is provided free to citizens by means of funds from the relevant budget, insurance contributions and other revenue.
(2)   In the Russian Federation federal programmes to protect and strengthen the population's health are financed, measures to develop state, municipal and private health care systems are taken, and activities conducive to the strengthening of people's health, the development of physical culture and sport, and ecological and sanitary and epidemiological well-being are encouraged.
(3)   The concealment by officials of facts and circumstances creating a threat to people's lives and health entails responsibility in accordance with federal law.

## Article 42

Each person has the right to a decent environment, reliable information about the state of the environment and compensation for damage caused to his health or property by ecological offences.

## Article 43

(1)   Each person has the right to education.
(2)   General access to free pre-school, basic general and secondary vocational education in state or municipal educational establishments and in enterprises is guaranteed.
(3)   Each person is entitled on a competitive basis to receive free higher education in a state or municipal educational establishment or in an enterprise.
(4)   Basic general education is compulsory. Parents or persons in loco parentis ensure that children receive basic general education.
(5)   The Russian Federation establishes federal state educational standards and supports various forms of education and self-education.

## Article 44

(1)   Each person is guaranteed freedom of literary, artistic, scientific, technical and other types of creation and teaching. Intellectual property is protected by law.
(2)   Each person has the right to participate in cultural life and use cultural institutions and to have access to cultural treasures.
(3)   Each person must display concern for preserving the historical and cultural heritage and look after historical and cultural monuments.

## Article 45

(1)   State protection of human and civil rights and freedoms in the Russian Federation is guaranteed.

(2) Each person is entitled to protect his rights and freedoms by any methods not prohibited by law.

## Article 46

(1) Each person is guaranteed judicial protection of his rights and freedoms.
(2) The decisions and actions (or inaction) of bodies of state power, bodies of local self-government, public associations and officials can be appealed in court.
(3) Each person is entitled, in accordance with the Russian Federation's international treaties, to appeal to interstate bodies for the protection of human rights and freedoms if all available means of legal protection inside the state have been exhausted.

## Article 47

(1) No one can be deprived of the right to have the case against him heard by the court and the judges to whose jurisdiction it is assigned by the law.
(2) Anyone accused of having committed a crime has the right to have the case against him heard by a court and jury as provided by federal law.

## Article 48

(1) Each person is guaranteed the right to receive qualified legal assistance. Legal aid is rendered free of charge as provided by law.
(2) Each detainee held in custody and accused of having committed a crime has the right to benefit from the assistance of a lawyer (defence attorney) from the moment of his detention, placing in custody, or indictment respectively.

## Article 49

(1) Each person accused of having committed a crime is presumed innocent until his guilt is proved as provided by federal law and established by means of a legitimate court sentence.
(2) The accused is not obliged to prove his innocence.
(3) Any undispelled doubts regarding the individual's guilt are interpreted in the accused's favour.

## Article 50

(1) No one can be tried a second time for the same crime.
(2) The use of any proof acquired in breach of the federal law is not permitted in the administration of justice.
(3) Each person sentenced for a crime has the right to have his sentence reviewed by a superior court as provided by federal law, as well as the right to appeal for pardon or a reduction of sentence.

*Article 51*

(1)  No one is obliged to testify against himself or against his spouse or close relatives, the range of the latter being defined by federal law.
(2)  Other instances when the obligation to give evidence is lifted can be laid down by federal law.

*Article 52*

The rights of the victims of crimes or of abuses of power are protected by law. The state guarantees the victims's access to justice and to compensation for damage caused.

*Article 53*

Each person has the right to compensation from the state for damage caused by the unlawful action (or inaction) of bodies of state power or their officials.

*Article 54*

(1)  No law establishing or mitigating liability can be retroactive.
(2)  No one can be held liable for any act which, at the time it was committed, was not considered to be in breach of the law. If liability for a breach of the law is abolished or mitigated after an act has been committed, the new law is applied.

*Article 55*

(1)  The listing of basic rights and freedoms in the constitution of the Russian Federation must not be interpreted as negating or diminishing other universally recognized human and civil rights and freedoms.
(2)  Laws abolishing or diminishing human and civil rights and freedoms must not be promulgated in the Russian Federation.
(3)  Human and civil rights and freedoms can be curtailed by federal law only to the extent to which is may be necessary for the purpose of protecting the foundations of the constitutional system, morality and the health, rights and legitimate interests of other individuals, or of ensuring the country's defence and the state's security.

*Article 56*

(1)  Individual restrictions of rights and freedoms can be introduced, with an indication of their extent and duration, in a state of emergency in order to ensure the safety of citizens and the protection of the constitutional system in accordance with federal constitutional law.
(2)  A state of emergency may be introduced throughout the territory of the Russian Federation or in individual localities thereof in the circumstances and according to the procedure provided by federal constitutional law.
(3)  The rights and freedoms contained in Articles 20, 21, 23 (Part 1), 24, 28, 34 (Part 1), 40 (Part 1) and 46–54 of the constitution of the Russian Federation may not be restricted.

*Article 57*

Each person is obliged to pay legitimately levied taxes and duties. Laws introducing new taxes or detrimental to the taxpayers' situation cannot be retroactive.

*Article 58*

Each person is obliged to protect nature and the environment and to show solicitude for natural wealth.

*Article 59*

(1)   The protection of the fatherland is the duty and obligation of citizens of the Russian Federation.
(2)   Citizens of the Russian Federation perform military service as provided by federal law.
(3)   In the event that the convictions or religious beliefs of a citizen of the Russian Federation are at odds with the performance of military service, as well as in other instances as provided by federal law, the citizen has the right to perform alternative civil service as a substitute.

*Article 60*

A citizen of the Russian Federation can autonomously exercise his rights and obligations in full from the age of 18 years.

*Article 61*

(1)   A citizen of the Russian Federation cannot be expelled from the Russian Federation or extradited to another state.
(2)   The Russian Federation guarantees the protection and patronage of its citizens outside its borders.

*Article 62*

(1)   A citizen of the Russian Federation can hold citizenship of a foreign state (dual citizenship) as provided by federal law or an international treaty of the Russian Federation.
(2)   The fact that a citizen of the Russian Federation holds citizenship of a foreign state does not diminish his rights and freedoms or exempt him from obligations stemming from Russian citizenship, unless otherwise provided by federal law or an international treaty of the Russian Federation.
(3)   Foreign citizens and stateless persons in the Russian Federation enjoy equal rights and bear equal obligations with citizens of the Russian Federation, except when otherwise provided by federal law or an international treaty of the Russian Federation.

*Article 63*

(1)   The Russian Federation offers political asylum to foreign citizens and stateless persons in accordance with universally recognized norms of international law.

(2)   The Russian Federation does not permit the extradition to other states of persons persecuted for their political beliefs or for actions (or inactions) which are not considered a crime in the Russian Federation. The extradition of persons accused of having committed a crime, or the extradition of sentenced persons to serve their sentence in other states, is performed on the basis of federal law or an international treaty of the Russian Federation.

*Article 64*

The provisions of this chapter comprise the foundations of the individual's legal status in the Russian Federation and cannot be amended except by the procedure established by the present constitution.

### Chapter 3 Federative structure

*Article 65*

(1)   The Russian Federation is made up of the following components:

(a)   the Republic of Adygeya (Adygea), the Republic of Altai, the Republic of Bashkortostan, the Republic of Buryatia, the Republic of Dagestan, the Republic of Ingushetia, the Kabardino-Balkar Republic, the Republic of Kalmykia, the Karachai-Cherkess Republic, the Republic of Karelia, the Republic of Komi, the Republic of Marii El, the Republic of Mordovia, the Republic of Sakha (Yakutia), the Republic of North Ossetia – Alania, the Republic of Tatarstan (Tatarstan), the Republic of Tyva, the Udmurt Republic, the Republic of Khakassia, the Chechen Republic, the Chuvash Republic – Chuvashia;

(b)   Altai krai, Kamchatka krai, Khabarovsk krai, Krasnodar krai, Krasnoyarsk krai, Maritime krai, Perm krai, Stavropol krai;

(c)   Amur oblast, Arkhangel oblast, Astrakhan oblast, Belgorod oblast, Bryansk oblast, Vladimir oblast, Volgograd oblast, Vologda oblast, Voronezh oblast, Ivanovo oblast, Irkutsk oblast, Kaliningrad oblast, Kaluga oblast, Kemerovo oblast, Kirov oblast, Kostromo oblast, Kurgan oblast, Kursk oblast, Leningrad oblast, Lipetsk oblast, Magadan oblast, Moscow oblast, Murmansk oblast, Nizhny Novgorod oblast, Novgorod oblast, Novosibirsk oblast, Omsk oblast, Orenburg oblast, Orel oblast, Penza oblast, Pskov oblast, Rostov oblast, Ryazan oblast, Samara oblast, Saratov oblast, Sakhalin oblast, Smolensk oblast, Sverdlovsk oblast, Tambov oblast, Tver oblast, Tomsk oblast, Tula oblast, Tyumen oblast, Ulyanovsk oblast, Chelyabinsk oblast, Chita oblast, Yaroslavl oblast;

(d)   Moscow, St Petersburg – cities of federal significance;

(e)   the Jewish Autonomous oblast;

(f)   the Aga Buryat Autonomous okrug, the Nenets Autonomous okrug, the Ust-Orda Buryat Autonomous okrug, the Khanty-Mansi Autonomous okrug – Yugra, the Chukotka Autonomous okrug, the Yamal-Nenetsk Autonomous okrug.

(2) The admission to the Russian Federation and the formation as part of the Russian Federation of a new component are carried out according to the procedure laid down by Federal constitutional law.

## Article 66

(1) The status of a republic is determined by the constitution of the Russian Federation and by the constitution of the republic.

(2) The status of a krai, oblast, city of federal significance, autonomous oblast and autonomous okrug is determined by the constitution of the Russian Federation and the charter of the krai, oblast, city of federal significance, autonomous oblast and autonomous okrug adopted by the legislative (representative) body of the relevant component of the Russian Federation.

(3) A federal law on the autonomous oblast or an autonomous okrug can be adopted upon submission by the legislative and executive bodies of the autonomous oblast or autonomous okrug.

(4) The relations of autonomous okrug forming part of a krai or oblast can be regulated by a federal law and treaty between the bodies of state power of an autonomous okrug and, accordingly, by the bodies of state power of a krai or oblast.

(5) The status of a component of the Russian Federation can be changed by the mutual consent of the Russian Federation and the component of the Russian Federation in accordance with federal constitutional law.

## Article 67

(1) The territory of the Russian Federation includes the territories of its components, inland stretches of water and territorial waters and the airspace over these.

(2) The Russian Federation possesses sovereign rights and exercises jurisdiction over the continental shelf and within the exclusive economic zone of the Russian Federation in accordance with the procedure defined by federal law and the norms of international law.

(3) The borders between components of the Russian Federation can be amended by their mutual consent.

## Article 68

(1) The Russian language is the state language of the Russian Federation throughout its territory.

(2) Republics are entitled to establish their own state languages. They are used alongside the state language of the Russian Federation in the bodies of state power, bodies of local self-government and state institutions of the republics.

(3) The Russian Federation guarantees all its peoples the right to retain their mother tongue and to create conditions for its study and development.

*Article 69*

The Russian Federation guarantees the rights of numerically small indigenous peoples in accordance with the generally recognized principles and norms of international law and the international treaties of the Russian Federation.

*Article 70*

(1)   The state flag, emblem and anthem of the Russian Federation, the description of these, and the procedure for their official use are established by federal constitutional law.

(2)   The capital of the Russian Federation is the city of Moscow. The status of the capital is established by federal law.

*Article 71*

The following fall within the jurisdiction of the Russian Federation:

(a)   the adoption and amendment of the constitution of the Russian Federation and federal laws, and the monitoring of compliance with them;

(b)   the federative system and territory of the Russian Federation;

(c)   the regulation and protection of human and civil rights and freedoms; citizenship of the Russian Federation; the regulation and protection of the rights of national minorities;

(d)   the establishment of a system of federal bodies of legislative, executive and judicial power, the procedure for their organization and activity; the formation of federal bodies of state power;

(e)   federal state property and the management thereof;

(f )   the establishment of the fundamentals of federal policy and federal programmes in the sphere of state, economic, ecological, social, cultural and national development of the Russian Federation;

(g)   the establishment of the legal foundations of the single market; financial, currency, credit and customs regulation, monetary emission and the foundations of pricing policy; federal economic services, including federal banks;

(h)   the federal budget; federal taxes and duties; federal regional development funds;

(i)   federal power systems, nuclear power generation, fissile materials; federal transport, railways, information and communications; activity in space;

(j)   the Russian Federation's foreign policy and international relations and the Russian Federation's international treaties; issues of war and peace;

(k)   the Russian Federation's foreign economic relations;

(l)   defence and security; defence production; the determination of the procedure for the sale and purchase of weapons, ammunition, military hardware and other military property; the production of toxic substances, narcotic substances and the procedure for their use;

(m)   the determination of the status and protection of the state border, territorial seas, airspace, the exclusive economic zone and the continental shelf of the Russian Federation;

(n)   the judicial system; the procurator's office; legislation in the field of criminal, criminal-procedure and criminal-executive law; amnesty and the granting of pardons; legislation in the field of civil law, the law of civil procedure and the law of arbitration procedure; the legal regulation of intellectual property;

(o)   federal law relating to the conflict of laws;

(p)   the meteorological service, standards and standard weights and measurements, the metric system and measurement of time; geodesy and cartography; geographic names; official statistical records and accounting.

(q)   state awards and honorary titles of the Russian Federation;

(r)   the federal civil service.

*Article 72*

(1)   The following fall within the joint jurisdiction of the Russian Federation and the components of the Russian Federation:

    (a)   the guaranteeing that the constitutions and laws of republics, and the charters, laws and other normative legal acts of krais, oblasts, cities of federal significance, the autonomous oblast and autonomous okrugs accord with the constitution of the Russian Federation and federal laws;

    (b)   the protection of human and civil rights and freedoms; the protection of the rights of national minorities; the guaranteeing of legality, law and order and public safety; the arrangements relating to border zones;

    (c)   issues relating to the ownership, use and disposal of land, mineral resources, water and other natural resources;

    (d)   the delimitation of state property;

    (e)   the use of the natural environment; environmental protection and the guaranteeing of ecological safety; natural sites under special protection; the protection of historical and cultural monuments;

    (f)   general issues of nurture, education, science, culture, physical fitness and sport;

    (g)   the coordination of questions of public health; the protection of the family, mothers, fathers and children; social protection, including social security;

    (h)   the implementation of measures for combating catastrophes, natural disasters and epidemics and the elimination of their consequences;

    (i)   the establishment of general principles of taxation and levying of duties in the Russian Federation;

    (j)   administrative, administrative-procedural, labour, family, housing, land, water and forestry legislation, and legislation on mineral resources and on environmental protection;

    (k)   personnel of judicial and law-enforcement bodies; attorneys and notaries;

    (l)   the protection of the primordial habitat and traditional way of life of numerically small ethnic communities;

    (m)   the establishment of the general principles for the organization of a system of bodies of state power and local self-government;

    (n)   the coordination of the international and foreign economic relations of components of the Russian Federation and the fulfilment of the Russian Federation's international treaties.

(2)   The provisions of this article apply in equal measure to the republics, krais, oblasts, cities of federal significance, the autonomous oblast and autonomous okrugs.

## *Article 73*

Outside the compass of the Russian Federation's jurisdiction and the powers of the Russian Federation as regards the terms of reference of the joint jurisdiction of the Russian Federation and the components of the Russian Federation, the components of the Russian Federation possess state power in its entirety.

## *Article 74*

(1)   The establishment of customs borders, duties, levies, and any other hindrances to the free movement of goods, services, and financial assets is not permitted on the territory of the Russian Federation.

(2)   Restrictions on the movement of goods and services can be introduced in accordance with federal law if this is essential for ensuring safety, the protection of the life and health of people, and the protection of nature and cultural assets.

## *Article 75*

(1)   The monetary unit in the Russian Federation is the rouble. Monetary emission is carried out exclusively by the Central Bank of the Russian Federation. The introduction and emission of other currencies is not permitted in the Russian Federation.

(2)   The protection and the guaranteeing of the stability of the rouble is the basic function of the Central Bank of the Russian Federation which it carries out independently of the other bodies of state power.

(3)   The system of taxes levied for the federal budget and the general principles of taxation and levies in the Russian Federation are established by federal law.

(4)   State loans are issued according to a procedure determined by federal law and are floated on a voluntary basis.

## *Article 76*

(1)   Federal constitutional laws and federal laws which operate directly throughout the territory of the Russian Federation are adopted with regard to the Russian Federation's areas of responsibility.

(2)   Federal laws, and the laws and other normative legal enactments of the components of the Russian Federation adopted in accordance with the aforesaid federal laws, are promulgated with regard to the areas of joint responsibility of the Russian Federation and components of the Russian Federation.

(3)   Federal laws cannot conflict with federal constitutional laws.

(4)   Outside the compass of the Russian Federation's jurisdiction and the joint jurisdiction of the Russian Federation and the components of the Russian Federation, the republics, krais, oblasts, cities of federal significance, the autonomous oblast and the autonomous okrugs exercise their own legal regulation, including the adoption of laws and other normative legal enactments.

(5)   The laws and other normative legal enactments of the components of the Russian Federation cannot conflict with federal laws adopted in accordance with the first and second parts of this article. In the event of conflicts between the federal law and another enactment promulgated in the Russian Federation, the federal law is to obtain.

(6)   In the event of conflict between the federal law and a normative legal enactment of a component of the Russian Federation promulgated in accordance with the fourth part of this article, the normative legal enactment of the component of the Russian Federation obtains.

*Article 77*

(1)   The system of bodies of state power of the republics, krais, oblasts, cities of federal significance, the autonomous oblast and autonomous okrugs is established by the components of the Russian Federation independently in accordance with the fundamentals of the constitutional system of the Russian Federation and the general principles of the organization of representative and executive bodies of state power established by federal law.

(2)   Within the areas of responsibility of the Russian Federation and the powers of the Russian Federation as regards the terms of reference of the joint jurisdiction of the Russian Federation and the components of the Russian Federation, the federal bodies of executive power and the bodies of executive power of the components of the Russian Federation form a unified system of executive power in the Russian Federation.

*Article 78*

(1)   In order to exercise their powers, the federal bodies of executive power can create their own territorial bodies and appoint the relevant officials.

(2)   The federal bodies of executive power, by agreement with the bodies of executive power of the components of the Russian Federation can transfer to them the implementation of some of their powers provided that this does not conflict with the constitution of the Russian Federation and federal laws.

(3)   By agreement with the federal bodies of executive power the bodies of executive power of the components of the Russian Federation can transfer to them the implementation of some of their powers.

(4)   The president of the Russian Federation and the government of the Russian Federation ensure in accordance with the constitution of the Russian Federation, the exercise of the powers of federal state authority throughout the territory of the Russian Federation.

*Article 79*

The Russian Federation can participate in interstate associations and hand over to them part of its powers in accordance with international treaties unless this entails the restriction of human and civil rights and freedoms and unless it conflicts with the fundamentals of the constitutional system of the Russian Federation.

### Chapter 4 President of the Russian Federation

*Article 80*

(1)    The president of the Russian Federation is the head of state.
(2)    The president of the Russian Federation is the guarantor of the constitution of the Russian Federation and of human and civil rights and freedoms. Within the procedure established by the constitution of the Russian Federation, he adopts measures to safeguard the sovereignty of the Russian Federation and its independence and state integrity and ensures the coordinated functioning and collaboration of bodies of state power.
(3)    The president of the Russian Federation, in compliance with the constitution of the Russian Federation and the federal laws, determines the basic guidelines of the state's domestic and foreign policy.
(4)    The president of the Russian Federation, in his capacity as head of state, represents the Russian Federation within the country and in international relations.

*Article 81*

(1)    The president of the Russian Federation is elected for four years by citizens of the Russian Federation on the basis of universal, equal and direct suffrage in a secret ballot.
(2)    A citizen of the Russian Federation who is at least 35 years of age and has been permanently resident in the Russian Federation for at least 10 years can be elected president of the Russian Federation.
(3)    One and the same person cannot hold the office of president of the Russian Federation for more than two consecutive terms.
(4)    The procedure of elections for president of the Russian federation is established by federal law.

*Article 82*

(1)    At his inauguration the president of the Russian Federation swears the following oath to the people:
"In exercising the powers of president of the Russian Federation I swear to respect and protect human and civil rights and freedoms, to observe and defend the constitution of the Russian Federation, to defend the state's sovereignty and independence and its security and integrity, and faithfully to serve the people."
(2)    The oath is administered in a ceremonial atmosphere in the presence of members of the Federation Council, deputies of the State Duma and justices of the Constitutional Court of the Russian Federation.

*Article 83*

The president of the Russian Federation:

(a)    appoints with the consent of the State Duma the head of the government of the Russian Federation;

(b)  has the right to chair sessions of the government of the Russian Federation;

(c)  adopts the decision on the dismissal of the government of the Russian Federation;

(d)  submits to the State Duma the candidate for appointment to the office of director of the Central Bank of the Russian Federation; raises before the State Duma the question of removing from office the director of the Central Bank of the Russian Federation;

(e)  at the proposal of the head of the government of the Russian Federation appoints and removes from office the deputy prime ministers of the government of the Russian Federation and federal ministers;

(f)  submits to the Federation Council candidates for appointment to the office of justices of the Constitutional Court of the Russian Federation, Supreme Court of the Russian Federation and Superior Court of Arbitration of the Russian Federation and also the candidate for general prosecutor of the Russian Federation; submits to the Federation Council the proposal on removing from office the procurator-general of the Russian Federation; appoints justices in other federal courts.

(g)  forms and heads the Security Council of the Russian Federation, whose status is defined by federal law;

(h)  approves the military doctrine of the Russian Federation;

(i)  forms the administration of the president of the Russian Federation;

(j)  appoints and removes plenipotentiary representatives of the president of the Russian Federation;

(k)  appoints and removes the high command of the Armed Forces of the Russian Federation;

(l)  appoints and recalls, following consultations with the relevant committees or commissions of the chambers of the Federal Assembly, diplomatic representatives of the Russian Federation in foreign states and international organizations.

## Article 84

The president of the Russian Federation:

(a)  schedules elections to the State Duma in accordance with the constitution of the Russian Federation and federal law;

(b)  dissolves the State Duma in instances and according to the procedure laid down by the constitution of the Russian Federation;

(c)  schedules referendums according to the procedure prescribed by federal constitutional law;

(d)  submits draft laws to the State Duma;

(e)  signs and promulgates federal laws;

(f)  delivers to the Federal Assembly annual messages on the state of the nation and on the basic guidelines of the state's domestic and foreign policy.

## Article 85

(1)  The president of the Russian Federation may use conciliation procedures to resolve disagreements between bodies of state power of the Russian Federation and bodies of state power of components of the Russian Federation, and also between bodies

of state power of components of the Russian Federation. In the event of failure to reach an agreed solution he may refer the resolution of the dispute for examination by the appropriate court.

(2)   Pending a resolution of the matter by the appropriate court, the president of the Russian Federation is entitled to suspend the operation of enactments by bodies of executive power of components of the Russian Federation if these enactments contravene the constitution of the Russian Federation and federal laws or the Russian Federation's international commitments or violate human and civil rights and freedoms.

*Article 86*

The president of the Russian Federation:

(a)   exercises leadership of the foreign policy of the Russian Federation;
(b)   conducts talks and signs international treaties of the Russian Federation;
(c)   signs instruments of ratification;
(d)   accepts the credentials and letters of recall of diplomatic representatives accredited to him.

*Article 87*

(1)   The president of the Russian Federation is the supreme commander-in-chief of the Armed Forces of the Russian Federation.
(2)   In the event of aggression against the Russian Federation or a direct threat of aggression the president of the Russian Federation introduces martial law on the territory of the Russian Federation or in individual localities of that territory and immediately notifies the Federation Council and State Duma of this.
(3)   The regime of martial law is defined by federal constitutional law.

*Article 88*

In the circumstances and according to the procedure laid down by federal constitutional law, the president of the Russian Federation introduces on the territory of the Russian Federation or in individual localities of that territory a state of emergency and immediately notifies the Federation Council and State Duma of this.

*Article 89*

The president of the Russian Federation:

(a)   decides questions of citizenship of the Russian Federation and of granting political asylum;
(b)   confers state awards of the Russian Federation and awards honorary titles of the Russian Federation and higher military and higher special ranks;
(c)   grants pardons.

*Article 90*

(1)   The president of the Russian Federation issues decrees and directives.
(2)   Implementation of the decrees and directives of the president of the Russian Federation is mandatory throughout the territory of the Russian Federation.
(3)   The decrees and directives of the president of the Russian Federation must not contravene the constitution of the Russian Federation and federal laws.

*Article 91*

The president of the Russian Federation enjoys immunity.

*Article 92*

(1)   The president of the Russian Federation begins exercising his powers from the moment he swears the oath and ceases exercising them upon the expiry of his term of office from the moment that the newly elected president of the Russian Federation swears the oath.
(2)   The president of the Russian Federation ceases the exercise of his powers early in the event of his resignation, persistent inability to exercise his powers for health reasons, or removal from office. Furthermore, the election of the president of the Russian Federation must take place no later than three months after the early cessation of the exercise of powers.
(3)   In all instances where the president of the Russian Federation is unable to perform his duties, they are temporarily carried out by the head of the government of the Russian Federation. The acting president of the Russian Federation does not have the right to dissolve the State Duma, schedule a referendum or submit proposals on amendments to and the revision of provisions of the constitution of the Russian Federation.

*Article 93*

(1)   The president of the Russian Federation can be removed from office by the Federation Council only on the basis of a charge of treason or commission of some other grave crime, filed by the State Duma and confirmed by a ruling of the Supreme Court of the Russian Federation that the actions of the president of the Russian Federation contain the elements of crime and a ruling by the Constitutional Court of the Russian Federation that the established procedure for filing the charge has been observed.
(2)   The decision by the State Duma on filing the charge and the decision by the Federation Council on removing the president from office must be adopted by a vote of two-thirds of the total membership of each chamber on the initiative of at least one-third of the deputies of the State Duma and provided there is a ruling by a special commission formed by the State Duma.
(3)   The decision by the Federation Council on removing the president of the Russian Federation from office must be adopted no later than three months following the filing of the charge against the president by the State Duma. If the decision by the

Federation Council is not adopted within this period of time, the charge against the president is deemed rejected.

### Chapter 5 Federal Assembly

*Article 94*

The Federal Assembly-parliament of the Russian Federation is the representative and legislative organ of the Russian Federation.

*Article 95*

(1)   The Federal Assembly consists of two chambers – the Federation Council and the State Duma.
(2)   The Federation Council consists of two representatives from each component of the Russian Federation; one each from the representative and executive bodies of state power.
(3)   The State Duma consists of 450 deputies.

*Article 96*

(1)   The State Duma is elected for a term of four years.
(2)   The procedure for forming the Federation Council and the procedure for electing deputies of the State Duma are established by federal laws.

*Article 97*

(1)   A citizen of the Russian Federation who has attained the age of 21 years and has the right to participate in elections can be elected a deputy of the State Duma.
(2)   One and the same person cannot simultaneously be a member of the Federation Council and a deputy of the State Duma. A deputy of the State Duma cannot be a deputy of any other representative bodies of state power or bodies of local self-government.
(3)   Deputies of the State Duma work on a full-time professional basis. Deputies of the State Duma cannot be in state service or engage in any other paid activity, apart from teaching, scientific or other creative activity.

*Article 98*

(1)   Members of the Federation Council and deputies of the State Duma enjoy immunity for the duration of their term of office. They cannot be detained, arrested or searched unless detained at the scene of a crime, nor can they be subjected to a body search except as provided by federal law in order to guarantee other people's safety.
(2)   Any question concerning the lifting of immunity is decided by the appropriate chamber of the Federal Assembly upon submission by the procurator-general of the Russian Federation.

*Article 99*

(1)  The Federal Assembly is a permanently functioning body.
(2)  The State Duma meets for its first session on the 30th day after its election. The president of the Russian Federation can convene a sitting of the State Duma prior to this date.
(3)  The first session of the State Duma is opened by the oldest deputy.
(4)  From the moment that the work of a newly elected State Duma begins, the powers of the previous State Duma are terminated.

*Article 100*

(1)  The Federation Council and the State Duma sit separately.
(2)  Sessions of the Federation Council and the State Duma are open. In instances stipulated by the standing orders of a chamber it is entitled to conduct closed sessions.
(3)  Chambers may convene jointly to hear messages from the president of the Russian Federation, messages from the Constitutional Court of the Russian Federation and speeches by the leaders of foreign states.

*Article 101*

(1)  The Federation Council elects from its membership the chair of the Federation Council and his/her deputies. The State Duma elects from its members the chair of the State Duma and his/her deputies.
(2)  The chair of the Federation Council and his/her deputies, and the chair of the State Duma and his/her deputies, chair sessions and control the internal procedures of the chamber.
(3)  The Federation Council and the State Duma form committees and commissions and conduct parliamentary hearings into matters under their jurisdiction.
(4)  Each of the chambers adopts its own standing orders and decides matters relating to the internal procedure governing its activity.
(5)  In order to monitor the implementation of the federal budget the Federation Council and the State Duma form an audit chamber whose composition and work procedure are determined by federal law.

*Article 102*

(1)  The jurisdiction of the Federation Council includes:

  (a)  confirming alterations to borders between components of the Russian Federation;
  (b)  confirming a decree of the president of the Russian Federation on the introduction of martial law;
  (c)  confirming a decree of the president of the Russian Federation on the introduction of a state of emergency;
  (d)  deciding the question of the possibility of the utilization of Russian Federation Armed Forces outside the borders of the territory of the Russian Federation;

(e)   scheduling elections for the president of the Russian Federation;

(f )   removing the president of the Russian Federation from office;

(g)   appointing justices of the Constitutional Court of the Russian Federation, the Supreme Court of the Russian Federation and the Superior Court of Arbitration of the Russian Federation;

(h)   appointing and removing from office the procurator-general of the Russian Federation;

(i)   appointing and removing from office the deputy head of the comptrollers office and half of its staff of auditors.

(2)   The Federation Council adopts decrees on matters designated as its area of responsibility by the constitution of the Russian Federation.

(3)   Decrees of the Federation Council are adopted by a majority of the votes of the total number of Federation Council members unless some other procedure for adopting a decision is stipulated by the constitution of the Russian Federation.

*Article 103*

(1)   The jurisdiction of the State Duma includes:

(a)   giving consent to the president of the Russian Federation for the appointment of the head of the government of the Russian Federation;

(b)   deciding a motion of confidence in the government of the Russian Federation;

(c)   appointing and removing from office the head of the Central Bank of the Russian Federation;

(d)   appointing and removing from office the head of the comptrollers office and half of its staff of auditors;

(e)   appointing and removing from office the commissioner for human rights, who operates in accordance with federal constitutional law;

(f )   declaring an amnesty;

(g)   filing a charge against the president of the Russian Federation to remove him from office.

(2)   The State Duma adopts decrees on matters designated as its area of responsibility by the constitution of the Russian Federation.

(3)   Decrees of the State Duma are adopted by a majority of the votes of the total number of deputies of the State Duma unless some other procedure for adopting a decision is stipulated by the constitution of the Russian Federation.

*Article 104*

(1)   The right of legislative initiative is vested in the president of the Russian Federation, the Federation Council, members of the Federation Council, deputies of the State Duma, the government of the Russian Federation and legislative (representative) bodies of components of the Russian Federation. The right of legislative initiative is also vested in the Constitutional Court of the Russian Federation, the Supreme Court of the Russian Federation and the Superior Court of Arbitration of the Russian Federation in matters under their jurisdiction.

(2)    Draft laws are submitted to the State Duma.
(3)    Draft laws on the introduction or abolition of taxes, exemption from the payment of taxes, the floating of state loans, the alteration of the financial obligations of the state and other draft laws envisaging expenditure funded out of the state budget can be submitted only when the government's findings are known.

## Article 105

(1)    Federal laws are adopted by the State Duma.
(2)    Federal laws are adopted by a majority of the votes of the total number of deputies of the State Duma unless otherwise stipulated by the constitution of the Russian Federation.
(3)    Federal laws adopted by the State Duma are passed to the Federation Council within five days for examination.
(4)    A federal law is deemed to have been approved by the Federation Council if more than half of the total number of members of this chamber have voted for it or if it has not been examined by the Federation Council within 14 days. In the event of the rejection of a federal law by the Federation Council the chambers may form a conciliation commission to overcome differences which have arisen, after which the federal law is subject to repeat examination by the State Duma.
(5)    In the event of disagreement by the State Duma with a decision of the Federation Council, a federal law is deemed to have been adopted if at least two-thirds of the total number of deputies of the State Duma vote for it in a repeat vote.

## Article 106

Federal laws adopted by the State Duma are subject to compulsory examination in the Federation Council when they concern questions of:

(a)    the federal budget;
(b)    federal taxes and levies;
(c)    financial, foreign currency, credit and customs regulation and money emission;
(d)    the ratification and denunciation of international treaties of the Russian Federation;
(e)    the status and protection of the state border of the Russian Federation;
(f )    war and peace.

## Article 107

(1)    A federal law that has been adopted is submitted within five days to the president of the Russian Federation for signing and promulgation.
(2)    The president of the Russian Federation signs and promulgates the federal law within 14 days.
(3)    If the president of the Russian Federation, within 14 days of receiving the federal law, rejects it, the State Duma and the Federation Council re-examine the said law in accordance with the procedure laid down by the constitution of the Russian Federation. If, after repeat examination, the federal law is approved by a majority of the votes of at least two-thirds of the total number of members of the Federation

Council and deputies of the State Duma in the wording previously adopted, it is to be signed by the president of the Russian Federation within seven days and promulgated.

*Article 108*

(1)  Federal constitutional laws are adopted on matters stipulated by the constitution of the Russian Federation.

(2)  A federal constitutional law is deemed to be adopted if it is approved by a majority of the votes of at least three-quarters of the total number of members of the Federation Council and at least two-thirds of the total number of deputies of the State Duma. A federal constitutional law that has been adopted is to be signed by the president of the Russian Federation and promulgated within 14 days.

*Article 109*

(1)  The State Duma may be dissolved by the president of the Russian Federation in the circumstances stipulated in Articles 111 and 117 of the constitution of the Russian Federation.

(2)  In the event of the dissolution of the State Duma, the president of the Russian Federation sets the date of elections so as to ensure that the newly elected State Duma is convened not later than four months from the date of dissolution.

(3)  The State Duma may not be dissolved on the grounds stipulated in Article 117 of the constitution of the Russian Federation for one year following its election.

(4)  The State Duma may not be dissolved from the moment it files a charge against the president of the Russian Federation, until the adoption of a corresponding decision by the Federation Council.

(5)  The State Duma may not be dissolved during the period of operation of a state of martial law or state of emergency on the whole territory of the Russian Federation, or within the six months preceding the expiry of the term of office of the president of the Russian Federation.

### Chapter 6 Government of the Russian Federation

*Article 110*

(1)  Executive power in the Russian Federation is exercised by the government of the Russian Federation.

(2)  The government of the Russian Federation consists of the head of the government of the Russian Federation, the deputy prime ministers of the government of the Russian Federation and the federal ministers.

*Article 111*

(1)  The head of the government of the Russian Federation is appointed by the president of the Russian Federation with the consent of the State Duma.

(2)  A proposal on the candidacy for the head of the government of the Russian Federation is submitted no later than two weeks following the entry into office of a newly

elected president of the Russian Federation or the resignation of the government of the Russian Federation or within a week following the rejection of a candidacy by the state Duma.

(3)    The State Duma examines the candidacy for the head of the government of the Russian Federation submitted by the president of the Russian Federation within a week of the day the candidacy proposal is submitted.

(4)    Following three rejections by the State Duma of candidacies submitted to head the government of the Russian Federation, the president of the Russian Federation appoints a head of the government of the Russian Federation, dissolves the State Duma and schedules new elections.

## Article 112

(1)    The head of the government of the Russian Federation, no later than one week following his appointment, submits to the president of the Russian Federation proposals on the structure of the federal bodies of executive power.

(2)    The head of the government of the Russian Federation proposes to the president of the Russian Federation candidacies for the posts of deputy prime ministers of the government of the Russian Federation and federal ministers.

## Article 113

The head of the government of the Russian Federation, in accordance with the constitution of the Russian Federation, federal laws and decrees of the president of the Russian Federation, defines the basic guidelines for the activity of the government of the Russian Federation and organizes its work.

## Article 114

(1)    The government of the Russian Federation:

(a)    drafts the federal budget, submits it to the State Duma and ensures its implementation; submits to the State Duma a report on the implementation of the federal budget;

(b)    ensures the implementation of a single fiscal, credit and monetary policy in the Russian Federation;

(c)    ensures the implementation of a single state policy in the Russian Federation in the sphere of culture, science, education, health, social security and ecology;

(d)    administers federal property;

(e)    implements measures to ensure the defence of the country, state security and the realization of the foreign policy of the Russian Federation;

(f)    implements measures to ensure the rule of law, civil rights and freedoms, the protection of property and public order, and the struggle against crime;

(g)    exercises other powers vested in it by the constitution of the Russian Federation, federal laws and decrees of the president of the Russian Federation.

(2)  The procedure for the activity of the government of the Russian Federation is defined by federal constitutional law.

*Article 115*

(1)  On the basis of and in implementation of the constitution of the Russian Federation, federal laws and normative decrees of the president of the Russian Federation, the government of the Russian Federation issues decrees and directives and ensures their implementation.
(2)  Decrees and directives of the government of the Russian Federation are mandatory in the Russian Federation.
(3)  Decrees and directives of the government of Russian Federation, in the event that they are at variance with the constitution of the Russian Federation, federal laws or decrees of the president of the Russian Federation, may be rescinded by the president of the Russian Federation.

*Article 116*

The government of the Russian Federation surrenders its powers to a newly elected president of the Russian Federation.

*Article 117*

(1)  The government of the Russian Federation may offer its resignation, which is accepted or rejected by the president of the Russian Federation.
(2)  The president of the Russian Federation may adopt a decision on the dismissal of the government of the Russian Federation.
(3)  The State Duma may express no confidence in the government of the Russian Federation. A decree of no confidence in the government of the Russian Federation is adopted by a majority of votes of the total number of deputies of the State Duma. Following an expression of no confidence by the State Duma in the government of the Russian Federation, the president of the Russian Federation is entitled to announce the dismissal of the government of the Russian Federation or to disagree with the decision of the State Duma. In the event that the State Duma expresses no confidence in the government of the Russian Federation for a second time within three months, the president of the Russian Federation announces the dismissal of the government or dissolves the State Duma.
(4)  The head of the government of the Russian Federation may submit to the State Duma a motion of confidence in the government of the Russian Federation. If the State Duma refuses its confidence, the president adopts a decision within seven days on the dismissal of the government of the Russian Federation or on the dissolution of the State Duma and the holding of new elections.
(5)  In the event of its resignation or the surrender of its powers, the government of the Russian Federation, on the instructions of the president of the Russian Federation, continues to act until the formation of the new government of the Russian Federation.

## Chapter 7 Judicial branch

*Article 118*

(1)  Justice in the Russian Federation is exercised only by the court.
(2)  Judicial power is exercised by means of constitutional, civil, administrative and criminal court proceedings.
(3)  The judicial system of the Russian Federation is established by the constitution of the Russian Federation and by federal constitutional law. The creation of emergency courts is not permitted.

*Article 119*

Citizens of the Russian Federation who have attained the age of 25 and have higher legal education and at least five years' experience in the legal profession may be judges. Additional requirements for judges in the courts of the Russian Federation may be imposed by federal law.

*Article 120*

(1)  Judges are independent and are subordinate only to the constitution of the Russian Federation and to federal law.
(2)  The court, having determined in the course of examining a case that an enactment of a state organ or other organ is not in accordance with the law, adopts a ruling in accordance with the law.

*Article 121*

(1)  Judges may not be removed.
(2)  A judge's powers may not be terminated or suspended except in accordance with the procedure and on the grounds laid down by federal law.

*Article 122*

(1)  Judges enjoy immunity.
(2)  A judge may not be subjected to criminal proceedings except in accordance with the procedure defined by federal law.

*Article 123*

(1)  The examination of cases in all courts is open. Hearing a case in closed session is permitted in circumstances stipulated in federal law.
(2)  The in absentia examination of criminal cases in the courts is not permitted, except in circumstances stipulated in federal law.
(3)  Court proceedings are carried out on the basis of the adversarial system and the equal rights of the parties.
(4)  In circumstances stipulated in federal law, court proceedings take place with the participation of jurors.

*Article 124*

The financing of courts is effected solely from the federal budget and must ensure the possibility of the complete and independent exercise of justice in accordance with federal law.

*Article 125*

(1)   The Constitutional Court of the Russian Federation consists of 19 judges.
(2)   The Constitutional Court of the Russian Federation, on the application of the president of the Russian Federation, the Federation Council, the State Duma, one-fifth of the members of the Federation Council or deputies of the State Duma, the government of the Russian Federation, the Supreme Court of the Russian Federation or the Superior Court of Arbitration of the Russian Federation, or bodies of legislative and executive power of the components of the Russian Federation, resolves cases relating to the compliance with the constitution of the Russian Federation of:

  (a)   federal laws and normative enactments of the president of the Russian Federation, the Federation Council, the State Duma or the government of the Russian Federation;
  (b)   the constitutions of republics and the charters of components of the Russian Federation and laws and other normative acts issued by them on matters falling within the jurisdiction of bodies of state power of the Russian Federation or the joint jurisdiction of bodies of state power of the Russian Federation and bodies of state power of components of the Russian Federation;
  (c)   treaties between bodies of state power of the Russian Federation and bodies of state power of components of the Russian Federation and treaties between bodies of state power of components of the Russian Federation;
  (d)   international treaties of the Russian Federation that have not entered into force.

(3)   The Constitutional Court of the Russian Federation resolves disputes over areas of jurisdiction:

  (a)   between federal bodies of state power;
  (b)   between bodies of state power of the Russian Federation and bodies of state power of components of the Russian Federation;
  (c)   between the highest state bodies of components of the Russian Federation.

(4)   The Constitutional Court of the Russian Federation, on the basis of complaints regarding the violation of citizens' constitutional rights and freedoms and at the request of judges, examines the constitutionality of the law that has been applied or is applicable in the specific case, in accordance with the procedure laid down by federal law.
(5)   The Constitutional Court of the Russian Federation, on the application of the president of the Russian Federation, the Federation Council, the State Duma,

the government of the Russian Federation or the bodies of legislative power of components of the Russian Federation, provides an interpretation of the constitution of the Russian Federation.

(6) Enactments or individual clauses that are deemed unconstitutional lose their force; international treaties of the Russian Federation that are not compatible with the constitution of the Russian Federation are not valid for entry into force or application.

(7) The Constitutional Court of the Russian Federation, on the application of the Federation Council, issues a ruling on whether the presentation of a charge against the president of the Russian Federation of treason or the commission of some other grave crime complies with established procedure.

*Article 126*

The Supreme Court of the Russian Federation is the highest judicial organ for civil, criminal, administrative or other cases under the jurisdiction of the courts of general jurisdiction, exercises judicial oversight over their activity within the procedural forms laid down by federal law and provides clarification on questions of judicial practice.

*Article 127*

The Superior Court of Arbitration of the Russian Federation is the highest judicial organ for the resolution of economic disputes and other cases examined by the courts of arbitration, exercises judicial oversight over their activity within the procedural forms laid down by federal law and provides clarification on questions of judicial practice.

*Article 128*

(1) Judges of the Constitutional Court of the Russian Federation, the Supreme Court of the Russian Federation and the Superior Court of Arbitration of the Russian Federation are appointed by the Federation Council on the submission of the president of the Russian Federation.

(2) Judges of other federal courts are appointed by the president of the Russian Federation in accordance with the procedure laid down by federal law.

(3) The powers and the procedure for the formation and activity of the Constitutional Court of the Russian Federation, the Supreme Court of the Russian Federation, the Superior Court of Arbitration of the Russian Federation and other federal courts are laid down by federal constitutional law.

*Article 129*

(1) The Russian Federation Procurator's Office is a single centralized system in which lower-level procurators are subordinate to higher-level procurators and to the procurator-general of the Russian Federation.

(2)   The procurator-general of the Russian Federation is appointed and released from office by the Federation Council on the submission of the president of the Russian Federation.

(3)   The procurators of components of the Russian Federation are appointed by the procurator-general of the Russian Federation by agreement with the Federation components.

(4)   Other procurators are appointed by the procurator-general of the Russian Federation.

(5)   The powers and the organization and procedure of activity of the Russian Federation Procurator's Office are defined by federal law.

### Chapter 8 Local self-government

*Article 130*

(1)   Local self-government in the Russian Federation ensures that the population autonomously resolves questions of local importance and the ownership, utilization and disposal of municipal property.

(2)   Local self-government is exercised by citizens by means of referendums, elections and other forms of direct expression of will and through elected and other bodies of local self-government.

*Article 131*

(1)   Local self-government in urban and rural settlements and other territories is exercised with due consideration for historical and other local traditions. The structure of local self-government bodies is autonomously determined by the population.

(2)   Changes to the borders of territories where local self-government is exercised are permitted with due consideration for the opinion of the population of the relevant territories.

*Article 132*

(1)   Bodies of local self-government autonomously manage municipal property, formulate, approve and implement the local budget, levy local taxes and duties, implement the protection of public order and also resolve other questions of local importance.

(2)   Individual state powers can be vested in bodies of local self-government by law, with the transfer of the material and financial resources necessary to exercise them. The exercise of delegated powers is monitorable by the state.

*Article 133*

Local self-government in the Russian Federation is guaranteed by the right to judicial protection, compensation for additional expenditure arising as a result of decisions adopted by bodies of state power, and the prohibition of the restriction of the rights of local self-government established by the constitution of the Russian Federation and federal laws.

## Chapter 9 Constitutional amendments and revision of the constitution

*Article 134*

Proposals to amend or revise provisions of the constitution of the Russian Federation can be submitted by the president of the Russian Federation, the Federation Council, the State Duma, the government of the Russian Federation, legislative (representative) bodies of components of the Russian Federation, and also by a group comprising at least one-fifth of members of the Federation Council or deputies of the State Duma.

*Article 135*

(1)  The provisions of Chapters 1, 2 and 9 of the constitution of the Russian Federation cannot be revised by the Federal Assembly.

(2)  If a proposal to revise the provisions of Chapters 1, 2 and 9 of the constitution of the Russian Federation is supported by a vote of three-fifths of the total number of members of the Federation Council and deputies of the State Duma then, in accordance with federal constitutional law, a Constitutional Assembly is convened.

(3)  The Constitutional Assembly either confirms the immutability of the constitution of the Russian Federation or elaborates a draft of a new constitution of the Russian Federation which is adopted by the Constitutional Assembly by a vote of two-thirds of the total number of its members or is submitted to a nationwide vote. If a nationwide vote is held, the constitution of the Russian Federation is considered adopted if votes for it are cast by more than one-half of voters casting their votes, provided that more than one-half of voters have cast their votes.

*Article 136*

Amendments to Chapters 3–8 of the constitution of the Russian Federation are adopted by the procedure envisaged for the adoption of federal constitutional law and come into force after they have been approved by the bodies of legislative power of at least two-thirds of the components of the Russian Federation.

*Article 137*

(1)  Amendments to Article 65 of the constitution of the Russian Federation, which determines the composition of the Russian Federation, are submitted on the basis of federal constitutional law relating to admission to the Russian Federation, to the formation of a new component of the Russian Federation within it and to the alteration of the constitutional-legal status of a component of the Russian Federation.

(2)  In the event of changes to the name of a republic, krai, oblast, city of federal significance, autonomous oblast or autonomous okrug, the new name of the component of the Russian Federation is to be incorporated in Article 65 of the constitution of the Russian Federation.

## Section two

### *Concluding and transitional provisions*

(1)   The constitution of the Russian Federation comes into force on the day of its official publication following the results of the nationwide vote.

    (a)   The day of the nationwide vote – 12th December 1993 – is deemed the day of the adoption of the constitution of the Russian Federation.

    (b)   The constitution (Basic Law) of the Russian Federation-Russia, adopted 12th April 1978 with its subsequent amendments and additions, simultaneously ceases to be in force.

    (c)   In the event of noncompliance with provisions of the constitution of the Russian Federation of provisions of the Federation Treaty – the treaty on the delimitation of areas of responsibility and powers between federal bodies of state power of the Russian Federation and bodies of state power of sovereign republics within the Russian Federation, the treaty on the delimitation of areas of responsibility and powers between federal bodies of state power of the Russian Federation and bodies of state power of krais, oblasts and the cities of Moscow and St Petersburg in the Russian Federation, the treaty on the delimitation of areas of responsibility and powers between federal bodies of state power of the Russian Federation and bodies of state power of the autonomous oblast and autonomous okrugs of the Russian Federation, as well as other treaties between federal bodies of state power of the Russian Federation and bodies of state power of components of the Russian Federation, and treaties between bodies of state power of components of the Russian Federation – the provisions of the constitution of the Russian Federation will prevail.

(2)   Laws and other legal enactments which were in force on the territory of the Russian Federation prior to the entry into force of the present constitution are applied to the extent to which they do not contravene the constitution of the Russian Federation.

(3)   From the day the present constitution comes into force, the president of the Russian Federation, elected in accordance with the constitution (Basic Law) of the Russian Federation-Russia, exercises the powers laid down by the present constitution until the expiry of the term for which he was elected.

(4)   From the day the present constitution comes into force, the Council of Ministers-government of the Russian Federation acquires the rights, obligations and responsibilities of the government of the Russian Federation established by the constitution of the Russian Federation and is thereafter known as the government of the Russian Federation.

(5)   Courts in the Russian Federation administer justice in compliance with the powers laid down by the present constitution.

After the constitution has come into force, the judges of all courts in the Russian Federation retain their powers until the expiry of the term for which they were elected. Vacancies are filled according to the procedure established by the present constitution.

(6) Pending the entry into force of the federal law laying down the procedure for the hearing of cases by a court with the participation of jurors, the existing procedure for judicial examination of such cases is retained.

    (a) The existing procedures for the arrest, holding in custody and detention of persons suspected of having committed a crime are retained until such time as the criminal procedure legislation of the Russian Federation is brought into line with the provisions of the present constitution.

(7) The first Federation Council and the first State Duma are elected for a two-year term.

(8) The Federation Council will convene for its first session on the 30th day following its election. The first session of the Federation Council will be opened by the president of the Russian Federation.

(9) A deputy of the first State Duma can simultaneously be a member of the government of the Russian Federation. The provisions of the present constitution on deputies' immunity as regards liability for actions (or inaction) associated with the performance of official duties do not extend to deputies of the State Duma who are members of the government of the Russian Federation.

    (a) Deputies of the first Federation Council perform their duties on a part-time basis.

# Notes

## 1 Soviet communism and its dissolution

1 Fyodor Dostoyevsky, 'One of Today's Falsehoods', 1875, in *A Writer's Diary, Volume 1, 1873–1876*, translated and annotated by Kenneth Lantz (London, Quartet Books, 1994), p. 288.
2 Ronald Grigor Suny, *The Soviet Experiment: Russia, the USSR, and the Successor States* (Oxford, Oxford University Press, 1998).
3 David Remnick, *Lenin's Tomb: The Last Days of the Soviet Empire* (London, Viking, 1993), pp. 294–5.
4 Mikhail Gorbachev, *Perestroika: New Thinking for Our Country and the World* (London, Collins, 1987), p. 10.
5 Gorbachev, *Perestroika*, p. 25.
6 This is the theme of E. A. Hewett, *Reforming the Soviet Economy: Equality vs Efficiency* (Washington, DC, Brookings, 1988).
7 László Póti, 'The Soviet Reform: Domestic Aspects and Implications for East-Central Europe', in *European Conference on 'Similarities and Differences in the Adaptation of the Countries of Central Europe to the European Community'* (Budapest, 28–30 November 1991, Euration), p. 32.
8 E.g., Graeme Gill, 'Liberalization and Democratization in the Soviet Union and Russia', *Democratization*, Vol. 2, No. 3, autumn 1995, pp. 313–36.
9 Neil Robinson, 'Gorbachev and the Place of the Party in Soviet Reform, 1985–91', *Soviet Studies*, Vol. 44, No. 3, 1992, pp. 423–44.
10 *Izvestiya*, 11 June 1989.
11 'Dekret o vlasti', *Argumenty i fakty*, No. 25, 23–9 June 1990, p. 1.
12 E.g. the First Secretary of the Komi Republic (Yu. Spiridonov) and the city Party leader in Kursk (N. Golovin).
13 Póti, 'The Soviet Reform', p. 32.
14 David Remnick, *New York Review of Books*, 17 May 1990, p. 3.
15 Nina Andreeva, 'I Cannot Forego My Principles', *Sovetskaya Rossiya*, 13 March 1988.
16 For a description of these events, see John Morrison, *Boris Yeltsin: From Bolshevik to Democrat* (London, Penguin Books, 1991), and for Yeltsin's own view, see *Against the Grain: An Autobiography* (London, Pan, 1991).
17 Estimate by V. Vorotnikov in *Pravda*, 26 March 1990, p. 2.
18 Brendan Kiernan, *The End of Soviet Politics* (Boulder, CO, Westview, 1993), p. 181.
19 L. Efimova, A. Sobyanin and D. Yur'ev, *Argumenty i fakty*, No. 29, 1990, p. 2.
20 Milovan Djilas, *The New Class: An Analysis of the Communist System* (New York, Praeger, 1957).
21 Yitzhak M. Brudny, *Reinventing Russia: Russian Nationalism and the Soviet State, 1953–1991* (Cambridge, MA, Harvard University Press, 1999).
22 Edward Allworth, 'Ambiguities in Russian Group Identity and Leadership of the RSFSR', in Allworth (ed.), *Ethnic Russia in the USSR* (New York, 1980), pp. 24–5.
23 Ruslan Khasbulatov, *The Struggle for Russia: Power and Change in the Democratic Revolution*, edited by Richard Sakwa (London and New York, Routledge, 1993), p. 46.

24 *Soviet News*, 2 August 1989, p. 260.

25 *Soviet News*, 30 August 1989, p. 288.

26 *Pravda* and *Sovetskaya Rossiya*, 7 June 1989, p. 2; also in John Dunlop, *The Rise of Russia and the Fall of the Soviet Empire* (Princeton, NJ, Princeton University Press, 1993), pp. 16–17.

27 *Sovetskaya Rossiya*, 31 May 1990.

28 'Deklaratsiya o gosudarstvennom suverenitete RSFSR', *Argumenty i fakty*, No. 24, 16–22 June 1990, p. 1.

29 Alexei Zverev, 'Qualified Sovereigny: The Tatarstan Model for Resolving Conflicting Loyalties', in Michael Waller, Bruno Coppieters and Alexei Malashenko (eds), *Conflicting Loyalties and the State in Post-Soviet Eurasia* (London, Frank Cass, 1998), p. 123.

30 M. S. Gorbachev, *On My Country and the World* (New York, Columbia University Press, 2000), p. 110.

31 Khasbulatov, *The Struggle for Russia*, p. 222.

32 'O mekhanizme narodovlastiya v RSFSR', *Argumenty i fakty*, No. 25, June 1990, p. 1.

33 Gordon M. Hahn, *Russia's Revolution from Above, 1985–2000: Reform, Transition, and Revolution in the Fall of the Soviet Communist Regime* (New Brunswick, NJ, Transaction Publishers, 2002), p. 246.

34 Khasbulatov, *The Struggle for Russia*, p. 36.

35 Steven L. Solnick, *Stealing the Soviet State: Control and Collapse in Soviet Institutions* (Cambridge, MA, Harvard University Press, 1998), p. 232 and *passim*.

36 Michael Urban, with Vyacheslav Igrunov and Sergei Mitrokhin, *The Rebirth of Politics in Russia* (Cambridge, Cambridge University Press, 1997).

37 For a study of the dilemmas facing the insurgency at this time and its state-centredness, see M. Stephen Fish, *Democracy from Scratch: Opposition and Regime in the New Russian Revolution* (Princeton, NJ, Princeton University Press, 1995).

38 *Pravda*, 28 May 1989, p. 1.

39 Gorbachev's most developed attempt to reconceptualise the role of the CPSU appeared in his 'Sotsialisticheskaya ideya i revolyutsionnaya *perestroika*', *Pravda*, 26 November 1989.

40 Michael Waller, *Democratic Centralism: An Historical Commentary* (New York, St Martin's, 1981).

41 The programme of the Marxist Platform was published in *Pravda*, 16 April 1990.

42 For an analysis of Gorbachev's attempts to reform the party, see Ronald J. Hill, 'The CPSU: Decline and Collapse', *Irish Slavonic Studies*, No. 12 (1991), pp. 97–119; and also his 'The Communist Party and After', in S. White, Alex Pravada and Zvi Gitelman (eds), *Developments in Soviet and Post-Soviet Politics* (London, Macmillan, 1992), pp. 68–87.

43 *Moscow News*, No. 27, 15 July 1990, p. 5.

44 Hill, 'The CPSU', pp. 113–14.

45 *Moscow News*, No. 24 (24 June 1990), pp. 8–9.

46 *Current Politics of the Soviet Union*, Vol. 1, No. 2 (1990), p. 173. At the Twenty-seventh Party Congress in February-March 1986 membership stood at 18.3 million full and 728,253 candidate members, a total of 19 million, *Izvestiya TsK KPSS*, No. 1, 1990.

47 By 259,605 (1.3%); of these, 136,600 left at their own request, a cumbersome procedure whereby communists had to write a formal letter of resignation and then seek permission to leave from a meeting of the local Party group, *Izvestiya TsK KPSS*, No. 2, 1989, p. 138, and No. 4, 1990, p. 113.

48 Report of the Central Auditing Commission to the 28th CPSU Congress, *Pravda*, 4 July 1990.

49 Oleg Vite, *Moscow News*, No. 24, 16 June 1991, p. 8.

50 *Izvestiya*, 10 July 1991, pp. 1, 3.

## 2 The disintegration of the USSR

1 Francis Bacon, *The Essays* (London, Odhams Press, nd), 'Of Empire', p. 74.

2 Cited by Boris Pankin, *Moscow Times*, 27 June 2001, p. 11.

3 *Izvestiya*, 22 July 1991, p. 1, and for Gorbachev's condemnation, *Pravda*, 26 July 1991.

4 The draft programme was later published in *Pravda*, 8 August, *Sovetskaya Rossiya*, 9 August 1991, under the title 'Socialism, Democracy, Progress'.

5   *Sovetskaya Rossiya*, 23 July 1991, p. 1; *Current Digest of the Soviet Press* (henceforth *CDSP*), Vol. 43, No. 30, 1991, pp. 8–10.

6   For an analysis of the coup, see Richard Sakwa, 'The Revolution of 1991 in Russia: Interpretations of the Moscow Coup', *Coexistence*, Vol. 29, No. 4, December 1992, pp. 27–67; and for a different version 'A Cleansing Storm: The August Coup and the Triumph of *Perestroika*', *Journal of Communist Studies*, Vol. 9, No. 1, spring 1993, pp. 131–49. Some of the more useful collections of materials on the coup include *Putch: khronika trevozhnykh dnei* (Moscow, Progress, 1991); *Avgust '91* (Moscow, Politicheskoi literatury, 1991); *Korichnevyi putch krasnykh avgust '91* (Moscow, Tekst, 1991); *Smert' zagovora: belaya kniga* (Moscow, Novosti, 1992); and an account by the investigators V. Stepankov and E. Lisov, *Kremlevskii zagovor* (Moscow, Ogonëk, 1992).

7   Mikhail Gorbachev, *The August Coup: The Truth and the Lessons* (London, Harper Collins, 1991), pp. 20–1.

8   Amy Knight, *Spies Without Cloaks: The KGB's Successors* (Princeton, NJ, Princeton University Press, 1996), p. 17. In her chapter 'The Myth of the August Coup', Knight marshals the evidence about Gorbachev's alleged complicity in the coup but the case against him remains circumstantial.

9   See Archie Brown, *The Gorbachev Factor* (Oxford, Oxford University Press, 1996), pp. 295–9.

10   *Izvestiya*, 10 October 1991.

11   Boris Yeltsin, 'To the Citizens of Russia', 19 August 1991, *CDSP*, Vol. 43, No. 33, 1991, pp. 6–7.

12   *Rossiiskaya gazeta*, 9 November 1991, p. 2.

13   See Ivan Bunich, *Zoloto partii* (St Petersburg, Shans, 1992); *Soviet Weekly*, 19 September 1991, p. 5; *Panorama*, BBC TV, 13 July 1992.

14   See Dmitrii Volkogonov, *Argumenty i fakty*, No. 6, February 1992, p. 4. For the links with the Communist Party of Great Britain, see Nina Fishman, 'Britain: the Road to the Democratic Left', in Martin J. Bull and Paul Heywood (eds), *West European Communist Parties after the Revolutions of 1989* (London, Macmillan, 1994), p. 170.

15   S. Akhromeev and G. Kornienko, *Glazami marshala i diplomata* (Moscow, Mezhdunarodnye otnosheniya, 1992).

16   Remnick, *Lenin's Tomb*, p. xi.

17   Gerd Ruge, *Der Putsch* (Frankfurt, Fischer, 1991), pp. 129, 185.

18   *Moscow News*, No. 37, 1991, p. 1.

19   Gorbachev, *The August Coup*, p. 38.

20   *Moscow News*, No. 37, 1991, p. 1.

21   *Izvestiya*, 7 September 1991.

22   Khasbulatov, *Rossiiskaya gazeta*, 29 October 1991, p. 3.

23   Khasbulatov, *The Struggle for Russia*, p. 223.

24   Boris El'tsyn, *Zapiski prezidenta* (Moscow, Ogonëk, 1994), pp. 165–6.

25   *Moscow News*, No. 37, 1991, p. 6.

26   M. S. Gorbachev, *On My Country and the World* (New York, Columbia University Press, 2000), p. 144.

27   The five Union Treaties were published in *Izvestiya*: 24 November 1990, 9 March, 27 June, 15 August and 25 November 1991.

28   Gorbachev, *On My Country and the World*, p. 145.

29   Roman Szporluk, *Russia, Ukraine and the Breakup of the Soviet Union* (Stanford, Hoover Institution Press, 2000), p. xxiv.

30   For Gorbachev's view of these events and his comments on Burbulis's long memorandum proposing the break-up of the USSR, see *Neokonchennaya istoriya: Besedy Mikhaila Gorbacheva s politologom Borisom Slavinym* (Moscow, Olma-Press, 2001), pp. 41–7, 54–5.

31   A point made by Yegor Ligachev, *Inside Gorbachev's Kremlin* (Boulder, CO, Westview Press, 1996), p. 372.

32   The idea of something approximating the (British) Commonwealth had first been proposed by Sakharov at the First USSR Congress of People's Deputies in May 1989, and had been promoted by Democratic Russia and Yeltsin.

33 Leonid Kravchuk interviewed in *Kyivska pravda*, 7 July 1995, cited in *Transition*, 11 August 1995, pp. 80–1, where he also notes that the name CIS was suggested by the Ukrainian delegation.

34 *Transition*, 11 August 1995, p. 81.

35 *Rossiiskaya gazeta*, 10 December 1991, p. 1.

36 *Rossiiskaya gazeta*, 24 December 1991, p. 1.

37 A number of books chart the dramatic personal relationship between Gorbachev and Yeltsin, for example *Rossiya segodnya: Politicheskii portret v dokumentakh, 1985–1990* (Moscow, Mezhdunarodnye otnosheniya, 1991), pp. 393–511; *Gorbachev-El'tsin: 1500 dnei politicheskogo protivosostoyaniya* (Moscow, Terra, 1992). Gorbachev's own harsh criticisms of Yeltsin's behaviour at this time are in Gorbachev, *On My Country and the World*, Part Two; while Yeltsin's views are presented in his *The View from the Kremlin* (London, Harper Collins, 1994), Chapter 3.

38 The proportion of those supporting Yeltsin to those not supporting him was 69:5, Shevardnadze 52:11, Khasbulatov 48:10, while Gorbachev's proportion was 19:37, *Rossiiskaya gazeta*, 13 December 1991, p. 2.

39 *Guardian*, 28 December 1991.

40 X (George Kennan), 'The Sources of Soviet Conduct', *Foreign Affairs*, July 1947, pp. 566–82, at p. 580.

41 In the west there are the Baltic, Black and Azov seas; the Arctic ocean contains the Barents, White, Karsk, Laptev, eastern Siberian and Chukotka seas; while the Pacific ocean has the Bering, Okhotsk and Japanese seas.

42 Speech to the Fifth Russian Congress of People's Deputies, *Rossiiskaya gazeta*, 29 October 1991, p. 1.

## 3 Phoney democracy, 1991–3

1 Alexander Solzhenitsyn, *Rebuilding Russia* (London, Harvill, 1991), p. 9.

2 For a 'revisionist' account of the legislature and an institutional explanation for its failure, see Joel M. Ostrow, *Comparing Post-Soviet Legislatures: A Theory of Institutional Design and Political Conflict* (Columbus, OH, Ohio State University Press, 2000).

3 See Stephen White, 'The Presidency and Political Leadership', in Peter Lentini (ed.), *Elections and Political Order in Russia* (Budapest, Central European University Press, 1995), pp. 202–25.

4 *Moscow News*, No. 25, 23 June 1991, p. 1.

5 Law on the Presidency, *Vedemosti S"ezda narodnykh deputatov RSFSR i verkhovnogo Soveta RSFSR*, No. 17, 1991, 512.

6 For details of the vote, including regional analysis, see D. Yurev, *Prezidentskie vybory* (Moscow, 1991).

7 *Rossiiskaya gazeta*, 31 October and 1 November 1991; *Izvestiya*, 2 and 4 November 1991.

8 *Demokraticheskaya gazeta*, 12, 15, 12–19 September 1991, p. 3.

9 Philippe C. Schmitter, 'Reflexions on Revolutionary and Evolutionary Transitions: The Russian Case in Comparative Perspective', in A. Dallin (ed.), *Political Parties in Russia* (Berkeley, CA, University of California Press, 1993), p. 31.

10 See Yitzhak M. Brudny, 'The Dynamics of "Democratic Russia", 1990–1993', *Post-Soviet Affairs*, Vol. 9, No. 2, 1993, pp. 141–70.

11 Article 104 of the amended 1978 constitution.

12 *Sed'moi s"ezd narodnykh deputatov Rossiiskoi Federatsii: Byulleten'*, No. 23, 14 December 1992, pp. 12–13.

13 For Nikolai Travkin's comments, see *Demokraticheskaya gazeta*, No. 8, July 1991, p. 2.

14 *Rossiiskaya gazeta*, 29 October 1991, p. 1.

15 'Ob izmeneniyakh i dopolneniyakh Konstitutsii (Osnovnogo Zakona) RSFSR', in *Rossiya segodnya: Politicheskii portret v dokumentakh, 1991–1992* (Moscow, Mezhdunarodnye otnosheniya, 1993), pp. 24–7.

16 *Izvestiya*, 12 March 1992, p. 1.

17 See Archie Brown, 'The October Crisis of 1993: Context and Implications', *Post-Soviet Affairs*, Vol. 9, No. 3, 1993, pp. 183–95.

18 By mid-1993 the constitution had been amended over 300 times, and the incremental nature of constitutional revision gave rise to numerous contradictions. Chief among them was the vesting of supreme power in both the legislative and executive.

19 For criticisms of Khasbulatov, see Otto Latsis, *Izvestiya*, 28 August 1992, p. 3; *Nezavisimaya gazeta*, 1 September 1992; Maria Bogatykh, *Rossiya*, No. 36, (94), 2 September 1992, p. 1; Georgi Ivanov-Smolenskii, *Izvestiya*, 3 September 1992, p. 2; interview with Sergei Yushenkov, coordinator of the Radical Democrats faction, *Rossiiskie vesti*, 10 September 1992, p. 2.

20 Article 104 of the amended 1978 constitution, *Konstitutsiya (osnovnoi zakon) RSFSR* (Moscow, Sovetskaya Rossiya), 1991, pp. 32–3.

21 Josephine T. Andrews, *When Majorities Fail: The Russian Parliament, 1990–1993* (Cambridge, Cambridge University Press, 2002).

22 The balance of forces was as follows: some 294 deputies were grouped under the umbrella of the Coalition of Reforms; 170 with the Bloc of Constructive Forces; some 269 independents with another 63 independent-minded deputies in the Sovereignty and Equality faction; and 290 in the oppositional bloc 'Russian Unity', A. A. Sobyanin (ed.), *VI s"ezd narodnykh deputatov Rossii: politicheskie itogi i perspektivy* (Moscow, Organisational Department of the Presidium of the Supreme Soviet of the Russian Federation, 1992), p. 11.

23 Viktor Sheinis, *Nezavisimaya gazeta*, 23 May 1992, p. 2.

24 *Izvestiya*, 11 June 1992.

25 *Rossiiskaya gazeta*, 30 July 1992, pp. 1–2.

26 Some 267 deputies were grouped under the umbrella of the Coalition of Reforms; 155 with the Bloc of Constructive Forces; some 208 independents with another 51 independent-minded deputies in the Sovereignty and Equality faction; and 359 in the oppositional bloc 'Russian Unity', *Sed'moi s"ezd narodnykh deputatov Rossiiskoi Federatsii: byulleten'*, No. 24, 14 December 1992, p. 15.

27 *Rossiiskaya gazeta*, 11 December 1992, pp. 1–2.

28 *Pravda*, 4 March 1993.

29 Khasbulatov, *The Struggle for Russia*, pp. 7–8 and *passim*.

30 *Izvestiya*, 13 August 1993, p. 2.

31 *Moscow News*, No. 39 (24 September 1993), pp. 1–2.

32 Julia Wishnevsky, 'Corruption Allegations Undermine Russia's Leaders', RFE/RL, *Research Report*, Vol. 2, No. 37, 17 September 1993, pp. 16–22.

33 *Rossiiskie vesti*, 2 September 1993, p. 1.

34 'O poetapnoi konstitutsionnoi reforme v Rossiiskoi Federatsii', *Konstitutsionnoe soveshchanie*, No. 2, October 1993, pp. 15–19; *Izvestiya*, 22 September 1993, p. 1.

35 *Izvestiya*, 22 September 1993, p. 1.

36 Described, for example, by Leon Aron, *Boris Yeltsin: A Revolutionary Life* (London, HarperCollins, 2000), pp. 540–8.

37 *Izvestiya*, 25 December 1993, p. 1.

38 Ulrich K. Preuss, 'The Political Meaning of Constitutionalism', in Richard K. Bellamy (ed.), *Constitutionalism, Democracy and Sovereignty: American and European Perspectives* (Aldershot, Avebury, 1996), pp. 22–4.

39 Max Weber, 'Bourgeois Democracy in Russia', in *The Russian Revolutions*, translated and edited by Gordon C. Wells and Peter Baehr (Oxford, Polity Press, 1995).

40 See Geoffrey Hosking, *The Russian Constitutional Experiment: Government and Duma, 1907–1914* (Cambridge, Cambridge University Press, 1973); also Lothar Schultz, 'Constitutional Law in Russia', in G. Katkov *et al.* (eds), *Russia Enters the Twentieth Century* (London, Temple Smith, 1971), pp. 34–59, esp. pp. 44–7.

41 Gorbachev, *On My Country and the World*, p. 21.

42 *Konstitutsiya (Osnovnoi Zakon) Soyuza Sovetskikh Sotsialisticheskikh Respublik* (Moscow, Yuridicheskaya literatura, 1980), p. 6.

43 See Aryeh L. Unger, *Constitutional Developments in the USSR: A Guide to the Soviet Constitutions* (London, Methuen, 1981).

44 Gorbachev introduced these ideas in his speech to the Nineteenth Party Conference on 28 June 1988, *Izbrannye rechi i stat'i*, Vol. 6, Moscow, 1989, pp. 373–76, and developed them

in his Supreme Soviet speech of 29 November 1988, 'K polnovlastiyu Sovetov i sozdaniyu sotsialisticheskogo pravovogo gosudarstvo', *Izbrannye rechi i stat'i*, Vol. 7, Moscow, 1990, pp. 150–75.

45 See L. V. Lazarev and A. Ya. Sliva, *Konstitutsionnaya reforma: pervyi etap* (Moscow, Znanie, 1989).

46 See Jon Elster, Claus Offe and Ulrich K. Preuss, *Institutional Design in Post-Communist Societies: Rebuilding the Boat in the Open Sea* (Cambridge, Cambridge University Press, 1997).

47 An extended version of this part of the chapter can be found in Richard Sakwa, 'The Struggle for the Constitution in Russia and the Triumph of Ethical Individualism', *Studies in East European Thought*, Vol. 48, Nos 2–4, September 1996, pp. 115–57.

48 *Argumenty i fakty*, No. 47, November 1990, whole issue; in *Konstitutsionnyi vestnik*, No. 4, 1990, pp. 55–120; a popular edition was published as *Konstitutsii Rossiiskoi Federatsii: proekt s kommentariyami* (Moscow and Krasnoyarsk, newspaper *Svoi golos* and Krasnoyarsk Press and Information Agency, 1991).

49 *Sovetskaya Rossiya*, 19 April 1991; an earlier version appeared in *Sovetskaya Rossiya*, 24 November 1990.

50 *Rossiiskaya gazeta*, 11 October 1991, special section, with an 'explanatory note' on p. 7.

51 Oleg Rumyantsev, 'Zachem nuzhna novaya konstitutsiya', *Konstitutsionnyi vestnik*, No. 8, 1991, pp. 3–7.

52 *Konstitutsionnyi vestnik*, No. 8, 1991, pp. 68–72.

53 *Konstitutsionnyi vestnik*, No. 8, 1991, p. 74; and pp. 84–148 for the revised draft of 24 October.

54 *Rossiiskaya gazeta*, 5 November 1991, p. 1.

55 *Argumenty i fakty*, No. 12, March 1992, whole issue; republished in *Proekt konstitutsii Rossiiskoi Federatsii: Sbornik materialov* (Moscow, Respublika, 1992), pp. 19–81.

56 Vladimir Kuznechevskii, *Rossiiskaya gazeta*, 3 April 1992, pp. 1–2.

57 The Federation Treaty was made up of three separate documents: an agreement (published in *Rossiiskaya gazeta*, 18 March 1992) signed by 18 out of the 20 republics, excluding the Chechen and Tatarstan republics; a document signed by Russia's *oblasts* and krais; and an agreement with the autonomous okrugs and the Jewish Autonomous *Oblast*. The Russian Federation was a separate signatory to the Treaty. *Federativnyi dogovor: Dokumenty, kommentarii* (Moscow, Respublika, 1992).

58 'O proekte konstitutsii Rossiiskoi Federatsii i poryadke dal'neishei raboty nad nim', 18 April 1992, in *Proekt konstitutsii Rossiiskoi Federatsii: Sbornik materialov*, pp. 3–4.

59 *Rossiiskaya gazeta*, 16 May 1992, pp. 3–5.

60 By that time seven laws making 340 amendments had been adopted: in 1990 there were 53 amendments and in 1991 29, Rumyantsev in *Konstitutsionnyi vestnik*, No. 15, March 1993, p. 8.

61 *Konstitutsionnyi vestnik*, No. 13, November 1992, pp. 25–115.

62 *Konstitutsionnyi vestnik*, No. 13, p. 7.

63 *Nezavisimaya gazeta*, 24 November 1993, p. 2.

64 This version was published as 'Konstitutsiya (osnovnoi zakon) Rossiiskoi Federatsii: Proekt' in *Izvestiya*, 30 April 1993, pp. 3–5; reprinted in *Konstitutsionnyi vestnik*, No. 16, May 1993, pp. 65–108.

65 *Izvestiya*, 13 May 1993, p. 1.

66 *Stolitsa*, No. 22 (132) (1993), pp. 6–7.

67 For example, Marina Shakina, 'Istoriya s konstitutsiei', *Novoe vremya*, No. 23, 1993, pp. 3–5.

68 *Konstitutsionnyi vestnik*, No. 16, May 1993, p. 202.

69 Shakhrai, for example, argued that it would be legal and constitutional for a Constituent Assembly to adopt a new constitution and declare new parliamentary elections, especially since presidential powers had been relegitimised in the referendum of 25 April 1993, *Izvestiya*, 30 April 1993, p. 2.

70 'Konstitutsiya Rossiiskoi Federatsii: proekt', *Konstitutsionnyi vestnik*, No. 16, May 1993, pp. 9–64.

71 *Nezavisimaya gazeta*, 26 June 1993, p. 1.

72 'O zavershenii raboty nad proektom Konstitutsii Rossiiskoi Federatsii', Supreme Soviet resolution of 29 April 1993, *Konstitutsionnyi vestnik*, No. 16, May 1993, pp. 201–2.
73 *Rossiiskaya gazeta*, 3 April 1992, pp. 1–2; *Nezavisimaya gazeta*, 26 January 1993, p. 5.
74 'O sozyve Konstitutsionnogo soveshchanie i zavershenii podgotovki proekta Konstitutsii Rossiiskoi Federatsii', *Konstitutsionnoe soveshchanii*, No. 1, August 1993, pp. 7–8.
75 The president nominated 50, there were 109 deputies (including all members of the Constitutional Commission), 352 representatives of regional executive and legislative author-ities (4 from each region), 26 from local government, and over 200 representatives of social and religious organisations.
76 *Konstitutsionnoe soveshchanie*, No. 1, pp. 12–20; *Rossiiskie vesti*, 8 June 1993, p. 2.
77 *Moskovskie novosti*, No. 25, 20 June 1993, p. A8.
78 Kronid Lyubarskii, 'Konets sovetskoi vlasti', *Novoe vremya*, No. 24, 1993, pp. 4–5.
79 B. A. Strashun, 'O "smeshannoi" forme pravleniya v proekte Konstitutsii Rossiiskoi Federatsii', *Konstitutsionnoe soveshchanie*, No. 2, 1993, pp. 51–7; and V. E. Chirkin, ' "Chistye" i "smeshannye" formy pravleniya: Plyusy i minusy razlichnykh sistem', ibid., pp. 57–65.
80 *Konstitutsionnoe soveshchanie: Informatsionnyi byulleten'*, No. 1, August 1993, pp. 109–57; *Rossiiskie vesti*, 15 July 1993.
81 The Assembly envisaged a broad process of consultation, in particular with the subjects of federation, and a referendum before the draft could be adopted, 'Zakon "O poryadke prinyatiya Konstitutsii Rossiiskoi Federatsii" (proekt)', *Konstitutsionnoe soveshchanie*, No. 1, August 1993, pp. 155–7.
82 *Izvestiya*, 14 August 1993, p. 1

# 4 Constitutionalism and the law

1 Alexander Pope, *Essay on Man*, Epistle 3.
2 *Izvestiya*, 24 September 1993, pp. 3–5.
3 Yeltsin's decree of 11 October allowed the election of the upper house ('O vyborakh v Sovet Federatsii Federal'nogo Sobraniya Rossiiskoi Federatsii'); and the decree of 6 November added yet another clause ensuring that a category of votes 'against all' was added to ballot papers, *Rossiiskaya Federatsiya*, No. 1 (13), 1993, pp. 7–20; *Moscow News*, No. 43, 22 October 1993, p. 1.
4 'O provedenii vsenarodnogo golosovaniya po proektu konstitutsii Rossiiskoi Federatsii'; accompanied on the same date by 'Polozhenie o vsenarodnom golosovanii po proektu konstitutsii Rossiiskoi Federatsii 12 dekabrya 1993 goda', in *Rossiiskaya Federatsiya*, No. 1 (13), 1993, pp. 22–4; *Rossiiskie vesti*, 21 October 1993. The word 'plebiscite' (*golosovanie*) was used rather than referendum.
5 The October 1990 RSFSR Referendum Law stipulated that matters affecting the constitution could be adopted by a simple majority of all registered voters, while non-constitutional matters could be decided by a simple majority of those participating in the referendum. A referendum would only be valid if turnout exceeded 50 per cent of registered voters, *Rossiiskaya gazeta*, 2 December 1990.
6 A trenchant critique of adopting the constitution by referendum was made by Rumyantsev, *Nezavisimaya gazeta*, 24 November 1993, p. 2.
7 These figures are given in *Rossiiskaya gazeta*, 21 December 1993, p. 1 and in full in *Byulleten' Tsentral'noi izbiratel'noi kommissii Rossiiskoi Federatsii* (henceforth *Byulleten' VTsIK*), No. 1 (12), 1994, p. 38.
8 Seven republics voted against the constitution: Adygeya, Bashkortostan, Chuvashia, Dagestan, Karachai-Cherkessia, Mordovia and Tuva; and 10 *oblasts*: Belgorod, Bryansk, Kursk, Lipetsk, Orël, Smolensk, Tambov, Penza, Volgograd and Voronezh, mainly south-west Russia where support for the Communist Party was strongest (*Byulleten' TsIK*, No. 1 (12), 1994, pp. 34–8). In Tatarstan the referendum was declared invalid since not enough turned up to vote, but of those who did 74% supported the constitution, *Nezavisimaya gazeta*, 18 December 1993, p. 1. No vote took place in the Chechen Republic.
9 *Rossiiskaya gazeta*, 25 December 1993.

10 Sergei S. Alekseev, *Demokraticheskie reformy i konstitutsiya* (Moscow, Pozitsiya, 1992), p. 4.

11 *Nezavisimaya gazeta*, 9 November 1993, p. 1.

12 *Segodnya*, 13 November 1993, p. 2.

13 *Moskovskie novosti*, No. 47, 21 November 1993, p. A13.

14 Cf. *Nezavisimaya gazeta*, 30 December 1993, p. 2.

15 Cf. Irina Koptel'skaya, 'Konstitutsionnue zakony – novoe yavlenie v zakonodatel'stve Rossii', *Konstitutsionnyi vestnik*, No. 1 (17), 1994, pp. 59–63.

16 *Rossiiskaya gazeta*, 17 December 1993, p. 1.

17 *Nezavisimaya gazeta*, 4 December 1993, p. 2.

18 *Stolitsa*, No. 50 (160), December 1993, p. 4.

19 *Pravda*, 19 January 1994.

20 *Financial Times*, 10 November 1993.

21 Since 1993 only Article 65 has been modified through five presidential decrees renaming regions (in 1996, 1996, 2001, 2003, 2004) and one federal constitutional law in 2004 to allow the creation of Perm krai (see Chapter 11), with more on their way.

22 For example, Vyacheslav Nikonov, *Nezavisimaya gazeta*, 23 December 1993, pp. 1, 2.

23 'Ob izmeneniyakh i dopolneniyakh Konstitutsii (Osnovnogo Zakona) RSFSR', in *Rossiya segodnya: Politicheskii portret v dokumentakh, 1991–1992* (Moscow, Mezhdunarodnye otnosheniya, 1993), pp. 24–27.

24 Wendy Slater, 'Head of Russian Constitutional Court Under Fire', *RFE/RL Research Report*, Vol. 2, No. 26, 25 June 1993, pp. 1–5.

25 *Sovetskaya Rossiya*, 23 September 1993, p. 1. On 30 September the Constitutional Court suspended the membership of three of the judges (one on health grounds), though the other two (Ernst Ametistov and Nikolai Vitruk) had already declared that they would no longer participate in the Court's work.

26 Cf. Robert Sharlet, 'The Russian Constitutional Court: The First Term', *Post-Soviet Affairs*, Vol. 9, No. 1, 1993, pp. 1–39.

27 See Robert Sharlet, 'Russian Constitutional Crisis: Law and Politics under Yel'tsin', *Post-Soviet Affairs*, Vol. 9, No. 4, 1993, pp. 314–36.

28 *Russkaya mysl'*, No. 4064, 9–15 February 1995, p. 20. Of the 'old' judges, nine had condemned the president's action in September 1993 (Nikolai Vedernikov, Valerii Zor'kin, Victor Luchin, Gadis Gadzhiev, Boris Ebzeev, Nikolai Seleznev, Oleg Tyunov, Vladimir Oleinik and Yurii Rudnik), four had supported the president (Ernst Ametistov, Tamara Morshchakova, Nikolai Vitruk and Anatolii Kononov), while the views of the six newcomers (Vladimir Tumanov, Olga Khokhryakova, Yurii Danilov, Vladimir Yaroslavtsev, Vladimir Strekozov and Marat Baglai, the last to be appointed) remained to be determined.

29 *Moskovskie novosti*, No. 17, 12–19 March 1995, p. 11.

30 Marie-Elisabeth Baudoin, 'Is the Constitutional Court the Last Bastion in Russia against the Threat of Authoritarianism?', *Europe–Asia Studies*, Vol. 58, No. 5, July 2006, pp. 679–99.

31 For a detailed analysis, see Robert Sharlet, 'Russia's Second Constitutional Court: Politics, Law, and Stability', in V. E. Bonnell and G. W. Breslauer (eds), *Russia in the New Century: Stability or Disorder?* (Boulder, CO, Westview, 2000), pp. 59–77.

32 Law of 24 October 1990, 'O deistvii aktov organov SSSR na territorii RSFSR', in *Sbornik zakonodatel'nykh aktov RSFSR o gosudarstvennom suverenitete, soyuznom dogovore i referendume* (Moscow, RSFSR Supreme Soviet, 1991), pp. 16–17.

33 'Law on the Procuracy', 1995 (*Sobranie Zakonodatel'stvo RF*, 1995, issue 47, No. 4472).

34 *Izvestiya*, 25 June 2007.

35 *Rossiiskaya gazeta*, 30 July 2006.

36 *Ugolovnyi kodeks Rossiiskoi Federatsii* (Moscow, 1997).

37 See Peter Solomon, 'Limits of Legal Order', *Post-Soviet Affairs*, Vol. 11, No. 2, 1995, pp. 89–114.

38 'Federal Constitutional Law on the Court System', 31 December 1996 (*SZ RF*, 1997, issue 1, No. 1).

39 *Soviet Weekly*, 24 October 1991, p. 2.

40 E.g., Genri Reznik, *Novaya ezhednevnaya gazeta*, 24 December 1993, p. 1; and this was repeated over the years.

41 *Russia: Country Rports on Human Rights Practices, 2006*, Bureau of Democracy, Human Rights, and Labor, US Department of State, released 6 March 2007, p. 10.
42 RFE/RL, *Newsline*, 26 June 2001.
43 *Nezavisimaya gazeta*, 15 December 2000, p. 8.
44 *Nezavisimaya gazeta*, 13 August 1992, p. 1.
45 *Moskovskie novosti* No. 17, 12–19 March 1995, p. 11.
46 Bill Bowring, 'Russia's Relations with the Council of Europe under Increasing Strain' (Brussels, Russia-EU Centre, 2007).
47 For example, Petr Orlov, 'Strasburgskii porog', *Rossiiskaya gazeta*, 14 May 2007, p. 2.
48 Edwin Rekosh, 'Remedies to Administrative Abuses: Setting the Stage for Action', *Local Government Brief*, Budapest, Summer 2003, pp. 2–7, at p. 2.
49 Vladimir Pastukhov, 'Law under Administrative Pressure in Post-Soviet Russia', *East European Constitutional Review*, Vol. 11, No. 3, summer 2002, pp. 66–74, at p. 68.
50 'Za chto v Rossii srok dayut', *Moskovskie novosti*, No. 47, 10–16 December 2004, p. 18.
51 'Subjugated Court System Stifles Battle with Corruption', *St. Petersburg Times*, 28 December 2004.
52 Greg Austin, *Political Change in Russia: Implications for Britain* (London, Foreign Policy Centre, November 2004), p. 18.
53 *Striving for Judicial Independence: A Report Into Proposed Changes to the Judiciary in Russia*, An International Bar Association Human Rights Institute Report (London, June 2005), Chapter 4.
54 Ralf Dahrendorf, *Reflections on the Revolution in Europe* (London, Chatto & Windus, 1990), pp. 79, 85.
55 The distinction is made by Hellmut Wollmann, 'Change and Continuity of Political and Administrative Elites from Communist to Post-Communist Russia', *Governance: An International Journal of Policy and Administration*, Vol. 6, No. 3, July 1993, pp. 325–40.
56 Valerii Zor'kin, 'Uroki oktyabrya-93', *Konstitutsionnyi vestnik*, No. 1 (17), 1994, p. 11.
57 For a theoretical discussion of the issues, see Giuseppe Di Palma, *To Craft Democracies: An Essay in Democratic Transition* (Berkeley, CA University of California Press, 1990).
58 Donald D. Barry (ed.), *Toward the 'Rule of Law' in Russia?: Political and Legal Reform in the Transition Period* (Armonk and London, M. E. Sharpe, 1992), p. xvi.
59 Cf. A. Walicki, *Legal Philosophies of Russian Liberalism* (Oxford, Oxford University Press, 1987), pp. 165–212. See also Jonathan Sutton, *The Religious Philosophy of Vladimir Solovyov* (London, Macmillan, 1988).
60 Ibid., p. 114.
61 See Barry (ed.), *Toward the 'Rule of Law' in Russia?*, p. 4.
62 A classic statement of this argument was made by M. J. C. Vile, *Constitutionalism and the Separation of Powers* (Oxford, Clarendon Press, 1967).
63 For an extended discussion of this issue, see Oleg Rumyantsev, *Osnovy konstitutsionnogo stroya Rossii* (Moscow, Yurist, 1994). See also, O. G. Rumyantsev, 'Osnovy konstitutsionnogo stroya: ponyatie, soderzhanie, otrazhenie v konstitutsii', *Gosudarstvo i pravo*, No. 10, 1993, pp. 3–15, and see note 54 above.
64 V. V. Leontovich, *Istoriya liberalizma v Rossii, 1762–1914* (Paris, YMCA Press, 1980), p. 539.
65 *Moscow News*, No. 46, 12 November 1993, p. 2.

## 5 Crime, corruption and security

1 Raymond Aron, *Democracy and Totalitarianism* (London, Weidenfeld & Nicolson, 1965), pp. 109–10.
2 Stephen Handelman, 'The Russian "Mafiya"', *Foreign Affairs*, Vol. 73, No. 2, March–April 1994, p. 90.
3 Stephen Handelman, *Comrade Criminal: The Theft of the Second Russian Revolution* (London, Michael Joseph, 1994), p. 8.
4 Georgii Podlesskikh and Andrei Tereshok, *Vory v zakone: brosok k vlasti* (Moscow, Khudozhestvennaya literatura, 1994), p.27.

5 Tanya Frisby, 'The Rise of Organised Crime in Russia: Its Roots and Social Significance', *Europe–Asia Studies*, Vol. 50, No. 1, 1998, p. 40.

6 RFE/RL, *Newsline*, 26 March 2001.

7 According to Moscow region police chief Alexander Kulikov, Interfax, 13 June 1997.

8 Andrew Osborn, 'Interior Ministry: "One-tenth of Russia under Criminal Control"', *Independent*, 15 March 2007.

9 Vadim Volkov, *Violent Entrepreneurs: The Use of Force in the Making of Russian Capitalism* (Ithaca, NY, Cornell University Press, 2002), p. 19.

10 *Nezavisimaya gazeta*, 21 April 1993, p. 2.

11 *Russia in Figures: 2006* (Moscow, Rosstat, 2006), p. 146.

12 *Nezavisimaya gazeta*, 11 April 1995, p. 1.

13 *Russia in Figures: 2006*, p. 146.

14 Vladimir Popov, 'Russia Redux?', *New left Review*, No. 44, March–April 2007, pp. 37–52, at pp. 46–7.

15 Some 289 in 1993 and 562 in 1994, *Nezavismaya gazeta*, 11 April 1995, p. 1; *The Observer*, 21 April 1995, p. 23.

16 *Moskovskie novosti*, No. 80, 19–26 November 1995, p. 21.

17 *Observer*, 26 March 1995, p. 6.

18 *Observer*, 16 April 1995, p. 21.

19 Phil Williams (ed.), *Russian Organized Crime: The New Threat* (London, Frank Cass, 1997).

20 RIA-Novosti, 2 July 1997.

21 Volkov, *Violent Entrepreneurs*, p. 19.

22 Handelman, *Comrade Criminal*.

23 *Rossiiskie vesti*, 23 July 1997.

24 Georgy Satarov, 'Corruption, Western and Russian', in Yuri Senokosov and Edward Skidelsky (eds), *Corruption in Russia*, issue 4 of *Russia on Russia* (Moscow and London, Moscow School of Political Studies and Centre for Post-Collectivist Studies, March 2001), pp. 8–9.

25 Yuri Levada, 'Corruption in Public Opinion', in ibid., pp. 49–58, at pp. 51–2.

26 Alena V. Ledeneva, *Russia's Economy of Favours: Blat, Networking and Informal Exchange* (Cambridge, Cambridge University Press, 1998).

27 For a powerful analysis, see Igor' Klyamkin and Lev Timofeev, *Tenevaya Rossiya: Ekonomiko-sotsiologicheskoe issledovanie* (Moscow, RGGU, 2000).

28 For the development of this argument, see my 'Russia: From a Corrupt System to a System with Corruption', in Robert Williams (ed.), *Party Finance and Political Corruption* (Basingstoke and London, Macmillan; New York, St Martin's Press, 2000), pp. 123–61.

29 The classic statement of this is Milovan Djilas, *The New Class* (New York, Praeger, 1957); with the profound political corruption described later by Mikhail Voslenskii, *Nomenklatura: Anatomy of the Soviet Ruling Class* (London, Bodley Head, 1984); and the social corruption by Konstantin Simis, *USSR: Secrets of a Corrupt Society* (London, Dent, 1982).

30 Leslie Holmes, *The End of Communist Power: Anti-corruption Campaigns and Legitimation Crisis* (Cambridge, Polity Press, 1993).

31 *Anticorruption in Transition: A Contribution to the Policy Debate* (Washington, DC, World Bank, 2000), pp. xv–xviii.

32 See Andrei Yakovlev, 'The Evolution of Business-State Interaction in Russia: From State Capture to Business Capture?', *Europe–Asia Studies*, Vol. 58, No. 7, November 2006, pp. 1033–56.

33 *Novaya gazeta*, No. 35, 1–7 September 1997.

34 *Novye izvestiya*, 6 November 1997.

35 Vladimir Gel'man, 'The Iceberg of Russian Political Finance', in Peter Burnell and Alan Ware (eds), *Funding Democratization* (Manchester, Manchester University Press, 1998), Chapter 8, pp. 158–79.

36 Rustam Narzikulov, *Nezavisimaya gazeta*, 11 March 1997.

37 Yeltsin declared an expenditure of 14.4 billion roubles (3.1 million dollars). See 'El'tsyn deneg ne zhalel', in *Ot El'tsina k... El'tsinu: Prezidentskaya gonka-96* (Moscow, Terra, 1997), pp. 547–9. For the full income reports of Yeltsin and the other 16 candidates, see *Deklaratsii o dokhodakh kandidatov v prezidenty na vyborakh 16 iyunya 1996*, compiled by

G. Belonuchkin (Moscow, Panorama, 1996). Zyuganov officially spent 11.3 billion roubles (2.1 million dollars).

38 Peter Reddaway, 'The West's Spoilt Russian Son', *New Statesman*, 22 August 1997, p. 26.
39 *Izvestiya*, 1 July 1997.
40 *Izvestiya*, 5 July 1997.
41 See Janine R. Wedel, *Collision and Collusion: The Strange Case of Western Aid to Eastern Europe 1989–1998* (Basingstoke and London, Macmillan, 1998), in particular Chapter 4.
42 In the event, perhaps taking advantage of his enforced leisure, Kokh did actually write a book, called appropriately *The Selling of the Soviet Empire*.
43 Yves Mény, 'Fin de Siècle Corruption', *International Social Science Journal*, No. 149, September 1996, p. 313.
44 John Girling, *Corruption, Capitalism and Democracy* (London, Routledge, 1997), p. vii.
45 For a discussion of the issue, see Natasha Kogan, 'Thinking about Corruption', *Transitions*, March 1998, pp. 46–9.
46 Leslie Holmes, 'Corruption and the Crisis of the Post-Communist State', *Crime, Law & Social Change*, Vol. 27, No. 3/4, 1997, pp. 1–23.
47 *Transitions*, March 1998, p. 61.
48 Jamestown Foundation, *Monitor*, 28 June 2001.
49 http://www.transparency.org/policy_and_research/surveys_indices/cpi/2005. The 2006 Index placed Russia in 121st place, a slight improvement.
50 *Diagnostika rossiiskoi korruptsii: Sotsiologicheskii analiz*, http://www.indem.ru
51 Natalya Alyakrinskaya, 'Inefficient Government Breeds Corruption', *Moscow News*, 11–17 January 2006.
52 Owen Matthews and Anna Nemsova, 'The New Feudalism', *Newsweek International*, 23 October 2006.
53 'Vo skol'ko raz uvelichilas' korruptsiya za 4 goda: rezul'taty novogo issledovaniya Fonda INDEM', http://www.indem.ru/russian.asp.
54 *Kommersant*, 31 October 2006.
55 Above all by Susan Rose-Ackerman, *Corruption: A Study in Political Economy* (New York, Academic Press, 1978).
56 In his analysis Federico Varese stresses precisely this, making reference to the 'tragedy of the commons' where the pursuit of individually rational goals leads to a less-than-optimal outcome, 'The Transition to the Market and Corruption in Post-socialist Russia', *Political Studies*, Vol. 45, No. 3, 1997, pp. 579–96.
57 Svetlana P. Glinkina, 'The Ominous Landscape of Russian Corruption', *Transitions*, March 1998, pp. 16–17.
58 Tsarist experience is discussed by William A. Clark, *Crime and Punishment in Soviet Officialdom: Combatting Corruption in the Political Elite, 1965–1990* (Armonk, NY, M. E. Sharpe, 1993), pp. 30–8.
59 This is a point made by Paul Goble in relation to anti-corruption campaigns in Kazakhstan, 'The Corruption of Power', *RFE/RL Newsline*, 14 July 1998.
60 *Moskovskii komsomolets*, 8 October 1997.
61 *OMRI Daily Digest*, 6 March 1997.
62 *RFE/RL Newsline*, 3 April 1998.
63 *RFE/RLNewsline*, 30 March 1998.
64 In the Czech Republic the ruling Civic Democratic Party (ODS) stood accused of corrupt financial deals whereby secret business donations were rewarded with political influence. It was even suggested that the prime minister himself, Vaclav Klaus, had built himself a villa in Switzerland out of party funds. An ironic twist in the story was that Klaus's arrogance had provoked some ODS leaders to expose the scandal (using *kompromat* that they had long known about) in order to unseat him and to take revenge on his dictatorial style of government that had humiliated them all.
65 For an analysis of Boldyrev's career, see 'Kontroler-ispytatel', *Figury i litsa: Nezavisimaya gazeta*, No. 11 (12), June 1998, pp. 9, 11.
66 See Brian Whitmore, 'Russia's Top Crime Fighter', *Transitions*, March 1998, pp. 35–9.
67 *Russia Journal*, 29 June–2 July 2001, p. 2.

68 Girling, *Corruption, Capitalism and Democracy*, p. xi.

69 Peter Rutland and Natasha Kogan, 'The Russian Mafia: Between Hype and Reality', *Transitions*, March 1998, p. 32.

70 It remains a moot point whether criminal ties subvert democracy. It has been alleged, for example, that up to a third of sitting MPs in India are criminals.

71 *RFE/RL Newsline*, 4 February 1998.

72 *Moscow News*, No. 47, 19 November 1993, p. 2.

73 For example, in the mid-1997 gubernatorial campaign in Nizhnii Novgorod State Duma deputy and Communist-backed candidate Gennadii Khodyrev charged that the Carnegie Endowment's Moscow Centre was financing the campaign of Ivan Sklyarov, then mayor of Nizhnii Novgorod city and ultimate victor in the campaign, *RFE/RL Newsline*, Vol. 1, No. 57, Part I, 20 June 1997.

74 Anders Aslund, 'Economic Causes of Crime in Russia', in Jeffrey D. Sachs and Katharina Pistor (eds), *The Rule of Law and Economic Reform in Russia* (Boulder, CO, Westview Press, 1997).

75 Diana Schmidt, 'Fighting against Corruption, and Struggling for Status', *Russian Analytical Digest*, No. 11, 5 December 2006, pp. 2–5.

76 Nabi Abdullaev, 'Putin Scores Points in Anti-graft Drive', *Moscow Times*, 23 June 2006.

77 *Rossiiskaya gazeta*, 7 November 2006.

78 Yves Mény, 'Politics, Corruption and Democracy: The 1995 Stein Rokkan Lecture', *European Journal of Political Research*, Vol. 30, No. 2 (1996), pp. 111–23. On the covert funding of parties and the like, see his *La corruption de la République* (Paris, Fayard, 1992).

79 For a stark description, see David Satter, *Darkness at Dawn: The Rise of the Russian Criminal State* (New Haven, CT, Yale University Press, 2003).

80 *Soviet Weekly*, 5 December 1991, p. 2.

81 Vadim Bakatin, appointed head of the KGB after the coup, describes the process in *Izbavlenie ot KGB* (Moscow, Novosti, 1992), pp. 197–220.

82 *Soviet Weekly*, 10 October 1991, p. 4.

83 *Rossiiskaya gazeta*, 11 August 1992, p. 4.

84 *Moskovskaya pravda*, 4 September 1992.

85 Victor Yasmann, 'Corruption in Russia: A Threat to Democracy?', *RFE/RL Research Report*, Vol. 2, No. 10, 5 March 1993, pp. 15–18.

86 See Alexander Rahr, 'Reform of Russia's State Security Apparatus', *RFE/RL Research Report*, Vol. 3, No. 8, 25 February 1994, pp. 19–30.

87 *Nezavisimaya gazeta*, 10 January 1995, p. 3.

88 *Rossiiskaya gazeta*, 28 May 1994, pp. 1, 4.

89 The law 'On Federal Security Service Bodies of the Russian Federation' of April 1995 introduced the name Federal Security Service; and a presidential decree of 23 June 1995 gave details on its implementation.

90 Bettina Renz, 'The Russian Force Structures', *Russian Analytical Digest*, No. 17, 20 March 2007, p. 6.

91 Victor Yasmann, 'Where Has the KGB Gone?', *RFE/RL Research Report*, Vol. 2, No. 2 (8 January 1993), pp. 17–20, at p. 18.

92 *Rossiiskaya gazeta*, 12 August 1992, p. 1.

93 *Rossiiskaya gazeta*, 12 July 2001.

94 J. Michael Waller, *Secret Empire: The KGB in Russia Today* (Oxford, Westview, 1994), p. 285.

95 *Moskovskie novosti*, No. 9, 5–12 February 1995, p. 6.

96 Amy Knight, *The Security Services and the Decline of Democracy in Russia: 1996–1999*, The Henry M. Jackson School of International Studies, The University of Washington, Seattle, The Donald W. Treadgold Papers, No. 23, October 1999, p. 8.

97 On the size and role of the *siloviki* in Putin's administration, see Olga Kryshtanovkaya and Stephen White, 'Putin's Militocracy', *Post-Soviet Affairs*, Vol. 19, No. 4, October-December 2003, pp. 289–306; and for updated figures, Ol'ga Kryshtanovkaya and Stephen White, 'Inside the Putin

98 Kryshtanovkaya and White, 'Putin's Militocracy', p. 294.

99 Kryshtanovkaya and White, 'Inside the Putin Court', pp. 1067–8.

100 Stephen White, 'The Domestic Management of Russia's Foreign and Security Policy', in Roy Allison, Margot Light and Stephen White, *Putin's Russia and the Enlarged Europe* (Oxford, Blackwell Chatham House Papers, 2006), p. 26.

101 Bettina Renz, 'Putin's Militocracy? An Alternative Interpretation of *Siloviki* in Contemporary Russian Politics', *Europe–Asia Studies*, Vol. 58, No. 6, 2006, pp. 903–24.

102 Sharon Werning Rivera and David W. Rivera, 'The Russian Elite under Putin: Militocratic or Bourgeois?', *Post-Soviet Affairs*, Vol. 22, No. 2, 2006, pp. 125–44, at p. 136.

103 Rivera and Rivera, 'The Russian Elite under Putin', p. 126.

104 A moving account of the travails of Oleg Korobeinichev, of the Institute of Chemical Kinetics and Combustion of the Siberian branch of the Russian Academy of Sciences, is in *Rossiiskaya gazeta*, 17 June 2007, as well as details of ten other cases. The fact that the official government newspaper provided a sympathetic report on the Korobeinichev case shows how far Russia is from being an authoritarian system, while the acts of courage in defence of Korobeinichev shows that plenty of people are willing to stand up to the undoubted elements of authoritarianism in the system.

105 *Nezavisimaya gazeta*, 29 May 2001.

106 Quoted in *The Moscow Times*, 13 March 2007.

107 *Newsline*, 12 July 2002.

108 F. M. Rudinsky (ed.), *Civil Human Rights in Russia: Modern Problems of Theory and Practice* (Piscataway, NJ, Transaction Publishers, 2007).

## 6 The executive

1 Thomas Paine, *Rights of Man* (London, Penguin, 1984), p. 191.

2 Following the October 1993 events, the government moved out of Old Square to the White House. Parliament in turn moved to new premises in Moscow city centre: the Duma to the former Gosplan building, and the Federation Council to an office block not far away.

3 Eugene Huskey, *Presidential Power in Russia* (Armonk, NY, M. E. Sharpe, 1999).

4 See Juan Linz, 'The Perils of Presidentialism', *Journal of Democracy*, Vol. 1, No. 1, winter 1990, pp. 72–84.

5 Arend Lijphart (ed.), *Parliamentary versus Presidential Government* (Oxford, Oxford University Press, 1992), p. 19.

6 Juan J. Linz, 'Presidential or Parliamentary Democracy: Does It Make a Difference?', in Juan J. Linz and Arturo Valenzuela (eds), *The Failure of Presidential Democracy: Comparative Perspectives* (Baltimore, Johns Hopkins University Press, 1994), p. 7.

7 *Rossiiskaya gazeta*, 8 April 1992, pp. 1–4.

8 Thomas M. Nichols, *The Russian Presidency: Society and Politics in the Second Russian Republic* (Basingstoke, Macmillan, 2000), p.7.

9 See Eugene Huskey, 'The State-Legal Administration and the Politics of Redundancy', *Post-Soviet Affairs*, Vol. 11, No. 2, 1995, pp. 115–43.

10 EastWest Institute, *Russian Regional Report*, Vol. 5, No. 13, 5 April 2000.

11 Strana.ru, 18 January 2001.

12 The core of the State Council consisted of 5 presidential advisers (also known as state councillors) and the heads of the 9 most important ministries.

13 Namely, state secretary of the RSFSR, secretary of the State Council (19 July 1991), state secretary of the Russian Federation (7 April 1992), state secretary to the president (8 May 1992), and finally, adviser without title (14 December 1992), Lesage, 'The Crisis of Public Administration in Russia', p. 129.

14 At the Institute of the USSR Ministry of Non-Ferrous Metallurgy.

15 *Rossiiskaya gazeta*, 11 June 1992, p. 5.

16 See Lieutenant-General Valeri Manilov's interview in *Moskovskie novosti*, No. 23, 5–12 June 1994, p. 11.

17 *Moskovskie novosti*, No. 63, 11–18 December 1994, p. 4.

18 *Rossiiskaya gazeta*, 16 July 1996, p. 4.

19 Eugene Huskey and Alexander Obolonsky, 'The Struggle to Reform Russia's Bureaucracy', *Problems of Post-Communism*, Vol. 50, No. 4, July/August 2003, pp. 22–33.

20 *Kommersant*, 14 April 2003.

21 http://www.president.kremlin.ru/text/appears/2003/05/44623.shtml

22 Andrei Kolesnikov, 'Vladimir Putin pozvolil sebe svobodu slov', *Kommersant*, 1 February 2006, p. 2.

23 Those in favour of the so-called 'project of the parliamentary majority' were allegedly the representatives of the 'family': Voloshin and his deputy Vladislav Surkov, backed by the oligarch Khodorkovsky, who may well have had ambitions to take on the premiership himself. At that time there was much speculation that after the end of his two terms as president allowed by the constitution, Putin would himself use the enhanced powers of the premiership to continue his leadership.

24 *Rossiiskaya gazeta*, 5 November 1991, p. 1.

25 Alexander Rahr, 'Liberal-Centrist Coalition Takes Over in Russia', *RFE/RL Research Report*, Vol. 1, No. 29, 21 August 1992, pp. 22–5, at p. 23.

26 *Nezavisimaya gazeta*, 26 May 1992.

27 *Rossiiskaya gazeta*, 7 November 1992, pp. 1, 5.

28 Matthew Campbell, 'The Invisible Coup', *Sunday Times*, 20 December 1992, p. 11.

29 OMRI Special Report: Russian Election Survey, No. 13, 12 December 1995.

30 Igor' Klyamkin and Liliya Shevtsova, *Vnesistemnyi rezhim Borisa II: nekotorye osobennosti politicheskogo razvitiya postsovetskoi Rossii* (Moscow, Carnegie Centre, 1999), p. 12.

31 In 1992–3 he was Deputy Minister of Foreign Economic Relations, in 1993–7 First Deputy Minister of Foreign Economic Relations, in 1997–8 Minister of Foreign Economic Relations, in 1999–2000 Minister of Trade, 2000–1 First Deputy Secretary of the Security Council.

32 See Michel Lesage, 'The Crisis of Public Administration in Russia', *Public Administration*, Vol. 71, spring/summer 1993, pp. 121–33.

33 *Literaturnaya gazeta*, 19 February 1992, p. 3.

34 T. H. Rigby, *The Changing Soviet System: Mono-organisational Socialism from its Origins to Gorbachev's Restructuring* (Aldershot, Edward Elgar, 1990).

35 S. Filatov, 'Power and Business', *Rossiiskaya gazeta*, 30 December 1992; *Rossiiskie vesti*, 30 December 1992.

36 See Aleksandr Obolonskii, 'Rossiiskoe chinovnichestvo i problemy ego reformirovaniya', *Konstitutsionnoe pravo: Vostochnoevropeiskie obozrenie*, No. 4 (33), 2000/No. 1 (34), 2001, pp. 2–9.

37 *Trud*, 27 July 1995.

38 Robert J. Brym and V. Gimpelson, 'The Size, Composition and Dynamics of the Russian State Bureaucracy in the 1990s', *Slavic Review*, Vol. 63, No. 1, spring 2004, pp. 90–113.

39 *Russia in Figures 2006* (Moscow, Rosstat, 2006), p. 50.

## 7 Party development

1 Joseph A. Schumpeter, *Capitalism, Socialism & Democracy* (London, Routledge, 1943/1992), p. 283.

2 Giovanni Sartori, *Parties and Party Systems: A Framework for Analysis* (Cambridge, Cambridge University Press, 1976) and his *The Theory of Democracy Revisited* (Chatham, Chatham House Publishers, 1987); see also Jean Blondel, *Comparative Government: An Introduction* (Hemel Hempstead, Simon & Schuster, 1990), Part II.

3 See Judith B. Sedaitis and Jim Butterfield (eds), *Perestroika From Below: Social Movements in the Soviet Union* (London, Westview, 1991). See also Gail Lapidus, 'State and Society: Toward the Emergence of Civil Society in the Soviet Union', in Alexander Dallin and Gail Lapidus (eds), *The Soviet System in Crisis* (Boulder, CO, Westview Press, 1991), pp. 130–47; Victoria Bonnell, 'Voluntary Associations in Gorbachev's Reform Program', also in *The Soviet System in Crisis*, pp. 151–60. Geoffrey A. Hosking, Jonathan Aves and Peter J. S. Duncan, *The Road to Post-Communism: Independent Political Movements in the Soviet Union* (London, Pinter Publishers, 1992).

4 Cf. Steven Fish, 'The Emergence of Independent Associations and the Transformation of Russian Political Society', *The Journal of Communist Studies*, Vol. 7, No. 3, September 1991, pp. 299–334.

5 For perhaps the best analysis of these problems, see Michael Urban, with Vyacheslav Igrunov and Sergei Mitrokhin, *The Rebirth of Politics in Russia* (Cambridge, Cambridge University Press, 1997).

6 A. V. Gromov, O. S. Kuzin, *Neformaly: kto est' kto?* (Moscow, mysl', 1990), pp. 11–15.

7 E.g. *Neformaly: kto oni? Kuda zovut?*, ed. V. A. Pecheneva (Moscow, Izd. politicheskoi literatury, 1990).

8 Vladimir Pribylovskii, *Dictionary of Political Parties and Organisations* (Moscow, PostFactum; Washington, DC, Center for Strategic and International Studies, 1992), pp. 28–32.

9 *Svobodnoe Slovo*, No. 5 (107), 1992, p. 1.

10 See Geoffrey Evans and Stephen Whitefield, 'Social and Ideological Cleavage Formation in Post-Communist Hungary', *Europe–Asia Studies*, Vol. 47, No. 7, 1995, pp. 1177–1204.

11 The figure comes from V. N. Berezovskii *et al.*, *Partii, assotsiatsii, soyuzy, kluby: spravochnik* (Moscow, RAU Press, 1991), Vol. 1 (1), p. 3, with a discussion of classification on pp. 5–9.

12 A survey of 100 political parties and groups is provided by Vladimir Pribylovskii in *Slovar' oppozitsii: novye politicheskie partii i organizatsii Rossii, Analiticheskie vestniki informatsionnogo agenstva Postfactum*, No. 4/5, April 1991.

13 Andranik Migranyan, 'Prospects for the Russian National Movement', *Nezavisimaya gazeta*, 14 November 1991, p. 5.

14 Cf. Michael Waller, 'Political Actors and Political Roles in East-Central Europe', *Journal of Communist Studies*, Vol. 9, No. 4, December 1993, pp. 21–36.

15 L. Gordon and E. Klopov (eds), *Novye sotsial'nye dvizheniya v Rossii* (Moscow, Progress-Kompleks, 1993), p. 25.

16 Michael Urban and Vladimir Gel'man, 'The Development of Political Parties in Russia', in Karen Dawisha and Bruce Parrott (eds), *Democratic Change and Authoritarian Reactions in Russia, Ukraine, Belarus and Moldova* (Cambridge, Cambridge University Press, 1997), pp. 175–219.

17 Vyacheslav Nikonov, *Nezavisimaya gazeta*, 7 August 1992, p. 5.

18 Giovanni Sartori, *Parties and Party Systems: A Framework for Analysis* (Cambridge, Cambridge University Press, 1976), p. 63.

19 *Narodnyi deputat*, No. 8, 1992, pp. 96–100, at p. 96.

20 *Izvestiya*, 20 April 1992, p. 2.

21 *Moscow News*, No. 22 (28 May 1993), p. 1.

22 Maurice Duverger, *Political Parties: Their Organization and Activity in the Modern State* (London, Methuen, 1954).

23 See V. G. Golovin, 'Ekonomicheskie vzglyady politicheskikh partii i blokov Rossii', in *Partii i partiinye sistemy sovremennoi evropy* (Moscow, INION, 1994), pp. 142–71.

24 *Izvestiya*, 24 August 1992.

25 See Yitzhak M. Brudny, 'The Dynamics of "Democratic Russia", 1990–1993', *Post-Soviet Affairs*, Vol. 9, No. 2, 1993, pp. 141–70; on the Civic Union, see Michael McFaul, 'Russian Centrism and Revolutionary Transitions', *Post-Soviet Affairs*, Vol. 9, No. 3 (1993), pp. 196–222.

26 *Izvestiya*, 3 August 1992, p. 3.

27 Alexander Vladislavlev of the Renewal League, *Nezavisimaya gazeta*, 11 July 1992, p. 4.

28 Vladimir Shumeiko, a co-founder of Renewal, in *Moscow News*, No. 24, 14 June 1992, p. 6.

29 *Segodnya*, 31 March 1994, p. 2.

30 Konstantin Medvedev, 'V Rossii vozmozhna smena kursa', *Nezavisimaya gazeta*, 7 December 1991, p. 2.

31 This characterised the Slavic Assembly (*Slavyanskii sobor*), an alliance of Soviet and Russian nationalists; the *Nashi* (Ours) movement which brought together Alexander Nevzorov, the presenter of the investigative Leningrad televison programme '600 Seconds', Victor Alksnis of the Soyuz group, and Sergei Kurginyan, one of the leading conservative intellectuals and leader of the '*Postperestroika*' group; and the Russian Popular Union (*Russkii obshchenarodnii soyuz*, ROS), led by Sergei Baburin and Nikolai Pavlov. A lawyer by training, Baburin insisted

that Russia *was* the former USSR and supported a strong state, collective property and mystical notions of Russian community.

32 *Obozrevatel'*, No. 2–3, 1992, prilozhenie, p. 21.
33 Including the writers Valentin Rasputin, V. Belov, A. Prokhanov, Academician I. Shafarevich, the well-known figures from the old Soviet Congress Viktor Alksnis and A. Makashov, as well as Baburin and Mikhail Astaf'ev (leader of the Constitutional Democratic Party). The core of the NSF was the oppositional parliamentary bloc 'Russian Unity'.
34 *Rossiya*, No. 27 (86), July 1992, p. 3.
35 Vyacheslav Nikonov, *Nezavisimaya gazeta*, 7 August 1992, p. 5.
36 The decree of 23 August 1991 halted the activity of the CPSU; the decree of 25 August confiscated its property; and the decree of 6 November banned the party in Russia. The appeal is in *Konstitutsionnyi vestnik*, No. 13, November 1992, pp. 221–5.
37 *Konstitutsionnyi vestnik*, No. 13, November 1992, pp. 226–42.
38 E.g. Sergei Shakhrai, *Moscow News*, No. 22, 31 May 1992, p. 2.
39 *Rossiiskaya gazeta*, 16 December 1992, p. 6.
40 Gavriil Popov, *Konstitutsionnoe soveshchanie*, No. 1, August 1993, p. 33.
41 Vera Tolz, 'The Civic Accord: Contributing to Russia's Stablity?', RFE/RL *Research Report*, Vol. 3, No. 19, 13 May 1994, pp. 1–5.
42 *Izvestiya*, 29 April 1994, p. 1.
43 NTV 19 December 1995, in *OMRI Daily Digest*, Part 1, 19 December 1995.
44 *Washington Post*, 8 September 2000.
45 Gleb Cherkasov, *Segodnya*, 9 December 1995, p. 2.
46 Robert G. Moser, *Unexpected Outcomes: Electoral Systems, Political Parties, and Representation in Russia* (Pittsburgh, PA, University of Pittsburgh Press, 2001).
47 *Izvestiya*, 18 August 2000.
48 For a discussion of the background to the law and various alternative drafts, see Z. Zotova, *Politicheskie partii Rossii: organizatsiya i deyatel'nost'* (Moscow, Rossiiskii tsentr obucheniya izbiratel'nym tekhnologiyam, 2001).
49 These criticisms were made by the Independent Expert Legal Council, *Novye Izvestiya*, 2 February 2001; RFE/RL, *Newsline*, 5 February 2001.
50 Herbert Kitschelt, Zdenka Mansfeldova, Radoslav Markowski and Gabor Toka, *Post-Communist Party Systems* (Cambridge, Cambridge University Press, 1999), p. 1.
51 Robert Michels, *Political Parties: A Sociological Study of the Oligarchical Tendencies of Modern Democracies* (New York, Free Press, 1962).
52 As reported by the Minister of Justice, Yuri Chaika, RFE/RL, *Newsline*, 25 January 2001. This number differs from other reports.
53 *Obshchaya gazeta*, No. 40 (1994), p. 8.
54 Richard Rose, Neil Munro and Stephen White, *The 1999 Duma Vote: A Floating Party System*, Studies in Public Policy Number 331 (Glasgow, University of Strathclyde, 2000), p. 7.
55 Luke March, 'The Contemporary Russian Left after Communism: Into the Dustbin of History?', *Journal of Communist Studies and Transition Politics*, Vol. 22, No. 4, December 2006, pp. 431–56.
56 *Izbiratel'nyi blok 'Rodina' (Narodno-patrioticheskii Soyuz): Programmnye dokumenty*, mimeo (on CEC website).
57 Vladislav Surkov, 'Suverenitet – eto politicheskii sinonim konkurentosposobnosti', *Moskovskie novosti*, No. 7, 3 March 2006.
58 Anatolii Khimenko, 'Partiinoe stroitel'stvo zamorozheno rossiiskimi "verkhami"', *Nezavisimaya gazeta*, 4 March 1993, p. 2.
59 Alexander Solzhenitsyn, *Rebuilding Russia: Reflections and Tentative Proposals* (London, Harvill, 1991), pp. 54–90, at p. 70.
60 S. M. Lipset and S. Rokkan, 'Cleavage Structures, Party Systems and Voter Alignments: An Introduction', in S. M. Lipset and S. Rokkan (eds), *Party Systems and Voter Alignments: Cross National Perspectives* (New York, The Free Press, 1967); see also S. Rokkan, *Citizens, Elections, Parties* (Oslo, Universitetsforlaget, 1970). For an attempt to apply Rokkanian analysis, see Maurizio Cotta, 'Building Party Systems after the Dictatorship: The East European Cases in a Comparative Perspective', in Geoffrey Pridham and Tatu Vanhanen (eds), *Democratization in Eastern Europe* (London, Routledge, 1994), pp. 99–127.

61  Mikhail Afanas'ev, *Klientelizm i rossiiskaya gosudarstvennost'* (Moscow, Moskovskii Obshchestvennyi Nauchnyi Fond, 1997).

62  Lipset and Rokkan, 'Cleavage Structures', pp. 50–1.

63  Cf. Geoffrey Evans and Stephen Whitefield, 'Identifying the Bases of Party Competition in Eastern Europe', *British Journal of Political Science*, Vol. 23, No. 4, 1993, pp. 521–48.

64  See, for example, Erwin Oberlander, 'The Role of the Political Parties', in K. Katkov *et al.* (eds), *Russia Enters the Twentieth Century* (London, Temple, Smith, 1971), pp. 60–84.

65  Cf. Terence Emmons, *The Formation of Political Parties and the First National Elections in Russia* (Cambridge, MA, Harvard University Press, 1983).

66  A. I. Zevelev (ed), *Istoriya politicheskikh partii Rossii* (Moscow, Vysshaya shkola, 1994); N. V. Orlova, *Politicheskie partii Rossii: stranitsy istorii* (Moscow, Yurist, 1994).

67  Igor' Malov and Maksim Khrustalev, 'Mnogopartiinost' v Rossii, 1917–1990', *Problemy vostochnoi evropy*, No. 31–2 (Washington, 1991), pp. 79–163.

68  E.g. Nikolai Biryukov and V. M. Sergeev, *Russia's Road to Democracy: Parliament, Communism and Traditional Culture* (Aldershot, Edward Elgar, 1993).

69  Stephen Welch, *The Concept of Political Culture* (Basingstoke, Macmillan, 1993).

70  This change is analysed by Richard Hofstadter, *The Idea of a Party System: The Rise of Legitimate Opposition in the United States, 1780–1840* (Berkeley, University of California Press, 1970). See also Robert Aldrich, *Why Parties? The Origin and Transformation of Political Parties in America* (Chicago and London, University of Chicago Press, 1995).

71  G. V. Golosov, 'Proiskhozhdenie sovremennykh rossiiskikh politicheskikh partii, 1987–1993', in V. Gel'man, G. Golosov and E. Meleshkina (eds), *Pervyi elektoral'nyi tsikl v Rossii, 1993–1996gg.* (Moscow, Ves' Mir, 2000), pp. 77–105. See also A. Panebianco, *Political Parties: Organisation and Power* (Cambridge, Cambridge University Press, 1998), p. 50.

72  M. Stephen Fish, *Democracy from Scratch: Opposition and Regime in the New Russian Revolution* (Princeton, NJ, Princeton University Press, 1995).

73  *Kommersant*, No. 48 (98) (16 December 1991), p. 23. A few groups favoured by Burbulis did get premises, but Yeltsin's reneging on this promise for the others was yet another reason for the bitter hostility against him of part of the new political elite.

74  A. Kulik and S. Pshizova (eds), *Political Parties in Post-Soviet Space* (London, Greenwood, 2005), p. 33.

75  *Sovetskaya Rossiya*, 31 May 1990.

76  Henry E. Hale, *Why Not Parties in Russia? Democracy, Federalism and the State* (Cambridge, Cambridge University Press, 2006); reference at p. 236.

77  V. Ya. Gel'man, 'Institutsional'nyi dizain: sozdavaya "pravila igry"', in V. Gel'man, G. Golosov and E. Meleshkina (eds), *Pervyi elektoral'nyi tsikl v Rossii, 1993–1996gg.* (Moscow, Ves' Mir, 2000), pp. 44–76.

78  *Moscow News*, No. 25 (18 June 1993), p. 2.

79  Sergei Mndoyants, Aleksei Salmin, *Moskovskie novosti*, No. 67, 1–8 October 1995, p. 6.

80  A. Kulik, 'Posttotalitarnye partii v politicheskom protsesse', *MEMO*, No. 2, 1994, pp. 27–38, at p. 29.

81  Vladimir Gel'man and Grigorii Golosov, 'Regional Party System Formation in Russia: The Deviant Case of Sverdlovsk *Oblast*', *Journal of Communist Studies and Transition Politics*, Vol. 14, No. 1/2, 1998, pp. 31–53.

82  Philippe C. Schmitter, 'Interest Systems and the Consolidation of Democracies', in G. Marks and L. Diamond (eds), *Reexamining Democracy* (London, Sage, 1992), pp. 156–81, at p. 160.

83  Fyodor Gavrilov, 'Russia's Right has to Decide What's Right', *St. Petersburg Times*, 23 July 1999.

84  See Evans and Whitefield, 'Identifying the Bases of Party Competition in Eastern Europe', op. cit.

85  Lyudmila Alekseeva, 'Nesvobodnye profsoyuzy', *Moskovskie novosti*, No. 3 (15–22 January 1995), p. 14.

86  This issue is discussed in the Eastern European context by Sten Berglund and Jan Ake Dellenbrant, 'The Evolution of Party Systems in Eastern Europe', *Journal of Communist Studies*, Vol. 8, No. 1, March 1992, pp. 148–59, esp. p. 154.

87 R. Inglehart, 'The Changing Structure of Political Cleavages in Western Societies', in R. J. Dalton *et al.* (eds), *Electoral Change in Advanced Industrial Democracies: Realignment or Dealignment?* (Princeton, Princeton University Press, 1984).

88 Richard S. Katz and Peter Mair, *How Parties Organise: Change and Adaptation in Party Organizations in Western Democracies* (London, Sage, 1994).

89 Alan Ware, *Political Parties and Party Systems* (Oxford, Oxford University Press, 1996), Chapter 7.

90 Daniel Bell, *The End of Ideology: On the Exhaustion of Political Ideas in the Fifties* (New York, Free Press of Glencoe, 1960).

91 Francis Fukuyama, 'The End of History', *The National Interest*, summer 1989, pp. 3–17; *The End of History and the Last Man* (New York, Free Press, 1992).

92 Cf. Richard Flacks, 'The Party's Over: So What is to Be Done?', *Social Research*, Vol. 60, No. 3, autumn 1993, pp. 445–70.

93 Cf. Andrew Wilson, *Virtual Politics: Faking Democracy in the Post-Soviet World* (New Haven, CT, Yale University Press, 2005).

94 Jacques Derrida, *Spectres of Marx* (London, Routledge, 1994); see also his 'Spectres of Marx', *New Left Review*, No. 205, May–June 1994, pp. 31–58.

## 8 Electoral politics

1 Vladislav Surkov, deputy head of the presidential administration, 'Russkaya politicheskaya kul'tura: Vzglyad iz utopii', http://www.er.ru/news.html?id=121456

2 See Jeffrey Hahn, 'An Experiment in Competition: The 1987 Elections to the Local Soviets', *Slavic Review*, Vol. 47, No. 2, 1988, pp. 434–47; and Stephen White, 'Reforming the Electoral System', *Journal of Communist Studies*, Vol. 4, No. 4, 1988, pp. 1–17.

3 The revised electoral law was published in *Izvestiya*, 28 October 1989.

4 An example of this is given for Yaroslavl region by Gavin Helf and Jeffrey Hahn, 'Old Dogs and New Tricks: Party Elites in the Russian Regional Elections of 1990', *Slavic Review*, Vol. 51, No. 3, fall 1992, p. 526.

5 See, for example, Stephen White, 'Democratizing Eastern Europe: The Elections of 1990', *Electoral Studies*, Vol. 9, No. 4, 1990, pp. 277–87; Vernon Bogdanor, 'Founding Elections and Regime Change', *Electoral Studies*, Vol. 9, No. 4, 1990, pp. 288–94.

6 *Izvestiya*, 4 May 1994, p. 4.

7 Rose *et al.* 'Voting in a Floating Party System'.

8 This argument is made by Salvatore d'Albergo and Pier Paolo Frassinelli, 'Electoral Typologies and Democracy', *Representation*, Vol. 36, No. 1, 1999, pp. 73–7.

9 Cited by Victor Sheinis in *ONS: Obshchestvennye nauki i sovremenost'*, No. 1, 1995, p. 9.

10 For a discussion of the manipulation of electoral systems, see Arend Lijphart, *Electoral Systems and Party Systems: A Study of Twenty-seven Democracies, 1945–1990* (Oxford, Oxford University Press, 1994).

11 *Moskovskie novosti*, No. 25, 20 June 1993, p. A9.

12 *Byulleten' Tsentral'noi izbiratel'noi kommissii*, 1 (12), 1994, p. 28.

13 Sergei Mdoyants, Aleksei Salmin, 'Vybor nakanune vyborov', *Nezavisimaya gazeta*, 30 March 1995, p. 3.

14 On this, see Richard Rose, Neil Munro and Stephen White, 'Voting in a Floating Party System: the 1999 Duma Election', *Europe–Asia Studies*, Vol. 53, No. 3, May 2001, pp. 419–43.

15 For a discussion of the issues, see Stephen White and Ian McAllister, 'Reforming the Russian Electoral System', *Journal of Communist and Transition Politics*, Vol. 15, No. 4, December 1999, pp. 17–40.

16 Anatolii Luk'yanov, 'Kontrol'naya nad demokratiya', *Nezavisimaya gazeta*, 2 March 2000, p. 3.

17 *O vyborakh deputatov Gosudarstvennoi Dumy Federal'nogo Sobraniya Rossiiskoi Federatsii: Federal'nyi zakon* (Moscow, Izdatel'stvo PRIOR, 1999).

18 Anastasiya Kornya, 'Partiinyi feminizm Aleksandr Veshnyakova', *Nezavisimaya gazeta*, 1 September 2004, pp. 1, 2.

19 *Rossiiskaya gazeta*, 24 May 2005, pp. 22–32.
20 Once again, Putin moved to deal with a problem that had long been tolerated elsewhere, notably in Italy. In that country's 13th parliament (1996–2001) 158 deputies had changed political allegiance, Tobias Jones, *The Dark Heart of Italy* (London, Faber and Faber, 2003), p. 188.
21 *Rossiiskaya gazeta*, 15 July 2006, p. 7.
22 *Nezavisimaya gazeta*, 15 November 2005, pp. 1, 2.
23 OSCE ODIHR 'Russia: Election Observation Mission Report', 27 January 2004, recommendation No. 14, http://www.osce.org/documents/odihr/2004/01/1947_en.pdf
24 *Rossiiskaya gazeta*, 23 November 2006; also 5 December 2006.
25 Gel'man, Vladimir, 'From "Feckless Pluralism" to "Dominant Power Politics"? The Transformation of Russia's Party System', *Democratization*, Vol. 13, No. 4, August 2006, p. 546.
26 Mikhail N. Afanas'ev, *Klientelizm i rossiiskaya gosudarstvennost'*, 2nd edn (Moscow, MONF, 2000), p. 17.
27 For a fuller analysis than can be given here, see Richard Sakwa, 'The Russian Elections of December 1993', *Europe–Asia Studies*, Vol. 47, No. 2, 1995, pp. 195–227.
28 *Rossiiskaya gazeta*, 11 December 1993, p. 1.
29 *Novoe vremya*, No. 7 (February 1994), pp. 8–12.
30 See A. A. Sobyanin and V. G. Sukhovolskii, *Demokratiya, ogranichennaya falsifikatsii* [*Democracy, Limited by Falsification*] (Moscow, Planning Group on Human Rights, 1995).
31 *Kommersant-Daily*, 18 November 1995.
32 *Nezavisimaya gazeta*, 16 November 1995.
33 *Moskovskie novosti*, No. 69, 8–15 October 1995, p. 6.
34 *Moskovskii komsomolets*, 19 December 1995.
35 *The Economist*, 7 October 1995, p. 55.
36 The term 'soft' backlash is from Urban, 'December 1993', p. 135, fn 19.
37 *Moskovskie novosti*, No. 44, 25 June–2 July 1995, p. 4.
38 *Nezavisimaya gazeta*, 27 April 1996.
39 Of the 441 deputies elected, 225 came from the party lists and 216 from single-member districts. A second round of voting was scheduled for the eight SMD seats where the majority of the electorate voted against all of the candidates on the ballot paper. Elections were not held in Chechnya, the ninth vacant seat.
40 *Izvestiya*, 25 February 2000, p. 5.
41 Yevgenia Borisova, 'And the Winner Is?', *Moscow Times*, 9 September 2000.
42 For a full analysis, see Richard Sakwa, 'The 2003–2004 Russian Elections and Prospects for Democracy', *Europe–Asia Studies*, Vol. 57, No. 3, May 2005, pp. 369–98, from which this section draws.
43 *Vybory deputatov gosudarstvennoi dumy federal'nogo sobraniya Rossiiskoi Federatsii 2003: elektoral'naya statistika*, Central Electoral Commission (Moscow, Ves' Mir, 2004), p. 194.
44 Full text at http://www.komitet2008.ru
45 Yavlinsky pointed to the events in Sverdlovsk *oblast*, where Yabloko and other independent candidates were refused registration for the *oblast* Duma elections on 14 March 2004 because UR (and the governor, Eduard Rossel) feared competition. *Novaya gazeta*, No. 9, 9–11 February 2004, p. 6.
46 RFE/RL, *(Un)Civil Societies*, Vol. 5, No. 1, 8 January 2004.
47 Alexei Titkov, *'Party Number Four' – Rodina: Whence and Why?* (Moscow, Panorama Centre, 2006), p. 18.
48 See Laura Belin, 'Glazev Gambles and Loses', RFE/RL, *Russian Political Weekly*, Vol. 4, No. 10, 17 March 2004.
49 Putin provided a broad analysis of the state of Russia when he came to power four years earlier, his achievements as president and his plans for the future, in a speech at Moscow State University on 12 February 2004, http://www.president.kremlin.ru/text/appears/2004/02/62215.shtml
50 Kabardino-Balkaria at 97.7 per cent led the field in turnout, followed by Ingushetia at 96.2 per cent and Mordovia came third with 94.5 per cent, followed by Dagestan at 94.09 per cent and Chechnya at 94 per cent. At the other end of the spectrum Krasnoyrask

came in with only 51.09 per cent, Irkutsk 52.4 per cent, Ivanovo 53.34 per cent, Novgorod 54.5 per cent and Sakhalin 54.8 per cent. Nowhere was there a turnout below 50 per cent (*Vybory prezidenta Rossiiskoi Federatsii 2004:elektoral'naya statistika*, Central Electoral Commission (Moscow, Ves' Mir, 2004), pp. 104–5). In Novgorod the governor, Mikhail Prusak, is no Putin enthusiast and had once called UR a 'mass grave'. It can be suggested that turnout can be a proximate index for the degree of authoritarianism and ability to mobilise 'administrative resources' and has little to do with the socio-economic characteristics of the region. Tatarstan's 83.2 per cent turnout suggests that the result was not manipulated outrageously (as in Kabardino-Balkaria and the other places listed above), but was probably affected by administrative intervention. The effort to achieve high turnout is also connected with the level of subsidy from the centre, although a cross-cutting factor is the personal attitude of the governor to the president.

51 Putin won 98.18 per cent of the vote in Ingushetiya, 96.49 per cent in Kabardino-Balkaria, while the lowest regions were Primorsk (59.37 per cent), Orenburg (58.79) and Belgorod at the bottom (54.82), *Vybory prezidenta Rossiiskoi Federatsii 2004*, p. 116.

52 For a discussion of the issue, see Andreas Auer (ed.), *Direct Democracy: The Eastern and Central European Experience* (Aldershot, Ashgate, 2001). On the broader issues of direct democracy, see also Ian Budge, *The New Challenge of Direct Democracy* (1997), and John Haskell, *Direct Democracy or Representative Government: Dispelling the Populist Myth* (Boulder, CO, Westview Press, 2000).

53 Article 37, sect. 2 of the law, *Sobranie Zakonodatel'stva RF 1995*, No. 42, pos. 3921.

54 Geoffrey Evans and Stephen Whitefield, 'Identifying the Bases of Party Competition in Eastern Europe', *British Journal of Political Science*, Vol. 23, No. 4, 1993, pp. 521–48.

55 See Stephen Whitefield and Geoffrey Evans, 'Class, Markets and Partisanship in Post-Soviet Russia', *Electoral Studies*, Vol. 18, No. 2, 1999, pp. 155–78.

56 Mikhail N. Afanas'ev, *Klientelizm i rossiiskaya gosudarstvennost'*, 2nd edn (Moscow, MONF, 2000), p. 17.

57 Cf. Sergei Mdoyants and Aleksei Salmin, 'Dozhivem li do "rutinoi" demokratii', *Moskovskie novosti*, No. 63, 17–24 September 1995, p. 6.

# 9 The legislature

1 Edmund Burke, 'Causes of Present Discontents', in *Edmund Burke on Revolution*, edited by Robert A. Smith (New York, Harper & Row, 1968), pp. 30–1.

2 Sergei Mdoyants, Aleksei Salmin, 'Pobedit sluchainyi', *Moskovskie novosti*, No. 71, 15–22 October 1995, p. 6.

3 *Nezavisimaya gazeta*, 12 January 1996, p. 2.

4 Ludmila Telen, *Moskovskie novosti*, No. 87, 1995, p. 8.

5 RFE/RL Newsline, 18 January 1999; Ol'ga Tropkina, 'Veshnyakov ne verit v massovye fal'sifikatsii na vyborakh', *Nezavisimaya gazeta*, 28 December 1999, p. 3 gave a slightly higher figure: 175.

6 *Vestnik Tsentral'noi izbiratel'noi komissii Rossiiskoi Federatsii*, No. 1 (91), 2000, p. 231.

7 Laura Belin, 'Early Presidential Election Secures Duma Majority for Putin', *RFE/RL Russian Election Report*, No. 8, 7 January 2000.

8 *Novye izvestiya*, 27 January 2004.

9 Alexei Titkov, *'Party Number Four' – Rodina: Whence and Why?* (Moscow, Panorama Centre, 2006), p. 64.

10 *Izvestiya*, 24 December 1993, pp. 1–2.

11 For his views, see Ivan Rybkin, *Gosudarstvennaya duma: Pytaya popytka* (Moscow, 1994); *My obrecheny na soglasie* (Moscow, Mezhdunarodnye otnosheniya, 1994).

12 *Segodnya*, 18 January 1996, p. 1.

13 Paul Chaisty, *Legislative Politics and Economic Power in Russia* (Basingstoke, Palgrave, 2006), pp. 83–5.

14 For an examination of the question of measuring significance, and a discussion of the contradiction between the actual productivity of the Duma and its poor image, see Paul Chaisty and

Petra Schleiter, 'Productive but Not Valued: The Russia State Duma, 1994–2001', *Europe–Asia Studies*, Vol. 54, No. 5, 2002, pp. 701–24.

15 Chaisty and Schleiter, 'Productive but Not Valued', p. 715.

16 Thomas Remington, 'Federal'noe Sobranie Rossiiskoi Federatsii (1994-2004)', *Sravnitel'noe konstitutsionnoe obozrenie*, No. 4 (53), 2005, pp. 40–52, at p. 45.

17 Henry E. Hale and Robert Orrtung, 'The Duma Districts: Key to Putin's Power', PONARS Policy Memo 290, September 2003.

18 Constitutional changes require not only a two-thirds majority in the Duma but also approval by three-quarters of the Federation Council and the endorsement of two-thirds of Russia's regional legislatures – as well as the signature of the president.

19 http://president.kremlin.ru/text/appears/2006/02/101129.shtml

20 Leonid Radzikhovskii, *Segodnya*, 6 February 2001.

21 Ivan Rodin, *Nezavisimaya gazeta*, 6 February 2001.

22 *Moskovskie novosti*, No. 69, 8–15 October 1995, p. 7.

23 Decree of 11 October, *Rossiiskaya Federatsiya*, No. 1 (13), 1993, p. 17.

24 Nikolai Ryabov, *Rossiiskaya gazeta*, 11 December 1993, p. 1.

25 OMRI, *Regional Report*, Vol. 1, No. 2, 4 September 1996, Part 1.

26 *Nezavisimaya gazeta*, 6 December 1995, p. 1.

27 *Rossiiskie vesti*, 24 January 1996, p.1.

28 *Nezavisimaya gazeta*, 19 May 2000.

29 The Jamestown Foundation, *Monitor*, 19 July 2000.

30 Sergei Sarychev, 'Stroev Deems Attempts to Reform Legislature Absurd', *Russian Regional Report*, Vol. 5, No. 28, 19 July 2000.

31 *Nezavisimaya gazeta*, 3 August 2000.

32 *Russian Regional Report*, Vol. 5, No. 29, 26 July 2000.

33 The head of the Northwest Federal District, Cherkesov (a close Putin ally), on 21 July 2000 did in fact suggest that in future the upper house could be elected, *Russian Regional Report*, Vol. 5, No. 29, 26 July 2000. Sergei Mironov in 2006 on several occasions suggested that direct elections to the FC would be appropriate.

34 Sarychev, 'Stroev Deems Attempts to Reform Legislature Absurd'.

35 *Nezavisimaya gazeta*, 3 August 2000.

36 *Nezavisimaya gazeta*, 26 February 2007.

37 Only Leonid Roketsky from Tyumen region and Magomedali Magomedov from Dagestan met this condition.

38 The public chamber of the Constitutional Assembly had opposed granting the FC rather than the Duma powers endorsing presidential decrees on a state of emergency, martial law and the deployment of troops abroad, but had been over-ruled, Viktor Sheinis, *Moscow News*, No. 46, 12 November 1993, p. 2.

## Part III  Nationalism, federalism and regionalism

1 S. A. Smith, 'Citizenship and the Russian Nation during World War I: A Comment', *Slavic Review*, Vol. 59, No. 2, summer 2000, pp. 316–35, at p. 322.

2 M. S. Gorbachev, *On My Country and the World* (New York, Columbia University Press, 2000), p. 164.

## 10  National identity and state-building

1 Valeri Tishkov, *Ethnicity, Nationalism and Conflict in and after the Soviet Union: The Mind Aflame* (London, Sage, 1996), p. 246.

2 Hans Kohn, *The Idea of Nationalism* (New York, Macmillan, 1945); see also his 'Western and Eastern Nationalism', in John Hutchinson and Anthony D. Smith (eds), *Nationalism* (Oxford, Oxford University Press, 1994), pp. 162–5.

3 *Vestnik statistiki*, No. 10, 1990, p. 72.

4 Mark R. Beissinger, 'The Persisting Ambiguity of Empire', *Post-Soviet Affairs*, Vol. 11, No. 2, 1995, pp. 149–84, at p. 158.
5 For an exploration of the tension between nation and empire, see Geoffrey Hosking, *People and Empire, 1552–1917* (London, Harper Collins, 1997).
6 Cited by Margot Light, 'Foreign Policy Thinking', in Neil Malcolm, Alex Pravda, Roy Allison and Margot Light (eds), *Internal Factors in Russian Foreign Policy* (London, RIIA /Oxford University Press, 1996), p. 36.
7 See Terry Martin, *The Affirmative Action Empire: Nations and Nationalism in the Soviet Union, 1923–1939* (Ithaca and London, Cornell University Press, 2001).
8 Geoffrey Hosking, *Rulers and Victims: The Russians in the Soviet Union* (Cambridge, MA, Harvard University Press, 2006).
9 For a good analysis of the rebirth of Russian nationalism, see Yitzhak M. Brudny, *Reinventing Russia: Russian Nationalism and the Soviet State, 1953–1991* (Cambridge, MA, Harvard University Press, 1999); Stephen K. Carter, *Russian Nationalism* (London, Pinter, 1990); and Peter Duncan, *Russian Messianism: Third Rome, Revolution, Communism and After* (London, Routledge, 2000).
10 Alexander Solzhenitsyn, *Letter to the Soviet Leaders* (New York, Harper and Row, 1974).
11 Igor Shafarevich, 'Separation or Reconciliation? The Nationalities Question in the USSR' and 'Does Russia Have a Future', in Alexander Solzhenitsyn (ed.), *From Under the Rubble* (London, Fontana, 1976), pp. 88–104, 279–94; and see also his 'Russofobiya', *Nash sovremennik*, No. 6, 1989; on allied questions see G. Popov and N. Adzhubei, 'Pamyat' i "Pamyat": o problemakh istoricheskoi pamyati i sovremennykh natsional'nykh otnoshenii', *Znamya*, No. 1, 1988.
12 The character of this apparent *mésalliance* is analysed, for example, by S. V. Cheshko, *Raspad Sovetskogo Soyuza: Entnopoliticheskii analiz*, 2nd edn (Moscow, Institut Etnologii RAN, 2000).
13 The roots of this thinking, the relationship between Nikolai Trubetskoi's anti-Western polemic *Europe and Humanity* (1921) and Nikolai Ustryalov's 'change of landmarks' (*smenovekhovtsy*) movement that endorsed the Bolshevik revolution since it appeared to augment Russian national power, are discussed by Jane Burbank, *Intelligentsia and Revolution* (Oxford, Oxford University Press, 1986), pp. 208–37.
14 Len Karpinskii, cited by Tony Barber 'Democracy Tears Russia to Shreds', *Independent on Sunday*, 22 March 1992.
15 E.g. Mykhailo Hrushevs'kyi in S. Frederick Starr (ed.), *The Legacy of History on the Foreign Policies of the New States of the Former Soviet Union* (New York, M. E. Sharpe, 1994).
16 Alexander Zinoviev, *Katastroika* (London, Claridge Press, 1990).
17 This was the view of the 'patriots' associated with the newspaper *Den'* (*Day*) edited by Prokhanov, sponsored by the Union of Russian Writers.
18 *Moscow News*, No. 37, 1991, p. 5.
19 Igor Klyamkin, *Ogonek*, No. 47, 1995, p. 19.
20 E. A. Pozdnyakov, *Natsiya, natsionalizm, natsional'nye interesy* (Moscow, Progress-kultura, 1994), p. 61.
21 Pozdnyakov, *Natsiya, natsionalizm, natsional'nye interesy*, p. 74.
22 Solzhenitsyn, *Rebuilding Russia*, p. 15.
23 Sergei Kondrashov, *Nationalism and the Drive for Sovereignty in Tatarstan, 1988–92* (New York, St Martin's Press, 2000).
24 Vladimir Ilyushenko, *Literaturnaya gazeta*, 19 February 1992, p. 11.
25 The term 'state-nation' is from Juan J. Linz and Alfred Stepan, 'Toward Consolidated Democracies', *Journal of Democracy*, Vol. 7, No. 1, April 1996, p. 27, where it is defined as 'those multicultural or even multinational states that nonetheless still manage to engender strong identification and loyalty from their diverse citizens', p. 27. The United States, Switzerland and India are cited as examples of state-nations.
26 Fadi Hakura, 'Emerging Identity: Turkey', *The World Today*, April 2007, pp. 25–7, at p. 26.
27 Nabi Abdullaev, 'Language of Lenin Losing Ground', *Moscow Times*, 25 October 2006.

28 For a good discussion of diaspora politics, with a measured analysis of the appropriate terminology, see Charles King and Neil J. Melvin, 'Diaspora Politics: Ethnic Linkages, Foreign Policy, and Security in Eurasia', *International Security*, Vol. 24, No. 3, winter 1999, pp. 108–38, esp. fn 30.

29 A point reiterated by Putin in his state of the nation speech on 10 May 2006, http://president. kremlin.ru/text/appears/2006/05/105546.shtml. See Vladimir Mukomel, 'Immigration and Russian Migration Policy: Debating the Future', *Russian Analytical Digest*, No. 7, 3 October 2006, pp. 2–8.

30 For a recent analysis, see Marléne Laruelle, *La question des Russes du proche-étranger en Russie (1991–2006)*, Les Etudes du CERI, No. 126, June 2006, Sciences Po, Paris.

31 Rogers Brubaker, *Nationalism Reframed: Nationhood and the National Question in the New Europe* (Cambridge, Cambridge University Press, 1996).

32 Pål Kolst?, *Russians in the Former Soviet Republics* (Bloomington, Indiana University Press, 1995), p. 50.

33 Cited by Roman Szporluk, 'The Imperial Legacy and the Soviet Nationalities Problem' in L. Hajda and M. Beissinger (eds), *The Nationalities Factor in Soviet Politics and Society* (Cambridge, Cambridge University Press, 1990), p. 13.

34 In Hajda and Beissinger (eds), *The Nationalities Factor in Soviet Politics and Society*, pp. 17–18.

35 See Vera Tolz, 'Forging the Nation: National Identity and Nation-Building in Post-Communist Russia', *Europe–Asia Studies*, Vol. 50, No. 6, 1998, pp. 993–1022.

36 E.g., Henry A. Kissinger, 'The New Russian Question', *Newsweek*, 10 February 1991, pp. 12–13, at p. 13.

37 Likhachev described his experiences in the 1988 film about the prison, *Solovetskii Power*.

38 Dmitrii S. Likhachev, *Reflections on Russia* (Boulder, Westview Press, 1991), quotation from p. 80; his popular works in Russian include *Proshloe-budushchemu: stat'i i ocherki* (Leningrad, Nauka, 1985) and *Ya vospominayu* (Moscow, Progress, 1991).

39 The history of the flag, emblem and anthem are described in B. A. Anikin (ed.), *Natsional'naya ideya Rossii* (Moscow, State Management University, 2002), with the words of the new anthem on p. 44, of earlier versions pp. 45–7.

40 *Moscow Times,* 19 July 2001.

41 V. V. Putin, *Razgovor s Rossiei: Stenogramma 'Pryamoi linii s Prezidentom Rossiiskoi Federatsii V. V. Putinym', 19 December 2002* (Moscow, Olma-Politizdat, 2003), pp. 86–7.

42 Itar-Tass, 12 June 2006.

43 Cf. Ronald Grigor Suny, 'States, Empires and Nations', *Post-Soviet Affairs*, Vol. 11, No. 2, 1995, pp. 185–96, at p. 190.

44 Vittorio Strada, 'Old and New Borders: Soviet and Russian Borders as a Phenomenon', *Nezavisimaya gazeta*, 6 November 1991.

45 Ken Jowitt, *New World Disorder: The Leninist Extinction* (Berkeley, University of California Press, 1992), pp. 319–26 analyses the 'civic/ethnic identity issue'.

46 *Politicheskii monitoring Rossiii*, No. 3, July-September 1992, p. 7.

47 *OMRI Daily Digest*, No. 11, Part I, 16 January 1996.

48 *Pravda*, 30 January 1992.

49 *Moscow News*, No. 37, 1991, p. 6.

50 *Soviet Weekly*, 10 October 1991, p. 5.

51 For details, see *Documents on British Foreign Policy, 1919–1939*, First Series, Vol. 11, *Upper Silesia, Poland, and the Baltic States, January 1920-March 1921* (London, HMSO, 1961), pp. 1–197.

52 Alexander Golts, *Krasnaya zvezda*, 18 July 1992, p. 2.

53 Andrei Kozyrev, 'Vneshnyaya politika preobrazhayushcheisya Rossii', *Voprosy istorii*, No. 1, 1994, p. 8.

54 Solzhenitsyn, *Rebuilding Russia*, p. 14.

55 Ibid.

56 Ibid., p. 24.

57 *Nezavisimaya gazeta*, 3 July 1992, p. 3; *CDSP*, Vol. 44, No. 27, 1992, pp. 11–12.

58 *Rossiiskaya gazeta*, 6 February 1992.
59 *Rossiiskaya gazeta*, 14 July 1993.
60 *Nezavismaya gazeta*, 16 December 2000, p. 3.
61 Lowell Barrington, 'The Domestic and International Consequences of Citizenship in the Soviet Successor States', *Europe–Asia Studies*, Vol. 47, No. 5, July 1995, pp. 731–63.
62 Bill Bowring, 'Austro-Marxism's Last Laugh? The Struggle for Recognition of National-cultural Autonomy for Rossians and Russians', *Europe–Asia Studies*, Vol. 54, No. 2, 2002, pp. 229–50.
63 See Paul Goble, RFE/RL, *Russian Federation Report*, 7 March 2001.
64 RFE/RL, *Newsline*, 3 January 2001.
65 Ryszard Kapuscinski, *Imperium*, translated from the Polish by Klara Glowczewska (London, Granta Books, 1994), p. 179.

## 11 Federalism and the new state

1 Niccolo Machiavelli, *Discourses on the First Decade of Titus Livius* (London, 1883), p. 175.
2 Cited in Paul Dukes, *The Last Great Game: USA versus USSR* (London, Pinter, 1989), p. 147.
3 E. H. Carr, *The Bolshevik Revolution, 1917–1921*, (London, Penguin, 1966), Vol. 1, p. 272.
4 On the creation of the USSR, see A. M. Salmin, *SNG: sostoyanie i perspektivy razvitiya* (Moscow, Gorbachev-Fond, 1992); Victor Swoboda, 'Was The Soviet Union Really Necessary?', *Soviet Studies*, Vol. 44, No. 5, 1992, pp. 761–84.
5 The primary units consisted of 16 Autonomous Soviet Socialist Republics (ASSR), 6 *krais* (territories), 49 *oblasts* (regions) and the cities of Moscow and St Petersburg, which ranked as *oblasts*. The 15 secondary units consisted of 5 autonomous *oblasts* within the *krais*, and 10 autonomous *okrugs* (districts), two of which were part of *krais* and the rest part of *oblasts*. There were also 1,834 rural *raions* (districts) and 1,067 cities, 13 with a population of over a million.
6 Alan P. Pollard (ed.), *USSR: Facts and Figures Annual*, Vol. 15 (Gulf Breeze, FL, Academic International Press, 1991), pp. 2, 504.
7 Ann Sheehy, 'Russia Republic's: A Threat to its Territorial Integrity?', *RFE/RL Research Report*, Vol. 2, No. 20, 14 May 1993, p. 36.
8 This certainly was the view of Khasbulatov, and in August 1990 he devised a constitution for a new federation of sovereign states, *The Struggle for Russia*, pp. 128–36.
9 Adygeya had been subordinate to Krasnodar *krai*; Gorno-Altai to Altai *krai*; Khakassia to Krasnoyarsk *krai*; and Karachai-Cherkessia to Stavropol *krai*.
10 The area of the RSFSR occupied by autonomous territories increased from 40.7 per cent in 1922 (27.7 per cent in the 1989 borders) to 53.3 per cent in 1989, Salmin, *SNG*, pp. 12, 19.
11 Titular nationalities were an absolute majority in Dagestan (80.2 per cent), Chechen-Ingushetia (70.7 per cent, Chechens alone comprised 58 per cent of Chechen-Ingushetia), Chuvashia (67.8 per cent), Tyva (64.3 per cent), Komi-Permyak *okrug* (60.2 per cent), Kabardino-Balkaria (57.7 per cent), Buryats of the Aga-Buryat autonomous okrug (54.9 per cent), North Ossetia (53.0 per cent). *All-Union Census of the Population of 1989* (Moscow, 1991), pp. 28–33.
12 Titular nationalities comprised comparative majorities in Tatarstan (48.5 per cent), Kalmykia (45.4 per cent), and Mari-El (43.3 per cent), *All-Union Census of the Population of 1989* (Moscow, 1991), pp. 28–33.
13 Calculations by A. I. Vdovin in A. S. Barsenkov *et al.*, *Towards a Nationalities Policy in the Russian Federation*, Centre for Soviet and East European Studies, University of Aberdeen, 1993, p. 16.
14 *Politicheskii monitoring Rossii*, No. 3, July–September 1992, pp. 44–5.
15 In 1993 the LDPR won 35.34 per cent of the party list vote in Mordovia, 22 per cent in Tatarstan, 27.45 per cent in Khakassia and 22.53 per cent in Chuvashia (*Byulleten' TsIK*, No. 1 (12), 1994, pp. 52–4). Zhirinovsky's support was strongest where identities were the most divided, as in Tatarstan, as well as among Russian soldiers in Tajikistan and the Russian population of Kaliningrad.

16 Ryszard Kapuscinski, *Imperium*, translated from the Polish by Klara Glowczewska (London, Granta Books, 1994), p. 172.

17 R. Khakim (Khakimov), *Sumerki imperii: k voprosu o natsii i gosudarstve* (Kazan, 1993), p. 16.

18 Khakimov, *Sumerki imperii*, p. 62. See also Alexei Zverev, 'Qualified Sovereigny: The Tatarstan Model for Resolving Conflicting Loyalties', in Michael Waller, Bruno Coppieters and Alexei Malashenko (eds), *Conflicting Loyalties and the State in Post-Soviet Eurasia* (London, Frank Cass, 1998), pp. 118–44 for a discussion of the features of the 'Tatarstan model'.

19 Kapuscinski, *Imperium*, pp. 162, 163.

20 EastWest Institute, *Russian Regional Report*, Vol. 5, No. 21, 31 May 2000.

21 On 5 October 1990 Adygeya raised its status to an autonomous republic; on 8 October the Koryak autonomous *okrug* declared itself sovereign; on 10 October Buryatia; on 11 October Bashkiria; on 16 October Yamalo-Nenets autonomous *okrug*; on 18 October Kalmykiya; on 22 October Mari ASSR; on 24 October Chuvashia; on 25 October Gorno-Altai; and so on until Dagestan on 13 May 1991 and, last of all and not to be left out, Birobidjan (Jewish autonomous *oblast*) on 5 November 1991 declared itself sovereign.

22 *Literaturnaya gazeta*, 15 August 1990.

23 Excerpts of Yeltsin's speech can be found in *Nezavisimaya gazeta*, 27 March 1992.

24 *Rossiiskaya gazeta*, 29 October 1991, p. 2.

25 Yelena Bonner, *Nezavisimaya gazeta*, 5 January 1992; *The Guardian*, 6 January 1992.

26 Shakhrai in *The Gubernatorskie novosti*, No. 9, March 1993, pp. 3–4.

27 Vladimir Lysenko, Deputy Chairman of the State Committee for Nationality Policy of the Russian Federation, *Rossiiskaya gazeta*, 1 December 1992, p. 4.

28 *Rossiiskaya gazeta*, 1 December 1992, p. 4.

29 See Susanna Rabow-Edling, 'The Decembrists and the Concept of a Civic Nation', *Nationalities Papers*, Vol. 35, No. 2, May 2007, pp. 369–91.

30 *Rossiiskaya gazeta*, 5 November 1991, p. 1.

31 The plan is explained at some length by Rumyantsev, *Rossiiskaya gazeta*, 11 October 1991, p. 7.

32 *Rossiiskaya gazeta*, 11 October 1991, p. 7.

33 *Nezavisimaya gazeta*, 27 November 1991.

34 *Federativnyi dogovor: dokumenty, kommentarii* (Moscow, Supreme Soviet of the Russian Federation, 1992).

35 The three Federal Treaties are in *Konstitutsiya (osnovnoi zakon) Rossiiskoi Federatsii-Rossii* (Moscow, Izvestiya, 1992), pp. 81–108.

36 *Nezavisimaya gazeta*, 1 April 1992, p. 1.

37 These points are made by Abdulatipov in his analysis of the treaties, *Federativnyi dogovor*, p. 4.

38 Abdulatipov insisted that the Federal Treaty gave the regions extensive economic and other powers that were not used by them, *Gubernatorskie novosti*, No. 9 (March 1993), p. 1.

39 *Izvestiya*, 14 August 1992; *Nezavisimaya gazeta*, 15 August 1992.

40 See M. Burgess and A. G. Gagnon (eds), *Comparative Federalism and Federation* (Hemel Hempstead, Harvester Wheatsheaf, 1993).

41 *Konstitutsiya respubliki Tatarstan*, adopted on 6 November 1992 (Kazan, Tatarskoe knizhnoe izd., 1993), p. 14.

42 The Seventh Congress failed to adopt a constitutional amendment that would have allowed the Constitutional Court to rescind legislative acts of the republics if it found them unlawful, *Moscow News*, No. 6 (4 February 1993), p. 3.

43 Sergei Khrushchev, 'The Political Economy of Russia's Regional Fragmentation', in Douglas Blum (ed.), *Russia's Future: Consolidation or Disintegration?* (Boulder, CO, Westview Press, 1994), pp. 93–4.

44 William H. Riker, *Federalism: Origin, Operation, Significance* (Boston, Little, Brown & Company, 1964), p. 11.

## 12  Segmented regionalism and the new federalism

1 Bertrand De Jouvenal, *Sovereignty: An Inquiry into the Political Good*, translated by J. F. Huntington (Cambridge, Cambridge University Press, 1957), p. 139.

2 A theme explored by Kathryn Stoner-Weiss, *Local Heroes: The Political Economy of Russian Regional Governance* (Princeton, NJ, Princeton University Press, 1997).

3 The decree establishing 'representatives of the presidium of the Supreme Soviet of the RSFSR' had already been drafted in mid–June, but was shelved until a more opportune moment, provided by the coup, *Demokraticheskya gazeta*, No. 12 (15), 12 September 1991, p. 3. Following the coup the 'temporary instructions' made them envoys of the president rather than parliament, causing parliament yet more umbrage.

4 For their responsibilities, see 'Glaza i ushi prezidenta', *Trud*, 30 January 1992, p. 3; *Izvestiya*, 11 January 1992, p. 2.

5 'Rasporyazhenie B. El'tsina o predstavitel'stve', *Izvestiya* and *Rossiiskaya gazeta*, 6 September 1991, p. 2.

6 *Rossiiskaya gazeta*, 6 September 1991, p. 2.

7 *Rossiiskaya gazeta*, 17 July 1997.

8 In Rostov *oblast*, for example, the governor was a former Party secretary who went on to appoint former *apparatchiki* as heads of administration, see A. Nikolenko, 'Vivat, nomenklatura?', *Narodny deputat*, No. 5, 1992. For accusations of betrayal, see *Zerkalo:Vestnik Obshchestvennyi Komitet Rossiiskikh Reform*, No. 2 , February 1992, p. 6.

9 Elections designated for 8 December 1991 were postponed by the Fifth CPD on 1 November 1991 to December 1992, and the president was granted the right to appoint heads of administration in the interim. Yeltsin conceded that new heads of administration would have to be approved by the corresponding soviet and MPs from that territory, *Rossiiskaya gazeta*, 5 November 1991, p. 1.

10 Robert Orttung, 'Resourceful Governors Able to Counter the Kremlin', EastWest Institute, *Russian Regional Report*, Vol. 5, No. 10, 15 March 2000; which contains an analysis of the advantages of incumbency.

11 'Ob obshchikh printsipakh organizatsii zakonodatel'nykh (predstavitel'nykh) i ispolnitel'nykh organov gosudarstvennoi vlasti sub'ektov Rossiiskoi Federatsii', *Rossiiskaya gazeta*, 19 October 1999, pp. 4–5.

12 The driving force behind the letter was governor Mikhail Prusak of Novgorod, and it was signed by Belgorod governor Evgenii Savchenko and Kurgan governor Oleg Bogomolov, 'I vlast', i ekonomika, i prezident na 7 let', *Nezavisimaya gazeta*, 25 February 2000, pp. 1, 4.

13 For an instructive comparative discussion, see Stein Rokkan, 'The Survival of Peripheral Identity', in *State Formation. Nation-Building, and Mass Politics in Europe: The Theory of Stein Rokkan*, Edited by Peter Flora with Stein Kuhle and Derek Urwin (Oxford, Oxford University Press, 1999), pp. 191–208.

14 'Titov protiv naznacheniya gubernatorov', *Nezavisimaya gazeta*, 3 March 2000; see also *Moscow Times*, 3 March 2000; and EastWest Institute, *Russian Regional Report*, Vol. 5, No. 9, 9 March 2000.

15 *Rossiiskaya gazeta*, 12 October 1993.

16 Mikhail A. Alexseev, 'Introduction: Challenges to the Russian Federation', in Mikhail A. Alexseev (ed.), *Center-Periphery Conflict in Post-Soviet Russia: A Federation Imperiled* (Basingstoke, Macmillan, 1999), p. 1.

17 *Izvestiya*, 4 November 1997; EastWest Institute, *Russian Regional Report*, Vol. 2, No. 38, 6 November 1997.

18 RFE/RL *Newsline*, 20 January 1998.

19 James Hughes, 'Moscow's Bilateral Treaties Add to Confusion', *Transition*, 20 September 1996, pp. 39–43, at p. 39.

20 *Rossiiskaya gazeta*, 5 November 1991, p. 1.

21 Politicheskii monitoring Rossii, No. 3, July–September 1992, p. 43; Sotsial'no-politicheskii monitoring Rossii, p. 28.

22 From West to East the economic regions are: Northern, North-Western, the Kaliningrad exclave (in effect part of the North-Western region but separated physically from Russia), Central, Central Black Earth, Volga, North Caucasian, Urals, Western Siberia, Eastern Siberia, and Far Eastern.

23 *Izvestiya*, 30 March 1992, p. 2.

24 Michael J. Bradshaw, 'Siberia Poses a Challenge to Russian Federalism', RFE/RL, *Research Report*, Vol. 1, No. 41, 16 October 1992, p. 6.

25 RIA Novosti, 9 March 2000, in Tacis, *The European Union's Project for Capacity Development in Election Monitoring*, 10 March 2000.

26 The issue is examined in A. Lavrov (ed.), *Federal'nyi byudzhet i regiony: opyt analiza finansovykh potokov* (Moscow, Dialog-MGU, 1999). See also S. D. Valentei (ed.), *Ekonomicheskie problemy stanovleniya Rossiiskogo federalizma* (Moscow, Nauka, 1999).

27 EastWest Institute, *Russian Regional Report*, Vol. 4, No. 20, 27 May 1999.

28 E.g. in Pskov, see Darrell Slider, 'Pskov Under the LDPR: Elections and Dysfunctional Federalism in One Region', *Europe–Asia Studies*, Vol. 51, No. 5, 1999, p. 764.

29 Daniel Treisman, 'The Politics of Intergovernmental Transfers in Post-Soviet Russia', *British Journal of Political Science*, Vol. 26, No. 3, July 1996, pp. 299–335. See also his 'Deciphering Russia's Federal Finance: Fiscal Appeasement in 1995 and 1996', *Europe–Asia Studies*, Vol. 50, No. 5, July 1998, pp. 893–906.

30 Daniel Treisman, *After the Deluge: Regional Crises and Political Consolidation in Russia* (Ann Arbor, MI, University of Michigan Press, 1999).

31 Alistair McAuley, 'The Determinants of Russian Federal-Regional Fiscal Relations: Equity or Political Influence', *Europe–Asia Studies*, Vol. 49, No. 3, May 1997, pp. 431–44.

32 A. M. Lavrov and Alexei G. Makushkin, with a foreword by Alexander G. Granberg, *The Fiscal Structure of the Russian Federation: Financial Flows Between the Centre and the Regions* (M. E. Sharpe, Armonk, New York and London, 2000).

33 Lavrov's study provides detailed analysis of regional differentiation, using comparisons based on the calculation Gross Regional Product (GRP), Lavrov and Makushkin, *The Fiscal Structure of the Russian Federation*.

34 Martin Nicholson, *Towards a Russia of the Regions*, Adelphi Paper 330 (London, International Institute for Strategic Studies, 1999), p. 35.

35 Julia Kusznir, 'The New Russian-Tatar Treaty and its Implications for Russian Federalism', *Russian Analytical Digest*, No. 16, 6 March 2007, pp. 2–5, at p. 2.

36 Kusznir, 'The New Russian-Tatar Treaty', p. 3.

37 Robert McIntyre, 'Regional Stabilisation Policy under Transitional Period Conditions in Russia: Price Controls, Regional Trade Barriers and Other Local-level Measures', *Europe–Asia* Studies, Vol. 50, No. 5, July 1998, pp. 859–72.

38 EastWest Institute, *Russian Regional Report*, Vol. 4, No. 24, 24 June 1999.

39 *Nezavisimaya gazeta*, 26 June 1999; *Izvestiya*, 30 June 1999.

40 *Kommersant-Daily*, 31 October 1997.

41 EWI, *Russian Regional Report*, Vol. 6, No. 4, 31 January 2001.

42 For example, in the case of Gorno-Altai, discussed below, *Rossiiskaya gazeta*, 21 June 2000, pp. 5–6.

43 Some of the arguments of this section were outlined in Richard Sakwa, 'Putin's New Federalism', EastWest Institute, *Russian Regional Report*, Vol. 5, No. 21, 31 May 2000, pp. 12–17.

44 Natalia Dinello, *What's So Great about Novgorod-The-Great: Trisectoral Cooperation and Symbolic Management* (Washington, DC, NCEEER, 2001), p. iii. For a more positive evaluation, see Nicolai Petro, 'The Novgorod Region: A Russian Success Story', *Post-Soviet Affairs*, Vol. 15, No. 3, 1999, pp. 235–61.

45 For a critique of this, see Grigorii Yavlinskii, 'The Last Phase of Agony', *Obshchaya gazeta*, 10–16 June 1999.

46 Vladimir Putin, *First Person: An Astonishingly Frank Self-portrait by Russia's President Vladimir Putin*, with Nataliya Gevorkyan, Natalya Timakova, and Andrei Kolesnikov, translated by Catherine A. Fitzpatrick (London, Hutchinson, 2000), pp. 182–3.

47 The material in this section amplifies the relevant part of Chapter 7 of my *Putin: Russia's Choice*, 2nd edn (London and New York, Routledge, 2007).

48 *Rossiiskaya gazeta*, 16 May 2000.

49 *Rossiiskaya gazeta*, 17 July 1997.

50 Petr Akopov and Svetlana Babaeva, *Izvestiya*, 15 May 2000.

51 The seven capitals of the new Federal Districts (FD) are: Moscow for the Central FD, St Petersburg for the Northwest FD, Rostov-na-Donu for the North Caucasus (later renamed the South Russia) FD, Nizhny Novgorod for the Volga FD, Ekaterinburg for the Urals FD, Novosibirsk for the Siberian FD and Khabarovsk for the Far East FD. The later merger of the Volga and Urals military districts accentuated the mismatch between the borders of the seven FDs and what had now become six military districts.

52 The full list is as follows: Sergei Kirienko, the former prime minister and one of the leaders of the Union of Rightist Forces (SPS) headed the Volga FD; CIS Affairs Minister and former Russian ambassador to Poland, Leonid Drachevsky, headed the Siberian FD (until replaced on 9 September 2004 by former head of the General Staff Anatoly Kvashnin); Victor Cherkesov, the First Deputy Director of the FSB, headed the Northwest FD (until replaced in March 2003 by Valentina Matvienko, until she in turn in October of that year was replaced by Ilya Klebanov); General Viktor Kazantsev, who had directed the latest onslaught against Chechnya, the North Caucasus (South Russian) FD (until replaced on 9 March 2004 by the former St Petersburg governor and former deputy prime minister Vladimir Yakovlev; he in turn was replaced on 13 September 2004 by Dmitry Kozak in move intended to focus the struggle against terrorism in the region); First Deputy Interior Minister Petr Latyshev, the Urals FD; former presidential representative to Leningrad *oblast* (and before that with years of service in the KGB), Georgy Poltavchenko, headed the Central FD; and Lieutenant-General Konstantin Pulikovsky, who had been a commander in the Chechen war of 1994–96, headed the Far East FD. On 14 November 2005 the head of the Volga FD, Sergei Kirienko, was replaced by Bashkortostan prosecutor Alexander Konovalov, and the head of the Far East FD, Konstantin Pulikovsky, was replaced by Kamil Iskhakov, the former mayor of Kazan, the capital of Tatarstan.

53 V. V. Cherkesov (ed.), *Institut general-guvernatorstva i namestnichestva v rossiiskoi imperii* (St Petersburg, Yuridicheskii Tsentr Press, 2003).

54 http:/www.president.kremlin.ru/events/34.html

55 Sarah Karush and Catherine Belton, 'Putin to Tighten Grip on Regions', *Moscow Times*, 18 May 2000.

56 *Newsline*, 18 May 2000.

57 Julie A. Corwin, 'The New Centralizer', *Newsline*, 21 June 2000.

58 'Postanovlenie Konstitutsionnogo Suda Rossiiskoi Federatsii po delu o proverke konstitutsionnosti otdel'nykh polozhenii Konstitutsii Respubliki Altai i Federal'nogo zakona "Ob obshchikh printsipakh organizatsii zakonodatel'nykh (predstavitel'nykh) i ispolnitel'nykh organov gosudarstvennoi vlasti sub"ektov Rossiiskoi Federatsii', *Rossiiskaya gazeta*, 21 June 2000, pp. 5–6.

59 See *Russian Regional Report*, Vol. 5, No. 25, 28 June 2000.

60 *Rossiiskaya gazeta*, 30 June 1999.

61 RFE/RL, Russian Federation Report, 4 July 2001.

62 *Nezavisimaya gazeta*, 30 June 2001, p. 3.

63 *Rossiiskaya gazeta*, 13 May 2000.

64 *Russian Regional Report*, Vol. 5, No. 19, 17 May 2000.

65 *Izvestiya*, 12 May 2000; *Nezavisimaya gazeta*, 12 May 2000; http://press.maindir.gov.ru

66 Kusznir, 'The New Russian-Tatar Treaty', p. 4.

67 See Robert Sharlet, 'Resistance to Putin's Campaign for Political and Legal Unification', in Robert Sharlet and Ferdinand Feldbrugge (eds), *Public Policy and Law in Russia: In Search of a Unified Legal and Political Space* (Leiden and Boston, Martinus Nijhoff Publishers, 2005), pp. 241–50.

68 http://www.kremlin.ru/text/appears/2006/03/103175.shtml

69 The announcement was made after a meeting with Putin on 16 March 2000.

70 EastWest Institute, *Russian Regional Report*, Vol. 6, No. 26, July 2001.

71 http://www.president.kremlin.ru/events/510/html

72 Nikolai Petrov, 'The Budget Nomenklatura', *Moscow Times*, 31 October 2006, updated.

73 *Izvestiya*, 20 July 2005.

74 V. V. Putin, *Razgovor s Rossiei: Stenogramma 'Pryamoi linii s Prezidentom Rossiiskoi Federatsii V. V. Putinym'*, 19 December 2002 (Moscow, Olma-Politizdat, 2003), p. 63.

75 *Rossiiskaya gazeta*, 15 December 2004.

76 *Rossiiskaya gazeta*, 29 December 2004.

77 *Rossiiskaya gazeta*, 2 July 2005.

78 The case was brought by an aggrieved citizen of Tyumen, Vladimir Grishkevich, who argued that the appointment of the regional governor (Sergei Sobyanin) violated his constitutional right to participate in elections at all levels. His complaint was supported by SPS. The Court refused to consider two other provisions of the law: the president's right to dismiss a governor; and the president's right to dissolve a regional legislature if it twice refused to support the proposed candidate. *Kommersant*, 22 December 2005.

79 Cf. Marie-Elisabeth Baudoin, 'Is the Constitutional Court the Last Bastion in Russia Against the Threat of Authoritarianism?', *Europe–Asia Studies*, Vol. 58, No. 5, July 2006, pp. 679–99.

80 In data published in December 2005, 66 per cent were for the election of governors, 26 per cent supported the new system, although 52 per cent agreed that even an elected governor should take a vow of loyalty to the president; http://www.levada.ru/press/2005122901.html. Accessed 5 January 2006.

81 Goode, 'The Puzzle of Putin's Gubernatorial Appointments', p. 382.

82 http://president.kremlin.ru/text/appears/2006/01/100848.shtml

83 Nikolai Petrov, 'Undercutting the Senators', *Moscow Times*, 30 May 2006.

84 A. S. Avtonomov, A. A. Zakharov and Ye. M. Orlova, *Regional'nye parlamenty v sovremennoi Rossii*, Nauchnye doklady No. 118 (Moscow, MONF, 2000).

85 See Alexander Kynev, 'The Role of Political Parties in Russia's 2002 Regional Elections', *Russia and Eurasia Review*, Vol. 2, 8, 15 April 2003.

86 For example, in Rostov, *Russian Regional Report*, 23 April 2003; Primorsky *krai*, *Russian Regional Report*, 7 May 2003.

87 For details, see Hutcheson, *Political Parties in the Russian Regions*.

88 Oleg Tsvetkov, 'Adygeya Leader Resigns, then Retracts Decision', *Russian Regional Report*, Vol. 11, No. 10, 14 April 2006.

89 The process did not stop, however, and a referendum on 11 March 2007 was held on the merger of the Chita region with the Agin-Buryat Autonomous *okrug* to create a new Transbaikal *krai*.

90 Viktor Yur'ev, 'Silovoi priglyad za milliardami', *Argumenty i fakty*, No. 15, 12 April 2006; Victor Yasmann, 'The Future of Russia's "Ethnic Republics"', RFE/RL, News and Analysis, 21 April 2006, http://www.rferl.org/featuresarticle/2006/04.

91 Kozak denied that this would be an outcome of the changes, 'Reforma vlasti: kak podelit' na troikh?', *Argumenty i fakty*, No. 16, April 2003, p. 6.

92 For details, see Tomila Lankina, *Governing the Locals: Local Self-government and Ethnic Mobilization in Russia* (Lanham, MD, Rowman & Littlefield, 2004); Tomila Lankina, 'President Putin's Local Government Reforms', in Peter Reddaway and Robert W. Orrtung (eds), *The Dynamics of Russian Politics: Putin's Reform of Federal-Regional Relations*, Vol. 2 (Lanham, MD, Rowman & Littlefield, 2005).

93 Some of the themes of this section have been examined in my 'Russian Regionalism, Policy-making and State Development', in Stefanie Harter and Gerald Easter (eds), *Shaping the Economic Space in Russia: Decision-Making Processes, Institutions and Adjustment to Change in the El'tsin Era* (Aldershot, Ashgate, 2000), Chapter 1, pp. 11–34.

94 For a useful discussion, see S. D. Valentei, *Federalizm: Rossiiskaya istoriya i Rossiiskaya real'nost'* (Moscow, Institute of the Economy, Centre for the Socio-Economic Problems of Federalism, RAS, 1998).

95 This is argued, for example, by James Hughes, 'Moscow's Bilateral Treaties Add to Confusion', *Transition*, 20 September 1996, pp. 39–43.

96 Richard Sakwa, 'The Republicanisation of Russia: Federalism and Democratization in Transition I', in Chris Pierson and Simon Tormey (eds), *Politics at the Edge, The PSA Yearbook 1999* (Basingstoke, Macmillan, 1999), Chapter 16, pp. 215–26. See also the Chapter by Cameron Ross in the same volume, pp. 227–40.

97 Kathryn Stoner-Weiss, 'Central Weakness and Provincial Autonomy: Observations on the Devolution Process in Russia', *Post-Soviet Affairs*, Vol. 15, No. 1, 1999, pp. 87–106.

98 *Izvestiya*, 4 July 2005.

99 *Rossiiskaya gazeta*, 4 July 2005.

100  Elena Chebankova, 'Putin's Struggle for Federalism: Structures, Operation, and the Commitment Problem', *Europe–Asia Studies*, Vol. 59, No. 2, March 2007, pp. 279–302, at p. 295.

## 13  Russian capitalism

1  Boris El'tsin, *Zapiski prezidenta* (Moscow, Ogonek, 1994), p. 300.

2  *The Economist*, 13 May 2000, p. 146.

3  *Transition Report: Economic Transition in Eastern Europe and the Former Soviet Union* (London, EBRD, October 1994), p. 45.

4  Anatolii B. Chubais and Sergei V. Vasil'ev, 'Privatisation as a Necessary Condition for Structural Change in the USSR', *Communist Economies and Economic Transformation*, Vol. 3, No. 1, 1991, pp. 57–62, at p. 57.

5  See, for example, Michael Ellman and Vladimir Kontorovich (eds), *The Destruction of the Soviet Economic System: An Insiders' History* (New York, M. E. Sharpe, 1998).

6  Armenia, Belarus, Kazakhstan, Kyrgyzstan, Russia, Tajikistan, Turkmenistan and Uzbekistan.

7  *Soviet Weekly*, 31 October 1991, pp. 6–7.

8  See Bert van Selm, *The Economics of Soviet Breakup* (London, Routledge, 1997).

9  Alistair McAuley, 'The Economic Consequences of Soviet Disintegration', *Soviet Economy*, Vol. 7, No. 3, 1991, pp. 189–214, suggests a high degree of interdependence.

10  V. Samonis, 'Who Subsidized Whom? The Distorted World of Baltic-Soviet Economic Relations', *Current Politics and Economics of Russia*, Vol. 2, No. 3, (1991), pp. 241–3.

11  *OECD Economic Surveys: The Russian Federation, 1995* (Paris, OECD, 1995), pp. 12–13.

12  *Soviet Weekly*, 5 December 1991, p. 10; John Tedstrom, 'Economic Crisis Deepens', RFE/RL,*Research Report*, Vol. 1, No. 1, 3 January 1992, pp. 22–6; Keith Bush, 'The Disastrous Last Year of the USSR', RFE/RL, *Research Report*, Vol. 1, No. 12, 20 March 1992, pp. 39–41.

13  Keith Bush, 'An Overview of the Russian Economy', RFE/RL, *Research Report*, Vol. 1, No. 25, 19 June 1992, p. 50.

14  *Soviet Weekly*, 10 October 1991, p. 11.

15  *Rossiiskaya gazeta*, 29 October 1991.

16  *Rossiiskaya gazeta*, 2 November 1991, p. 1.

17  Janos Kornai, *The Road to a Free Economy: Shifting from a Socialist System: The Example of Hungary* (New York, Norton, 1990).

18  John Kenneth Galbraith, 'Revolt in Our Time: The Triumph of Simplistic Ideology', in Gwyn Prins (ed.), *Spring in Winter: The 1989 Revolutions* (Manchester, Manchester University Press, 1990), pp. 1–12.

19  *Moskovskie novosti*, No. 78, 12–19 November 1995, p. 5.

20  For their views, see Alec Nove, 'New Thinking on the Soviet Economy', in Archie Brown (ed.), *New Thinking in Soviet Politics* (London, Macmillan, 1992), pp. 29–38.

21  *Russian Economic Trends*, Vol. 1, No. 1, 1992, p. 5.

22  *Ekonomika i zhizn'*, No. 51, 1991, p. 1.

23  Chubais and Vasil'ev, 'Privatisation', p. 59.

24  *OECD Economic Surveys*, p. 8.

25  Anders Aslund, 'Reform vs. "Rent-Seeking" in Russia's Economic Transformation', *Transition*, 26 January 1996, p. 13.

26  Joel S. Hellman, 'Winners Take All: The Politics of Partial Reform in Postcommunist Transitions', *World Politics*, Vol. 50, 1998, pp. 203–34.

27  Dmitrii S. L'vov, 'The Social and Economic Problems of *perestroika*', *Communist Economies and Economic Transformation*, Vol. 4, No. 1, 1992, pp. 75–83, at pp. 78–9.

28  Vladimir Capelik, 'The Development of Antimonopoly Policy in Russia', RFE/RL, *Research Report*, Vol. 1, No. 34, 28 August 1992, pp. 66–70.

29  *OECD Economic Reviews*, p. 88. In Russia small firms (1–249 employees) made up 53 per cent of the total, in the USA 98 per cent.

30  *Rossiiskaya gazeta*, 10 January 1992, pp. 3–4, with an appendix on 15 January, p. 2.

31 See Alexander Bim *et al.*, 'Privatization in the Former Soviet Union and the New Russia', in Saul Estrin (ed.), *Privatization in Central and Eastern Europe* (London, Longman, 1994), pp. 252–78.

32 *OECD Economic Surveys*, p. 72; Bim *et al.*, pp. 262–7.

33 'Interview with Richard Layard', in Keith Bush, *From the Command Economy to the Market: A Collection of Interviews* (Aldershot, Dartmouth Publishing, 1991), pp. 142–7, at p. 143.

34 'Interview with Anders Aslund', in Bush, *From the Command Economy to the Market*, pp. 7–12, at p. 8.

35 'Interview with Milton Friedman', in Bush, *From the Command Economy to the Market*, pp. 49–57, at p. 51.

36 For a discussion of these issues, see Elizabeth Teague (ed.), 'Is Equity Compatible with Efficiency?', RFE/RL, *Research Report*, Vol. 1, No. 17, 1992, pp. 9–14.

37 Ivan Ustinov, *Nezavisimaya gazeta – politekonomiya*, 17 April 2001, cited in RFE/RL, *Newsline*, 18 April 2001.

38 EastWest Institute, *Russian Regional Report*, 16 July 2001.

39 See *Russian Analytical Digest*, No. 24, 3 July 2007.

40 RFE/RL, *Newsline*, 14 February 2001.

41 *Moscow Times*, 2 May 2007.

42 Vladimir Popov, 'Russia Redux?', *New Left Review*, No. 44, March–April 2007, pp. 37–52, at pp. 40, 43.

43 These were figures given by Sergei Dubinin, then head of the Central Bank, in July 1997. For details, see 'Krupneiskie banki Rossii', *Finansovye izvestiya*, No. 58 (508), 11 August 1998.

44 RFE/RL, *Newsline*, 4 January 2001.

45 *Moscow News*, No. 37, 1991, p. 2.

46 RFE/RL, *Newsline*, 3 January 2001.

47 Reported by finance minister Alexei Kudrin, *Rossiiskie vesti*, No. 40, 3 November 2006; Itar-Tass, 20 November 2006; with updated figures from deputy prime-minister Alexander Zhukov, Interfax, 20 December 2006.

48 *Kommersant-Vlast'*, 8 May 2006, p. 10.

49 Reported by Andrew E. Kramer, 'Russia Called too Reliant on Petroleum', *New York Times*, 18 April 2006.

50 Peter Rutland, 'Russia and the WTO: One Step Forward, One Step Back', *Russian Analytical Digest*, No. 24, 3 July 2007, pp. 2–4, at p. 3.

51 Natalya Volchkova, 'Russia and the WTO: A Russian View', *Russian Analytical Digest*, No. 24, 3 July 2007, pp. 5–7.

52 *Izvestiya*, 10 April 2006.

53 Miriam Elder, 'US, Russia Sign 800-Page WTO Deal', *Moscow Times*, 20 November 2006.

54 This is made explicit by Pavel Felgenhauer, 'US Green Lights Russian WTO Membership, Seeks Agreement on Iran', *Eurasia Daily Monitor*, Vol. 3, No. 212, 15 November 2006.

55 *The Independent*, 23 August 2006.

56 Gérard Roland, 'The Russian Economy in the Year 2005', *Post-Soviet Affairs*, Vol. 22, No. 1, 2006, pp. 90–8, at p. 92.

57 Charles Wolf, 'A Mighty Country's Progress and Regress', http://www.rand.org/commentary/010407PS.html

58 Total number of SMEs from *Russia in Figures: 2006* (Moscow, Rosstat, 2006), p. 168.

59 Vyacheslav Shironin, 'Not All Big Business', *Russia Profile*, Vol. 3, No. 10, December 2006, pp. 13–15, at p. 13.

60 *Izvestiya*, 12 July 2007.

61 The Jamestown Foundation, *Monitor*, 5 July 2001.

62 Tedstrom, 'Russia: Progress Report on Industrial Privatization', p. 49.

63 The phrase comes from Roy D. Laird and Edward Crowley (eds), *Soviet Agriculture: The Permanent Crisis* (New York, Praeger, 1965). See also Stefan Hedlund, *Crisis in Soviet Agriculture* (New York, St Martin's Press, 1985). For a discussion of the historical context and Gorbachev's approach to agriculture, see the special issue of *Studies in Comparative Communism*, Vol. 23, No. 2, summer 1990.

64 George F. Kennan, 'America and the Russian Future', *Foreign Affairs*, Vol. 29, No. 3, April 1951, pp. 351–70, at p. 355.

65 The words are those of a speaker at the founding congress of the USSR Peasants' Union in June 1990, *Pravitel'stvennyi vestnik*, No. 25 (51), June 1990, p. 5.

66 Stephen K. Wegren, 'Private Farming and Agrarian Reform in Russia', *Problems of Communism*, Vol. 41, No. 3, May–June 1992, pp. 107–21.

67 *Pravda*, 7 March 1990.

68 *Sovetskaya Rossiya*, 17 March 2001, p. 2.

69 *Monitor*, 5 January 2001.

70 *Russia in Figures: 2006*, pp. 170–1.

71 *Russia in Figures: 2006*, p. 231.

72 Dariusz Rosati *et al.*, *Transition Countries in the First Quarter 1998: Widening Gap Between Fast and Slow Reformers*, Vienna Institute for Comparative Economic Studies, Research Report No. 248, Vienna, June 1998, p. 25.

73 Ruslan Grinberg, 'Desyat' let sistemnoi transformatsii', *Nezavismaya gazeta*, 22 December 1999, p. 4.

74 Sergei Rogov, 'Rossiya i SShA na poroge XXI veka', *Svobodnaya mysl'*, No. 4, 1997, p.34.

75 *OECD Economic Surveys*, p. iii.

76 Yeltin press conference, 21 August 1992.

77 Marshall I. Goldman, *Lost Opportunity: Why Economic Reforms in Russia Have Not Worked* (London, Norton, 1995).

78 See Douglass North, *Institutions, Institutional Change, and Economic Performance* (Cambridge, Cambridge University Press, 1990), p. 1 and *passim*.

79 Peter Evans, *Embedded Autonomy: States and Industrial Transformation* (Princeton, Princeton University Press, 1995).

80 Jude Wanniski, 'The Future of Russian Capitalism', *Foreign Affairs*, Vol. 71, No. 2, spring 1992, pp. 17–25, at p. 17.

81 'Nefteglobalizatsiya', *Nezavisimaya gazeta*, 23 April 2003, pp. 1, 3.

82 *Moscow Times*, 23 April 2003, pp. 1–2.

83 Wolf, 'A Mighty Country's Progress and Regress'.

84 *Vedemosti VUZ*, No. 3 (11), April 2007, p. 4.

85 Vladimir Ryzhkov, *Christian Science Monitor*, 17 May 2007.

86 *Izvestiya*, 12 July 2007.

87 Mancur Olson, *Power and Prosperity: Outgrowing Communist and Capitalist Dictatorships* (New York, Basic Books, 1999).

## 14 Society and social movements

1 Adam Smith, *The Wealth of Nations* (London, Penguin, 1970), p. 8.

2 Solzhenitsyn, *Rebuilding Russia*, p. 33.

3 *Soviet Weekly*, 24 October 1991, p. 5.

4 Solzhenitsyn, *Rebuilding Russia*, p. 33.

5 Barrington Moore, Jr, *Social Origins of Dictatorship and Democracy: Lord and Peasant in the Making of the Modern World* (Harmondsworth, Peregrine, 1967), p. 418.

6 Report to State Duma on 17 November 2000 by Aleksandr Pochinok, minister of labour and social development, in Paul Goble, 'Compounding a Demographic Disaster', *Monitor*, 20 November 2000.

7 In 1960 there were 23.2 births per 1,000, 7.4 deaths per 1,000, giving a natural growth of 15.8 per 1,000, and the figure declined thereafter, Pockney, *Soviet Statistics since 1950*, p. 74.

8 *Nezavisimaya gazeta*, 26 January 1993, p. 1.

9 *Demograficheskii ezhegodnik RF, 1993* (Moscow, Goskomstat, 1994), p. 83; *Pravda*, 28 November 1995.

10 The Russian fertility rate is comparable to that in Estonia (1.44), Germany (1.39), Greece (1.35) and Italy (1.25), while in the former GDR it fell to 0.98 in 1991, Penny Morvant, 'Alarm over Falling Life Expectancy', *Transition*, 20 October 1995, p. 41.

11 *Independent*, 9 November 1992. In 1991 the birth rate fell from 12.1 to 11.1 per 1,000, while the death rate increased from 11.4 to 11.9 per 1,000, *Nezavisimaya gazeta*, 26 January 1992, p. 1.

12  *Rossiya v tsifrakh: 2000*, p. 70. Part of the reason for the peak is that in 1993 Russia adopted international standards of measurement.

13  RFE/RL, *Russian Political Weekly*, Vol. 6, No. 11, 25 May 2006.

14  RFE/RL, *Newsline*, 8 January 2001.

15  E.g., Vadim Pervyshin, 'Genotsid kak sistema', *Den'*, No. 36 (51), 6 September 1992, p. 3; see also Boris Khodov in *Pravda*, 30 March 1995. The theme is reflected in Stanislav Govorukhin's film of 1994, *The Russia That We Have Lost*.

16  RFE/RL, *Newsline*, 22 June 2001; *Rossiya v tsifrakh: 2000*, p. 70.

17  Victoria Clark, *The Observer*, 26 November 1995, p. 26.

18  *Rossiya v tsifrakh: 2000*, p. 71.

19  *Monitor*, 5 January 2001.

20  *Komsomolskaya pravda*, 25 July 1995. Hungary still has the highest suicide rate out of 84 developed countries, but Russia now comes in third.

21  *The Guardian*, 15 June 2007.

22  *The Guardian*, 12 April 2007, p. 22.

23  On the anti-alcohol campaign, see Stephen White, *Russia Goes Dry: Alcohol, State and Society* (Cambridge, Cambridge University Press, 1995).

24  Stephen White, 'Hangover Cure for the Bear with a Sore Head', *Times Higher Educational Supplement*, 28 July 1995, pp. 17, 19.

25  *Russia in Figures: 2006*, p. 74.

26  This issue is discussed by several contributors in Murray Yanovitch (ed.), *New Directions in Soviet Social Thought* (New York, M. E. Sharpe, 1989).

27  A. Putko, *Soviet Weekly*, 5 December 1991, p. 4.

28  B. P. Pockney, *Soviet Statistics since 1950* (Aldershot, Dartmouth, 1991), pp. 63, 67.

29  A study by the Economic Analysis Bureau, reported in *Finansovaya Rossii*, No. 4, 2001, cited in RFE/RF, *Newsline*, 13 February 2001.

30  Cf. Dietwald Claus, 'Looking for Russia's Middle Class', *Moscow News*, 4–10 May 2007.

31  Stephen Castles and Mark J. Miller, *The Age of Migration: International Population Movements in the Modern World* (London, Macmillan, 1993).

32  For detailed studies, see Hilary Pilkington, *Migration, Displacement and Identity in Post-Soviet Russia* (London and New York, Routledge, 1998); V. A. Tishkov (ed.), *Vynuzhdennye migranty: integratsiya i vozvrashchenie* (Moscow, Institute of Ethnology and Anthropology, RAS, 1997).

33  See Benedict Anderson, *Imagined Communities: Reflections on the Origin and Spread of Nationalism* (London, Verso, 1983).

34  *Nezavisimaya gazeta: NG regiony*, 23 July 2007, p. 9.

35  King and Melvin, 'Diaspora Politics', p. 123.

36  *The Independent*, 19 April 1995, p. 8.

37  *OECD Economic Surveys*, p. 130.

38  Konstantin Zatulin, 'We May Not Ignore These Problems', *Delovoi mir*, 2 December 1995, p. 6.

39  *Rossiiskie vesti*, 5 May 1994, p. 4.

40  *Monitor*, 5 January 2001.

41  *Rossiya*, No. 19, 18–24 May 1994, p. 4.

42  *Izvestiya*, 9 July 1992, p. 3.

43  The Jamestown Foundation, *Prism*, June 2001.

44  Gaidar's report to parliament, 22 September 1992.

45  *Rossiiskaya gazeta*, 5 May 1994, p. 4.

46  *Independent*, 8 May 1992.

47  *Rezultaty sotsiologicheskogo issledovaniya 'Sotsial'no-aktivnye sily Rossii: usloviya i puti ikh konsolidatsii* (Moscow, Institut sotsial'nykh i politicheskikh tekhnologii, 1991), pp. 10–11.

48  For a detailed sociological study of the differentiated outcomes, see L. Gordon and E. Klopov, *Poteri i obreteniya v Rossii 90-kh: istoriko-sotsiologicheskie ocherki ekonomicheskogo polozheniya narodnogo bol'shinstva*, Vol. 1, *Menyayushchayasya strana v menyayushchem-sya mire: predposylki peremen v usloviyakh truda i urovnya zhizni* (Moscow, Editorial URSS, 2000).

49 *Rossiiskaya gazeta*, 12 July 2001.

50 *Russia's Regions: Goals, Challenges and Achievements* (New York, UNDP, 2007), www.undp.ru

51 Cf. Christopher M. Davies, 'Eastern Europe and the Former USSR: An Overview', RFE/RL, *Research Report*, Vol. 2, No. 40, 8 October 1993, pp. 31–43.

52 RIA Novosti, 15 May 2007.

53 S. A. Sidorenko, 'Moskovskie bezdomnye – pervye shagi v izuchenii problemy', *Ekonomicheskie i sotsial'nye peremeny: monitoring obshchestvennogo mneniya*, No. 4, July–August 1995, p. 46.

54 Sheila Marnie, 'Economic Reform and the Social Safety Net', RFE/RL, *Research Report*, Vol. 2, No. 17, 23 April 1993, p. 2.

55 Sheila Marnie, 'The Social safety Net in Russia', RFE-RL, *Research Report*, Vol. 2, No. 17, 23 April 1993, pp. 17–23.

56 Khasbulatov, *The Struggle for Russia*, p. 96.

57 *Soviet Weekly*, 3 October 1991, p. 7.

58 *Obshchaya gazeta*, 15 February 2001.

59 Figures cited by Putin at his press conference on 4 June 2007, Kremlin.ru

60 See Richard Rose, 'The Value of Fringe Benefits in Russia', RFE/RL, *Research Report*, Vol. 3, No. 15, 15 April 1994, pp. 16–21.

61 Details of presidential decrees, governmental acts and laws on social policy are in *Sotsial'naya politika v Rossii: Sbornik dokumentov* (Moscow, Respublika, 1992).

62 RFE/RL, *Newsline*, 27 June 2001.

63 *Trud*, 5 January 2001; RFE/RL, *Newsline*, 8 January 2001.

64 *Ekonomika i zhizn'*, No. 22, 1991.

65 *OMRI Daily Digest*, No. 19, Part I, 26 January 1996.

66 RFE/RL, *Newsline*, 25 June 2001.

67 *The Economist*, 20 November 1993, pp. 47–48.

68 *Rossiiskie vesti*, 5 May 1994, p. 4.

69 Alexander Shokhin, 'Labour Market Regulation in the USSR', *Communist Economies*, Vol. 3, No. 4 (1991), pp. 499–509, at p. 505.

70 *Vremya*, 19 March 2001, p. 1.

71 For details, see Sheila Marnie, 'How Prepared Is Russia for Mass Unemployment?', RFE/RL, *Research Report*, Vol. 1, No. 48, 4 December 1992, pp. 44–50; see also her 'Who and Where Are the Russian Unemployed?', ibid. Vol. 2, No. 33, 20 August 1993, pp. 36–42.

72 Linda J. Cook, *The Soviet Social Contract and Why it Failed: Welfare Policy and Workers' Politics from Brezhnev to Yeltsin* (Cambridge, MA, Harvard University Press, 1993).

73 See, for example, Russell Bova, 'Worker Activism: The Role of the State', in Judith B. Sedaitis and Jim Butterfield (eds), *Perestroika from Below: Social Movements in the Soviet Union* (Boulder, CO, Westview Press, 1991), pp. 29–42.

74 For details on each union, see *Kto est' chto: politicheskaya Moskva 1993* (Moscow, Catallaxy, 1993), pp. 501–624; *Kyo est' chto*, Vol. 2 *Profsoyuznye ob"edineniya i tsentry* (Moscow, 1994).

75 *Soviet Weekly*, 17 October 1991, p. 4.

76 For details of this, see Aleksandr Lebedev, 'Ot kogo nezavisimy nezavisimye profsoyuzy?', *Izvestiya*, 16 May 2007, p. 3.

77 Linda Cook, *Labor and Liberalization: Trade Unions in the New Russia* (New York, Twentieth Century Press, 1997).

78 For details, see Linda J. Cook, 'Russia's Labor Relations', in D. W. Blum (ed.), *Russia's Future* (Boulder, CO, Westview, 1994), pp. 69–89.

79 Stephen Crowley, 'Barriers to Collective Action: Steelworkers and Mutual Dependence in the Former Soviet Union', *World Politics*, Vol. 46, No. 4 (July 1994), pp. 589–615.

80 See John Thirkell, Richard Scase and Sarah Vickerstaff (eds), *Labour Relations and Political Change in Eastern Europe: A Comparative Perspective* (London, UCL Press, 1995).

81 See Bela Greskovits, *The Political Economy of Protest and Patience: East European and Latin American Transformations Compared* (Budapest, Central European University Press, 1998).

82  See Boris Kagarlitskii, 'Profsoyuzy stoyat pered vyborom', *Nezavisimaya gazeta*, 25 August 1994, p. 4.

83  The most influential were the Independent Miner's Union, Sotsprof, the Kuzbas Confederation of Labour, and the trade unions for dockers, sailors, pilots, air traffic controllers, and locomotive railway workers, Lyudmila Alekseeva, 'Nesvobodnye profsoyuzy', *Moskovskie novosti*, No. 3, 22 January 1995, p. 14.

84  For an early study, see Matthew Wyman, *Public Opinion in Postcommunist Russia* (London, Macmillan, 1996), pp. 116–19.

85  See E. B. Gruzdeva and E. S. Chertikhina, 'Polozhenie zhenshchiny v obshchestve: konflikt rolei', in *Obshchestvo v raznykh izmereniyakh: sotsiologi otvechayut na voprosy*, compiled by V. E. Gimpel'son and A. K. Nazimova (Moscow, Moskovskii rabochii, 1990), pp. 147–67.

86  Pockney, *Soviet Statistics since 1950*, pp. 48–49.

87  Pockney, *Soviet Statistics since 1950*, p. 47.

88  For a detailed study, see M. K. Gorshkova and N. E. Tikhonova (ed.), *Zhenshchina novoi Rossii: kakaya ona? kak zhivet? k chemu stremitsya?* (Moscow, Rosspen, 2002). For a full-scale comparative study, see N. M. Stepanova and E. V. Kochkina (eds), *Genderaya rekonstruktsiya politicheskikh sistem* (St Petersburg, Aleteiya, 2004), in particular Part 5, 'Gendernye problemy rossiiskoi demokratii', pp. 477–676.

89  Grigorii Gendler and Marina Gildingersh, 'A Socioeconomic Portrait of the Unemployed in Russia', RFE/RL, *Research Report*, Vol. 3, No. 3, 21 January 1994, p. 35.

90  *Rossiiskaya gazeta*, 18 February 1994.

91  Mikhail Gorbachev, *Perestroika: New Thinking for Our Country and the World* (London, Collins, 1987), p. 117.

92  Penny Morvant, 'Bearing the "Double Burden" in Russia', *Transition*, 8 September 1995, pp. 4–9.

93  RFE/RL, *Newsline*, 25 October 2000.

94  In 1970 the figure was 30 out of 100, and in 1980 40, *Naselenie Rossii* (Moscow, Goskomstat, 1993).

95  *Russia in Figures: 2006.* p. 75.

96  Viktor Perevedentsev, *Moskovskie novosti*, No. 49, 5 December 1993, p. 6.

97  Valentina Bodrova, 'The Russian Family in Flux', *Transition*, 8 September 1995, pp. 10–11.

98  *Izvestiya*, 2 December 1993, p. 4.

99  Peter Lentini, 'Women and the 1989 Elections to the USSR Congress of People's Deputies', *Coexistence*, Vol. 31, 1994, pp. 1–28.

100  *Rossiiskaya gazeta*, 3 December 1992, p. 1; women comprised 8.9 per cent of the Supreme Soviet.

101  Wendy Slater, 'Female Representation in Russian Politics', RFE/RL, *Research Report*, Vol. 3, No. 22, 3 June 1994, pp. 27–33.

102  S. V. Polenina, 'Zhenshchiny, vlast', demokratiya', *Byulleten' TsIK*, No. 1 (27), 1995, p. 15.

103  See Svetlana Aivazova, 'Zhenskoe dvizhenie v Rossii: traditsii i sovremennost'', *ONS*, No. 2 (1995), pp. 121–30.

104  *Nezavisimaya gazeta*, 12 January 1996, p. 2.

105  *Vek*, No. 15, 2000.

106  For an analysis of this, see Valerie Sperling, *Organizing Women in Contemporary Russia: Engendering Transition* (Cambridge, Cambridge University Press, 1999).

107  Cited in *Itogovyi otchet o rabote i nezavisimogo zhenskogo foruma* (Moscow, 1991), p. 7.

108  Elzbieta Matynia, 'Women after Communism: A Bitter Freedom', *Social Research*, Vol. 62, No. 2, summer 1994, pp. 351–77.

109  See Rebecca Kay, *Russian Women and their organisation: Gender, Discrimination and Grassroots Women's Organisations, 1991–96* (Basingstoke, Macmillan, 2000).

110  Cf. Mira Marody, 'Why I Am Not a Feminist', *Social Research*, Vol. 60, No. 4, winter 1993, pp. 853–64.

111  David Holloway, 'The Politics of Catastrophe', *The New York Review of Books*, 10 June 1993, p. 36.

112  Mark Popovskii, *Delo akademika Vavilova* (Moscow, Kniga, 1991).

113 Douglas Weiner, *Models of Nature: Ecology, Conservation, and Cultural Revolution in Soviet Russia* (Bloomington, Indiana University Press, 1988).

114 See Charles E. Ziegler, 'Environmental Politics and Policy under *Perestroika*', in Sedaitis and Butterfield (eds), *Perestroika from Below*, pp. 113–32.

115 *Soviet Weekly*, 31 October 1991, p. 4.

116 For more details see Georgii S. Golitsyn, 'Ecological Problems in the CIS During the Transitional Period', RFE/RL, *Research Report*, Vol. 2, No. 2, 8 January 1993, pp. 33–46; on the Caspian Sea, *Izvestiya*, 11 December 1993, p. 15; on sunken nuclear reactors, *Independent*, 10 November 1993; and on whaling, *The Guardian*, 12 February 1994, p. 12.

117 *Soviet Weekly*, 31 October 1991, p. 4.

118 William Millinship, *Observer*, 31 May 1992, p. 49. For details of the crisis, see Murray Feshbach and Alfred Friendly, *Ecocide in the USSR: Health and Nature under Siege* (New York, Basic Books, 1992).

119 Jonathan D. Oldfield, *Russian Nature: Exploring the Consequences of Societal Environmental Change* (Aldershot, Ashgate, 2005).

120 Divish Petrof, 'Siberian Forests under Threat', *The Ecologist*, Vol. 22, No. 6, 1992, pp. 267–70.

121 *Moscow News*, No. 6, 4 February 1993, p. 3.

122 In 2005 Shell had signed a draft asset swap agreement with Gazprom whereby the latter planned to acquire a quarter of Sakhalin Energy in exchange for half of Zapolyarnoe, a large Western Siberian gas field. A few days after the agreement, Shell disclosed that Sakhalin's costs had doubled to $20billion, an announcement that incensed the Russian government, since its share of revenues from the project were indefinitely postponed. Carl Mortishead, 'Putin Signals End to Overseas Ownership of Russian Energy', *The Times*, 12 December 2006.

123 Oldfield, *Russian Nature*, pp. 71–81.

124 See Zhores Medvedev, *The Legacy of Chernobyl* (Oxford, Blackwell, 1991); see also Piers Paul Reed, *Ablaze: The Story of the Heroes and Victims of Chernobyl* (New York, Random House, 1992).

125 See David R. Marples, 'Nuclear Power in the CIS: A Reappraisal', RFE/RL, *Research Report*, Vol. 3, No. 22, 3 June 1994, pp. 21–6.

126 *Independent*, 25 January 1992.

127 Cf. Jeremy Russell, *Energy and Environmental Conflicts in East/Central Europe: The Case of Power Generation* (London, RIIA/World Conservation Union, 1991).

128 http://president.kremlin.ru/text/appears/2007/04/125401.shtml

129 *The Observer*, 26 March 1995, p. 1.

130 Cf. Duncan Fisher, *Paradise Deferred: Environmental Policymaking in Central and Eastern Europe* (London, RIIA-Ecological Studies Institute, 1992).

131 *Vedemosti S"ezda narodnykh deputatov Rossiiskoi Federatsii i Verkhovhogo Soveta Rossiiskoi federatsii*, No. 10, 5 March 1992, pp. 592–630.

132 D. J. Peterson, 'The Environment in the Post-Soviet Era', RFE/RL, *Research Report*, Vol. 2, No. 2, 8 January 1993, pp. 43–46.

133 *Russian Conservation News*, No. 3, May 1995, p. 4. As of 30 March 1995 Russia had 89 *Zapovedniki* covering a total area of 29.1 million hectares (1.42 per cent of Russia's territory), and 29 National Parks, covering 6.6 million hectares, or 0.38 per cent of the Federation, with the final total expected to settle at about 100, ibid., p. 11.

134 Cf. M. Waller and F. Millard, 'Environmental Politics in Eastern Europe', *Environmental Politics*, Vol. 2, 1992, p. 171.

135 See Guillermo O'Donnell, 'Horizontal Accountability in New Democracies', *Journal of Democracy*, Vol. 9, No. 3, 1998, pp. 112–26; also in Andreas Schedler, Larry Diamond and Marc F. Plattner (eds), *The Self-restraining State: Power and Accountability in New Democracies* (Boulder, CO, Lynne Rienner Publishers, 1999); and discussed in Guillermo O'Donnell, Jorg Vargas Cullell and Osvaldo M. Iazzetta (eds), *The Quality of Democracy* (Notre Dame, IN, University of Notre Dame Press, 2004).

136 Cf. F. Riggs, 'The Survival of Presidentialism in America: Para-constitutional Practices', *International Political Science Review*, Vol. 9, No. 4, 1988, pp. 247–78.

137 For a discussion of these issues, see Hans Oversloot, 'Reordering the State (without Changing the Constitution): Russia under Putin's Rule, 2000–2008', *Review of Central and East European Law*, Vol. 32, 2007, pp. 41–64, in particular pp. 61–3.
138 'Ob Obshchestvennoi Palate Rossiiskoi Federatii', http://document.kremlin.ru/index.asp
139 The term is from Jeremy Bransten, 'Public Chamber Criticized as "Smokescreen"', *RFE/RL Russian Political Weekly*, Vol. 5, No. 13, 1 April 2005.
140 *Izvestiya*, 18 November 2005.
141 'O vnesenii izmenenii v nekotorye zakonodatel'nye akty Rossiiskoi Federatsii', *Rossiiskaya gazeta*, 17 January 2006.

## 15 Cultural transformation

1 Alexei Podberezkin, leader of the 'Spiritual Heritage' movement, quoted by Eric Black, 'Russia's Heritage Sets It Apart', *Star Tribune*, 29 October 1999, in *Johnson's Russia List*, No. 3595/6.
2 For a discussion of the re-evaluation of history, see R. W. Davies, *Soviet History in the Gorbachev Revolution* (Basingstoke, Macmillan, 1989); the story is taken further in his *Soviet History in the Yeltsin Era* (Basingstoke, Macmillan, 1997).
3 *Soviet Weekly*, 10 October 1991, p. 3.
4 For a more recent study, see George Sanford, *Katyn and the Massacre of 1940: Truth, Justice and Memory* (London, Routledge, 2005).
5 *Rossiiskaya gazeta*, 8 February 1992, pp. 3–4.
6 RFE/RL, *Newsline*, 15 June 2001.
7 Oksana Yablokovo, 'Newspapers Passing into Hands of Kremlin Allies', *Moscow Times*, 7 June 2006. Berezovsky sold his share to Badri Patarkatsishvili, his Georgian business partner, in February 2006 to try to insulate the paper from Kremlin pressure. It was rumoured later that year that Patarkatsishvili sold it on to Roman Abramovich's investment company, Millhouse, for $120 million (£65 million).
8 See Sarah Oates, *Television, Democracy and Elections in Russia* (London, Routledge, 2006).
9 Dmitry Vinogradov, 'Russian Internet Remains an Island of Free Speech and Civil Society', *Russian Analytical Digest*, No. 9, 2006, pp. 12–16, at p. 12.
10 Robert Orttung, 'Kremlin Systematically Shrinks Scope of Russian Media', *Russian Analytical Digest*, No. 9, 2006, pp. 2–5, at p. 2.
11 http://www.rsf.org/article.php3?id_article=19388
12 *Partiinaya zhizn'*, No. 18, September 1991, p. 3.
13 Stjepan G. Mestrovic, 'Series Editor's Statement', in Joseph Gibbs, *Gorbachev's Glasnost: The Soviet Media in the First Phase of Perestroika* (College Station, Texas A & M University Press, 1999), p. x.
14 RFE/RL, *Newsline*, 26 January 2001.
15 http://www.scrf.gov.ru/
16 Rosalind Marsh, 'The Death of Soviet Literature: Can Russian Literature Survive?', *Europe–Asia Studies*, Vol. 45, No. 1, 1993, pp. 115–39.
17 *Rossiiskaya gazeta*, 29 October 1991, p. 2.
18 For a discussion of plans, see *Nezavisimaya gazeta*, 28 June 2001, p. 8.
19 *Literaturnaya gazeta*, 22 July 1992, p. 5.
20 Leon Aron, 'A Champion for the Bourgeoisie: Reinventing Virtue and Citizenship in Boris Akunin's Novels', *The National Interest*, spring 2004.
21 On the role of the intelligentsia from a different perspective, see K. G. Barbakova and V. A. Mansurov, *Intelligentsiya i vlast'* (Moscow, Institute of Sociology, 1991).
22 *The Guardian*, 3 December 1992.
23 This was the view of Kozyrev, *Izvestiya*, 30 June 1992.
24 *Rossiya*, No. 1 (9), 4–10 January 1991, p. 1.
25 *Religion in Communist Dominated Areas*, Vol. 30, No. 1, 1991, p. 9.
26 John B. Dunlop, 'KGB Subversion of Russian Orthodox Church', RFE/RL, *Research Report*, Vol. 1, No. 12, 20 March 1992, pp. 51–3; Oxana Antic, 'Orthodox Church Reacts to Criticism of KGB Links', RFE/RL, *Research Report*, Vol. 1, No. 23, 5 June 1992, pp. 61–3.

27 See Edwin Bacon, 'Religion and Politics in Russia, in Mike Bowker and Cameron Ross (eds), *Russia after the Cold War* (Harlow, Longman, 2000), pp. 185–98, at p. 188.

28 RFE/RL, 'Russian Orthodox Churches Unite', 17 May 2007.

29 Deacon Andrei Kurayev, *Moscow News*, No. 7, 11 February 1993, p. 11.

30 RFE/RL, *Newsline*, 30 May 2001.

31 According to Mikhail Tul'skii (*Nezavisimaya gazeta – religii*, April 2001), there were 10,913 Orthodox congregations, 3,048 Muslim groups, 197 Jewish communities, and 193 Buddhist temples. The growth of Protestant groups was marked, with 2,910 Evangelical churches, 330 Jehovah's Witness groups, 213 Presbytarian congregations and 476 other communities. In addition, there were 106 registered Hare Krishna groups, 20 Bahai communities and 17 Unification Church branches.

32 *Russia in Figures: 2006*, p. 55.

33 Max Weber, *The Protestant Ethic and the Spirit of Capitalism* (London, Allen & Unwin, 1976); R. H. Tawney, *Religion and the Rise of Capitalism* (London, Pelican, 1938).

34 Zoe Knox, *Russian Society and the Orthodox Church: Religion in Russia after Communism* (London, RoutledgeCurzon, 2005).

35 See Harry Eckstein, Frederic J. Fleron Jr., Erik P. Hoffmann, and William M. Reissinger, *Can Democracy Take Root in Post-Soviet Russia? Explorations in State-Society Relations* (Lanham, MD, Rowman & Littlefield Publishers, Inc., 1998).

36 G. A. Almond and S. Verba, *The Civic Culture: Political Attitudes and Democracy in Five Nations* (Princeton University Press, 1963); G. A. Almond and S. Verba (eds), *The Civic Culture Revisited* (Boston, Little, Brown, 1980); L. W. Pye and S. Verba (eds), *Political Culture and Political Development* (Princeton, NJ, Princeton University Press, 1965).

37 Nikolai Biryukov and V. M. Sergeev, *Russia's Road to Democracy: Parliament, Communism and Traditional Culture* (Aldershot, Edward Elgar, 1993); see also their *Russian Politics in Transition: Institutional Conflict in a Nascent Democracy* (Aldershot, Ashgate Publishing, 1997).

38 Alexander Lukin, *Political Culture of Russian Democrats* (Oxford, Oxford University Press, 1999), p. 298.

39 The classic example of this approach was the comparative analysis of the past and present of several communist countries in Archie Brown and Jack Gray (eds), *Political Culture and Change in Communist Systems* (London, Macmillan, 1977). See also Archie Brown (ed.), *Political Culture and Communist Studies* (London, Macmillan, 1984), and Stephen White, *Political Culture and Soviet Politics* (London, Macmillan, 1979).

40 For a recent discussion of Russian political culture and methodological issues, see Stephen Whitefield (ed.), *Political Culture and Post-Communism* (Basingstoke, Palgrave, 2005).

41 Robert D. Putnam, *Making Democracy Work: Civic Traditions in Modern Italy* (Princeton, NJ, Princeton University Press, 1993).

42 For a review of the literature and the debate, see Robert Bideleux, Robert, '"Making Democracy Work" in the Eastern Half of Europe: Explaining and Conceptualising Divergent Trajectories of Post-Communist Democratisation', *Perspectives on European Politics and Society*, Vol. 8, No. 2, June 2007, pp. 109–30.

43 See, for example, Sergei Pushkarev, *Self-government and Freedom in Russia* (Boulder, CO, Westview Press, 1988); Nicolai N. Petro (ed.), *Christianity and Russian Culture in Soviet Society* (Boulder, CO, Westview Press, 1990).

44 Letter to the author, 18 November 1992. This is the core of his argument in Nicolai N. Petro, *The Rebirth of Russian Democracy: An Interpretation of Russian Political Culture* (Cambridge, MA, Harvard University Press, 1995).

45 J. R. Millar (ed.), *Politics, Work and Daily Life in the USSR* (Cambridge, Cambridge University Press, 1987).

46 Some 18,000 people were questioned in 25 regions of Russia, including a representative sample from Moscow, *Rezultaty sotsiologicheskogo issledovaniya 'Sotsial'no-aktivnye sily Rossii: usloviya i puti ikh konsolidatsii'* (Moscow, Institut sotsial'nykh i politicheskikh tekhnologii, 1991), p. 7.

47 *Rezultaty sotsiologicheskogo issledovaniya*, p. 12.

48 Study conducted by the Russian Independent Institute for Social and Nationality Problems, *Nezavisimaya gazeta*, 8 August 1992, p. 2.

49  Weekly poll conducted by the independent Institute of the Sociology of Parliamentarianism, *Izvestiya*, 17 August 1992, p. 2.

50  This trend is reflected in numerous polls and traced in those conducted by the Media and Opinion Research (MOR) Department of the RFE/RL Research Institute: RFE/RL, *Research Report*, Vol. 1, No. 19 (8 May 1992), pp. 57–8; No. 25 (19 June 1992), pp. 72–3; No. 41 (16 October 1992), pp. 64–5; Vol. 2, No. 3 (15 January 1993), pp. 42–4.

51  Jeffrey W. Hahn, 'Continuity and Change in Russian Political Culture', *British Journal of Political Science*, Vol. 21, 1991, pp. 393–412.

52  Jeffrey W. Hahn, 'Yaroslavl' Revisited: Assessing Continuity and Change in Russian Political Culture Since 1990', in Whitefield (ed.), *Political Culture and Post-Communism*, Chapter 8, pp. 148–79.

53  For an investigation of the issue, see Richard Rose, Richard and Neil Munro, *Elections without Order: Russia's Challenge to Vladimir Putin* (Cambridge, Cambridge University Press, 2002).

54  In February 1992, 33 per cent out of 1985 agreed that the market was 'our only salvation', whereas 20 per cent saw it as 'the cause of our destruction', and in the same poll 43 per cent saw more negative than positive in the transition, and only 22 per cent saw more positive, *Mir mnenii i mneniya o mire*, No. 8, August 1992, pp. 4–5.

55  *Soviet Weekly*, 10 October 1991, p. 6.

56  Leonid Gordon and Natal'ya Pliskevich, 'Lyudi ustali ot nasiliya', *Nezavisimaya gazeta*, 7 December 1991, p. 2.

57  *Rezultaty sotsiologicheskogo issledovaniya*, pp. 21–2.

58  For earlier discussions of social justice, see David S. Mason and Svetlana Sidorenko, 'Perestroika, Social Justice and Soviet Public Opinion', *Problems of Communism*, Vol. 34, No. 6, November-December 1990, pp. 34–43.

59  V. A. Kolosov (ed.), *Mir glazami rossiyan: Mify i vneshnyaya politika* (Moscow, Institut fonda 'Obshchestvennoe mnenie', 2003).

60  Leonid Gordon and Natal'ya Pliskevich, 'Lyudi ustali ot nasiliya', *Nezavisimaya gazeta*, 7 December 1991, p. 2.

61  James Gibson, 'A Mile Wide but an Inch Deep? The Structure of Democratic Commitments in the Former USSR', *American Journal of Political Science*, Vol. 40, No. 2, May 1996, pp. 396–420.

62  Leonid Sedov, *Nezavisimaya gazeta – Stsenarii*, No. 5, 2000.

63  For a report on a detailed survey of the question, see *Izvestiya*, 30 June 2001, p. 4.

64  William L Miller, Stephen White and Paul Heywood, *Values and Political Change in Postcommunist Europe* (Basingstoke, Macmillan, 1998), p. 28.

65  Timothy J. Colton and Michael McFaul, *Are Russians Undemocratic?* (Carnegie Endowment for International Peace, Russian Domestics Politics Project, Russian and Eurasian Program, Working Paper No. 20, June 2001), p. 8.

66  Ibid., p. 11.

67  Ibid., pp. 15–16.

68  Ibid., p. 22.

69  Alexander Zinoviev, *The Yawning Heights* (Harmondsworth, Penguin, 1981), p. 621.

70  'Yeltsin Call for "Unifying National Idea"', Itar-Tass 12 July 1996. See Michael Urban, 'Remythologising the Russian State', *Europe–Asia Studies*, Vol. 50, No. 6, 1998, pp. 969–92.

71  Putin, *First Person*, p. 213; Sakwa, *Putin*, p. 256.

72  Interfax, 3 November 1999.

73  Itar-Tass, 22 December 1999.

74  Putin, *First Person*, p. 214; Sakwa, *Putin*, p. 256.

75  M. Steven Fish, 'Putin's Path', *Journal of Democracy*, Vol. 12, No. 4, October 2001, p. 73.

76  Putin's defended his synthetic approach in *Komsomol'skaya pravda*, 6 December 2000.

77  For a discussion of how these practices operate in the post-communist era, see Alena V. Ledeneva, *How Russia Really Works: The Informal Practices that Shaped Post-Soviet Politics and Business* (Ithaca, NY, and London, Cornell University Press, 2006).

78  This is one of the questions posed by Karl Marx, and paradoxically the fall of communism might well have made his analysis, if not his solutions, more relevant to Russian society than before.

## Part V Foreign, security and neighbourhood policy

1 *Trud*, 11 January 2001.
2 *Medium Term Strategy for the Development of Relations between the RF and the EU (2000–2010)*, mimeo 1999, point 1.1.

## 16 Foreign policy

1 G. P. Fedotov, *Russia, Europe and Us: Collected Essays*, Vol. 2 (Paris, YMCA Press, 1973), p. 232.
2 On the ambiguous relationship between Russia and Europe, see Martin Malia, *Russia under Western Eyes: From the Bronze Horseman to the Lenin Mausoleum* (Cambridge, MA, Belknap, 2000).
3 A. V. Kozyrev, 'Vneshnyaya politika preobrazhayushcheisya Rossii', *Voprosy istorii*, No. 1, 1994, p. 4.
4 Boris Pankin, *The Last Hundred Days of the Soviet Union* (London, I. B. Tauris, 1996), p. 104.
5 Cited in Kozyrev, 'Vneshnyaya politika', *Voprosy istorii*, No. 1, 1994, p. 6.
6 Andrei Kozyrev, 'Russia: A Chance of Survival', *Foreign Affairs*, spring 1992, pp. 1–16, at p. 4.
7 E.g. *Izvestiya*, 30 June 1992.
8 Pavel Baev, *The Russian Army in a Time of Trouble* (London, Sage, 1996).
9 *Nezavisimaya gazeta*, 28 March 1992. Andranik Migranyan later claimed to have rediscovered the notion of the Monroe Doctrine for Russia, 'Russia and the Near Abroad', *Nezavisimaya gazeta*, 12 January 1994.
10 'A Strategy for Russia', *Nezavisimaya gazeta*, 19 August 1992, p. 4.
11 Suzanne Crow, 'Russia Seeks Leadership in Regional Peacekeeping', RFE/RL, *Research Report*, Vol. 2, No. 15, 9 April 1993.
12 Kozyrev, 'Vneshnyaya politika', p. 3.
13 *Izvestiya*, 8 October 1993.
14 See Andrei Kozyrev, 'Partnership or Cold Peace?', *Foreign Policy*, No. 99, summer 1995, pp. 3–14.
15 E.g., Andranik Migranyan, *Nezavisimaya gazeta*, 10 December 1994.
16 *Moskovskie novosti*, No. 63, 11–18 December 1994, pp. 4, 6.
17 *Izvestiya*, 10 February 1996, p. 3.
18 *Independent*, 13 January 1996, p. 9.
19 RFE/RL, *Newsline*, 27 March 2000.
20 http://www.mid.ru/mid/eng/econcept.htm, in English.
21 http://www.president.kremlin.ru/events/145.html
22 *Soviet Weekly*, 26 September 1991, p. 6.
23 *Diplomaticheskii vestnik*, No. 16, 31 March 1992.
24 *Rossiiskaya gazeta*, 31 March 1995, p. 5.
25 Konstantin Eggert, *Izvestiya*, 16 December 1995, p. 3.
26 *Izvestiya*, 30 June 1992.
27 *Nezavisimaya gazeta*, 27 May 1994, p. 5.
28 Cited in Suzanne Crow, 'Russia Prepares to Take a Hard Line on "Near Abroad"', RFE/RL, *Research Report*, Vol. 1, No. 32, 1992, pp. 21–4.
29 *Nezavisimaya gazeta*, 19 August 1992, p. 4.
30 *Nezavisimaya gazeta*, 27 May 1994, pp. 4–5.
31 S. A. Karaganov (ed.), *Strategiya dlya Rossii: Povestka dnya dlya prezidenta-2000* (Moscow, Vagrius/SVOP, 2000), abstract.
32 'O koordinatsii mezhdunarodnykh i vnesheekonomicheskikh svyazei sub"ektov Rossiiskoi Federatsii', 4 January 1999, *Rossiiskay gazeta*, 16 January 1999.
33 For example, in the case of Gorno-Altai, discussed below, *Rossiiskaya gazeta*, 21 June 2000, pp. 5–6.
34 *Nezavisimaya gazeta*, 27 May 1994, p. 4.

35  Cf. the testimony of the former deputy foreign minister from October 1991 to October 1992, Fedor Shelov-Kovedyaev, *Segodnya*, 31 August 1993.

36  Vladimir Zubok, 'Tyranny of the Weak: Russia's New Foreign Policy', *World Policy Journal*, Vol. 9, No. 2, spring 1992, pp. 191–218.

37  *Moscow News*, No. 52, 31 December 1993, p. 1.

38  *Pravda*, 29 June–2 July 2001, p. 3.

39  Cf. V. P. Lukin, 'Rossiya i ee interesy', *Diplomaticheskii vestnik*, No. 21–2, 15–30 November 1992, pp. 48–53.

40  Sergei Stankevich, *Nezavisimaya gazeta*, 28 March 1992, p. 4.

41  Cf. Elgiz Pozdnyakov, 'National, State, and Class Interests in International Relations', in *MEMO: New Soviet Voices on Foreign and Economic Policy*, edited by Steve Hirsch (Washington, D.C., Bureau of National Affairs, 1989), pp. 471–90; originally in *MEMO*, No. 5, May 1988.

42  E.g., Sergei Goncharov, head of the Sino-Russian relations department at the Institute of the Far East, RAN, *Izvestiya*, 25 February 1992, p. 6.

43  Pozdnyakov, *Natsiya, natsionalizm, natsional'nye interesy*, p. 78.

44  Sergei Stankevich, 'A Power in Search of Itself', *Nezavisimaya gazeta*, 28 March 1992, p. 4. See also Alexander Rahr, 'Atlanticists versus Eurasians in Russian Foreign Policy', RFE/RL, *Research Report*, Vol. 1, No. 22, 1992, pp. 17–22.

45  Tibor Szamuely, *The Russian Tradition*, (London, Fontana, 1988), p. 10.

46  Szamuely, *The Russian Tradition*, p. 10.

47  Dmitrii Likhachev, *Reflections on Russia* (Boulder, CO, Westview Press, 1991), p. 80.

48  See Elgiz Pozdnyakov, 'The Problem of Returning the Soviet Union to European Civilisation', *Paradigms: The Kent Journal of International Relations*, Vol. 5, No. 1/2, 1991, pp. 45–57. See also Milan Hauner, *What Is Asia for Us? Russia's Asian Heartland Yesterday and Today* (London, Unwin Hyman, 1990); and Mark Bassin, 'Russia between Europe and Asia: The Ideological Construction of Geographical Space', *Slavic Review*, Vol. 50, No. 1, spring 1991, pp. 1–17.

49  Assen Ignatow, *Der 'Eurasismus' und die Suche nach einer neuen russischen Kulturidentitat. Die Neubelebung des 'Jewrasijstwo'-Mythos* (Cologne, Berichte des BIOst 15, 1992).

50  Halford J. Mackinder, 'The Geographical Pivot of History', in his *Democratic Ideals and Reality* (New York, W. W. Norton & Co., 1962).

51  Cited in John M. Letiche and Basil Dmytryshyn, *Russian Statecraft: The Politika of Iurii Krizhanich* (Oxford, Basil Blackwell, 1985), p. 128.

52  Sergei N. Goncharov, 'Russia's Special Interests: What Are They?', *Izvestiya*, 25 February 1992, p. 6.

53  P. Ya. Chaadaev, *Polnoe sobranie sochinenii i izbrannye pis'ma* (Moscow, Nauka, 1991), pp. 320–39.

54  Elgiz Pozdnyakov, 'Russia is a Great Power', *International Affairs* (Moscow), No. 1, 1993, pp. 3–5.

55  Alan Ingram, 'Aleksander Dugin: Geo-politics and Neo-fascism in Post-Soviet Russia', *Political Geography*, Vol. 20, No. 8, 2001, pp. 1029–51; A. G. Dugin, 'Evraziya prevyshe vsego: Manifest sovremennogo evraziiskogo dvizheniya', *Osnovy Evraziistva* (Moscow, Arktogeya tsentr, 2002).

56  Paradorn Rangsimaporn, 'Interpretations of Eurasianism: Justifying Russia's Role in East Asia', *Europe–Asia Studies*, Vol. 58, No. 3, May 2006, pp. 371–89.

57  Zhan Parvulesko (Jean Parvulesco), *Putin i evraziiskaya imperiya*, Translated from French (St. Petersburg, Amfora, 2006).

58  Dmitri Trenin, *The End of Eurasia: Russia on the Border Between Geopolitics and Globalization* (Moscow, Carnegie Moscow Center, 2001).

59  Dmitry Trenin, *Integratsiya i identichnost': Rossiya kak 'novyi zapad'* (Moscow, Evropa, 2006).

60  Andrei Zagorsky, 'Russia and Europe', *International Affairs* (Moscow), No. 1, 1993, pp. 43–51.

61  *The Observer*, 10 September 1995, p. 23.

62  A point made already under Gorbachev by, for example, Jack Snyder, 'International Leverage on Soviet Domestic Change', *World Politics*, Vol. 42, No. 1, 1990, pp. 1–30.

63 For a general discussion of the 'democratic peace' hypothesis, see, *inter alia*, Michael Brown, Sean Lynn-Jones and Steven Miller (eds), *Debating the Democratic Peace* (Cambridge, MA, MIT Press, 1996); John Oneal and Bruce Russett, 'The Classical Liberals were Right: Democracy, Interdependence and Conflict, 1950–1985', *International Studies Quarterly*, Vol. 41, No. 2, 1997, pp. 267–94; Michael W. Doyle, *Ways of War and Peace* (New York, W. W. Norton, 1997); Randall Schweller, 'Domestic Structure and Preventive War: Are Democracies More Pacific?', *World Politics*, Vol. 44, No. 2, pp. 235–69; Tarak Barkawi and Mark Laffey (eds), *Democracy, Liberalism, and War: Rethinking the Democratic Peace Debate* (London, Lynne Rienner, 2001).

64 The link between democratisation and war was suggested by E. Mansfield and J. Snyder, 'Democratization and the Danger of War', *International Security*, Vol. 20, No. 1, 1995, pp. 26–31. It was challenged by Neil Malcolm and Alex Pravda, 'Democratization and Russian Foreign Policy', *International Affairs*, Vol. 72, No. 3, 1996, pp. 537–52. See also B. F. Braumoeller, 'Deadly Doves: Liberal Nationalism and the Democratic Peace in the Soviet Successor States', *International Studies Quarterly*, Vol. 41, 1997, pp. 375–402; Michael McFaul, 'A Precarious Peace: Domestic Politics in the Making of Russian Foreign Policy', *International Security*, Vol. 22, No. 3, 1998, pp. 5–35. Snyder develops his argument in his *From Voting to Violence: Democratization and Nationalist Conflict* (New York, W. W. Norton, 2000).

65 Errol A. Henderson, *Democracy and War: The End of an Illusion?* (Boulder, CO, Lynne Rienner, 2002).

66 James M. Goldgeier and Michael McFaul, 'Russians as Joiners: Realist and Liberal Conceptions of Postcommunist Europe', in Michael McFaul and Kathryn Stoner-Weiss (eds), *After the Collapse of Communism: Comparative Lessons of Transition* (New York, Cambridge University Press, 2004), Chapter 7, pp. 232–56.

67 Thomas Ambrosio, *Challenging America's Global Preeminence: Russia's Quest for Multi-polarity* (Ashgate, Aldershot, 2005).

68 Tsygankov, Andrei P., 'Vladimir Putin's Vision of Russia as a Normal Great Power', *Post-Soviet Affairs*, Vol. 21, No. 2, 2005, pp. 132–58, at p. 133.

69 'The Foreign Policy Concept of the Russian Federation', http://www.mid.ru/mid/eng/econcept.htm

70 For an overview, see Alexander J. Motyl, Blair A. Ruble and Lilia Shevtsova (eds), *Russia's Engagement with the West: Transformation and Integration in the Twenty-first Century* (New York, M. E. Sharpe, 2003).

71 *Independent*, 18 June 1992.

72 For example, Stephen F. Cohen, *Failed Crusade: America and the Tragedy of Post-Communist Russia* (New York, W. W. Norton, 2000).

73 On the long-standing concerns of the Europeans, see Evgenii Grigor'ev, '"Bunt" evropeitsev: Politiki starogo kontinenta ne khotyat igrat' role' satellitov SShA', *Nezavisimaya gazeta*, 15 February 2002, p. 6.

74 John C. K. Daly, *Eurasia Daily Monitor*, Vol. 4, No. 42, 1 March 2007.

75 Andrew Kuchins, Vyacheslav Nikonov and Dmitri Trenin, *U.S.-Russian Relations: The Case for an Upgrade* (Moscow, Moscow Carnegie Centre, 2005), p. 2.

76 Kuchins *et al.*, *U.S.-Russian Relations*, p. 2

77 *Russia's Wrong Direction: What the United States Can and Should Do*, Independent Task Force Report No. 57, John Edwards and Jack Kemp (Chairs), Stephen Sestanovich (Project Director), (New York, Council on Foreign Relations, 2006).

78 Vitalii Ivanov and Konstantin Simonov, 'Vernyi put' Rossii: chto khotyat sdelat' SShA?', *Nezavisimaya gazeta*, 28 April 2006, p. 10.

79 Press release of the Office of the Vice President, White House, 4 May 2006.

80 Dmitri Trenin, *Reading Russia Right*, Carnegie Endowment for International Peace, Policy Brief, Special Edition 42, October 2005, p. 8.

81 *Frankfurter Allgemeine Zeitung*, 31 July 1998, cited in *The Guardian*, 15 April 1999, p. 19.

82 *Russkaya mysl'*, 19 April 1991.

83 *The Independent*, 18 March 1995.

84 *The Independent*, 16 February 1995.

85 *The Common Strategy of the EU on Russia*, 4 June 1999, at http://europa.eu.int/council/ off/conclu/June 1999/annexe_en.htm#a2. The Madrid European Council of December 1995 had commissioned the *European Action Plan for Russia* of May 1996 (*Bulletin of the European Union*, No. 5, 1996) that had already outlined five priorities for Russia-EU relations: the promotion of Russia's democratic reforms, economic cooperation, cooperation in the areas of justice and home affairs, security in Europe and foreign policy.
86 These four points are discussed in Hannes Adomeit *et al.*, *Russia's Futures: Assessment of the CPN Russia Team as of February 2000* (Brussels, Conflict Prevention Network (CPN), 2000), pp. 14–15.
87 For further details, see Jackie Gower, 'Russia and the European Union', in Mark Webber (ed.), *Russia and Europe: Conflict and Cooperation* (Basingstoke, Macmillan, 2000), pp. 66–98.
88 *Nezavisimaya gazeta*, 17 November 2004.
89 Hanna Smith, 'Russian Foreign Policy', in Osmo Kuusi, Hanna Smith and Paula Tiihonen (eds), *Russia 2017: Three Scenarios* (Helsinki, Parliament of Finland, The Committee for the Future, 2007), pp. 67–75, at p. 68.
90 RFE/RL, *Newsline*, 3 July 2001.
91 'Wider Europe – Neighbourhood: Proposed New Framework for Relations with the EU's Eastern and Southern Neighbours', March 2003 Communication of the Commission to the Council.
92 Vladimir Putin, '50 Years of the European Integration and Russia', *Sunday Times*, 25 March 2007; also in CEPS, *European Neighbourhood Watch*, issue 25, March 2007, pp. 2–4, at p. 3.
93 Watanabe Koji, 'Introduction', in W. Koji (ed.), *Engaging Russia in Asia Pacific* (Tokyo, Japan Center for International Exchange, 1999), p. 13.
94 Zbigniew Brzezinski, *The Grand Chessboard: American Primacy and Its Geostrategic Imperatives* (New York, Basic Books, 1997).
95 Akino Yutaka, 'Welcome for a New Russia', in Koji (ed.), *Engaging Russia*, p. 162.
96 V. I. Lenin, *Polnoe sobranie sochinenii*, 5th edn (Moscow, 1958–70), Vol. 30, p. 236.
97 See Millan Hauner, *What Is Asia for Us? Russia's Asian Heartland Yesterday and Today* (London, Unwin Hyman, 1990).
98 *Russkaya mysl'*, 19 April 1991.
99 See E. Valkenier, *The Soviet Union and the Third World: The Economic Bind* (New York, Praeger, 1983); J. F. Hough, *The Struggle for the Third World: Soviet Debates and American Options* (Washington, DC, Brookings, 1986).
100 Solzhenitsyn, *Rebuilding Russia*, p. 27.
101 *Nezavisimaya gazeta*, 1 April 1992, p. 3.

## 17  Defence and security policy

1 Osip Mandelstam, cited by Vasily Grossman, *Life and Fate* (London, Harvill Press, 1995), p. 267.
2 Paul Hirst, 'The State, Civil Society and the Collapse of Soviet Communism', *Economy and Society*, Vol. 20, No. 2, pp. 217–42. For a discussion of the size of the defence sector, see *Kommunist*, No. 1, 1991, pp. 54–64.
3 On the economic burden, see Clifford G. Gaddy, *The Price of the Past: Russia's Struggle with the Legacy of a Militarized Economy* (Washington, DC, Brookings, 1996).
4 William E. Odom, *The Collapse of the Soviet Military* (New Haven, CT, Yale University Press, 1998), Chapter 16.
5 For a discussion of the army's ambiguous legal status at this time, see *Nezavisimaya gazeta*, 2 February 1992, p. 1.
6 The defence minister, Konstantin Morozov, argued that the decision was prompted by Moscow's refusal to release around 20,000 officers of Ukrainian origin serving outside the republic who had asked to return to serve in Ukraine's armed forces, *Independent*, 8 June 1992.
7 *The Military Balance 1994-1995* (London, Brasseys for the International Institute for Strategic Studies, 1994), p. 104.
8 *Soviet Weekly*, 19 September 1991, p. 2.

9 Shaposhnikov observed 'I am a citizen of Russia ... whom do I serve if not Russia? But it is Russia whose vital interests are conjugated with the interests of the other CIS nations ...', *Moscow News*, No. 6, 4 February 1993, p. 4.

10 *Izvestiya*, 3 July 1992, pp. 1–2.

11 RFE/RL, *Research Report*, Vol. 1, No. 42, 23 October 1992, p. 41.

12 *Krasnaya zvezda*, 9 May 1992.

13 *Moscow News*, No. 7, 11 February 1993, p. 3.

14 *Nezavisimoe voennoe obozrenie*, No. 17, 1 June 2007.

15 Viktor Litovkin, 'Russia Has an Unknown Number of Troops Outside the Defense Ministry', *Russian Profile*, Vol. 4, No. 5, 2007, pp. 35–6, at p. 35.

16 Cf. Adrian Karatnycky, 'The Ukrainian Factor', *Foreign Affairs*, Vol. 71, No. 3, summer 1992, p. 94.

17 *The Military Balance 1994–1995*, p. 108.

18 'Poslanie Federal'nomu Sobraniyu Rossiiskoi Federatsii', 26 April 2007, http://president.kremlin.ru/text/appears/2007/04/125401.shtml

19 *Krasnaya zvezda*, 17 February 1993, p. 1.

20 Dzintra Bungs, 'Soviet Troops in Latvia', RFE/RL, *Research Report*, Vol. 1, No. 34, 28 August 1992, pp. 18–28.

21 Stephen Foye, 'Russia's Defense Establishment in Disarray', RFE/RL, *Research Report*, Vol. 2, No. 36, 10 September 1993, pp. 49–54.

22 RFE/RL, *Research Report*, Vol. 1, No. 31, 31 July 1992, p. 61.

23 *The Military Balance 1994–1995*, p. 109.

24 *Nezavisimaya gazeta*, 21 February 2001.

25 *Moscow News*, No. 5, 28 January 1993, p. 4.

26 Scott McMichael, 'Russia's New Military Doctrine', RFE/RL, *Research Report*, Vol. 1, No. 40, 9 October 1992, p. 45. For a fascinating discussion of Soviet military doctrine, see A. A. Kokoshin, *Armiya i politika: Sovetskaya voenno-politicheskaya i voenno-strategichsekaya mysl', 1918–1991* (Moscow, Mezhdunarodnye otnosheniya, 1995).

27 The draft was published in a special issue of *Voennaya mysl'*, May 1992, pp. 4–7.

28 The document was discussed by the Security Council on 3 March and 6 October 1993, and accepted at its session of 2 November, on which date the president decreed its adoption, 'Osnovnye polozheniya voennoi doktriny Rossiiskoi Federatsii', special issue of *Voennaya mysl'*, November 1993, also in *Izvestiya*, 18 November 1993, pp. 1, 4.

29 Available at the Security Council's website: www.scrf.gov.ru/documents

30 *Vedemosti*, 6 March 2007.

31 Rod Thornton, 'Toothless Bear?', *The World Today*, June 2007, pp. 16–17, at p. 16.

32 *Rossiiskaya gazeta*, 5 May 1992.

33 'Kontseptsiya national'noi bezopasnosti Rossiiskoi Federatsii', www.scrf.gov.ru/documents/decree/24-1.html

34 For a comparison of the two versions, see Jakub M. Godzimirski, 'Russian National Security Concepts 1997 and 2000: A Comparative Analysis', *European Security*, Vol. 9, No. 4, winter 2000, pp. 73–91.

35 See V. N. Tsygichko, 'Geopolitical Aspects of Shaping Russia's Nuclear Policy', *Military Thought/Voennaya Mysl'*, No. 3, March 1994, pp. 2–9.

36 According to one report the Soviet nuclear arsenal included 45,000 warheads at its peak in 1986, 12,000 more than had been thought, *The Independent*, 27 September 1993.

37 Stephen Van Evera, 'Managing the Eastern Crisis: Preventing War in the Former Soviet Empire', *Security Studies*, Vol. 1, No. 3, spring 1992.

38 Bohdan Nahaylo, 'The Shaping of Ukrainian Attitudes towards Nuclear Arms', RFE/RL, *Research Report*, Vol. 2, No. 8, 19 February 1993, pp. 21–33.

39 *Nezavisimaya gazeta*, 7 December 1991, p. 1.

40 See John W. R. Lepingwell, 'Ukraine, Russia, and the Control of Nuclear Weapons', RFE/RL, *Research Report*, Vol. 2, No. 8, 19 February 1993, pp. 4–20.

41 RIA Novosti, 31 July 2006.

42 Keir A. Lieber and Daryl G. Press, 'The Rise of U.S. Nuclear Primacy', *Foreign Affairs*, Vol. 85, No. 2, March/April 2006, pp. 42–54.

43  29 May 2007, http://president.kremlin.ru/text/appears/2007/05/131976.shtml

44  *Vek*, 23 February 2001.

45  *Izvestiya*, 25 June 2001.

46  Dale R. Herspring, 'Rebuilding the Russian Military', *Russian Profile*, Vol. 4, No. 5, pp. 37–40, at p. 37.

47  *Moscow News*, No. 30, 1990, p. 11.

48  *The Independent*, 12 May 1992.

49  Editorial, *Vedemosti*, 16 February 2006.

50  Anne White, *Democratization in Russia under Gorbachev 1985–91: The Birth of a Voluntary Sector* (Basingstoke, Macmillan, 1999), p. 123.

51  E.g. V. K. Demedyuk and Yu. S. Kortunenko, 'On Organizational Structure of the Armed Forces', *Military Thought/Voennaya mysl'*, No. 5 (May 1994), pp. 2–6, who had defended a separate ADF.

52  Douglas L. Clarke, 'Rusting Fleet Renews Debate on Navy's Mission', RFE/RL, *Research Report*, Vol. 2, No. 25, 18 June 1993, p. 30.

53  Sergei Parkhomenko, *Segodnya*, 19 November 1994.

54  25 October 2006 hot line with the people, http://president.kremlin.ru/text/appears/2006/10/112959.shtml

55  Roger McDermott, 'Russian Military "Modernizing", Not Reforming – Ivanov', *Eurasia Daily Monitor*, Vol. 4, No. 32, 14 February 2007.

56  Victor Yasmann, 'Russia: Reviving the Army, Revising Military Doctrine', RFE/RL, 12 March 2007.

57  Chris Donnelly, 'Civil-Military Relations in the New Democracies', in David Betz and John Löwenhardt (eds), 'Army and State in Postcommunist Europe', special issue of *Journal of Communist Studies and Transition Politics*, Vol. 17, No. 1, March 2001, p. 9.

58  Stephen Foye, 'The Defense Ministry and the New Military "Opposition" ', RFE/RL, *Research Report*, Vol. 2, No. 20, 14 May 1993, pp. 68–73.

59  *Moscow News*, No. 7, 11 February 1992, p. 1.

60  RFE/RL, *Research Report*, Vol. 1, No. 36, 11 September 1992, p. 72. According to unofficial figures, some 25,000 officers had been dismissed by the end of 1992 for disagreeing with the government, *The Guardian*, 13 January 1993.

61  Chris Donnelly, 'Evolutionary Problems in the Former Soviet Armed Forces', *Survival*, autumn 1992, p. 37.

62  *Moscow News*, No. 5 (28 January 1993), p. 4.

63  For Yeltsin's vivid depiction of these events, see his *Zapiski prezidenta*, pp. 382–7.

64  *The Independent*, 28 October 1995, p. 11.

65  *The Independent*, 28 October 1995, p. 11.

66  Andrei Nikolaev, *Rossiya na perelome* (Moscow, Sovremennyi pisatel', 1999).

67  For a detailed analysis, see Sven Gunnar Simonsen, 'Marching to a Different drum? Political Orientations and Nationalism in Russia's Armed Forces', in Betz and Löwenhardt (eds), pp. 43–64.

68  *Moskovskie novosti*, No. 59, 3–10 September 1995, p. 7.

69  Benjamin S. Lambeth, 'Russia's Wounded Military', *Foreign Affairs*, Vol. 74, No. 2 (March/April 1995), pp. 86–7.

70  Pavel K. Baev, 'The Russian Armed Forces: Failed reform Attempts and Creeping Regionalization', in Betz and Löwenhardt (eds), p. 23.

71  Andrei Zagorskii, 'Khel'sinki: budushchee v tumane', *Moskovskie novosti*, No. 13, 29 March 1991, p. 5.

72  http://president.kremlin.ru/text/appears/2007/02/118109.shtml

73  *Rossiiskaya gazeta*, 28 February 2007.

74  http://president.kremlin.ru/text/appears/2007/04/125401.shtml

75  The 2000 US National Security Strategy (NSS), drafted under Clinton, stressed the key role that the OSCE had 'in enhancing Europe's stability', whereas Bush's NSS 2002 does not mention the OSCE at all, while NSS 2006 mentions it once in a list of organisations that could help America advance 'effective democracy'.

76 See Donald D. Asmus *et al.*, 'NATO Expansion: The Next Steps', *Survival*, Vol. 37, No. 1, spring 1995.
77 For a concise overview, see Caroline Kennedy-Pipe, 'Russia and the North Atlantic Treaty Organization', in Mark Webber (ed.), *Russia and Europe: Conflict or Cooperation?* (Basingstoke, Macmillan, 2000), pp. 46–65.
78 Kozyrev, 'Partnership or Cold Peace?, p. 13.
79 Yuliya Timoshenko, 'Containing Russia', *Foreign Affairs*, Vol. 86, No. 3, May–June 2007, pp. 69–82.
80 *Soviet Weekly*, 31 October 1991, p. 4.
81 *Izvestiya*, 6 September 1994.
82 RFE/RL, *Newsline*, 3 July 2001.
83 For details, see J. L. Black, *NATO Expansion: Bearing Gifts or Bearing Arms?* (Lanham MD, Rowman & Littlefield, 2000).
84 Oleg Varfolomeyev, 'Is Ukraine Ready to Join NATO?', *Russia and Eurasia Review*, Vol. 1, No. 4, 16 July 2002.
85 The Basic Document of the EAPC, adopted at Sintra, Portugal, on 30 Yay 1997, is in *NATO Review*, No. 4, July–August 1997, special insert.
86 *NATO Review*, No. 3, May 1995, p. 5.
87 'Founding Act on Mutual Relations, Cooperation and Security between NATO and the Russian Federation', *NATO Review*, Vol. 45, No. 4, 1997 (special insert, pp. 7–10).
88 Andrei Zagorski, 'Great Expectations', *NATO Review*, Vol. 49, spring 2001, pp. 24–7, at p. 25.
89 *The Guardian*, 8 June 2006, p., 20.
90 'Question and Answer at the State Duma Session, 7 June 2006', www.fednews.ru
91 The impact of enlargement on Russian domestic opinion is discussed extensively by Black, *NATO Expansion*.
92 *Nezavisimaya gazeta*, 3 February 1995; see also the CFDP's theses on how Russia should respond to NATO expansion, *Nezavisimaya gazeta*, 21 June 1995, reproduced in *Transition*, 15 December 1995, pp. 27–32.

## 18 Commonwealth, community and fragmentation

1 Elie Kedourie, *Nationalism*, 4th edn (Oxford, Blackwell, 1993), p. xvii.
2 For an overview, see Richard Sakwa and Mark Webber, 'The Commonwealth of Independent States, 1991–1998: Stagnation and Survival', *Europe–Asia Studies*, Vol. 51, No. 3, May 1999, pp. 379–415.
3 *Pravda*, 27 November 1991.
4 The Alma Ata agreements of 21 December are in *Rossiiskaya gazeta*, 24 December 1991, p. 1.
5 Mikhail Gorbachev, 'Mir na perelome', *Svobodnaya mysl'*, No. 16, 1992, pp. 3–18, at p. 9.
6 Andrei Zagorskii *et al.*, *The Commonwealth of Independent States: Developments and Prospects* (Moscow, Centre for International Studies, MGIMO, 1992), p. 6.
7 See Andrei Zagorskii, *SNG: ot dezintegratsii k reintegratsii?* (Moscow, MGIMO, 1994).
8 *Literaturnaya gazeta*, 19 August 1992, p. 11.
9 *Nezavisimaya gazeta*, 18 August 1992, p. 2. Gorbachev remained consistent in this view, developed at length in his *Dekabr'–91: moya pozitsiya* (Moscow, Novosti, 1992).
10 Erica Marat, 'Kulov Continues to Advocate Russian-Kyrgyz Confederation', *Eurasia Daily Monitor*, Vol. 4, No. 130, 5 July 2007.
11 Valerii Vyzhutovich, 'Kursovaya ustoichivost', *Rossiiskaya gazeta*, 12 May 2007, p. 3.
12 *Nezavisimaya gazeta*, 9 October 1992, p. 3.
13 Andrei Zagorskii, 'Reintegration in the Former USSR?', *Aussenpolitik*, No. 3, 1994, pp. 263–72.
14 Robert Cottrell, 'In Search of a Policy', *Financial Times*, 21 February 2001.
15 *Nezavisimaya gazeta*, 1 September 1992.
16 Suzanne Crow, 'Russia's Relations with Members of the Commonwealth', RFE/RL, *Research Report*, Vol. 1, No. 19, 8 May 1992, pp. 8–12, at p. 11.
17 *Rossiiskaya gazeta*, 23 September 1995, p. 4.

18  Survey conducted by the 'Obshchestvennoe mnenie' agency, reported in *Sovetskaya Rossiya*, 17 March 2001, p. 1.
19  *Rossiiskaya gazeta*, 25 April 2005.
20  For example, 1 February 2007 press conference, http://www.fednews.ru/
21  Yuri Shishkov, *Argumenty nedeli*, No. 23, 7 June 2007.
22  http://www.fednews.ru/
23  The text is in Stephen Foye, 'The Soviet Legacy', *RFE/RL Research Report*, Vol. 2, No. 25, 18 June 1993, pp. 4–5.
24  Roy Allison, Stephen White and Margot Light, 'Belarus between East and West', *Journal of Communist Studies and Transition Politics*, Vol. 21, No. 4, December 2005, pp. 487–511, at p. 494.
25  Putin's speech to the Security Council, 29 January 2005, Kremlin.ru, in *Johnson's Russia List* 9040/8.
26  *Eurasia Daily Monitor*, Vol. 3, No. 102, 25 May 2006.
27  *CEPS Neighbourhood Watch*, issue 16, May 2006, p. 8.
28  For an early exposition of elements of this strategy, see his Zbigniew Brzezinski, 'The Premature Partnership', *Foreign Affairs*, Vol. 73, No. 2, 1994, pp. 67–82.
29  *The Guardian*, 5 May 2006, p. 18.
30  *The Moscow Times*, 5 May 2006, p. 4.
31  http://president.kremlin.ru/text/appears/2006/05/105546.shtml
32  Kolosov (ed.), *Mir glazami rossiyan,* p. 159.
33  David Marples, 'The Isolation of Europe's Last Dictator', *Russia and Eurasia Review*, 17 December 2002.
34  Alexander Baturo and Slava Mikhailov, "I Love You, You Pay My Rent": Belarusian-Russian Integration', in David Dusseault (ed.), *The CIS: Form or Substance?*, Aleksanteri Papers 2/2007 (Helsinki, Aleksanteri Institute, 2007), pp. 98–130.
35  *Newsline*, 14 June 2002.
36  Lobatch, Andrei, 'Peculiarities of the Integration Process Between Belarus and the Russian Federation: Economic and Political Aspects', in Kimitaka Matsuzato (ed.), *Emerging Meso-areas in the Former Socialist Countries: Histories Revised or Improvised?* (Sapporo, Slavic Research Center, Hokkaido University, 2005), pp. 155–76, at p. 172.
37  Putin, *Razgovor s Rossiei*, 19 December 2002, p. 108.
38  Roy Allison, Stephen White and Margot Light, 'Belarus between East and West', *Journal of Communist Studies and Transition Politics*, Vol. 21, No. 4, December 2005, pp. 487–511, at p. 495.
39  *Moskovskii komsomolets*, No. 11, 20 January 2006.
40  Michael Mainville, 'A Potential Rival for NATO', *The Toronto Star*, 3 June 2006.
41  Hsiu-Ling Wu and Chien-Hsun Chen, 'The Prospects for Regional Economic Integration between China and the Five Central Asian Countries', *Europe–Asia Studies*, Vol. 56, No. 7, November 2004, pp. 1059–80.
42  David Wall, 'Shanghai Cooperation Organisation', *The World Today*, June 2006, pp. 20–1.

## 19  Problems of transition

1  Vladimir Putin meeting with representatives of non-governmental organisations on 12 June 2001, at which he noted that many had 'a more effective influence on society than do political parties', RFE/RL, *Newsline*, 13 June 2001.
2  'The Case of the Russian Archives: An Interview with Iurii N. Afanas'ev', *Slavic Review*, Vol. 52, No. 2, summer 1993, p. 315.
3  For an evaluation of Western 'Sovietology' and the debate over the Soviet collapse, see Michael Cox (ed.), *Rethinking Soviet Collapse: Sovietology, the Death of Communism and the New Russia* (London and New York, Pinter, 1998).
4  For an excellent overview, see Archie Brown, *Seven Years that Changed the World: Perestroika in Perspective* (Oxford, Oxford University Press, 2007).
5  Paul Kennedy, *The Rise and Fall of the Great Powers: Economic Change and Military Conflict from 1500 to 2000* (London, Unwin Hyman, 1988).

6 Cf. Philip G. Roeder, *Red Sunset: The Failure of Soviet Politics* (Princeton, NJ, Princeton University Press, 1993).

7 Roeder, *Red Sunset*.

8 For a defence of the concept of totalitarianism, see William E. Odom, 'Soviet Politics and After: Old and New Concepts', *World Politics*, Vol. 45, No. 1, 1992, pp. 66–98; and for the view that the so-called 'totalitarianism' versus 'pluralism' debate obscured as much as it revealed, George Breslauer, 'In Defense of Sovietology', *Post-Soviet Affairs*, Vol. 8, No. 3, 1992, pp. 197–238, esp. pp. 216–22.

9 Max Weber, *The Russian Revolutions*, translated and edited by Gordon C. Wells and Peter Baehr (Oxford, Polity Press, 1995).

10 Robert O. Crummey, 'Introduction', in Crummey (ed.), *Reform in Russia and the USSR: Past and Prospects* (Urbana, IL, University of Illinois Press, 1989), p. 9.

11 Ibid.

12 See, for example, Ian Kershaw and Moshe Lewin (eds), *Stalinism and Nazism: Dictatorships in Comparison* (Cambridge, Cambridge University Press, 1997).

13 See, for example, Tim Mason, *Social Policy in the Third Reich: The Working Class and the National Community* (Providence, RI, Berg, 1993); and his *Nazism, Fascism and the Working Class* (Cambridge, Cambridge University Press, 1994). During the transition to NEP, as we have seen, Lenin, fearing for the stability of the regime, intensified the political dictatorship.

14 Ralf Dahrendorf, *Society and Democracy in Germany* (London, Weidenfeld and Nicolson, 1968), p. 342.

15 The problem of Russia's 'asocial subjectivity' and allied issues are discussed in my 'Subjectivity, Politics and Order in Russian Political Evolution', *Slavic Review*, Vol. 54, No. 4, winter 1995, pp. 943–64.

16 For a discussion of history and time, see Robert C. Tucker, 'Kakoe vremya pokazyvayut seichas chasy Rossiiskoi istorii' ('What Time Is It In Russia's History'), *Problemy vostochnoi evropy*, No. 31–2, 1991, pp. 58–78. For a broad discussion, see Stephen E. Hanson, *Time and Revolution: Marxism and the Design of Soviet Institutions* (Chapel Hill, NC, University of North Carolina Press, 1997).

17 John Miller, *Mikhail Gorbachev and the End of Soviet Power* (London, Macmillan, 1993), p. 8.

18 *Political Archives of the Soviet Union*, Vol. 2, No 2, 1991, p. 119.

19 Petro, *The Rebirth of Russian Democracy*, Chapter 2.

20 N. Berdyaev *et al.*, *Vekhi: sbornik statei o Russkoi intelligentsii* (Moscow, 1909; reprinted Frankfurt, Posev, 1967).

21 Geoffrey Hosking, *The Russian Constitutional Experiment: Government and Duma, 1907–1914* (Cambridge, Cambridge University Press, 1973).

22 Richard Pipes, *Russia under the Old Regime* (London, Weidenfeld & Nicolson, 1974).

23 *Izvestiya*, 16 November 1993.

24 Reddaway, Peter and Dmitri Glinski, *The Tragedy of Russia's Reforms: Market Bolshevism against Democracy* (Washington, DC, United States Institute of Peace Press, 2001).

25 See, for example, Sergei Pushkarev, *Self-government and Freedom in Russia* (Boulder, CO, Westview Press, 1988); Nicolai N. Petro (ed.), *Christianity and Russian Culture in Soviet Society* (Boulder, CO, Westview Press, 1990).

26 A. V. Obolenskii, 'Mekhanizm tormozheniya: chelovecheskoe izmerenie', *Sovetskoe gosudarstvo i pravo*, No. 1, 1990, pp. 80–7; see also his 'Russian Politics in the Time of Troubles', in Amin Saikal and William Maley (eds), *Russia in Search of its Future* (Cambridge, Cambridge University Press, 1995), pp. 12–27.

27 Petro, *The Rebirth of Russian Democracy*, pp. 2–3 and passim.

28 E.g. at the State Conference on 12–15 August 1917 in speeches by Georgi Plekhanov ('There can be no bourgeois revolution in which the bourgeoisie do not take part. There can be no capitalism in which there are no capitalists'), and Alexander Guchkov, a leader of the Octobrist Party, who urged the establishment of a strong government, *Moscow News*, No. 24, 16 June 1991, p. 9.

29 *Izvestiya*, 16 November 1993.

30  Alexander Yakovlev, 'Wake up Brother Russia', *The Guardian*, 6 May 1992.
31  For recent assessments of 1917 in Russia, see Edward Acton, *Rethinking the Russian Revolution* (London, Edward Arnold, 1990); Edith Rogovin Frankel, Jonathen Frankel and Baruch Knei-Paz (eds), *Revolution in Russia: Reassessments of 1917* (Cambridge, Cambridge University Press, 1992). The best of recent analyses of the intelligentsia in revolution includes Jane Burbank, *Intelligentsia and Revolution: Russian Views of Bolshevism, 1917–1922* (Oxford, Oxford University Press, 1986); Christopher Read, *Culture and Power in Revolutionary Russia: The Intelligentsia and the Transition from Tsarism to Communism* (London, Macmillan, 1990).
32  For a discussion of the issue, see Luc Huyse, 'Justice after Transition: On the Choices Successor Elites Make in Dealing with the Past', *Law and Social Enquiry*, Vol. 20, No. 1, winter 1995, pp. 51–78.
33  Solzhenitsyn, *Rebuilding Russia*, p. 29.
34  Gerd Ruge, *Der Putsch* (Frankfurt, Fischer, 1991), p. 153.
35  Gorbachev, *The August Coup*, p. 48.
36  *Zerkalo, Vestnik Obshchestvennyi Komitet Rossiiskikh Reform*, No. 2, February 1992, pp. 1–2. This is the approach argued most forcefully by Vladimir Bukovsky.
37  *Moscow News*, No. 5, 28 January 1993, p. 13.
38  See Tina Rosenberg, 'Overcoming the Legacies of Dictatorship', *Foreign Affairs*, Vol. 74, No. 3, May–June 1995, pp. 134–52.
39  Cf. Geoffrey Best, *War and Law Since 1945* (Oxford, Clarendon, 1994).
40  C. Charles Bertschi, 'Lustration and the Transition to Democracy: The Cases of Poland and Bulgaria', *East European Quarterly*, Vol. 28, No. 4 (January 1995), pp. 435–51.
41  Knight, *Spies Without Cloaks*, p. 204.
42  For the reasons why West Germany pursued the issue so aggressively in the East, see A. James McAdams, 'Reappraising the Conditions of Transitional Justice in Unified Germany" *East European Constitutional Review*, winter 2001, pp. 53–9.
43  Amos Elon, 'East Germany: Crime and Punishment', *The New York Review of Books*, 14 May 1992, pp. 6–11.
44  Peggy Morvant, 'Yakovlev on Communist Repression of Religion', *OMRI Daily Digest*, No. 230, Part I, 28 November 1995.
45  See Vladimir Wozniuk, 'In Search of Ideology: The Politics of Religion and Nationalism in the New Russia (1991–1996)', *Nationalities Papers*, Vol. 25, No. 2, 1997, p. 201.
46  For a painful reconstruction of mutual incomprehension, see Eva-Clarita Onken, 'The Baltic States and Moscow's 9 May Commemoration: Analysing Memory Politics in Europe', *Europe–Asia Studies*, Vol. 59, No. 1, January 2007, pp. 23–46.
47  Nanci Adler, 'The Future of the Soviet Past Remains Unpredictable: The Resurrection of Stalinist Symbols amidst the Exhumation of Mass Graves', *Europe–Asia Studies*, Vol. 57, No. 8, December 2005, pp. 1093–1119, at p. 1110.
48  *Moscow News*, No. 5, 28 January 1993, p. 13.
49  Zdeněk Mlynář, *Can Gorbachev Change the Soviet Union? The International Dimension of Political Reform* (Boulder, CO, Westview Press, 1990).
50  Francis Fukuyama, 'The End of History', *The National Interest*, summer 1989, pp. 3–17; *The End of History and the Last Man* (New York, Free Press, 1992).
51  Giuseppe Di Palma, *To Craft Democracies: An Essay in Democratic Transition* (Berkeley, University of California Press, 1990); Jon Elster, Claus Offe and Ulrich K. Preuss, *Institutional Design in Post-Communist Societies: Rebuilding the Ship at Sea* (Cambridge, Cambridge University Press, 1998); A. E. Dick Howard (ed.), *Constitution Making in Eastern Europe* (Baltimore, MD, Johns Hopkins University Press); Arend Lijphart and Carlos Waisman (eds), *Institutional Design in New Democracies: Eastern Europe and Latin America* (Boulder, CO, Westview Press, 1996).
52  Arend Lijphart, *Democracies: Patterns of Majoritarian and Consensus Government in Twenty-one Countries* (New Haven, Yale University Press, 1984); Arend Lijphart, *Electoral Systems and Party Systems* (Oxford, Oxford University Press, 1994).
53  G. Sartori, *Parties and Party Systems: A Framework for Analysis* (Cambridge, Cambridge University Press, 1976); A. Ware, *Political Parties and Party Systems* (Oxford, Oxford

University Press, 1996); G. Pridham and P. Lewis (eds), *Stabilising Fragile Democracies: Comparing New Party Systems in Southern and Eastern Europe* (London and New York, Routledge, 1996).

54 G. O'Donnell, 'On the State, Democratization and Some Conceptual Problems (A Latin American View with Glances at Some Post-Communist Countries)', *World Development*, Vol. 21, No. 8, August 1993, pp. 1355–70; Juan J. Linz, 'The Perils of Presidentialism', *Journal of Democracy*, Vol. 1, No. 1, winter 1990, pp. 72–84; Juan J. Linz and Arturo Valenzuela (eds), *The Failure of Presidential Democracy: Comparative Perspectives* (Baltimore, Johns Hopkins University Press, 1994); Arend Lijphart (ed.), *Parliamentary versus Presidential Government* (Oxford, Oxford University Press, 1992); S. Mainwaring, 'Presidentialism, Multipartism, and Democracy', *Comparative Political Studies*, Vol. 26, No. 2, 1993, pp. 198–228; M. Shugart and J. M. Carey, *Presidents and Assemblies* (Cambridge, Cambridge University Press, 1992).

55 T. A. Baylis, 'Presidents Versus Prime Ministers', *World Politics*, Vol. 48, 1996, pp. 297–323.

56 Samuel P. Huntington, *The Third Wave: Democratization in the Late Twentieth Century* (Norman: University of Oklahoma Press, 1991); see also his 'How Countries Democratize', *Political Science Quarterly*, Vol. 106, No. 4, 1991–2, pp. 579–616.

57 Thomas Carothers, 'The End of the Transition Paradigm', *Journal of Democracy*, Vol. 13, No. 1, January 2002, pp. 5–21.

58 Samuel P. Huntington, 'After Twenty Years: The Future of the Third Wave', *Journal of Democracy*, Vol. 8, No. 1, January 1997, pp. 111–26.

59 For a sustained analysis of methodological problems from a Russian perspective, see Andrei Yu. Melvil', *Demokraticheskie tranzity (teoretiko-metodologicheskie in prikladnye aspekty)* (Moscow, 1999); and one of the most sustained attempts to apply political science approaches to the Russian transition, Vladimir Gel'man, *Transformatsiya v Rossii: politicheskii rezhim i demokraticheskaya oppozitsiya* (Moscow, 1999).

60 G. O'Donnell, P. Schmitter and L. Whitehead (eds), *Transitions from Authoritarian Rule* (Baltimore, Maryland, Johns Hopkins University Press, 1986), Vol. 4, *Tentative Conclusions about Uncertain Democracies*, pp. 15–36.

61 Alfred Stepan, 'Paths toward Redemocratisation: Theoretical and Comparative Considerations', in O'Donnell *et al.* (eds), *Comparative Perspectives*, pp. 64–84.

62 The classic statement is Samuel Huntington, *Political Order in Changing Societies* (New Haven, CT, Yale University Press, 1968).

63 Dankwart Rustow, 'Transitions to Democracy: Toward a Dynamic Model', *Comparative Politics*, Vol. 2, No. 3, 1970, pp. 337–63, at pp. 352–61.

64 Claus Offe, 'Capitalism by Democratic Design? Democratic Theory Facing the Triple Transition in East Central Europe', *Social Research*, Vol. 58, No. 4, 1991, pp. 876–92. Also in Claus Offe, *Varieties of Transition: The East European and East German Experience* (Cambridge, Polity Press, 1996), Chapter 3, pp. 29–49.

65 For an extended discussion of the various spheres, see Juan J. Linz and Alfred Stepan, *Problems of Democratic Transition and Consolidation: Southern Europe, South America, and Post-Communist Europe* (Baltimore, Johns Hopkins University Press, 1996), esp. Chapter 1.

66 Valerie Bunce, 'Should Transitologists be Grounded?', *Slavic Review*, Vol. 54, No. 1, spring 1995, pp. 111–27. See also Valerie Bunce, 'Comparing East and South', *Journal of Democracy*, Vol. 6, No. 3, 1995, pp. 87–100.

67 On the idea of a fourth wave, see Klaus von Beyme, *Transition to Democracy in Eastern Europe* (London, Macmillan, 1996), p. 3; cf. M. Stephen Fish, 'Russia's Fourth Transition', in Larry Diamond and Marc F. Plattner (eds), *The Global Resurgence of Democracy* (Baltimore, MD, Johns Hopkins University Press, 1996).

68 The issue was debated by Sarah Meiklejohn Terry, 'Thinking about Post-Communist Transitions: How Different Are They?', *Slavic Review*, Vol. 52, No. 2, summer 1993, pp. 333–7; Philippe C. Schmitter with Terry Lynn Karl, 'The Conceptual Travails of Transitologists and Consolidologists: How Far East Should They Attempt to Go?', *Slavic Review*, Vol. 53, No. 1, spring 1994, pp. 173–85; Terry Lynn Karl and Philippe C. Schmitter, 'From an Iron Curtain to a Paper Curtain: Grounding Transitologists or Students of Postcommunism?', *Slavic Review*, Vol. 54, No. 4, winter 1995, pp. 965–87.

69 Rustow, 'Transitions to Democracy', p. 337.

70 Rustow, 'Transitions to Democracy', p. 352, Adam Przeworski, 'Some Problems in the Study of the Transition to Democracy', Guillermo O'Donnell *et al.* (eds), *Comparative Perspectives*, pp. 47–63, at p. 58, and Giuseppe Di Palma, *To Craft Democracies: An Essay in Democratic Transitions* (Berkeley, CA, University of California Press, 1990), pp. 54ff.

71 Cf. Joseph Schumpeter, *Capitalism, Socialism and Democracy* (London, 1942/76); for a discussion of Schumpeter's relevance to the post-communist transitions, see Richard Bellamy, 'Schumpeter and the Transformation of Capitalism, Liberalism and Democracy', *Government and Opposition*, Vol. 26, No. 4, 1991, pp. 500–19.

72 For a discussion of mismodernisation, see Richard Sakwa, *Postcommunism* (Milton Keynes, Open University Press, 1999), pp. 24–5.

73 *Rossiiskaya gazeta*, 29 October 1991, p. 1.

74 Michel Foucault, 'The Politics of Health in the Eighteenth Century', in Colin Gordon (ed.), *Power/Knowledge: Selected Interviews and Other Writings, 1972–1977* (London, Harvester Wheatsheaf, 1980), p. 171.

75 Vladimir Putin, 'Russia at the Turn of the Millennium', in Richard Sakwa, *Putin: Russia's Choice*, 2nd edn (London, Routledge, 2007), pp. 321–33, at p. 323.

76 Seymour Martin Lipset, 'Some Social Requisites of Democracy', *American Political Science Review*, Vol. 53, No. 1, March 1959, pp. 69–105; 'Economic Development and Democracy', in S. M. Lipset, *Political Man* (London, Mercury Books, 1963), pp. 45–76; 'The Social Requisites of Democracy Revisited', *American Sociological Review*, Vol. 59, No. 1, February 1994, pp. 1–22; 'On the General Conditions for Democracy', in Lisa Anderson (ed.), *Transitions to Democracy* (New York, Columbia University Press, 1999).

77 Lucian W. Pye, 'Political Science and the Crisis of Authoritarianism', *American Political Science Review*, Vol. 84, No. 1, March 1990, pp. 3–19.

78 For a sophisticated attempt to analyze the relationship between modernisation and political development, see Andrew C. Janos, 'Social Science, Communism, and the Dynamics of Political Change', *World Politics*, Vol. 44, No. 1, October 1991, pp. 81–112.

79 See Boris Kapustin, *Sovremmenost' kak predmet politicheskoi teorii* (Moscow, Rosspen, 1998).

80 Dankwart Rustow, 'Democracy: A Global Revolution', *Foreign Affairs*, Vol. 69, No. 4, fall 1990, p. 75.

81 Clifford G. Gaddy and Barry W. Ickes, 'Russia's Virtual Economy', *Foreign Affairs*, September-October 1998, pp. 53–67.

82 Karl Polanyi, *The Great Transformation: The Political and Economic Origins of Our Times* (New York, Rinehart, 1944).

83 For a stimulating comparison of the governmental technologies of the Bolsheviks and the early modern police, see Agnes Horvath and Arpad Szakolczai, *The Dissolution of Communist Power: The Case of Hungary* (London, Routledge, 1992), esp. ch. 8.

84 Guillermo O'Donnell and Philippe Schmitter, *Transitions from Authoritarian Rule: Tentative Conclusions about Uncertain Democracies* (Baltimore, MD, Johns Hopkins University Press, 1986).

85 For a classic example of the maturation argument, see Moshe Lewin, *The Gorbachev Phenomenon: A Historical Interpretation* (London, Hutchinson Radius, 1988).

86 Chris Brown, '"Really Existing Liberalism" and International Order', *Millennium*, Vol. 21, No. 3, 1992, pp. 313–28; see also his *International Relations Theory: New Normative Approaches* (Hemel Hempstead, Harvester Wheatsheaf, 1992).

87 Moore, *Social Origins of Dictatorship and Democracy,* p. 418.

88 For example, Charles Lindblom, *Politics and Markets* (New York, Basic Books, 1977); John Freeman, *Democracy and Markets* (Ithaca, NY, Cornell University Press, 1989).

89 For a stimulating discussion of the weakness of post-communist liberalism and its 'economistic' turn, see Jerzy Szacki, *Liberalism after Communism* (Budapest, Central European University Press, 1995).

90 For a challenging analysis of 'populist' and 'pluralist' definitions of democracy and the emergence of parliamentarianism in Russia, see Biryukov and Sergeev, *Russia's Road to Democracy.*

91 Rustow, 'Democracy: A Global Revolution', p. 79.

92 For a perceptive attempt to 'deconstruct' the discursive framework of the globalisation paradigm, see Colin Hay and David Marsh (eds), *Demystifying Globalization* (Basingstoke, Macmillan, 2000). See also Justin Rosenberg, 'Globalization Theory: A Post-mortem', *International Politics*, Vol. 42, No. 1, 2005, pp. 2–74.

93 *Financial Times*, 14 May 2001, p. 21.

94 Jadwiga Staniszkis, *The Dynamics of Breakthrough in Eastern Europe* (Berkeley, CA, California University Press, 1991).

95 Samuel P. Huntington, 'The Clash of Civilizations?', *Foreign Affairs*, Vol. 72, No. 3, summer 1993, pp. 22–49; Zyuganov's views are in 'Rossiya i mir', in *Sovremennaya Russkaya ideya i gosudarstvo* (Moscow, Obozrevatel', 1995), pp. 10–26; see also his *Za gorizontom* (Moscow, 1995), p.8 and *passim*; and his collected essays *Postizhenie Rossii* (Moscow, Mysl', 2000), Part III.

96 Jadwiga Staniszkis, 'The Worrying Power Shift in the Kremlin', *European Brief*, Vol. 2, No. 4, 1993, pp. 73–4.

97 Laurence Whitehead, 'International Aspects of Democratisation', in Guillermo O'Donnell, Philippe Schmitter and Laurence Whitehead (eds), *Transitions from Authoritarian Rule: Comparative Perspectives* (Baltimore, MD, Johns Hopkins University Press, 1986), pp. 3–46.

98 Frank Field review of Ronald H. Preston, *Religion and the Ambiguities of Capitalism* (London, SCM, 1992), *Independent*, 4 June 1992.

99 See, for example, Michael Bratton and Nicolas van de Walle, *Democratic Experiments in Africa: Regime Transitions in Comparative Perspective* (Cambridge, Cambridge University Press, 1997); Richard Joseph (ed.), *State, Conflict, and Democracy in Africa* (Boulder and London, Lynne Rienner Publishers, 1999). For a general discussion, see Robin Luckham and Gordon White (eds), *Democratization in the South: The Jagged Wave* (Manchester, Manchester University Press, 1996).

100 Joel Migdal, *Strong Societies and Weak States: State-Society Relations and State Capacities in the Third World* (Princeton, NJ, Princeton University Press, 1988).

101 Melvin Croan *et al.*, 'Is Latin America the Future of Eastern Europe?', *Problems of Communism*, Vol. 41, No. 3, May–June 1992, pp. 44–57.

## 20  Democracy in Russia

1 Max Weber, 'Bourgeois Democracy in Russia', in *The Russian Revolutions*, edited and translated by Gordon C. Wells and Peter Baehr (Cambridge, Polity Press, 1995), p. 109.

2 Moore, *Social Origins of Dictatorship and Democracy*, p. 414.

3 Alexis de Tocqueville, *Democracy in America* (New York, Random House, 1981).

4 Bo Petersson, *National Self-images and Regional Identities in Russia* (Aldershot, Ashgate, 2001), p. 146.

5 Larry Diamond, *Developing Democracy: Towards Consolidation* (Baltimore and London, Johns Hopkins University Press, 1999).

6 See V. B. Pastukhov, 'Stanovlenie Rossiiskoi gosudarstvennosti i konstitutsionnyi protsess: politologicheskii aspekt', *Gosudarstvo i pravo*, No. 2, 1993, pp. 89–96, at p. 89.

7 For a collection of Rigby's articles on the Soviet system see T. H. Rigby, *The Changing Soviet System: Mono-Organisational Socialism from its Origins to Gorbachev's Restructuring* (Aldershot, Edward Elgar, 1990).

8 Guillermo O'Donnell, 'Delegative Democracy', *Journal of Democracy*, Vol. 5, No. 1, January 1994, pp. 55–69.

9 Guillermo O'Donnell, 'On the State, Democratization and Some Conceptual Problems (A Latin American View with Glances at Some Postcommunist Countries)', *World Development*, Vol. 21, No. 8, 1993, pp. 1355–69, at p. 1367.

10 See Adam Przeworski, *Democracy and the Market: Political and Economic Reforms in Eastern Europe and Latin America* (Cambridge, Cambridge University Press, 1991); John F. Helliwell, 'Empirical Linkages between Democracy and Economic Growth', *British Journal of Political Science*, Vol. 24, No. 2, 1994, pp. 225–48.

11  For example, V. Gel'man, S. Ryzhenkov, M. Bri (eds), *Rossiya regionov: transformatsiya politicheskikh rezhimov* (Moscow, Ves' Mir, 2000).

12  Fareed Zakaria, 'The Rise of Illiberal Democracy', *Foreign Affairs*, Vol. 76, No. 6, November/December 1997, pp. 22–43.

13  A similar distinction is made by Igor' Klyamkin and Liliya Shevtsova, *Vnesistemnyi rezhim Boris II: nekotorye osobennosti politicheskogo razvitiya postsovetskoi Rossii* (Moscow, Carnegie Centre, 1999), although operationalised in a different way. For an earlier approach to the question, see my 'The Regime System in Russia', *Contemporary Politics*, Vol. 3, No. 1, 1997, pp. 7–25.

14  Michael Mann, 'The Autonomous Power of the State: Its Origins, Mechanisms and Results', in John A. Hall (ed.), *States in History* (Oxford, Basil Blackwell, 1986).

15  Cf. David Woodruff, *Money Unmade: Barter and the Fate of Russian Capitalism* (Ithaca and London, Cornell University Press, 1999).

16  John Laughland, *The Death of Politics under Mitterrand* (London, Michael Joseph, 1994).

17  W. M. Reissinger, A. H. Miller and V. L. Hesli, 'Political Norms in Rural Russia', *Europe–Asia Studies*, Vol. 47, No. 6, September 1995, p. 1030.

18  *Nezavisimaya gazeta*, 23 June 1994, p. 2.

19  RFE/RL, *Newsline*, 3 January 2000.

20  Viktor Sheinis, 'Posle bitvy: itogi parlamentskikh vyborov i novaya Gosudarstvennaya Duma', *Nezavisimaya gazeta*, 29 December 1999, p. 8.

21  Anthony Giddens, *The Third Way: The Renewal of Social Democracy* (Cambridge, Polity Press, 1998).

22  Vladimir Putin, 'Rossiya na rubezhe tysyacheletii', *Nezavisimaya gazeta*, 30 December 1999, p. 4; www.pravitelstvo.gov.ru. See also his book of interviews, Vladimir Putin, *First Person: An Astonishingly Frank Self-portrait by Russia's President Vladimir Putin*, with Nataliya Gevorkyan, Natalya Timakova, and Andrei Kolesnikov, translated by Catherine A. Fitzpatrick (London, Hutchinson, 2000), pp. 209–19.

23  'Yeltsin and Russia: Two Views', *The New York Review of Books*, 22 April 1993, p. 17.

24  Sergei Stankevich, 'Russia's Lost Decade of Reforms', *Transitions*, March 1999, pp. 61–2.

25  Gordon A. Craig, 'Demonic Democracy', *New York Review of Books*, 13 February 1992, pp. 39–43, at p. 43; see also Wolfgang J. Mommsen, *Max Weber and German Politics, 1890–1920*, translated by Michael S. Steinberg (Chicago, University of Chicago Press, 1984).

26  Ken Jowitt, *New World Disorder: The Leninist Extinction* (Berkeley, CA, University of California Press, 1992), p. 293.

27  *Izvestiya*, 4 May 1994, p. 5; *The Observer*, 29 May 1994.

# Select bibliography

Adelman, Jonathan A., *Torrents of Spring: Soviet and Post-Soviet Politics* (New York, McGraw-Hill, 1995).

Aron, Leon, *Boris Yeltsin: A Revolutionary Life* (London, HarperCollins, 2000).

Bacon, Edwin and Matthew Wyman, *Contemporary Russia* (Basingstoke, Palgrave, 2005).

Barany, Zoltan and Robert G. Moser (eds), *Russian Politics: Challenges of Democratization* (Cambridge, Cambridge University Press, 2001).

Barner-Barry, Carol and Cynthia Hody, *The Politics of Change: The Transformation of the Former Soviet Union* (London, Macmillan, 1995).

Beyme, Klaus Von, *Transition to Democracy in Eastern Europe* (London, Macmillan, 1996).

Bjorkman, Tom, *Russia's Road to Deeper Democracy* (Washington, DC, Brookings Institution Press, 2003).

Billington, James H., *Russia Transformed: Breakthrough to Hope* (New York, Free Press, 1993).

Blum, Douglas W., *Russia's Future: Consolidation or Disintegration?* (Boulder, CO, Boulder Press, 1994).

Bonnell, Victoria E. and George W. Breslauer (eds), *Russia in the New Century: Stability or Disorder?* (Oxford and Boulder, CO, Westview Press, 2000).

Bova, Russell (ed.), *Russia and Western Civilization: Cultural and Historical Encounters* (Armonk, New York, M. E. Sharpe, 2003).

Bowker, Mike and Cameron Ross (eds), *Russia after the Cold War* (Harlow, Longman, 2000).

Breslauer, George W., *Gorbachev and Yeltsin as Leaders* (Cambridge, Cambridge University Press, 2002).

Brown, Archie (ed.), *Contemporary Russian Politics: A Reader* (Oxford University Press, 2001).

Brudny, Yitzhak, Jonathan Frankel, and Stefani Hoffman (eds), *Restructuring Post-Communist Russia* (New York, Cambridge University Press, 2004).

Buckley, Mary, *Redefining Russian Society and Polity* (Oxford, Westview Press, 1993).

Clark, Bruce, *An Empire's New Clothes: The End of Russia's Liberal Dream* (London, Vintage, 1997).

Cohen, Ariel, *Russian Imperialism: Development and Crisis* (New York, Praeger Publishers, 1998).

Cohen, Stephen F., *Failed Crusade: America and the Tragedy of Post-Communist Russia* (New York, W. W. Norton, 2000).

Colton, Timothy J. and Stephen Holmes (eds), *The State after Communism: Governance in the New Russia* (Lanham, MD, Rowman & Littlefield, 2006).

Danks, Catherine, *Russian Politics and Society* (Harlow, Longman, 2001).

Davies, R. W., *Soviet History in the Yeltsin Era* (London, Macmillan, 1996).

Dawisha, Karen and Bruce Parrott, *Russia and the New States of Eurasia: The Politics of Upheaval* (Cambridge, Caubrdge University Press, 1994).

DeBardeleben, Joan, *Russian Politics in Transition*, 2nd edn (Abingdon, Houghton Mifflin, 1997).

Devlin, Judith, *The Rise of the Russian Democrats: The Causes and Consequences of the Elite Revolution* (Aldershot, Edward Elgar, 1995).

Dunlop, John B., *The Rise of Russia and the Fall of the Soviet Empire* (Princeton, NJ, Princeton University Press, 1993).

Eckstein, Harry, Frederic J. Fleron Jr., Erik P. Hoffmann and William M. Reissinger, *Can Democracy Take Root in Post-Soviet Russia? Explorations in State-Society Relations* (Lanham, MD, Rowman & Littlefield, 1998).

Ellison, Herbert J., *Boris Yeltsin and Russia's Democratic Transformation* (Seattle and London, University of Washington Press, 2006).

Fish, M. Steven, *Democracy Derailed in Russia: The Failure of Open Politics* (Cambridge, Cambridge University Press, 2005).

Freeland, Chrystia, *Sale of the Century: Russia's Wild Ride from Communism to Capitalism* (New York, Crown Business, 2000).

Gill, Graeme, *The Collapse of a Single-party System* (Cambridge, Cambridge University Press, 1994).

Gill, Graeme and Roger D. Markwick, *Russia's Stillborn Democracy? From Gorbachev to Yeltsin* (Oxford, Oxford University Press, 2000).

Gustafson, Thane, *Capitalism Russian-style* (Cambridge, Cambridge University Press, 1999).

Hahn, Gordon M., *Russia's Revolution from above, 1985–2000: Reform, Transition, and Revolution in the Fall of the Soviet Communist Regime* (New Brunswick, NJ, Transaction Publishers, 2002).

Harter, Stefanie and Gerald Easter (eds), *Shaping the Economic Space in Russia: Decision-Making Processes, Institutions and Adjustment to Change in the El'tsin Era* (Aldershot, Ashgate, 2000).

Hedlund, Stefan, 'Vladimir the Great, Grand Prince of Muscovy: Resurrecting the Russian Service State', *Europe–Asia Studies*, Vol. 58, No. 5, July 2006, pp. 775–801.

Hesli, Vicki L. *Governments and Politics in Russia and the Post-Soviet Region* (Boston, Houghton Mifflin Company, 2007).

Hesli, Vicki L. and William M. Reissinger (eds), *Elections, Parties and the Future of Russia* (Cambridge, Cambridge University Press, 2003).

Hoffman, David E., *The Oligarchs: Wealth and Power in the New Russia* (New York, PublicAffairs, 2002).

Isakova, Irina, *Russian Governance in the Twenty-first Century: Geo-strategy, Geopolitics and Governance* (London, Frank Cass, 2004).

Isham, Heyward (ed.), *Remaking Russia: Voices from Within* (New York, M. E. Sharpe, 1995).

Isham, Heyward, with Natan M. Shklyar (eds), *Russia's Fate Through Russian Eyes: Voices of a New Generation* (Boulder, CO, Westview Press, 2000).

Jones, Mark, *Russia in the Emergent World System* (London, Pluto Press, 1999).

Kagarlitsky, Boris, *Mirage of Modernisation* translated by Renfrey Clarke, (London, Verso, 1995).

Kagarlitsky, Boris, *Restoration in Russia: Why Capitalism Failed*, translated by Renfrey Clarke (London, Verso, 1995).

Kagarlitsky, Boris, *Russia under Yeltsin and Putin: Neo-liberal Autocracy* translated by Renfrey Clarke, (London, Verso, 2001).

Kampfner, John, *Inside Yeltsin's Russia* (London, Cassell, 1994).

Klein, Lawrence and Marshall Pomer (eds), *The New Russia: Transition Gone Awry* (Cambridge, Cambridge University Press, 2001).

Kolstø, Pål, *Political Construction Sites: Nation Building in Russia and the Post-Soviet States* (Boulder, CO, Westview Press, 2000).

Kuchins, Andrew C. (ed.), *Russia after the Fall* (Washington, DC, Carnegie Endowment, 2002).

Lane, David (ed.), *Russia in Transition: Politics, Privatisation and Inequality* (Harlow, Longman, 1995).

Lane. David (ed.), *The Legacy of State Socialism and the Future of Transformation* (Lanham, MD, Rowman & Littlefield, 2002).

Lapidus, Gail W. (ed.), *The New Russia: Troubled Transformation* (Boulder, CO, Westview Press, 1994).

Ledeneva, Alena V., *Russia's Economy of Favours: Blat, Networking and Informal Exchange* (Cambridge, Cambridge University Press, 1998).

Ledeneva, Alena V., *Unwritten Rules: How Russia Really Works* (London, Centre for European Reform, 2001).

Ledeneva, Alena V., *How Russia Really Works: The Informal Practices that Shaped Post-Soviet Politics and Business* (Ithaca, NY, and London, Cornell University Press, 2006).

Lloyd, John, *Rebirth of a Nation: An Anatomy of Russia* (London, Michael Joseph, 1998).

Löwenhardt, John, *The Reincarnation of Russia: Struggling with the Legacy of Communism, 1990-94* (Harlow, Longman, 1995).

Lupher, Mark, *Power Restructuring in China and Russia* (Boulder, Westview, 1996).

Lynch, Allen C., *How Russia Is Not Ruled: Reflections on Russian Political Development* (Cambridge, Cambridge University Press, 2005).

McCauley, Martin, *Bandits, Gangsters and the Mafia: Russia, the Baltic States and the CIS Since 1991* (Harlow, Longman, 2001).

McFaul, Michael, *Post-Communist Politics: Democratic Prospects in Russia and East Europe* (Washington, DC, Centre for Strategic and International Studies, 1993).

McFaul, Michael, *The Troubled Birth of Russian Democracy* (Stanford, Hoover Press, 1993).

McFaul, Michael, *Russia's Unfinished Revolution: Political Change from Gorbachev to Putin* (Ithaca and London, Cornell University Press, 2001).

McFaul, Michael and Kathryn Stoner-Weiss (eds), *After the Collapse of Communism: Comparative Lessons of Transition* (New York, Cambridge University Press, 2004).

McFaul, Michael, Nikolai Petrov and Andrei Ryabov, *Between Dictatorship and Democracy: Russian Post-Communist Political Reform* (Washington, DC, Carnegie Endowment for International Peace, 2004).

Marsh, Christopher, *Russia at the Polls: Voters, Elections, and Democratization* (Washington, DC, CQ Press, 2002).

Marsh, Christopher, *Unparalleled Reforms: China's Rise, Russia's Fall, and the Interdependence of Transition* (Lanham, MD, Rowman & Littlefield, 2005).

Matsuzato, Kimitaka (ed.), *Emerging Meso-areas in the Former Socialist Countries: Histories Revised or Improvised?* (Sapporo, Slavic Research Center, Hokkaido University, 2005).

Mau, Vladimir and Irina Starodubrovskaya, *The Challenge of Revolution: Contemporary Russia in the History of Revolutions* (Oxford, Oxford University Press, 2001).

Medvedev, Roy, *A Journey through the Yeltsin Era* (New York, Columbia University Press, 2000).

Meier, Sndrew, *Black Earth: Russia After the Fall* (London, HarperCollins, 2004).

Morrison, John, *Boris Yeltsin: From Bolshevik to Democrat* (London, Penguin Books, 1991).

Murray, Donald, *A Democracy of Despots* (Boulder, CO, Westview Press, 1996).

Murrell, G. D. G., *Russia's Transition to Democracy: An Internal Political History, 1989–1996* (Brighton, Sussex Academic Press, 1997).

Nelson, Lynn D. and Irina Kuzes, *Radical Reform in Yeltsin's Russia: What Went Wrong?* (Armonk, NY, M. E. Sharpe, 1995).

Nogee, Joseph L. and R. Judson Mitchell, *Russian Politics: The Struggle for Order* (Hemel Hempstead, Allyn & Bacon, 1997).

Orlovsky, Daniel (ed.), *Beyond Soviet Studies* (Washington, The Woodrow Wilson Center Press, 1995).

Petro, Nicolai N., *The Rebirth of Russian Democracy: An Interpretation of Political Culture* (Cambridge, MA, Harvard University Press, 1995).

Poe, Marshall T., *The Russian Moment in World History* (Princeton, NJ, Princeton University Press, 2003).

Politkovskaya, Anna, *Putin's Russia* (London, Harvill, 2004).

Politkovskaya, Anna, *A Russian Diary* (London, Harvill Secker, 2007).

Pravda, Alex (ed.), *Leading Russia: Putin in Perspective* (Oxford, Oxford University Press, 2005).

Ra'anan, Uri (ed.), *Flawed Succession: Russia's Power Transfer Crises* (Lanham, MD, Rowman & Littlefield, 2005).

Ragsdale, Hugh, *The Russian Tragedy: The Burden of History* (New York, M. E. Sharpe, 1996).

Reddaway, Peter and Dmitri Glinski, *The Tragedy of Russia's Reforms: Market Bolshevism against Democracy* (Washington, DC, United States Institute of Peace Press, 2001).

Remington, Thomas, *Politics in Russia*, 3rd edn (London, Pearson Longman, 2004).

Remnick, David, *Resurrection: The Struggle for a New Russia* (New York, Random House, 1997).

Robinson, Neil, *Russia: A State of Uncertainty* (London and New York, Routledge, 2002).

Robinson, Neil (ed.), *Institutions and Political Change in Russia* (Basingstoke, Macmillan, 2000).

Rose, Richard and Neil Munro, *Elections without Order: Russia's Challenge to Vladimir Putin* (Cambridge, Cambridge University Press, 2002).

Rose, Richard, William Mishler and Neil Munro, *Russia Transformed: Developing Popular Support for a New Regime* (Cambridge, Cambridge University Press, 2006).

Rosefielde, Steven, *Russia in the 21st Century: The Prodigal Superpower* (Cambridge, Cambridge University Press, 2005).

Ross, Cameron (ed.), *Russian Politics under Putin* (Manchester, Manchester University Press, 2004).

Rutland, Peter (ed.), *Business and the State in Contemporary Russia* (Boulder, CO, Westview Press, 2001).

Saikal, Amin and William Maley (eds), *Russian in Search of its Future* (Cambridge, Cambridge University Press, 1995).

Saivetz, Carol R., and Anthony Jones (eds), *In Search of Pluralism: Soviet and Post-Soviet Politics* (Boulder, CO, Westview, 1994).

Sakwa, Richard, *Putin: Russia's Choice*, 2nd edn (London, Routledge, 2007).

Satter, David, *Darkness at Dawn: The Rise of the Russian Criminal State* (New Haven, CT, Yale University Press, 2003).

Service, Robert, *Russia: Experiment with a People, from 1991 to the Present* (Basingstoke, Palgrave, 2002).

Shaw, D. J. B., *The Post-Soviet Republics: A Systematic Geography* (London, Longman, 1995).

Shevchenko, Iulia, *The Central Government of Russia: From Gorbachev to Putin* (Aldershot, Ashgate, 2004).

Shleifer, Andrei, *A Normal Country: Russia after Communism* (Cambridge, MA, Harvard University Press, 2005).

Shleifer, Andrei and Daniel Treisman, 'A Normal Country', *Foreign Affairs*, Vol. 83, No. 2, March–April 2004, pp. 20–39.

Simes, Dmitri K., *After the Collapse: Russia Seeks Its Place as a Great Power* (New York, Simon & Schuster, 1999).

Smith, Gordon B., *State-building in Russia: The Yeltsin Legacy and the Challenge of the Future* (Armonk, NY, M. E. Sharpe, 1998).

Smith, Graham, *The Post-Soviet States: Mapping the Politics of Transition* (London, Arnold, 1999).

Solzhenitsyn, Alexander, *Rebuilding Russia: Reflections and Tentative Proposals* (London, Harvill Press, 1991).

Solzhenitsyn, Alexander, *The Russian Question at the End of the Twentieth Century* (London, Harvill Press, 1995).

Sperling, Valerie (ed.), *Building the Russian State: Institutional Crisis and the Quest for Democratic Governance* (Boulder, CO, Westview Press, 2000).

Starr, S. Frederick (ed.), *The Legacy of History in Russia and the New States of Eurasia* (New York, M. E. Sharpe, 1994).

Steele, Jonathan, *Eternal Russia* (London, Faber, 1994).

Stoner-Weiss, Kathryn, *Resisting the State: Reform and Retrenchment in Post-Soviet Russia* (Cambridge, Cambridge University Press, 2006).

Surovell, Jeffrey, *Capitalist Russia and the West* (Aldershot, Ashgate, 2000).

Thatcher, Ian (ed.), *Regime and Society in Twentieth Century Russia* (London, Macmillan, 1997).

Tikhomirov, Vladimir (ed.), *Russia after Yeltsin* (Aldershot, Ashgate, 2001).

Tismaneanu, Vladimir (ed.), *Political Culture in Russia and the New States of Eurasia* (New York, M. E. Sharpe, 1995).

Truscott, Peter, *Russia First: Breaking with the West* (London, I. B. Tauris, 1997).

Waller, Michael, *Russian Politics Today: The Return of a Tradition* (Manchester, Manchester University Press, 2005).

Wegren, Stephen K. (ed.), *Russia's Policy Challenges: Security, Stability and Development* (Armonk, NY, M. E. Sharpe, 2003).

Weigle, Marcia A., *Russia's Liberal Project: State-Society Relations in the Transition from Communism* (University Park, PA, Penn State University Press, 2000).

White, Stephen, *Russia's New Politics: The Management of a Postcommunist Society* (Cambridge, Cambridge University Press, 2000).

White, Stephen, Graeme Gill and Darrell Slider *The Politics of Transition: Shaping a Post-Soviet Future* (Cambridge, Cambridge University Press, 1993).

White, Stephen, Richard Rose and Ian McAllister, *How Russia Votes* (Chatham, NJ, Chatham House Publishers, 1996).

White, Stephen, Zvi Gitelman and Richard Sakwa (eds), *Developments in Russian Politics 6* (Basingstoke, Palgrave Macmillan, 2005).

Wilson, Andrew, *Virtual Politics: Faking Democracy in the Post-Soviet World* (New Haven, CT, Yale University Press, 2005).

Yergin, Daniel and Thane Gustafson, *Russia 2010 and What it Means for the World* (New York, Random House, 1993).

Zwass, Adam, *From Failed Communism to Underdeveloped Capitalism: Transformation of Eastern Europe, the Post-Soviet Union, and China* (New York, M. E. Sharpe, 1995).

# Index

Printed in the USA/Agawam, MA
January 10, 2013

571824.111